PRENTICE HALL
WRITING COACH

Upper Saddle River, New Jersey
Boston, Massachusetts
Chandler, Arizona
Glenview, Illinois

WRITING COACH

WELCOME TO Writing COACH

Seven Great Reasons to Learn to Write Well

Acknowledgments appear on page R55, which constitute an extension of this copyright page.

PEARSON

0-13-253140-2

978-0-13-253140-5

9 10 V063 14 13

1 Writing is hard, but hard is **rewarding**.

2 Writing helps you **sort things out**.

3 Writing helps you **persuade** others.

4 Writing makes you a **better reader**.

5 Writing makes you **smarter**.

6 Writing helps you get into and through **college**.

7 Writing **prepares you** for the world of work.

AUTHORS

The contributing authors guided the direction and philosophy of *Prentice Hall Writing Coach*. Working with the development team, they helped to build the pedagogical integrity of the program and to ensure its relevance for today's teachers and students.

Program Authors

Jeff Anderson

Jeff Anderson has worked with struggling writers and readers for almost 20 years. His works integrate grammar and editing instruction into the processes of reading and writing. Anderson has written articles in NCTE's *Voices from the Middle, English Journal*, and *Educational Leadership.* Anderson won the NCTE Paul and Kate Farmer Award for his *English Journal* article on teaching grammar in context. He has published two books, *Mechanically Inclined: Building Grammar, Usage, and Style into Writer's Workshop* and *Everyday Editing: Inviting Students to Develop Skill and Craft in Writer's Workshop* as well as a DVD, *The Craft of Grammar.*

Grammar gives me a powerful lens through which to look at my writing. It gives me the freedom to say things exactly the way I want to say them.

Kelly Gallagher

Kelly Gallagher is a full-time English teacher at Magnolia High School in Anaheim, California. He is the former co-director of the South Basin Writing Project at California State University, Long Beach. Gallagher is the author of *Reading Reasons: Motivational Mini-Lessons for the Middle and High School, Deeper Reading: Comprehending Challenging Texts 4–12, Teaching Adolescent Writers,* and *Readicide.* He is also featured in the video series, *Building Adolescent Readers.* With a focus on adolescent literacy, Gallagher provides training to educators on a local, national and international level. Gallagher was awarded the Secondary Award of Classroom Excellence from the California Association of Teachers of English—the state's top English teacher honor.

The best swimmers swim the most; the best writers write the most. There's only one way to become a good writer: write!

Contributing Authors

Evelyn Arroyo

Evelyn Arroyo is the author of **A+RISE**, Research-based Instructional Strategies for ELLs (English Language Learners). Her work focuses on closing the achievement gap for minority students and English language learners. Through her publications and presentations, Arroyo provides advice, encouragement, and practical success strategies to help teachers reach their ELL students.

> Your rich, colorf... cultural life expe... are unique and c... easily be painte... through words. ... experiences defi... who you are toda... writing is one way... begin capturing y... history. Become a... taker and fall in l... with yourself thro... your own words.

> When you're learning a new language, writing in that language takes effort. The effort pays off big time, though. Writing helps us generate ideas, solve problems, figure out how the language works, and, above all, allows us to express ourselves.

Jim Cummins, Ph.D.

Jim Cummins is a Professor in the Modern Language Centre at the University of Toronto. A well-known educator, lecturer, and author, Cummins focuses his research on bilingual education and the academic achievement of culturally diverse students. He is the author of numerous publications, including **Negotiating Identities: Education for Empowerment in a Diverse Society.**

Grant Wiggins, Ed.D.

Grant Wiggins is the President of Authentic Education. He earned his Ed.D. from Harvard University. Grant consults with schools, districts, and state education departments; organizes conferences and workshops; and develops resources on curricular change. He is the co-author, with Jay McTighe, of **Understanding By Design,** the award-winning text published by ASCD.

> I hated writing as a student—and my grades showed it. I grew up to be a writer, though. What changed? I began to think I had something to say. That's ultimately why you write: to find out what you are really thinking, really feeling, really believing.

> Concepts of grammar can sharpen your reading, communication, and even your reasoning, so I have championed its practice in my classes and in my businesses. Even adults are quick to recognize that a refresher in grammar makes them keener— and more marketable.

Gary Forlini

Gary Forlini is managing partner of the School Growth initiative **Brinkman—Forlini—Williams,** which trains school administrators and teachers in Classroom Instruction and Management. His recent works include the book **Help Teachers Engage Students** and the data system **ObserverTab** for district administrators, **Class Acts: Every Teacher's Guide To Activate Learning**, and the initiative's workshop **Grammar for Teachers**.

WRITING

WRITING GAME PLAN

> *Writing without grammar only goes so far. Grammar and writing work together. To write well, grammar skills give me great tools.*

CORE WRITING CHAPTERS

WRITING COACH

Online

Interactive Writing Coach™

Interactive Graphic Organizer

Interactive Model

Online Journal

Resources

Video

GRAMMAR

Writing COACH

How to Use This Program

This program is organized into two distinct sections: one for WRITING and one for GRAMMAR.

In the **WRITING** section, you'll learn strategies, traits, and skills that will help you become a better writer.

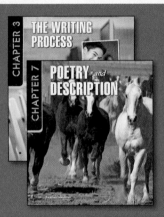

In the **GRAMMAR** section, you'll learn the rules and conventions of grammar, usage, and mechanics.

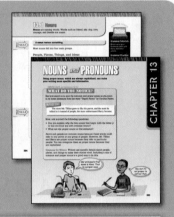

What DIGITAL writing and grammar resources are available?

The Writing Coach Online boxes will indicate opportunities to use online tools.

In **Writing,** use the **Interactive Writing Coach™** in two ways to get personalized guidance and support for your writing.
- Paragraph Feedback and
- Essay Scorer

WRITING COACH

Online
www.phwritingcoach.com

Interactive Writing Coach™
- Choosing from the Topic Bank gives you access to the Interactive Writing Coach™.
- Submit your writing and receive instant personalized feedback and guidance as you draft, revise, and edit your writing.

WRITING COACH

Online
www.phwritingcoach.com

Grammar Tutorials
Brush up on your grammar skills with these animated videos.

Grammar Practice
Practice your grammar skills with Writing Coach Online.

Grammar Games
Test your knowledge of grammar in this fast-paced interactive video game.

In **Grammar,** view grammar tutorials, practice your grammar skills, and play grammar video games.

What will you find in the WRITING section?

Writing Genre

Each chapter introduces a different **writing genre.**

Learn about the key characteristics of the **genre** before you start writing.

Focus on a single form of the genre with the **Feature Assignment**.

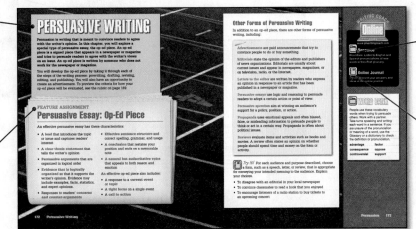

Writing Coach Online

- View the **Word Bank** words in the eText glossary, and hear them pronounced in both English and Spanish.

- Use your **Online Journal** to record your answers and ideas as you respond to *Try It!* activities.

Mentor Text and Student Model

The **Mentor Text** and **Student Model** provide examples of the genre featured in each chapter.

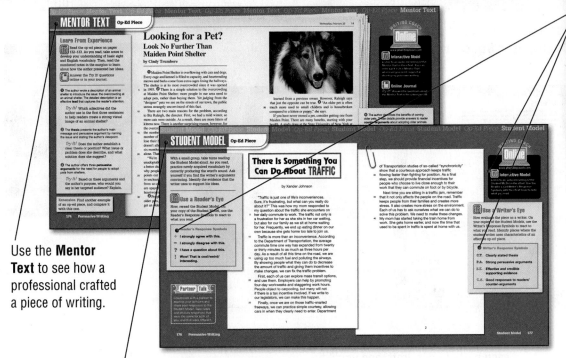

Writing Coach Online

- Use the **Interactive Model** to mark the text with Reader's and Writer's Response Symbols.

- Listen to an audio recording of the **Mentor Text** or **Student Model.**

Use the **Mentor Text** to see how a professional crafted a piece of writing.

Review the **Student Model** as a guide for composing your own piece.

The **Topic Bank** provides prompts for the **Feature Assignment.**

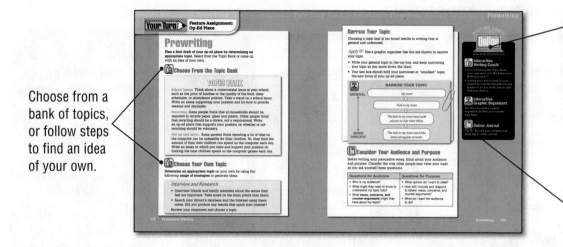

Choose from a bank of topics, or follow steps to find an idea of your own.

Writing Coach Online

- As you narrow your topic, get the right type of support! You'll find three different forms of graphic organizers—one model, one with step-by-step guidance, and one that is blank for you to complete.

- Use *Try It!* ideas to practice new skills. Use *Apply It!* activities as you work on your own writing.

Whether you are working on your essay drafts online or with a pen and paper, an **Outline for Success** can get you started.

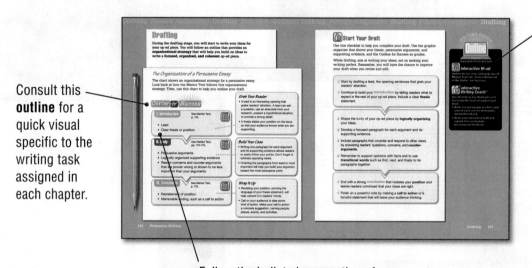

Consult this **outline** for a quick visual specific to the writing task assigned in each chapter.

Follow the bulleted suggestions for each part of your draft, and you'll be on your way to success.

Writing Coach Online

- Start with just a paragraph and build up to your essay draft, or if you are ready, go straight to submitting your essay. The choice is yours!

You can use the **Revision RADaR** strategy as a guide for making changes to improve your draft.

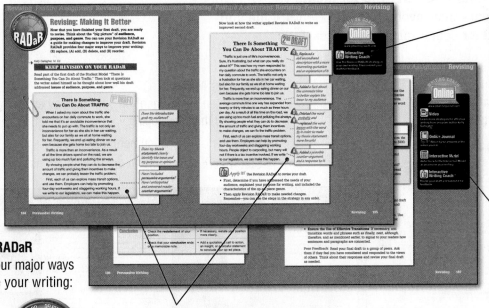

Revision RADaR

provides four major ways to improve your writing:
- **R**eplace
- **A**dd
- **D**elete
- **R**eorder

Check out these example drafts to see how to apply **Revision RADaR.**

Writing Coach Online

- With **Interactive Writing Coach™,** submit your paragraphs and essays multiple times. View your progress in your online writing portfolio. Feel confident that your work is ready to be shared in peer review or teacher conferencing.

- View **videos** with strategies for writing from program author **Kelly Gallagher.**

In the editing stage, **What Do You Notice?** and **Mentor Text** help you zoom in on powerful sentences.

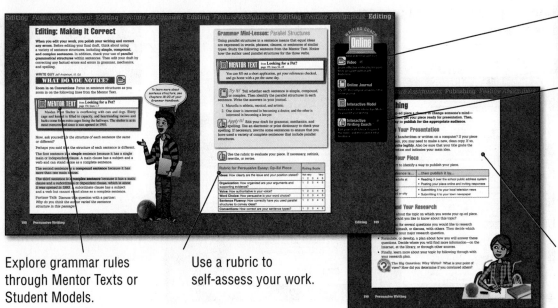

Explore grammar rules through Mentor Texts or Student Models.

Use a rubric to self-assess your work.

Find the best way to share your writing with others.

Writing Coach Online

- View **videos** with strategies for writing from program author **Jeff Anderson.**

- Submit your essay for feedback and a score.

How do end-of-chapter features help you apply what you've learned?

21st Century Learning

In **Make Your Writing Count** and **Writing for Media** you will work on innovative assignments that involve the 21st Century life and career skills you'll need for communicating successfully.

Make Your Writing Count
Work collaboratively on project-based assignments and share what you have learned with others. Projects include:

• Debates
• TV Talk Shows
• News Reports

Writing for Media
Complete an assignment on your own by exploring media forms, and then developing your own content. Projects include:

• Blogs   • Documentary Scripts
• Storyboards   • Multimedia Presentations

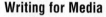

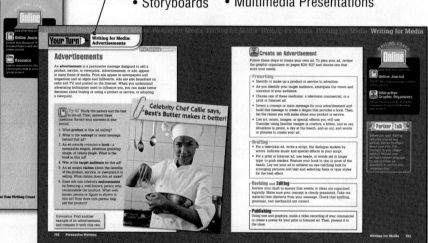

Test Prep

The **Writing for Assessment** pages help you prepare for important standardized tests.

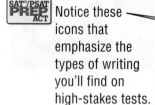
Notice these icons that emphasize the types of writing you'll find on high-stakes tests.

Use **The ABCDs of On-Demand Writing** for a quick, memorable strategy for success.

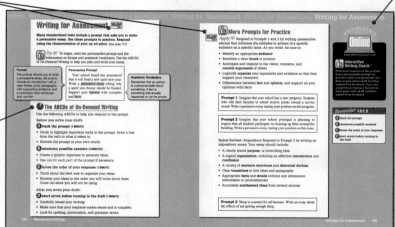

Writing Coach Online
Submit your essay for feedback and a score.

What will you find in the GRAMMAR section?

The **Find It/Fix It** reference guide helps you fix the **20** most common errors in student writing.

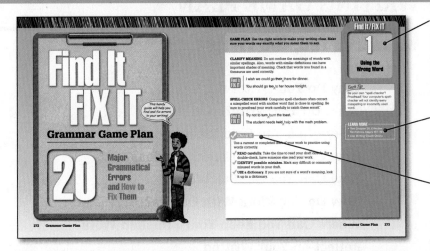

Study each of the 20 common errors and their corrections, which are clearly explained on each page.

Follow cross-references to more instruction in the grammar chapters.

Review the **Check It** features for strategies to help you avoid these errors.

Each grammar chapter begins with a **What Do You Notice?** feature and **Mentor Text.**

Use the **Mentor Text** to help you zoom in on powerful sentences. It showcases the correct use of written language conventions.

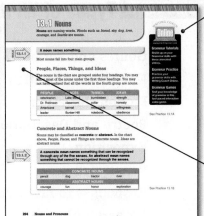

Writing Coach Online
The **Writing Coach Online** digital experience for Grammar helps you focus on just the lessons and practice you need.

Use the grammar section as a quick reference handbook. Each **grammar rule** is highlighted and numbered.

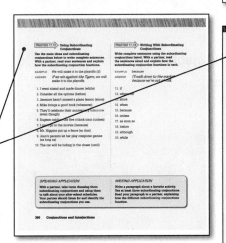

Try **Practice** pages and **Test Warm-Ups** to help you check your progress.

CONTENTS

WRITING

WRITING GAME PLAN

WRITING COACH

Online

www.phwritingcoach.com

All content available online

- Interactive Writing Coach™
- Interactive Graphic Organizer
- Interactive Models
- Online Journal
- Resources
- Video

WRITING

Connect to the Big Questions

- **What do you think?**
  Which experiences shape our sense of ourselves?

- **Why write?**
  What should we put in and leave out to be accurate and honest?

Connect to the Big Questions

- **What do you think?**
  What can we learn from playing games?

- **Why write?**
  What can fiction do better than nonfiction?

WRITING COACH

Online

www.phwritingcoach.com

All content available online
- Interactive Writing Coach™
- Interactive Graphic Organizer
- Interactive Models
- Online Journal
- Resources
- Video

WRITING

Connect to the Big Questions

THE BIG QUESTION

- **What do you think?**
  How can we communicate what we see?

- **Why write?**
  How does one best convey feelings through words on a page?

CHAPTER 8 **Exposition** **144**

Connect to the Big Questions

- **What do you think?**
  What can we learn from similarities and differences?

- **Why write?**
  What should we tell and what should we describe to make information clear?

WRITING COACH

Online

www.phwritingcoach.com

All content available online
- Interactive Writing Coach™
- Interactive Graphic Organizer
- Interactive Models
- Online Journal
- Resources
- Video

WRITING

Connect to the Big Questions

- **What do you think?**
  Which responsibilities are most important?

- **Why write?**
  What is your point of view? How will you know if you've convinced others?

Connect to the Big Questions

• **What do you think?**
How does literature shape who we become?

• **Why write?**
What should you write about to make others interested in a text?

WRITING COACH

Online

www.phwritingcoach.com

All content available online
• Interactive Writing Coach™
• Interactive Graphic Organizer
• Interactive Models
• Online Journal
• Resources
• Video

WRITING

Connect to the Big Questions

- **What do you think?**
  What is the best way to find important information about a topic?

- **Why write?**
  Do you understand a subject well enough to write about it? How will you find out what the facts are?

Connect to the Big Questions

- **What do you think?**
  When is it most important to communicate clearly with teammates?

- **Why write?**
  What do daily workplace communications require of format, content, and style?

WRITING COACH
Online
www.phwritingcoach.com

All content available online
- Interactive Writing Coach™
- Interactive Graphic Organizer
- Interactive Models
- Online Journal
- Resources
- Video

GRAMMAR GAME PLAN

Find It/Fix It
The 20 Errors

GRAMMAR

WRITING COACH

Online

www.phwritingcoach.com

All content available online
- Grammar Tutorials
- Grammar Practice
- Grammar Games

GRAMMAR

WRITING COACH
Online
www.phwritingcoach.com
All content available online
• Grammar Tutorials
• Grammar Practice
• Grammar Games

GRAMMAR
USAGE

WRITING COACH

Online

www.phwritingcoach.com

All content available online

- Grammar Tutorials
- Grammar Practice
- Grammar Games

GRAMMAR

WRITING COACH

Online

www.phwritingcoach.com

All content available online
- Grammar Tutorials
- Grammar Practice
- Grammar Games

STUDENT RESOURCES

NONFICTION NARRATION *Personal Narrative* FICTION NARRATION *Re*

ntrast Essay PERSUASION *Persuasive Essay* RESPONSE TO LITERATURE

w-To Essay, Thank You Letter, Friendly Letter NONFICTION NARRATIO

em and Haiku EXPOSITION *Compare-and-Contrast Essay* PERSUASION

nal Research Report WORKPLACE WRITING *How-To Essay, Thank You Let*

ON Realistic Short Story POETRY *Rhyming Poem and Haiku* EXPOSITION

RE Letter to an Author RESEARCH *Informational Research Report* WORKPL

ON Personal Narrative FICTION NARRATION *Realistic Short Story* POE

ON Persuasive Essay RESPONSE TO LITERATURE *Letter to an Author* RES

Writing

CHAPTER 1

YOU, THE WRITER

Why Do You Write?

Writing well is one of the most important life skills you can develop. Being a good writer can help you achieve success in school and beyond. Most likely, you write for many reasons. You write:

To Share

You probably often write to **share** your experiences with others. Writing can be an easy way to **reach out** to people and connect with them.

To Persuade People

Writing can also be an effective way to **persuade** people to consider your opinions. For example, you may find it's easier to convince someone of your point of view when you've effectively organized your thoughts in an essay or a letter.

To Inform

Another reason to write is to **inform.** Perhaps you want to tell an audience how you built your computer network or how you finally got your e-mail to function properly.

To Enjoy

Personal fullfillment is another important motivation for writing, since writing enables you **to express** your thoughts and feelings. In addition, writing can also help you recall an event, or let you escape from everyday life.

Fortunately, writing well is a skill you can learn and one that you can continue to improve and polish. This program will help you improve your writing skills and give you useful information about the many types of writing.

What Do You Write?

Writing is already an important part of your everyday life. Each day is full of opportunities to write, allowing you to capture, express, think through and share your thoughts and feelings, and demonstrate what you know. Here are some ways you might write.

- Recording thoughts in a journal
- Texting friends or posting on social networking sites
- E-mailing thank-you notes to relatives
- Creating lists of things to do or things you like
- Writing research reports, nonfiction accounts, fiction stories, and essays in school

How Can You Find Ideas?

The good news is that ideas are all around you. You just need to be aware of the rich resources that are available.

By Observing

Observing is a good way to start to find ideas. Did you see anything interesting on your way to school? Was there something unusual about the video game you played last night?

By Reading

Reading is another useful option— look through newspaper articles and editorials, magazines, blogs, and Web sites. Perhaps you read something that surprised you or really made you feel concerned. Those are exactly the subjects that can lead to the ideas you want to write about.

By Watching

Watching is another way to get ideas— watch online videos or television programs, for example.

WRITING COACH

Online

www.phwritingcoach.com

 Online Journal

Try It! Record your notes, answers, and ideas in the online journal. You can also record and save your answers and ideas on pop-up sticky notes in the eText.

❝ Writer to Writer ❞

I write when I want to be heard or connect. Writing lets me be a vital part of my community and reach outside it as well. All the while, I get to be me—my unique self.

—Jeff Anderson

How Can You Keep Track of Ideas?

You may sometimes think of great writing ideas in the middle of the night or on the way to math class. These strategies can help you remember those ideas.

Start an Idea Notebook or a Digital Idea File

Reserving a small **notebook** to record ideas can be very valuable. Just writing the essence of an idea, as it comes to you, can later help you develop a topic or essay. A **digital idea file** is exactly the same thing—but it's recorded on your computer, cell phone, or other electronic device.

Keep a Personal Journal

Many people find that keeping a **journal** of their thoughts is helpful. Then, when it's time to select an idea, they can flip through their journal and pick up on the best gems they wrote—sometimes from long ago.

Maintain a Learning Log

A **learning log** is just what it sounds like—a place to record information you have learned, which could be anything from methods of solving equations to computer shortcuts. Writing about something in a learning log might later inspire you to conduct further research on the same topic.

Free Write

Some individuals find that if they just let go and write whatever comes to mind, they eventually produce excellent ideas. **Free writing** requires being relaxed and unstructured. This kind of writing does not require complete sentences, correct spelling, or proper grammar. Whatever ends up on the paper or on the computer screen is fine. Later, the writer can go back and tease out the best ideas.

How Can You Get Started?

Every writer is different, so it makes sense that all writers should try out techniques that might work well for them. Regardless of your writing style, these suggestions should help you get started.

Get Comfortable

It's important to find and create an environment that encourages your writing process. Choose a spot where you'll find it easy to concentrate. Some writers prefer quiet. Others prefer to work in a room with music playing softly.

Have Your Materials Ready

Before starting to write, gather all the background materials you need to get started, including your notes, free writing, reader's journal, and portfolio. Make sure you also have writing tools, such as a pen and paper or a computer.

Spend Time Wisely

Budgeting your available writing time is a wise strategy. Depending on your writing goal, you may want to sketch out your time on a calendar, estimating how long to devote to each stage of the writing process. Then, you can assign deadlines to each part. If you find a particular stage takes longer than you estimated, simply adjust your schedule to ensure that you finish on time.

			◀ October ▶			
SUNDAY	MONDAY	TUESDAY	WEDNESDAY	THURSDAY	FRIDAY	SATURDAY
		1 Start Research	2 Finish Research	3 Write Outline	4	5
6	7	8 Finish First Draft	9 Finish Revising	10 Finish Proof-reading	11	12
13	14 DUE DATE	15	16	17	18	19
20	21	22	23	24	25	26
27	28	29	30	31		

How Do You Work With Others?

If you think of writing as a solitary activity, think again. Working with others can be a key part of the writing process.

Brainstorming

Brainstorming works when everyone in a group feels free to suggest ideas, whether they seem commonplace or brilliant.

Cooperative Writing

Cooperative writing is a process in which each member of a group concentrates on a different part of an assignment. Then, the group members come together to discuss their ideas and write drafts.

Peer Feedback

Peer feedback comes from classmates who have read your writing and offered suggestions for improvements. When commenting, it's important to provide constructive, or helpful, criticism.

21st Century Learning

Collaborate and Discuss

In **collaborative writing,** each group member takes a role on a writing project. The goal is to work and rework the writing until all members feel they have produced the best result.

Possible Roles in a Collaborative Writing Project

LEADER
Initiates the discussion by clearly expressing group goals and moderates discussions

FACILITATOR
Works to move the discussion forward and clarify ideas

COMPROMISER
Works to find practical solutions to differences of opinion

LISTENER
Actively listens and serves to recall details that were discussed

Using Technology

Technology allows collaboration to occur in ways that were previously unthinkable.

- By working together on the Internet, students around the world have infinite opportunities to collaborate online on a wide-range of projects.

- Collaboration can range from projects that foster community cooperation, such as how to improve debates during local elections, to those that increase global awareness, such as focusing on how to encourage more recycling.

- Being able to log in and to contribute to media, such as journals, blogs, and social networks, allows you to connect globally, express your views in writing, and join a world-wide conversation.

 # Where Can You Keep Your Finished Work?

A **portfolio,** or growing collection of your work, is valuable for many reasons. It can serve as a research bank of ideas and as a record of how your writing is improving. You can create a portfolio on a computer or in a folder or notebook. You'll learn more about managing a portfolio in chapter 3.

A **Reader's Journal,** in which you record quotes and ideas from your reading, can also be used to store original ideas. Your journal can be housed on a computer or in a notebook.

Reflect on Your Writing

Analyzing, making inferences, and drawing conclusions about how you find ideas can help you become a better, more effective writer. Find out more about how you write by asking yourself questions like these:

- Which strategies have I found most effective for finding good ideas for writing?

- What pieces of writing represent my best work and my weakest work? What do the pieces in each group have in common?

With a partner, talk about your collaborative writing experiences. Be sure to share your responses to such questions as these: What project did you work on as a collaborative effort? What did you learn that you might not have discovered if you were developing a writing project by yourself?

CHAPTER 2

TYPES *of* WRITING

Genres and Forms

Genres are types, or categories, of writing.

- Each genre has a specific **purpose,** or goal. For example, the purpose of persuasive writing is to convince readers to agree with the writer's point of view.

- Each genre has specific **characteristics.** Short stories, for example, have characters, a setting, and a plot.

In this chapter, you will be introduced to several genres: nonfiction narratives, fiction narratives, poetry and descriptive writing, expository writing, persuasive writing, responses to literature, and workplace writing.

Forms are subcategories of genres that contain all the characteristics of the genre plus some unique characteristics of their own. For example, a mystery is a form of short story. In addition to plot, characters, and setting, it has a mystery to be solved.

Selecting Genres

In some writing situations, you may need to select the correct genre for conveying your intended meaning.

- To **entertain,** you may choose to write a short story or a humorous essay.

- To **describe** an emotion, writing a poem may be best.

- To **persuade** someone to your point of view, you may want to write a persuasive essay or editorial.

Each genre has unique strengths and weaknesses, and your specific goals will help you decide which is best.

Nonfiction Narration

Nonfiction narratives are any kind of literary text that tells a story about real people, events, and ideas. This genre of writing can take a number of different forms but includes well-developed conflict and resolution, interesting and believable characters, and a range of literary strategies, such as dialogue and suspense. Examples include Gary Soto's "The Drive-In Movies"; Avi's "Superpatriot."

Personal Narratives

Personal narratives tell true stories about events in a writer's life. These types of writing are also called **autobiographical essays.** The stories may tell about an experience or relationship that is important to the writer, who is the main character. They have a clearly defined focus and communicate the reasons for actions and consequences.

Biographical Narratives

In a **biographical narrative,** the writer shares facts about someone else's life. The writer may describe an important period, experience, or relationship in that other person's life, but presents the information from his or her own perspective.

Blogs

Blogs are online journals that may include autobiographical narratives, reflections, opinions, and other types of comments. They may also reflect genres other than nonfiction such as expository writing, and they may include other media, such as photos, music, or video.

Diary and Journal Entries

Writers record their personal thoughts, feelings, and experiences in **diaries** or **journals.** Writers sometimes keep diaries and journals for many years and then analyze how they reacted to various events over time.

Eyewitness Accounts

Eyewitness accounts are nonfiction writing that focus on historical or other important events. The writer is the narrator and shares his or her thoughts about the event. However, the writer is not the main focus of the writing.

Memoirs

Memoirs usually focus on meaningful scenes from writers' lives. These scenes often reflect on moments of a significant decision or personal discovery. For example, many modern U.S. presidents have written memoirs after they have left office. These memoirs help the public gain a better understanding of the decisions they made while in office.

Reflective Essays

Reflective essays present personal experiences, either events that happened to the writers themselves or that they learned about from others. They generally focus on sharing observations and insights they had while thinking about those experiences. Reflective essays often appear as features in magazines and newspapers.

Try It! With a small group, discuss which of the narrative nonfiction forms would be the best choice for each of these purposes. For each, identify two ideas you would expect the writing to address. Discuss your ideas and report your decisions.

- To tell about seeing a championship kite-flying tournament
- To write about one of the first astronauts to walk in space
- To record personal thoughts about a favorite teacher

Fiction Narration

Fiction narratives are literary texts that tell a story about imagined people, events, and ideas. They contain elements such as characters, a setting, a sequence of events, and often, a theme. As with nonfiction narratives, this genre can take many different forms, but most forms include well-developed **conflict** and **resolution.** They also include **interesting and believable elements** and a range of **literary strategies,** such as dialogue and suspense. Examples include Cynthia Rylant's "Stray"; Laurence Yep's "The Homecoming"

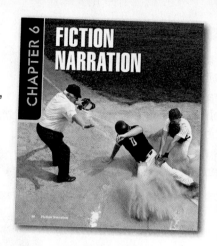

Realistic Fiction

Realistic fiction portrays invented characters and events in everyday situations. Because the focus is on everyday life, realistic fiction often presents problems that many people face and solutions they devise to solve them.

Fantasy Stories

Fantasy stories stretch the imagination and take readers to unreal worlds. Animals may talk, people may fly, or characters may have superhuman powers. Good fantasy stories manage to keep the fantastic elements believable.

Historical Fiction

Historical fiction is about imaginary people living in real places and times in history. Usually, the main characters are fictional people who know and interact with famous people and participate in important historical events.

Mystery Stories

Mystery stories present unexplained or strange events that characters try to solve. These stories are often packed full of suspense and surprises. Some characters in mystery stories, such as Sherlock Holmes, have become so famous that many people think of them as real people.

Myths and Legends

Myths and **legends** are traditional stories, told in cultures around the world. They were created to explain natural events that people could not otherwise explain or understand. They may, for example, tell about the origin of fire or thunder. Many myths and legends include gods, goddesses, and heroes who perform superhuman actions.

Science Fiction

Science fiction stories tell about real and imagined developments in science and technology and their effects on the way people think and live. Space travel, robots, and life in the future are popular topics in science fiction.

Tall Tales

You can tell a **tall tale** from other story types because it tells about larger-than-life characters in realistic settings. These characters can perform amazing acts of strength and bravery. One very famous hero of tall tales is Pecos Bill, who could ride just about anything—even a tornado!

Try It! Think about what you've read about narrative fiction and narrative nonfiction genres. Then, discuss in a group which **genre** would be best if you were planning a first draft and had these purposes in mind. Select the correct genre for conveying your intended meaning to your audiences. Then, identify two or three ideas that you would expect to include in a first draft. Be sure to explain your choices.

- To tell about a Texas rancher who can lasso lightning
- To share a true story about a famous person
- To tell the story of your most exciting day at school

Poetry and Description

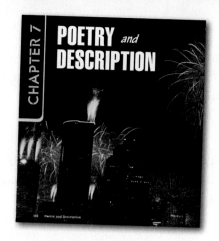

Poetry and other kinds of descriptive literature express ideas and feelings about real or imagined people, events, and ideas. They use rhythm, rhyme, precise language, and sensory details—words that appeal to the senses—to create vivid images. In addition, they use figurative language—writing that means something beyond what the words actually say—to express ideas in new, fresh, and interesting ways.

Structural elements, such as line length and stanzas, also help the poet express ideas and set a mood. Some examples of poetry include Lewis Carroll's "The Walrus and the Carpenter"; Langston Hughes's "April Rain Song."

Ballad

A **ballad** is a form of lyric poetry that expresses the poet's emotions toward someone or something. Ballads rhyme, and some have refrains that repeat after each stanza, which makes them easy to translate into songs.

In many places, traditional folk ballads were passed down as oral poems or songs and then later written. Some ballads tell about cultural heroes. Other ballads tell sad stories or make fun of certain events.

Free Verse

Free verse is poetry that has no regular rhyme, rhythm, or form. Instead, a free verse poem captures the patterns of natural speech. The poet writes in whatever form seems to fit the ideas best. A free verse poem can have almost anything as its subject.

Partner Talk

Think about an example of fiction that you've especially enjoyed reading. Then, choose a partner and report your choices to each other. Be sure to explain what made the fiction piece so enjoyable, interesting, or exciting.

Prose Poem

A **prose poem** shares many of the features of other poetry, but it takes the form of prose, or non-verse writing. Therefore, a prose poem may look like a short story on a page.

Sonnet

The **sonnet** is a form of rhyming lyric poetry with set rules. It is 14 lines long and usually follows a rhythm scheme called iambic pentameter. Each line has ten syllables and every other syllable is accented.

Haiku

Haiku is a form of non-rhyming poetry that was first developed in Japan hundreds of years ago. Typically, the first line has seven syllables, the second line has five syllables, and the third line has seven syllables. Haiku poets often write about nature and use vivid visual images.

Other Descriptive Writing

Descriptive writing includes descriptive essays, travel writing, and definition essays.

- **Descriptive essays** often use words that involve the senses to create a clear picture of a subject.
- A **travel essay** uses sensory words to describe a place.
- A **definition essay** can draw on a writer's emotional experience to describe something abstract, like friendship or happiness.

   Description can be used in other types of writing. For example, a short story may include strong description.

Try It! Now that you've learned more about poetry and description, discuss which specific **genre** would be best for each of these purposes. Select the correct genre for conveying your intended meaning to your audiences. Then, identify two or three types of information that you would want to include in a first draft. Be ready to explain your thinking.

- To tell about a trip to a beach in Mexico
- To describe a drop of rain
- To tell the story of a character who lives in the wilderness

Exposition

Exposition is writing that seeks to communicate ideas and information. It relies on facts to inform or explain.

- Effective expository writing includes effective introductory paragraphs, body paragraphs, and concluding paragraphs.
- In addition, good expository writing uses a variety of sentence structures and rhetorical devices—deliberate uses of language for specific effects.

Examples of expository writing include "Destructive Scratching in Cats"; William Scheller's "Race to the End of the Earth"

Analytical Essay

An **analytical essay** explores a topic by supplying relevant information in the form of facts, examples, reasons, and valid inferences to support the writer's claims.

- An **introductory paragraph** presents a thesis statement, the main point to be developed.
- The **body of the essay** provides facts about the topic, using a variety of sentence structures and transitions.
- The **concluding paragraph** sums up ideas.

Compare-and-Contrast Essay

A **compare-and-contrast** essay explores similarities and differences between two or more things for a specific purpose. As with other expository essays, the compare-and-contrast essay offers clear, factual details about the subject.

Cause-and-Effect Essay

A **cause-and-effect essay** traces the results of an event or describes the reasons an event happened. It is clearly organized and gives precise examples that support the relationship between the cause and effect.

"Writer to Writer"

Expository forms can shape my thinking and help my writing gel. I find the expository patterns clarifying my thoughts and filling in gaps that I may have otherwise missed.

—Jeff Anderson

Partner Talk

Choose a different partner this time. Discuss a poem that you've read in class. Share your thoughts about the poem and describe what made the piece successful.

Classification Essay

In a **classification essay,** a writer organizes a subject into categories and explains the category into which an item falls.

- An effective classification essay **sorts** its subjects—things or ideas—into several categories.

- It then offers **examples** that fall into each category. For example, a classification essay about video games might discuss three types of video games—action, adventure, and arcade.

- The essay might conclude with a statement about how the items classified are different or about how they are similar.

Problem-Solution Essay

A **problem-solution essay** presents a problem and then offers solutions to that problem. This type of essay may contain opinions, like a persuasive essay, but it is meant to explain rather than persuade.

- An effective problem-solution essay presents a clear statement of the problem, including a summary of its causes and effects.

- Then, it proposes at least one realistic solution and uses facts, statistics, or expert testimony to support the solution.

- The essay should be clearly organized, so that the relationship between the problem and the solution is obvious.

Pro-Con Essay

A **pro-con essay** examines arguments for and against an idea or topic.

- It has a topic that has two sides or points of view. For example, you might choose the following as a topic: Is it right to keep animals in zoos?

- Then, you would develop an essay that tells why it's good to keep animals in zoos, as well as why it's harmful to keep animals in zoos.

- It's important to be sure to give a clear analysis of the topic.

Newspaper and Magazine Articles

Newspaper and **magazine articles** offer information about news and events. They are typically factual and do not include the writer's opinions. They often provide an analysis of events and give readers background information on a topic. Some articles may also reflect genres other than the analytical essay, such as an editorial that aims to persuade.

Internet Articles

Articles on the **Internet** can supply relevant information about a topic.

- They are often like newspaper or magazine articles but may include shorter sentences and paragraphs. In addition, they include more visuals, such as charts and bulleted lists. They may also reflect genres other than analytical essays.
- It's always wise to consider the source when reading Internet articles because only the most reputable sources should be trusted to present correct facts.

On-Demand Writing

Because essay questions often appear on school tests, knowing how to write to **test prompts**, especially under time limits, is an important skill.

Test prompts provide a clear topic with directions about what should be addressed. The effective response to an essay demonstrates not only an understanding of academic content but also good writing skills.

 *Try It!* Think about what you've learned about expository writing and consider the other genres you've discussed. Then, discuss in a group which **genre** would be best if you were planning a first draft with these purposes in mind. Select the correct genre for conveying your intended meaning to your audiences. Then, identify two or three key ideas that you would want to include in a first draft. Be sure to explain your choices.

- To weigh the benefits of two kinds of pets
- To imagine what life would be like on the moon

> ### Partner Talk
> Share your experiences with writing expository essays with a partner. Talk about strategies that worked well for you, as well as those that weren't as successful. Be sure to include your analysis of why certain strategies worked better than others.

Persuasion

Persuasive writing aims to influence the attitudes or actions of a specific audience on specific issues. A strong persuasive text is logically organized and clearly describes the issue. It also provides precise and relevant evidence that supports a clear thesis statement. Persuasive writing may contain diagrams, graphs, or charts. These visuals can help to convince the reader. Examples include Richard Durbin's "Preserving a Great American Symbol"; Krystin Oliphant's "Astros Welcome Instant Replay."

Persuasive Essays or Argumentative Essays

A **persuasive essay** or **argumentative essay** uses logic and reasoning to persuade readers to adopt a certain point of view or to take action. A strong persuasive essay starts with a clear thesis statement and provides supporting arguments based on evidence. It also anticipates readers' counter-arguments and responds to them as well.

Persuasive Speeches

Persuasive speeches are presented aloud and aim to win an audience's support for a policy, position, or action. These speeches often appeal to emotion and reason to convince an audience. Speakers sometimes change their script in order to address each specific audience's concerns.

Editorials

Editorials state the opinion of the editors and publishers of news organizations. Editorials usually present an opinion about a current issue, starting with a clear thesis statement and then offering strong supporting evidence.

Op-Ed Pieces

An **op-ed, or opposite-editorial, piece** is an essay that tries to convince readers to agree with the writer's views on an issue. The writer may not work for the publication and is often an expert on the issue or has an interesting point of view.

Letters to the Editor

Readers write **letters to editors** at print and Internet publications to express opinions in response to previously published articles. A good letter to the editor gives an accurate and honest representation of the writer's views.

Reviews

Reviews evaluate items and activities, such as books, movies, plays, and music, from the writer's point of view. A review often states opinions on the quality of an item or activity and supports those opinions with examples, facts, and other evidence.

Advertisements

Advertisements in all media—from print to online sites to highway billboards—are paid announcements that try to convince people to buy something or do something. Good advertisements use a hook to grab your attention and support their claims. They contain vivid, persuasive language and multimedia techniques, such as music, to appeal to a specific audience.

Propaganda

Propaganda uses emotional appeals and often biased, false, or misleading information to persuade people to think or act in a certain way. Propaganda may tap into people's strongest emotions by generating fear or attacking their ideas of loyalty or patriotism. Because propaganda appears to be objective, it is wise to be aware of the ways it can manipulate people's opinions and actions.

Partner Talk

Share your experiences with various types of persuasive texts with a partner. Talk about the types of persuasive text that you think are most effective, honest, and fair. Be sure to explain your thinking.

Try It! Think about what you have learned about exposition, description, and persuasion. Form a group to discuss and draw conclusions about which **genres** would be best if you were planning a first draft with each of these intentions in mind. Select the correct genre for conveying your intended meaning to your audiences. Then, identify two or three types of information that you would want to include in a first draft.

- To explain how an event happened
- To describe a beautiful landscape
- To encourage teens to buy teeth-whitening toothpaste

Responses to Literature

Responses to literature analyze and interpret an author's work. They use clear **thesis statements** and **evidence from the text using embedded quotations to support the writer's ideas.** They also evaluate how well authors have accomplished their goals. Effective responses to literature extend beyond literal analysis to evaluate and discuss how and why the text is effective or not effective.

Critical Reviews

Critical reviews evaluate books, plays, poetry, and other literary works. Reviews present the writer's opinions and support them with specific examples. The responses may analyze the aesthetic effects of an author's use of language in addition to responding to the content of the writing.

Compare-and-Contrast Essays

Compare-and-contrast essays explore similarities and differences between two or more works of literature. These essays provide relevant evidence to support the writer's opinions.

Letters to Authors

Readers write **letters to authors** to share their feelings and thoughts about a work of literature directly.

Blog Comments

Blog comments on an author's Web site or book retailer pages let readers share their ideas about a work. Readers express their opinions and give interpretations of what an author's work means.

Try It! As a group, decide which **genre** would be most appropriate if you were planning a first draft for each of these purposes. Select the correct genre for conveying your intended meaning to your audiences. Then, identify two or three key questions that you would want to answer in a first draft.

- To tell an author why you think her book is excellent
- To write an opinion about a newspaper article
- To imagine how a certain landform came to be

> **Partner Talk**
>
> Interview your partner about his or her experiences writing interpretative responses. Be sure to ask questions such as these:
>
> - How did you support your opinion of the author's work?
> - How did you choose evidence, such as quotes, to support your analysis or opinion?

Research Writing

Research writing is based on factual information from outside sources. Research reports organize and present ideas and information. They present evidence in support of a clear thesis statement.

Research Reports and Documented Essays

Research reports and **documented essays** present information and analysis about a topic that the writer has studied. Start with a clear thesis statement. Research reports often include graphics and illustrations. Documented essays are less formal research writing that show the source of every fact, quote, or borrowed idea in parentheses.

Experiment Journals and Lab Reports

Experiment journals and **lab reports** focus on the purposes, procedures, and results of a lab experiment. They often follow a strict format that includes dates and specific observation notes.

Statistical Analysis Reports

A **statistical analysis report** presents numerical data. Writers of this type of report must explain how they gathered their information, analyze their data, tell what significance the findings may have, and explain how these findings support their thesis.

Annotated Bibliographies

An **annotated bibliography** lists the research sources a writer used. It includes the title, author, publication date, publisher, and brief notes that describe and evaluate the source.

 *Try It!* Discuss which kinds of reports you might write if you were planning a first draft for these purposes. **Select the correct form** for conveying your intended meaning to your audiences. Then, identify two or three key questions that you would want to answer in a first draft. Explain your choices.

- To accompany a project you plan to enter in a science fair
- To write about a poll taken to predict the results of an election

Partner Talk

Share with a partner the kinds of research writing you've done in school. Explain which projects you've enjoyed and why.

Workplace Writing

Workplace writing is writing done on the job or as part of a job, often in an office setting. It usually communicates details about a particular job or work project. This type of writing features organized and accurately conveyed information and should include reader-friendly formatting techniques, such as clearly defined sections and enough blank space for easy reading.

Business Letters and Friendly Letters

A **business letter** is a formal letter written to, from, or within a business. It can be written to make requests or to express concerns or approval. For example, you might write to a company to ask about job opportunities. Business letters follow a specific format that includes an address, date, formal greeting, and closing.

In contrast, a **friendly letter** is a form of correspondence written to communicate between family, friends, or acquaintances. For example, you might write a thank-you note for a gift.

Memos

Memos are short documents usually written from one member of an organization to another or to a group. They are an important means of communicating information within an organization.

E-mails

E-mail is an abbreviation for "electronic mail" and is a form of electronic memo. Because it can be transmitted quickly allowing for instant long-distance communication, e-mail is a very common form of communication that uses a computer and software to send messages.

Forms

Forms are types of workplace writing that ask for specific information to be completed in a particular format. Examples include applications, emergency contact information forms, and tax forms.

Instructions

Instructions are used to explain how to complete a task or procedure. They provide clear, step-by-step guidelines. For example, recipes and user manuals are forms of instructions.

Project Plans

Project plans are short documents usually written from one member of an organization to another. They outline a project's goals and objectives and may include specific details about how certain steps of a project should be achieved.

Résumés

A **résumé** is an overview of a person's experience and qualifications for a job. This document lists a person's job skills and work history. Résumés can also feature information about a person's education.

College Applications

College applications are documents that ask for personal information and details about someone's educational background. College administrators use this information to decide whether or not to accept a student.

Job Applications

Job applications are similar to résumés in that they require a person to list work experience and educational background. Most employers will require a completed job application as part of the hiring process.

Try It! As a group, discuss which form of workplace writing would be best for each of these purposes. Select the correct form for conveying your intended meaning to your audiences. Identify two or three types of information you would expect to include in a first draft.

- To inform the company that made your cell phone that it does not work properly
- To prepare information about your qualifications for a job search
- To create a plan for your group assignment in science class

Partner Talk

Share with a partner your experience with workplace and procedural writing. For example, have you ever written instructions, created a résumé, or completed a job application? What do you find are particular challenges with this type of writing?

Writing for Media

The world of communication has changed significantly in recent years. In addition to writing for print media such as magazines and books, writers also write for a variety of other **media,** in forms such as:

- Scripts for screenplays, video games, and documentaries
- Storyboards for graphic novels and advertisements
- Packaging for every kind of product
- Web sites and blogs

Scripts

Scripts are written for various media, such as documentaries, theater productions, speeches, and audio programs. Movies, television shows, and video games also have scripts.

- A good script focuses on a clearly expressed or implied **theme** and has a specific **purpose.**
- It also contains interesting details, which contribute to a definite **mood or tone.**
- A good script also includes a clear **setting, dialogue,** and well-developed **action.**

Blogs

Blogs address just about every purpose and interest. For example, there are blogs about local issues, pets, or food.

Advertisements

Advertisements are designed to persuade someone to buy a product or service. Advertisements use images, words, and music to support their message. Writers write the content of advertisements. In addition, they may help create music and design the sound and the images in the ad.

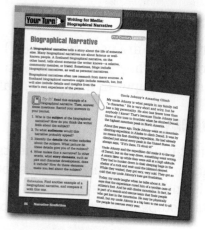

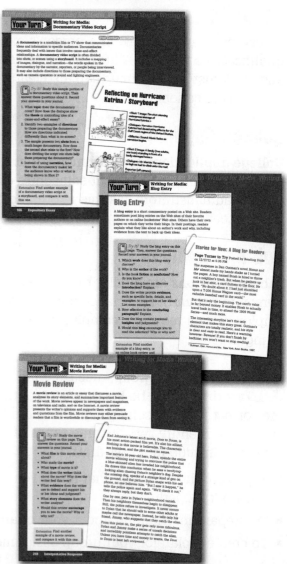

Creating Multimedia Projects

A **multimedia project** or presentation uses sound, video, and other media to convey a point or entertain an audience. No matter what type of project you choose as your own multimedia project, it is important to follow these steps:

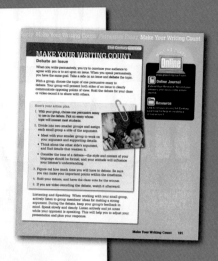

- Decide on the project's **purpose** and your target **audience.**

- Choose **media** that will effectively convey your **message.**

- **Plan** your presentation. Will you work alone or with a partner or group? If you work with others, how you will assign the tasks?

- What **equipment** will you need? Will you produce artwork, record audio, and take photographs? Should you produce a storyboard to show the sequence of details in your presentation? Be sure to allow enough time to produce the text and all the other elements in your project.

- Keep the **writing process** in mind. There should be working and reworking along the way.

- **Assess** the progress of the project as you work. Ask questions, such as: Does my project incorporate appropriate writing genres? Will the presentation interest my audience? Have I kept my purpose in mind?

- **Rehearse!** Before presenting your project, be sure to do several "practice runs" to weed out and correct any errors.

- Keep an electronic record of your presentation for future reference.

- After your presentation, have others assess the project. Their critique will help you to do an even better job next time!

Partner Talk

Share with a partner your experience with writing for media or multimedia projects. Have you created a Web site or contributed to one? Have you had to complete multimedia projects for a class assignment or for a personal project on which you worked? Talk about how writing for media presents different challenges from more traditional writing and how you have dealt with those challenges.

Reflect on Your Writing

Learning more about the different types of writing can help you focus on the characteristics of each type so you can keep improving your own writing. Think about what you've learned in Chapter 2 as you answer these questions:

- What type of writing most interests you?
- What type of writing do you think is most useful? Why?

CHAPTER 3

THE WRITING PROCESS

Writing Traits

Good writing has specific qualities, or traits. In this chapter you will learn about these traits and how to use rubrics to evaluate them. You will also learn how to apply traits during the stages of the writing process.

Ideas

Good writing sends a strong message or presents a clear "angle" or point of view on a subject. It is also informative. The ideas are well developed, or explained with examples and other details.

Organization

A well-organized paper has an obvious plan. You will want to make sure that your ideas move from sentence to sentence and paragraph to paragraph in a logical way. For example, events in a story often appear in the order in which they occurred.

Voice

Voice is the combination of word choice and personal writing style that makes your writing unique. Voice connects a reader to the writer. It can show your personality or "take" on a story.

Word Choice

Your choice of words can help you achieve your purpose. Precise word choice means choosing the word that says exactly what you mean to say. Vivid word choice involves choosing words that create pictures for readers, describing how a subject looks, sounds, smells, and so on.

Sentence Fluency

Good writing is like a song—it has fluency, or a rhythm and a flow. By varying sentence patterns, writers ensure that the rhythm of their writing stays interesting.

Conventions

By following the rules of spelling, capitalization, punctuation, grammar, and usage, you help readers understand your ideas.

Overview of Writing Traits	
Ideas	• Significant ideas and informative details • Thorough development of ideas • Unique perspective or strong message
Organization	• Obvious plan • Clear sequence • Strong transitions
Voice	• Effective word choice • Attention to style
Word Choice	• Precise, not vague, words • Vivid, not dull, words • Word choices suited to audience and purpose
Sentence Fluency	• Varied sentence beginnings, lengths, and structures • Smooth sentence rhythms
Conventions	• Proper spelling and capitalization • Correct punctuation, grammar, usage, and sentence structure

WRITING COACH

Online

www.phwritingcoach.com

Online Journal

Try It! Record your answers and ideas in the online journal. You can also record and save your answers and ideas on pop-up sticky notes in the eText.

"Writer to Writer"

Good writing is a symphony of traits—all coming together to make the paper sing.

—Kelly Gallagher

Rubrics and How To Use Them

You can use rubrics to evaluate the traits of your writing. A rubric allows you to score your writing on a scale in different categories. You will use a six-point rubric like this to help evaluate your writing in chapters 5–12.

Writing Traits	Rating Scale					
Ideas: How interesting, significant, or original are the ideas you present? How well do you develop ideas?	Not very 1	2	3	4	5	Very 6
Organization: How logically is your piece organized? Do your transitions, or movements from idea to idea, make sense?	1	2	3	4	5	6
Voice: How authentic and original is your voice?	1	2	3	4	5	6
Word Choice: How precise and vivid are the words you use? To what extent does your word choice help achieve your purpose?	1	2	3	4	5	6
Sentence Fluency: How well do your sentences flow? How strong and varied is the rhythm they create?	1	2	3	4	5	6
Conventions: How correct is your punctuation? Your capitalization? Your spelling?	1	2	3	4	5	6

Each trait appears in the first column. The rating scale appears in the second column. The higher your score for a trait, the better your writing exhibits that trait.

Using a Rubric on Your Own

A rubric can be a big help in assessing your writing while it is still in process. Imagine you've just started writing a piece of narrative fiction. You know that narrative fiction should have characters, a setting, and a conflict and resolution. You can check the rubric as you write to make sure you are on track. For example, you may use the rubric and decide that you have not developed the conflict well. You can revise to improve your writing and get a better score.

Narrative Fiction Elements	Rating Scale					
	Not very				Very	
Interesting characters	1	2	3	4	5	6
Believable setting	1	2	3	4	5	6
Literary strategies	1	2	3	4	5	6
Well-developed conflict	1	2	3	4	5	6
Well-developed resolution	1	2	3	4	5	6

 Try It! If you checked your story against the rubric and rated yourself mostly 1s and 2s, what actions might you want to take next?

Using a Rubric With a Partner

In some cases, building your own rubric can help you ensure that your writing will meet your expectations. For example, if your class has an assignment to write a poem, you and a partner might decide to construct a rubric to check one another's work. A rubric like the one shown here can help point out whether you should make any changes. Extra lines allow room for you to add other criteria.

Poetry Elements	Rating Scale					
	Not very				Very	
Good sensory details	1	2	3	4	5	6
Colorful adjectives	1	2	3	4	5	6
	1	2	3	4	5	6
	1	2	3	4	5	6
	1	2	3	4	5	6

Try It! What other elements might you add to the rubric?

Using a Rubric in a Group

It is also helpful to use a rubric in a group. That way you can get input on your writing from many people at the same time. If the group members' ratings of your piece are similar, you will probably have an easy time deciding whether to make changes. If the responses vary significantly, you might want to discuss the results with the group. Then, analyze what led to the differing opinions and make careful judgments about what changes you will make.

WRITING COACH

Online

www.phwritingcoach.com

Online Journal

Try It! Record your answers and ideas in the online journal. You can also record and save your answers and ideas on pop-up sticky notes in the eText.

What Is the Writing Process?

The five steps in the writing process are prewriting, drafting, revising, editing, and publishing. Writing is a process because your idea goes through a series of changes or stages before the product is finished.

Study the diagram to see how moving through the writing process can work. Remember, you can go back to a stage in the process. It does not always have to occur in order.

Prewriting

In prewriting, you will:
- Explore ideas
- Choose a purpose and an audience
- Gather details
- Sequence ideas

Drafting

In drafting, you will:
- Put ideas down
- Develop a thesis or controlling idea
- Structure ideas in a sustained way

In publishing, you will:
- Produce a final polished copy of your writing
- Share your writing

Publishing

In the editing phase, you will:
- Check the accuracy of facts
- Correct errors in spelling, grammar, usage, and mechanics

In revising, you will:
- Re-read draft to see what works and what does not
- Use a rubric to evaluate
- Analyze what you want to change or improve
- Make changes

Revising

Editing

Why Use the Writing Process?

Writing involves careful thinking, which means you will make changes as you write. Even professional writers don't just write their thoughts and call it a finished work of art. They use a process. For example, some writers keep going back to the revising stage many times, while others feel they can do the revision in just one step. It is up to each writer to develop the style that works best to produce the best results.

You might find that the writing process works best for you when you keep these tips in mind:

- Remember that the five steps in the writing process are equally important.
- Think about your audience as you plan your paper and develop your writing.
- Make sure you remember your topic and stick to your specific purpose as you write.
- Give your writing some time to "rest." Sometimes it can be good to work on a piece, walk away, and look at it later, with a fresh eye and mind.

The following pages will describe in more detail how to use each stage of the writing process to improve your writing.

WRITING COACH

Online

www.phwritingcoach.com

Online Journal

Try It! Record your answers and ideas in the online journal. You can also record and save your answers and ideas on pop-up sticky notes in the eText.

"Writer to Writer"

Writing process gives us the freedom to write like mad, tinker like an engineer, evaluate like a judge—playing different roles at different stages. Most importantly it gives us the freedom to get our words out of our heads and into the world.

—Jeff Anderson

Prewriting

Prewriting

Drafting

Revising

Editing

Publishing

No matter what kind of writing you do, planning during the prewriting stage is crucial. During prewriting, you determine the topic of your writing, its purpose, and its specific audience. Then, you narrow the topic and gather details.

Determining the Purpose and Audience

What Is Your Purpose?

To be sure your writing communicates your ideas clearly, it is important to clarify why you are writing. Consider what you want your audience to take away from your writing. You may want to entertain them, or you may want to warn them about something. Even when you write an entry in a private journal, you're writing for an audience—you!

Who Is Your Audience?

Think about the people who will read your work and consider what they may already know about your topic. Being able to identify this group and their needs will let you be sure you are providing the right level of information.

Choosing a Topic

Here are just a few of the many techniques you can use to determine an appropriate topic.

- **Brainstorm**
  You can brainstorm by yourself, with a partner, or with a group. Just jot down ideas as they arise, and don't rule out anything. When brainstorming in a group, one person's idea often "piggy-backs" on another.

- **Make a Mind Map**
  A mind map is a quick drawing you sketch as ideas come to you. The mind map can take any form. The important thing is to write quick notes as they come to you and then to draw lines to connect relationships among the ideas.

- **Interview**
  A fun way to find a writing topic is to conduct an interview. You might start by writing interview questions for yourself or someone else. Questions that start with *what*, *when*, *why*, *how*, and *who* are most effective. For example, you might ask, "When was the last time you laughed really hard?" "What made you laugh?" Then, conduct the interview and discover the answers.

- **Review Resources and Discuss Ideas**
  You can review resources, such as books, magazines, newspapers, and digital articles, to get ideas. Discussing your initial ideas with a partner can spark even more ideas.

Narrowing Your Topic

Once you have settled on a topic idea you really like, it may seem too broad to tackle. How can you narrow your topic?

- **Use Graphic Organizers**
  A graphic organizer can help narrow a topic that's too broad. For example, you might choose "Animals" as a topic. You might make your topics smaller and smaller until you narrow the topic to "The Habitat of Emperor Penguins."

WRITING COACH

Online

www.phwritingcoach.com

Online Journal

Try It! Record your answers and ideas in the online journal. You can also record and save your answers and ideas on pop-up sticky notes in the eText.

"Writer to Writer"

Put something down. Anything. Then, magic will happen.

—Jeff Anderson

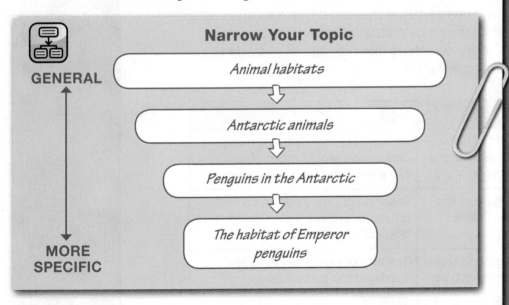

Narrow Your Topic

GENERAL

Animal habitats

↓

Antarctic animals

↓

Penguins in the Antarctic

↓

The habitat of Emperor penguins

MORE SPECIFIC

Prewriting

Drafting

Revising

Editing

Publishing

Prewriting (continued)

- **Use Resource Materials**

  The resource materials you use to find information can also help you narrow a broad topic. Look up your subject online in an encyclopedia or newspaper archive. Scan the resources as you look for specific subtopics to pursue.

Gather Details

After you decide on a topic, you will want to explore and develop your ideas. You might start by looking through online resources again, talking with people who are knowledgeable about your topic, and writing everything you already know about the topic. It will be helpful to gather a variety of details. Look at these types:

- Facts
- Statistics
- Personal observations
- Expert opinions

- Examples
- Descriptions
- Quotations
- Opposing viewpoints

After you have narrowed your topic and gathered details, you will begin to plan your piece. During this part of prewriting, you will develop your essay's thesis or controlling idea—its main point.

As you plan your piece, you can use a graphic organizer. Specific kinds of graphic organizers can help structure specific kinds of writing. For example, a pro-con chart like this one can clarify the reasons for and against an idea.

Pro	Con
Adding funds to the school music budget would allow more students to learn to play instruments.	Giving more money to the music department would mean other programs would get less money.
Research shows that music helps the brain become more flexible.	Other programs, such as sports, are important in keeping students physically healthy.
Band members could stop selling gift-wrap materials at holiday time.	The school board has already approved the current budget allocations.

Drafting

In the drafting stage, you get your ideas down. You may consult an outline or your prewriting notes as you build your first draft.

Prewriting
Drafting
Revising
Editing
Publishing

WRITING COACH

Online

www.phwritingcoach.com

Online Journal

Try It! Record your answers and ideas in the online journal. You can also record and save your answers and ideas on pop-up sticky notes in the eText.

The Introduction

Most genres should have a strong introduction that immediately grabs the reader's attention and includes the thesis. Even stories and poems need a "hook" to grab interest.

Try It! Which of these first sentences are strong openers? Read these examples of first sentences. Decide which ones are most interesting to you. Explain why they grab your attention. Then, explain why the others are weak.

- Have you ever wondered what it would be like to wake up one morning to find you're someone else?
- There are many ways to paint a room.
- Autumn is a beautiful season.
- On Sunday, we went to the store.
- When I woke up that morning, I had no idea that it would be the best day of my life.

The Body

The body of a paper develops the main idea and details that elaborate on and support the thesis. These details may include interesting facts, examples, statistics, anecdotes or stories, quotations, personal feelings, and sensory descriptions.

The Conclusion

The conclusion typically restates the thesis and summarizes the most important concepts of a paper.

Revising: Making It Better

Prewriting

Drafting

Revising

Editing

Publishing

No one gets every single thing right in a first draft. In fact, most people require more than two drafts to achieve their best writing and thinking. When you have finished your first draft, you're ready to revise.

Revising means "re-seeing." In revising, you look again to see if you can find ways to improve style, word choice, figurative language, sentence variety, and subtlety of meaning. As always, check how well you've addressed the issues of purpose, audience, and genre. Carefully analyze what you'd want to change and then go ahead and do it. Here are some helpful hints on starting the revision stage of the writing process.

Take a Break

Do not begin to revise immediately after you finish a draft. Take some time away from your paper. Get a glass of water, take a walk, or listen to some music. You may even want to wait a day to look at what you've written. When you come back, you will be better able to assess the strengths and weaknesses of your work.

Put Yourself in the Place of the Reader

Take off your writer's hat and put on your reader's hat. Do your best to pretend that you're reading someone else's work and see how it looks to that other person. Look for ideas that might be confusing and consider the questions that a reader might have. By reading the piece with an objective eye, you may find items you'd want to fix and improve.

Read Aloud to Yourself

It may feel strange to read aloud to yourself, but it can be an effective technique. It allows you to hear the flow of words, find errors, and hear where you might improve the work by smoothing out transitions between paragraphs or sections. Of course, if you're more comfortable reading your work aloud to someone else, that works, too.

Share Your Work to Get Feedback

Your friends or family members can help you by reading and reacting to your writing. Ask them whether you've clearly expressed your ideas. Encourage them to tell you which parts were most and least interesting and why. Try to find out if they have any questions about your topic that were not answered. Then, evaluate their input and decide what will make your writing better.

Use a Rubric

A rubric might be just what you need to pinpoint weaknesses in your work. You may want to think about the core parts of the work and rate them on a scale. If you come up short, you'll have a better idea about the kinds of things to improve. You might also use a rubric to invite peer review and input.

21st Century Learning

Collaborate and Discuss

When presenting and sharing drafts in the revision stage with a small group, it may be wise to set some ground rules. That way, the group is more likely to help each other analyze their work and make thoughtful changes that result in true improvements.

Here are some suggestions for reviewing drafts as a group:

- Cover the names on papers the group will review to keep the work anonymous.
- Print out copies for everyone in the group.
- Show respect for all group members and their writing.
- Be sure all critiques include positive comments.
- While it is fine to suggest ways to improve the work, present comments in a positive, helpful way. No insults are allowed!
- Plan for a second reading with additional input after the writer has followed selected suggestions.

WRITING COACH

Online

www.phwritingcoach.com

Online Journal

Try It! Record your answers and ideas in the online journal. You can also record and save your answers and ideas on pop-up sticky notes in the eText.

Partner Talk

After a group revision session, talk with a partner to analyze each other's feelings on how the session went. Discuss such issues as these: Did the group adhere to the ground rules? What suggestions could you and your partner make to improve the next session?

Revision RADaR

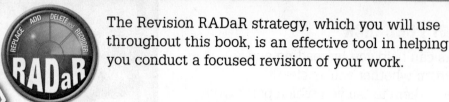

The Revision RADaR strategy, which you will use throughout this book, is an effective tool in helping you conduct a focused revision of your work.

Prewriting

Drafting

Revising

Editing

Publishing

You can use your Revision RADaR to revise your writing. The letters **R**, **A**, **D**, and **R** will help you remember to **r**eplace, **a**dd, **d**elete, and **r**eorder.

To understand more about the Revision RADaR strategy, study the following chart.

R	**A**	**D** and	**R**
Replace . . .	**Add . . .**	**Delete . . .**	**Reorder . . .**
• Words that are not specific • Words that are overused • Sentences that are unclear	• New information • Descriptive adjectives and adverbs • Rhetorical or literary devices	• Unrelated ideas • Sentences that sound good, but do not make sense • Repeated words or phrases • Unnecessary details	• So most important points are last • To make better sense or to flow better • So details support main ideas

 Replace

You can strengthen a text by replacing words that are not specific, words that are overused, and sentences that are unclear. Take a look at this before and after model.

BEFORE
I kicked the soccer ball hard into the goal.

AFTER
With amazing power, I slammed the soccer ball into the goal.

Apply It! **How did the writer replace the overused word *kicked*? What other replacement do you see? How did it improve the text?**

Add

You can add new information, descriptive adjectives and adverbs, and rhetorical or literary devices to make your piece more powerful. Study this before and after model.

BEFORE
I was happy when I won the award.
AFTER
I was beyond thrilled when I won the Science Fair award.

Apply It! **How did the second sentence make you feel, compared with the first? Explain. What information was added to the second sentence?**

 Delete

Sometimes taking words out of a text can improve clarity. Analyze this before and after model.

BEFORE
I knew the test would be difficult, so I should have studied harder for the test before the test day.
AFTER
I knew the test would be difficult, so I should have studied harder for it.

Apply It! **Describe the revision you see. How did taking out unnecessary repetition of the word *test* help the sentences flow more naturally?**

 Reorder

When you reorder, you can make sentences flow more logically.

BEFORE
Today, I have band practice, but yesterday I didn't.
AFTER
I didn't have band practice yesterday, but today I do.

Apply It! **Which of the models flows more logically? Why?**

WRITING COACH
Online
www.phwritingcoach.com

Online Journal

Try It! Record your answers and ideas in the online journal. You can also record and save your answers and ideas on pop-up sticky notes in the eText.

USING TECHNOLOGY

Most word processing programs have a built-in thesaurus tool. You can use the thesaurus to find descriptive words that can often substitute for weaker, overused words.

Revision RADaR (continued)

Read the first draft of the Student Model—a review of the novel *End Game*. Think about how you might use your Revision RADaR to improve the text in a second draft.

Kelly Gallagher, M. Ed.

Prewriting
Drafting
Revising
Editing
Publishing

KEEP REVISION ON YOUR RADaR

End Game Fails to Thrill `1ST DRAFT`

I like detective stories. So when my favorite writer, Mary O'Reilly, published a new detective novel, I bought it. Unfortunately, the novel, *End Game,* was incredibly disappointing.

In the story, an online video gamer disappears. A detective, Katherine, tries to track down the missing man through gaming Web sites. But here's where O'Reilly really messed up. It's clear that she didn't research the technology involved in online gaming. For example: "Katherine waited while her dial-up modem connected her to the virtual world."

The cheesy and ridiculous dialogue made my reading experience even worse. The errors in the book were bad enough! For example, the suspect says to Katherine, "I'm gonna get you, copper!" Now, this is the year 2010. A modern-day criminal would never use such outdated, silly lines. Instead of making the story exciting, the dialogue made it laughably bad.

O'Reilly has written many great books. My favorites were *On the High Seas* and *Danger in Denver.* They were great. I loved them! But I think it's time for O'Reilly to put down her pen. She clearly doesn't have what it takes any more to be a great writer. And as for *End Game*…don't waste your money!

> Is my introduction interesting? Does it grab my readers' attention?

> Have I fully analyzed and explained my examples from the text?

> Is my information logically ordered?

> Is my information relevant to the thesis? Have I included only necessary information?

After writing a draft, the student asked questions like these:

- What could I **replace**?
- What could I **add**?
- What words might I **delete**?
- Should I **reorder** anything?

The student writer created this second draft.

2ND DRAFT

End Game Fails to Thrill

The suspense and high-paced action in detective stories are so thrilling! I simply can't get enough of these books. So when my favorite writer, Mary O'Reilly, published a new detective novel, I ran to the store to buy my copy. Unfortunately, the novel, *End Game,* was incredibly disappointing.

In the story, an online video gamer disappears. A detective, Katherine, tries to track down the missing man through gaming Web sites. But here's where O'Reilly really messed up. It's clear that she didn't research the technology involved in online gaming. For example: "Katherine waited while her dial-up modem connected her to the virtual world." Dial-up modems aren't fast enough to do serious online gaming!

Although the errors in the book were bad enough, the cheesy and ridiculous dialogue made my reading experience even worse. For example, the suspect says to Katherine, "I'm gonna get you, copper!" Now, this is the year 2010. A modern-day criminal would never use such outdated, silly lines. Instead of making the story exciting, the dialogue made it laughably bad.

I think it's time for O'Reilly to put down her pen. She clearly doesn't have what it takes any more to be a great writer. And as for *End Game*…don't waste your money!

R *Replaced dull first line with a more engaging opening.*

A *Added a sentence to better explain to my audience why the information from the text was incorrect.*

R *Reordered text so that the information about the errors connected the ideas in the second and third paragraphs.*

D *Deleted unnecessary information.*

Try It! What other words did the writer replace? Add? Delete? Reorder?

WRITING COACH

Online

www.phwritingcoach.com

Online Journal

Try It! Record your answers and ideas in the online journal. You can also record and save your answers and ideas on pop-up sticky notes in the eText.

Partner Talk

Work with a partner to come up with a list of words that describe detective stories. For example, you might use "high-paced action" or "thrilling." Then discuss the value of using more specific words in your writing.

Editing: Making It Correct

Editing is the process of checking the accuracy of facts and correcting errors in spelling, grammar, usage, and mechanics. Using a checklist like the one shown here can help ensure you've done a thorough job of editing.

Prewriting

Drafting

Revising

Editing

Publishing

Editing Checklist	
Task	**Ask Yourself**
Check your facts and spelling	❏ Have I checked that my facts are correct? ❏ Have I used spell check or a dictionary to check any words I'm not sure are spelled correctly?
Check your grammar	❏ Have I written any run-on sentences? ❏ Have I used the correct verbs and verb tenses? ❏ Do my pronouns match their antecedents, or nouns they replace?
Check your usage	❏ Have I used the correct form of irregular verbs? ❏ Have I used object pronouns, such as *me*, *him*, *her*, *us*, and *them* only after verbs or prepositions? ❏ Have I used subject pronouns, such as *I*, *he*, *she*, *we*, and *they* correctly—usually as subjects?
Check for proper use of mechanics	❏ Have I used correct punctuation? ❏ Does each sentence have the correct end mark? ❏ Have I used apostrophes in nouns but not in pronouns to show possession? ❏ Have I used quotation marks around words from another source? ❏ Have I used correct capitalization? ❏ Does each sentence begin with a capital letter? ❏ Do the names of specific people and places begin with a capital letter?

Using Proofreading Marks

Professional editors use a set of proofreading marks to indicate changes in a text. Here is a chart of some of the more common proofreading marks.

Proofreader's Marks

(b.f.)	boldface
⌐	break text start new line
(Caps)	capital letter
⊃	close up
e	deletes
a/	insert ^ word
˙/	insert ^ comma
=/	insert ^ hyphen
+/	insert letter
⊙/	insert period
(ital)	italic type
(Stet)	let stand as is
(l.f.)	lightface
(l.c.)	lower case letter
⌐	move left
⌐	move right
¶	new paragraph
(rom)	roman type
	run text up
(sp)	spell out whole word
	transpose

WRITING COACH

Online

www.phwritingcoach.com

Online Journal

Try It! Record your answers and ideas in the online journal. You can also record and save your answers and ideas on pop-up sticky notes in the eText.

USING TECHNOLOGY

Many word processing programs have automatic spelling and grammar checks. While these tools can be helpful, be sure to pay attention to any suggestions they offer. That's because sometimes inappropriate substitutes are inserted automatically!

Editing: Making It Correct (continued)

WRITE GUY *Jeff Anderson, M. Ed.*

WHAT DO YOU NOTICE?

Using an editing checklist is a great way to check for correct grammar. However, using a checklist is not enough to make your writing grammatically correct. A checklist tells you what to look for, but not how to correct mistakes you find. To do that, you need to develop and apply your knowledge of grammar.

Looking closely at good writing is one way to expand your grammar know-how. The *What Do You Notice?* feature that appears throughout this book will help you zoom in on passages that use grammar correctly and effectively.

As you read this passage, from "Jobs for Kids," zoom in on the sentences in the passage.

I have a paper route. After school, I deliver newspapers on my bike to my neighbors. I love this job because I get exercise, and I get to be outside.

Now, ask yourself: *What do you notice about the sentences in this passage?*

Maybe you noticed that the writer uses sentences of varying lengths and with different structures.

After asking a question that draws your attention to the grammar in the passage, the *What Do You Notice?* feature provides information on a particular grammar topic. For example, following the passage and question, you might read about simple and complex sentences, which are both used in the passage.

The *What Do You Notice?* feature will show you how grammar works in actual writing. It will help you learn how to make your writing correct.

Prewriting

Drafting

Revising

Editing

Publishing

WRITING COACH

Online

www.phwritingcoach.com

Jobs for Kids

I like having my own money. That way, I can buy things I want and can also save money for my future. But here's the problem: How can we, as kids, make money? There are many types of jobs for kids, but each job has pluses and minuses.

I have a paper route. After school, I deliver newspapers on my bike to my neighbors. I love this job because I get exercise, and I get to be outside. This job isn't for everyone, though. Some kids have a lot of after-school activities, so they don't go straight home. Because papers have to be delivered on time, this can be challenging.

A friend of mine babysits because she has fun with and loves taking care of children. To be a babysitter, you have to find out if your state has a law about how old you have to be before you can babysit. You also have to be a patient, responsible person who is good with children. Finally, it helps to know first-aid, just in case a child gets injured.

My brother does yard work for neighbors. He rakes leaves, weeds gardens, and mows lawns. He loves to be outside and doesn't mind getting dirty. However, there are certain safety issues involved. For example, you have to know how to handle a lawnmower properly and wear protective gear.

What type of job is right for you? What are your interests? Get creative, and start making some money!

Online Journal

Try It! Record your answers and ideas in the online journal. You can also record and save your answers and ideas on pop-up sticky notes in the eText.

" Writer to Writer "

If I wonder how to write any kind of writing, I look at models—well-written examples of the kind of writing I want to do. Models are the greatest how-to lesson I have ever discovered.

—Jeff Anderson

Try It! Read "Jobs for Kids." Then, zoom in on two more passages. Write a response to each question in your journal.

1. What do you notice about the pronouns (*you, he*) in the fourth paragraph?

2. How does the writer use transitions, such as the word *finally*, to connect ideas in the third paragraph?

Publishing

Prewriting

Drafting

Revising

Editing

Publishing

When you publish, you produce a final copy of your work and present it to an audience. When publishing you'll need to decide which form will best reach your audience, exhibit your ideas, show your creativity, and accomplish your main purpose.

To start assessing the optimal way to publish your work, you might ask yourself these questions:

- What do I hope to accomplish by sharing my work with others?
- Should I publish in print form? Give an oral presentation? Publish in print form and give an oral presentation?
- Should I publish online, in traditional print, or both?
- What specific forms are available to choose from?

The answers to most of these questions will most likely link to your purpose for writing and your audience. Some choices seem obvious. For example, if you've written a piece to contribute to a blog, you'll definitely want to send it electronically.

Each publishing form will present different challenges and opportunities and each will demand different forms of preparation. For example, you may need to prepare presentation slides for a speech, or you may want to select music and images if you will be posting a video podcast online.

Ways to Publish

There are many ways to publish your writing. This chart shows some of several opportunities you can pursue to publish your work.

Genre	Publishing Opportunities	
Narration: Nonfiction	• Blogs • Book manuscript • Audio recording	• Private diary or journal entries • Electronic slide show
Narration: Fiction	• Book manuscript • Film	• Audio recording • Oral reading to a group
Poetry and Description	• Bound collection • Visual display	• Audio recording • Oral reading to a group
Exposition and Persuasion	• Print or online article • Web site • Slide show • Visual display	• Film • Audio recording • Oral reading or speech
Response to Literature	• Print or online letters • Visual displays	• Blogs • Slide show
Research Writing	• Traditional paper • Print and online experiment journals	• Multimedia presentation

Reflect on Your Writing

Think about what you learned in Chapter 3 as you answer these questions:

- What did you learn about the writing process?
- What steps in the writing process do you already use in your writing?
- Which stage do you think is the most fun? Which one may be most challenging for you? Explain.

WRITING COACH

Online

www.phwritingcoach.com

Online Journal

Try It! Record your answers and ideas in the online journal. You can also record and save your answers and ideas on pop-up sticky notes in the eText.

Discuss the chart on this page with a partner. If there are ways to publish that neither of you has ever tried, talk about how you might go about experimenting with those forms.

SENTENCES, PARAGRAPHS, *and* COMPOSITIONS

Good writers know that strong sentences and paragraphs help to construct effective compositions. Chapter 4 will help you use these building blocks to structure and style excellent writing. It will also present ways to use rhetorical and literary devices and online tools to strengthen your writing.

The Building Blocks: Sentences and Paragraphs

A **sentence** is a group of words with two main parts: a subject and a predicate. Together, these parts express a complete thought.

A **paragraph** is built from a group of sentences that share a common idea and work together to express that idea clearly. The start of a new paragraph has visual clues—either an indent of several spaces in the first line or an extra line of space above it.

In a good piece of writing, each paragraph supports, develops, or explains the main idea of the whole work. Of course, the traits of effective writing—ideas, organization, voice, word choice, sentence fluency, and conventions—appear in each paragraph as well.

Writing Strong Sentences

To write strong paragraphs, you need strong sentences. While it may be your habit to write using a single style of sentences, adding variety will help make your writing more interesting. Combining sentences, using compound elements, forming compound sentences, and using subordination all may help you make your sentences stronger, clearer, or more varied.

Combine Sentences

Putting information from one sentence into another can make a more powerful sentence.

BEFORE	Basketball is a fun game. It takes a lot of skill and practice.
AFTER	Basketball, which takes a lot of skill and practice, is a fun game.

Use Compound Elements

You can form compound subjects, verbs, or objects to help the flow.

BEFORE	Students enjoy many different hobbies. Some play sports. Some write poetry. Some paint.
AFTER	Students enjoy many different hobbies, such as playing sports, writing poetry, and painting.

Form Compound Sentences

You can combine two sentences into a compound sentence.

BEFORE	Some people enjoy skateboarding. It can be a dangerous hobby.
AFTER	Some people enjoy skateboarding, but it can be a dangerous hobby.

Use Subordination

Combine two related sentences by rewriting the less important one as a subordinate clause.

BEFORE	Horseback riding allows you to be outside in the fresh air. That is good for you.
AFTER	Horseback riding allows you be outside in the fresh air, which is good for you.

WRITING COACH
Online
www.phwritingcoach.com

Online Journal
Try It! Record your answers and ideas in the online journal. You can also record and save your answers on pop-up sticky notes in the eText.

LEARN MORE
For more on sentence combining see Chapter 20.

Writing Strong Paragraphs

If all the sentences in a paragraph reflect the main idea and work together to express that idea clearly, the result will be a strong paragraph.

Express Your Main Idea With a Clear Topic Sentence

A **topic sentence** summarizes the main idea of a paragraph. It may appear at the beginning, middle, or end of a paragraph. It may even be unstated. When the topic sentence comes at the beginning of a paragraph, it introduces the main idea and leads the reader naturally to the sentences that follow it. When it appears at the end of a paragraph, it can draw a conclusion or summarize what came before it. If the topic sentence is unstated, the rest of the paragraph must be very clearly developed, so the reader can understand the main idea from the other sentences.

Think about the topic sentence as you read this paragraph.

> There is no question that computer skills are necessary to have today. Without these skills, it will be difficult to get a college degree and find a good job. Most assignments in college must be done on a computer. Much research in college is done on the Internet, and many libraries have switched from a paper card catalog to a digital catalog. In addition, many companies won't hire someone who has no computer skills. After all, if you can't send e-mails and create important documents in word processing programs, how will you be able to properly do many jobs?

 Try It! Look back at the sample paragraph to answer these questions.

1. What is the topic sentence?
2. Does the topic sentence introduce the main idea or draw a final conclusion? Explain.
3. What makes this topic sentence strong?

Write Effective Supporting Sentences

A clear topic sentence is a good start, but it needs to be accompanied by good details that support the paragraph's main idea. Your supporting sentences might tell interesting facts, describe events, or give examples. In addition, the supporting sentences should also provide a smooth transition, so that the paragraph reads clearly and logically.

Think about the topic sentences and supporting details as you read this paragraph.

> Owning a dog can be hard work, but it is well worth it! A dog owner must be very responsible and take good care of her pet. She has to feed and walk the dog every day and bathe it regularly. Every dog also needs a lot of play time with its owner! All of this takes a great deal of time and energy. However, a dog can be your best friend. It will love you and protect you, and sometimes make you laugh! Plus, what could be better than snuggling up with a sweet, loving dog?

 Try It! Look at the paragraph and answer these questions.

1. What is the topic sentence of the paragraph?
2. Do you think it's an effective topic sentence? Why or why not?
3. What supporting details does the writer provide?
4. If you were the writer, what other supporting details might you add to strengthen the paragraph?

www.phwritingcoach.com

Online Journal

Try It! Record your answers and ideas in the online journal. You can also record and save your answers on pop-up sticky notes in the eText.

Writing Strong Paragraphs 51

Include a Variety of Sentence Lengths, Structures, and Beginnings

To be interesting, a paragraph should include sentences of different lengths, types, and beginnings. Similarly, if every sentence has the same structure—for example, article, adjective, noun, verb—the paragraph may sound boring or dry.

21st Century Learning

Collaborate and Discuss

With a group, study this writing sample.

On the night of the school concert, I didn't think I'd survive my stage fright. My hands felt cold and clammy, and a lump was stuck in my throat. A trickle of sweat slipped between my shoulder blades and down my back. I was so nervous! As the band began playing the opening notes of the first song and I stepped up to the microphone, the glare of the bright lights blinded me. I closed my eyes, took a deep breath, and belted out the song without even thinking. When the song was over, the audience responded with deafening applause. I had done it!

Discuss these questions about the paragraph.

1. What is the topic sentence? How does it draw in the reader?

2. What details support the topic sentence in each paragraph?

3. Point out some examples of varying sentence lengths and beginnings.

4. What examples can you find of sentences with a variety of sentence structures?

USING TECHNOLOGY

It's often better to use the tab key, rather than the space bar, to indent a paragraph. Using the tab key helps to ensure that the indents in all paragraphs will be uniform.

Composing Your Piece

You've learned that the building blocks of writing are strong sentences and paragraphs. Now it's time to use those building blocks to construct a composition. While the types of writing vary, most types have a definite structure with clearly defined parts.

The Parts of a Composition

Writers put together and arrange sentences and paragraphs to develop ideas in the clearest way possible in a composition. Some types of writing, such as poetry and advertisements, follow unique rules and may not have sentences and paragraphs that follow a standard structure. However, as you learned in Chapter 3, most compositions have three main sections: an introduction, a body, and a conclusion.

I. Introduction

The introduction of a composition introduces the focus of the composition, usually in a thesis statement. The introduction should engage the reader's interest, with such elements as a question, an unusual fact, or a surprising scene.

II. Body

Just as supporting statements develop the ideas of a topic sentence, the body of a composition develops the thesis statement and main idea. It provides details that help expand on the thesis statement. The paragraphs in the body are arranged in a logical order.

III. Conclusion

As the word implies, the conclusion of a composition concludes or ends a piece of writing. A good way to ensure the reader will remember your thesis statement is to restate it or summarize it in the conclusion. When restating the thesis, it's usually most effective to recast it in other words. Quotations and recommendations are other ways to conclude a composition with memorable impact. The conclusion should provide a parting insight or reinforce the importance of the main idea.

"Writer to Writer"

Strong, varied sentences and unified paragraphs are the building blocks of effective writing.

—Kelly Gallagher

Rhetorical and Literary Devices

Like any builders, good writers have a set of tools, or devices, at their fingertips to make their writing interesting, engaging, and effective. Writers can use the rhetorical devices of language and their effects to strengthen the power of their style. This section presents some tools you can store in your own writing toolbox to develop effective compositions.

Sound Devices

Sound devices, which create a musical or emotional effect, are most often used in poetry. The most common sound devices include these:

- **Alliteration** is the repetition of consonant sounds at the beginning of words that are close to one another.

  Example: The sweet sound of singing swam in the breeze.

- **Assonance** is the repetition of vowel sounds in words that are close to one another.

  Example: We see shells on the beach, by the sea.

- **Consonance** is the repetition of consonants within or at the end of words.

  Example: The doctor checked the sick patient at three o'clock.

Structural Devices

Structural devices determine the way a piece of writing is organized. Rhyme and meter are most often used to structure poetry, as are stanzas and many other structural devices.

- **Rhyme** is the repetition of sounds at the ends of words. Certain poetry forms have specific rhyme schemes.
- **Meter** is the rhythmical pattern of a poem, determined by the stressed syllables in a line.
- **Visual elements**, such as stanzas, line breaks, line length, fonts, readability, and white space, help determine how a piece of writing is read and interpreted. These elements can also affect the emotional response to a piece.

Other Major Devices

You can use these devices in many forms of writing. They help writers express ideas clearly and engage their readers.

Device	Example
Figurative language is writing that means something beyond what the words actually say. Common forms of figurative language include these: • A **simile** compares two things using the words *like* or *as*. • A **metaphor** compares two things by mentioning one thing as if it is something else. It does not use *like* or *as*. • **Personification** gives human characteristics to a non-human object.	*His voice sounded like nails on a chalkboard.* *The trapeze artist was a bird in flight.* *The sun smiled down on us.*
Hyperbole is exaggeration used for effect.	*I felt stronger than a superhero!*
Irony is a contradiction between what happens and what is expected.	In a famous story, a wife cuts her hair to buy her husband a watch fob, and he sells his watch to buy her a brush.
Paradox is a statement that contains elements that seem contradictory, but could be true.	Mother Teresa said, "…if you love until it hurts, there can be no more hurt, only more love."
An **oxymoron** is word or phrase that seems to contradict itself.	The movie was seriously funny!
Symbolism is an object that stands for something else.	The American flag is often considered a symbol of freedom.
An **allegory** is a narrative that has a meaning other than what literally appears.	Some say the story of the sinking ship is an allegory for the effects of pride.
Repetition (or tautology) occurs when content is repeated, sometimes needlessly—for effect.	The band's song was loud, loud and far too long.

WRITING COACH

Online

www.phwritingcoach.com

Online Journal

Try It! Record your answers and ideas in the online journal. You can also record and save your answers on pop-up sticky notes in the eText.

USING TECHNOLOGY

Most word processing programs have a built-in thesaurus tool. You can use the thesaurus to find descriptive words that can often substitute for weaker, overused words.

Partner Talk

There are many online tools that can help you strengthen your writing. For example, you can search for examples of figurative language and sound devices. Then you can model your own writing after the samples. Just be sure that you don't plagiarize or copy the written work of others.

Using Writing Traits to Develop an Effective Composition

You read about rubrics and traits in Chapter 3. Now it's time to look at how they function in good writing.

Ideas

A good writer clearly presents and develops important information, a strong message, and original ideas.

As you read the sample, think about the ideas it presents.

Achoo!

Achoo! The common cold can be a major downer. Who wants to be home with a runny nose and sore throat? It happens more often than you might think, though. According to the Mayo Clinic, students can get as many as six to ten colds a year! If you understand the causes of the common cold and take precautions, you can successfully avoid catching a cold.

A common cold is caused by a virus. Many different viruses could be responsible for your runny nose, but all of them have one thing in common: they're very contagious. A common-cold virus can spread in the air when a sick person coughs, sneezes, or even talks.

Once you know how colds spread, you can see that avoiding a cold is fairly easy, if you follow some simple rules. Wash your hands often. Keep doorknobs and countertops clean. Don't share drinking glasses or silverware. Most importantly, avoid being around sick people. If you do happen to catch a cold, sneeze or cough into your elbow to help keep your cold from spreading to others. No one likes to be sick!

Try It! Think about ideas in the writing sample as you answer this question.

What is the writer's message? List three details that clearly convey or give support for this message.

Organization

A well-organized composition flows easily from sentence to sentence and paragraph to paragraph. It clearly shows relationships between ideas. The paper also avoids needless repetition.

Think about organization as you reread "Achoo!" on page 56.

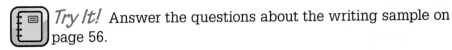 *Try It!* Answer the questions about the writing sample on page 56.

1. Which sentence introduces the topic of the piece?
2. Why must the second paragraph appear before the third?
3. List three details in the third paragraph. Explain how each supports the first sentence in the paragraph.

Voice

Voice is the individual "sound" of a writer's writing, reflecting the writer's personality or perspective. A successful paper has a definite voice expressing the writer's individuality.

Read the writing sample. Think about voice as you read.

> I'll never forget the day my parents got home with 4-month-old Liang. I was sitting on the couch, waiting for them. My stomach was doing flip-flops. Then Mom and Dad walked through the door, carrying this little bundle wrapped in a blanket. Mom sat on the couch with me and introduced me to my new brother. I expected him to totally freak out—to scream and cry. Instead, he just looked up at me with his big, brown eyes and smiled. His tiny hand reached out and grabbed my finger. He had a pretty strong grip!
>
> I found out that while babies are sometimes loud, smelly, and drooly, all of that stuff didn't matter. I loved my little brother, and I couldn't wait till he grew up, so I could teach him how to use that strong grip to hold a football!

Try It! Consider the writer's voice as you answer this question.

Which words and phrases give you a clear sense of the writer's personality and perspective? Explain.

WRITING COACH

Online

www.phwritingcoach.com

Online Journal

Try It! Record your answers and ideas in the online journal. You can also record and save your answers on pop-up sticky notes in the eText.

Partner Talk

Analyze the composition about colds on page 56 with a partner. Discuss how well it might score on the traits of ideas and organization—from ineffective (1), to somewhat effective (2), to fairly effective (3), to effective (4), to highly effective in parts (5), to highly effective throughout (6).

Word Choice

By choosing words with precision, good writers give their writing energy and help readers picture exactly what they are talking about. Think about word choice as you read these two drafts:

> Bob got into Ted's car. As he sat down, he realized he was hearing something familiar. "That's right," Ted said. "I finally put our stuff on CD. It sounds so nice on this system!"

> Bob climbed over chrome fittings into Ted's customized SUV. As Bob eased into the leather-upholstered seat, he recognized the crunching guitar chords that came crashing through the car stereo's speakers. "That's right," Ted said. "I finally mixed our band's songs down to a CD. They sound so crisp on this system!"

 Try It! Answer these questions about the two drafts.

1. List two vague or imprecise words in the first draft.
2. What do the precise words in the second draft help you understand?

Sentence Fluency

In the best writing, sentences have rhythm. They flow smoothly when read aloud, rather than sounding awkward. To control rhythm, good writers use a variety of sentence structures. Think about the rhythm of the writer's sentences as you read this draft:

> After six years of weekly lessons, I can say I have done my best to master the cello. I may not have been good enough for the All-County Orchestra last year, but this year will be different. This year, my dedication will pay off!

 Try It! Respond to this prompt about the draft.

Describe the rhythm of the sentences in the passage.

Conventions

If a piece of writing reflects a good command of spelling, capitalization, punctuation, grammar, usage, and sentence structure, it is much more likely to communicate clearly to readers.

Pay attention to spelling, capitalization, punctuation, grammar, usage, and sentence structure as you read this first draft.

If your an action-movie fan, you have to run—not walk—to see *Welcome to Mars!* This movie is non-stop action, from start to finish. Me and my friend were blown away by the battle scenes, special effects, and suspense.

The movie has a great message, too: Understanding can lead to peace. In one very tense moment, the lead scientist on Mars is captured by aliens. I was so sure they would kill her! Instead, she stayed with them learning their language and to learn, their ways of life. This led to peace between the humans and the aliens.

Now, read this section of the reviewer's second draft.

If you're an action-movie fan, you have to run—not walk—to see *Welcome to Mars!* This movie is non-stop action, from start to finish. My friend and I were blown away by the battle scenes, special effects, and suspense.

The movie has a great message, too: Understanding can lead to peace. In one very tense moment, the lead scientist on Mars is captured by aliens. I was so sure they would kill her! Instead, she stayed with them, learning their language and their ways of life. This led to peace between the humans and the aliens.

 Try It! Answer these questions about both drafts.

1. What errors in convention did the writer correct in the second draft?

2. Why is the next-to-last sentence easier to read in the second draft?

WRITING COACH

Online

www.phwritingcoach.com

Online Journal

Try It! Record your answers and ideas in the online journal. You can also record and save your answers on pop-up sticky notes in the eText.

Using Interactive Writing Coach

As you learned in Chapter 3, you can use rubrics and your Revision RADaR to check how well your paragraphs and essays read. With Writing Coach, you also have another tool available to evaluate your work: the Interactive Writing Coach.

The Interactive Writing Coach is a program that you can use anywhere that you have Internet access. Interactive Writing Coach functions like your own personal writing tutor. It gives you personalized feedback on your work.

The Interactive Writing Coach has two parts: **Paragraph Feedback** and **Essay Scorer**.

- Paragraph Feedback gives you feedback on individual paragraphs as you write. It looks at the structure of sentences and paragraphs and gives you information about specific details, such as sentence variety and length.

- Essay Scorer looks at your whole essay and gives you a score and feedback on your entire piece of writing. It will tell you how well your essay reflects the traits of good writing.

This chart shows just a few questions that Paragraph Feedback and Essay Scorer will answer about your writing. The following pages explain Paragraph Feedback and Essay Scorer in more detail.

Sentences	• Are sentences varied in length? • Do sentences have varied beginnings? • Which sentences have too many ideas? • Are adjectives clear and precise? • Is the sentence grammatically correct? • Is all spelling correct in the sentence?
Paragraphs	• Does the paragraph support its topic? • Does the paragraph use transitions? • Does the paragraph contain the right amount of ideas and information?
Compositions	• Does the essay reflect characteristics of the genre? • Does it demonstrate the traits of good writing? • Is the main idea clear? • Is the main idea well supported? • Is the essay cohesive—does it hold together?

Interactive Writing Coach and the Writing Process

You can begin to use Essay Scorer during the drafting section of the writing process. It is best to complete a full draft of your essay before submitting to Essay Scorer. (While you are drafting individual paragraphs, you may want to use Paragraph Feedback.) Keep in mind, however, that your draft does not need to be perfect or polished before you submit to Essay Scorer. You will be able to use feedback from Essay Scorer to revise your draft many times. This chart shows how you might use the Interactive Writing Coach and incorporate Essay Scorer into your writing process.

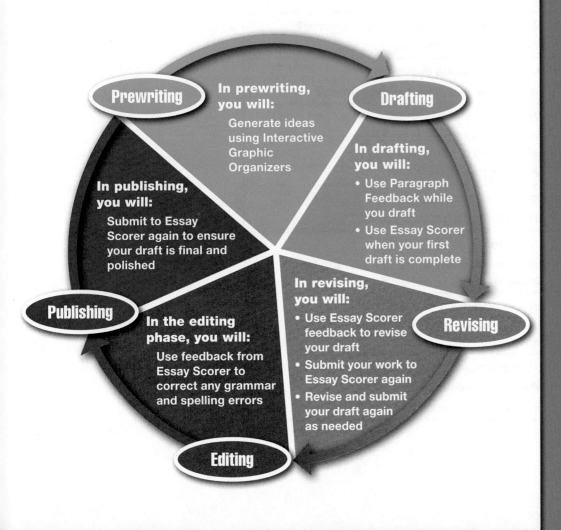

Prewriting

In prewriting, you will:

Generate ideas using Interactive Graphic Organizers

Drafting

In drafting, you will:

- Use Paragraph Feedback while you draft
- Use Essay Scorer when your first draft is complete

In publishing, you will:

Submit to Essay Scorer again to ensure your draft is final and polished

In revising, you will:

- Use Essay Scorer feedback to revise your draft
- Submit your work to Essay Scorer again
- Revise and submit your draft again as needed

Revising

Publishing

In the editing phase, you will:

Use feedback from Essay Scorer to correct any grammar and spelling errors

Editing

Paragraph Feedback With Interactive Writing Coach

Paragraph Feedback assesses the ideas and topic support for each paragraph you write. You can enter your work into Paragraph Feedback one paragraph at a time. This makes it easy to work on individual paragraphs and get new feedback as you revise each one. Here are some things that Paragraph Feedback will be able to tell you.

Overall Paragraph Support	• Does the paragraph support the main idea? • Which sentences do not support the main idea?
Transitions	• Which sentences contain transition words? • Which words are transition words?
Ideas	• How well are ideas presented? • Which sentences have too many ideas?
Sentence Length and Variety	• Which sentences are short, medium, and long? • Which sentences could be longer or shorter for better sense or variety? • Are sentences varied?
Sentence Beginnings	• How do sentences begin? • Are sentence beginnings varied?
Sentence Structure	• Are sentence structures varied? • Are there too many sentences with similar structures?
Vague Adjectives	• Are any adjectives vague or unclear? • Where are adjectives in sentences and paragraphs?
Language Variety	• Are words repeated? • Where are repeated words located? • How can word choice be improved?

Essay Scoring With Interactive Writing Coach

Essay Scorer assesses your essay. It looks at the essay as a whole, and it also evaluates individual paragraphs, sentences, and words. Essay Scorer will help you evaluate the following traits.

WRITING COACH

Online

www.phwritingcoach.com

Interactive Writing Coach™

Interactive Writing Coach provides support and guidance to help you improve your writing skills.
- Select a topic to write about from the Topic Bank.
- Use the interactive graphic organizers to narrow your topic.
- Go to Writing Coach Online and submit your work, paragraph by paragraph or as a complete draft.
- Receive immediate, personalized feedback as you write, revise, and edit your work.

Ideas	• Are the ideas significant or original? Is a clear message or unique perspective presented? • Is the main idea clearly stated? • Is the main idea supported by informative details?
Organization	• Is the organization logical? • Is the introduction clear? Is the conclusion clear? • What transitions are used, and are they effective?
Voice	• Does the writing have a unique, individual "sound" showing the personality or perspective of the writer? • Does the tone match the audience and purpose?
Word Choice	• Are precise words used? • Are vivid words used? • Do the word choices suit the purpose and audience?
Sentence Fluency	• Are sentence beginnings, lengths, and structures varied? • Do the sentences flow smoothly?
Conventions	• Is spelling correct? • Is capitalization used properly? • Is all punctuation (ending, internal, apostrophes) accurate? • Do subjects and verbs agree? • Are pronouns used correctly? • Are adjectives and adverbs used correctly? • Are plurals formed correctly? • Are commonly confused words used correctly?

Whenever you see the Interactive Writing Coach icon, you can go to Writing Coach Online and submit your writing, either paragraph by paragraph or as a complete draft, for personalized feedback and scoring.

CHAPTER 5

NONFICTION NARRATION

What Do You Remember?

Why are memories important? What might make memories interesting to other people?

To tell a story about a favorite memory, you will need to remember details of the experience. Using vivid details to describe your memories will make them more interesting to others.

Try It! Think about one of your favorite memories. Consider these questions as you participate in an extended discussion with a partner. Take turns expressing your ideas and feelings.

- What happened?
- Where were you?
- Who was there?
- How did you feel during the experience?
- What did you see, smell, touch, feel, and hear during the experience?

Review your list, and then think about how you would include these details when telling someone a story, or personal narrative, about your memory. Tell your story to a partner. As you listen to your partner's story, see if you can answer the questions.

What's Ahead

In this chapter, you will review two strong examples of a personal narrative: a Mentor Text and a Student Model. Then using the examples for guidance, you will write a personal narrative of your own.

WRITING COACH

Online

www.phwritingcoach.com

Online Journal
Try It! Record your answers and ideas in the online journal.

You can also record and save your answers and ideas on pop-up sticky notes in the eText.

Connect to the Big Questions

THE BIG QUESTION

Discuss these questions with your partner:

1 What do you think? Which experiences shape our sense of ourselves?

2 Why write? What should we put in and leave out to be accurate and honest?

NARRATIVE NONFICTION

In this chapter, you will explore a special type of narrative nonfiction: the personal narrative. In a personal narrative, you tell a story about YOU. By sharing a personal experience, you can let readers know something about who you are, and you can encourage them to look inside themselves, too.

You will develop the personal narrative by taking it through each of the steps of the writing process: prewriting, drafting, revising, editing, and publishing. You will also have an opportunity to use your personal narrative to create a biographical narrative. To preview the criteria for how your personal narrative will be evaluated, see the rubric on page 83.

FEATURE ASSIGNMENT

Narrative Nonfiction: Personal Narrative

An effective narrative nonfiction essay has these characteristics:

- An interesting story with a clear focus, or main point

- A sequence of events told in chronological, or time, order

- A well-developed plot that tells the reasons for and consequences of characters' actions

- Sensory details, or details that appeal to the senses of sight, sound, touch, smell, and taste

- Narrative devices to enhance the plot, such as dialogue and suspense

- Effective sentence structure and correct spelling, grammar, and usage

A personal narrative also includes:

- Specific details about your personal experiences

- Strong descriptions of characters, who are real people, including yourself

- A way for the reader to connect to your story

Other Forms of Narrative Nonfiction

In addition to personal narratives, there are other forms of narrative nonfiction, including:

Biographical narratives are stories that share facts about someone else's life. These stories can include the writer's ideas and feelings about the subject of the narrative.

Blogs, or comments that writers share in online forums, may include autobiographical narratives (short or long), reflections, opinions, and other types of comments. Blogs often invite responses, and they usually are not considered a "permanent" form of writing.

Diary entries, which are highly personal, include experiences, thoughts, and feelings—but the audience is private, unless writers choose to share the entries.

Memoirs contain a writer's reflections on an important person or event from his or her own life. Book-length memoirs by famous people often are quite popular.

Narrative essays use one or more biographical or autobiographical narratives to illustrate or prove a point (the main idea).

Reflective essays present personal experiences (either events that happened to the writers themselves or that they learned about from others), but they focus more on sharing the observations and insights that writers had while thinking about those experiences. Reflective essays often appear as features in magazines and newspapers.

Try It! For each audience and purpose described, choose a form, such as a diary entry, blog, or biographical narrative, that is appropriate for conveying your intended meaning to the audience. Explain your choices.

- To express your feelings about a family situation
- To comment about your experiences volunteering at the local food bank and invite community members' responses
- To tell the story of the life of the person you most admire

MENTOR TEXT

Personal Narrative

Learn From Experience

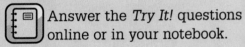 After reading the personal narrative on pages 68–69, read the numbered notes in the margins to learn about how the author presented his ideas.

Answer the *Try It!* questions online or in your notebook.

---

1 Here, the general topic, Jim, is narrowed to a clearly defined **focus**. That focus is a specific situation involving Jim.

Try It! What situation is the focus of the narrative? Describe it in your own words.

2 The author uses **chronological order** to describe what he and his brother did. That means events are given in the order in which they actually happened.

Try It! What does the author do first? What does his brother do next?

3 The author uses **dialogue** to help tell his story and let you know what his brother was like.

Try It! What does this dialogue tell you about Jim?

4 The author uses vivid **sensory details** to help readers imagine how things looked and even **smelled.**

Try It! What does the dark blue shirt smell like? How does this description help you imagine the scene?

Roommates

by Jon Scieszka

1 Jim was a pretty good roommate because he was neat and not too much of a pain in the neck like the little brothers. But man, could Jim talk.

5 I think Jim knew from the time he was four that he was going to be a lawyer. He was always trying to win an argument or make a case why you should agree with him. Jim would talk and talk and then talk some more.

His best pitch ever was the time he tried to sell me my own shirt.

10 **2** I was looking for a clean shirt to wear. Most of my clothes were in a pile on the floor of my closet. I was digging through the pile, sniffing for one that was not too smelly.

Jim pulled a clean, folded, short-sleeved shirt out of his dresser drawer.

15 "I really should save this shirt, Jon. But because you need it, I'm going to give you a deal," said Jim.

I found a shirt with only a couple of grass stains on the elbows. "What's that?" I said.

3 "This is an excellent shirt, a clean shirt, a lightweight
20 shirt, a short-sleeved shirt," said Jim. "But because you need it, I'm going to give it to you for a bargain price."

I held up a pretty good-looking dark blue shirt. **4** It smelled like the two-week-old socks still hanging on it.

"Look at this shirt. It's a great shirt. Probably the best
25 shirt," said Jim. "And I'm going to let you have it, while I wear my same old shirt, for only fifty cents."

I looked at the shirt. It was a great shirt.

"It's perfectly clean," said Jim.

He was right. It was perfectly clean.

30 I checked my pockets.

"I've only got twenty-five cents," I said.

Jim put the shirt back in his drawer.

35 "I'm afraid I can't go any lower than forty cents. It's my only clean shirt. I'm going to need it soon. I was going to do you a favor, but I can see it's not going to work out."

I tried on a brown shirt. It smelled even worse than the green shirt.

"Maybe I can get twenty-five cents off Tom," I said. "Let me see the shirt."

40 Jim handed it over. I tried it on. It fit perfectly. It was so clean. It was so . . . familiar.

"Hey," I said. "This is my shirt."

"It was in my drawer," said Jim. "You owe me fifty cents."

45 "I do not."

"You do too."

"Do not."

"Take it off."

"Make me."

50 Our legal debate quickly turned into a wrestling match. Jim jumped on me. I got him in a choke hold. We rolled around on the bedroom floor.

❺ So I think it was really me who made Jim a better, stronger lawyer.

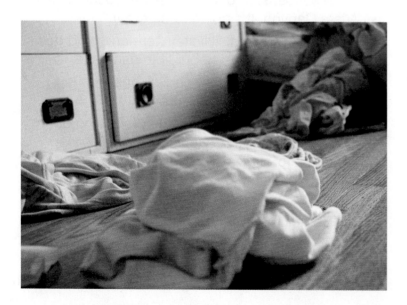

WRITING COACH

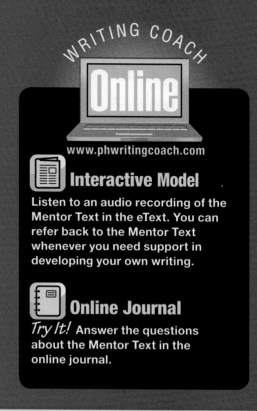

Online

www.phwritingcoach.com

Interactive Model

Listen to an audio recording of the Mentor Text in the eText. You can refer back to the Mentor Text whenever you need support in developing your own writing.

Online Journal

Try It! Answer the questions about the Mentor Text in the online journal.

❺ The surprise ending is a **narrative device** that makes the story more interesting.

Try It! Did the ending surprise you? Explain why or why not.

Extension Find another example of a personal narrative from classical or contemporary literature and compare it with this one. How are their structures and themes similar and different?

STUDENT MODEL Personal Narrative

With a small group, take turns reading this Student Model aloud. As you read, practice newly acquired vocabulary by correctly producing the word's sound. Notice how the writer mixes action with thoughts and dialogue. Also notice how the story unfolds and holds your interest. Afterward, write down a few notes that describe what you learned about yourself, others, or the world from the reading.

Use a Reader's Eye

Now, reread the Student Model. On your copy of the Student Model, use the Reader's Response Symbols to react to what you read.

Reader's Response Symbols

+ **I like where this is going.**

- **This isn't clear to me.**

? **What will happen next?**

! **Wow! That is really cool/weird/ interesting!**

Discuss the theme of the Student Model with a partner, and express your opinions, ideas, and feelings about it. Note and discuss responses that were the same for both of you, as well as responses that were different.

The BRIDGE

by Thomas Waylan

What are you afraid of? Spiders? Dogs? Writing essays? I have always been afraid of heights. I never slid down the tallest slide, climbed a tree, or went off the high diving
5 board. Or at least I didn't before last summer.

Last summer, my family drove to Canyon State Park. Now, canyons tend to involve cliffs, otherwise known as heights, and I'm afraid of heights. On the last day, my dad told
10 us, "This morning, we're going on a special, guided hike. It's called the 'Bridge Hike.'"

"What kind of bridge?" I asked, already sensing that I wasn't going to like it.

"A suspension bridge, over the spectacular
15 Vista Canyon. It's going to be great."

"No way," I said. "I'll stay here and hold down the fort." I gestured to our little campsite.

My mom shook her head. "Honey, you can't stay here by yourself."

20 So, there I was an hour later, following our guide, Alejandro, through some of the most beautiful forest I've ever seen. Sunlight fell through the branches as Alejandro pointed out hawks overhead and coyote tracks along the trail.

25 "So, tell me about this bridge we're going to cross," I said to Alejandro.

"Don't worry," he said, with a Spanish accent, looking me straight in the eye. "You can walk with

1

me. Just hold your head up, instead of looking
30 down. Trust me—you'll love it. The vista is beautiful!"

Yeah, right, I thought.

At last we came out of the forest, and I could
see a huge canyon stretching out in front of
us. And across that canyon was a narrow
35 bridge, suspended by what looked like little
wires. I stopped in my tracks. I felt sick and
weak in the knees just looking at the bridge,
but somehow I knew that I had to do it.

"You ready, son?" my dad asked.

40 I let out a big sigh and nodded. "Let's go," I
said, walking straight toward the bridge, holding
my head high as Alejandro had suggested.

When I stepped out onto the bridge I could feel
it swing slightly beneath me, but I kept going. With
45 each step, there was a slight bounce. I didn't look
down. I looked straight ahead, looking at the colors
of the canyon wall—oranges and reds—against
the bright blue of the sky. I put one foot in front of
the other, and then I was across. I had done it!

50 Ever since then, I've known that my fear of heights
would never stop me again. It wouldn't stop me
from climbing a tree or going off the high dive.

2

WRITING COACH

Online

www.phwritingcoach.com

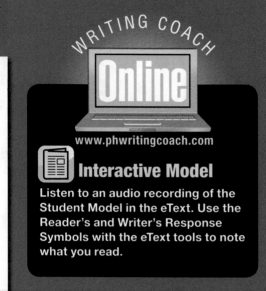

Interactive Model

Listen to an audio recording of the
Student Model in the eText. Use the
Reader's and Writer's Response
Symbols with the eText tools to note
what you read.

Use a Writer's Eye

Now evaluate the piece as a writer. On
your copy of the Student Model, use the
Writer's Response Symbols to react to
what you read. Identify places where the
student writer uses characteristics of an
effective personal narrative.

> **Writer's Response Symbols**
>
> **E.S.**   **Engaging story**
>
> **C.R.**   **Clear, well-developed conflict and resolution**
>
> **B.C.**   **Believable characters**
>
> **S.D.**   **Specific and vivid details**

Your Turn

**Feature Assignment:
Personal Narrative**

Prewriting

Plan a first draft of your personal narrative **by determining an appropriate topic.** You may select from the Topic Bank or come up with an idea of your own.

Choose From the Topic Bank

TOPIC BANK

What Are You Going to Wear? Clothing can be associated with particular events or circumstances, such as a lucky hat or a sweatshirt you always bring on a family trip. Identify a piece of clothing you associate with a special event in your life. In an autobiographical narrative, tell the story of what makes this piece of clothing special.

Gifted Think of a gift that you have been given that has special meaning for you. Write a personal narrative in which you describe the gift and why it is so important to you.

WOW! Think about an exciting experience you had. Write a personal narrative that describes your experience and explains why it was so exciting.

Choose Your Own Topic

Determine an appropriate topic on your own by using the following **range of strategies** to generate ideas.

Talk and Reflect

- Talk to some friends about things that have happened in your life. Then, ask your friends which experience they feel is the most interesting. Monitor their spoken language by asking follow-up questions to confirm your understanding.

- If you post to social networking sites, review what you have posted lately. Could you develop a post into a story starring you?

Review your responses and choose a topic.

Narrow Your Topic

Narrowing your topic will help ensure that your personal narrative has a clearly defined focus, or main point.

Apply It! Use a graphic organizer like the one shown to narrow your topic.

- Record your general topic—your broadest story idea—in the top box; then narrow your topic as you move down the chart.
- Your final box should hold your narrowest story idea, the new focus of your personal narrative.

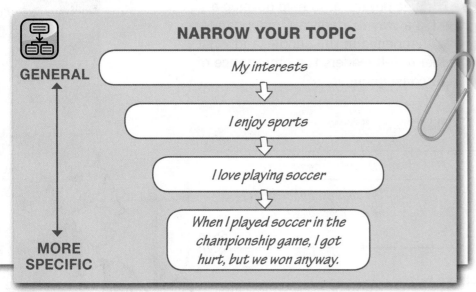

NARROW YOUR TOPIC

GENERAL

> My interests

> I enjoy sports

> I love playing soccer

> When I played soccer in the championship game, I got hurt, but we won anyway.

MORE SPECIFIC

Consider Your Audience and Purpose

Before writing, think about your audience and purpose. Consider how your narrative will convey the intended meaning to this audience. Consider the views of others as you ask these questions.

Questions for Audience	Questions for Purpose
• Who are the people in my audience? • What might the audience want to know about me—and why? • How can I communicate the importance of my experience?	• What is my purpose? Do I want my writing to be humorous, thought-provoking, or something else? • How much about myself do I want to share?

Record your answers in your writing journal.

Plan Your Piece

You will use a graphic organizer like the one shown to identify your characters and setting, and to organize your story's plot details. When it is complete, you will be ready to write your first draft.

Develop Your Focus To develop a **clearly defined focus** for your personal narrative, think about what you learned from the experience or what you want your audience to learn. In a personal narrative, your focus should be on the importance of the experience and what it taught you.

Map Out Your Story Use a graphic organizer to help develop a draft that tells what happened in a way readers can understand. Tell what happened first, what happened in the middle, and what happened at the end. Remember to tell readers **the importance of or reason for actions and their consequences.**

Plan Your Story	
Characters:	*Me and my teammates*
Setting:	*The championship game at Hart Stadium*
Beginning (Introduce the problem.)	
Middle (Tell how the problem got worse.)	*I got hurt just after halftime when somebody accidentally kicked my leg instead of the ball.*
End (Tell how the problem was resolved and why events were important.)	

Gather Details

To develop their ideas in a personal narrative, writers use some of the kinds of details shown in these examples.

- **Actions and Their Consequences:** *I thought that my teammates depended on me to win. I felt a lot of pressure, so I played more aggressively than usual. This might have led to my injury.*

- **Sensory Details:** *A shooting pain raced up my leg, and I crumpled to the ground.*

- **Dialogue:** *Coach said, "Lupita, you can't play on that leg. You're going to have to sit out the rest of the game."*

- **Suspense:** *The other team was still four points ahead. Could we catch up before the game ended?*

Good writers use a variety of strategies to engage readers and to tell their stories.

Try It! Read the Student Model excerpt and identify how the author's opening engages the readers' interest and defines the focus.

WRITING COACH

Online

www.phwritingcoach.com

Interactive Graphic Organizers

Use the interactive graphic organizers to help you create a plan for your writing.

Interactive Model

Refer back to the Interactive Model in the eText as you plan your writing.

> **STUDENT MODEL** from **The Bridge**
> page 70; lines 1–5
>
> What are you afraid of? Spiders? Dogs? Writing essays? I have always been afraid of heights. I never slid down the tallest slide, climbed a tree, or went off the high diving board. Or at least I didn't before last summer.

Apply It! Review the kinds of details that writers of personal narratives often use. Then identify at least one detail for the beginning, middle, and end of your story. Be sure to also identify details to describe the characters and setting of your personal narrative.

- Decide which details help you to show the focus of your narrative. They will be details that help to show the importance of the story's events.

- Add these details to your graphic organizer, matching each detail to the right part of the story.

- Determine which narrative devices, such as suspense and dialogue, you will use to enhance the plot, or make it stronger.

Drafting

During the drafting stage, you will start to write your ideas for your personal narrative. You will follow an outline that provides an **organizational strategy** that will help you build on ideas to write a **focused, organized, and coherent** personal narrative.

The Organization of a Personal Narrative

The chart shows an organizational strategy for a personal narrative. Look back at how the Mentor Text follows this organizational strategy. Then, use this chart to help you outline your draft.

Outline for Success

I. Beginning

See Mentor Text, p. 68.

- Interesting opening
- Introduce focus, or main idea

Grab Your Reader

- An interesting opening, such as a question or a vivid detail, will catch the reader's attention.
- A personal narrative should have a clear focus. The focus suggests why the story you are going to tell is important.

II. Middle

See Mentor Text, pp. 68–69.

- Sequence of events in chronological order, or time order
- Development of interesting plot, setting, and characters
- Narrative devices, including suspense and dialogue
- Details that appeal to the senses of sight, touch, hearing, and smell

Develop Your Plot

- Readers will be better able to understand your story if events are presented in chronological order. In this section, readers get to experience why characters do things and what the consequences of those actions are. Narrative devices, such as suspense, will help to further develop the plot.
- Readers are better able to identify with characters if dialogue to make the characters true to life is included.
- Vivid sensory details—about the characters, setting, and action—help readers feel a part of the story. These details strengthen the focus of your narrative.

III. Conclusion

See Mentor Text, p. 69.

- Resolution
- Ending that reflects the focus

Wrap It Up

- The resolution shows how the problem was solved.
- The ending shows the importance of the events that took place in the story and how those events affected you.

Start Your Draft

Use the checklist below to help complete your draft. Use the graphic organizer that shows your characters, setting, and plot outline, and the Outline for Success as guides.

While drafting, aim at writing your ideas, not on making your writing perfect. Remember, you will have the chance to improve your draft when you revise and edit.

√ Start by drafting an attention-getting **opening** sentence.

√ Continue your **beginning** by giving details that introduce the **focus** of your narrative and make the story interesting. Make your readers want to read on!

√ Develop the **middle** of your personal narrative. Introduce interesting, believable characters and develop the conflict.

√ Present specific actions and events in **chronological** order.

√ Show the **reasons** for each action—and the consequences. Sharpen the focus of the narrative by suggesting why events are important.

√ Use narrative **devices,** such as suspense and dialogue, and include plenty of sensory details to describe actions, setting, and characters.

√ At the **end** of your narrative, show the **resolution** of the conflict, or how the events worked out.

√ Finish by reflecting on why the experience was important—the **focus** of your personal narrative.

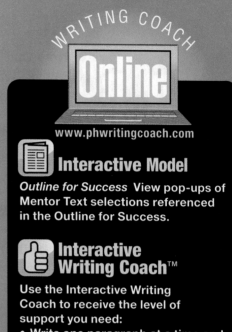

WRITING COACH

Online

www.phwritingcoach.com

Interactive Model

Outline for Success View pop-ups of Mentor Text selections referenced in the Outline for Success.

Interactive Writing Coach™

Use the Interactive Writing Coach to receive the level of support you need:
- Write one paragraph at a time and submit each one for immediate, detailed feedback.
- Write your entire first draft and submit it for immediate, personalized feedback.

Revising: Making It Better

Now that you have finished your first draft, you are ready to revise. Think about the "big picture" of **audience, purpose, and genre.** You can use the Revision RADaR strategy as a guide for making changes to improve your draft. Revision RADaR provides four major ways to improve your writing: (R) replace, (A) add, (D) delete, and (R) reorder.

Kelly Gallagher, M. Ed.

KEEP REVISION ON YOUR RADaR

Read part of the first draft of the Student Model, "The Bridge." Then look at questions the writer asked himself as he thought about how well his draft addressed issues of **audience, purpose, and genre.**

The Bridge

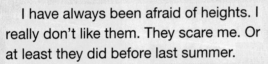

I have always been afraid of heights. I really don't like them. They scare me. Or at least they did before last summer.

Last summer my family drove to Canyon State Park. Now, canyons tend to involve cliffs, otherwise known as heights, and I am afraid of heights. I like camping and sleeping in a tent, but I wished that there were some video games to play. Until the last day when my dad told us, "This morning, we're going on a special, guided hike. It's called the 'Bridge Hike.'"

Bridges are usually very high up from the ground. I was terrified! I told my parents that there was no way I was going to go. I wanted to stay at our campsite, but they wouldn't let me.

So, there I was an hour later, following our guide, Alejandro, through some of the most beautiful forest I've ever seen.

Have I grabbed my audience's attention?

Have I included details that introduce a clearly defined focus for my personal narrative?

Have I kept the focus of my narrative sharp?

Have I included enough narrative devices to keep the story interesting?

Now look at how the writer applied Revision RADaR to write an improved second draft.

The BRIDGE

2ND DRAFT

What are you afraid of? Spiders? Dogs? Writing essays? I have always been afraid of heights. I never slid down the tallest slide, climbed a tree, or went off the high diving board. Or at least I didn't before last summer.

A *Added questions to grab the audience*

Last summer, my family drove to Canyon State Park. Now, canyons tend to involve cliffs, otherwise known as heights, and I'm afraid of heights. On the last day, my dad told us, "This morning, we're going on a special, guided hike. It's called the 'Bridge Hike.'"

R *Replaced general information with specific details*

"What kind of bridge?" I asked, already sensing that I wasn't going to like it.

D *Deleted details that didn't directly relate to the focus*

"A suspension bridge, over the spectacular Vista Canyon. It's going to be great."

 "No way," I said. "I'll stay here and hold down the fort." I gestured to our little campsite.

A *Added dialogue to develop characters and build suspense*

My mom shook her head. "Honey, you can't stay here by yourself."

So, there I was an hour later, following our guide, Alejandro, through some of the most beautiful forest I've ever seen.

 Apply It! Use your Revision RADaR to revise your draft.

- First, make sure you have included a clearly defined focus and have communicated the importance of your story's events.
- Then, apply the Revision RADaR strategy to make needed changes. Remember—you can use the steps in any order.

Look at the Big Picture

Use the chart and your analytical skills to evaluate how well each section of your personal narrative addresses **purpose, audience, and genre.** When necessary, use the suggestions in the chart to revise your narrative.

Section	Evaluate	Revise
Beginning	• Decide whether your **opening** sentence is interesting, making your audience want to read on.	• Add a question or vivid detail that engages readers' curiosity.
	• Make sure that your **focus** is clearly defined. Readers should know why you're writing about this experience.	• Add a sentence and/or details that introduce and explain the focus of your narrative.
Middle	• Review the **plot** of your narrative. Are the events clearly presented in chronological order? Have you used narrative devices, such as suspense?	• Rearrange events to ensure chronological, or time, order. Add, change, or even take out details to keep readers in suspense about the outcome.
	• Underline details that show your characters in action in one or more settings. Do **sensory details** make the characters and settings interesting and believable?	• To help readers identify with your characters and settings, add sensory details about both. Also consider adding or revising dialogue to make the characters more real.
	• Look at the middle as a whole and evaluate whether you have shown the reasons for **actions** and their consequences and importance.	• Add details and sentences that clarify meaning, showing why things happen and why they are important.
End	• Check for a well-developed **resolution**—one that clearly illustrates the focus of the narrative.	• Add or revise details to show how the problem was solved and why events were important to you.
	• Evaluate your **closing** to see if it reflects the beginning and brings the narrative full circle.	• Add or substitute language that reminds readers of the problem and shows how it was solved.

Focus on Craft: Sentence Variety

Think about **sentence variety** when you write. Sentences should have different lengths. A paragraph or essay composed of all short, simple sentences will be choppy. Using too many long, compound sentences will make your essay difficult to follow. Try to vary sentences by including both simple and compound sentences to create a rhythm and emphasize important points.

Think about variety in sentence length as you read the following sentences from the Student Model.

 **STUDENT MODEL** from **The Bridge,** page 71; lines 45–49

> I didn't look down. I looked straight ahead, looking at the colors of the canyon wall—oranges and reds—against the bright blue of the sky. I put one foot in front of the other, and then I was across. I had done it!

 Try It! Now, ask yourself these questions:

- Are the sentences in this passage different lengths? Does the rhythm of the sentences reflect the rhythm of the actions described?
- What is the impact of a short sentence followed by a long one?

 ## Fine-Tune Your Draft

Apply It! Use the revision suggestions to prepare your final draft **after rethinking how well questions of purpose, audience, and genre have been addressed.**

- **Ensure Sentence Variety** Raise the interest level by including both long, compound sentences with two main clauses with their own subjects and verbs and short, simple sentences with only one clause.
- **Clarify Meaning** Add words and phrases that clarify meaning by adding transition words that show the sequence of events and the relationship among them, such as *first, later,* and *on the other hand.*

Teacher Feedback Show your final draft to your teacher. Ask for his or her feedback and revise as necessary.

WRITING COACH

 www.phwritingcoach.com

 Video

Learn more strategies for effective writing from program author Kelly Gallagher.

Online Journal

Try It! Record your answers in the online journal.

 Interactive Model

Refer back to the Interactive Model as you revise your writing.

 Interactive Writing Coach™

Revise your draft and submit it for feedback.

Editing: Making It Correct

When you edit your work, you polish your writing and correct errors.

Before you edit, make sure that you have used a **consistent verb tense,** and have not included multiple verb tenses without a reason. Then edit your draft by correcting any errors in **grammar, mechanics, and spelling.**

WRITE GUY *Jeff Anderson, M. Ed.*

WHAT DO YOU NOTICE?

Zoom in on Conventions Focus on verb tenses as you zoom in on these lines from the Mentor Text.

 **MENTOR TEXT** from **Roommates**
pages 68–69, lines 10–12

> Most of my clothes were in a pile on the floor of my closet. I was digging through the pile, sniffing for one that was not too smelly.

> To learn more about consistent verb tense, see Chapter 14 of your Grammar Handbook.

Now, ask yourself: *When did the events in each sentence occur?*

Perhaps you said that both sentences show actions that happened in the past. You probably noticed right away that the verb *were* in the first sentence is the past tense of the verb *are.* The verb *was digging* in the second sentence is a little more unusual.

A **progressive tense** verb shows that an action is or was happening for a period of time. Progressive tense verbs consist of a form of the helping verb *be,* such as *is, are, was,* or *were,* with the present participle of the main verb, which ends in *-ing.* The past progressive tense "was digging" shows the action the author was completing for a period of time.

Partner Talk Discuss this question with a partner: *Why do you think the author used a progressive tense verb in this passage?*

Grammar Mini-Lesson: Consistent Tenses

To learn more, see page 284.

Usually, you should use one verb tense for consistency. Sometimes, though, you must change tense to show the sequence of events. For example, a writer may use the past tense when the narrator discusses events, but change to the present tense when characters speak in dialogue. **Consistent verb tense** is especially important in sentences that have more than one action and more than one clause. "She *went* to Africa, and she *will go* to India." Notice how the past tense is used consistently in the Student Model.

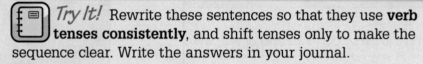 **STUDENT MODEL** from **The Bridge** page 70; lines 3–5

> I never <u>slid</u> down the tallest slide, <u>climbed</u> a tree, or <u>went</u> off the high diving board.

 Try It! Rewrite these sentences so that they use **verb tenses consistently**, and shift tenses only to make the sequence clear. Write the answers in your journal.

1. Lightning frightens me, but it's thunder that scared my dog!
2. Bowling sounds like a fun activity for the birthday party, but we went last week.

Apply It! Edit your draft for grammar, mechanics, and spelling. Check that you have used verb tenses correctly and consistently.

Use the rubric to evaluate your piece. If necessary, rethink, rewrite, or revise.

Rubric for Nonfiction Narration: Personal Narrative	Rating Scale
Ideas: How focused is your narrative on a single, important event?	Not very Very 1 2 3 4 5 6
Organization: How logical is your sequence of events?	1 2 3 4 5 6
Voice: How authentic and engaging is your voice?	1 2 3 4 5 6
Word Choice: How vivid is your word choice?	1 2 3 4 5 6
Sentence Fluency: How varied are your sentence beginnings?	1 2 3 4 5 6
Conventions: How correct is your usage of verb tenses?	1 2 3 4 5 6

Publishing

Share your experiences by publishing your personal narrative. First, get your narrative ready for presentation. Then, choose ways to **publish it for appropriate audiences**.

Wrap Up Your Presentation

Is your personal narrative handwritten or written on a computer? If your narrative is handwritten, you may need to make a new, clean copy. If so, be sure to **write legibly.** Also, be sure the title to your narrative grabs the reader's attention.

Publish Your Piece

Use the chart to identify ways to publish your personal narrative for appropriate audiences.

If your audience is...	...then publish it by...
Classmates and teachers at school	• Reading it aloud • Submitting it to the school newspaper or Web site
People in your town or around the world that you may never meet	• Posting it to a blog for people who share your interests • Submitting it to a print or online magazine that publishes first-person, true-life accounts

Reflect on Your Writing

Now that you are done with your personal narrative, read it over and use your writing journal to answer the following questions. Use specific details to describe and explain your reflections. Increase the specificity of your details based on the type of information requested.

- Does your final product accurately express your emotions?

- Are any parts weak—dull, for example, or unrealistic? If so, what can you focus on in your next writing assignment?

- In what ways did your narrative work well? How can you apply these strengths in future writing assignments?

 The Big Question: Why Write? What did you decide to put in or leave out to be accurate and honest?

Manage Your Portfolio You may wish to include your published personal narrative in your writing portfolio. If so, consider what your narrative reveals about your writing and your growth as a writer.

MAKE YOUR WRITING COUNT

Create a Storyboard for a Personal Narrative

Personal narratives can take many forms. True-life stories are often compelling enough to transfer to the movie screen. Plan a movie version of a personal narrative written by one of your peers.

Create a **storyboard,** which is a drafting tool used by filmmakers as they plan a movie. A storyboard is a series of sketches containing the elements of each scene to be filmed. Your storyboard should have a clear focus and details that communicate the importance of the event.

Your storyboard can be created with pen and ink. Present each frame on a large poster or scan each frame into presentation software.

WRITING COACH

Online
www.phwritingcoach.com

Online Journal
Reflect on Your Writing Record your answers and ideas in the online journal.

Resource
Link to resources on 21st Century Learning for help in creating a group project.

Here's your action plan.

1. Choose group roles, such as illustrator, dialogue writer, and a producer who puts the final storyboard together.

2. Working with your group to evaluate your personal narratives, choose one that you would like to make into a movie. Consider the narrative's action, characters, dialogue, and ending.

3. Create the storyboard to tell the story visually, scene by scene.

   - Find example storyboards online.
   - Make a separate frame for each scene. Include the characters, setting, and action, as well as text that describes the action and the dialogue.
   - Place the frames in the correct sequence.

4. Present the storyboard to the class, either as a series of posters or as a set of slides in a presentation software application.

Listening and Speaking Work as a team to present the storyboard in a dynamic way. For example, act out dialogue and include music and sound effects for each scene. Explain the creative process and the solid reasoning behind each scene. Afterward, ask the audience for feedback about improving the storyboard's flow.

21st Century Learning

Biographical Narrative

A **biographical narrative** tells a story about the life of someone
else. Many biographical narratives are about famous or well-
known people. A firsthand biographical narrative, on the
other hand, tells about someone the writer knows—a relative,
community member, or friend. Sometimes, blogs include
biographical narratives, as well as personal narratives.

Biographical narratives often use research from many sources. A
firsthand biographical narrative might include research, too, but
will also include details and insights from the
writer's own experience of the person.

Try It! Read this example of a
biographical narrative. Then, answer
these questions. Record your answers in
your journal.

1. Who is the **subject** of the biographical
   narrative? How do you think the writer
   feels about the subject?

2. To what **audiences** would this
   narrative probably appeal?

3. Identify the **details** the writer includes
   about the subject. What picture do
   these details give you of the subject?

4. What makes this a narrative? In other
   words, what **story elements**, such as
   plot and character development, does
   it include? How do these elements
   make you feel about the subject?

Extension Find another example of a
biographical narrative, and compare it
with this one.

Uncle Johnny's Amazing Climb

My uncle Johnny is what people in my family call
"a character." He is very short and wiry, but he
has a big personality. He also has fewer toes than
anybody I know! That's because Uncle Johnny lost
three of his toes to frostbite when he climbed Denali,
the highest mountain peak in North America.

About five years ago, Uncle Johnny went on a mountain-
climbing expedition in Alaska to climb Denali. It was by
no means his first climbing expedition. He had already
climbed just about every peak in the United States. He
always says, "If it's there, I'll climb it!"

Uncle Johnny and the expedition did make it to the top
of Denali, but on the way down, something went wrong.
A storm blew up while they were still at a high altitude.
They had to hunker down in their sleeping bags in the
shelter of a rock and wait until the blizzard cleared.
While they waited, they got very, very cold. They got so
cold that my uncle Johnny's toes got frostbitten.

Today, my uncle laughs when he talks about it. He
says that the experience cured him of a terrible case of
athlete's foot. And he still climbs mountains. In fact, he
is part of a search-and-rescue team that finds people
who get lost in the mountains. He may be physically
small, but my uncle Johnny is a big hero to me and to all
the people he rescues every year.

Create a Biographical Narrative

Follow these steps to create your own biographical narrative. To plan your biographical narrative, review the graphic organizers on pages R24–R27 and choose one that suits your needs.

Prewriting

- Choose a subject. Take a few minutes to note the names of people you know who are interesting or have qualities you admire.

- Review your list and choose the person you find most interesting or whom you think your audience would find most interesting.

- Decide what aspect of the person's life you would like to focus on and write an outline for your narrative. Jot down key events, traits, and details.

Drafting

- As you begin to draft, write a sentence that states your main idea about your subject—the focus of your essay.

- Look at the outline you made and write your narrative, organizing events and details in a logical order, such as chronological, or time order.

- Use specific details to write your ideas and feelings.

Revising and Editing

- Make sure you have identified the subject of your biography and clearly expressed your thoughts about the subject.

- Check to see if your ideas are organized in a way that makes sense so that readers can follow your narrative.

- Check that spelling, grammar, and mechanics are correct.

Publishing

- Add photographs or illustrations to your biographical narrative and create a booklet to share with others who are interested in your subject or with the subject him- or herself.

- You might also want to publish your biographical narrative as a multimedia presentation that includes text, video, and pictures of your subject. Your presentation would make a wonderful tribute to your subject.

WRITING COACH

Online

www.phwritingcoach.com

Online Journal

Try It! Record your answers in the online journal.

Interactive Graphic Organizers

Choose from a variety of graphic organizers to plan and develop your project.

Partner Talk

Before you start drafting, describe and explain the details of your biographical narrative to a partner and ask for feedback. What does your partner want to know more about?

Writing for Assessment

Many standardized tests include a prompt that asks you to write an essay about a personal experience. Respond using the characteristics of a personal narrative. (See page 66.)

 Try It! Read the **narrative nonfiction** prompt and the information on format and academic vocabulary. Use the ABCDs of On-Demand Writing to help you plan and write your essay.

Format
The prompt directs you to write a *personal narrative.* A beginning sets the scene; a middle narrates a sequence of events; and an end tells why the events were important.

Narrative Nonfiction Prompt
We all have special days we will never forget. Write a personal narrative about a day you shared with a favorite family member or friend. Describe the sequence of events and why the day was so special.

Academic Vocabulary
Remember to include a *sequence of events,* a series of related events told in chronological order, or the order in which they happened in time. Your personal narrative should include a sequence of events.

The ABCDs of On-Demand Writing

Use the following ABCDs to help you respond to the prompt.

Before you write your draft:

A ttack the prompt [1 MINUTE]

- Circle or highlight important verbs in the prompt. Draw a line from the verb to what it refers to.
- Rewrite the prompt in your own words.

B rainstorm possible answers [4 MINUTES]

- Create a graphic organizer to generate ideas.
- Use one for each part of the prompt if necessary.

C hoose the order of your response [1 MINUTE]

- Think about the best way to organize your ideas.
- Number your ideas in the order you will write about them. Cross out ideas you will not be using.

After you write your draft:

D etect errors before turning in the draft [1 MINUTE]

- Carefully reread your writing.
- Make sure that your response makes sense and is complete.
- Look for spelling, punctuation, and grammar errors.

More Prompts for Practice

Apply It! Respond to Prompts 1 and 2 by writing **personal narratives** that each have a **clearly defined focus** and that **communicate the importance of or reason for actions and/or consequences.** As you write, be sure to:

- Identify an appropriate audience for your intended purpose
- Organize the sequence of events in chronological order
- Fully develop the plot, setting, and characters
- Include narrative devices, such as suspense and dialogue
- Include sensory details

Prompt 1 Write a personal narrative about a family celebration. It could be a special holiday, family dinner, or trip to the park. Tell what happened and why this event was meaningful or important.

Prompt 2 What day stands out as the best day in your life so far? Why? Write a personal narrative about that day. Tell what happened and what made it so great. Include sensory details and your thoughts about the day.

More Strategies for Writing for Assessment

- Consider several possible topics and quickly list details that you might use in your response. Then, choose the topic for which you have the strongest ideas.
- If you do not understand any words in the prompt, use context clues to help you determine the meaning.
- Be sure to follow the ABCDs of writing to a prompt. Planning is an important part of writing. Don't just start writing right away.
- Make sure to reread your piece after you have completed it. This will give you time to find and correct errors. If you are in a timed situation, be sure to leave enough time for this step.

WRITING COACH

Online

www.phwritingcoach.com

Interactive Writing Coach™

Plan your response to the prompt. If you are using the prompt for practice, write one paragraph at a time or your entire draft and then submit it for feedback. If you are using the prompt as a timed test, write your entire draft and then submit it for feedback.

Remember **ABCD**

Attack the prompt

Brainstorm possible answers

Choose the order of your response

Detect errors before turning in the draft

CHAPTER 6

FICTION NARRATION

What's the Story?

What is happening in the baseball game? What story can you tell about what happened shortly before this photograph was taken?

Many stories have realistic settings. Believable details about setting, such as the weather or specifics about the baseball field, help get the reader interested and add to the story. Conflict is also important. It is the central problem of the story.

Try It! Think about how each of the people in the photograph reacted in the moments before the photograph was taken. Write notes about each of their reactions.

Consider these questions as you participate in an extended discussion with a partner. Take turns expressing your ideas and feelings.

- What details can you tell about the setting of the game?
- What is the conflict during this part of the game?
- Who are the characters here and what are they like?

Review your notes. Use your notes to tell a story about how each player reacted to the situation. Be sure to use details to make your story believable.

What's Ahead

In this chapter, you will review two strong examples of a short story: a Mentor Text and a Student Model. Then, using the examples as guidance, you will write a short story of your own.

WRITING COACH

Online

www.phwritingcoach.com

 Online Journal
Try It! Record your answers and ideas in the online journal.

You can also record and save your answers and ideas on pop-up sticky notes in the eText.

Connect to the Big Questions

Discuss these questions with your partner:

1 **What do you think?** What can we learn from playing games?

2 **Why write?** What can fiction do better than nonfiction?

SHORT STORY

A short story is a brief work of fiction that presents characters in a conflict that is first developed and then resolved. In this chapter, you will explore a special type of short story, realistic fiction. Like other kinds of fiction, realistic fiction is untrue. However, the characters, setting, and conflict should all feel true to life. Realistic fiction closely resembles real life and often takes place in the present.

You will develop a realistic short story by taking it through each of the steps of the writing process: prewriting, drafting, revising, editing, and publishing. You will also have an opportunity to create an audio script. To preview the criteria for how your realistic short story will be evaluated, see the rubric on page 111.

FEATURE ASSIGNMENT

Short Story: Realistic Short Story

An effective short story has these characteristics:

- **Characters** who are well-developed and interesting. Well-developed characters have realistic thoughts and actions.

- A believable **setting,** or the time and place in which a story takes place, created using **sensory details.** Sensory details use the five senses to help readers experience the story.

- A clearly defined **focus,** or main idea, and **plot,** or events in the story centered on a **conflict,** or problem

- A definite **point of view,** or perspective from which the story is told. Stories usually use the first-person or third-person point of view.

- **Dialogue** that develops the story and moves the action along

- **Effective sentence structure** and correct spelling, grammar, and usage

A realistic short story also includes:

- Characters, setting, and dialogue that seem real and a plot that could actually happen

- A contemporary **setting** that most readers will recognize

Other Forms of Fiction

In addition to realistic short stories, there are other forms of fiction, including:

Fantasy stories stretch the imagination and take readers to unreal worlds. Animals may talk, people may fly, or characters may have superhuman powers.

Historical fiction tells about imaginary people living in real places and times in history. Usually, the main characters are fictional people who know and interact with famous people in history and participate in important historical events.

Mystery stories focus on unexplained or strange events that one of the characters tries to solve. These stories are often full of suspense and surprises.

Myths and legends are traditional stories that different cultures have told to explain natural events, human nature, or the origins of things. They often include gods and goddesses from ancient times and heroes who do superhuman things.

Science fiction stories focus on real or imagined developments in science and technology and their effects on the way people think and live. Space travel, robots, and life in the future are popular topics for science fiction.

Try It! For each audience and purpose described, choose a form, such as historical fiction, science fiction, or fantasy, that is appropriate for conveying your intended meaning to the audience. Explain your choices.

- To tell your social studies classmates the events of a significant historical event
- To show your science classmates what life on the moon is like
- To tell how a teenager might handle moving to a new community

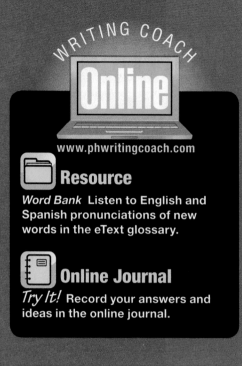

MENTOR TEXT

Realistic Short Story

Learn From Experience

 Read the realistic short story on pages 94–97. As you read, take notes to develop your understanding of basic sight and English vocabulary. Then, read the numbered notes in the margins to learn about how the author presented her ideas.

Answer the *Try It!* questions online or in your notebook.

---

❶ This **clearly defined focus** tells what has happened and how it affects the characters. The focus sparks interest in reading more and makes it easier to understand the story.

Try It! Sum up what happened before the story began. Why is the mother busy tidying up the farm?

❷ Throughout the story, the narrator, or voice telling the story, is the daughter of a family living on a farm. The narrator tells what happens from her **point of view.**

Try It! Is the story told in the first-person point of view or the third-person point of view? How can you tell?

Extension Find another example of a realistic short story, and compare it with this one. Analyze what the selections tell you about the cultural contexts in which they were written.

From
A Gentleman's Agreement

by Elizabeth Jolley

❶ Grandpa was an old man and though his death was expected it was unexpected really and it was a shock to Mother to find she suddenly had eighty-seven acres to sell. And there was the house too. She had a terrible lot
5 to do as she decided to sell the property herself and, at the same time, she did not want to let down the people at South Heights. There was a man interested to buy the land, Mother had kept him up her sleeve for years, ever since he had stopped once by the bottom paddock to ask if it was for
10 sale. At the time Mother would have given her right arm to be able to sell it and she promised he should have first refusal if it ever came on the market.

We all three, Mother and myself and my brother, went out at the weekend to tidy things up. We lost my brother
15 and then we suddenly saw him running and running and shouting, his voice lifting up in the wind as he raced up the slope of the valley.

"I do believe he's laughing! He's happy!" Mother just stared at him and she looked so happy too.
20 ❷ I don't think I ever saw the country look so lovely before.

The tenant was standing by the shed. The big tractor had crawled to the doorway like a sick animal and had stopped there, but in no time my brother had it going.

25 ❸ It seemed there was nothing my brother couldn't do. Suddenly after doing nothing in his life he was driving the tractor and making fire breaks, he started to paint the sheds and he told Mother what fencing posts and wire to order. All these things had to be done before the sale could go
30 through. We all had a wonderful time in the country. I kept wishing we could live in the house, all at once it seemed lovely there at the top of the sunlit meadow. But I knew that however many acres you have they aren't any use unless you have money too. I think we were all thinking this but
35 no one said anything though Mother kept looking at my brother and the change in him.

There was no problem about the price of the land, this man, he was a doctor, really wanted it and Mother really needed the money.

40 "You might as well come with me," Mother said to me on the day of the sale. "You can learn how business is done." So we sat in this lawyer's comfortable room and he read out from various papers and the doctor signed things and Mother signed. Suddenly she said to them, "You know my
45 father really loved his farm but he only managed to have it late in life and then he was never able to live there because of his illness." The two men looked at her.

❹ "I'm sure you will understand," she said to the doctor, "with your great love of the land, my father's love for his
50 valley. I feel if I could live there just to plant one crop and stay while it matures, my father would rest easier in his grave."

"Well I don't see why not." The doctor was really a kind man. The lawyer began to protest, he seemed quite angry.

"It's not in the agreement," he began to say. But the
55 doctor silenced him, he got up and came round to Mother's side of the table.

"I think you should live there and plant your one crop and stay while it matures," he said to her. "It's a gentleman's agreement," he said.

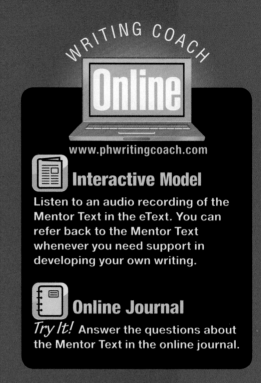

WRITING COACH

Online

www.phwritingcoach.com

Interactive Model

Listen to an audio recording of the Mentor Text in the eText. You can refer back to the Mentor Text whenever you need support in developing your own writing.

Online Journal

Try It! Answer the questions about the Mentor Text in the online journal.

❸ The author focuses on the **character** of the brother in this passage. Both the narrator and her mother notice a change in him.

Try It! What was the brother like in the past? What is he like now?

❹ In a gentleman's agreement, people promise to keep an agreement out of a sense of honor. This **dialogue** about the agreement introduces a twist in the plot.

Try It! What deal does the mother work out in the agreement? What does the agreement suggest about the culture, or traditions, of the people in the story?

⑤ The **plot line,** or sequence of events in the story, seems to move toward a happy ending here, but the story is not over yet.

Try It! Why is each person who is part of the agreement satisfied with it?

⑥ The author uses **sensory details** in this paragraph to help readers picture the **setting,** or where the story takes place.

Try It! Describe where the story takes place. Then give two specific details that describe the boxes of seedlings.

⑦ The **plot** moves toward the climax, or moment of highest tension, when the mother explains what she plans to plant.

Try It! Why has the mother chosen to plant jarrah forest seedlings?

60 "That's the best sort," Mother smiled up at him and they shook hands.

"I wish your crop well," the doctor said, still shaking her hand.

⑤ The doctor made the lawyer write out a special clause
65 which they all signed. And then we left, everyone satisfied. Mother had never had so much money and the doctor had the valley at last but it was the gentleman's agreement that was the best part.

My brother was impatient to get on with improvements.
70 "There's no rush," Mother said.

"Well one crop isn't very long," he said.

"It's long enough," she said.

⑥ So we moved out to the valley and the little weatherboard cottage seemed to come to life very quickly
75 with the pretty things we chose for the rooms.

"It's nice whichever way you look out from these little windows," Mother was saying and just then her crop arrived. The carter set down the boxes along the edge of the verandah and, when he had gone, my brother began
80 to unfasten the hessian coverings. Inside were hundreds of seedlings in little plastic containers.

"What are they?" he asked.

"Our crop," Mother said.

⑦ "Yes I know, but what is the crop? What are these?"
85 "Them," said Mother, she seemed unconcerned, "oh they're a jarrah forest," she said.

"But that will take years and years to mature," he said.

"I know," Mother said. "We'll start planting tomorrow. We'll pick the best places and clear and plant as we
90 go along."

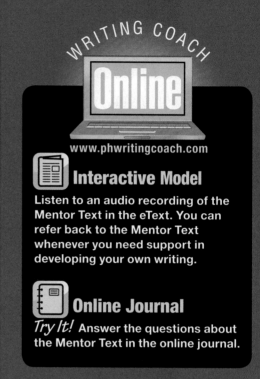

WRITING COACH

Online

www.phwritingcoach.com

Interactive Model

Listen to an audio recording of the Mentor Text in the eText. You can refer back to the Mentor Text whenever you need support in developing your own writing.

Online Journal

Try It! Answer the questions about the Mentor Text in the online journal.

8 The author returns to the **character** of the doctor in this paragraph as the narrator imagines how he might respond to the mother's clever trick.

Try It! How does the narrator imagine the doctor will respond?

9 The story ends with a twist as the final outcome is revealed in the **resolution.**

Try It! How does the ending of this story compare to that of other stories you have read? Who is the true "gentleman" in the agreement: the mother or the doctor? Explain.

"But what about the doctor?" I said. **8** Somehow I could picture him pale and patient by his car out on the lonely road which went through his valley. I seemed to see him looking with longing at his paddocks and his meadows and at his
95 slopes of scrub and bush.
9 "Well he can come on his land whenever he wants to and have a look at us," Mother said. "There's nothing in the gentleman's agreement to say he can't."

STUDENT MODEL

Realistic Short Story

With a small group, take turns reading this Student Model aloud. As you read, identify the elements of fiction. Look out for realistic ideas, characters, and events in the story.

 ## Use a Reader's Eye

Now, reread the Student Model. On your copy of the Student Model, use the Reader's Response Symbols to react to what you have read.

Reader's Response Symbols

+ That is a good description.

− This isn't clear to me.

! This is really cool/weird/ interesting!

? What will happen next?

Review the Student Model and participate in an extended discussion with a partner. Express your opinions and share your responses to the Student Model. Pay close attention to how the writer introduces characters, setting, and plot.

Playing to Win

by Monica LaRocque

"Wow, Lara. For someone who won the Most Valuable Player Award last year, you sure blew it today," said Tony, pulling off his sweaty mitt.

5 "Yeah. Thanks for helping us lose the game, Lara," said Suze, as she stomped off the hot, dusty field.

"Geez! I'm the best player on this team. I was just having an off day," Lara mumbled. "What crummy friends! They don't have to be so rude." Sure, Tony had called the fly ball, but going after 10 everything was what made Lara the best. If Tony hadn't been in the way, they wouldn't have run into each other and Lara would have made a really great catch. And they had the nerve to be mad at *her!*

Later that day, Lara and her little brother were 15 playing Total Athlete 3 in their cozy and sunny living room. The smell of their dad's famous meatballs came from the kitchen. They had already passed the track-and-field level and were now working together to beat the game at doubles 20 tennis. They were losing pretty badly. Gary kept going for the balls in Lara's part of the court.

"Gary, cut it out! You can't play your position and my position," Lara snapped. "We have to play together. You have to trust that I'll cover my zone!"

25 "Geez, Lara!" Gary replied. "I was just having fun trying to get to all the balls."

Lara looked at Gary, and suddenly it hit her: She had been the one at fault at the baseball game earlier in the day. She had been the one who 30 was showing off. And she had been the one who hadn't trusted her teammate to make the catch.

1

WRITING COACH

Online

www.phwritingcoach.com

Interactive Model

Listen to an audio recording of the Student Model in the eText. Use the Reader's and Writer's Response Symbols with the eText tools to note what you read.

At the game the following week, Lara stood in the outfield in the sweltering afternoon sun, a trickle of sweat dripping down her back. At the top of the 35 ninth with two outs, Lara caught a line drive deep in left field. She threw the ball to Suze at shortstop. Suze made a great throw to the catcher and got an out at home plate to win the game. The crowd roared, and Suze and Tony ran over to Lara.

40 "I thought for sure you were going to try to make that throw to home plate yourself!" exclaimed Tony.

"Nah," Lara said, a little embarrassed. "Great play, Suze. And look, Tony, I'm really sorry about the other day. I was way out of line. Thanks for not 45 holding it against me."

"Of course not!" Tony said.

At the exact same time, Suze said, "We're teammates, aren't we?"

They all laughed as they walked back across 50 the field.

Use a Writer's Eye

Now, evaluate the piece as a writer. On your copy of the Student Model, use the Writer's Response Symbols to react to what you have read. Identify places where the student writer uses characteristics of an effective realistic short story.

Writer's Response Symbols

R.D. Realistic and believable dialogue

S.D. Vivid sensory details that create and suggest mood

W.C. Well-developed, interesting characters

E.S. Engaging story

2

Your Turn

Feature Assignment:
Realistic Short Story

Prewriting

Plan a first draft of your realistic short story by **determining an appropriate topic.** You can select from the Topic Bank or come up with an idea of your own.

Choose From the Topic Bank

TOPIC BANK

Achieving a Goal Think about all the hard work that goes into achieving a goal. Write a realistic short story about a character who accomplishes a goal in the face of many problems.

A Misunderstanding Even friends misunderstand one another. Sometimes people cannot see eye to eye. Write a realistic short story about two friends who have a misunderstanding.

Learning a Lesson Lessons are not always learned in school. They can be learned in very unlikely places. Sometimes surprising lessons are the best ones. Write a realistic short story about a character who learns a lesson he or she was not expecting.

Choose Your Own Topic

Determine an appropriate topic on your own by using the following **range of strategies** to generate ideas.

List and Discuss

- Jot down notes about some of the best stories you have read. What were they about? What were some of the problems the characters in the stories had to face?
- Write a list of some of the funny, sad, or exciting things you have experienced. How did those experiences change you?
- With a group of classmates, talk about ideas, events, and characters you would like to see in a story.

Review your responses and choose a topic.

Narrow Your Topic

It is important that the topic of your story be focused. A focused topic will help you choose only necessary characters and events.

Apply It! Use a graphic organizer like the one shown to narrow your topic.

- Write your general topic in the top box, and keep narrowing your topic as you move down the chart.
- Your last box should hold your narrowest or "smallest" topic, the new focus of your story.

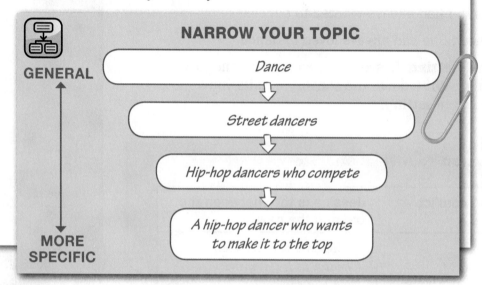

NARROW YOUR TOPIC

GENERAL

Dance

↓

Street dancers

↓

Hip-hop dancers who compete

↓

A hip-hop dancer who wants to make it to the top

MORE SPECIFIC

Consider Your Audience and Purpose

Before writing, think about your audience and purpose. Ask yourself what your audience needs and wants to know about your realistic short story.

Questions for Audience	Questions for Purpose
• Who will read my story? • What kinds of story lines will my audience find realistic? • What background information will my audience need to understand my realistic fiction story?	• Why am I writing this story? What do I want my audience to question, notice, or learn? • How can I keep my audience's attention? • What point of view is best for this story?

Record your answers in your writing journal.

Plan Your Piece

You will use a graphic organizer like the one shown to establish a setting, characters, and plot events for your imaginative story. When it is complete, you will be ready to write your first draft.

Outline Your Story Use a graphic organizer like this one to map out an interesting story with a clearly defined **focus, plot, and point of view**. The plot or action should move toward an ending that makes sense. Be sure to decide the **point of view** for your story. Will the main character be the narrator, or will the narrator be a voice outside of the story? Look at these examples:

First-person point of view: I had always wanted to dance.

Third-person point of view: She had always loved to dance.

Develop Characters and Setting Leave space on your outline to plan for realistic characters. Write down the **sensory details** you will use to create a **believable setting**.

Develop Your Realistic Story

Main character and conflict	Jessica is torn between the old and the new.
Beginning *Introduce an interesting conflict and a clear setting.*	• *Jessica is torn between her ballet training and hip-hop dancing.* • *The story takes place…*
Middle *Use sensory details and dialogue to describe the story's events.*	• *First…* • *Then…*
End *Show what happens after the problem is solved and how the characters are changed by the story.*	• *Jessica starts a hip-hop dance class at her ballet school.* • *The characters learn that there is value in both the old and the new.* • *Jessica wins the top competition with her new friends while her old friends cheer them on.*

Gather Details

Writers use a variety of different literary devices to enhance their short stories. Look at these examples.

- **Dialogue:** *"Jess, I can't believe what you're saying to me," Callie whispered. "I know, Cal. I can hardly believe it myself."*
- **Interesting Comparisons:** *Jessica felt a thousand butterflies fluttering in her stomach, and she wished they would settle down.*
- **Descriptions:** *The tiny community center was nothing like the academy's high-tech studios.*

Sensory details help readers feel like they are "in the story." Look at these examples.

- **Sight:** *She squinted her eyes against the bright sun.*
- **Smell:** *Kate wrinkled her nose at the stench of the garbage.*
- **Sound:** *The constant tap, tap, tapping made his brain rattle.*
- **Taste:** *Julio thought of home and cinnamon peach pie.*
- **Touch:** *The fabric was so rough that it felt like sandpaper.*

Try It! Read the Student Model excerpt and identify which kinds of details the author uses.

 **STUDENT MODEL** from **Playing to Win**
page 98; lines 1–5

> "Wow, Lara. For someone who won the Most Valuable Player Award last year, you sure blew it today," said Tony, pulling off his sweaty mitt.
>
> "Yeah. Thanks for helping us lose the game, Lara," said Suze, as she stomped off the hot, dusty field.

Apply It! Review the types of details a short story writer can use. Then use **sensory details** and **dialogue,** as well as other literary devices, to develop each section of your story.

- Use these elements to create a **clear focus, plot,** and **point of view** and to **develop the story** through the beginning, middle, and end of the story.
- Then add these details to your graphic organizer. Be sure to **use sensory details to help create a specific and believable setting** and interesting characters.

WRITING COACH

Online

www.phwritingcoach.com

Interactive Graphic Organizers

Use the interactive graphic organizers to help you create a plan for your writing.

Interactive Model

Refer back to the Interactive Model in the eText as you plan your writing.

Drafting

During the drafting stage, you will start to write your ideas for your realistic short story. You will follow an outline that provides an appropriate **organizational strategy** that will help you build on ideas to write a **focused, organized, and coherent** realistic short story.

The Organization of a Realistic Short Story

The chart shows an organizational strategy for a short story. Look back at how the Mentor Text follows this organizational strategy. Then, use this chart to help you outline your draft.

Outline for *Success*

Beginning See Mentor Text, p. 94.

- Focus and plot
- Clear point of view
- Setting and characters

Middle See Mentor Text, pp. 94–96.

- Events keep the plot moving toward a climax
- Engaging dialogue
- Climax, when the problem is faced and solved

End See Mentor Text, pp. 96–97.

- Resolution
- The effect of the outcome

Set the Tone

- The focus and plot of the story tells the main character's goal.
- The point of view of your story determines if you will have a narrator tell the story about the characters or if you will have one of the characters tell the story.
- The setting often provides specific details about the time and place of your story as well as information about each character.

Build Suspense

- The plot moves toward a climax when the main character tries and fails to solve the problem a few times.
- Dialogue can show the characters' actions and thoughts in a lively way.
- The climax is the most interesting part of the story. It builds intensity by keeping readers unsure of what will happen.

Wrap it Up

- The resolution satisfies readers' curiosity by showing that the problem has been resolved.
- Readers will enjoy a sense of closure if they have a description of the outcome and its effects on the characters.

Start Your Draft

Use the checklist to help you complete your draft. Use the graphic organizer that shows the plot and setting, and the Outline for Success as guides.

While drafting, aim at writing your ideas, not on making your writing perfect. Remember, you will have the chance to improve your draft when you revise and edit.

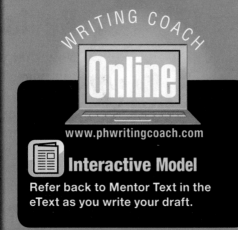

WRITING COACH

Online

www.phwritingcoach.com

Interactive Model
Refer back to Mentor Text in the eText as you write your draft.

√ Start drafting with the **beginning** of your realistic short story. Decide on a topic and a perspective from which to tell the story in order to clearly define the focus and **point of view.**

√ Use sensory details to create a specific and **believable setting** and characters.

√ Introduce the character's **goal** and problem.

√ Create a well-defined **plot** in the **middle.** Build suspense by dropping hints about what will happen next. As you draft, use realistic details to help readers feel like they are "in the story."

√ Use literary devices such as **dialogue** to develop the story and keep the reader interested.

√ Keep the action moving with events that are linked to solving the **problem** in the story. Make the reader feel the importance of finding a solution to the problem.

√ Make the **climax** emotional.

√ **End** by showing what happens after the problem has been **solved.**

√ Describe how the characters' **decisions** and actions have taught them something or changed their lives.

Revising: Making It Better

Now that you have finished your first draft, you are ready to revise. Think about the "big picture" of **audience, purpose, and genre.** You can use your Revision RADaR as a guide for making changes to improve your draft. Revision RADaR provides four major ways to improve your writing: (R) replace, (A) add, (D) delete, and (R) reorder.

Kelly Gallagher, M. Ed.

KEEP REVISION ON YOUR RADAR

Read part of the first draft of the Student Model, **"Playing to Win"**. Then look at questions the writer asked herself as she thought about how well her draft addressed issues of **audience, purpose, and genre**.

Playing to Win

1ST DRAFT

Later that day, Lara and her little brother were playing Total Athlete 3. They had already passed the track-and-field level and were now working together to beat the game at doubles tennis. They were losing pretty badly. Gary kept going for the balls in her part of the court.

Gary was really annoying Lara. He was playing all the positions and hogging the ball.

"Geez, Lara!" Gary replied. "I was just having fun trying to get to all the balls."

Lara looked at Gary, and suddenly it hit her: She had been the one at fault at the baseball game earlier in the day. I had been the one who was showing off. And I had been the one who hadn't trusted my teammate to make the catch. I didn't believe he could do it without me.

> *Do I show readers a believable setting?*

> *Can I use dialogue here to help move the story forward?*

> *Is my point of view clear?*

Now, look at how the writer applied Revision RADaR to write an improved second draft.

Playing to Win

2ND DRAFT

Later that day, Lara and her little brother were playing Total Athlete 3 in their cozy and sunny living room. The smell of their dad's famous meatballs came from the kitchen. They had already passed the track-and-field level and were now working together to beat the game at doubles tennis. They were losing pretty badly. Gary kept going for the balls in her part of the court.

"Gary, cut it out! You can't play your position and my position," Lara snapped. "We have to play together. You have to trust that I'll cover my zone!"

"Geez, Lara!" Gary replied. "I was just having fun trying to get to all the balls."

Lara looked at Gary, and suddenly it hit her: She had been the one at fault at the baseball game earlier in the day. She had been the one who was showing off. And she had been the one who hadn't trusted her teammate to make the catch.

A *Added sensory details to create a specific setting*

R *Replaced narration with dialogue to tell the story in a more interesting way*

R *Replaced first-person pronouns for third-person pronouns to keep a consistent point of view*

D *Deleted unnecessary sentence*

WRITING COACH

Online

www.phwritingcoach.com

Video

Learn more strategies for effective writing from program author Kelly Gallagher.

Apply It! Use your Revision RADaR to revise your draft.

- First, determine if you have established a clearly defined focus, plot, and point of view.
- Check that you have built a specific setting through sensory details. Look for places to strengthen your story with dialogue.
- Then, apply the Revision RADaR strategy to make needed changes. Remember—you can use the steps in the strategy in any order.

Look at the Big Picture

Use the chart and your analytical skills to evaluate how well each section of your realistic short story addresses **purpose, audience, and genre.** When necessary, use the suggestions in the chart to revise your piece.

Section	Evaluate	Revise
Beginning	• Check the opening. Is the story's **focus** clear?	• Rewrite sentences to create a clearly defined focus. Use strong nouns and verbs to describe the problem and main character.
	• Is the **point of view** both clear and consistent?	• Avoid confusing your reader—make sure that you are using only one point of view throughout the story.
	• Have sensory details been used to establish the **setting**?	• Add descriptive language to create a specific, believable setting that will engage the reader's interest.
	• Have well-developed **characters** been introduced?	• Introduce interesting characters that are realistic and believable.
Middle	• Check that the **action** is related to the problem and creates emotion in the reader.	• To strengthen your plot, show the character struggling to make a decision.
	• Underline details that build **suspense.** Draw a line from each one to the climax.	• Rearrange details and events to keep your reader interested and guessing. Take out or replace details that don't help build up to the climax.
	• Use **dialogue** and other literary devices that develop the story.	• Delete scenes or dialogue that do not move the story forward. Replace dull narration with dialogue.
End	• Check that the **problem** has been solved.	• Wrap up loose ends by explaining the result of what the character did.
	• Make sure you described how the character's actions have affected the **resolution.**	• Answer questions such as *Has the character been changed in some way? What has he or she learned from the experience?*

Focus on Craft: Improve Transitions

Clear **transitions,** or changes, from one idea to another allow readers to follow the plot line. Transition words like *first, after,* and *before* are like signals that tell the reader what kind of information is coming. Transitions help with the organization of a story and telling events in order. Look at these examples:

- The word *next* signals to readers that something is about to happen.
- The word *or* signals a choice.

Transitions can connect ideas within a sentence or paragraph, between sentences or paragraphs, or between sections of a story.

 STUDENT MODEL from **Playing to Win**
page 98; lines 14–20

Later that day, Lara and her little brother were playing Total Athlete 3 in their cozy and sunny living room. They had already passed the track-and-field level and were now working together to beat the game at doubles tennis. They were losing pretty badly.

 Try It! Read the passage. Then, ask yourself these questions. Record your answers in your journal.

- What do the words *later, already,* and *now* signal to readers?
- How would the reader's understanding change if the last sentence was moved to the beginning of the passage?

Fine-Tune Your Draft

Apply It! Use the revision suggestions to prepare your final draft after rethinking how well questions of **purpose, audience, and genre** have been addressed.

- **Improve Transitions** Use transitions to organize your imaginative story. Add, delete, combine, or rearrange sentences or paragraphs to improve transitions.

- **Enhance Style** Your style is the unique way you communicate. Improve the style of your writing by adding interesting comparisons or sentence patterns.

Peer Feedback Read your final draft to a group of peers. Ask them to comment on your plot and characters. Think about their responses and revise your final draft as needed.

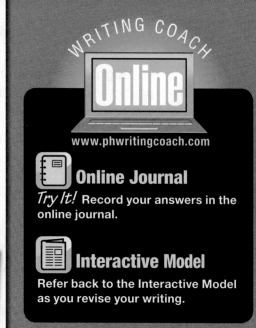

WRITING COACH

Online

www.phwritingcoach.com

Online Journal

Try It! Record your answers in the online journal.

Interactive Model

Refer back to the Interactive Model as you revise your writing.

Editing: Making It Correct

Editing means polishing your writing. It can be helpful to read your draft out loud to listen for places where the writing needs correction.

Before you edit, think about using **prepositional phrases to convey location, time, and direction or to provide details**. They can also be used as **transitions**. Then correct any errors in **grammar, mechanics, and spelling**.

WRITE GUY *Jeff Anderson, M. Ed.*

WHAT DO YOU NOTICE?

Zoom in on Conventions Focus on prepositional phrases as you zoom in on this sentence from the Mentor Text.

MENTOR TEXT from **A Gentleman's Agreement** page 95; lines 40–41

> "You might as well come with me," Mother said to me on the day of the sale.

Now ask yourself: *Which of the phrases in the sentence expresses time?*

Perhaps you said that *on the day* shows time.

In this sentence, *on* is a **preposition**. A preposition relates one word to another in a sentence in order to convey, or express, information about location, time, or direction or provide details.

A **prepositional phrase** contains a preposition and a noun or pronoun that is the object of the preposition, plus its modifiers. The prepositional phrases in the Mentor Text are *with me, to me, on the day,* and *of the sale*. The phrases *with me* and *to me* convey direction, *on the day* conveys time, and *of the sale* provides a detail.

Partner Talk Discuss this question with a partner: *How might an author use prepositions to describe the setting of a short story?*

To learn more about prepositional phrases, see Chapter 19 of your Grammar Handbook.

Grammar Mini-Lesson:
Prepositional Phrases

Prepositional phrases can also be used as **transitions** between ideas. A transition appears at the beginning of a sentence and is followed by a comma. Notice how the Student Model author uses a prepositional phrase as a transition.

 **STUDENT MODEL** | from **Playing to Win**
page 99; lines 32–34

At the game the following week, Lara stood in the outfield in the sweltering afternoon sun, a trickle of sweat dripping down her back.

 Try It! Copy each sentence into your journal. Underline the prepositional phrases in each sentence, and then place a comma after each phrase used as a transition.

In the meantime a new game had started in Field Park.

Since the season ended the players have more time for other activities.

Apply It! Edit your draft for grammar, mechanics, and spelling. If necessary, rewrite some sentences to ensure that you have used prepositional phrases as transitions to organize your writing.

Use the rubric to evaluate your piece. If necessary, rethink, rewrite, or revise.

Rubric for Short Story: Realistic Short Story	Rating Scale
Ideas: How well have you developed your characters and plot?	Not very　　Very 1　2　3　4　5　6
Organization: How clearly organized are the events in your story?	1　2　3　4　5　6
Voice: How well does your style engage the reader?	1　2　3　4　5　6
Word Choice: How effective is your word choice in creating setting and characters?	1　2　3　4　5　6
Sentence Fluency: How well have you used transitions to help readers follow the plot?	1　2　3　4　5　6
Conventions: How correct are your prepositional phrases?	1　2　3　4　5　6

To learn more, see Chapter 19.

WRITING COACH

 Online

www.phwritingcoach.com

 Video
Learn effective editing techniques from program author Jeff Anderson.

Online Journal
Try It! Record your answers in the online journal.

Interactive Model
Refer back to the Interactive Model as you edit your writing.

Publishing

Share your realistic story with others by publishing it. First, get the story ready to present. Then choose a way to **publish your work for an appropriate audience.**

Wrap Up Your Presentation

Is your short story handwritten or written on a computer? If you use a computer, be sure to choose a readable font. Even though a font can be used to communicate style, the purpose in publishing is to share your writing with readers. That means you must choose a plain, easy-to-read font.

Publish Your Piece

Use this chart to identify a way to publish your written work.

If your audience is...	...then publish it by...
Family or friends	• Presenting it as an audio or video recording of a drama • Reading it aloud at a family and friend gathering
Students or adults in your school	• Posting it to a literary blog and allowing peer and teacher responses • Creating a class Web site of realistic stories for the school library

Reflect on Your Writing

Now that you are done with your short story, read it over and use your writing journal to answer these questions. Use specific details to describe and explain your reflections. Increase the specificity of your details based on the type of information requested.

- What did you most enjoy about writing a realistic short story? Why?
- What did you find to be the most difficult? Why?

The Big Question: Why Write? What can fiction do better than non-fiction?

Manage Your Portfolio You may wish to include your published realistic short story in your writing portfolio. If so, consider what this piece reveals about your writing and your growth as a writer.

MAKE YOUR WRITING COUNT

Give a Dramatic Reading of a Realistic Story

Realistic fiction often tells dramatic stories about life in the modern world. Bring the world of a short story to life for classmates by performing a **dramatic reading** of realistic fiction.

Working as team, choose a realistic short story to perform in a dramatic reading for your classmates. During the planning, rehearsal, and performance, be open to each group member's perspective, ideas, and input. Perform your dramatic reading live, or record it as an audiobook.

WRITING COACH

Online

www.phwritingcoach.com

Online Journal

Reflect on Your Writing Record your answers and ideas in the online journal.

Resource

Link to resources on 21st Century Learning for help in creating a group project.

Here's your action plan.

1. Choose roles, such as editor, director, narrator, and actors.

2. With your group, review your peers' short stories. Choose one with multiple characters and plenty of dialogue.

3. Analyze the story. Your group must understand it in order to perform it well.

4. Search online for audio clips of dramatic readings to use as models for your own performance.

5. Mark up the story text to show where to pause, emphasize words, and change speakers. Then, practice reading the story in a group.

   - Make your voice express appropriate emotions.
   - Pause when a character or narrator would pause.
   - Use louder voices to indicate the climax.

6. Perform your reading for the class. You may wish to record your performance, and make it available online for students to download.

Listening and Speaking Work as a team to rehearse for your presentation. Ask group members to listen critically during rehearsal. Take notes to help you improve your performance. During your dramatic reading for the class, use your notes. Speak clearly and in the appropriate tones. After the performance, listen for reactions from your classmates.

Writing for Media: Audio Script

Audio Script

An **audio script** is a piece of writing that is made especially for radio, podcast, or online listening. Just like a film or stage script, it has a plot, lines for characters, settings, and directions. However, an audio script depends on dialogue with sensory details, music, and sound effects because its audience will not be able to see the characters and setting or read about them on a page. Like other stories, audio script drama have a focus, point of view, plot, setting, and characters.

Try It! Study the script. Then, answer these questions in your journal.

1. Which details help you to get a sense of the drama's **focus**?
2. What evidence of a **problem** do you see?
3. How would you describe the **characters**?
4. Which **sensory details** add to the description?
5. Do you think the **setting** is realistic? Explain.
6. Identify **sound effects** and **directions** used in the script. How do they support the story?

Extension Find another example of a radio drama or audio script and compare it with this one.

Maribelle Strikes Again!

[Scene: A county fairground. JEFF and his sister CAITLYN are walking through the carnival grounds on the way to one of the livestock barns. The sounds of footsteps as well as carnival music can be heard in the background.]

LOUDSPEAKER. The judges will be in the livestock barns in 15 minutes to judge the animals.

JEFF. I didn't realize it was so late, Caitlyn! Hurry!

[Sound of running footsteps and heavy breathing]

CAITLYN. [Out of breath] Do you think Maribelle will win?

JEFF. [Out of breath] Yes. [pause] Whew! We made it.

[Sounds of footsteps slow to a walk. Various animal sounds are in the background—goats and sheep.]

JEFF. [Gasps] Oh no! Where's Maribelle? Caitlyn, she's not in her pen! Why would someone steal Maribelle?!

CAITLYN. I don't see her, Jeff! I bet she escaped again. How does she do it? [chuckles] Let's go see if we can find her, but I bet we won't be able to find her in time for the judges.

[Sound of judges' discussions in the distance.]

JEFF. How much do you want to bet...? Let's go!

[Sound of running footsteps]

WOMAN. [Shrieking] Where did this goat come from? It's eating my prize-winning pie!

CAITLYN. [Calmly] Ma'am, I'm really very sorry. Okay, Maribelle. Let's go, you little escape artist!

CAITLYN. I bet we still have time to get her back to her pen for the judging. Let's go, Jeff!

Create an Audio Script

Follow these steps to create your own audio script. To plan your script, review the graphic organizers on pages R24–R27 and choose one that suits your needs.

Prewriting

- Write a list of possible ideas for your audio script and select the one that would suit a play best.
- Identify the focus of the script and its point of view. For example, will your play be funny, serious, scary, or something else? Will you use third- or first-person narration?
- Decide the setting. Remember, you will have to use dialogue with sensory details to help listeners imagine the setting.
- Write descriptions of the script's characters.
- Before you draft, summarize the events of the script. Be sure to tell a full narrative. Introduce a conflict and then resolve it.

Drafting

- Use language that reflects who the characters are. Think about their backgrounds as you create dialogue.
- Make sure the conflict and resolution are well-developed.
- Be sure to provide helpful directions to the performers. Keep in mind that your audio script is meant for actors.

Revising and Editing

- Review your draft to make sure events are organized logically. Make sure the problem and the outcome of the story are clear.
- Use the Revision RADaR strategy to improve your draft.
- Check that spelling, grammar, and mechanics are correct.

Publishing

- Make an audio recording of your script. Use a music player and sound effects to create more realistic scenes. Make posters to advertise your script.
- Perform your audio script for the class. Create a division in the classroom that prevents your classmates from seeing you and allows them to just listen.

Online Journal

Try It! Record your answers in the online journal.

Interactive Graphic Organizers

Choose from a variety of graphic organizers to plan and develop your project.

Partner Talk

Before you start drafting, use specific details to describe and explain the theme of your audio script to a partner. Ask for feedback about your theme. For example, will your story sustain reader interest?

Writing for Assessment

You may have to write to a prompt that asks you to write creatively. Use the prompts on these pages to practice. Respond using the characteristics of your realistic short story. (See page 92.)

Try It! To begin, read the realistic **short story** prompt and the information on format and academic vocabulary. Use the ABCDs of On-Demand Writing to help you plan and write your short story.

Format

The prompt directs you to write a *short story.* Start with a beginning that introduces the conflict. Include a middle that develops the problem. Finish by showing what happens after the climax.

Short Story Prompt

Write a short story about a character who wins the lottery. Describe the events of the story using sensory details. Establish a believable setting, interesting characters, and events that move toward a solution. Use dialogue to develop your story.

Academic Vocabulary

Remember that *dialogue* is the conversation between two or more characters.

 ## The ABCDs of On-Demand Writing

Use the following ABCDs to help you respond to the prompt.

Before you write your draft:

Attack the prompt [1 MINUTE]

- Circle or highlight important verbs in the prompt. Draw a line from the verb to what it refers to.
- Rewrite the prompt in your own words.

Brainstorm possible answers [4 MINUTES]

- Create a graphic organizer to generate ideas.
- Use one for each part of the prompt if necessary.

Choose the order of your response [1 MINUTE]

- Think about the best way to organize your ideas.
- Number your ideas in the order you will write about them. Cross out ideas you will not be using.

After you write your draft:

Detect errors before turning in the draft [1 MINUTE]

- Carefully reread your writing.
- Make sure that your response makes sense and is complete.
- Look for spelling, punctuation, and grammar errors.

More Prompts for Practice

Apply It! Respond to Prompts 1 and 2 by writing imaginative **short stories** with engaging story lines that keep the reader's interest.

- Create a **specific, believable setting** through the use of **sensory details**.
- Create **characters** that are realistic and interesting.
- Decide on a single **point of view**.
- Determine a topic to define the **focus** and **plot**.
- Show the **results** of the characters' actions.
- Include **dialogue** that develops the action of the story.

> **Prompt 1** Write a short story about something that happens in a park. Be sure to include the following fiction elements: believable setting and characters, clear point of view and focus, engaging plot, and dialogue. Use sensory details to bring your story to life.

> **Prompt 2** Write a short story about a family vacation. Make sure your setting and characters are interesting and believable and that your plot is engaging. Include a problem and solution in your story and use sensory details to define the focus.

Spiral Review: Narrative Respond to Prompt 3 by writing a **personal narrative**. Make sure it reflects all of the characteristics described on page 66. Your essay should include these elements:

- A **clearly defined focus**
- The **importance of or reasons for actions and/or consequences**

> **Prompt 3** Write a personal narrative about a time you took part in a competition. Think about the reasons for decisions you made and how you acted. Discuss the importance of the consequences, or the outcome of your choices.

WRITING COACH

www.phwritingcoach.com

Interactive Writing Coach™

Plan your response to the prompt. If you are using the prompt for practice, write one paragraph at a time or your entire draft and then submit it for feedback. If you are using the prompt as a timed test, write your entire draft and then submit it for feedback.

Remember **ABCD**

Attack the prompt

Brainstorm possible answers

Choose the order of your response

Detect errors before turning in the draft

CHAPTER 7

POETRY and DESCRIPTION

What Do You See?

People see different things when they look at something. Some people may look at this photograph and see fireworks. Others may look at it and see power or beauty.

People also use different words to describe what they see. Words can be a powerful way to capture a moment or feeling.

Try It! Take a few minutes to list what you see in the fireworks photograph. Remember, you might describe the actual image or you might describe how it makes you feel.

Consider these questions as you participate in an extended discussion with a partner. Take turns expressing your ideas and feelings.

- What details do you see in the photograph?
- What emotions does this photograph make you feel?
- What might you feel if you were near the fireworks?
- What do the fireworks mean to you?

Review the list you made. Use your list to describe to a partner what you see in this photograph.

What's Ahead

In this chapter, you will review some strong examples of poems: Mentor Texts and Student Models. Then, using the examples as guidance, you will write a poem of your own.

WRITING COACH

Online

www.phwritingcoach.com

Online Journal

Try It! Record your answers and ideas in the online journal.

You can also record and save your answers and ideas on pop-up sticky notes in the eText.

Connect to the Big Questions

Discuss these questions with your partner:

1 **What do you think?** How can we communicate what we see?

2 **Why write?** How does one best convey feeling through words on a page?

POETRY AND DESCRIPTION

In this chapter, you will focus on writing a poem. Poetry is different from other kinds of writing. Rather than using sentences and paragraphs, poets write in lines and stanzas to convey their emotions and ideas. Because poems tend to be short, poets must choose their words carefully, using language that is vivid, precise, and pleasing to the ear. They may use rhythm and rhyme to add a musical quality to the work. Most writing includes description, but this type of language is especially important in poetry. Poets use sensory details to help readers imagine how things look, smell, sound, feel, and taste.

You will develop a poem by taking it through each stage of the writing process: prewriting, drafting, revising, editing, and publishing. To preview the criteria for how your poem will be evaluated, see the rubric on page 137. You will also have an opportunity to use your descriptive writing skills in an essay about a place you have visited.

FEATURE ASSIGNMENT

Poem

An effective poem has these characteristics:

- A clear **focus, topic, theme,** or **controlling idea**

- **Poetic techniques** that create a musical quality, emphasize words, or enhance the rhythm

- **Figurative language** that expresses ideas imaginatively

- **Sensory details** and **imagery** that allow the reader to see, smell, hear, taste, and feel what the poet describes

- Attention to **graphic elements,** such as line length or capital letters

A **rhyming poem** also has these characteristics (see pages 129–130):

- **Rhyming words** that fall within or at the ends of lines

- A strong, regular **rhythm**

A **haiku** also has these characteristics (see pages 129–130):

- A set **structure** of 17 syllables arranged in three lines of 5, 7, and 5 syllables

- A clear **image,** often of nature, that creates an emotional response in the reader

Forms of Poetry and Description

There are many forms of poetry and description, including:

Ballads are poems that tell a story and are usually meant to be sung. Ballads often contain repetition and have a simple, regular rhyme pattern and meter, or "beat."

Descriptive essays use imagery and vivid details to help readers imagine a person, place, thing, or event. Like all essays, they are made up of an introduction, body, and conclusion.

Free verse is poetry that imitates the rhythms of everyday speech. It has no set rhythm and rhyme patterns and uses poetic devices to convey ideas and feelings.

Haiku are three-line poems that originated in Japan. In a haiku, the first and last lines consist of five syllables, and the middle line consists of seven syllables.

Lyric poems express a speaker's feelings about a particular person, place, thing, or event. Unlike ballads, lyric poems usually do not tell a story.

Prose poems look like prose, or regular text you might find in a story or essay, but use poetic techniques to create a memorable description of a person, place, thing, or event.

Sonnets are 14-line poems written in a regular meter and pattern of rhyme. One kind of sonnet has three four-line stanzas and a final couplet, or two rhyming lines. In each stanza, alternating lines usually rhyme.

Try It! For each audience and purpose described, choose a form, such as a sonnet, descriptive essay, or lyric poem, that is appropriate for conveying your intended meaning to the audience. Explain your choices.

- To describe a special trip to classmates
- To express feelings about a beloved pet
- To impress your reader with your use of regular meter and rhyme

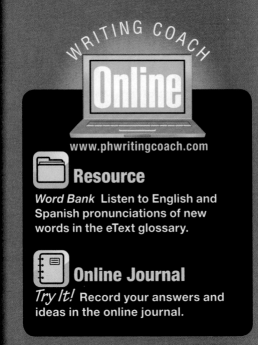

MENTOR TEXT

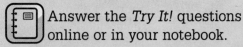

Rhyming Poem and Haiku

Learn From Experience

Read the rhyming poem and haiku on pages 122–123. As you read, take notes to develop your understanding of basic sight and English vocabulary. Then, read the numbered notes in the margins to learn about how the poets presented their ideas.

Answer the *Try It!* questions online or in your notebook.

❶ There is a **clear focus** to the poem from the start. Knowing what the poem will be about helps readers understand it.

Try It! Write a sentence that tells what the focus is.

❷ The poet uses **onomatopoeia**, or words that imitate sounds, to make the poem more vivid and funny.

Try It! Which word imitates a sound made by a computer?

❸ Regular **rhyme** creates pleasing sounds when the poem is read aloud and supports the humor in the poem.

Try It! Which words rhyme in lines 9–12?

Baby Ate a Microchip
by Neal Levin

❶ Baby ate a microchip,
Then grabbed a bottle, took a sip.
❷ He swallowed it and made a beep,
And now he's thinking pretty deep.

5 He's downloading his ABCs
And calculating 1-2-3s.
He's memorizing useless facts
While doing Daddy's income tax.

❸ He's processing, and now he thrives
10 On feeding his internal drives.
He's throwing fits, and now he fights
With ruthless bits and toothless bytes.

He must be feeling very smug.
But hold on, Baby caught a bug.
15 Attempting to reboot in haste,
He accidentally got erased!

Three Haiku

by Julienne Marlaire

The Journey

Snail inches across
The garden, never stopping.
Where is he going?

Nighttime in Winter

❹ Falling snow blankets,
Making silent, still music—
A sweet lullaby.

Sunrise

❺ Sunlight floods the land,
Glistening on dewy grass.
A new day begins!

WRITING COACH

Online

www.phwritingcoach.com

Interactive Model

Listen to an audio recording of the Mentor Text in the eText. You can refer back to the Mentor Text whenever you need support in developing your own writing.

Online Journal

Try It! Answer the questions about the Mentor Text in the online journal.

❹ The poet uses **personification** when she describes the falling snow. This helps readers picture snow in a fresh, new way.

Try It! Which human characteristics or actions does she give to the snow? How did this figurative language make you feel when you read the poem? Explain.

❺ The poems follow the traditional haiku structure of **three lines** made up of words that total 17 syllables.

Try It! How does the length of the poem affect you as a reader? Explain.

STUDENT MODEL

Rhyming Poem and Haiku

With a small group, take turns reading each Student Model aloud. As you read, note the structure and elements of the poems. You may want to take a look at the Poet's Toolbox on page 129. Ask yourself how the images and poetic language affect your emotions.

 Use a Reader's Eye

Now, reread the Student Models. On your copies of the Student Models, use the Reader's Response Symbols to react to what you read.

Reader's Response Symbols

+ **I can picture this.**

− **This image could be stronger.**

? **I wonder what this means.**

! **This is cool!**

 **Partner Talk**

Participate in an extended discussion with a partner. Express your opinions and share your responses to the Student Model. About what do you agree? How do your feelings about the poems differ?

The Game

A Rhyming Poem by Justine Margolis

Players maneuver in and out
Like lions on the prowl.
Pass, run, shoot, and shout,
Never fumble, never foul.

5 Guard and block, assist, rebound,
The team works all as one.
Fans create a wall of sound
As the other team comes undone.

    Grace in action, strength, and power
10 So much more than play.
Fighting to the final hour,
We'll win this game today.

1

Changing Seasons

A Haiku by Renee Baker

The summer tree's leaves
are greener than autumn's, but
spring's are the greenest.

Autumn

A Haiku by Renee Baker

Red and yellow leaves
Like fire climbing in the sky
Flaunt autumn's beauty.

2

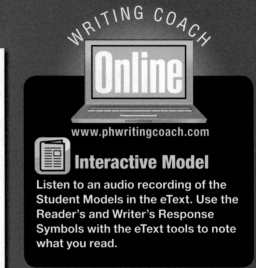

WRITING COACH

Online

www.phwritingcoach.com

Interactive Model

Listen to an audio recording of the Student Models in the eText. Use the Reader's and Writer's Response Symbols with the eText tools to note what you read.

Use a Writer's Eye

Now, evaluate the poems as a writer. On your copies of the Student Models, use the Writer's Response Symbols to react to what you read. Identify places where the student writers use characteristics of an effective rhyming poem or haiku.

Writer's Response Symbols

R.R. Rhythm or rhyme, if present, fits poem's form

S.D. Effective use of sound devices

F.L. Figurative language conveys a mood

I.D. Images and details appeal to the senses

Prewriting

Plan a first draft of your poem by **determining an appropriate topic.** First, decide which form of poetry you will write—a rhyming poem, haiku, or other form of poetry. Then, select a topic from the Topic Bank or come up with an idea of your own.

Choose From the Topic Bank

TOPIC BANK

Memorable Day Think of a day that was memorable because of the weather, such as a day with a summer thunderstorm. In a poem, describe the weather and the mood the weather created.

Hero Write a poem about one of your personal heroes, such as your favorite author, singer, or leader. Be sure to be specific and detailed in your explanation about what makes the person heroic to you.

Special Place Write a poem about a place you go to have fun or relax. Describe the place so that readers can picture it in their minds.

Choose Your Own Topic

Determine an appropriate topic of your own by using the following **range of strategies** to generate ideas.

Observe and Discuss

- Walk through your neighborhood, a local park, or an area of natural beauty. What images catch your eye?
- Look through photos of the people and events of your life. What ideas do they spark?
- List ideas you gathered through observation and discuss them with a partner. Circle the topic that is the most interesting.

Review your responses and choose a topic.

Narrow Your Topic

Choosing a topic that is too broad may result in a poem that lacks focus.

Apply It! Use a graphic organizer like the one shown to narrow your topic.

- Write your general topic in the top box, and keep narrowing your topic as you move down the chart.
- Your last box should hold your narrowest or "smallest" topic, the new focus or central image of your poem.

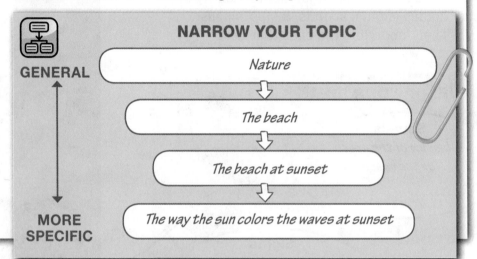

NARROW YOUR TOPIC

GENERAL

Nature

The beach

The beach at sunset

MORE SPECIFIC

The way the sun colors the waves at sunset

Consider Your Audience and Purpose

Before writing, think about your audience and purpose. Think about how others may see things as you ask yourself these questions.

Questions for Audience	Questions for Purpose
• Who might enjoy my poem? My teacher? Readers of the school paper? My online friends? • What form of poetry would best convey my meaning to my audience? • How will I help readers visualize my images?	• Do I want to entertain my audience, make them feel emotions, or something else? • What kinds of poetic techniques will help me fulfill my purpose? • What figurative language and graphic elements will help me fulfill my purpose?

Record your answers in your writing journal.

Plan Your Piece

You will use a graphic organizer like the one shown to organize your details. When it is complete, you will be ready to write your first draft.

Develop a Topic, Theme, or Controlling Idea To focus your poem, review your notes and write a clear statement of your topic, theme, or controlling idea. Name the most important idea or feeling you would like to communicate. Add your statement to your graphic organizer.

Develop Ideas and Details Use the graphic organizer to identify ideas, feelings, and sensory details (sights, sounds, tastes, smells, touch) related to your topic. Then, underline the ones that best fulfill your purpose.

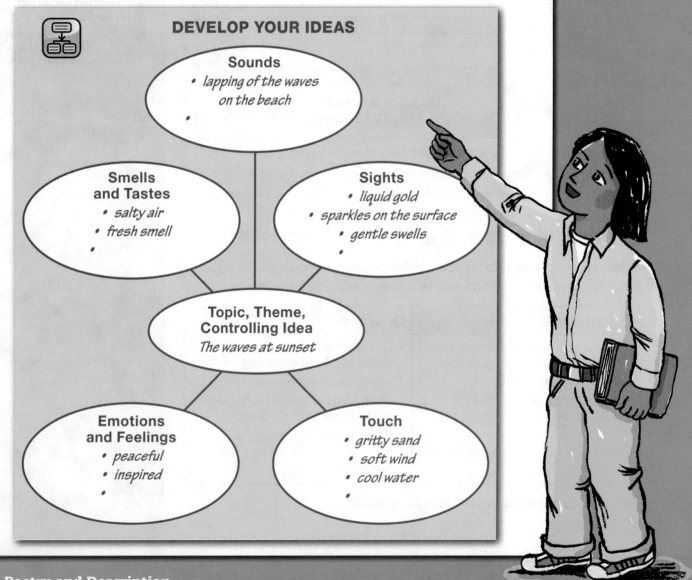

DEVELOP YOUR IDEAS

Sounds
- *lapping of the waves on the beach*

Smells and Tastes
- *salty air*
- *fresh smell*

Sights
- *liquid gold*
- *sparkles on the surface*
- *gentle swells*

Topic, Theme, Controlling Idea
The waves at sunset

Emotions and Feelings
- *peaceful*
- *inspired*

Touch
- *gritty sand*
- *soft wind*
- *cool water*

Poet's Toolbox

Writers use a variety of poetic techniques and literary devices to convey ideas, create images, and appeal to readers' emotions. Here are some techniques you might use in your poem.

Figurative language is writing that means something beyond what the words actually say.	
Simile: comparison using *like* or *as*	*The waves are like gentle hills, rolling in the distance.*
Metaphor: comparison made by saying that one thing is something else	*The beach is my home.*
Personification: human characteristics applied to non-human objects	*The wind whispers quietly.*
Symbols add depth and insight to poetry.	
An object that stands for something else	*The gulls soaring overhead might be symbols of freedom.*
Sound Devices create a musical or emotional effect.	
Alliteration: repetition of consonant sounds at the beginning of nearby words	**S**unshine **s**parkles on the **s**ea.
Assonance: repetition of vowel sounds in nearby words	*Winds bl**ow** and waves gr**ow** in an endless fl**ow**.*
Consonance: repetition of consonants in the middle or at the end of words	*I wat**ch** as ea**ch** bea**ch**ed wave rea**ch**es out to me.*
Structural Elements help build the framework for poetic language.	
Rhyme: repetition of sounds at the ends of lines of poetry	*"Sunshine sparkles on the **sea** As the wind whispers quiet**ly**."*
Meter: rhythmical pattern of a poem. It is determined by stressed syllables in a line. Some forms of poetry have specific patterns of stressed syllables.	**Sun**shine **spark**les **on** the **sea** (Stressed syllables in poetry are marked with a ´, while unstressed syllables are marked with a ˘.)
Graphic Elements position the words on the page.	
Arrangement of words on a page	capital letters, line spacing, and line breaks

WRITING COACH

Online

www.phwritingcoach.com

Interactive Graphic Organizers

Use the interactive graphic organizers to help you create a plan for your writing.

Interactive Model

Refer back to the Interactive Model in the eText as you plan your writing.

 Apply It! Review the ideas and details you added to your prewriting graphic organizer.

- First, confirm the poetic form you will develop.
- Then, decide what techniques from the Poet's Toolbox you would like to use in your poem. Keep in mind that some poetic techniques must be used in specific forms, while other techniques are optional.

Drafting

During the drafting stage, you will start to write your ideas for your rhyming poem, haiku, or other poetic form you chose. First, **choose an appropriate organizational strategy,** based on the form of poem you choose to write. Then, **build on the ideas** you developed in your graphic organizer to **write a focused, organized, and coherent** poem.

Drafting a Rhyming Poem or Haiku

Each poetic form has specific characteristics. You will write your poem using these characteristics, the techniques from the Poet's Toolbox, and the ideas, feelings, and sensory details you developed in your graphic organizer. The charts show the characteristics of each form. Review the characteristics. Then, answer the questions in the right column as you draft your poem.

Rhyming Poem Characteristics	Questions to Answer While Drafting
• Varied number of lines • Varied number of stanzas • Rhyme at the ends of lines • Poetic techniques used • Figurative language likely used • Vivid descriptions	• How long will my poem be? • How will I break the lines into stanzas? **Tip:** Stanzas should focus on a single idea or image. • Will each stanza have the same number of lines? • What words will I rhyme in each stanza? **Tip:** Consult a rhyming dictionary. • What poetic techniques will I use? • How can I use figurative language? • How will I make my descriptions vivid?

Haiku Characteristics	Questions to Answer While Drafting
• One central image, often from nature • 3 lines of 5, 7, and 5 syllables each • Feeling or emotion conveyed • Precise wording • Typically does not include rhyme • Figurative language may be used • Poetic techniques may be used	• What image will I choose? • How can I choose the best words with the correct number of syllables? **Tip:** Consult a thesaurus. • What feelings or emotions will I express? • What figurative language or poetic techniques will I use?

Start Your Draft

Writing poetry is different than creating most other genres. The process is more open. Use the graphic organizer that shows your topic, ideas, and details, and the Poet's Toolbox as guides, but be open to experimenting with your draft.

While developing your poem, aim at writing your ideas, not on making your writing perfect. Remember, you will have the chance to improve your poem when you revise and edit.

WRITING COACH

Online

www.phwritingcoach.com

Interactive Model

Refer back to Mentor Text in the eText as your write your draft.

Before You Write

√ Begin by thinking about the main message you'd like your poem to convey. This message is the poem's **theme,** or controlling idea.

√ Review the **ideas** and details you listed in your prewriting graphic organizer. Decide which ideas and details will work with your theme.

√ Choose a **main image** or several images to include in the poem. Find **sensory details** that will make your image(s) easy for your readers to "see."

While You Write

√ Use **vivid verbs** and details that appeal to sight, sound, smell, touch, and taste. Use a rhyming dictionary and thesaurus to choose the best words.

√ Include figurative language, **poetic techniques**, and graphic elements that support your message and your poem's form. If you experiment with a technique that does not seem to work, try another.

√ Pay attention to the sound and **rhythm** of the language you use.

Revising: Making It Better

Now that you have finished your draft, you are ready to revise. Think about the "big picture" of **audience, purpose, and genre.** You can use your Revision RADaR as a guide for making changes to improve your draft. Revision RADaR provides four major ways to improve your writing: (R) replace, (A) add, (D) delete, and (R) reorder.

Kelly Gallagher, M. Ed.

KEEP REVISION ON YOUR RADaR

Read the first draft of the Student Model "The Game." Then look at questions the writer asked herself as she thought about how well the draft **addressed issues of audience, purpose, and genre.**

The Game

1ST DRAFT

Players maneuver in and out
Like lions on the prowl.
Pass, run, shoot, and shout,
Never mess up, do not foul.

Guard and block, assist, rebound,
The team works all as one.
Players continue to run around
As the other team comes undone.

In the hallway, friends say 'bye
It's over, time to go.
Our parents wait in cars nearby
To drive us through the snow.

Do I use effective poetic techniques, such as alliteration?

Does this line present a vivid image?

Do these lines clearly develop my theme or controlling idea?

Now, look at how the writer applied Revision RADaR to write an improved second draft.

The Game

Players maneuver in and out
Like lions on the prowl.
Pass, run, shoot, and shout,
Never fumble, never foul. · · · · · · · · · · · · · **A** *Added words to build alliteration*

Guard and block, assist, rebound,
The team works all as one.
Fans create a wall of sound · · · · · · · · · **R** *Replaced a less interesting description with a vivid image*
As the other team comes undone.

Grace in action, strength, and power · · · · · **D** *Deleted a stanza that was unrelated to my theme and*
So much more than play.
Fighting to the final hour. **R** *replaced it with a stanza that keeps the focus on the big game*
We'll win this game today.

Apply It! Now, revise your draft after rethinking how well questions of purpose, audience, and genre have been addressed.

- First, determine whether you have included the characteristics of a rhyming poem or a haiku.

- Then apply your Revision RADaR to make needed changes. Focus specifically on enhancing your poem's style by using **poetic techniques, figurative language,** and **graphic elements.** Remember—you can use the steps in Revision RADaR in any order.

Look at the Big Picture

Use the chart and your analytical skills to evaluate how well your poem **addresses purpose, audience, and genre.** When necessary, use the suggestions in the chart to revise your poem.

	Evaluate	Revise
Topic and Focus	• Make sure your controlling idea or **theme** is clear.	• Think about your poem's message. Add words or images to convey your theme.
	• Check that your **sensory details** all support the controlling idea or theme.	• Delete sensory details that do not support the theme and replace them with details that help paint a clearer picture.
	• Consider your **audience.** Who will be reading the poem? What language will appeal to them?	• Adapt your language to your audience.
Structural Devices	• Check the **rhyme** and rhythm if you are writing a rhyming poem.	• Use a rhyming dictionary to substitute rhymes. • Tap out the rhythm and reorder words to fix any awkward spots.
	• If you are writing a haiku, check that your lines contain the correct number of **syllables.**	• Count your syllables and add or delete words as necessary.
Poetic Techniques	• Make sure your **figurative language** and word choices help convey your meaning.	• Replace dull or vague words with figurative language, vivid words, and sensory details.
	• Make sure to include effective **sound devices.**	• Read your poem aloud to hear the way it sounds. Use a dictionary or thesaurus to find words to create alliteration or onomatopoeia.

Focus on Craft: Enhance Style

Every author has his or her own **style,** or unique way of communicating. Style is made up of many elements, including the way a writer uses poetic techniques, figurative language, and graphic elements. Emily Dickinson, for example, is known for her style of using graphic elements like capitalization, while Henry Wadsworth Longfellow is known for his strong rhythms.

Think about the poet's style as you read the following lines from the Student Model.

 **STUDENT MODEL** from **The Game**
page 124; lines 11–12

Fighting to the final hour,

We'll win this game today.

 Try It! Now, ask yourself these questions. Record your answers in your journal.

- How does the poet use alliteration in these lines?
- How would the poem's effect be different if the first line read *Fighting to the last hour*?

Fine-Tune Your Draft

Apply It! Now, prepare your final draft after rethinking how well questions of purpose, audience, and genre have been addressed.

- **Improve Your Style** Add alliteration or other **poetic devices** to your poem. Use a dictionary or thesaurus to find words that sound the best. Substitute **figurative language** for words and phrases that do not convey your meaning or enhance the poem's mood. Add **graphic elements,** such as capitalization or special punctuation, for emphasis.
- **Improve Your Imagery** Add sensory details to help readers fully experience your poem's topic.

Teacher Feedback Read your poem aloud to your teacher. Ask if you have conveyed the meaning you intended. Think about his or her response and revise your final draft in response to your teacher's feedback.

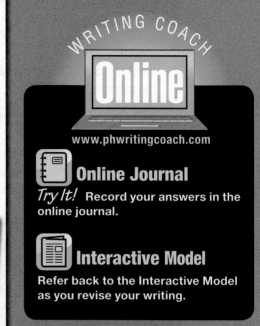

WRITING COACH

Online

www.phwritingcoach.com

Online Journal
Try It! Record your answers in the online journal.

Interactive Model
Refer back to the Interactive Model as you revise your writing.

Editing: Making It Correct

Editing means polishing your work by checking for spelling and grammar errors.

Before you edit, think about your use of **predicate adjectives**, which are adjectives that come after a linking verb and describe the subject. Sometimes, a predicate adjective needs to be in its **comparative or superlative form**. Then edit your final draft for any errors in **grammar, mechanics, and spelling.**

WRITE GUY *Jeff Anderson, M. Ed.*

WHAT DO YOU NOTICE?

Zoom In On Conventions Focus on adjectives as you zoom in on these lines from the Mentor Text.

 **MENTOR TEXT** from **Baby Ate a Microchip**
page 122; lines 13–14

> He must be feeling very smug.
> But hold on, Baby caught a bug.

Now ask yourself: *Which word describes how the subject He is feeling?*

Perhaps you said that the adjective *smug* describes how the subject is feeling. In this sentence *smug* is a predicate adjective. A **predicate adjective** follows a linking verb and describes the subject of the sentence.

A linking verb connects a subject with a word that describes or identifies it. The most common linking verbs are forms of the verb *be*. Other linking verbs are forms of the verbs *appear, become, feel, look, seem,* and *sound*. In the Mentor Text, *smug* is connected to the subject *He*, or Baby, by the linking verb *must be feeling.*

Partner Talk Discuss this question with a partner: *How can predicate adjectives add descriptive details to poetry?*

> To learn more about adjectives, see Chapter 15 of your Grammar Handbook.

Grammar Mini-Lesson: Adjective Forms

To learn more, see Chapter 24.

When using **predicate adjectives**, use the **comparative form** to compare two things and the **superlative form** to compare three or more things. For most one- and two-syllable adjectives, add *-er* to form the comparative and *-est* to form the superlative. For longer adjectives, use *more* to form the comparative and *most* to form the superlative. Notice how the Student Model uses adjective forms.

STUDENT MODEL from **Changing Seasons**
page 125; lines 1–3

> The summer tree's leaves
>
> are greener than autumn's, but
>
> spring's are the greenest.

 Try It! In your journal, write the correct comparative or superlative form of each predicate adjective in parentheses.

1. Of the three heroes, Achilles was (fast) and (strong).
2. Of all the flowers in the garden, to me the rose seems (pretty).

Apply It! Edit your draft for grammar, mechanics, and spelling. Make sure you have used the correct comparative and superlative forms of predicate adjectives.

Use the rubric to evaluate your piece. If necessary, rethink, rewrite, or revise.

Rubric for Poetry: Rhyming Poem or Haiku	Rating Scale
Ideas: How well do your ideas develop your poem's subject or controlling idea?	Not very Very 1 2 3 4 5 6
Organization: How clearly are your ideas organized?	1 2 3 4 5 6
Voice: How effectively do you use figurative language and poetic techniques to create a unique voice?	1 2 3 4 5 6
Word Choice: How well does your word choice create vivid images?	1 2 3 4 5 6
Sentence Fluency: How effective is the rhythm and sound of your poem?	1 2 3 4 5 6
Conventions: How correct is your usage of adjectives?	1 2 3 4 5 6

Publishing

Now it's time to let others enjoy your poem. First, get it ready for publication. Then, choose a way to **publish your poem for appropriate audiences.**

Wrap Up Your Presentation

Is your poem handwritten or written on a computer? If your poem is handwritten, you may need to make a new, clean copy. If so, be sure to **write legibly.** Also check to see that your title grabs the reader's attention and indicates your poem's topic.

Publish Your Piece

Use this chart to identify a way to publish your poem.

If your audience is...	...then publish it by...
Family, friends, or others who enjoy poetry	• Memorizing and reciting it on a special occasion, with appropriate gestures and expression • Recording it with background music as a podcast and sending it to your friends • Submitting it to an online literary journal for kids
Teachers and students at your school	• Reading it aloud to your classmates • Writing it on a poster for a hallway poetry display • Posting it on a class or school blog

 **Reflect on Your Writing**

Now that you are done with your poem, read it over and use your writing journal to answer these questions. Use specific details to describe and explain your reflections. Increase the specificity of your details based on the type of information requested.

- Which parts of the poem do you think you wrote particularly well?
- Do any parts of the poem seem weaker than others? If so, what can you work on to improve in your next writing assignment?

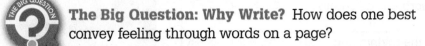 **The Big Question: Why Write?** How does one best convey feeling through words on a page?

Manage Your Portfolio You may wish to include your published poem in your writing portfolio. If so, consider what this poem reveals about your writing and your growth as a writer.

MAKE YOUR WRITING COUNT

Share the Vision of Your Poetry Using Multimedia

Poems, such as haiku, use language to create images. Bring your poetic vision to life for your classmates by creating a **poetry presentation**.

With a group, produce a **multimedia presentation** with text, graphics, and audio. Group members will enhance their poems with visuals and sound. The group will then present the work to the class, either as a live poetry reading or in an electronic slideshow presentation.

WRITING COACH

Online

www.phwritingcoach.com

Online Journal
Reflect on Your Writing Record your answers and ideas in the online journal.

Resource
Link to resources on 21st Century Learning for help in creating a group project.

Here's your action plan.

1. With your group, read through the poems and haiku that you created. Brainstorm possible titles for the presentation. Vote on the best title.

2. Find or create photos or drawings that support the imagery in each poem.

3. Support the imagery with sounds, such as music or special effects, you can create or play from a recording.

3. Create a poster or electronic slide for each poem.

- Write each poem legibly, or type it into slideshow presentation software.
- Illustrate the text of each poem with your visuals.
- Plan for instruments and sound effects to play live or include as audio files.

4. Practice reading your poems aloud, clearly and with emotion. If presenting a slideshow, you may record your readings in an audio file as well.

5. Perform your poetry presentation, whether live or as a slideshow, for your classmates to see.

Listening and Speaking Listen to group members as they rehearse reading their poems aloud. Be respectful as you provide positive suggestions to others. For live presentations, rehearse staging the readings along with the visual elements.

Your Turn

**Writing for Media:
Descriptive Essay**

Descriptive Essays

An essay is a short work of nonfiction that presents the author's point of view on a topic. Like poetry, some essays rely on description to convey a message. In **descriptive essays,** writers use sensory details and precise word choice to create vivid images or a certain mood. Like all essays, descriptive essays focus on a single topic and have a clear sense of purpose. Descriptive essays can cover a wide range of topics, from describing a character's flaws in the latest hit movie to painting a word picture of a gorgeous vacation spot.

Try It! Study the sample descriptive essay. Then answer the questions. Record your answers in your journal.

1. What **topic** does this essay describe?

2. Good descriptive essays have a clear focus and sense of **purpose**. What are the focus and purpose of this essay?

3. Who is the **audience** for this essay?

4. Writers of descriptive essays share their **ideas** or feelings about a specific person, place, event, or idea. What is the writer's opinion of Café Delight?

5. Writers of descriptive essays use **sensory details** to create vivid **images.** To what senses does the writer appeal in this essay? Give an example of one sensory detail.

6. Descriptive essays are **organized** with an introduction, body, and conclusion. How does the writer conclude this piece?

Extension Find another example of a descriptive essay, and compare it with this one.

Café Delight

Dining out with the whole family can be tricky. After all, what restaurant can please parents, kids, babies, and even grandparents? Café Delight attempts to do just that. I visited Café Delight last week and brought the whole family along. From the moment we stepped in the door and smelled the fresh-baked bread, I knew we had found a special place.

The décor at Café Delight is simple, yet pleasing, with bright colors on the walls and large black-and-white photos showing families of every shape and size. Swingy jazz plays softly over hidden speakers. To order, you step up to a large front counter and choose from a varied menu of mostly American and Italian dishes. Kids' favorites like macaroni and cheese are offered along with more grown-up fare, such as lobster and shrimp ravioli.

The food arrived quickly. My lasagna was rich and satisfying, with a slightly spicy tomato sauce, flavorful spinach and ricotta cheese, and homemade pasta noodles. My family enjoyed their winter salads—a blend of greens, apples, pears, and pecans, with a surprisingly tasty maple syrup vinaigrette dressing—as well as the creamy macaroni and cheese.

But the best part of Café Delight has to be its game room. Along the south wall, the restaurant has set aside a room that includes nearly every game a kid could want. And it is enclosed in glass so parents can keep an eye on their kids, while still being able to enjoy some adult conversation. My family and I will be returning soon, and I recommend that you join us!

Create a Descriptive Essay

Follow these steps to write your own descriptive essay. To plan your essay, review the graphic organizers on pages R24–R27 and choose one that suits your needs.

Prewriting

- Identify a place that you have visited, either with your family or with your class, and that you'd like to describe.

- Identify a specific audience. For instance, you might be writing your essay for students in another class to read. Consider the audience's interests as you plan your essay.

- Identify your purpose and the focus of your essay.

- Brainstorm for sensory details that describe your place. Try to come up with descriptions that appeal to all five senses.

Drafting

- Write a thesis, or main idea statement, identifying the place you are describing and your thoughts about it.

- Draft an opening that grabs your audience.

- Present your description with interesting and helpful details and strong images. Keep your information clear, specific, and accurate.

- In the conclusion sum up your ideas or feelings about the place.

Revising and Editing

Review your draft to ensure that the description is logically organized and the details and images help readers imagine the place you are describing. Take out details that do not support your purpose. Make sure your ideas and feelings have been made clear. Check that your spelling, grammar, and mechanics are correct.

Publishing

Create a **multimedia presentation** of your essay. Use **graphics** including images that are related to your topic. Also include some of the **text** of your essay. Add music to help set the mood. Share your presentation with your class.

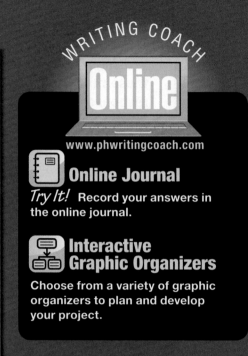

WRITING COACH

Online

www.phwritingcoach.com

Online Journal

Try It! Record your answers in the online journal.

Interactive Graphic Organizers

Choose from a variety of graphic organizers to plan and develop your project.

Partner Talk

Before you start drafting, describe the place to your partner using vivid sensory details. Ask for feedback about your description. For example, can your partner summarize your main ideas and feelings about the place? Monitor his or her spoken language by asking follow-up questions to confirm your understanding.

Writing for Assessment

Writing a good poem can take a lot of practice. You can use these prompts to do just that—practice writing poems. Your responses should include the same characteristics as your rhyming poem or haiku. (See page 120.)

Try It! To begin, read the prompt and the information on the format and academic vocabulary. Then, use the ABCDs of On-Demand Writing to help you plan and write your poem.

Format
The prompt directs you to write a *poem*. Develop your topic, theme, or controlling idea by deciding on ideas and sensory details you would like to use.

Poetry Prompt
Write a poem describing a person who has made a strong impression on you. Choose language to convey your feelings. Use a variety of sensory details in your description.

Academic Vocabulary
Remember that a *poem* is a piece written in verse. Poets use *sensory details* that convey sight, sound, touch, taste, and smell to convey their ideas.

The ABCDs of On-Demand Writing

Use the following ABCDs to help you respond to the prompt.

Before you write your draft:

A ttack the prompt [1 MINUTE]

- Circle or highlight important verbs in the prompt. Draw a line from the verb to what it refers to.
- Rewrite the prompt in your own words.

B rainstorm possible answers [4 MINUTES]

- Create a graphic organizer to generate ideas.
- Use one for each part of the prompt if necessary.

C hoose the order of your response [1 MINUTE]

- Think about the best way to organize your ideas.
- Number your ideas in the order you will write about them. Cross out ideas you will not be using.

After you write your draft:

D etect errors before turning in the draft [1 MINUTE]

- Carefully reread your writing.
- Make sure that your response makes sense and is complete.
- Look for spelling, punctuation, and grammar errors.

More Prompts for Practice

WRITING COACH

Online

www.phwritingcoach.com

Apply It! Respond to Prompt 1 by writing a **poem**. As you write, be sure to:

- Develop a clear, specific focus, theme, or controlling idea
- Use **poetic techniques, figurative language,** and **graphic elements** to make your writing come alive for your readers
- Choose your words carefully, using sensory details and imagery
- Use characteristics specific to your poetic form

> **Prompt 1** Write a poem about an adventure you have had. Use vivid imagery to give life to your description.

Spiral Review: Narrative If you choose to respond to Prompt 2 by writing a **personal narrative,** make sure your story reflects all of the characteristics described on page 66.

> **Prompt 2** Think about a place in nature that is special to you, such as a tree you love to climb or a park you enjoy visiting. Write a personal narrative describing that place, why it means so much to you, and an experience you may have had there.

Spiral Review: Short Story If you choose to write a **short story** in response to Prompt 3, make sure your **engaging story** reflects all of the characteristics described on page 92, including:

- **A clearly defined focus, plot, and point of view**
- **A specific, believable setting created through the use of sensory details**
- **Dialogue that develops the story**
- **Communicates reasons for actions and/or consequences**

> **Prompt 3** Write an imaginative short story about a private detective and a case he or she is working on. What sensory details might help you build suspense? What point of view will best reveal the action of the story? What is the best setting for such a story?

Interactive Model

Plan your response to the prompt. If you are using the prompt for practice, write one paragraph at a time or your entire draft and then submit it for feedback. If you are using the prompt as a timed test, write your entire draft and then submit it for feedback.

Remember **ABCD**

Attack the prompt

Brainstorm possible answers

Choose the order of your response

Detect errors before turning in the draft

CHAPTER 8

EXPOSITION

How Can You Explain This?

What do you know about dogs? What ideas and information about dogs could you share with others?

Information can be presented many ways. For example, you can compare two things, you can discuss causes and effects, or you can present a problem and a solution.

Try It! How could you explain the differences between these two dogs?

Consider these questions as you participate in an extended discussion with a partner. Take turns expressing your ideas and feelings.

- How are these two dogs similar?
- How are these two dogs different?
- What details would you use to describe the dogs?

Review the ideas you wrote. Discuss your comparison with a partner.

What's Ahead

In this chapter, you will review two strong examples of an analytical essay: a Mentor Text and a Student Model. Then, using the examples as guides, you will write an analytical essay in the compare and contrast form.

WRITING COACH

Online
www.phwritingcoach.com

Online Journal
Try It! Record your answers and ideas in the online journal.

You can also record and save your answers and ideas on pop-up sticky notes in the eText.

THE BIG QUESTION

Connect to the Big Questions

Discuss these questions with your partner:

1 What do you think? What can we learn from similarities and differences?

2 Why write? What should we tell and what should we describe to make information clear?

EXPOSITORY ESSAY

An expository essay gives readers information about a topic. In this chapter, you will learn to write a type of expository essay known as a compare-and-contrast essay. A compare-and-contrast essay organizes this information by showing similarities and differences. Compare-and-contrast essays often present different points of view on an issue or information about many products.

You will develop the compare-and-contrast essay by taking it through each of the steps of the writing process: prewriting, drafting, revising, editing, and publishing. You will also have an opportunity to develop a consumer report, which provides information about products. To preview the criteria for how your compare-and-contrast essay will be evaluated, see the rubric on page 163.

FEATURE ASSIGNMENT

Expository Essay: Compare-and-Contrast Essay

An effective expository essay has these characteristics:

- Detailed **information** and **explanations** about a specific topic to guide and inform the reader's understanding of key ideas and evidence

- An effective **introduction** that states the main idea and **conclusion** that wraps up the essay

- An **organized structure** that logically follows the writer's points

- A **variety of sentence structures** to keep readers interested and **transitions** to connect ideas

- **Effective sentence structure** and correct spelling, grammar, and usage

A compare-and-contrast essay also includes:

- A **thesis** statement that sets up the compare/contrast points

- Specific **facts, details,** and **examples** to support the thesis

Other Forms of Expository Writing

In addition to compare-and-contrast essays, there are other forms of expository writing, including:

Cause-and-effect essays trace the results of an event or the reasons an event happened.

Classification essays organize a subject into categories or explain the category into which an item falls.

Newspaper and magazine articles that are printed or published on the Internet supply relevant information about a particular topic by analyzing the topic's elements. They may also reflect genres other than analytical essays—for example, persuasive writing, or narrative nonfiction writing.

Pro/con essays examine the arguments for and against a particular action or decision.

Problem/solution essays explore a particular problem and present one or more possible solutions to it. They may address concerns related to personal issues; businesses or consumers; or the local, national, or global community.

Try It! For each audience and purpose described, choose a form, such as a speech, essay, or review, that is appropriate for conveying your intended meaning to the audience. Explain your choices.

- To tell your friends the reasons for and against buying a particular video game
- To inform your community about ways to fix a local pollution problem
- To inform classmates about a new scientific discovery

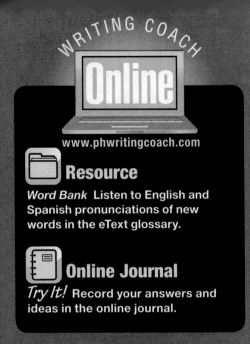

WRITING COACH
Online
www.phwritingcoach.com

Resource

Word Bank Listen to English and Spanish pronunciations of new words in the eText glossary.

Online Journal

Try It! Record your answers and ideas in the online journal.

WORD BANK

People often use these basic and content area vocabulary words when they talk about expository writing. Work with a partner. Take turns saying each word aloud. Then write one sentence using each word. If you are unsure of the meaning or pronunciation of a word, use the Glossary or a dictionary to check the definition or pronunciation.

compare	example
contrast	inform
evidence	similar

MENTOR TEXT

Learn From Experience

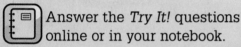 After reading the expository essay on pages 148–149, read the numbered notes in the margins to learn about how the author presented ideas. Later you will read a Student Model, which shares these characteristics and also has the characteristics of a compare-and-contrast essay.

Answer the *Try It!* questions online or in your notebook.

---

❶ The **introduction** describes teen activities, including volunteer jobs. Specific details like these **grab readers' interest** and let readers know the topic of the essay.

> *Try It!* What do you think the essay will be about, and why do you think so?

❷ The author states her **controlling idea** here.

> *Try It!* What is the controlling, or main, idea of the essay? Put it in your own words.

❸ Specific **facts, details,** and **quotations** from experts **support** the controlling idea.

> *Try It!* Which fact, detail, or quotation do you think most strongly supports the author's thesis? Why?

Extension Find another example of an expository essay, and compare it with this one.

Profiles in Caring

by Kirsten Weir

❶ Between school, sports, clubs, and friends, today's teens have plenty to keep them busy. But that doesn't stop many young people from adding volunteer jobs to their to-do lists.

❷ There are many reasons to volunteer. Young people
5   involved in community service are more likely to get good grades, graduate from high school, and go to college, says Steve Culbertson, president of Youth Service America (YSA). They also gain valuable skills that help them shine in paid jobs down the line.

10   **❸** Notably, 61 percent of 13 - to 25-year-olds feel personally responsible for making a difference in the world, according to a study by the companies Cone Inc. and AMP Insights. Eighty-one percent of those surveyed had volunteered within the past year. "In the last two decades," Culbertson says, "the
15   number of teenagers volunteering has doubled in the United States. Kids [today] are exposed much more to the problems of the world and [are] more likely to help."

Volunteering is rewarding in its own right. But donating your time can also give you a head start down your future
20   career path. Volunteers discover new talents, learn new skills, build real-world experience, and test potential career fields. Read on for stories of three teens who make community service part of their routines. As they have learned, volunteering is fun and loaded with benefits—for
25   the community as well as the volunteer.

❹ Community Building

In the summer of 2006, Arizona native Leena Patel, now 17, traveled to North Carolina for a 13-day volunteer mission. As part of a team of 14 teens, Leena helped build
30 homes through Habitat for Humanity, an organization that serves families who need safe, affordable housing.

Working eight hours every day, Leena's team built homes for four families. "I had never done construction before," Leena says. She quickly learned to install doors and windows,
35 attach baseboards, and put up vinyl siding. After all her hard work, the biggest reward was meeting the families who would live in the homes. "They were so genuine and so thankful," she says. "I didn't expect them to be just like me."

❹ Birds on the Brain

40 Kaleigh Gerlich has a cool volunteer job—literally. She's a penguin keeper's assistant at the Denver Zoo. The 18-year-old has volunteered at the zoo for three years. "People always think it's crazy; they say the penguins smell like fish," she says. "But they're just so much fun. They have the greatest personalities."
45 Gerlich worked at the zoo every Sunday throughout high school. In the summers, she spent even more time there. Last summer, she logged 150 volunteer hours cleaning the penguin enclosures and preparing food for penguins and other birds. As a teen leader, Gerlich also helped coordinate
50 other teen volunteers and pitched in with office work.

❹ Bake a Difference

Daniel Feldman, 17, of Linwood, N.J., has a big goal: ending child hunger in the United States. It's not far-fetched for someone who practically grew up volunteering. Since
55 age 7, Daniel has worked with Peer Partners, a youth volunteer organization his sister founded. Daniel started his own organization, Kids Feeding Kids. The group holds bake sales, plant sales, and other community fundraisers to fight child hunger. In the past four years, Kids Feeding Kids
60 has raised nearly $40,000, as well as "pounds upon pounds of food for the local food bank," he says.

Daniel hopes that his success will inspire others. ❺ "Find a cause you think is worthy, and go for it," he says. "The smallest things can make the biggest difference."

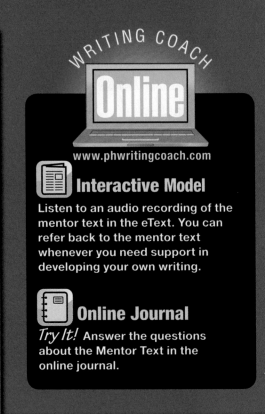

WRITING COACH

Online

www.phwritingcoach.com

📰 Interactive Model

Listen to an audio recording of the mentor text in the eText. You can refer back to the mentor text whenever you need support in developing your own writing.

📓 Online Journal

Try It! Answer the questions about the Mentor Text in the online journal.

❹ The essay has a **clear, logical organization.** Headings set off the three supporting **examples,** marking the **transition** from one teen's story to the next.

> *Try It!* How does each teen's story support the author's thesis? Write a sentence or two comparing the experiences of the teen volunteers.

❺ In the conclusion, the author **quotes** the last student's words to wrap up the essay.

> *Try It!* How do the last quotations support the controlling idea of the essay?

STUDENT MODEL
Compare-and-Contrast Essay

With a small group, take turns reading this Student Model aloud. As you read, practice newly acquired vocabulary by correctly producing the word's sound. Think about the author's purpose and main ideas. Look for evidence, such as facts and details, in the text.

 ## Use a Reader's Eye

Now, reread the Student Model. On your copy of the Student Model, use the Reader's Response Symbols to react to what you read.

Reader's Response Symbols

+ **Aha! That makes sense to me.**

− **This isn't clear to me.**

? **I have a question about this.**

! **Wow! That is cool/weird/ interesting.**

Take turns reading the Student Model aloud to a partner. Then discuss how the writer organizes the three points of comparison. Decide how this organization helps the author identify main ideas and achieve a purpose.

Do We Still Need to Talk FACE-TO-FACE?

by Travis Barry

I just read an awesome science fiction story in which people live below ground and rarely meet face-to-face. Instead, they communicate through a machine. Could humans really live that way?
5   The story made me think about why we need both e-mail and face-to-face communication.

E-mail is a great way to keep in touch. It's fast, it connects people around the world, and it makes it easy to share information. For example, my uncle
10   lived in Japan for two years. When I had to do a report on Japanese art, he asked an artist he knew if I could e-mail him some questions. The artist agreed. I sent the questions and got his answers the next day. Doing an e-mail interview this way
15   was much faster than if I'd had to travel all the way to Japan to do the interview face-to-face. I was also able to contact the artist immediately and directly, even though I didn't know him.

Although e-mail is so fast and easy that people
20   send over 200 billion e-mails every day, talking face-to-face is sometimes better. For one thing, e-mail is so fast that it can make people feel they have to reply quickly, which can stress out some people. Although getting together can be slower,
25   it gives people time to think. Another problem is that although connecting by e-mail is easy, it can be hard to build trust. When we meet face-to-face, we can use smiles and gestures to show how we

1

feel about what we say. When we read an e-mail,
30 we can't see the sender's face or hear a voice.
So it's easy to misunderstand a joke or to think
someone who is just slightly annoyed is really angry.

If you want to end a disagreement or share
bad news, do it face-to-face. On the other hand,
35 if you need to send information to someone far
away, use e-mail. E-mail is fast and convenient,
but it can send the wrong message about how
someone feels. That's why e-mail will never
completely replace face-to-face communication.

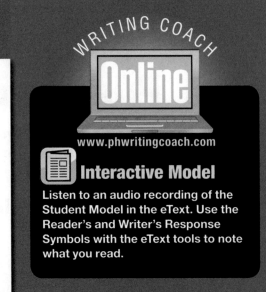

www.phwritingcoach.com

Interactive Model

Listen to an audio recording of the
Student Model in the eText. Use the
Reader's and Writer's Response
Symbols with the eText tools to note
what you read.

Use a Writer's Eye

Now evaluate the piece as a writer. On
your copy of the Student Model, use the
Writer's Response Symbols to react to
what you read. Identify places where the
student writer uses characteristics of an
effective **compare-and-contrast essay.**

Writer's Response Symbols	
C.T.	**Clearly stated thesis**
I.C.	**Effective introduction and conclusion**
T.W.	**Transition words show how ideas are alike or different**
S.E.	**Effective supporting evidence**

2

Your Turn > **Feature Assignment:**
Compare-and-Contrast Essay

Prewriting

Plan a first draft of your compare-and-contrast essay. Select from the Topic Bank or think of an idea of your own.

👍 Choose From the Topic Bank

TOPIC BANK

Ethnic Foods All nationalities have special foods. Burritos and tacos are two popular Mexican foods. Ravioli and lasagna are famous Italian dishes. Compare any two international food favorites and describe the ingredients, appearance, and taste.

Rules Think about the rules you have at home and at school. They may be rules about helping with household chores or about bedtimes. They may be rules about being quiet while your teacher is talking or about running in the hallways. Write an essay in which you compare and contrast the rules you have to follow at home with the rules you have to follow at school.

Buildings Choose two buildings in your city or town. Think about how they are alike and how they are different. Think about the way they look, their age, how they are used, and who uses them. Write an essay in which you compare and contrast these two buildings.

👍 Choose Your Own Topic

Generate your own ideas or topics with these strategies.

Make Comparisons and Organize

- Write a list of five people, things, or activities you know well. Then, next to each, list a different type of related thing or activity. For example, you could write *soccer* and *football*.

- Next, draw two circles that overlap. Label each circle with your two related points.

Review your responses and choose a topic.

Narrow Your Topic

Choosing a topic that is too broad will make it hard to find similarities and differences to compare and contrast.

Apply It! Use a graphic organizer like the one shown to narrow your topic.

- Write a category in the top box.
- Use the next box to list interesting people, things, or ideas in that category.
- Finally, choose two items from the list to compare and contrast.

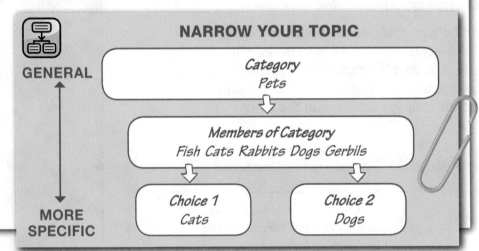

NARROW YOUR TOPIC

GENERAL

Category
Pets

Members of Category
Fish Cats Rabbits Dogs Gerbils

Choice 1
Cats

Choice 2
Dogs

MORE SPECIFIC

Consider Your Audience and Purpose

Before writing, think about your audience and purpose. Ask yourself what your audience needs and wants to know about your compare-and-contrast essay.

Questions for Audience	Questions for Purpose
• Who is my audience? • What does my audience already know about what I'm comparing and contrasting? • What kinds of ideas will grab and keep my audience's attention?	• Which people, things, or ideas do I want to compare and contrast? • Which similarities and differences do I want to include in my essay? What evidence will I need? • What do I want people to learn through this comparison and contrast?

Record your answers in your writing journal.

WRITING COACH

Online

www.phwritingcoach.com

Interactive Writing Coach™

- Choosing from the Topic Bank gives you access to the Interactive Writing Coach™.
- Submit your writing and receive instant personalized feedback and guidance as you draft, revise, and edit your writing.

Interactive Graphic Organizers

Use the interactive graphic organizers to help you narrow your topic.

Online Journal

Try It! Record your answers and ideas in the online journal.

Plan Your Piece

You will use a graphic organizer like this one to state your thesis, organize your arguments, and identify details. When it is complete, you will be ready to write your first draft.

Develop a Clear Thesis List similarities and differences between what you're comparing. These are your points of comparison and contrast. For example, you could compare dogs and cats according to levels of care, sociability, and trainability. Use these points to **develop your thesis.** Then, think about how you will use the information from your thesis to create an **effective introduction and conclusion.**

Logically Organize Your Points You can use **point-by-point organization** as in the model—care, sociability, and trainability, discussing both cats and dogs in each section. You can also use **block organization** for the topics of cats and dogs—first explain cats' care, sociability, and trainability; then explain the same elements about dogs.

Develop Your Points of Comparison/Contrast

Clear Thesis	*Both cats and dogs can make great pets, but there are many differences between the two.*
First Point of Comparison/ Contrast	*Cats are easier to care for than dogs.*
Supporting Evidence/Details	
Second Point of Comparison/ Contrast	*Cats tend to be less sociable than dogs.*
Supporting Evidence/Details	
Third Point of Comparison/ Contrast	*Dogs can be trained more easily than cats.*
Supporting Evidence/Details	
Conclusion	*Knowing the differences between cats and dogs will help you choose the right pet.*

Gather Details

To provide supporting evidence for their points, writers use these kinds of details. Look at these examples.

- **Facts:** *With American pet owners dogs are slightly more popular than cats.*
- **Examples:** *Cats quickly learn to use a litter box.*
- **Expert Opinions:** *Our veterinarian says that dogs are pack animals, so they are very sociable.*
- **Personal Observations:** *When we moved, our dog quickly made friends with the neighbors. Our cat was more interested in exploring her new home.*

Try It! Read the excerpt from the Student Model and identify which types of details the author used to support his points.

STUDENT MODEL · from **Do We Still Need to Talk Face-to-Face?** page 150; lines 7–14

E-mail is a great way to keep in touch. It's fast, it connects people around the world, and it makes it easy to share information. For example, my uncle lived in Japan for two years. When I had to do a report on Japanese art, he asked an artist he knew if I could e-mail him some questions. The artist agreed. I sent the questions and got his answers the next day.

 *Apply It!* Review the types of support the writer of a compare-and-contrast essay can use. Then, identify at least one supporting detail for each of your points. Evaluate each detail and determine if it will support your thesis.

- Make sure your evidence includes **specific facts, details, and examples.** Review your details to decide which ones will be best to **guide and inform your reader's understanding of the key ideas and evidence.**
- Then, add these details to your graphic organizer. Match each detail to the right point of comparison/contrast to create an **appropriately organized structure.**

WRITING COACH

Online

www.phwritingcoach.com

Interactive Graphic Organizers

Use the interactive graphic organizers to help you create a plan for your writing.

Interactive Model

Refer back to the Interactive Model in the eText as you plan your writing.

Drafting

During the drafting stage, you will start to write your ideas for your compare-and-contrast essay. You will follow an outline that provides an **organizational strategy** that will help you build on ideas to write a **focused, organized, and coherent** compare-and-contrast essay.

The Organization of a Compare-and-Contrast Essay

The chart shows an organizational strategy for a compare-and-contrast essay. Look back at how the Mentor Text follows this organizational strategy. Then use this chart to help you outline your draft.

I. Introduction

See Mentor Text, p. 148.

- Interesting opening to grab readers' interest
- Clear thesis

Grab Your Reader

- An interesting opening can ask a question, use an anecdote, or use a strong detail.
- A clear thesis, or the main point you are making, states what you are comparing or contrasting.

II. Body

See Mentor Text, pp. 148–149.

- Points of comparison and contrast
- Logical organization of points

Point-by-Point
- Point 1: Topic A and B
- Point 2: Topic A and B
- Point 3: Topic A and B

Block Organization
- Topic A: Points 1, 2, and 3
- Topic B: Points 1, 2, and 3

Compare and contrast

- Full development of each point of comparison and contrast provides supporting evidence that explains the main point and informs your readers.
- The organizational strategy—point-by-point (see page 154) or block organization—helps readers follow your ideas more easily. Block organization works best if you have only one or two points of comparison, otherwise use point-by-point.

III. Conclusion

See Mentor Text, p. 149.

- Restatement of thesis
- Ending that shows why this topic matters

Wrap It Up

- Restating your thesis reinforces your main points and briefly summarizes your points of comparison and contrast.
- A powerful sentence at the end of your essay leaves readers thinking that your main point matters.

Start Your Draft

Use the checklist to help complete your draft. Use the graphic organizer that shows your thesis, points of comparison and contrast, and supporting details, and the Outline for Success as guides.

While drafting, aim at writing your ideas down, not on making your writing perfect. Remember, you will have the chance to improve your draft when you revise and edit.

√ Identify your **topics** of comparison and contrast.

√ Create an **effective** introduction by beginning with an interesting opening and your thesis statement.

√ Shape the **body** of your essay by using an appropriate organizational strategy for comparing and contrasting, such as **point-by-point** or **block organization**.

√ Include **evidence** such as specific facts, details, and examples to inform your reader's understanding of your key ideas.

√ Use both long and short sentences. A **variety of sentence structures** keeps your writing interesting and lively.

√ Use **transitions** such as *however, in contrast, similarly,* or *in the same way* to connect and build on ideas between sentences and paragraphs. This will help you be sure that your essay is focused, organized, and coherent.

√ End with an **effective** conclusion that summarizes your main points.

√ Help readers to remember your ideas by ending with a **powerful thought**.

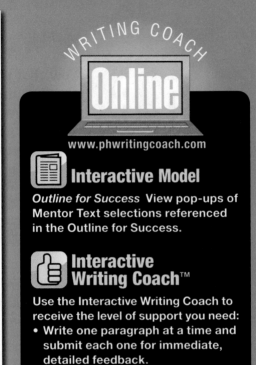

WRITING COACH

Online

www.phwritingcoach.com

Interactive Model

Outline for Success View pop-ups of Mentor Text selections referenced in the Outline for Success.

Interactive Writing Coach™

Use the Interactive Writing Coach to receive the level of support you need:
- Write one paragraph at a time and submit each one for immediate, detailed feedback.
- Write your entire first draft and submit it for immediate, personalized feedback.

Revising: Making It Better

Now that you have finished your first draft, you are ready to revise. Think about the "big picture" of **audience, purpose, and genre.** You can use the Revision RADaR strategy as a guide for making changes to improve your draft. Revision RADaR provides four major ways to improve your writing: (R) replace, (A) add, (D) delete, and (R) reorder.

Kelly Gallagher, M. Ed.

KEEP REVISION ON YOUR RADaR

Read part of the first draft of the Student Model "Do We Still Need to Talk Face-to-Face?" Then look at questions the writer asked himself as he thought about how well his draft **addressed issues of audience, purpose, and genre.**

Do We Still Need to Talk Face-to-Face?

E-mail is a great way to keep in touch. It's fast. It connects people around the world. It makes it easy to share information. My uncle lived in Japan for two years. When I had to do a report on Japanese art, he asked an artist he knew if I could e-mail some questions. The artist agreed. I sent the questions and got his answers the next day.

E-mail is so fast and easy that people send many e-mails every day. Talking face-to-face is sometimes better. For one thing, e-mail is so fast that it can make people feel they have to reply quickly, which can stress out some people. Although getting together can be slower, it gives people time to think. Another problem is that although connecting by e-mail is easy, it can be hard to build trust. When we meet face to face, we can use smiles and gestures to show how we feel...

Have I used a variety of sentence structures? Have I included transitions to connect ideas?

Have I explained my points to help guide and inform my readers?

Have I used transitions between paragraphs to link ideas and set up comparisons and contrasts? Have I included specific facts, details, and examples?

Now, look at how the writer applied Revision RADaR to write an improved second draft.

Do We Still Need to Talk FACE-TO-FACE? 2ND DRAFT

E-mail is a great way to keep in touch. It's fast, it connects people around the world, and it makes it easy to share information. For example, my uncle lived in Japan for two years. When I had to do a report on Japanese art, he asked an artist he knew if I could e-mail some questions. The artist agreed. I sent the questions and got his answers the next day. Doing an e-mail interview this way was much faster than if I'd had to travel all the way to Japan to do the interview face-to-face. I was also able to contact the artist immediately and directly, even though I didn't know him.

Although e-mail is so fast and easy that people send over 200 billion e-mails every day, talking face-to-face is sometimes better. For one thing, e-mail is so fast that it can make people feel they have to reply quickly, which can stress out some people. Although getting together can be slower, it gives people time to think. Another problem is that although connecting by e-mail is easy, it can be hard to build trust. When we meet face to face, we can use smiles and gestures to show how we feel...

R *Reordered short, choppy sentences by combining them into one longer, more complex sentence*

A *Added the transition for example to help connect ideas*

A *Added several sentences to more fully explain my point to my audience*

A *Added the transition Although to connect ideas between paragraphs and to set up a contrast between e-mailing and face-to-face communication*

R *Replaced the general word many with a fact*

 Apply It! Use your Revision RADaR to revise your draft.

- First, determine if you have organized your points of comparison and contrast clearly, provided supporting evidence for each point, and used transitions to link ideas between sentences and paragraphs.

- Then, apply Revision RADaR to make needed changes. Remember—you can use the steps in the strategy in any order.

Look at the Big Picture

Use the chart and your analytical skills to evaluate how well each section of your compare-and-contrast essay addresses **purpose, audience, and genre.** When necessary, use the suggestions in the chart to revise your piece.

Section	Evaluate	Revise
Introduction	• Check the **opening** sentence. Will it grab readers' attention and make them want to read more?	• Make your introduction more interesting by adding a question, anecdote, quotation, or strong detail.
	• Does the thesis identify the topics I'm comparing and contrasting to create an effective **introduction?**	• To check your thesis sentence, circle each topic and underline the point you're making about them. Add or delete information as needed.
Body	• Check that you have **organized** your essay in an easy-to-follow way.	• Make sure you have used either a point-by-point or block organization consistently.
	• Underline specific facts, details, and **examples** that provide support and help to guide and inform the reader's understanding of your key ideas and evidence.	• Rearrange a detail that is not in the same paragraph as the point it supports. When necessary, add or take out details.
	• Place a check mark by each **transition** you have used.	• If necessary, add words such as *in contrast* and *similarly* to show how your ideas are related.
	• Make sure you have a mixture of simple and compound **sentences.**	• Avoid too many of the same type of sentences. Rearrange words to include a variety of structures.
Conclusion	• Check that you have restated your thesis and provided a brief **summary** of your main points.	• If necessary, restate your thesis more clearly to create an **effective conclusion.**
	• Make sure you have ended your essay in a way that helps readers understand your **points.**	• Add a quotation or a forceful statement to conclude your essay on a memorable point. It is not enough to show comparison and contrast—tell readers why it matters.

Focus on Craft: Improve Transitions

In a compare-and-contrast essay, you show both similarities and differences. The information can get confusing for readers unless you use transitions. **Transitions** are signal words that show how ideas are related. They link ideas between sentences and paragraphs. To show similarities, you can use transitions such as *in the same way*, *similarly*, or *likewise*. To show differences, you can use transitions such as *on the other hand*, *but*, or *however*.

Think about transitions as you read the following sentences from the Student Model.

 **STUDENT MODEL** from **Do We Still Need to Talk Face to Face?** page 151; lines 33–36

> If you want to end a disagreement or share bad news, do it face-to-face. On the other hand, if you need to send information quickly to someone far away, use e-mail.

 Try It! Now, ask yourself these questions:

- What transition is used to show contrast?
- Would the second sentence be more or less effective if there were no transition? Explain.

 Fine-Tune Your Draft

Apply It! Use the revision suggestions to prepare your final draft **after rethinking how well questions of purpose, audience, and genre have been addressed.**

- **Improve Transitions** Make the transitions that link ideas and paragraphs stronger by adding, deleting, combining, and rearranging sentences.
- **Improve Sentences** Simple sentences include only a main clause—a subject, a verb, and their objects and modifiers. Avoid too many short, simple sentences.

Peer Feedback Read your final draft to a group of peers. Ask classmates to tell you about your comparisons and contrasts. Think about their responses and revise your final draft as needed.

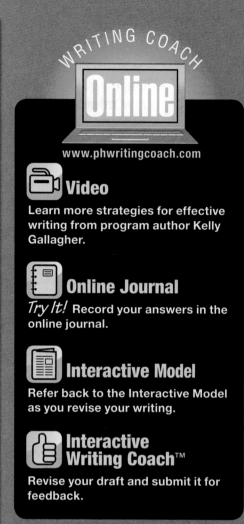

WRITING COACH

Online

www.phwritingcoach.com

Video

Learn more strategies for effective writing from program author Kelly Gallagher.

Online Journal

Try It! Record your answers in the online journal.

Interactive Model

Refer back to the Interactive Model as you revise your writing.

Interactive Writing Coach™

Revise your draft and submit it for feedback.

Editing: Making It Correct

Once you have your final draft the way you want it, spend a few minutes doing a careful edit. Read your draft sentence by sentence to check it thoroughly.

When editing your final draft, think about using **subordinating conjunctions**. These elements of writing will connect your ideas and improve the flow of your essay. Then edit your final draft for factual errors and errors in **grammar, mechanics, and spelling**.

 **WRITE GUY** *Jeff Anderson, M. Ed.*

WHAT DO YOU NOTICE?

Zoom In On Conventions Focus on words that connect ideas as you zoom in on this sentence from the Student Model.

 **STUDENT MODEL** from **Do We Still Need to Talk Face-to-Face?** page 150; lines 16-18

> I was also able to contact the artist immediately and directly, even though I didn't know him.

Now, ask yourself: *Which words connect different ideas in the sentence?*

Perhaps you said that *even though* connects different ideas.

Even though is a subordinating conjunction. A **subordinating conjunction** connects two ideas by making one idea dependent on the other. Common subordinating conjunctions include *after, even though, if, since, until,* and *when.*

The ideas that subordinating conjunctions connect are expressed in clauses. A clause is a group of words with its own subject and verb. A main clause can stand by itself as a sentence, but a subordinate clause cannot. In the Student Model, the subordinate clause is *even though I didn't know him.*

Partner Talk Discuss this question with a partner: *Why do you think the author chooses to connect ideas using subordinating conjunctions instead of writing separate sentences?*

> To learn more about subordinating conjunctions, see Chapter 17 of your Grammar Handbook.

Grammar Mini-Lesson: Commas With Clauses

To learn more, see Chapter 25.

If a subordinate clause occurs at the beginning of the sentence, place a comma at the end of the clause. If a subordinate clause occurs at the end of the sentence, a comma may or may not be placed before the main and subordinate clause. Notice how the author of the Student Text placed a comma after an introductory subordinate clause.

 STUDENT MODEL from **Do We Still Need to Talk Face-to-Face?** page 151; lines 29–30

> When we read an e-mail, we can't see the sender's face or hear a voice.

 Try It! Identify the subordinating clause in each sentence. Then tell if a comma is needed and where it should go. Write the answers in your journal.

1. Mia stood at the bus stop until it began to rain.
2. After Jill hung up the phone she sat patiently and waited for her friend to arrive.

 Apply It! Edit your draft for grammar, mechanics, and spelling. If necessary, rewrite sentences to include **subordinating conjunctions**. Place commas before or after subordinate clauses as needed.

 Use the rubric to evaluate your piece. If necessary, rethink, rewrite, or revise.

Rubric for Expository Writing: Compare-and-Contrast Essay	Rating Scale					
Ideas: How well do you explain the similarities and differences of your topics?	Not very					Very
	1	2	3	4	5	6
Organization: How well do you organize the similarities and differences of your topic?	1	2	3	4	5	6
Voice: How well do you engage the reader?	1	2	3	4	5	6
Word Choice: How clearly do your words convey your ideas?	1	2	3	4	5	6
Sentence Fluency: How effectively do you use transitions?	1	2	3	4	5	6
Conventions: How correct is your usage of commas in clauses?	1	2	3	4	5	6

WRITING COACH

Online

www.phwritingcoach.com

Video

Learn effective editing techniques from program author Jeff Anderson.

Online Journal

Try It! Record your answers in the online journal.

Interactive Model

Refer back to the Interactive Model as you edit your writing.

Interactive Writing Coach™

Edit your draft. Check it against the rubric and then submit it for feedback.

Publishing

Share your ideas with a wider audience. Get your essay ready for presentation. Then, choose a way to **publish it for the appropriate audiences.**

Wrap Up Your Presentation

Adding images to your expository essay can provide readers with visual support to illustrate the evidence you presented. Think of some images you can include to bring your compare-and-contrast essay to life.

Publish Your Piece

Use the chart to find a way to publish your essay.

If your audience is...	...then publish it by...
Students or adults at school	• Reading it aloud during a writer's workshop • Posting your essay online and inviting responses
Your local community	• Submitting it to a local newspaper • Posting it on a community Web site

Extend Your Research

Think more about the topic on which you wrote your compare-and-contrast essay. What else would you like to know about this topic?

- Brainstorm for several questions that you would like to research and then consult, or discuss, with others. Then, decide which question is your major research question.

- Formulate, or develop, a plan about how you will answer these questions. Decide where you will find more information—on the Internet, at the library, or through other sources.

- Finally, learn more about your topic by following through with your research plan.

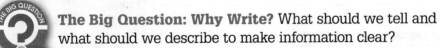 **The Big Question: Why Write?** What should we tell and what should we describe to make information clear?

Manage Your Portfolio You may wish to include your published compare-and-contrast essay in your writing portfolio. If so, consider what this piece reveals about your writing.

MAKE YOUR WRITING COUNT

Write and Present the Results of a Survey

Compare-and-contrast essays identify and explain similarities and differences between people, things, or issues. Identify your classmates' preferences by using a **survey** to determine what people, things, or issues are important to them.

With a group, create a paper or electronic survey for students at your school. The goal of the survey is to evaluate what your peers consider to be important. Then, present the results in a **multimedia presentation** including text and graphics. Present the results orally to a group. Support your presentations with charts and graphs made using available technology or with handmade posters.

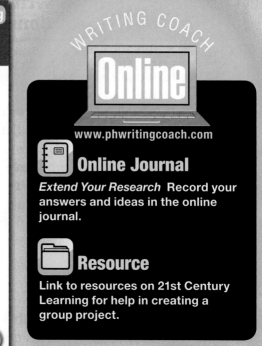

WRITING COACH

Online

www.phwritingcoach.com

Online Journal

Extend Your Research Record your answers and ideas in the online journal.

Resource

Link to resources on 21st Century Learning for help in creating a group project.

Here's your action plan.

1. Choose roles, such as writer and graphics creator.

2. Review your compare-contrast essays for topics. Choose appropriate people, things, or issues to present in your survey.

3. Look at sample surveys online. Then, prepare a brief survey following these guidelines:

   - Ask questions that can be answered with yes or no, or ask multiple-choice questions.
   - Write your questions legibly or type them.
   - Distribute copies by hand or electronically.

4. Analyze the completed surveys. Create a graph of the results by hand or with software.

5. Produce a multimedia presentation that includes the survey, a verbal summary of the results, and a graph showing the results visually. Share it with the school.

Listening and Speaking After you collect the results, work in a group together to discuss conclusions you can draw about the answers. Listen for disagreements about the data and resolve them. Then, rehearse your group oral presentation. Make sure your graphics will be clearly visible to the audience. During your presentation, sum up the overall meaning of your survey results.

Writing for Media:
Consumer Comparison

Consumer Comparison

21st Century Learning

A **consumer comparison** is a review intended to help people choose the best product. Some reviews are based on formal tests and are published in magazines. Others are more informal—they are posted on Web sites by people who have purchased a product and want to let others know how they liked it. When you write a consumer comparison, you choose criteria you will use to compare and contrast products. You also provide supporting details to show whether a product meets each criterion.

Try It! Study the table on this page. Then, answer these questions. Record the answers in your journal.

1. What two things are being compared and contrasted?

2. What is the **purpose** of this consumer comparison?

3. Who is the target **audience** for this comparison?

4. Will the points of comparison and contrast chosen help the **audience** choose the best product?

5. How do the **supporting details** help readers make the right choice?

6. Are there enough **supporting details** to write a fair and balanced comparison? Why or why not?

7. How does the **organization** of the table make it easier to understand how the restaurants are alike and different?

Extension Find another example of a consumer comparison, and compare it with this one.

Report on: Taco Shack and Gourmet Garden

Date of visit: Nov. 10

Observations:

- Long line moved quickly at the Taco Shack.
- Gourmet Garden ran out of what I wanted, so they gave me a free dessert.

Points of Comparison/ Contrast	Taco Shack	Gourmet Garden
Price	• From $.99 to $5.99 • Generous portions	• From $15.99 to $35.99 • Small portions
Atmosphere	• Typical strip mall • Casual • Family friendly	• Upscale • Formal • Not family friendly
Food quality	• Mexican fast food • Fresh ingredients • Many items • Consistent quality	• Dishes from all over the world • Fresh ingredients • Only a few specials • Inconsistent quality

Create a Consumer Comparison

Follow these steps to create your own consumer comparison. To plan your consumer report, review the graphic organizers on pages R24–R27 and choose one that suits your needs.

Prewriting

- Choose a topic for your review. Consider stores, video games, restaurants, or any other product or service you often use.
- Identify your target audience. How are they likely to use this comparison? What will they want to know about the product?
- Determine your points of comparison and contrast. If you review two restaurants, you might compare price, atmosphere, and quality of food.
- List supporting details for each point of comparison and contrast.

Drafting

- Decide whether you are going to organize your review with a point-by-point or block organization. For example, you could start by comparing prices at both restaurants. Another approach would be to discuss the price, atmosphere, and food at one restaurant, then address each of these points at the other.
- Consider organizing your information into a table to make it easier to read.

Revising and Editing

- Review your draft to ensure that your points of comparison and contrast are organized logically.
- Consider whether your comparison is fair. Do you support your opinion with accurate details? Also check that you have included the same amount of detail for each topic. Remove any biased points.
- Check that spelling, grammar, and mechanics are correct.

Publishing

- Submit your comparison to your student newspaper.
- Turn your comparison into a multimedia presentation. In a slideshow, make an opening that includes text titles, and add music and images to help support your ideas.

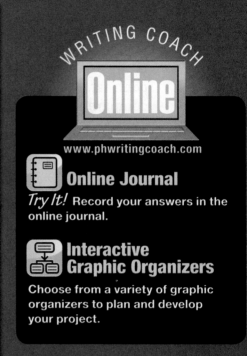

WRITING COACH

Online

www.phwritingcoach.com

Online Journal

Try It! Record your answers in the online journal.

Interactive Graphic Organizers

Choose from a variety of graphic organizers to plan and develop your project.

Partner Talk

Explain your review to a partner. While explaining, increase the specificity of your details based on the type of information you are discussing. Describe your main points and ask whether your consumer report is clear and fair. Consider your partner's responses when you revise your report.

Writing for Assessment

Many tests include a prompt that asks you to compare and contrast. Respond using the characteristics of an effective compare-and-contrast essay. (See page 146.)

 Try It! To begin, read the **expository** prompt and the information on format and academic vocabulary. Use the ABCDs of On-Demand Writing to help you plan and write your essay.

Format
The prompt directs you to write a *compare-and-contrast essay*. Be sure to include an introduction that identifies who you are comparing, a body with supporting evidence, and a conclusion that restates your main ideas.

Compare-and-Contrast Prompt
Choose two celebrities and write a compare-and-contrast essay about how they are alike and different. Choose at least two points of comparison/contrast. Use an organized structure that's easy for readers to follow.

Academic Vocabulary
Each similarity or difference you write about is *a point of comparison/contrast*. An *organized structure* is the way you organize your points—such as point-by-point or block organization.

The ABCDs of On-Demand Writing

Use the following ABCDs to help you respond to the prompt.

Before you write your draft:

Attack the prompt [1 MINUTE]

- Circle or highlight important verbs in the prompt. Draw a line from the verb to what it refers to.
- Rewrite the prompt in your own words.

Brainstorm possible answers [4 MINUTES]

- Create a graphic organizer to generate ideas.
- Use one for each part of the prompt if necessary.

Choose the order of your response [1 MINUTE]

- Think about the best way to organize your ideas.
- Number your ideas in the order you will write about them. Cross out ideas you will not be using.

After you write your draft:

Detect errors before turning in the draft [1 MINUTE]

- Carefully reread your writing.
- Make sure that your response makes sense and is complete.
- Look for spelling, punctuation, and grammar errors.

More Prompts for Practice

Apply It! Respond to Prompts 1 and 2 by writing **compare-and-contrast essays** that convey information about your topics. As you write, be sure to:

- Include effective **introduction** and **conclusion** paragraphs.
- Include specific **facts, details,** and **examples** to support your ideas.
- Establish points of comparison and contrast.
- Include **explanations** that will guide and inform your reader's understanding of your key ideas and evidence.
- Use an **organizing structure** appropriate for comparing and contrasting.
- Vary your **sentence structure.**
- Use **transitions** to link paragraphs.

Prompt 1 Many different beautiful places in nature exist all over the world. Write a composition that compares and contrasts two places in nature. Make sure that you use facts and details that will guide and inform your reader's understanding of your key ideas.

Prompt 2 Life in the country can be very different from life in a city. Write a composition that compares and contrasts an urban place and a rural place. Remember to think about ways these places are similar and different so that you can find a basis for comparison.

Spiral Review: Poetry Respond to Prompt 3 by writing a **poem**. Make sure your poem reflects all of the characteristics described on page 120. Include **poetic techniques** such as rhythm and rhyme. Also, consider including **figurative language** such as similes and metaphors to bring the language to life. Your poem should also make use of **graphic elements,** such as line length.

Prompt 3 Think about your school. What are your favorite things about your school? What are the best things that have happened here? Write a poem expressing your ideas and feelings about your school.

WRITING COACH

Online
www.phwritingcoach.com

Interactive Writing Coach™

Plan your response to the prompt. If you are using the prompt for practice, write one paragraph at a time or your entire draft and then submit it for feedback. If you are using the prompt as a timed test, write your entire draft and then submit it for feedback.

Remember **ABCD**

Attack the prompt

Brainstorm possible answers

Choose the order of your response

Detect errors before turning in the draft

PERSUASION

Persuasion

What Do You Think?

Some teenagers have responsibilities around their homes. For example, this girl brushes the horse on her family farm. Should teenagers have to show responsibility by doing chores? Or is working on homework and going to school responsibility enough?

What is your opinion about this topic? Once you have your opinion, you may want to convince someone to share it. When you use words to convince people to think or act in a certain way, you are using persuasion.

Try It! List reasons why teenagers should and should not have to do household chores to show they can handle responsibilities.

Consider these questions as you participate in an extended discussion with a partner. Take turns expressing your ideas and feelings.

- What are some ways teenagers can show responsibility?
- What are the benefits of doing household chores?
- What are some of the reasons why teenagers should not have to do household chores?

Review the list you made. Choose a position on the issue by deciding which side to take. Write a sentence that states which position, or side, you will take. Then, take turns talking about your ideas and positions with a partner.

What's Ahead

In this chapter, you will review two strong examples of a persuasive essay: a Mentor Text and a Student Model. Then, using the examples as guidance, you will write a persuasive essay of your own.

www.phwritingcoach.com

Online Journal
Try It! Record your answers and ideas in the online journal.

You can also record and save your answers and ideas on pop-up sticky notes in the eText.

Connect to the Big Questions

Discuss these questions with your partner:

1 What do you think? Which responsibilities are most important?

2 Why write? What is your point of view? How will you know if you've convinced others?

PERSUASIVE ESSAY

In this chapter, you will explore a type of persuasive writing called the persuasive essay. The writer of a persuasive essay presents his or her view on an issue. Then the writer tries to persuade the reader to agree with that view. The writer supports his or her position with detailed evidence. Using sound reasoning, the writer shows why his or her point of view is stronger than other points of view.

You will develop the persuasive essay by taking it through each of the steps of the writing process: prewriting, drafting, revising, editing, and publishing. You will also have an opportunity to create a magazine cover. To preview the criteria for how your persuasive essay will be evaluated, see the rubric on page 189.

FEATURE ASSIGNMENT

Persuasive Essay

An effective persuasive essay has these characteristics:

- A **clear thesis** to **establish a position** on an issue that has at least two sides

- **Sound reasoning** to establish a position and create a convincing argument

- **Powerful language** to appeal to the emotion and reason of an appropriate audience

- **Detailed and relevant evidence,** such as facts and examples

- Consideration of **alternatives and counter-arguments,** or the ideas of people who do not share your opinions

- **Clear organization,** including an introduction, a body, and a conclusion

- A **conclusion** that restates your view and provides a memorable ending

- **Effective sentence structure** and correct spelling, grammar, and usage

- **Other types of evidence**, such as quotes from an expert on the topic

Other Forms of Persuasive Writing

In addition to the persuasive essay, there are other forms of persuasive writing, including:

Advertisements are paid announcements that try to convince people to do or buy something.

Editorials state the opinion of the editors and publishers of news organizations. Editorials are usually about current issues. They appear in newspapers and magazines, or on television, radio, or the Internet.

Letters to the editor are written by readers of a newspaper or magazine. The letters express an opinion in response to an article in the newspaper or magazine.

Op-ed pieces, or opinion editorials, try to persuade readers of a newspaper or magazine to agree with the writer's views on an issue. Op-eds differ from editorials in two ways. Op-eds are signed, while editorials are usually unsigned. Op-ed pieces are often written by people who do not work for the newspaper or magazine.

Persuasive speeches aim at winning an audience's support for a policy, position, or action.

Propaganda tries to persuade people to think or act in a certain way. This type of persuasive writing uses emotional appeals and often biased, false, or misleading information. Propaganda is often about political issues.

Reviews evaluate items and activities, such as books and movies. A review often states an opinion on whether people should spend time and money on the item or activity.

 Try It! For each audience and purpose described, choose a form, such as an advertisement, a letter, or a review, that is appropriate for conveying your intended meaning to the audience. Explain your choices.

- To express your support for an editorial in your local newspaper
- To encourage your friends and family to go see the school play
- To convince people to donate money or to volunteer for an important cause

MENTOR TEXT

Persuasive Essay

Learn From Experience

 Read the persuasive essay on pages 174–175. As you read, take notes to develop your understanding of basic sight and English vocabulary. Then, read the numbered notes in the margins to learn about how the author presented her ideas.

Answer the *Try It!* questions online or in your notebook.

---

❶ Vivid language in the **introduction** helps get readers' attention and make readers aware of the litter problem.

Try It! In your opinion, which descriptions of littering are the most vivid in the introduction?

❷ The author gives specific **examples** of litter that she found on the ground. These examples support her position that litter is ruining a city park.

Try It! What is the effect of listing so many specific examples of litter?

❸ In the **thesis**, the author makes her position clear.

Try It! Put the thesis in your own words. What is the purpose of the essay? Who do you think is the audience?

Extension Find another example of a persuasive essay, and compare it with this one.

Individuals Can Make a Difference

by **Martha M. Everett**

---

❶ Two weeks ago, I cleaned up a city block along a fine old city park, the edge of which has become a forgotten no-man's land. It's in my neighborhood, and I pass it by car or on foot nearly every day. It is littered with trash, its quiet
5 green grass dotted with the belch of brown cardboard and silver aluminum. What should be an oasis among the city's brick and asphalt had become an eyesore the city doesn't clean. I couldn't stand it any longer. I put on latex gloves and took a lawn bag to the spot on Loughborough Avenue. With
10 cars speeding past spewing carbon monoxide, I bent and hauled and scraped up everything I could. In 90 minutes, the huge green bag was filled with trash.

❷ There was an empty medicine vial, a cut-up credit card (why bother to cut it up if you're going to throw it
15 on the street?), an Xbox game case, pieces of broken CDs, ribbons of cassette tape, pennies, plastic bottles, a ripped-up photo of a young woman, . . . and lots of things I could not (or preferred to not) identify or decipher.

For a few days, it was lovely. I passed the area and
20 enjoyed the view. But within a week, the block once again was littered with garbage. I felt defeated and powerless.

During the time I spent bent over retrieving what others had discarded, I had ample time to think. And I started thinking about that phrase people say so often: One person
25 can't make a difference. I don't know if they believe that or if it's just a convenient excuse to not take action, but the line kept ringing in my head. And the more trash I picked up, the more ridiculous the statement seemed to me.

❸ Of course an individual can make a difference. As
30 simplistic as it sounds, the world is made up of individuals.

4 The CEO of a multimillion-dollar corporation is an individual, as are the people on its board of directors. Presidents are individuals. The Founding Fathers were individuals, and look what they accomplished.

35 What I was doing—as an individual—was making a difference; it's just that the effect of it was temporary. If every individual who tosses waste on the street chose not to do so, collectively they would make a lasting difference. And if those people were the ones along this block of my
40 South St. Louis neighborhood, they would make a true, permanent difference. And the area would thrive.

I'm not the most dedicated environmentalist. I recycle when I can, although the city doesn't make it convenient. And I try to conserve water and plant trees.

45 **5** Public areas are shared treasures. As Voltaire's Candide said, we must tend our own garden. The Earth is our garden. On a list of sins against the planet, littering may not rank high, but littering certainly is not tending.

Maintaining our garden is an individual responsibility
50 for the good of the whole. And as individuals, we can make a difference.

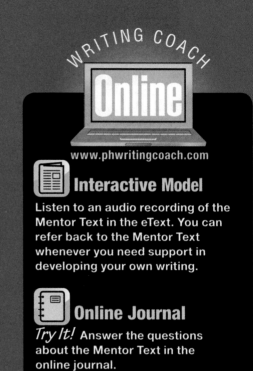

WRITING COACH

Online

www.phwritingcoach.com

Interactive Model

Listen to an audio recording of the Mentor Text in the eText. You can refer back to the Mentor Text whenever you need support in developing your own writing.

Online Journal

Try It! Answer the questions about the Mentor Text in the online journal.

4 The author supports her position with **sound reasoning** and **examples.**

Try It! Do you think the reasoning and examples are persuasive? Explain.

5 The **conclusion** contains **language that appeals to both emotion and reason**.

Try It! Quote a sentence that stirs your emotions, or feelings. Which statement or statements seem especially reasonable to you?

STUDENT MODEL

Persuasive Essay

With a small group, take turns reading this Student Model aloud. Ask yourself if you find the author's arguments convincing.

Use a Reader's Eye

Now, reread the Student Model. On your copy of the Student Model, use the Reader's Response Symbols to react to what you read.

Reader's Response Symbols

+ **I strongly agree with this.**

− **I strongly disagree with this.**

? **I have a question about this.**

! **Wow! That is cool/weird/ interesting.**

Participate in an extended discussion with a partner. Express your opinions and share your responses to the Student Model. Take notes and discuss responses that were the same for both of you, and that were different.

Raise Your Hand for School Uniforms

by Jane Scott

Every morning, my mother puts on her uniform of carefully ironed navy blue pants and a light blue shirt. Then she is ready to go to work as a city bus driver. Meanwhile, in homes all over town,
5 kids are wondering what to wear to school. If we had a uniform, it would save a lot of time. More importantly, wearing uniforms would help students take their studies more seriously and encourage better behavior. The school district should
10 require all students to wear a school uniform.

First, wearing uniforms could help students take school more seriously. Dressing differently often makes people act differently. When I wear a skirt and a blouse, I feel more grown-up than when I
15 wear jeans and a sweatshirt. By wearing "school clothes" instead of "play clothes," kids will come to school ready to learn. When a school district in Washington State began requiring school uniforms, fewer students skipped school or were late to class.

20 Despite the evidence that uniforms can help students, some people don't want a uniform policy. They say that uniforms are too expensive for families. However, uniforms are sold at much lower prices than trendy clothes. The school district could also
25 help those families that are unable to afford uniforms.

Another reason to promote school uniforms is to encourage good behavior. Clothes can be a major distraction in school. Some kids like to gossip about people's outfits. Students who can't afford trendy
30 clothes sometimes get teased. If everyone wore the

1

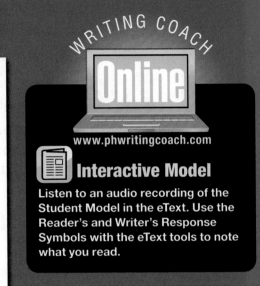

WRITING COACH

Online

www.phwritingcoach.com

Interactive Model

Listen to an audio recording of the Student Model in the eText. Use the Reader's and Writer's Response Symbols with the eText tools to note what you read.

same clothes, fashion and cost would matter much less. Kids would get along better. We could focus on what's on the inside instead of the outside.

35   However, many kids like thinking about what's on the outside. They believe that choosing their outfits is a form of creativity. These students don't want the school to limit their self-expression. But school offers many more important ways for students to express themselves: through their art, writing, and thinking.

40   School uniforms can have positive effects on learning and behavior. One year after students began wearing uniforms in a school district in California, the district had 36 percent less school crime. If you are in favor of a school uniform policy,
45   write to the school board. Let's help schools focus on what's important: education, not fashion.

Use a Writer's Eye

Now, evaluate the piece as a writer. On your copy of the Student Model, use the Writer's Response Symbols to react to what you read. Identify places where the student writer uses characteristics of an effective persuasive essay.

Writer's Response Symbols	
C.T.	**Clearly stated thesis**
P.A.	**Good persuasive arguments**
S.E.	**Effective supporting evidence**
C.A.	**Good responses to readers' counter-arguments**

2

Your Turn

**Feature Assignment:
Persuasive Essay**

Prewriting

Plan a first draft of your persuasive essay by determining an appropriate topic. You can select from the Topic Bank or come up with an idea of your own.

 Choose From the Topic Bank

TOPIC BANK

Pets Anyone who has ever owned a pet has an opinion on which animal makes the best pet. Take a stand on which kind of animal makes the best pet. Write an essay using reasons and examples to support your choice.

Community Issues Think about issues affecting your community, such as littering or the use of cell phones while driving. Choose the issue that you feel is the most important. Write a persuasive essay in which you state and explain your opinion on the issue.

Persuade Your Parents Think of an item that you would like to buy or an activity you would like to do. Write an essay in which you identify the item or activity and persuade your parent or caregiver to give his or her permission.

 Choose Your Own Topic

To determine an appropriate topic on your own, use the following **range of strategies** to generate ideas before you plan a first draft.

Discussion and Research

- With your friends and family, discuss the issues that interest you. Ask about their views. Take notes on your conversations.

- Review your notes. Circle key words and phrases that describe the issues you want to learn more about.

- Search your library's database and the Web for the key words and phrases from your notes. Keep records of any sources you may use.

Review your responses and choose a topic.

Narrow Your Topic

If your topic is too broad, your essay will be vague. A narrow topic helps you write a clear thesis statement and build a strong argument.

Apply It! Use a graphic organizer like the one shown to narrow your topic.

- Write your general topic in the top box. Make your topic more specific as you move down the chart.
- Use the last box to establish a position on your chosen issue. This is the topic for your persuasive essay.

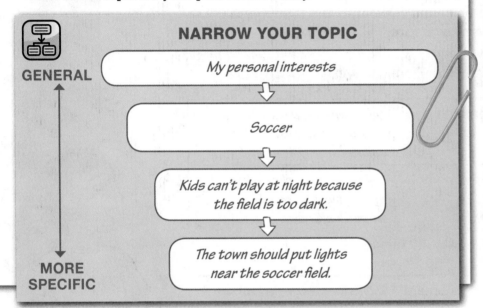

NARROW YOUR TOPIC

GENERAL

My personal interests

Soccer

Kids can't play at night because the field is too dark.

The town should put lights near the soccer field.

MORE SPECIFIC

Consider Your Audience and Purpose

Before writing, think about your audience and purpose. Consider the views of others and **alternatives to your position** as you ask yourself these questions.

Questions for Audience	Questions for Purpose
• Who is in my audience, and what do they need to know to understand my topic? • What counter-arguments might they have? How will I respond to those arguments?	• What is my **position** on my chosen issue? • What do I want the audience to do?

Record your answers in your writing journal.

Plan Your Piece

You will use the graphic organizer to state your thesis, organize your arguments, and identify details. When it is complete, you will be ready to write your first draft.

Develop a Clear Thesis Make sure the audience knows which side of the issue you support. Write a **thesis statement**—one sentence in which you **establish a position** on the issue. Add your thesis statement to a graphic organizer like the one shown.

Organize Your Arguments Fill in the graphic organizer to arrange your arguments from least to most important. Make sure each argument is based on **sound reasoning** and is supported with **detailed and relevant evidence.**

Develop Your Persuasive Arguments	
Clear Thesis Statement	*Our town should place lights near the soccer field so teams can play at night.*
First Persuasive Argument	*Lights will make the park around the soccer field safer for everyone.*
Supporting Evidence/ Details	
Second Persuasive Argument	*Lights will allow more kids to participate in soccer.*
Supporting Evidence/ Details	
Alternative Arguments	*Installing lights will be expensive. The town doesn't want kids to use the field at night without supervision.*
Response to Alternative Arguments	

Gather Details

To support their arguments, writers gather information that is relevant, or important, to their topic. Look at these examples of types of information:

- **Sound Reasoning:** There are not enough daylight hours to allow the participation of all the kids who want to play soccer. Lights on the soccer field would increase the number of hours in which games could be played. Therefore, we could form more teams and allow more kids to play.

- **Facts:** Kids who play sports are healthier on average than kids who do not.

- **Examples:** Since lighting its sports fields, a nearby town no longer has a waiting list to join soccer teams.

- **Expert Opinions:** Police Chief Reyes says that lights on the soccer field would also reduce crime in the area around the field.

Try It! Read the Student Model excerpt and identify which details the author used to support her argument.

 STUDENT MODEL from **Raise Your Hand for School Uniforms** pages 176–177; lines 26–33

> Another reason to promote school uniforms is to encourage good behavior. Clothes can be a major distraction in school. Some kids like to gossip about people's outfits. Students who can't afford trendy clothes sometimes get teased. If everyone wore the same clothes, fashion and cost would matter much less. Kids would get along better. We could focus on what's on the inside instead of the outside.

Apply It! Review the types of support a persuasive writer can use. Then identify at least one detail for each of your arguments.

- Remember to find evidence to use in your **consideration of alternatives,** where you address the views of people who disagree with you.

- Then add these details to your graphic organizer. Reread your arguments and supporting details to check that they support your thesis.

WRITING COACH

Online

www.phwritingcoach.com

Interactive Graphic Organizers

Use the interactive graphic organizers to help you create a plan for your writing.

Interactive Model

Refer back to the Interactive Model in the eText as you plan your writing.

Drafting

During the drafting stage, you will start to write your ideas for your persuasive essay. You will follow an outline that provides an **organizational strategy** that will help you build on ideas to write a **focused, organized, and coherent** persuasive essay.

The Organization of a Persuasive Essay

The chart shows an organizational strategy for a persuasive essay. Look back at how the Mentor Text follows this organizational strategy. Then, use this chart to help you outline your draft.

Outline for Success

I. Introduction

See Mentor Text p. 174.

- Interesting opening
- Clear thesis statement

Grab Your Reader

- An interesting opening will grab the reader's attention with a "hook." Your hook could be an interesting fact, an unusual detail, or a thoughtful question.
- The thesis statement establishes your position on the issue.

II. Body

See Mentor Text pp. 174–175.

- Logically organized arguments
- Relevant evidence
- Consideration of alternatives

Build Your Case

- Arguments should be organized so that they make sense to the reader. The most important idea should be saved for last.
- Relevant evidence means the facts, statistics, quotations, and other details you use that are important and closely related to your topic and point of view.
- Not everyone will agree with your point of view. Considering alternatives means thinking about how others view the issue.

III. Conclusion

See Mentor Text p. 175.

- Restatement of position
- Memorable ending

Wrap It Up

- A strong conclusion restates the thesis in a way that leaves a lasting impression.
- A memorable ending tells the readers what they should do to support your position. For example, a call to action might tell readers which events to attend or organizations to join or contact.

 **Start Your Draft**

Use the checklist below to help complete your draft. Use the graphic organizer that shows your thesis, persuasive arguments, and supporting evidence, and the Outline for Success as guides.

While drafting, aim at writing your ideas, not on making your writing perfect. Remember, you will have the chance to improve your draft when you revise and edit.

√ First, draft your **opening** sentences. These first few sentences should interest your audience and make them want to keep reading.

√ Continue your **introduction** by summarizing your most important arguments. Establish your position in your thesis statement.

√ Shape the **body** of your persuasive essay.

√ Write one paragraph for each argument. Organize your **arguments** logically. Start with the second-strongest argument and end with the strongest argument.

√ Use detailed and relevant **evidence** and sound reasoning to support each argument.

√ Address counter-arguments. Use evidence to explain why readers should agree with your point of view instead of the **alternative views**.

√ Use **transition** words, such as *first, next,* and *finally* to connect ideas and help readers follow your arguments.

√ End with a strong **conclusion** that restates your position.

√ Call your readers to **action** by telling them what you want them to do or think about the issue.

WRITING COACH

www.phwritingcoach.com

Interactive Model

Outline for Success View pop-ups of Mentor Text selections referenced in the Outline for Success.

 **Interactive Writing Coach™**

Use the Interactive Writing Coach to receive the level of support you need:

• Write one paragraph at a time and submit each one for immediate, detailed feedback.

• Write your entire first draft and submit it for immediate, personalized feedback.

Revising: Making It Better

Now that you have finished your first draft, you are ready to revise. Think about **the "big picture" of audience, purpose, and genre.** You can use the Revision RADaR strategy as a guide for making changes to improve your draft. Revision RADaR provides four major ways to improve your writing: (R) replace, (A) add, (D) delete, and (R) reorder.

Kelly Gallagher, M. Ed.

KEEP REVISION ON YOUR RADaR

Read part of the first draft of the Student Model "Raise Your Hand for School Uniforms." Then look at questions the writer asked herself as she thought about how well her draft **addressed issues of audience, purpose, and genre**.

Raise Your Hand for School Uniforms

Many adults wear uniforms to work every day. On some days, I have trouble deciding what to wear to school. If we had a uniform, it would save a lot of time. More importantly, wearing uniforms would help students take their studies more seriously and encourage better behavior. School uniforms might be one way to improve our education.

First, wearing uniforms could help students take school more seriously. Dressing differently often makes people act differently. When I wear a skirt and a blouse, I feel more grown-up than when I wear jeans and a sweatshirt. By wearing "school clothes" instead of "play clothes," kids will come to school ready to learn.

Does the introduction get my audience's attention?

*Does my **thesis statement** establish a clear position?*

Have I used persuasive arguments? Have I supported them with evidence?

Now look at how the writer applied Revision RADaR to write an improved second draft.

Raise Your Hand for School Uniforms [2ND DRAFT]

Every morning, my mother puts on her uniform of carefully ironed navy blue pants and a light blue shirt. Then she is ready to go to work as a city bus driver. Meanwhile, in homes all over town, kids are wondering what to wear to school. If we had a uniform, it would save a lot of time. More importantly, wearing uniforms would help students take their studies more seriously and encourage better behavior. The school district should require all students to wear a school uniform.

First, wearing uniforms could help students take school more seriously. Dressing differently often makes people act differently. When I wear a skirt and a blouse, I feel more grown-up than when I wear jeans and a sweatshirt. By wearing "school clothes" instead of "play clothes," kids will come to school ready to learn. When a school district in Washington State began requiring school uniforms, fewer students skipped school or were late to class.

R *Replaced opening sentences with a personal story to add interest*

D *Deleted an unclear sentence* **A** *and added a thesis statement to clarify meaning*

A *Added a piece of evidence to support my argument*

 Apply It! Use your Revision RADaR to revise your draft.

- First, consider how well you have **addressed the needs of your audience, explained your purpose** for writing, and included the characteristics of the persuasive writing **genre**.

- Then apply your Revision RADaR to make needed changes. Remember—you can use the steps in Revision RADaR in any order.

Look at the Big Picture

Use the chart and your analytical skills to evaluate how well each section of your persuasive essay addresses **purpose, audience, and genre**. When necessary, use the suggestions in the chart to revise your piece.

Section	Evaluate	Revise
Introduction	• Check the **introduction.** Will it draw your readers in and keep them reading?	• To make your introduction more interesting, add a question, personal story, or strong statement.
	• Does the thesis clearly establish your **position** on the issue?	• Replace weak language with more forceful language to express your opinion strongly.
Body	• Check that the organization of your persuasive **arguments** makes the strongest case for your view.	• Reorder your paragraphs to support strong reasoning. Put your second-strongest argument first, the weaker arguments in the middle, and the strongest argument last.
	• Make sure that your supporting evidence is detailed and **relevant.** Draw a line from each detail to the argument it supports.	• Delete evidence that is not relevant. Delete any detail that is not in the same paragraph as the argument it supports.
	• Review **alternatives** and counter-arguments. Be certain that you have answered each one.	• Add information to prove that alternative views are less strong than your view.
Conclusion	• Check your **thesis** restatement.	• Restate the important points of your thesis using slightly different words, and make sure the meaning is clear.
	• Make sure that your essay has a memorable **ending.**	• Add a call to action, question, or prediction to strengthen your conclusion.

Focus on Craft: Enhance Style

Style is the way a writer chooses to use language. In order to convince readers, your language should be interesting and persuasive. Vivid language helps persuade your audience to agree with you. By using language more effectively, you will draw the reader to your purpose. Think about style as you read the following sentences from the Student Model.

 STUDENT MODEL from **Raise Your Hand for School Uniforms** page 176; lines 13–17

> When I wear a skirt and a blouse, I feel more grown-up than when I wear jeans and a sweatshirt. By wearing "school clothes" instead of "play clothes," kids will come to school ready to learn.

Try It! Now, ask yourself these questions. Record your answers in your journal.

- What is the main idea of this passage? Does the writer have a casual or formal attitude about the subject? Explain.
- Would the last sentence be more or less convincing if it read *By wearing uniforms instead of casual clothes, kids will come to school ready to learn*? Explain.

Fine-Tune Your Draft

Apply It! First, **rethink how well questions of purpose, audience, and genre have been addressed** in your essay. Then use the ideas for revision to prepare your final draft.

- **Enhance Style** Add language that is more vivid and appealing.
- **Clarify Meaning** Look for confusing sentences and add explanations as needed.
- **Improve Transitions** To connect ideas, add, delete, combine, or rearrange sentences by using words like *next* and *in contrast*.

Peer Feedback Read your final draft to a group of peers. Ask if you have **considered and answered alternative viewpoints**. Think about your group's responses and revise your draft as needed.

WRITING COACH
Online
www.phwritingcoach.com

 Video
Learn more strategies for effective writing from program author Kelly Gallagher.

 Online Journal
Try It! Record your answers in the online journal.

 Interactive Model
Refer back to the Interactive Model as you revise your writing.

Interactive Writing Coach™
Revise your draft and submit it for feedback.

Editing: Making It Correct

To edit your work, read your draft carefully to correct errors in spelling and grammar.

Review pronouns you have used in your writing. Each **pronoun** must have a clear **antecedent,** or a clearly stated person, place, or thing that the pronoun later replaces. Look at these sentences:

Karen and Walter missed the bus. They were late for school.
(The pronoun *they* clearly refers to Karen and Walter.)

I am going away for the weekend with my family. It should be fun.
(The antecedent for *it* is unclear. The second sentence could be corrected this way: *The trip should be fun.*)

WRITE GUY *Jeff Anderson, M. Ed.*

WHAT DO YOU NOTICE?

Zoom in on Conventions Focus on the use of pronouns as you read these lines from the Student Model.

 **STUDENT MODEL** from **Raise Your Hand for School Uniforms** page 176; lines 1–6

> Every morning, my mother puts on her uniform of carefully ironed navy blue pants and a light blue shirt. Then she is ready to go to work as a city bus driver. Meanwhile, in homes all over town, kids are wondering what to wear to school. If we had a uniform, it would save a lot of time.

Now, ask yourself: *Which pair of sentences contains a vague pronoun reference?*

Perhaps you chose the second pair of sentences, which contains a vague pronoun reference. The antecedent of the pronoun *we* is unclear. To correct this vague pronoun reference, the sentences would read: *Meanwhile, in homes all over town, kids like my friends and me are wondering what to wear to school. If we had a uniform, it would save a lot of time.*

The first pair of sentences has correct pronoun-antecedent usage. Since only one woman, *my mother,* is mentioned in the first sentence, the pronoun *she* clearly takes the place of that antecedent. There is no way that the pronoun could refer to any other person.

> To learn more about pronoun-antecedent agreement see Chapter 23 of your Grammar Handbook.

Grammar Mini-Lesson: Vague Pronoun References

To learn more, see page 276.

Look at these other examples of vague pronoun references and their corrections:

Vague: *When we got to the stadium,* they *showed us to our seats.*
Correct: *When we got to the stadium,* the ushers *showed us to our seats.*
Vague: *My favorite player made a goal.* It *was great!*
Correct: *My favorite player made a goal.* His kick *was great!*

Notice how the pronoun *they* in these lines from the Student Model has a clear antecedent.

 **STUDENT MODEL** from **Raise Your Hand for School Uniforms** page 177; lines 34–36

However, many kids like thinking about what's on the outside. They believe that choosing their outfits is a form of creativity.

Try It! Tell whether each of these items has a clear pronoun reference. If a reference is vague, rewrite the sentence to make the clear. Write the answers in your journal.

1. Kari is a huge soccer fan, so she never misses a game.
2. At the games, Kari loves to watch them play.

Apply It! Edit your draft for **grammar, mechanics, and spelling**. Be sure to check each pronoun reference to make sure that its antecedent is clear. Revise sentences, if necessary.

Use the rubric to evaluate your piece. If necessary, rethink, rewrite, or revise.

Rubric for Persuasive Essay	Rating Scale					
	Not very					Very
Ideas: How clearly are the issue and your position stated?	1	2	3	4	5	6
Organization: How organized are your arguments and supporting evidence?	1	2	3	4	5	6
Voice: How authoritative is your voice?	1	2	3	4	5	6
Word Choice: How persuasive is your word choice?	1	2	3	4	5	6
Sentence Fluency: How smooth are your transitions?	1	2	3	4	5	6
Conventions: How clear are your pronoun references?	1	2	3	4	5	6

WRITING COACH

Online

www.phwritingcoach.com

 Video
Learn effective editing techniques from program author Jeff Anderson.

 Online Journal
Try It! Record your answers in the online journal.

 Interactive Model
Refer back to the Interactive Model as you edit your writing.

 Interactive Writing Coach™
Edit your draft. Check it against the rubric and then submit it for feedback.

Publishing

Give your persuasive essay a chance to influence someone—publish it! First, get your essay ready for presentation. Then, choose a way to **publish it for the appropriate audience**.

Wrap Up Your Presentation

Is your persuasive essay handwritten or written on a computer? If your essay is handwritten, you may need to make a new, clean copy. If so, be sure to **write legibly.**

Publish Your Piece

Use the chart to identify a way to publish your persuasive essay for the appropriate audience.

If your audience is...	...then publish it by...
Students or adults at school	• Submitting it to your school newspaper • Posting it on your school's Web site and asking for responses
People in your city	• Submitting it to your local newspaper • Recording it and submitting it to a local radio station

Extend Your Research

Think more about the topic on which you wrote your persuasive essay. What else would you like to know about this topic?

▪ Brainstorm for several questions you would like to research and then consult, or discuss, with others. Then decide which question is your major research question.

▪ Formulate, or develop, a plan about how you will answer these questions. Decide where you will find more information—on the Internet, at the library, or through other sources.

▪ Finally, learn more about your topic by following through with your research plan.

The Big Question: Why Write? What is your point of view? How did you determine if you convinced others?

MAKE YOUR WRITING COUNT

Debate an Issue

When you write persuasively, you try to convince your audience to agree with you or to act upon an issue. When you speak persuasively, you have the same goal. Take a side on an issue and **debate** the topic.

With a group, choose the topic of one persuasive essay to debate. Your group will present both sides of an issue to clearly communicate opposing points of view. Hold the debate for your class or video-record it to share with others.

Here's your action plan.

1. With your group, choose one persuasive essay to use in the debate. Pick an essay whose topic will interest most students.

2. Divide into two smaller groups and assign each small group a side of the argument.

   - Meet with your smaller group to work on your argument and supporting details.

   - Think about the other side's argument, and find details that weaken it.

   - Consider the tone of a debate—the style and content of your language should be formal, and your attitude will influence your listener's understanding.

3. Figure out how much time you will have to debate. Be sure you can make your important points within the timeframe.

4. Hold your debate, and have the class vote for the winner.

5. If you are video-recording the debate, watch it afterward.

Listening and Speaking When working with your small group, actively listen to group members' ideas for making a strong argument. During the debate, keep your group's feedback in mind. Speak slowly and clearly. Listen actively and jot notes while your opponent is speaking. This will help you to adjust your presentation and plan your response.

WRITING COACH

Online

www.phwritingcoach.com

Online Journal

Extend Your Research Record your answers and ideas in the online journal.

Resource

Link to resources on 21st Century Learning for help in creating a group project.

Your Turn

**Writing for Media:
Magazine Covers**

21st Century Learning

Magazine Covers

A **magazine cover** is a persuasive message designed to sell the magazine. A magazine cover has just a few seconds to grab a shopper's attention. So, magazine covers often carry eye-catching photos and graphics. But you should not believe everything you see! Cover photos have often been altered to make them more appealing. Sometimes the text on the cover makes the stories inside sound more interesting or exciting than they really are. When you understand how advertising is used to influence you, you can make better decisions about buying or using a product.

Try It! Study the picture and the text on the magazine cover. Then, answer the questions. Record your answers in your journal.

1. Read the **title** of the magazine. What does the title tell you about it?

2. The **layout** is the arrangement of all the words and pictures on the cover. What feeling does the layout create?

3. How would you describe the people shown in the main image? Does this image seem **realistic?** Why or why not?

4. The short descriptions of the stories inside the magazine are called **cover lines.** Do the cover lines make the stories sound appealing to people who might read this magazine? Explain.

5. Describe the type of person this magazine wants to **target,** or reach. Is the typical reader male or female? How old? What are his or her interests?

Extension Find another example of a magazine cover, and compare it with this one.

Discovery Girls

Twelve-year-old Girls Find Ancient Treasure

The World's Youngest Detectives

You Can Find Your Way in the Wilderness

Volume 4, Issue 1

Create a Magazine Cover

Follow these steps to create your own magazine cover.

Prewriting

- Think about what type of magazine your cover will advertise. For example, you could choose news, sports, or fashion.
- Establish a position on your magazine's topic. For example, you could create the cover for a cooking magazine. Then think of an appropriate title for the magazine.
- Identify your target audience. Decide if your readers are male or female or both, and how old they are, along with other traits.
- Decide what types of stories and images are appropriate for your target audience.
- Brainstorm a list of articles that will be in your magazine and a list of images you might use on the cover.

Drafting

- Write the cover lines for your stories. Brainstorm several cover lines for each story. Then, consider the alternatives you have developed and choose the most interesting one.
- Choose one or more images that will grab readers' attention.
- Lay out your cover. Decide where the title, the image(s), and the cover lines will go, and how large each will be. Choose fonts or type styles for the title and cover lines. Try different layouts to achieve an eye-catching look.

Revising and Editing

- Review your draft. Make sure that your cover lines and pictures are relevant to your target audience. Check that the most important and appealing elements are the largest.
- Check that spelling, grammar, and mechanics are correct.

Publishing

- Make a multimedia version of your magazine cover. Include both your text **and graphics** to enhance the main ideas.
- Present your multimedia cover to the class.

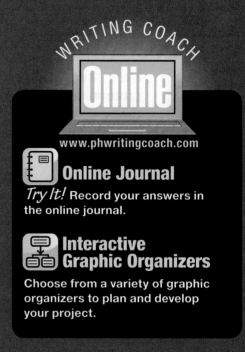

WRITING COACH

Online

www.phwritingcoach.com

Online Journal

Try It! Record your answers in the online journal.

Interactive Graphic Organizers

Choose from a variety of graphic organizers to plan and develop your project.

Partner Talk

Before you start drafting, describe your magazine cover to a partner. Use specific details to describe and explain your ideas. Increase the specificty of your details based on the type of information you are discussing. Ask for feedback about your plan. For example, will your cover lines appeal to your target audience?

Writing for Assessment [SAT®/PSAT PREP ACT]

Many standardized tests include writing prompts. Use the prompts on these pages to practice. Your responses should include the same characteristics as your persuasive essay. (See page 172.)

👍 *Try It!* Read the prompt and the information on format and academic vocabulary. Then write an essay using the ABCDs of On-Demand Writing.

Format
The prompt asks you to write a *persuasive essay.* Be sure to include an introduction, body paragraphs with supporting evidence, and a conclusion.

Persuasive Prompt
Some students and teachers think that the school day is too long. Write a persuasive essay to convince your principal to shorten the school day. Support your opinion with evidence.

Academic Vocabulary
Remember that an *opinion* is a personal belief about something. *Evidence* helps prove something is true. Facts and examples are often used as evidence.

◔ The ABCDs of On-Demand Writing

Use the following ABCDs to help you respond to the prompt.

Before you write your draft:

Attack the prompt [1 MINUTE]

- Circle or highlight important verbs in the prompt. Draw a line from the verb to what it refers to.
- Rewrite the prompt in your own words.

Brainstorm possible answers [4 MINUTES]

- Create a graphic organizer to generate ideas.
- Use one for each part of the prompt if necessary.

Choose the order of your response [1 MINUTE]

- Think about the best way to organize your ideas.
- Number your ideas in the order you will write about them. Cross out ideas you will not be using.

After you write your draft:

Detect errors before turning in the draft [1 MINUTE]

- Carefully reread your writing.
- Make sure that your response makes sense and is complete.
- Look for spelling, punctuation, and grammar errors.

More Prompts for Practice

SAT®/PSAT PREP ACT

Apply It! Respond to Prompts 1 and 2 by writing **persuasive essays** that influence your readers' opinions or actions. As you write, be sure to:

- Identify an appropriate audience
- Establish a **clear position or thesis**
- Use **sound reasoning** to make your arguments convincing
- Provide **consideration of alternative arguments**
- Include **detailed and relevant evidence** to support your view

> **Prompt 1** Think of a place you would like to visit or an activity you would like to take part in. Imagine that on a specific occasion, you would prefer not to go to this place or do this activity alone. Write a persuasive essay to convince a friend to go with you.

> **Prompt 2** Do your parents or guardians have any rules that you think are unfair? Choose one rule that you would like to change. In a persuasive essay, make the case to your parents or guardians that the rule is unfair and should be changed.

Spiral Review: Expository Respond to Prompt 3 by writing a compare-and-contrast **expository essay**. Make sure your essay reflects all the characteristics described on page 146, including an **effective introduction and concluding paragraphs; specific facts, details, and examples in an appropriately organized structure; and a variety of sentence structures and transitions to link paragraphs.** Your essay should also **guide and inform the reader's understanding of key ideas and evidence.**

> **Prompt 3** Think about the many different kinds of workers who make your school a great place to be: teachers, cafeteria workers, the principal, and so on. Write an expository essay that compares and contrasts the jobs of two kinds of school workers.

WRITING COACH

Online

www.phwritingcoach.com

Interactive Writing Coach™

Plan your response to the prompt. If you are using the prompt for practice, write one paragraph at a time or your entire draft and then submit for immediate feedback. If you are using the prompt as a timed test, write your entire draft and then submit it for feedback.

Remember ABCD

- **A**ttack the prompt
- **B**rainstorm possible answers
- **C**hoose the order of your response
- **D**etect errors before turning in the draft

What Do You Think?

Think back to your first experiences reading. Did a teacher read to you? What were your favorite books and authors? What did those authors do to interest you?

Part of being an active reader is thinking about how an author uses words and ideas to affect a reader.

Try It! Think about a book you had read to you when you were younger. Then, write notes about that book and why it was meaningful to you.

Consider these questions as you participate in an extended discussion with a partner. Take turns expressing your ideas and feelings.

- What was the book about?
- How did the author keep your interest?
- What was unique, or special, about the book?

Review your list. Then, think about other books you have read recently. What was powerful or interesting about those books?

What's Ahead

In this chapter, you will review two strong examples of an interpretative response essay: a Mentor Text and a Student Model. Then, using the examples as guides, you will write an interpretative response essay of your own.

WRITING COACH

Online

www.phwritingcoach.com

 Online Journal

Try It! Record your answers and ideas in the online journal.

You can also record and save your answers and ideas on pop-up sticky notes in the eText.

Connect to the Big Questions

Discuss these questions with your partner:

1 **What do you think?** How does literature shape who we become?

2 **Why write?** What should you write about to make others interested in a text?

INTERPRETATIVE RESPONSE

An interpretative response analyzes an author's work. In this chapter, you will explore a special kind of interpretative response, a letter to an author. In a letter to an author, you analyze that person's work and describe your reactions to it. You also share your thoughts and feelings and tell what the work meant to you. If you liked the author's style or sense of humor, for example, you might discuss that.

You will develop your letter to an author by taking it through each of the steps of the writing process: prewriting, drafting, revising, editing, and publishing. You will also have an opportunity to write a blog entry, or short commentary posted on a Web site, about one of your favorite books, poems, or stories. To preview the criteria for how your letter to an author will be evaluated, see the rubric on page 215.

FEATURE ASSIGNMENT
Interpretative Response: Letter to an Author

An effective interpretative response has these characteristics:

- A **clear thesis or controlling idea** that expresses the main idea of your response to the work

- An **analysis** of your ideas about what happens in the work, with conclusions about what the work means

- **Details and evidence from the text** that show understanding of the work

- **Personal insights and evaluations** of the meaning and quality of the work

- A discussion of how **literary elements,** such as plot, setting, and character, affect the quality and interest of the selection

A letter to an author also includes:

- A greeting and closing

- Polite and professional language

- Questions or requests

Other Forms of Interpretative Response

In addition to a letter to an author, there are other forms of interpretative response, including these:

Blog comments posted on an author's Web site are a way to share ideas about an author's work. Readers express their opinions and give their interpretations of what an author's work means.

Comparison essays explore similarities and differences between two or more works of literature. For example, a comparison essay may compare how major characters in two different stories handle a similar problem.

Critical reviews discuss the quality of books, plays, poetry, and other literary works. Reviews appear in newspapers and magazines, on television and radio, and on the Internet. These works state the writer's opinions and support them with specific examples.

Response to literature essays analyze and interpret an author's work. Such essays examine what an author states and what those statements mean. Essay writers also evaluate how well an author has accomplished what he or she has set out to do.

Try It! For each audience and purpose described, choose a form, such as a critical review or a blog, that is appropriate for the audience you wish to reach. Explain your choices.

- To convince readers that a play is worth reading
- To demonstrate to a classmate how two plots are alike
- To explain to online readers why a story that seems simple actually has a deeper meaning

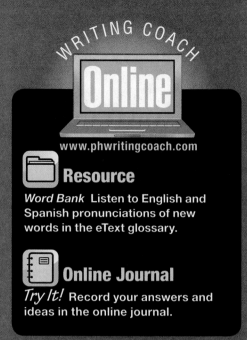

MENTOR TEXT

Book Review

Learn From Experience

 After reading the review on pages 200–201, read the numbered notes in the margins to learn about how the reviewer presented her ideas. Later you will read a Student Model, which shares these characteristics and also has the characteristics of a letter to an author.

Answer the *Try It!* questions online or in your notebook.

---

❶ The unusual **introduction** gives interesting details about the parents of Nick, the main **character** in the book. The reviewer does this to capture readers' attention.

Try It! From the introduction, what do you think Nick's parents are like? Do the details about the parents make you want to read the book? Explain.

❷ The reviewer gives more **details** about the **plot**, or what happens in the book.

Try It! Why do you think the reviewer chose to tell readers about this scene in the book?

❸ The reviewer **identifies the work** and its author. She also takes the **position** that the author is worth reading.

Try It! What is the title of the book being reviewed, and who wrote it? How can you tell the reviewer enjoys the author's work?

Search for Boy and Giant Chicken Will Charm Young and Old

by Sandy Bauers

❶ They have decided Nick needs a dose of urban reality. The first day, his bicycle is stolen. His room is sweltering. Worse, . . . his father speaks with an affected British accent and calls people "old chap" and exclaims "Odds 5 bodkins!" and the like.

His mother is the kind who says with delight, as Nick tells her he's going out to interview street bums, "Oh, another urban experience!"

("I simply tolerate these weirdnesses," Nick notes.)

10 ❷ One day, as Nick is exploring the dark basement, he hears voices on the other side of the wall. He creeps closer and speaks through a crack: "I am Edmond Dantes and I have been unjustly imprisoned by my enemies."

A voice responds: "I am the Abbé Faria . . . also unjustly 15 imprisoned in the Chateau d'If."

Naturally, they are kids just like Nick. And they all know the lines to Dumas' *Count of Monte Cristo* because they're fans of classic comics.

And so a friendship is born.

20 ❸ If you haven't met author Daniel Pinkwater yet, now's the time. The comic curmudgeon, perhaps best described as a National Public Radio raconteur, turns his offbeat sights to children's books from time to time, and the story of Nick and his buddies, *Looking for Bobowicz*, is his latest.

25 About the name *Bobowicz:* The children find an old scrapbook with tales of a giant chicken that rampaged through Hoboken years before. It turned out to be the 266-pound pet of a boy named Arthur Bobowicz.

WRITING COACH

Online

www.phwritingcoach.com

Interactive Model

Listen to an audio recording of the mentor text in the eText. You can refer back to the mentor text whenever you need support in developing your own writing.

Online Journal

Try It! Answer the questions about the Mentor Text in the online journal.

30 Well, of course, they just happen to be the very same chicken and Bobowicz in Pinkwater's 1977 book, *The Great Hoboken Chicken Emergency.*

It's been getting laughs for 27 years now. Harper recorded it in 1999, and has now reissued it to go with a recording of the sequel. . . .

35 Pinkwater reads both, but his debut on *The Great Hoboken Chicken Emergency* is a disappointment. He reads too fast. And he rarely pauses. I wanted a performance, not a pell-mell gushing. But his reading on the sequel is much better.

❹ Both books are wonderfully, humorously, endearingly
40 kooky. Pinkwater is witty and mischievous to the core. Parents and children can listen together and all get a kick out of it.

Nick and his buddies decide they have to know more, of course, and they set out on a search for Bobowicz, during
45 which they spot a phantom, are aided and abetted by a librarian in a cape, and are almost asphyxiated by sauerkraut.

They also befriend the DJ of the pirate radio station WRJR (Radio Jolly Roger). His name is Vic Trola, and he plays corny oldies that go, "I gave you my heart in a
50 diamond, and you clubbed me with a spade."

❺ I don't think I'm giving anything away by revealing that they find Bobowicz. After all, it's a children's book and things pretty much have to turn out right.

But that's all I'm saying.

❹ This **controlling idea** sums up the reviewer's opinion of *Looking for Bobowicz* as well as *The Great Hoboken Chicken Emergency.*

> *Try It!* What is the reviewer's main message about the book? What is her purpose for writing, and for what audience do you think she wrote the review?

❺ The reviewer **includes important information** about the book but does not tell everything that happens.

> *Try It!* Why do you think the reviewer says she does not want to tell more about what happens in the book?

Extension Find another example of a book review, and compare it with this one.

STUDENT MODEL   Letter to an Author

With a small group, take turns reading this Student Model aloud. As you read, practice newly acquired vocabulary by correctly producing the word's sound. Together, determine which elements make it a strong letter to an author. Look for evidence in the text, such as facts and details, that supports your conclusions.

Use a Reader's Eye

Now, reread the Student Model. On your copy of the Student Model, use the Reader's Response Symbols to react to what you read.

Reader's Response Symbols

+   **I agree with this point.**

−   **This isn't clear to me**

?   **I have a question about this.**

!   **Well said!**

Express your ideas about the Student Model. Discuss whether or not you feel that the letter is well-written and whether or not the writer supports her ideas. Monitor your partner's spoken language by asking follow-up questions to confirm your understanding.

I. B. Singer's "Zlateh the Goat"

Dear Mr. Singer:

I really liked reading your story "Zlateh the Goat." At first, it seemed like a very simple tale about a boy and a goat caught in a storm. Then, I realized it was
5   really a great story about survival and friendship.

The description of how Zlateh and Aaron begin their adventure really got me interested in what was going to happen. When you wrote that Zlateh was going to be sold because she was
10   not producing milk anymore, I felt sorry for her, especially because she trusted the family: "She knew that they always fed her and never did her any harm." I also felt bad for the family because I could tell that it wasn't an easy decision to send
15   Zlateh away. For example, the mother and the little sisters all shed tears for Zlateh. I was glad you told us that they had cared for Zlateh for twelve years and were having a hard time making money from the fur business because of the weather. This
20   information helped me to understand the family and their choice better. I liked this beginning because it made me think about the relationship people have with animals. Animals can help feed us and give us clothes, but they can also be our friends.

25   The middle of the story is my favorite part because it is so suspenseful and shows good survival thinking. I really liked how the storm was so unexpected. When Aaron and Zlateh start their trip, the day is sunny. The sudden change
30   in the weather made things exciting because I knew Aaron wasn't prepared for a storm like this. You tell us that Aaron had "never experienced a snow like this one." I also like the way you show

1

Aaron making good decisions. First, he looks for
35 shelter and finds the haystack, and then, he digs
a warm cave. He even remembers to make a large
enough air hole so he and Zlateh can breathe.
Each problem and solution kept me interested
in reading to see what would happen next.

40   This part of the story is also a good example of
how animals help humans. During the storm, Zlateh
made milk, even though she wasn't supposed to
be able to anymore. Aaron was able to survive
off of it. Zlateh also keeps him warm and from
45 feeling too alone. I was relieved that in the end
of the story Zlateh was saved and loved by the
family for the rest of her life. She had definitely
shown that she was more than a working animal.

This story really showed how danger can be
50 avoided through smart thinking and teamwork.
The boy and the goat both needed and helped
each other. Neither of them would have
survived the blizzard without each other.

Thank you for writing this story. It really made
55 me think about making smart choices and how
I treat animals. I will read it many more times.

Sincerely,

Denise Jenkins

2

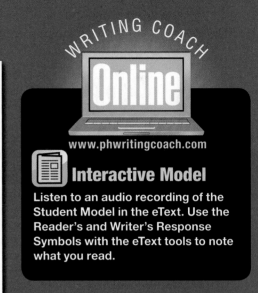

WRITING COACH

Online

www.phwritingcoach.com

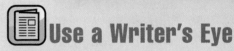

Interactive Model

Listen to an audio recording of the
Student Model in the eText. Use the
Reader's and Writer's Response
Symbols with the eText tools to note
what you read.

Use a Writer's Eye

Now, evaluate the piece as a writer. On
your copy of the Student Model, use the
Writer's Response Symbols to react to
what you read. Identify places where the
student writer uses characteristics of an
effective letter to an author.

Writer's Response Symbols

C.T.   **Clearly stated thesis**

I.A.   **In-depth analysis**

S.E.   **Effective supporting evidence**

E.Q.   **Effective quotations**

Your Turn

**Feature Assignment:
Letter to an Author**

Prewriting

Plan a first draft of your letter to an author **by determining an appropriate topic.** You can select from the Topic Bank or come up with an idea of your own.

 ## Choose From the Topic Bank

TOPIC BANK

Review of a Short Story Write an entry for a reader's response journal for "Greyling" by Jane Yolen. The entry should focus on whether you liked or disliked the story. Include specific examples from the literature to back up your opinions.

Response to a Plot Think about a book or short story you enjoyed reading. Write a letter to the author explaining why you enjoyed the plot of the book or short story.

Response to a Mentor Text Read "Roommates" by John Scieszka on page 68. Write a letter to the author telling how you felt about the the two main characters.

Choose Your Own Topic

Determine an appropriate topic on your own by using the following **range of strategies** to generate ideas.

Discussion and Personal Interests

- Think about your favorite work by an author. Discuss with a partner reasons why this work has special meaning for you.
- Consider questions that you had about an author's work. Think about whether the answers to these questions are directly stated or just hinted at in the work. Brainstorm for ideas.

Review your responses and choose a topic.

Narrow Your Topic

Choosing a topic that is too broad results in writing that is too general and unfocused.

Apply It! Use a graphic organizer like the one shown to narrow your topic.

- Write your general topic in the top box, and keep narrowing your topic as you move down the chart.
- Your last box should hold your narrowest or "smallest" topic, the focus of your letter to the author.

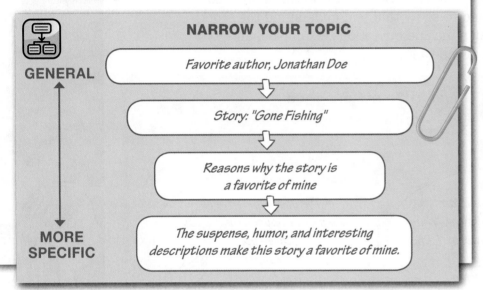

NARROW YOUR TOPIC

GENERAL

Favorite author, Jonathan Doe

Story: "Gone Fishing"

Reasons why the story is a favorite of mine

MORE SPECIFIC

The suspense, humor, and interesting descriptions make this story a favorite of mine.

Consider Your Audience and Purpose

Before writing, think about your audience and purpose. Consider the views of others as you ask yourself these questions.

Questions for Audience	Questions for Purpose
• Who will read my letter: My teacher? Classmates? The author? All of them? • What will make my reaction to the work interesting and convincing?	• What do I want my readers to know about the work? • What thoughts and feelings do I want to share in my letter? • What response do I want to get from readers?

Record your answers in your writing journal.

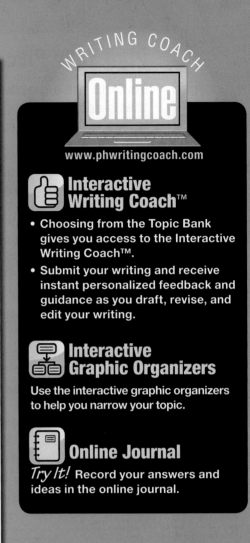

WRITING COACH

Online

www.phwritingcoach.com

Interactive Writing Coach™

- Choosing from the Topic Bank gives you access to the Interactive Writing Coach™.
- Submit your writing and receive instant personalized feedback and guidance as you draft, revise, and edit your writing.

Interactive Graphic Organizers

Use the interactive graphic organizers to help you narrow your topic.

Online Journal

Try It! Record your answers and ideas in the online journal.

Plan Your Piece

You will use a graphic organizer like the one shown to state your thesis and organize your evidence. When it is complete, you will be ready to write your first draft.

Develop a Clear Thesis Think about your reaction to the author's work. Then state your feelings and thoughts in a **clear thesis**. Add your thesis to a graphic organizer like this one.

Organize Your Supporting Evidence Use a graphic organizer to help you logically organize evidence from the author's work to support your response and to show that you understand the work. Evidence from the text can include quotations, examples, and other specific details from the work.

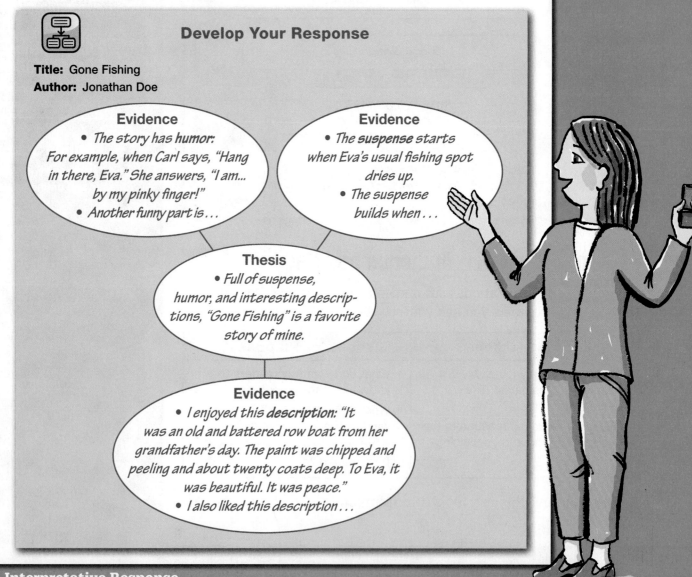

Develop Your Response

Title: Gone Fishing
Author: Jonathan Doe

Evidence
• *The story has **humor**: For example, when Carl says, "Hang in there, Eva." She answers, "I am... by my pinky finger!"*
• *Another funny part is . . .*

Evidence
• *The **suspense** starts when Eva's usual fishing spot dries up.*
• *The suspense builds when . . .*

Thesis
• *Full of suspense, humor, and interesting descriptions, "Gone Fishing" is a favorite story of mine.*

Evidence
• *I enjoyed this **description**: "It was an old and battered row boat from her grandfather's day. The paint was chipped and peeling and about twenty coats deep. To Eva, it was beautiful. It was peace."*
• *I also liked this description . . .*

Gather Details

To support their ideas, writers provide evidence from the text. Look at these examples:

- **Quotations:** *"I don't understand it," Eva said. "My family has been fishing here for generations."*

- **Examples:** *A scary situation occurs when Eva and Carl realize that they are the only people around for miles and miles.*

- **Descriptive Details:** *In the cabin, "he noticed that there wouldn't be enough food to live off of if they couldn't count on fish as a food source."*

- **Personal Observations:** *What makes the story so interesting is that you expect the characters to behave one way but they act another way.*

Try It! Read the Student Model excerpt and identify the evidence that the author uses to support her ideas.

WRITING COACH

Online

www.phwritingcoach.com

Interactive Graphic Organizers

Use the interactive graphic organizers to help you create a plan for your writing.

Interactive Model

Refer back to the Mentor Text in the eText as you plan your writing.

STUDENT MODEL from **I. B. Singer's "Zlateh the Goat"**
page 202; lines 8–13

When you wrote that Zlateh was going to be sold because she was not producing milk anymore, I felt sorry for her, especially because she trusted the family: "She knew that they always fed her and never did her any harm."

 *Apply It!* Review the types of supporting evidence that can be used in a letter to an author. Then identify and write one piece of relevant evidence of each type.

- Review your evidence to make sure it supports your thesis. Be sure to include one or more pieces of each kind of **evidence from the text to demonstrate your understanding.**

- Add your supporting evidence to your graphic organizer.

Drafting

During the drafting stage, you will start to write your ideas for your letter to an author. You will follow an outline that provides an **organizational strategy** that will help you build on ideas to write a **focused, organized, and coherent** letter to an author.

The Organization of an Interpretative Response

The chart shows an organizational strategy for interpretative response. Look back at how the Mentor Text follows this organizational strategy. Then use this chart to help you outline your draft.

Outline for Success

I. Introduction
See Mentor Text, p. 200.

- Interesting opening statement
- Name of work
- Clear thesis

Grab Your Reader

- A strong statement, question, or reference to a character or event in the work will create an interesting opening and grab the reader's attention.
- The introduction mentions the title of the work being discussed.
- A clear thesis statement gives the main idea of your response.

II. Body
See Mentor Text, pp. 200–201.

- Thoughtful analysis and interpretation
- Supporting details and evidence from the text
- Logically organized statements

Develop Your Ideas

- The information in the body goes beyond just a summary or a retelling of the work. It shows a clear understanding and analysis of the work.
- Each idea presented is supported by evidence from the text, such as quotations, examples, and details.
- Each new idea has a new paragraph. The sentences and paragraphs are arranged so that they flow logically, with one idea building on another.

III. Conclusion
See Mentor Text, p. 201.

- Restatement of thesis or main points
- Explanation of the significance of those points, such as what the writer has learned

Wrap It Up

- The thesis and main points are briefly restated in the conclusion.
- To leave readers with a clear idea of the writer's ideas, the importance of the main points should be made clear.

Start Your Draft

Use this checklist to help you complete your draft. Use the graphic organizer that shows your thesis and evidence from the text, and the Outline for Success as guides.

While drafting, aim at writing your ideas, not on making your writing perfect. Remember, you will improve the draft when you revise and edit.

> √ A **salutation** to the author, such as "Dear Ms. Barnes," should start your letter.
>
> √ Your **introduction** should identify the work about which you're writing.
>
> √ Present your thesis statement.

> √ Use the **body** of your letter to develop your ideas. Write a response that explains your understanding of the work and how the author's work affected you.
>
> √ To create a focused and **organized** letter to an author, choose an appropriate organizational strategy that builds on ideas in a logical way.
>
> √ Include only information that is related to your thesis. Make sure your letter is **coherent**—it should flow well, and all the details should support your main idea.
>
> √ Support your ideas with specific **evidence** from the text, including examples and quotations, to demonstrate your understanding of the text. Provide specific and detailed explanations to show how the evidence supports your ideas.

> √ In your **conclusion**, restate or summarize your thesis.
>
> √ Include a memorable **final statement** that clearly tells your opinions.
>
> √ End your letter with a **closing,** such as "Sincerely," and sign your name.

WRITING COACH

www.phwritingcoach.com

Interactive Model

Outline for Success View pop-ups of Mentor Text selections referenced in the Outline for Success.

Interactive Writing Coach™

Use the Interactive Writing Coach to receive the level of support you need:

• Write one paragraph at a time and submit each one for immediate, detailed feedback.

• Write your entire first draft and submit it for immediate, personalized feedback.

Revising: Making It Better

Now that you have finished your first draft, you are ready to revise. Think about the "big picture" of **audience, purpose, and genre**. You can use your Revision RADaR as a guide for making changes to improve your draft. Revision RADaR provides four major ways to improve your writing: (R) replace, (A) add, (D) delete, and (R) reorder.

Kelly Gallagher, M. Ed.

KEEP REVISION ON YOUR RADaR

Read part of the first draft of the Student Model "I. B. Singer's 'Zlateh the Goat.'" Then look at questions the writer asked herself as she thought about how well her draft **addressed issues of audience, purpose, and genre**.

I. B. Singer's "Zlateh the Goat"

1ST DRAFT

I read your story "Zlateh the Goat." It was a great story of how a goat saved a boy's life.

The description of how Zlateh and Aaron begin their adventure really got me interested in what was going to happen. When you wrote that Zlateh was going to be sold because she was not producing milk for the family anymore I felt sorry for her. I also felt bad for the family because I could tell that it wasn't an easy decision to send Zlateh away. For example, the mother and the little sisters all shed tears for Zlateh. Aaron's dad is a furrier. This winter is a very dry season and people are not buying furs. If no one buys furs, Aaron's family needs to get money from somewhere else like selling Zlateh. Animals can help feed us and give us clothes, but they can also be our friends.

*Does the introduction grab my reader's attention? Does my **thesis statement** clearly express my overall response?*

*Have I included relevant **evidence**, such as quotations, to support my opinions?*

*Have I included an **analysis** of the work that is not simply a summary or a retelling?*

Now look at how the writer applied Revision RADaR to write an improved second draft.

Interactive Writing Coach™

Use the Revision RADaR strategy in your own writing. Then submit your paragraph or draft for feedback.

I. B. Singer's "Zlateh the Goat"

2ND DRAFT

At first it seemed like a very simple tale about a boy and a goat caught in a storm. Then I realized it was really a great story about survival and friendship.

> **A** *Added specific information so that the opening is more interesting and the thesis statement more clearly expresses my main idea*

The description of how Zlateh and Aaron begin their adventure really got me interested in what was going to happen. When you wrote that Zlateh was going to be sold because she was not producing milk anymore, I felt sorry for her, especially because she trusted the family: "She knew that they always fed her and never did her any harm." I also felt bad for the family because I could tell that it wasn't an easy decision to send Zlateh away. For example, the mother and the little sisters all shed tears for Zlateh. I was glad you told us that they had cared for Zlateh for twelve years and were having a hard time making money from the fur business because of the weather. This information helped me to understand the family and their choice better. I liked this beginning because it made me think about the relationship people have with animals. Animals can help feed us and give us clothes, but they can also be our friends.

> **A** *Added a quotation to support my idea with evidence from the work*

> **D** *Deleted a simple retelling of the events of the story*

> **R** *Replaced it with personal insights*

Apply It! Now, revise your draft after rethinking how well questions of **purpose**, **audience**, and **genre** have been addressed.

- First, determine if you have clearly stated your ideas and supported them with **evidence** from the text to show your understanding.

- Then, apply your Revision RADaR to make needed changes. Focus especially on working to **clarify your meaning** to your audience. You can use the steps in RADaR in any order.

Look at the Big Picture

Use the chart and your analytical skills to evaluate how well each section of your letter to an author **addresses purpose, audience, and genre**. When necessary, use the suggestions in the chart to revise your letter.

Section	Evaluate	Revise
Introduction	• Check the **opening.** It should grab readers' attention and make them want to read on.	• Make your opening more interesting by writing a strong first sentence or asking a question.
	• Make sure the **thesis** clearly expresses the main idea of your response.	• Ask yourself if you have made important points that are not covered in the thesis. If so, rewrite the thesis to cover all your points.
Body	• Check that you have presented **evidence** from the text to support your ideas and to demonstrate your understanding.	• Skim the story to find and add more examples and quotations that explain and support your ideas.
	• Make sure your **analysis** goes beyond summarizing and retelling.	• Don't just tell what happens in the story. Also describe, specifically and with detail, why it happens or what you think it means.
	• Check your letter's **coherence**— be sure that you have ordered sentences and paragraphs so that they flow logically.	• Reorder text as needed to improve flow. You can add, delete, combine, or reorder sentences to make them sound better.
	• Check that you have developed an **analysis** —make sure you have analyzed specific elements of the work.	• Identify something that you think the author did especially well. Then, tell how that "something" makes the work enjoyable.
Conclusion	• Check the restatement of your **thesis**.	• If necessary, discuss your restatement with a classmate and ask for suggestions.
	• Check that your conclusion leaves readers with a new **insight** and a clear understanding of your feelings.	• Add a final statement that sums up how you feel about the work or why it is important to you.

Focus on Craft: Clarify Meaning

When writing, it is important to **clarify your meaning,** or to clearly state your views. Simple, direct language without unnecessary repetition is a good way to communicate meaning to readers. Using precise words and transitions such as *then* and *next* will help you to state your ideas in a logical, clear way.

Think about clarifying meaning as you read the following sentences from the Student Model.

STUDENT MODEL from **I. B. Singer's "Zlateh the Goat"**
page 203; lines 49-53

> This story really showed how danger can be avoided through smart thinking and teamwork. The boy and the goat both needed and helped each other. Neither of them would have survived the blizzard without each other.

Try It! Now, ask yourself these questions:

- How does the following version of the text differ from the example? *This story is a tale about how teamwork and working together to overcome the odds can be achieved through smart thinking about good decisions.*
- Which version is simpler and more interesting to read? Explain.

Fine-Tune Your Draft

Apply It! Use the revision suggestions to prepare your final draft after again rethinking how well questions of **purpose, audience,** and **genre** have been addressed.

- **Clarify Meaning** Use simple language and avoid unnecessarily repeating ideas. Cut words that are not needed, and make sure to say exactly what you mean.
- **Improve Transitions** You can improve your transitions from one idea to another by adding, deleting, combining, and rearranging sentences or larger units of text.

Teacher Feedback Submit your final draft to your teacher and revise it based on his or her feedback.

WRITING COACH

Online

www.phwritingcoach.com

 Video
Learn more strategies for effective writing from program author Kelly Gallagher.

 Online Journal
Try It! Record your answers in the online journal.

 Interactive Model
Refer back to the Interactive Model as you revise your writing.

 Interactive Writing Coach™
Revise your draft and submit it for feedback.

Editing: Making It Correct

Editing means checking your draft for errors in spelling, grammar, and punctuation.

When editing your draft, make sure you use **proper punctuation and spacing for quotations.** Also, use **parentheses, brackets, and ellipses to indicate missing text, interruptions, or incomplete statements.** Then correct any other errors in **grammar, mechanics, and spelling.**

WRITE GUY *Jeff Anderson, M. Ed.*

WHAT DO YOU NOTICE?

Zoom in on Conventions Focus on the quotation marks as you zoom in on this sentence from the Mentor Text.

> **MENTOR TEXT** from **Search for Boy and Giant Chicken Will Charm Young and Old** page 200; lines 14–15
>
> A voice responds: "I am the Abbé Faria… also unjustly imprisoned in the Chateau d'If."

Now ask yourself: *How does the use of quotation marks help make the writer's meaning clear?*

Perhaps you said that **quotation marks** help make it clear exactly what the voice is responding to and what the writer has quoted directly from the text.

When using quotations, place quotation marks before the first word of the quote and after the last word. The end punctuation, such as a period, goes inside the quotation marks. A comma or a colon is usually used to set off the direct quotation from the rest of the sentence. When the quotation cannot stand alone, it is not set off by a comma.

If you are quoting a passage of more than four lines, set it off in a block of its own. Add a line of **spacing** above and below it. Indent the whole passage, but don't use quotation marks.

To learn more about quotations, see Chapter 25 of your Grammar Handbook.

Grammar Mini-Lesson: Editing Quotations

To learn more, see Chapter 25.

Use **ellipses**, a series of three or four periods, to show omitted, incomplete, or interrupted text. Use **parentheses** to set off loosely related information. Use **brackets** to show explanations, replacements for pronouns, or changes to capitalization and punctuation. Notice the edits to the Mentor Text.

 MENTOR TEXT from **Search for Boy and Giant Chicken Will Charm Young and Old** page 200; lines 6–7

[Nick's] mother is the kind who says… "Oh, another urban experience!"

("I simply tolerate these weirdnesses," Nick notes.)

 Try It! Rewrite the sentences, using ellipses to shorten the quotation and brackets to identify the furrier's name as Paul. Enclose the second sentence in parentheses.

"It was a very bad year for a furrier such as him," the story states. It was for many others, too.

 Apply It! Edit your draft for grammar, mechanics, and spelling. Use proper punctuation and spacing for **quotations.** Use parentheses, brackets, and ellipses to show omitted, missing, or interrupted text.

Use the rubric to evaluate your piece. If necessary, rethink, rewrite, or revise.

Rubric for Interpretative Response: Letter to an Author	Rating Scale
Ideas: How well does your response present a focused statement about the work?	Not very Very 1 2 3 4 5 6
Organization: How clearly organized is your analysis?	1 2 3 4 5 6
Voice: How well have you engaged the reader and sustained his or her interest?	1 2 3 4 5 6
Word Choice: How clearly do your words state your views?	1 2 3 4 5 6
Sentence Fluency: How well have you used transitions to improve the flow of your writing?	1 2 3 4 5 6
Conventions: How correct is your punctuation for quotations?	1 2 3 4 5 6

WRITING COACH

Online

www.phwritingcoach.com

 Video

Learn effective editing techniques from program author Jeff Anderson.

Online Journal

Try It! Record your answers in the online journal.

Interactive Model

Refer back to the Interactive Model as you edit your writing.

Interactive Writing Coach™

Edit your draft. Check it against the rubric and then submit it for feedback.

Publishing

Share the feelings and thoughts expressed in your letter to an author—publish it! First, get your letter ready for presentation. Then, choose a way to **publish it for the appropriate audience**.

Wrap Up Your Presentation

Now that you have finished your draft, add the final details. Make a final draft that is neat and is easy for others to read. Be sure to include page numbers on each page of your letter.

Publish Your Piece

Use the chart to identify a way to publish your letter for the appropriate audience.

If your audience is...	...then publish it by...
A living author	• Mailing or e-mailing it to the author through his or her publishing company • Submitting it to the author's Web site
Students at school	• Reading it aloud in English class • Submitting it to your school newspaper • Posting your piece online and inviting responses

 Extend Your Research

Think more about the topic on which you wrote your letter to an author. What else would you like to know about this topic?

- Brainstorm several questions that you would like to research and then consult, or discuss, with others. Then, decide which question is your major research question.

- Formulate, or develop, a plan about how you will answer these questions. Decide where you will find more information—on the Internet, at the library, or through other sources.

- Finally, learn more about your topic by following through with your research plan.

 The Big Question: Why Write? What should you write about to make others interested in a text?

21st Century Learning

MAKE YOUR WRITING COUNT

Share Letters With the School Community

The mail is just one of the many ways you can share a letter with others, such as an author. For example, newspapers and magazines have a Letters to the Editor page and blogs and Web sites have places to post your ideas and opinions. What ways can you think of to share your letters with other students in your school or elsewhere?

With a group, decide on a way to use technology to publish the letters for your audience, in this case other students and teachers in the school. Your group will come up with a plan and present it to the teacher or principal to explain how it can be done. If possible, publish the letters applying the chosen technology.

Here's your action plan.

1. With your group, identify roles such as leader and notetaker.

2. With your group, brainstorm for different ways to use technology, such as a Web site, group e-mail, or a blog, to publish and share your letters.

3. Use the Internet to research additional technology options for sharing letters.

4. Review the ideas you have brainstormed, and vote for the best one.

5. Create a plan that explains how you will use the technology to share the letters.

   - Use poster paper or a bulletin board to display a flowchart illustrating the process.
   - Include an explanation of the technology in your plan.

6. If possible, use your plan to publish your letters.

Listening and Speaking Come to your group's brainstorming session with an open mind. Listen actively and effectively to your group members' ideas and offer your own ideas as part of the discussion, as well. As you plan your presentation, consult with others to ask for advice on ways to improve your plan. Incorporate this advice and feedback as you give your presentation.

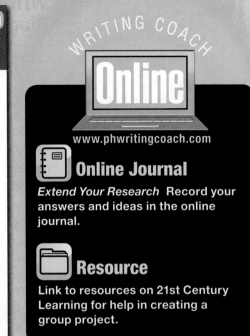

WRITING COACH

Online

www.phwritingcoach.com

Online Journal

Extend Your Research Record your answers and ideas in the online journal.

Resource

Link to resources on 21st Century Learning for help in creating a group project.

Your Turn ✏️ **Writing for Media: Blog Entry**

Blog Entry

A **blog entry** is a short commentary posted on a Web site. Readers sometimes post blog entries on the Web sites of their favorite authors or on online bookstores' Web sites. Others have their own pages on which they write their blogs. In their postings, readers explain what they like about an author's work and why, including evidence from the text to back up their ideas.

Try It! Study the blog entry on this page. Then, answer the questions. Record your answers in your journal.

1. Which **work** does this blog entry discuss?

2. Who is the **author** of the work?

3. Is the book **fiction** or **nonfiction?** How do you know?

4. Does the blog have an effective **introduction**? Explain.

5. Does the writer provide **evidence**, such as specific facts, details, and examples, to support his or her ideas? List some examples.

6. How effective is the **concluding paragraph**? Explain.

7. Does the blog contain personal **insights** and judgments?

8. Would this **blog** encourage you to read the selection? Why or why not?

Extension Find another example of a blog entry, or an online book review and compare it with this one.

Stories for Now: A Blog for Readers

Page Turner to Try Posted by Reading Dude on 12/17/12 at 5:35 PM

The suspense in Dan Gutman's novel *Honus and Me*[1] almost made my hands shake as I turned the pages. A boy named Stosh is hired to throw out a neighbor's trash. But when he gathers up junk in her attic, a card flutters to the floor. He says. "No doubt about it. I had just stumbled upon a T-206 Honus Wagner card—*the most valuable baseball card in the world.*"

But that's only the beginning. The card's value is far beyond money. It enables Stosh to actually travel back in time, to attend the 1909 World Series—and much more.

The interesting storyline isn't the only element that makes this story great. Gutman's characters are totally realistic, and his style is clear and easy to read. Here's a warning, however: Beware! If you don't finish by bedtime; you won't want to stop reading!

[1] Gutman, Dan. *Honus and Me.* New York: Avon Books, 1997.

Create a Blog Entry

Follow these steps to create your own blog entry. Review the graphic organizers on pages R24–R27 and choose one that suits your needs.

Prewriting

- Choose a book that you have recently read and enjoyed. Then, think about which readers are sure to like the book as well as which readers *might* enjoy it.

- Think about how best to grab readers' attention. For example, you might begin with a question or start with an exciting passage.

- Jot down ideas about the author's style, the selection's message, and what quotations or details you might include.

- Review your notes and decide the main insight you'd like to convey about the work.

Drafting

- Begin with a strong opening statement to grab your reader's attention. Then, write a brief summary that makes the book sound appealing to the target audience. Take your writing further by adding the insight you will develop.

- Provide evidence from the text to demonstrate your understanding of it and to support your ideas. Use this evidence to persuade others to read the book.

- Describe the author's style and tell why it is effective.

Revising and Editing

Review your draft to ensure that your ideas flow logically and that you have presented them in a persuasive way. Be sure that you have used a positive tone and done all you can to "sell" the book and the author. Edit your draft for errors in grammar, mechanics, and spelling.

Publishing

Post your blog entry on a school Web site, and invite your classmates to read and respond to the entry.

WRITING COACH

Online

www.phwritingcoach.com

Online Journal

Try It! Record your answers in the online journal.

Interactive Graphic Organizers

Choose from a variety of graphic organizers to plan and develop your project.

Partner Talk

Before you start drafting, describe and fully explain your ideas for your planned blog entry to a partner. Be specific and detailed, and ask your partner for feedback. For example, you might ask whether your blog entry ideas are persuasive enough or if you have included enough evidence to support your ideas.

Writing for Assessment

You may see a prompt that asks you to write an essay in which you respond to literature. Use these prompts to practice. Respond using the characteristics in your letter to an author. (See page 198.)

 Try It! To begin, read the **interpretative response** prompt and the information on format and academic vocabulary. Use the ABCDs of On-Demand Writing to help you plan and write your essay.

Format

The prompt directs you to write a *critical review* of a story, book, or poem. Your introduction should include a clear thesis. The body of your essay should provide supporting evidence from the text. The conclusion should strongly support your thesis.

Interpretative Response Prompt

Write an essay that is a critical review of a short story, book, or poem you have read. Analyze and evaluate the work. Support your analysis and opinions with specific details, such as examples and quotations from the work. [30 minutes]

Academic Vocabulary

When you *analyze* a story, book, or poem, you study and respond to its elements. When you *evaluate* a work of literature, you state and support your opinion about its strengths and weaknesses.

The ABCDs of On-Demand Writing

Use the following ABCDs to help you respond to the prompt.

Before you write your draft:

Attack the prompt [1 MINUTE]

- Circle or highlight important verbs in the prompt. Draw a line from the verb to what it refers to.
- Rewrite the prompt in your own words.

Brainstorm possible answers [4 MINUTES]

- Create a graphic organizer to generate ideas.
- Use one for each part of the prompt if necessary.

Choose the order of your response [1 MINUTE]

- Think about the best way to organize your ideas.
- Number your ideas in the order you will write about them. Cross out ideas you will not be using.

After you write your draft:

Detect errors before turning in the draft [1 MINUTE]

- Carefully reread your writing.
- Make sure that your response makes sense and is complete.
- Look for spelling, punctuation, and grammar errors.

More Prompts for Practice

Try It! Respond to Prompts 1 and 2 by writing **interpretative responses**. As you write, be sure to:

- Express the main idea of your response in a clear thesis statement
- Include effective introductory and concluding paragraphs
- Include supporting details and **evidence from the text**
- Go beyond a simple retelling to include a careful analysis of the work
- **Demonstrate your understanding of the text** and what it means to you
- Clearly convey meaning through an appropriately organized structure

> **Prompt 1** Write an interpretative essay comparing and contrasting two characters from two different books or short stories. Support your ideas and opinions with specific details and examples from the texts.

> **Prompt 2** Write an essay interpreting a theme or central insight in a short story, book, or poem you have read. Analyze how well the author demonstrates the theme and discuss what the theme means to you.

SAT/PSAT PREP ACT **Spiral Review: Persuasive** Respond to Prompt 3 by writing a **persuasive essay** **for appropriate audiences**. Make sure your persuasive essay reflects all of the characteristics described on page 172, including:

- **establish a clear position**
- **demonstrate sound reasoning**
- **provide detailed and relevant evidence**
- **include a consideration of alternative views**

> **Prompt 3** Write an essay to persuade the mayor of your town to start a new community program, such as a recycling program or an after-school program at a local community center.

WRITING COACH

Online

www.phwritingcoach.com

Interactive Writing Coach™

Plan your response to the prompt. If you are using the prompt for practice, write one paragraph at a time or your entire draft and then submit it for feedback. If you are using the prompt as a timed test, write your entire draft and then submit it for feedback.

Remember **ABCD**

Attack the prompt

Brainstorm possible answers

Choose the order of your response

Detect errors before turning in the draft

CHAPTER 11

RESEARCH WRITING

What Do You Want To Know?

How do people find out more information about interesting topics? They do research. Research writing is a way to gather, organize, and present information in a report that others can read.

One of the first steps of research is to identify a topic that interests you and then develop research questions. For example, if you want to find out more about jellyfish, like the kind shown in the photograph, you would first decide what you want to know about them.

Try It! Take a few minutes to brainstorm for some things you want to know about jellyfish. Write them in a list.

Consider these questions as you participate in an extended discussion with a partner. Take turns expressing your ideas.

- What do you want to know about where jellyfish live?
- What do you want to know about their bodies?
- What do you want to know about how jellyfish survive?
- Where could you find information about jellyfish?

Review your list of questions with your partner. Compare your lists to determine if any ideas overlap or how you might build off each other's ideas. Then, discuss where you would go to research answers to your questions.

What's Ahead

In this chapter, you will review a strong example of an informational research report. Then, using the examples as guidance, you will develop a research plan and write your own informational research report.

Connect to the Big Questions

Discuss these questions with your partner:

1 **What do you think?** What is the best way to find important information about a topic?

2 **Why write?** Do you understand a subject well enough to write about it? How will you find out what the facts are?

RESEARCH WRITING

Research writing is a way to gather information, and then synthesize, or combine, that information into a report for others to read. In this chapter, you will write an informational research report. Your report will provide information about a topic that interests you. Before you write, you will search for information about your topic in different kinds of sources. You will decide which facts and details to use in your report, and organize your ideas clearly for your audience.

You will develop your informational research report by taking it through each of the steps of the writing process: prewriting, drafting, revising, editing, and publishing. You will also have an opportunity to use your informational research report in an oral or multimedia presentation that uses text and graphics to share what you have learned. To preview the criteria for how your research report will be evaluated, see the rubric on page 247.

FEATURE ASSIGNMENT

Research Writing: Informational Research Report

An effective informational research report has these characteristics:

- A specific **topic sentence** or thesis statement that identifies a major research topic

- Information from a variety of **reliable, accurate, and relevant sources** to support the main ideas

- Information that is compiled from **multiple sources** and that is **accurate, relevant, valid, and current**

- **Evidence**, including facts, details, examples, quotations, and explanations, that supports conclusions

- Clear presentation that **summarizes findings**

- A **bibliography with citations** to credit others for their work according to a standard format

- **Effective sentence structure** and correct spelling, grammar, and usage

Other Forms of Research Writing

In addition to an informational research report, there are other forms of research writing, including:

Biographical profiles give specific details about the life and work of a real person. The person may be living or dead, someone famous, or someone familiar to the writer.

Documentaries are filmed reports that focus on a specific topic. These multimedia presentations use spoken and written text as well as photographs, videos, music, and other sound effects.

Health reports present the latest information, data, and research about a specific disease or health-related issues.

Historical reports give in-depth information about a past event. These kinds of reports focus on a narrow topic and may discuss causes and effects.

I-Search reports blend informational and personal writing. In an I-search report, you tell the story of your research and investigations, including the dead-ends and small victories, in addition to presenting the results of your research.

Scientific reports analyze information and data concerning a scientific issue or problem. A lab report describes a scientific experiment, including observations and conclusions.

Try It! For each research report described, brainstorm for possible topics with other students. Then, consult with one another to choose a major research topic for each report and write a research question for each topic. As you write, keep your audience and purpose in mind.

- A biographical profile of an important member of your community
- A lab report about the results of a scientific experiment
- A historical report about an event in the history of your state

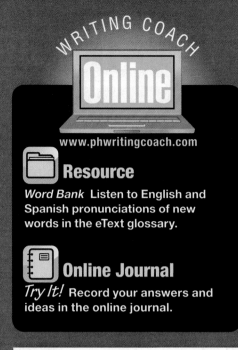

WRITING COACH

Online

www.phwritingcoach.com

Resource

Word Bank Listen to English and Spanish pronunciations of new words in the eText glossary.

Online Journal

Try It! Record your answers and ideas in the online journal.

WORD BANK

People use these basic and content-based words when they talk about writing that reports information. Work with a partner. Take turns saying and writing each word in a sentence. If you are unsure of the meaning of a word, use the Glossary or a dictionary to check the definition.

accuracy	logical
analysis	standard
document	summarize

STUDENT MODEL
Informational Research Report

Use a Reader's Eye

Read the Student Model on pages 226–229. Then, use the symbols to react to what you've read.

Reader's Response Symbols

√ **OK. I understand this. It's very clearly explained.**

? **I don't follow what the writer is saying here.**

+ **I think the writer needs more details here.**

— **This information doesn't seem relevant.**

! **Wow! That is cool/weird/interesting.**

Learn From Experience

Read the numbered notes in the margins as you reread the Student Model to learn about how the writer presented his ideas.

Answer the *Try It!* questions online or in your notebook.

❶ The writer uses **proper formatting** for heads and pagination according to a style manual.

❷ The **topic sentence** identifies the major research topic and gives the main ideas.

❸ The writer uses a **quotation** from an expert as **evidence** to explain an important idea.

Try It! What is the major research topic of the report? What open-ended questions might this writer have asked about this topic as he was creating his report?

❶ John Butler
Mrs. Harker
English 101
21 December 2009

❶Big Mountain, Big Challenge

When you reach the summit of Mount Everest, you stand on top of the world. At 29,035 feet tall, the mountain is the highest point on earth ("Everest, Mount"). Everest has fascinated many climbers. Between 2000 and 2006, 4,886 people attempted
5 the climb, and 38 climbers died ("Everest Expedition"). ❷ While climbing Mount Everest can be dangerous, an understanding of science basics such as altitude, air pressure, and simple machines can help climbers stay safe.

Everest is at a very high altitude. The word *altitude*
10 means how far above sea level something is. The higher up you go, the less oxygen there is (Platt 12). Because people need oxygen to breathe, they may get altitude sickness as they climb to higher altitudes. ❸ "Because of the lack of oxygen," explains British mountaineer Graham Ratcliffe,
15 "you get nausea and bad headaches and suffer from loss of appetite" ("Double Feat"). These are the most common symptoms of altitude sickness.

To lessen altitude sickness, climbers go up the mountain in stages (see figure 1) ("Everest, Mount"). Climbers spend
20 about a month adjusting to higher altitudes before trying to reach the top. But it is impossible to avoid altitude sickness completely. At 25,000 feet begins the "death zone." Here, the level of oxygen in the air drops sharply. To make it through the death zone to the summit, almost all climbers
25 carry containers of oxygen to help them breathe (Leahy).

Climbers spend about four weeks acclimatizing, or getting used to the altitude, before trying to reach the top. At first, they stay in Base Camp. Then, they carry supplies to Camp I

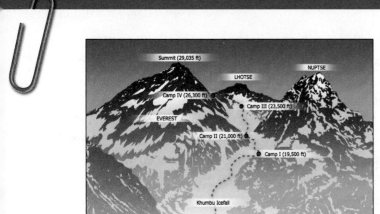

Butler 2

4 Figure 1. Southern Climbing Route; based on information from Jean Ricard, "About Everest," *Everest for Kids,* (Everest for Kids: 2007). Web. 15 Dec. 2009.

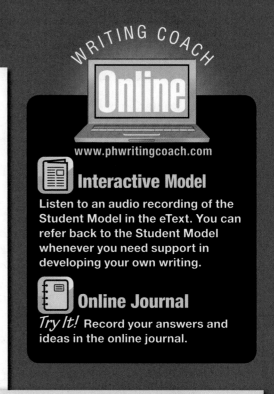

WRITING COACH

Online

www.phwritingcoach.com

Interactive Model
Listen to an audio recording of the Student Model in the eText. You can refer back to the Student Model whenever you need support in developing your own writing.

Online Journal
Try It! Record your answers and ideas in the online journal.

and return to Base Camp to sleep, then climb to Camp II and
30 return to Base Camp, and so on ("Everest, Mount").

5 One symptom of severe altitude sickness is confused thinking (Platt 12). Climbers may hallucinate—see or feel things that are not really there. Frozen climbers have been found on Everest without their coats or gloves. They removed
35 their protective clothing after hallucinating that they were in a warm place (Viesturs). Climbers know that if they become too sick, they must descend to a lower altitude where there is more oxygen ("Everest, Mount").

Another danger of climbing Everest is the evil weather,
40 which includes storms and high winds. **6** Storms are caused by changes in air pressure. Air moves to an area of lower pressure near Earth's surface, and the air rises and cools. If there is enough moisture in the air, snow can fall (Williams, "What's Happening"). Differences in air pressure also cause
45 wind. Air flows from an area of high pressure to an area of low pressure (Williams, "Pressure Differences").

Forecasting storms and winds on Everest is difficult. The mountain's vast size affects different weather patterns. Therefore, precautions must be taken. First, climbers schedule
50 climbs in the spring and fall, when the weather is best (Platt 17). They also receive frequent weather forecasts. Forecasters take information on air pressure and other conditions from satellites and computer models. They

4 This **graphic** is relevant to the written explanation of how climbers lessen altitude sickness.

5 The writer compiles relevant information from **multiple sources** to support the main ideas.

Try It! How does using information from a variety of sources make research writing stronger?

6 Facts are pieces of information that can be proven. Facts like this one are an important type of **evidence** in a research report.

Try It! Which sentence(s) in this paragraph contain facts? Which include a statement or opinion that cannot be proven true?

STUDENT MODEL

Informational Research Report *(continued)*

7 A long **quotation** of 4 lines or more is set off from the rest of the text, indented without quotation marks.

Try It! Is this quotation a strong piece of supporting evidence? Why or why not?

8 This **photo** helps the reader picture the tool discussed in the text.

Try It! How does the figure reference to a graphic help you locate information you need?

9 Throughout the report, the writer cites, or gives credit to, the source of his data.

Try It! Why is it important to use and cite a valid and reliable source? What are the dangers of using weak sources?

10 The report ends with a conclusion and a final thought on the topic.

Try It! Is this information from research or the writer's own ideas? How do you know?

11 The Works Cited list provides proper **documentation** by listing publication information for each source. The **formatting** of the list follows an appropriate style.

Try It! Study the Works Cited list. Why is it helpful to readers to list sources in alphabetical order?

Extension Locate one of the sources from the Works Cited page, and write a brief synopsis of it in your own words.

---

55 combine this data with their experience from years of watching the weather on the mountain.

But no forecaster can be one hundred percent right. The weather can change quickly. For example, the morning of May 10, 1996, was clear. A large number of Everest climbers decided to try for the top. Famous American climber Ed 60 Viesturs was on the mountain. He described what he could and could not see of the summit from his location:

7 That day dawned perfect, so there was no reason for them not to go. We had a telescope in camp with us to monitor the climbers' progress…. Then, the big storm 65 rolled in. The summit disappeared, the clouds lowered, swallowing up more and more of the upper mountain until finally our visibility was cut off…. It wasn't until 10 p.m. that we got any news. Paula radioed up to us and said, "Only half the people who left the South Col 70 this morning have made it back." … By May 12 five climbers from the two teams were dead.

To cope with conditions on the mountain, climbers need the right equipment. Simple machines are the basis of some important climbing tools. One example is 75 the ice axe (see figure 2). The slopes of Everest are covered in glaciers. A glacier is a mass of ice that exists year-round. The ice axe has a pick on one end. A pick is a kind of wedge. When the climber 80 swings the axe, the inclined planes of the pick split the ice, driving the point deep inside (Tomecek). Climbers use the pick to stop themselves if they begin to fall down the glacier (Platt 39).

8 Figure 2. Ice axe is a wedge. Courtesy of Jupiter Images.

85 **9** Over time, glaciers move. Cracks form in the ice. Deep cracks are called crevasses (Platt 11). Crevasses are very dangerous for climbers. Another simple machine called a pulley can help if a person falls into a crevasse. Other climbers can use a pulley system to get the stranded person out. Pulleys

Butler 4

90 multiply the force applied to a rope ("How Pulleys Work"). The climbers attach a rope to the stranded person. With the advantage provided by the pulleys, the other climbers—who may be weak and tired themselves—can lift the stranded person to safety (Tyson and Clelland 130).

95 In 1923, British climber George Mallory was asked why he wanted to climb Everest. Mallory said, "Because it's there" (Golden 72). Mallory died on the mountain. No one knows if he reached the summit (Platt 19). The conditions on Everest mean that climbing this mountain will never be completely 100 free of danger. However, increased understanding of altitude, air pressure, and simple machines makes climbing Everest safer today than it was in Mallory's time. **❿** Perhaps only one thing is certain: As long as there are those who, like Mallory, want to test their limits, people will climb Everest.

⓫ Works Cited

"Double Feat Proved the Peak of Achievement." *Evening Chronicle*, [Newcastle, UK], 21 May 2003, ed. 1, sec. 01A: 28. Print.

"Everest Expedition Statistics 2000–2006." *AdventureStats.com.* ExplorersWeb, n.d. Web. 17 Dec. 2009.

"Everest, Mount." *Encyclopaedia Britannica Online Library Edition.* Encyclopaedia Britannica, 2009. Web. 17 Dec. 2009.

Golden, Frederic. "Who Got There First?" *Time* 17 May 1999: 72+. Print.

"How Pulleys Work." *NASA's Our World.* NASA, n.d. Web. 19 Dec. 2009.

Leahy, Michael. "The Dark Side of the Mountain." *Washington Post* 28 Nov. 2004, final ed.: W12. Print.

Platt, Richard. *Everest: Reaching the World's Highest Peak.* New York: Dorling Kindersley, 2000. Print.

Tomecek, Steve. "Simple Machines: The Wedge." *Dirtmeisters's Science Reporters.* Scholastic, n.d. Web. 19 Dec. 2009.

Tyson, Andy and Mike Clelland. *Glacier Mountaineering: An Illustrated Guide to Glacier Travel and Crevasse Rescue.* Helena, Montana: Falcon, 2009. Print.

Viesturs, Ed. "Ed Viesturs on 1996: Turn Around, Guys!" *National Geographic Online.* National Geographic, n.d. Web. 17 Dec. 2009.

Williams, Jack. "Pressure Differences Get the Wind Going." *USATODAY. com.* USA Today. 20 May 2005. Web. 15 Dec. 2009.

—. "What's Happening Inside Highs and Lows." *USATODAY.com.* USA Today, n.d. Web. 15 Dec. 2009.

WRITING COACH

Online

www.phwritingcoach.com

Interactive Model

Listen to an audio recording of the Student Model in the eText. You can refer back to the Student Model whenever you need support in developing your own writing.

Use a Writer's Eye

Now go back to the beginning of the Student Model and evaluate the piece as a writer. On your copy of the Student Model, use the Writer's Response Symbols to react to what you read. Identify places where the student writer uses characteristics of an effective informational research report.

Writer's Response Symbols

T.S.	**Clear topic sentence**
S.E.	**Supporting evidence**
R.G.	**Relevant graphic**
D.S.	**Proper documentation of sources**

Your Turn

Feature Assignment:
Informational Research Report

Prewriting

Begin to plan a first draft by **choosing an appropriate topic.** You can select from the Topic Bank or come up with an idea of your own.

 Choose From the Topic Bank

TOPIC BANK

Conservation Counts Research ways that you can help conserve energy at home and reasons why your efforts matter. How do small steps add up to big savings?

How Did It Happen? What causes a natural disaster such as an earthquake, tsunami, or cyclone? Research the science behind one of these events: the 2004 Sri Lankan tsunami, the Great Tangshan Earthquake of 1976, or the 1970 Bhola cyclone in Bangladesh. Also, find out how the disaster affected safety measures and ways people prepare for emergencies in the country where it took place.

Special Delivery—Music Technology has changed the music industry in the past 20 years. What changes have occurred in the ways in which music is delivered? How has listening to music changed? Which technologies have had the greatest impact on the industry?

 Choose Your Own Topic

Determine a topic of your own by using these strategies.

Brainstorm and Browse

- **Consult** with a partner to **brainstorm** for a list of topics.
- **Formulate open-ended questions** about your topics. Circle key words in your questions. Use your key words to browse your library's research resources.
- Search the Internet, using the same key words. Work with your partner to decide which topic provides results that interest you.
- Review your work and choose a topic.

Formulate Your Research Question

A topic that is too broad is almost impossible to research well. It also makes writing a report more difficult. Plan to do some research to help narrow your topic and then formulate your research question.

 *Apply It!* Use a printed or online graphic organizer like the one shown to narrow your topic.

- Write your general topic in the top box, and keep narrowing your topic by **refining** your **research questions**. You may need to develop a secondary set of questions to guide you as you move down the chart.

- Your last box should hold your narrowest or most refined research question. This will be the focus of your report.

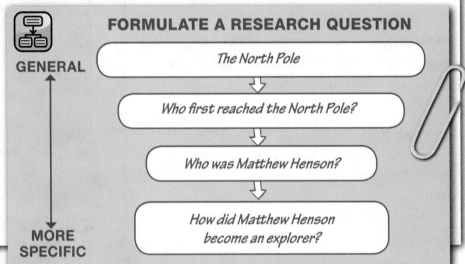

FORMULATE A RESEARCH QUESTION

GENERAL

The North Pole

Who first reached the North Pole?

Who was Matthew Henson?

How did Matthew Henson become an explorer?

MORE SPECIFIC

Consider Your Audience and Purpose

Before researching for your informational research report, think about your audience and purpose. Ask yourself these questions. Then, think about the kinds of information you'll look for in order to meet your audience's needs and your purpose.

Questions About Audience	Questions About Purpose
• Who is my audience: My teacher? My classmates? Someone else? • What does my audience need and want to know about my topic? • What vocabulary will I need to explain to my audience?	• Why am I writing the report: To inform? To make my audience want to learn more about the topic? Something else? • How do I want my audience to react as they read my report?

Record your answers in your writing journal.

Make a Research Plan

Once you have written your major research question, you are ready to make a research plan. As part of your plan, you will create a timeline for finishing your report. You will also find and evaluate sources of information.

Find Multiple Relevant Sources For your report, you will need to collect data, or gather information. You should **compile,** or gather, important information from a range of print and electronic resources, including expert interviews and multimedia resources. Follow these guidelines:

Print Resources

- Find print resources in libraries and bookstores.
- Use encyclopedias, magazines, newspapers, and textbooks.
- Search for print resources using electronic databases or with help from a reference librarian.

Electronic Resources

- Find electronic resources using search engines on the Internet.
- Choose only authoritative reliable sites, such as those ending in:
  .edu (educational institution)
  .gov (government group)
  .org (not-for-profit organization; these may be biased toward a specific purpose)
- If you are not sure that a site is reliable and unbiased, do not use it.

Interviews with Experts

- Ask questions of an expert on your topic.
- Set up a short in-person, e-mail, or telephone interview.
- Record the interview and take good notes.

Multimedia Resources

- Watch movies about your topic.
- Listen to podcasts or seminars related to the topic.
- Search for relevant photos, diagrams, charts, and graphs.

Evaluate Your Sources Do not assume that all sources of information on your topic are useful or trustworthy. Use the checklist to evaluate sources of information you find. The more questions that you can answer with a yes, the more likely you should use the source.

Checklist for Evaluating Sources

Does the source of information:

- ❏ Contain **relevant** information that answers your research question?
- ❏ Give facts and details at a level you can understand?
- ❏ Tell all sides of a story, including opposing viewpoints, so that it is **unbiased**?
- ❏ Provide **valid and reliable** information written or gathered by experts?
- ❏ Have a **recent** publication date, indicating that it provides current information?

WRITING COACH

Online

www.phwritingcoach.com

Online Journal

Record your answers and ideas in the online journal.

Differentiate Between Types of Sources As you research, you will discover two kinds of sources: primary sources and secondary sources. Your teacher may require that you use both kinds.

- **A primary source** is an original document that provides direct, firsthand knowledge. Examples of primary sources include speeches such as Abraham Lincoln's *Gettysburg Address* and journals such as *The Diary of Anne Frank.*

- **A secondary source** is a source that gives indirect or secondhand understanding of a subject. For example, a book about the Gettysburg Address is a secondary source. In a secondary source, the writer may include his or her opinion about the subject.

Apply It! Generate a **research plan** and timeline for finishing your report, and list at least four print and electronic sources of information, including expert and multimedia resources, that you plan to use.

- Work with your teacher to determine the dates by which you need to finish your research, your drafting, and your final report.
- For each source you plan to use, give full publication information.
- Tell whether each source is primary or secondary.
- **Evaluate the relevance and reliability** of each source by using the Checklist for Evaluating Sources. For each source, explain why you answered yes or no.

Change Your Plan If Necessary After you begin to follow your research plan and collect data, you may find that you need to refine, or change, your research question. If you cannot find answers to a research question, you may decide to change the focus of your topic.

Collect and Organize Your Data

For your informational research report, you will need to use **multiple** sources of information. Notes will help you **record data** and see the **relationships between ideas.** Notes will also help you keep track of the sources of your information. There are different forms of notes from which you can choose. You can keep handwritten notes on note cards, or utilize available **technology** such as **word processors** to keep electronic notes on a computer.

Keep Track of Multiple Sources A good way to stay organized is to create a source card for each one of your sources. Give each source its own number. Then, note the full publishing information for the source, including the author, title, city of publication, publisher, and copyright date. Here is a source card that the writer of the Student Model made. Notice that he recorded the information in the same MLA style he used on his Works Cited page.

Take Notes When you take notes on a source, follow these guidelines.

- Note only facts and details you might use.
- Organize the notes using headings that sum up the main ideas of each group of notes.
- Be very careful to use your own words. You can also use abbreviations.
- If you want to quote someone, enclose the exact words in large quotation marks. They will remind you that these are someone else's words—not your own.

Apply It! Take written notes to record data that is relevant to your research question. As you work, effectively organize the information on note cards or on the computer.

- Group related information together and consider using software or graph paper to turn your notes into a chart, graph, or map. These techniques will help you see the **relationships** between ideas.
- Paraphrase or summarize the information in your own words. Convert data from charts, diagrams, or timelines into your own words. If you want to quote, carefully copy the original and enclose the quotation in quotation marks. **Identify each source** you use and record its bibliographic information according to a standard.

> ### Source 1
>
> Platt, Richard. *Everest: Reaching the World's Highest Peak.* New York: Dorling Kindersley, 2000. Print.

> ### Notes From Source 1
>
> *Diagram of human body: effects of altitude sickness p. 12*
>
> - Shows all systems of body and how affected by altitude
> - Brain: Altitude makes person dizzy, trouble concentrating/thinking/ sleeping, can lead to person becoming unconscious

Avoid Plagiarism

Presenting someone else's words or ideas as your own is plagiarism. You must always document the source of your information. When you quote someone, you must clearly show that you are using another person's words. Plagiarism is a serious error with severe consequences. Do not plagiarize.

Careful Note-taking Matters You can accidentally set yourself up to plagiarize by not taking good notes. The student who wrote this note card made two mistakes. She followed the original source too closely, and she forgot to include full publication information.

WRITING COACH

Online

www.phwritingcoach.com

Online Journal
Record your answers and ideas in the online journal.

The modern ice axe is safer and lighter because of new materials, and the shape of the axe has also changed.

Original Source

> ## Notes From Source 3
>
> ### Tools
>
> *New materials have made the modern ice axe safer and lighter. The shape of the axe has changed, too.*
> *from Everest: Reaching the World's Highest Peak by Richard Platt, p. 39*

Plagiarized Notes

Partner Talk

Review taking notes with a partner. Explain why each of these is important:
- Citing valid and reliable sources
- Your own words to summarize ideas
- Large quotation marks for direct quotations

Use these strategies to avoid plagiarism.

- **Paraphrase** When you paraphrase, you put a writer's idea in your own words. Read a passage and think about what it means. Then, write it as you might explain it to someone else.

- **Summarize** In your own words, state the most important ideas in a long passage. A summary should be shorter than the original passage.

- **Direct Quotation** Enclose the writer's exact words in quotation marks, and tell who said it. (See page 247.)

Try It! Look at the *Notes From Source 3* in the example you just read. Highlight the parts that are plagiarizing rather than paraphrasing the original. Now, write a new note based on the original source. Be sure to avoid plagiarizing the content. Why is it important to cite valid and reliable sources?

Document Your Sources

When you write a research report, you have to use a standard style to tell your readers where you found information. You need to cite all researched information that is not common knowledge, and cite it according to a standard format.

Works Cited On the Works Cited page at the end of your report, list all the sources that you used to write your report. Do not include sources you looked into but did not use. Follow the format shown in a standard style manual, such as that of the Modern Language Association (MLA). Your teacher will be able to tell you which standard format style you should use.

Look at the example citations shown. Use these and the MLA Style for Listing Sources on page R16 as guides for writing your citations. Pay attention to formatting, including italics, abbreviations, and punctuation.

Book

Author's last name, author's first name followed by the author's middle name or initial (if given). *Full title of book.* City where book was published: Name of publisher, date of publication. Print.

Tyson, Andy and Mike Clelland. *Glacier Mountaineering: An Illustrated Guide to Glacier Travel and Crevasse Rescue.* Helena, Montana: Falcon, 2009. Print.

Newspaper Article

Author's last name, author's first name followed by author's middle name or initial (if given). "Title of article." *Title of newspaper* followed by date on which article appeared, edition in which it appeared, section letter and page number on which it appeared. Print.

Leahy, Michael. "The Dark Side of the Mountain." *Washington Post* 28 Nov. 2004, final ed., W12. Print.

Web Page

Author's last name, author's first name followed by author's middle name or initial (if given). "Name of page." Publisher or N.p. if none given, date page was posted or n.d. if none given. Web. Date on which you used the page.

Tomecek, Steve. "Simple Machines: The Wedge." *Dirtmeister's Science Reporters.* Scholastic, n.d. Web. 19 Dec. 2009.

Parenthetical Citations Use parenthetical citations in the text of your report. Parenthetical citations briefly identify the source where you found each piece of information. These citations give the author's last name and the page number on which the information is located. If the author is mentioned in the sentence, only the page number is given in parentheses. Look at this citation from the Student Model.

STUDENT MODEL from **"Big Mountain, Big Challenge"** page 227; lines 49–51

First, climbers schedule climbs in the spring and fall, when the weather is best (Platt 17).

When the author's name is not available, use a word from the title:

At 29,035 feet tall, the mountain is the highest point on earth ("Everest, Mount").

 Try It! Use MLA style to create a short Works Cited page based on the sources described.

- A Web page called "Going High: The Early Pioneers." No information about the author or publisher is available, and the page has no date. The Web site name is pbs.org.
- A two-page magazine article titled "You're Alive" by Gail Skroback Hennessey. The article appeared in the May 1999 issue of *Boys' Life.* The article starts on page 44.

Critique Your Research Process

At every step in the research process, be prepared to modify or change your research plan. If you can't find enough information to write your topic sentence or thesis statement, try rewording your research question. Don't get bogged down in the research step. It's essential that you stick to your **timetable.** You're ready to wrap up the prewriting part of your research paper and start drafting your paper.

Apply It! Write entries on your Works Cited page to identify all the sources you have used in your research report. Record the bibliographic information for each source according to a standard format. Confirm that you have researched enough information to begin writing your draft. Then, use your journal to write a clear topic sentence or thesis statement that summarizes the main ideas for your research report.

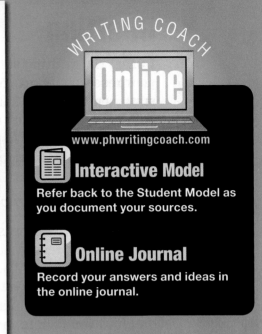

 **Partner Talk**

Get together with a partner to discuss research sources. Where have you looked for information on your topic? How have you been keeping track of sources? Monitor spoken language by asking follow-up questions to confirm your understanding.

Drafting

During the drafting stage, you will start to write your ideas for your research report. You will **develop a topic sentence** or thesis statement. You will follow an outline that will help you write an organized research report that **presents your findings in a consistent format.** As you write your draft or prepare your notes for an oral presentation, remember to keep your audience in mind.

The Organization of an Informational Research Report

The Outline for Success chart shows an organizational strategy for a research report. Look back at how the Student Model follows this same strategy. Then, create a detailed outline for your report. Use the outline template on page R26 as a guide. Organize your evidence and ideas in a logical order, and note any graphics you plan to include. Refer to the Outline for Success as you work.

Outline for Success

I. Introduction
See Student Model, p. 226.

- Clear topic sentence, or thesis statement
- Attention-grabbing introduction

II. Body
See Student Model, pp. 226–229.

- Synthesis of information from multiple sources
- Evidence to support conclusions
- A logical progression of ideas
- Graphics and illustrations that support your topic.

III. Conclusion
See Student Model, p. 229.

- Summary of findings
- Memorable ending

Introduce Your Topic Sentence

- A topic sentence or thesis statement is often the last sentence in the introduction and identifies your major research topic.
- An interesting fact, detail, or example at the beginning of your report will make your reader want to keep going.

Support Your Topic Sentence

- The main ideas from your notes are placed in a logical order. You and your reader should be able to see the relationships between ideas.
- Each paragraph covers one main idea. Evidence, such as facts, statistics, examples, and quotations, supports each main idea. Relevant photos, charts, or other visuals help explain complicated information.

Add a Final Thought

- The concluding paragraph is made up of several sentences that summarize your findings on your research topic.
- A noteworthy fact, detail, quotation, or other piece of evidence leaves your reader with something to think about.

 # Start Your Draft

Use the checklist below to help complete your draft. Use the graphic organizer that shows your topic sentence; the outline that shows the order of your ideas and evidence, your graphics; and the Outline for Success as guides.

While drafting, aim at writing your ideas, not on making your writing perfect. Remember, you will have the chance to improve your draft when you revise and edit.

√ Start your introduction by drafting an attention-getting sentence.

√ End the introduction with a clearly worded **topic sentence** that is based on your research question. Your topic sentence, or thesis statement, should be the roadmap for your report.

√ Develop the **body** one paragraph at a time.

√ Start by drafting the first sentence of each paragraph. This sentence states the main idea.

√ Then, write the rest of the paragraph, using only the best **evidence**, including quotations, to support the main idea and your conclusions. **Compile** important supporting information from multiple sources.

√ Use an appropriate form of documentation, such as parenthetical references, to **acknowledge your sources** and give credit to others' ideas.

√ Draft a **conclusion** that **summarizes** your findings and adds a final thought.

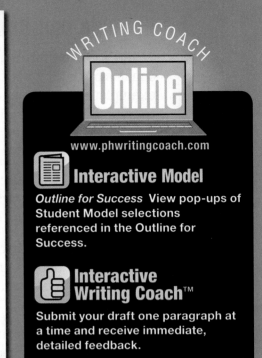

WRITING COACH

Online

www.phwritingcoach.com

Interactive Model

Outline for Success View pop-ups of Student Model selections referenced in the Outline for Success.

Interactive Writing Coach™

Submit your draft one paragraph at a time and receive immediate, detailed feedback.

Provide and Document Evidence

While you are drafting, you will compile **evidence** to support your conclusions about your topic. Your evidence may include facts, examples, explanations, and quotations. Evidence must come from multiple valid and reliable sources. **Document** other people's words and ideas when you provide evidence.

Give Facts and Statistics Facts are convincing because they can be proven true. Statistics, or facts stated in numbers, are also convincing when they come from reliable and current sources. Be sure to give the source of facts that are not common knowledge.

Give Examples Make complicated ideas clear by providing examples. You do not need to document examples from personal experience, but you do need to document examples from a particular source.

Give Explanations Complex ideas may require you to describe how they work. For example, you can help your reader understand a process, system, or technology by explaining it. Document any information that doesn't come from your knowledge or experience.

Use Quotations Direct quotations from experts are also convincing evidence. Make sure a quotation fits smoothly into your paragraph, and use your own words to identify the expert.

 **STUDENT MODEL** from **"Big Mountain, Big Challenge"** page 229; lines 95–96

In 1923, British climber George Mallory was asked why he wanted to climb Everest. Mallory said, "Because it's there" (Golden 72).

Remember to follow these guidelines:
- Do not quote if paraphrasing is just as clear.
- Separate and inset a quote of four lines or more.
- Identify who wrote the quote and why that person is an expert.
- Be sure to punctuate quotes correctly. (See page 247.)
- Follow quotes with a proper parenthetical citation.

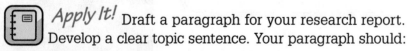 *Apply It!* Draft a paragraph for your research report. Develop a clear topic sentence. Your paragraph should:
- **Compile information** from multiple sources
- **Summarize** the main ideas of your findings
- Use evidence, including at least one fact and one **direct quotation,** to support the main idea and your conclusions
- Use in-text citations to **acknowledge sources** of information

Use Graphics and Illustrations

Some ideas are more easily explained by a graphic than by a written account. For example, the diagram on page 227 in the Student Model helps the reader understand a climber's route up the mountain. While drafting, consider how you can present evidence in a diagram or type of graphic. If you copy an existing graphic, you will need permission from the copyright holder if you publish your work for use outside school. Always label your visuals with a figure or table number, caption, and source information. Number the tables or figures in numerical order and refer to it in your text.

- **Photographs** Use a photograph to show your audience how something looks. For example, a photo of a tool could help the reader understand how it works. If you use a photograph, include a caption, or brief sentence explaining what the photo shows.

- **Charts, Tables, and Graphs** Create a chart, table, or graph to provide information in a more visual or organized way. Give each a title. Include a citation for the source of information you used to create it. Put the citation below after the word Source and a colon.

Table 1. Typical gear needed for mountain climbing.

Mountain Climbing Gear	
Equipment	**Purpose**
Backpack	Carries equipment and food
Clothing (climbing suit, gloves, boots)	Prevents climber from freezing
Crampons	Attach to boots to provide grip on ice
Ice axe	Assists in climbing; prevents falls
Oxygen tank and mask	Lessens altitude sickness
Radio	Allows climbers to stay in touch with each other and base camp
Ropes and pulleys	Prevent falls; used for rescue

Source: Steve Jenkins, *The Top of the World: Climbing Mount Everest.* Boston: Houghton Mifflin Company, 1999. Print.

- **Maps** A map can show where a place is or where an event occurred. Always include a legend and a compass with your map, in addition to the figure number, caption, and source.

Try It! Study the diagram of the Mount Everest climbing route on page 227. Then, write in your own words all of the information that the diagram conveys. Evaluate the diagram for its clarity and usefulness. Could the diagram be improved? Explain.

Apply It! Brainstorm for two graphics that you might use in your informational research report. Be sure to identify the type of information each graphic would explain. Give your graphics titles, and document your sources.

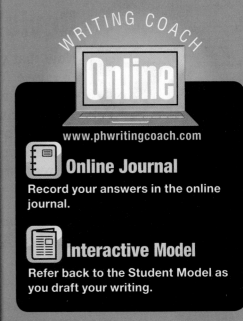

WRITING COACH

Online

www.phwritingcoach.com

Online Journal
Record your answers in the online journal.

Interactive Model
Refer back to the Student Model as you draft your writing.

Partner Talk

With a partner, discuss the paragraph you wrote for the *Try It!*. Use the information on page 240 to evaluate your writing. Ask and answer these questions:

- Does the paragraph have a topic sentence that states the main idea?
- Is the main idea supported by at least one fact and one direct quotation?
- Is the quotation introduced and punctuated correctly?
- Are sources of information properly documented?

Revising: Making It Better

Now that you have finished your draft, you are ready to revise. Think about the "big picture" of **audience, purpose, and genre.** You can use the Revision RADaR strategy as a guide for making changes to improve your draft. Revision RADaR provides four major ways to improve your writing: (R) replace, (A) add, (D) delete, and (R) reorder.

Kelly Gallagher, M. Ed.

KEEP REVISION ON YOUR RADaR

Read part of the first draft of the Student Model "Big Mountain, Big Challenge." Then, look at questions the writer asked himself as he thought about how well his draft addressed issues of audience, purpose, and genre.

Big Mountain, Big Challenge `1ST DRAFT`

When you reach the summit of Mount Everest, you stand on top of the world. At 29,035 feet tall, the mountain is the highest point on earth ("Everest, Mount"). Everest has fascinated many climbers. Between 2000 and 2006, 4,886 people attempted the climb ("Everest Expedition Statistics"). This undertaking can be dangerous. An understanding of science is important for climbers on Mount Everest.

The higher up you go on the mountain, the less oxygen there is. Everest is at a very high *altitude*. The word *altitude* means how far above sea level something is. People need oxygen to breathe. The lack of oxygen on Everest causes altitude sickness. "Because of the lack of oxygen," explains British mountaineer Graham Ratcliffe, "you get nausea and bad headaches and suffer from loss of appetite" ("Double Feat"). If you experience altitude sickness, you may feel like you have a case of the flu and have trouble sleeping ("Altitude Sickness Cure").

*Have I used evidence to support my **conclusions**?*

*Have I developed my **topic sentence** effectively?*

Is information well organized?

*Have I properly evaluated the relevance and reliability of my **sources**?*

Now look at how the writer applied Revision RADaR to write an improved second draft.

Big Mountain, Big Challenge

When you reach the summit of Mount Everest, you stand on top of the world. At 29,035 feet tall, the mountain is the highest point on Earth ("Everest, Mount"). Everest has fascinated many climbers. Between 2000 and 2006, 4,886 people attempted the climb. This undertaking can be dangerous—38 climbers died ("Everest Expedition Statistics"). While climbing Mount Everest can be dangerous, an understanding of science basics such as altitude, air pressure, and simple machines can help climbers stay safe.

Everest is at a very high altitude. The word *altitude* means how far above sea level something is. The higher up you go, the less oxygen there is (Platt 26). Because people need oxygen to breathe, they may get altitude sickness as they climb to higher altitudes. "Because of the lack of oxygen," explains British mountaineer Graham Ratcliffe, "You get nausea and bad headaches and suffer from loss of appetite" ("Double Feat"). These are the most common symptoms of altitude sickness.

A *Added a fact that helps prove my conclusion that climbing Everest is dangerous*

R *Replaced weak topic sentence with a topic sentence developed with more specific details*

R *Reordered a detail, moving it further down to where it supports the main idea, which is now the first sentence of the paragraph*

D *Deleted the sentence with information from an unreliable source (a Web site selling a product)*
R *Replaced it with a concluding sentence that summarizes my findings*

WRITING COACH
Online

www.phwritingcoach.com

Video
Learn more strategies for effective writing from program author Kelly Gallagher

Interactive Writing Coach™
Use the Revision RADaR strategy in your own writing. Then, submit your draft paragraph by paragraph for feedback.

Apply It! Use your Revision RADaR to revise your draft.

- First, ask yourself if you have addressed the needs of your audience, explained your ideas clearly and logically, and included the characteristics of an informational research report. If necessary, make changes to **clarify meaning** in your report.

- Then, apply Revision RADaR to make needed changes. Remember—you can use the steps in the strategy in any order.

Look at the Big Picture

Use the chart and your analytical skills to evaluate how well each section of your informational research report addresses **purpose, audience, and genre.** When necessary, use the suggestions in the chart to revise your piece.

Section	Evaluate	Revise
Introduction	• Check that the opening paragraph grabs your reader's attention. It should make the reader want to learn the answers to your **research question.**	• Add an interesting fact, anecdote, brief story, or quotation.
	• Make sure you have a well-developed **topic sentence**, or thesis statement, that identifies the major ideas your report will explore.	• Clarify your topic sentence, or thesis statement. Rearrange your introduction so that the topic sentence comes at the end.
Body	• Make sure each body paragraph clearly develops one **main idea.** Present your findings in a consistent format.	• Add a sentence to the beginning of each paragraph that states the main idea. Use a style manual to check your report's formatting.
	• Check that the information in each paragraph is **well organized,** and that the body of the report presents your ideas in the most effective order.	• Reorder words, sentences, and paragraphs to communicate information and ideas in a logical manner.
	• Make sure you have given enough **evidence** to support your conclusions.	• Use quotations and information compiled from multiple sources to support important points.
	• Make sure quotations and facts that are not common knowledge are **documented** and presented according to a style manual.	• Identify the source of each quotation. Add parenthetical citations, following the style specified in a style manual. Set off long quotes.
Conclusion	• Check that your conclusion **summarizes** your findings.	• Briefly restate the main points from the body of your report.
	• Make sure your research report leaves the reader with a **final thought.**	• Add a quotation or fact, or restate your topic sentence, to create a satisfying conclusion.
Works Cited/ Bibliography	• Make sure your Works Cited page or Bibliography is complete and uses **an appropriate style.**	• Add any missing sources, and format your list according to the correct style manual. • Add parenthetical citations that are missing.

Focus on Craft: Sentence Variety

A simple sentence has only one independent clause (group of words that can stand on its own). A compound sentence has two or more independent clauses. However, compound sentences may also contain one or more dependent clauses. Using a variety of simple and compound sentences will add interest to your writing. It will also help to create a pleasing rhythm for the reader. Think about sentence variety as you read these sentences from the Student Model.

 **STUDENT MODEL** from **"Big Mountain, Big Challenge"** page 227; lines 39–43

> Another danger of climbing Everest is the evil weather, which includes storms and high winds. Storms are caused by changes in air pressure. Air moves to an area of lower pressure near Earth's surface, and the air rises and cools.

 Try It! Now, ask yourself these questions:

- The second sentence is a simple sentence. How could the writer create variety in this sentence?
- Divide the last sentence, which is compound, into two simple sentences. How does this change the effect of the writing?

Fine-Tune Your Draft

Apply It! Use the revision suggestions to prepare your final draft. Make sure you keep your audience, purpose, and genre in mind as you focus on making your report read smoothly.

- **Focus on Sentence Variety** Review your draft for passages that sound choppy or dull. Vary sentence types to include simple and compound sentences and make your writing livelier.
- **Use the Best Sentence Structure** Think about the purpose of and audience for your research report. Then, revise sentence structures to clarify meaning. For example, you might connect two related simple sentences with a conjunction to make a compound sentence.

Teacher and Family Feedback Share your draft with your teacher or a family member. Carefully review the comments you receive and revise your final draft as needed.

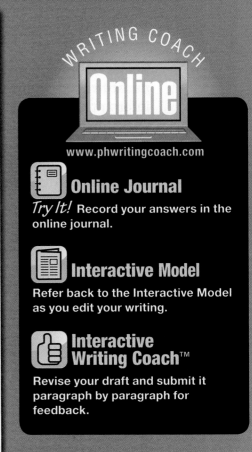

WRITING COACH

Online

www.phwritingcoach.com

Online Journal
Try It! Record your answers in the online journal.

Interactive Model
Refer back to the Interactive Model as you edit your writing.

Interactive Writing Coach™
Revise your draft and submit it paragraph by paragraph for feedback.

Editing: Making It Correct

Before editing your final draft, think about how you have **paraphrased, summarized, quoted,** and **cited** all researched information. Then, edit your draft using a **style manual,** such as *MLA Handbook for Writers of Research Papers,* to accurately **document sources** and format the materials, including quotations. Finally, edit your final draft for errors in **grammar, mechanics, and spelling.**

WRITE GUY *Jeff Anderson, M. Ed.*

WHAT DO YOU NOTICE?

Zoom in on Conventions Focus on quotations as you zoom in on these lines from the Student Model.

> **STUDENT MODEL** from **"Big Mountain, Big Challenge"**
> page 228; lines 59–71
>
> Famous American climber Ed Viesturs was on the mountain. He described what he could and could not see of the summit from his location:
>
> > That day dawned perfect. . . . Then, the big storm rolled in. The summit disappeared, the clouds lowered, swallowing up more and more of the upper mountain until finally our visibility was cut off. . . .
> > It wasn't until 10 p.m. that we got any news. Paula radioed up to us and said, "Only half the people who left the South Col this morning have made it back." ... In all, five climbers would die as a result of the storm that day.

To learn more about integrating quotations, see Grammar Game Plan Error 18, page 290.

Now, ask yourself this question: *How well has the writer worked the long quotation into his report?*

Perhaps you noted the writer used these helpful techniques to surround the quotation. The writer:

- Provides a lead-in to the quotation
- Tells us whom he is quoting
- Uses ellipses to let us know when he has left out irrelevant information
- Omits quotation marks and insets the quotation per MLA style for extended quotes

Partner Talk Discuss this question with a partner: *Why is it particularly easy to figure out which words from the Student Model are the student's and which words are not the student's?*

Grammar Mini-Lesson: Punctuation

To learn more, see Chapter 25.

Punctuating Quotations With Citations Quotations follow specific punctuation rules. Study this sentence from the Student Model. Notice how the writer punctuated the quotation and the information about its source. Parenthetical citations occur after the quote but before the period.

 **STUDENT MODEL** from **"Big Mountain, Big Challenge"** page 229; lines 95–97

> In 1923, British climber George Mallory was asked why he wanted to climb Everest. Mallory said, "Because it's there" (Golden 72).

 Try It! Which of these sentences uses correct punctuation for the quotation and for the citation in the parentheses? Write the answers in your journal.

1. Ken Burns and Stephen Ives, the filmmakers, have said "America without the West is unthinkable now." *(New Perspectives on the West.)*
2. Ken Burns and Stephen Ives, the filmmakers, have said, "America without the West is unthinkable now" *(New Perspectives on the West).*

 Apply It! Edit your draft for grammar, mechanics, and spelling. If necessary, rewrite sentences so that quotations work well next to your own words. Also correctly punctuate and acknowledge sources.

 Use the rubric to evaluate your piece. If necessary, rethink, rewrite, or revise.

Rubric for Informational Research Report	Rating Scale					
Ideas: How focused and supported is your thesis statement?	Not very 1	2	3	4	5	Very 6
Organization: How logical is the progression of your ideas?	1	2	3	4	5	6
Voice: How clearly is your personal point of view expressed?	1	2	3	4	5	6
Word Choice: How effectively does your word choice explain your thesis statement?	1	2	3	4	5	6
Sentence Fluency: How well have you varied the sentence types in your report?	1	2	3	4	5	6
Conventions: How correctly are your sources formatted?	1	2	3	4	5	6

WRITING COACH

Online

www.phwritingcoach.com

Video
Learn effective editing techniques from program author Jeff Anderson.

Online Journal
Try It! Record your answers in the online journal.

Interactive Model
Refer to the Student Model as you edit your writing.

Interactive Writing Coach™
Edit your draft and check it against the rubric. Submit it paragraph by paragraph for feedback.

Publishing

Share your knowledge! When you're happy with the final draft of your research report, publish it for an appropriate audience.

Wrap Up Your Presentation

Your teacher may require that you provide a typed final draft of your paper. Prepare a cover sheet, and number the pages according to your style manual. Also be sure to add a title that indicates what your report is about.

Publish Your Piece

Use the chart to identify a way to publish your informational research report for the appropriate audience. You might publish a written report. You could also present your report as an oral or **multimedia presentation** that uses **text, graphics, and sound.**

If your audience is...	...then publish it by...
Students or adults at school	• Displaying your written report in the school library, along with books about your topic • Recording a podcast of your report and posting it on a school Web site where others can download it
A local group with a special interest in your topic	• Presenting a multimedia report at a group meeting and answering questions about your research • Posting your written report on the group's Web site and inviting comments

 Reflect on Your Writing

Now that you are done with your informational research report, read it over and use your writing journal to answer these questions.

- Which parts of your research report are you proudest of? Which parts do you think are weak?

- What will you do differently the next time you are assigned a research report?

The Big Question : Why Write? Do you understand a subject well enough to write about it? How did you find out what the facts were?

Manage Your Portfolio You may include your published informational research report in your writing portfolio. If so, consider what this piece reveals about your writing and your growth as a writer.

MAKE YOUR WRITING COUNT

Get Your Message Out in a Magazine or eZine

Research reports answer questions about how the world works. Share information with your classmates by creating a **magazine.**

A magazine is a regularly published group of articles based on a theme, such as news, sports, or current research. An eZine is a magazine published on the Web. (The *e* stands for *electronic.*) Both use text and images to share information. eZines also use graphics, audio, and video. Create articles based on your research reports. Then, organize them into a print or electronic magazine. Share your work in a **multimedia presentation.**

www.phwritingcoach.com

Online Journal

Reflect on Your Writing Record your answers and ideas in the online journal.

Resource

Link to resources on 21st Century Learning for help in creating a group project.

Here's your action plan.

1. With your group, set goals and choose roles, such as writer, editor, image finder, and page designer.

2. Review your research reports. Assign topics. Write short articles reporting on each other's research. Each article should answer the *5Ws and an H* questions.

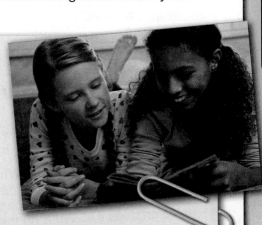

3. Read magazines and view eZines online. Notice how the pages are designed.

4. Edit and arrange your articles. Create or find visuals and graphics. Name your magazine.

5. Your magazine should include:
   - Several informative articles
   - Text, images, and graphics arranged in an eye-catching way
   - Audio or visual links, if possible

6. Rehearse your multimedia presentation, highlighting each medium you used. Then, present your work to the class.

Listening and Speaking Meet with your group to discuss how to present your magazine to the class. Consider making a poster of your magazine pages or showing a Web site. Then, practice your presentation. Ask listeners for feedback on volume, pacing, and word choice. Keep their responses in mind as you present your magazine.

**Writing for Media:
I-Search Report**

21st Century Learning

I-Search Report

In an **I-search report,** writers examine and tell their readers about their research process as well as their findings about their topic. There are four main steps to writing an I-search report:

1) Choose a topic by thinking about your interests, brainstorming, and browsing resources.

2) Research by creating questions, finding sources (usually including an interview), and keeping a log of your research process.

3) Analyze the information in your sources and take notes.

4) Create a final product that includes the six parts shown in the model.

Try It! Study the excerpt from the I-search report outline shown on this page. Then, answer these questions. Record your answers in your journal.

1. What do you think is the writer's **purpose?** Who do you think is the intended **audience?**

2. What information does this writer provide about the research process?

3. How do the writer's **sources** provide evidence that answers the research questions? Why is it important to cite valid and reliable sources?

4. What types of **visuals** do you think would enhance the writer's I-search report on this topic? Explain.

Protecting Grizzly Bears

I. Why I Chose My Topic
I saw a grizzly bear when I visited Yellowstone National Park. It was cool!

II. What I Already Know/What I Want to Learn
A park ranger told me that the government is trying to increase the number of bears in the United States. I wonder why. I wonder where else grizzlies live. What do they eat? How long do they live?

III. The Search: Steps I Took/The Interview
I started my search online. At first I found a lot of information on sports teams named the Grizzlies. I found better information when I used "grizzly bear" as a search term. My interview with zookeeper Rob Singer gave me great information.

IV. What I Learned
I learned that the grizzly bear is a threatened species in the United States. This means that grizzly bears could become an endangered species if they are not protected. That's why the government is trying to increase the number of grizzlies (U.S. Fish and Wildlife Service). I also learned that this type of brown bear lives mainly in western North America, although a few are still found in Europe and Asia (Singer).

V. Conclusion/Reflection
People need to work to protect grizzlies. It would be too bad if people who went to national parks could no longer see this fierce yet beautiful animal.

VI. References
"Grizzly Bear Recovery." *Endangered Species.* U.S. Fish and Wildlife Service. n.d. Web. 5 Jan. 2010.
Singer, Rob. Personal interview. 1 Jan. 2010.

Create an I-Search Report

Follow these steps to create your own **I-search report.** Review the graphic organizers on R24–R27 and choose one that suits your needs.

Prewriting

- Consult your peers to brainstorm for a list of topics. When you've finished, circle the topic you have decided to use.

- Be sure to identify the target **audience** and your purpose for your online report. Are you writing to **inform** an audience of students? Families with children? Older adults?

- It's important to generate a **research plan** for gathering sources and information. To guide your research, choose an open-ended **research question** related to your topic that your report will try to answer. Then, follow your plan.

- You'll need to get information from a range of **print and electronic sources,** including data and quotations from experts on your topic.

- **Evaluate** every source you consider using. Before using it, evaluate the source to make sure it is **relevant** and **reliable.** Remember, as you gather data you should reflect on what you're learning and **refine the research question** as needed to get better search results.

- To identify the source of your notes, record information on note cards, in a learning log, or through an online application. Make a source card for each source. Record bibliographic information according to a standard format and note whether it's a **primary or secondary source.**

- As you take notes, look for similarities and differences in how the multiple texts present information. Be sure to **summarize** information. Take written notes on graphic and visual sources as well. If you use a **direct quotation,** enclose it in big quotation marks to remind you to cite it later.

- Check your notes to make sure you have paraphrased or quoted but not **plagiarized.**

- Use graph paper or technology to record your data as graphs or charts. This can help you to better see the relationships between certain ideas.

- Think of **audio-visual support** you can add to your report. Be sure to record source information for any you intend to use.

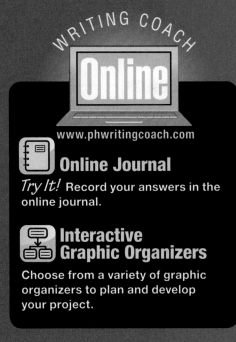

Partner Talk

Summarize your findings for a partner. Ask for feedback on your research plan. Did you gather enough data? Did you cite valid and reliable sources? Discuss why this is important and make adjustments as needed.

Your Turn

Writing for Media:
I-Search Report (*continued*)

Drafting

- Create an I-Search outline to help you organize your information. Think about an introduction, decide what main ideas you will cover in the body, and consider how you will conclude the report.

- Once you know the main ideas of your report, develop a topic **sentence** for each paragraph.

- **Compile** your notes from all of your sources and organize the information according to your outline. Then, start writing.

- Think about why someone would want to read or hear your report. Use your ideas to begin your report with an attention-grabbing opening.

- Choose **important information** and **evidence,** such as facts or quotations, to **support** your main ideas and conclusions. Summarize complex ideas and findings so that your audience can understand them.

- Remember, presenting someone else's words or ideas as your own is plagiarism. Use your own words, or enclose direct quotations in quotation marks.

- Think about how to include visuals and sound in your multimedia report. You might want to project a screen from your computer during your presentation, so write text that would make that work smoothly.

- **Acknowledge** your **sources** as needed in context or in a credits section.

Revising

Use Revision RADaR techniques as you review your draft carefully.

- **Replace** general terms with vivid details and unclear explanations with precise ideas.

- **Add** specific details or missing information to support your argument. **Delete** information that does not support your thesis or develop your argument.

- **Reorder** sentences and paragraphs to present ideas clearly and logically.

- Read aloud your report to make sure it reads smoothly and presents your findings in a consistent format.

Editing

Now take the time to check your I-search report carefully before you present it to the class. Focus on each sentence and then on each word. Look for these common kinds of errors:

- Errors in subject-verb agreement
- Errors in pronoun usage
- Run-on sentences and sentence fragments
- Spelling and capitalization mistakes
- Omitted punctuation marks
- Problems with appropriate documentation and quotations

Publishing

- Give your report to other classes or community groups who might be interested in learning more about Internet research.
- Turn your report into a slide presentation and post it on your school's Web site so that other students can view it.
- Post the text of your I-search report as a blog entry. Search for a Web site that allows users to create a free blog.
- With your classmates, compile your I-search reports into a complete guide to Internet searching. Print it for classroom display or for your school library.

Extension Find another example of an I-Search report and compare it with the one you are writing.

WRITING COACH

www.phwritingcoach.com

Online Journal

Record your answers in the online journal.

Interactive Graphic Organizers

Choose from a variety of graphic organizers to plan and develop your project.

> Partner Talk

Before you present your I-search report to the class, practice with a partner. Critique each other's presentations. Think about the speed of the presentation and how well it uses media.

Writing for Assessment

Many tests include a prompt that asks you to write or critique a research plan. Use these prompts to practice. Respond using the characteristics of your Internet-research report. (See page 224.)

 Try It! Read the prompt and create a **research plan.** Use the ABCDs of On-Demand Writing to help you plan and write your research plan.

Format

Write your *research plan* in the form of an outline. List all the steps you would follow. Put the steps in the order you would do them. Under some main headings, you may have subheadings.

Research Plan Prompt

Write a research plan about a person, battle, or event related to the Civil War. First, ask open-ended questions about the topic to help you decide on a major research question. Then, tell how you will go about researching your question. What kinds of primary and secondary sources will you use? What other steps will you take before you start drafting your report? [30 minutes]

Academic Vocabulary

Primary sources are first-hand accounts from people who experienced the events they are telling about. *Secondary sources* provide analysis of primary sources. As you list possible sources of information, consider whether the information in them will be relevant (directly related to your research question) and valid (true).

The ABCDs of On-Demand Writing

Use these ABCDs to help you respond to the prompt.

Before you write your draft:

Attack the prompt [1 MINUTE]

- Circle or highlight important verbs in the prompt. Draw a line from the verb to what it refers to.
- Rewrite the prompt in your own words.

Brainstorm for possible answers [4 MINUTES]

- Create a graphic organizer to generate ideas.
- Use one for each part of the prompt if necessary.

Choose the order of your response [1 MINUTE]

- Think about the best way to organize your ideas.
- Number your ideas in the order you will write about them. Cross out ideas you will not be using.

After you write your draft:

Detect errors before turning in the draft [1 MINUTE]

- Carefully reread your writing.
- Make sure that your response makes sense and is complete.
- Look for spelling, punctuation, and grammar errors.

 More Prompts for Practice

Apply It! Work with a partner to **critique the research plan** in Prompt 1. In a written response, make specific suggestions to improve the plan.

- Has the research plan covered all of the Prewriting steps?
- Is there a limited topic appropriate for the audience and purpose?
- Is the writer planning to find enough sources? Are they varied?
- Does the writer plan to include graphics?
- Does the research plan say anything about evaluating sources?

Prompt 1 Alana wrote this research plan. Explain what she did well and what needs improvement.

My Topic: My research question is, *Can people ride on zebras, and why or why not?*

My Research: I'm going to search the Internet and the databases at the library. I'll also look for print sources there. I'll interview a zookeeper who works with zebras.

My Writing: I'll start writing when I find the perfect book.

Spiral Review: Narrative If you choose to respond to Prompt 2, write a **personal narrative**. Make sure your story reflects the characteristics described on page 66.

Prompt 2 Write a personal narrative about a time you went someplace you had never been to before. Include details about how you felt and what you heard and saw. Were there surprises? Disappointments? Would you recommend that someone else go there as well?

Spiral Review: Response to Literature If you choose to write a **response to literature** in response to Prompt 3, make sure it reflects all of the characteristics on page 198. Your interpretative response essay should provide **evidence from the text** to support your ideas and show your **understanding of the work**.

Prompt 3 People in life, as well as characters in literary texts, often face tasks that require great courage. Write a response to a literary text or an expository or nonfiction text that describes such a situation. Provide evidence from the text to demonstrate your understanding.

WRITING COACH

www.phwritingcoach.com

Interactive Writing Coach™

Plan your response to the prompt. If you are using the prompt for practice, write one paragraph at a time or your entire draft and then submit it for feedback. If you are using the prompt as a timed test, write your entire draft and then submit it for feedback.

Remember **ABCD**

Attack the prompt

Brainstorm for possible answers

Choose the order of your response

Detect errors before turning in the draft

CHAPTER 12

WORKPLACE WRITING

What's Ahead

In this chapter, you will learn how you can write procedural documents, which explain how something works or is done. You will also learn how to write other practical forms of writing, including letters and various workplace documents important in business. All of these functional documents should present organized information that is written and presented in a reader-friendly format.

Characteristics of Writing

Effective workplace and practical writing has these characteristics:

- **Information** that is well-organized and accurate
- A clear **purpose** and intended audience
- **Formal, polite** language
- **Reader-friendly formatting techniques,** such as sufficient white or blank space and clearly defined sections
- Correct **grammar, punctuation,** and **spelling** appropriate to the form of writing

Forms of Writing

Forms of workplace writing include:

How-to essays are used to explain how something works or how to do something. These essays are written in a step-by-step format.

Thank-you letters are formal or informal correspondence written to express gratitude.

Business letters are formal correspondence written to, from, or within a business. They can be written for various reasons, including to make requests and to express concerns or approval.

Memos are short documents usually written from one member of a group to another, or to another group. They assume some background knowledge of the topic.

Other forms of practical writing include:

Friendly letters are informal letters written to a friend or acquaintance. They can be written for various reasons, including to ask how someone is doing or just to say hello.

 Try It! For each audience and purpose described, select the appropriate form of writing such as a thank-you letter, friendly letter, how-to essay, or business letter. Explain your choices.

- To thank a relative for a birthday gift
- To explain how to order supplies

 Connect to the Big Questions

Discuss these questions:

1 What do you think? When is it most important to communicate clearly with teammates?

2 Why write? What do daily workplace communications require of format, content, and style?

WORD BANK

These vocabulary words are often used with workplace writing. Use the Glossary or a dictionary to check the definitions.

communicate	instructions
document	technical

STUDENT MODEL | How-To Essay

Learn From Experience

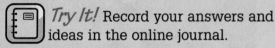 After reading the how-to essay on this page, read the numbered notes in the margin to learn about how the writer presented his ideas. As you read, practice newly acquired vocabulary by correctly producing the word's sound.

Try It! Record your answers and ideas in the online journal.

---

❶ In the first paragraph, the writer makes the **audience** and **purpose** clear.

❷ **Transition words** like *first* and *second* help the reader understand what to do first, next, and so on.

❸ **Sentences in the body,** or main part of the essay, **explain important information.** Notice that the writer explains how to avoid a possible problem.

❹ The last paragraph **brings the essay to a logical end** by explaining the last step in the process.

Try It!

- Why is it helpful to state the purpose of a work-related document, such as a how-to-essay?

- What transition words besides *first* and *second* are used in the essay?

- Do you think the essay clearly explains how to write an e-mail? Explain.

How To Write an E-mail

by Jimmy Dixon

❶ E-mail is an easy way to send messages over the Internet. If you are new to e-mail, follow these steps to write a message.

❷ First, open your e-mail program, and click on the command for writing mail. It will be "New Mail," "Write," or something similar to that. After you click, you will get a blank e-mail.

❷ Second, fill in the "To" field, or blank, at the top of the e-mail. Type the e-mail address of the person who will receive your message. ❸ Then, read the address to make sure it is right. Even one little mistake will keep your e-mail from being sent.

Next, fill in the "Subject" field. Think of a short, clear way to say why you are writing, and type that in the blank. Now, write your message. Type it in the blank space below the "To" and "Subject" fields. Keep it short and clear. After you have typed your message, read it to make sure your message is clear and to see if you made any mistakes. If you did, fix them.

❹ Finally, click on "Send." Away your e-mail goes! It really is that easy to write and send an e-mail!

**Your Turn** **Feature Assignment: How-To Essay**

Prewriting

- Plan a first draft of your **how-to essay**. You can select from the Topic Bank or come up with an idea of your own.

TOPIC BANK

Hobby Time Many people have hobbies. Choose a hobby, such as skateboarding or collecting baseball cards. Write an essay explaining how to get started in this hobby.

Hit the Books Think about the ways that students can successfully study and review material before a test. Explain one of your favorite ways to prepare for a test.

- Brainstorm for a list of ideas for your how-to essay. Sketch out the steps of the process you will include in your explanation.
- Read your step-by-step list aloud to a partner. Ask your partner to help you identify any steps you may have left out.

## Drafting

- Use reader-friendly formatting techniques, including all the features of a how-to essay. Use an **active voice** when writing out the steps. For example, write *Hammer three nails* instead of *Three nails should be hammered.*
- Include the **important information** so that the purpose is clearly stated early in the essay and so that each step is clearly explained.
- Accurately **convey ideas** by using logical steps in your essay.

Revising and Editing

- Before you revise, review your draft to ensure that information is presented accurately and concisely.
- After rethinking purpose and audience, revise the draft to use appropriate conventions, such as spelling, capitalization, and bullets.

Publishing

- Print your essay and share it with a partner or the whole class.
- Post your essay to a Web site or blog on a similar topic.

Interactive Model
Listen to an audio recording of the Student Model.

Online Journal
Try It! Record your answers and ideas in the online journal.

Interactive Writing Coach
Submit your writing and receive personalized feedback and support as you draft, revise, and edit.

Video
Learn strategies for effective revising and editing from program authors Jeff Anderson and Kelly Gallagher.

**Partner Talk**

Work with a partner to edit your how-to essay. Read your draft to your partner. Then, ask him or her to retell the steps of the process to you. Decide whether or not you need to include more steps.

STUDENT MODEL

Thank-You Letter

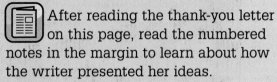
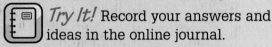

Learn From Experience

After reading the thank-you letter on this page, read the numbered notes in the margin to learn about how the writer presented her ideas.

Try It! Record your answers and ideas in the online journal.

---

1 The writer begins with the date and a salutation, or **greeting,** that is appropriate for the recipient. The greeting is followed by a comma.

2 In the first paragraph, the writer makes the **purpose** of the letter clear.

3 Here and elsewhere in the **body** of the letter, the writer fulfills the purpose by **developing ideas.** Notice that she gives an example of something she especially enjoyed.

4 The writer ends the letter with an appropriate **closing.** She might use a more formal closing, like *Sincerely,* if the letter were for a teacher or someone else outside her family.

Try It!

- How would you describe the tone, or "sound," of the thank-you letter? Friendly? Informal? Happy? Something else?
- Which words help create that tone?
- Is the tone appropriate for the audience and purpose of the letter? Explain.

---

1 May 21, 2010

Dear Auntie Amita,

2 I am writing to thank you for the big birthday surprise. I was so happy to see you last Saturday. I did not know you were planning to make the trip all the way from Michigan.

How did you know that a day at the amusement park was exactly what I wanted? **3** I had so much fun on the rides. I especially liked the roller coaster. It was so exciting!

The surprise waiting for me at home was the best of all. I never guessed that you got me out of the house so Mom could set up a party for me. I was shocked when I walked in the house and saw all my friends.

Everyone had a great time. Thanks to you, I will never forget my 12th birthday.

4 Love,

Farah

 **Your Turn** ▶ **Feature Assignment: Thank-You Letter**

Prewriting

- Plan a first draft of your **thank-you letter.** You can select from the Topic Bank or come up with an idea of your own.

> ### TOPIC BANK
>
> **School Spirit** Write to your student council thanking them for something they have done for your school in the past year.
>
> **Class Act** Write to your favorite teacher thanking him or her for teaching or sharing something interesting or important with the class.

- Brainstorm for a list of things that your letter's recipient will need to know about you and your purpose for writing the letter.
- Use a telephone directory or online resources to find the accurate contact information for the letter's recipient.

 Drafting

- Use reader-friendly formatting techniques, including all the **conventions** of an informal letter.
- Use a salutation that matches your relationship with the recipient.
- Include the **important information** so that the purpose of your letter is clearly stated.
- Demonstrate a sense of **closure** in your final paragraph by summing up the purpose of your letter.

Revising and Editing

As you revise, review your draft to ensure that your ideas are conveyed accurately and concisely. Ask yourself if the **purpose and audience** for your letter are clearly identified and addressed. After rethinking purpose and audience, revise to clarify meaning, and edit for appropriate use of conventions.

Publishing

- If you plan to mail the letter, print the letter or write it neatly on paper or stationery suitable for the recipient.
- If you plan to e-mail the letter, confirm the correct e-mail address and attach your letter to a message as a Portable Document Format (PDF).

 WRITING COACH

 Interactive Model

Listen to an audio recording of the Student Model.

Online Journal

Try It! Record your answers and ideas in the online journal.

Interactive Writing Coach

Submit your writing and receive personalized feedback and support as you draft, revise, and edit.

Video

Learn strategies for effective revising and editing from program authors Jeff Anderson and Kelly Gallagher.

 **Partner Talk**

Work with a partner to revise your letter. Ask for feedback about the content and organization of your letter.

STUDENT MODEL **Friendly Letter**

① June 15, 2010

① Dear Mallari Family,

② Welcome to the neighborhood! Now that you are settled in, we'd like to invite you to our annual block party.

③ The party will take place on Nightingale Street on Sunday, July 4, from 11 a.m. to 7 p.m. Each family brings its own picnic lunch and one extra snack or dessert to share. The Nightingale Block Party Committee sets up picnic tables on the street for everyone to use.

③ In the afternoon, there will be games and races for the younger children, and a baseball game for the older kids. The party breaks up in the evening so that families can get ready for the fireworks show in Elmtown Park.

③ We hope that you can join us for the celebration. Everyone is looking forward to getting to know you! Please let me know by June 25 if you will be able to attend. My telephone number is (690) 555-1011. Or, leave me a note if you prefer.

Sincerely,

④ *Vito Santos*

Vito Santos

Your Turn **Feature Assignment: Friendly Letter**

Prewriting

- Plan a first draft of your **friendly letter.** You can select from the Topic Bank or come up with an idea of your own.

- Make a list of the ideas you want to include in your letter.

- Use a telephone directory or online resources to find the accurate contact information for the letter's recipient.

Camp Days Imagine that you've just spent a week at a summer camp. Write a friendly letter to your grandparents or another relative telling them about your experiences at camp.

Far and Away Write a friendly letter to a pen pal in another country. Start by identifying the place where your imaginary pen pal lives. What will you share with your pen pal about life in the United States?

 Drafting

- Use reader-friendly formatting techniques, including all the **conventions** of an informal letter.

- Use a greeting that matches your relationship with the recipient.

- Include **important information** so that the purpose is clearly stated.

- **Demonstrate a sense of closure** in your final paragraph by summing up the purpose of your letter.

Revising and Editing

As you revise, review your draft to ensure that information is concisely and **accurately conveyed**. Then, revise the draft according to teacher and peer feedback.

Publishing

- If you plan to mail the letter, print the letter or write it neatly on paper or stationery suitable for the recipient.

- If you plan to e-mail the letter, confirm the correct e-mail address and attach your letter to a message as a PDF.

WRITING COACH

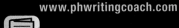

www.phwritingcoach.com

 **Interactive Model**
Listen to an audio recording of the Student Model.

Online Journal
Try It! Record your answers and ideas in the online journal.

Interactive Writing Coach
Submit your writing and receive personalized feedback and support as you draft, revise, and edit.

Video
Learn strategies for effective revising and editing from program authors Jeff Anderson and Kelly Gallagher.

Partner Talk

Read your final draft to a partner. Ask your partner to listen for correct grammar and usage. Revise your final draft as needed.

MAKE YOUR WRITING COUNT

Present a Research Report on Making Connections

How-to essays communicate important information to specific audiences. These workplace documents may involve ideas or activities that could be further developed by research. Write a **research report** and presentation about ideas for ways to connect with family, friends, and community.

With a group, **brainstorm for** topics from among your work in this chapter that you can explore further. Have a discussion with others to **decide upon a topic** that will be helpful to someone thinking about making connections with other people. Work together to **formulate an open-ended research question** that will help you produce a research report about the topic.

Consider topics like planning a family reunion, having a neighborhood block party, or starting an annual day-in-the park event in your town.

Group members should **consult** one another and **critique the process** as you work. Be prepared to **refine** the research question and adjust the plan as needed. Remember that a research report should:

- Include a specific thesis statement or topic sentence
- Meet the needs of audience and purpose
- Express a clear point of view
- Provide supporting evidence
- Present ideas in a logical way
- Document sources using correct formatting

Then, present your research results to students in your school. Your report should be a **multimedia presentation** that uses text and graphics. You may use posters or presentation software.

Here's your action plan.

1. Research takes time. In a group, make a plan for several group meetings. Set objectives and choose roles for each member.

2. Work together to create a **research plan** that includes:

   - Locating and exploring **print and electronic resources,** data from experts, and **quotations**

   - Using **software** or graph paper to turn data into graphs or charts in order to make connections and see big ideas

   - Interpreting visuals by recording their data as **written notes**

   - Checking that your sources are **reliable and relevant**

   - Collecting supporting evidence and **documenting sources** appropriately. Record **bibliographic information** according to a standard format.

   - Noting whether a source is **primary** (firsthand account) or **secondary** (interpretation of events or data)

3. Discuss your findings. **Evaluate the sources,** discussing the importance of citing valid and relevant sources. Reject weak sources. Work together to create a clear thesis statement or **topic sentence** that conveys the main idea of the research.

4. Outline the content of the report. Assign sections of the outline to each group member. Be sure to **summarize** your findings, and cite sources.

5. Work together to write a rough draft by **compiling** collected information. As a group, discuss the difference between **plagiarism** and **paraphrasing.** Remember to use citations to acknowledge all sources.

6. Revise and edit to ensure the thesis statement and conclusions are well-supported by evidence and that the findings are presented in a **consistent format.**

7. Add appropriate audio and visuals to support the topic.

8. Present your report to students, counselors, and teachers.

Listening and Speaking Practice the presentation in front of another group or each other. Listen to feedback to help you make improvements. When you present, speak clearly and confidently.

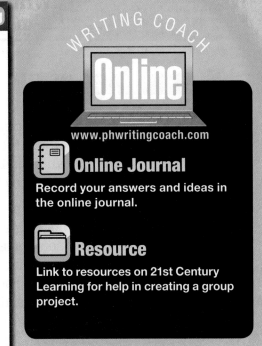

WRITING COACH

Online

www.phwritingcoach.com

Online Journal

Record your answers and ideas in the online journal.

Resource

Link to resources on 21st Century Learning for help in creating a group project.

Your Turn → **Writing for Media: E-mail Message**

E-mail Message

An **e-mail message** can be formal or informal, depending on the relationship of the writer and recipient and the purpose of the message. For example, an e-mail message from a student to the editor of a school magazine may be informal.

Magazines frequently feature a "Letters to the Editor" page or a "Letters from our Readers" page. This section is devoted to letters from readers who have sent messages—either by mail or by e-mail—to the magazine about a story it published. The **Letters section of a magazine** is the place where readers can see their opinions published for all to read.

Try It! Read the e-mail message on this page. Then, answer these questions. Record your answers in your journal.

1. How does the **subject line** help the reader know what the e-mail will be about?

2. What is the **purpose** of this e-mail message? How does the writer introduce the purpose?

3. Who is the intended **audience** for this e-mail? How does the writer address the audience?

4. Is the writer of the **e-mail message** in favor of or critical of the article he discussed? What **details** in the message support your response?

Extension Look at the formatting of this e-mail. How is it the same or different from that of a friendly letter?

To: MagazineEditor@example.com
From: BenNorth@example.com
Subject: Letter to the Editor on Skateboarding Article
Date: October 5, 2011

Dear Editor,

Thanks for your article about the popularity of skateboarding! Your coverage of famous boarders was the best I've read in our school's magazine.

I also enjoyed the feature "Best Places to Board." I was especially excited to see our town on the map. It also gave me good ideas for other places in our area to board.

The school magazine has changed for the better by including stories that truly interest the students. Thanks for listening to us, and keep up the good work.

Sincerely,
Ben North

Create an E-mail Message

Follow these steps to create your own informal **e-mail message** to the editor of a school publication, such as the school newspaper or magazine. Review the graphic organizers on R24–R27 and choose one that suits your needs.

Prewriting

- Brainstorm for a list of school publications you like to read. Include details about some recent stories you have read.

- Choose one story to which you would like to respond.

- Consider the needs of your specific audience. What would you say to the editor of this magazine in your e-mail message?

Drafting

- Organize your ideas and include **important information,** so that the purpose is clearly stated early in the e-mail message and so that each paragraph has a clear purpose.

- Use reader-friendly formatting techniques, including all the **conventions** of an e-mail message, such as a clear subject line.

- Accurately **convey ideas** by double-checking your ideas.

Revising and Editing

- As you revise, review your draft to ensure that information is presented accurately and concisely and that the message has a sense of **closure.**

- Ask yourself if the purpose and audience for your e-mail message are clearly identified and addressed.

- After rethinking purpose and audience, revise the draft to improve your style.

Publishing

- Type the message in an e-mail program. Be sure to include a subject in the subject line.

- Confirm that you have the recipient's correct e-mail address.

- Send the e-mail message. Check your "sent messages" list to confirm the message was sent successfully.

WRITING COACH

Online

www.phwritingcoach.com

 **Online Journal**

Try It! Record your answers and ideas in the online journal.

 **Interactive Graphic Organizers**

Use the graphic organizers to plan your e-mail message.

Partner Talk

Exchange e-mail messages with a partner. Have your partner answer these questions: Whom is this e-mail message for? What is the purpose of the message? Monitor your partner's spoken language by asking follow-up questions to confirm your understanding.

Writing for Assessment

Many tests include a prompt that asks you to write a procedural text. Your responses should include most of the same characteristics as your how-to-essay. (See pages 258–259.)

 Try It! Read the **procedural text** prompt and the information on format and academic vocabulary. Use the ABCDs of On-Demand Writing to help you plan and write your response.

Format

The prompt directs you to write a *procedural text*. Describe the purpose of the text in the first section. Be sure to include steps with organized information such as a numbered list or materials list.

Procedural Text Prompt

Your friend wants to learn to use an MP3 player. He would like to read written instructions. Write a procedural text that includes stepped-out instructions on how to operate an MP3 player. [30 minutes]

Academic Vocabulary

A procedural text is a kind of text that tells somebody how to perform a task. *Stepped-out instructions* have numbered lists that provide details in the order they are used.

The ABCDs of On-Demand Writing

Use the following ABCDs to help you respond to the prompt.

Before you write your draft:

Attack the prompt [1 MINUTE]

- Circle or highlight important verbs in the prompt. Draw a line from the verb to what it refers to.
- Rewrite the prompt in your own words.

Brainstorm possible answers [4 MINUTES]

- Create a graphic organizer to generate ideas.
- Use one for each part of the prompt if necessary.

Choose the order of your response [1 MINUTE]

- Think about the best way to organize your ideas.
- Number your ideas in the order you will write about them. Cross out ideas you will not be using.

After you write your draft:

Detect errors before turning in the draft [1 MINUTE]

- Carefully reread your writing.
- Make sure that your response makes sense and is complete.
- Look for spelling, punctuation, and grammar errors.

More Prompts for Practice

 *Apply It!* Respond to Prompt 1 by writing a **procedural text.** As you write, be sure to:

- Consider what your **audience** knows and needs to know
- Organize **information** into steps or paragraphs
- Define any **terms** that your audience may not know

> **Prompt 1** You are writing a cookbook. Choose your favorite sandwich and write a procedural text for the cookbook. Include stepped-out instructions for making your favorite sandwich.

Spiral Review: Expository If you choose to respond to Prompt 2, write a compare-and-contrast **expository essay.** Make sure your essay reflects the characteristics described on page 146.

> **Prompt 2** In some communities you are required to reduce, reuse, or recycle certain materials. Write an expository essay that compares and contrasts two ways to conserve the same item or material.

Spiral Review: Research Plan If you choose to respond to Prompt 3, write a **critique of the research plan.** Make sure your critique evaluates all of the characteristics described on page 224. Your critique should determine if the research plan:

- Contains a **narrowed topic,** and is appropriate for the **audience**
- Includes enough **primary** and **secondary sources,** and says something about **evaluating** sources

> **Prompt 3** Juana wrote the following research plan. Explain what she did well and what needs improvement.
> *My Topic:* Altitude sickness.
> *My Research:* I'm going to search the Internet, talk to the reference librarian, and look for print sources. I know that Mount Everest is at a very high altitude, so I'll look for articles and stories about people who have climbed it.
> *My Drafting:* After a week of research, I will use my notes to write my draft. Then, I'll show my teacher before revising it.

WRITING COACH

Online

www.phwritingcoach.com

Interactive Writing Coach™

Plan your response to the prompt. If you are writing the prompt for practice, write one paragraph at a time or your entire draft and submit it for feedback. If you are using the prompt for a timed test, write your entire draft and submit it for feedback.

Remember **ABCD**

Attack the prompt

Brainstorm possible answers

Choose the order of your response

Detect errors before turning in the draft

Grammar

Find It FIX IT

Grammar Game Plan

This handy guide will help you find and fix errors in your writing!

20

Major Grammatical Errors and How to Fix Them

Using the Wrong Word

GAME PLAN Use the right words to make your writing clear. Make sure your words say exactly what you mean them to say.

CLARIFY MEANING Do not confuse the meanings of words with similar spellings. Also, words with similar definitions can have important shades of meaning. Check that words you found in a thesaurus are used correctly.

Do you know the ~~affect~~ effect of skipping breakfast?

The bookstore was having a book sale for the whole ~~weak~~ week.

SPELL-CHECK ERRORS Computer spell-checkers often correct a misspelling with a different, similarly spelled word. Be sure to proofread your work carefully to catch these errors. In each of the following examples, the word with a strikethrough represents an inappropriate spell-checker correction.

Sally asked if he ~~sent~~ went to the movie.

The teacher chose Emilio to be the class helper for the ~~say~~ day.

Use a current or completed draft of your work to practice using words correctly.

✔ **READ carefully.** Take the time to read your draft closely. For a double-check, have someone else read your work.

✔ **IDENTIFY possible mistakes.** Mark any difficult or commonly misused words in your draft.

✔ **USE a dictionary.** If you are not sure of a word's meaning, look it up in a dictionary.

Tech Tip

Be your own "spell-checker"! Proofread! Your computer's spell-checker will not identify every misspelling or incorrectly used word.

LEARN MORE
- See Chapter 20, Effective Sentences, pages 461–465
- See Writing Coach Online

2

Missing Comma After Introductory Element

LEARN MORE
- See Chapter 25, Punctuation, pages 561, 564
- See Writing Coach Online

GAME PLAN Place a comma after the following introductory elements in your work.

WORDS Place a comma after introductory words.

Dana,ⱯWould you like some help with that?

Yes,Ɐplease carry the boxes for me.

PHRASES Place a comma after introductory prepositional phrases. If the prepositional phrase has only two words, a comma is not necessary.

From top to bottom,Ɐyour outfit looks great.

Upon arriving on our street,Ɐyou need to turn left.

Before bed we turn off the lights.

CLAUSES Introductory adverbial clauses should be followed by a comma.

Because she missed the bus,Ɐshe was late for school.

Whenever her friend is in town,Ɐshe meets her for dinner.

✔ Check It

Use a current or completed draft of your work to practice placing commas after introductory clauses.

✔ **SCAN your draft.** Look for introductory words, phrases, and clauses.

✔ **IDENTIFY missing commas.** Mark sentence starters that might need a comma.

✔ **USE your textbook.** Check the grammar section of your textbook if you are not sure whether or not to use a comma.

GAME PLAN Provide complete citations for borrowed words and ideas. Use the citation style (such as MLA) that your teacher recommends.

MISSING CITATIONS Cite sources of direct quotes and statistics. Remember–when in doubt, cite the source.

The scientist said, "This animal was unusual in many ways"ʌ(Gaspard 8).

Mr. Cleaver identified twelve new species of plant life ʌ(Brooks 24).

INCOMPLETE CITATIONS Make sure your citations include complete source information. This information will vary depending on the source and the citation style. It often includes the author's name, the source's title, and the page numbers. You may use the shortened version you see here if your paper includes a bibliography where the reader can get the title of the source and the author's first name.

The author's newest book has been called "a terrific read" (ʌCho 25).

A 12 percent drop in sales was reported in January (Alberts ʌ31).

Use a current or completed draft of your work to practice documenting your sources.

✔ **REVIEW your notes.** Look for introductory words, phrases, and clauses.

✔ **USE a style guide.** Check the correct format for your citations in the style guide your teacher recommends.

Tech Tip

When researching for an assignment on the Internet, be sure to use only reputable sources that cite their information. Then, use the correct citation style for Internet sources, which often includes the Web site URL and date visited.

LEARN MORE
• See Chapter 11, Research Writing, pages 234–237
• See Writing Coach Online

4

Vague Pronoun Reference

LEARN MORE
- See Chapter 5, Nonfiction Narration, pages 82–83
- See Writing Coach Online

GAME PLAN Create clear pronoun-antecedent relationships to make your writing more accurate and powerful.

VAGUE IDEA Pronouns such as *which, this, that,* and *these* should refer to a specific idea. To avoid a vague reference, try changing a pronoun to an adjective that modifies a specific noun.

Amaya bought new running shoes for her upcoming races. These_∧shoes will be important for many months.

UNCLEAR USE OF *IT, THEY,* AND *YOU* Be sure that the pronouns *it, they,* and *you* have a clearly stated antecedent. Replacing the personal pronoun with a specific noun can make a sentence clearer.

My best friend's dad drove us to the baseball game yesterday. ~~It~~_∧The game was a lot of fun.

The teachers asked the students ~~if they could~~ _∧to help with plans for the class play.

Every morning ~~you~~_∧students should get to class on time.

Use a current or completed draft of your work to practice identifying vague pronoun references.

✔ **READ** carefully. Read your draft slowly to locate pronouns.

✔ **IDENTIFY** possible errors. Mark any vague pronoun references.

✔ **REVISE** your draft. Rewrite sentences with vague pronoun-antecedent relationships.

GAME PLAN Spelling errors can change the meaning of a sentence. Proofread your work after spell-checking to be sure you have used the correct words.

SPELL-CHECK ERRORS Computer spell-checkers often replace misspelled words with others close in spelling but different in meaning. Proofread your work carefully to correct these errors.

When we go camping, my dad likes to make a ~~tire~~∧fire to cook our food.

Nicolas took us on a ~~talk~~∧walk to the local forest preserve.

HOMOPHONES Words that are pronounced the same but have different spellings and meanings are called homophones. Check that you have used the correct homophones to convey your meaning.

Hiroshi ~~red~~∧read to his younger brother yesterday.

We want to go ~~their~~∧there for vacation.

Use a current or completed draft of your work to practice spelling words correctly.

✔ **READ** carefully. Read your draft word by word looking for spelling errors.

✔ **IDENTIFY** possible mistakes. Mark any incorrect words or words that are misspelled.

✔ **USE** a dictionary. If you are not certain how to spell a word or think a homophone has been used incorrectly, check a dictionary.

Tech Tip

Proper nouns are not checked by a computer spell-checker. Proofread to make sure that you have spelled people's names correctly.

LEARN MORE

- See Chapter 20, Effective Sentences, pages 461–465
- See Writing Coach Online

6

Punctuation Error With a Quotation

LEARN MORE

• See Chapter 25, Punctuation, pages 579–583
• See Writing Coach Online

GAME PLAN Quotation marks are used to identify direct quotations. Correct punctuation helps to identify quotations and relate them to your work.

DIRECT AND INDIRECT QUOTATIONS A direct quotation is enclosed in quotation marks. Indirect quotations do not need quotation marks.

"How short do you want your hair cut?" the barber asked.

The barber asked me how short I wanted my haircut.

QUOTATION MARKS WITH OTHER PUNCTUATION When commas or periods end a quotation, the punctuation goes inside the quotation marks. Question marks and exclamation marks go either inside or outside the quotation marks, depending on the sentence structure.

The park ranger said, **"**To your left, you'll see redwood trees**."**

"The trees are so tall**!"** Jules exclaimed.

Did he just say, **"**The trees are so small**"?**

✓ Check It

Use a current or completed draft of your work to practice punctuating quotations correctly.

✔ **READ** carefully. If you used indirect quotations, make sure you did not put them in quotation marks.

✔ **IDENTIFY** direct quotations. Mark each direct quotation in your work. Is each quotation punctuated correctly?

✔ **REVISE** your sentences. Correct all punctuation errors in your quotations.

GAME PLAN Before you insert a comma, think about how your ideas relate to one another. Make sure the comma is necessary.

APPOSITIVES If an appositive is essential to the meaning of a sentence, it is *not* set off by commas.

My neighbor, Mrs. Romero, knows a lot about nature.

PARTICIPIAL PHRASES If a participial phrase is essential to the meaning of a sentence, it should *not* be set off by commas.

The student, studying trees for her research paper, asked if Mrs. Romero knew anything about maple trees.

ADJECTIVAL CLAUSES Essential adjectival clauses should *not* be set off by commas.

The tree, that gives us maple syrup, is the maple tree!

Tech Tip

Remember to add or delete commas as needed when you cut and paste and move text.

LEARN MORE
• See Chapter 25, Punctuation, pages 563, 565
• See Writing Coach Online

✔ *Check It*

Use a current or completed draft of your work to practice correctly punctuating essential elements.

✔ **SCAN** Mentor Texts. Notice how professional writers use commas.

✔ **IDENTIFY** essential elements. Did you incorrectly use commas to indicate these elements?

✔ **REVISE** your sentences. Delete any commas that set off essential elements.

Find It/FIX IT

8

Unnecessary or Missing Capitalization

Tech Tip

Sometimes word processors will automatically capitalize any word that follows a period, even if the period is part of an abbreviation. Proofread carefully for incorrectly capitalized words.

LEARN MORE
- See Chapter 26, Capitalization, pages 608–627
- See Writing Coach Online

GAME PLAN Follow the rules of capitalization. For example, capitalize proper nouns, the first word of a sentence, and titles of works of art.

PROPER NOUNS Names, geographical locations, organizations, abbreviations, and acronyms are examples of nouns that should be capitalized.

Abby showed her friends all of the badges she received from the Girl Scouts.

Micha lives in Texas near the Rio Grande.

There are many shows on TV about the FBI.

TITLES OF WORKS OF ART The first word and all other key words in the titles of books, poems, stories, plays, paintings, and other works of art are capitalized.

Have you read any of the poems in Shel Silverstein's book *Where the Sidewalk Ends*?

The book *The Polar Express* was made into a movie.

 Check It

Use a current or completed draft of your work to practice correctly capitalizing words.

✔ **SCAN** your draft. Look for words that are capitalized.

✔ **IDENTIFY** errors in capitalization. Mark words that might be capitalized incorrectly.

✔ **USE** your textbook. Check the grammar section of your textbook if you are not sure if a word should be capitalized.

9

Missing Word

GAME PLAN Make sure there are no missing words in a text so that your ideas flow smoothly and are clear to readers.

ARTICLES To make sure that ideas flow smoothly, you must proofread your work. A missing word, even a missing article (*a, an, the*), can confuse a reader.

> After we went ice-skating, I wanted∧a warm drink.

KEY IDEAS When copying and pasting text, you might miss moving a word in a sentence. If that word is part of the main idea of the sentence, your meaning could be lost.

> Isabelle told her teacher that she∧was moving to Florida.
>
> When asked why she had to move, she said her∧dad got a new job in Florida.

✔ Check It

Use a current or completed draft of your work to practice proofreading.

✔ **READ** carefully. Read your draft word by word to make sure that you did not leave out a word.

✔ **IDENTIFY** unclear sentences. Mark any sentences you find that do not make sense. Are they unclear because of a missing word?

✔ **REVISE** your sentences. Add words to your sentences to make the meaning clear.

Tech Tip

When cutting and pasting sentences, you may use the same word twice by mistake. Proofread to be sure your sentences read correctly.

LEARN MORE
- See Editing sections in the writing chapters
- See Writing Coach Online

10

Faulty Sentence Structure

Tech Tip

Be careful when you cut one part of a sentence and paste it in another. Check that the new sentence structure is correct.

LEARN MORE
- See Chapter 20, Effective Sentences, pages 438–442
- See Writing Coach Online

GAME PLAN Sentences should express complex ideas clearly. Combine two main clauses with similar ideas to form a compound sentence.

JOINING CLAUSES When you have two sentences that express a similar idea, you can join them using a comma and a coordinating conjunction (e.g., *and, or, but, nor, yet, so*). Make sure that the ideas expressed are expressed in a similar way.

The county fair has rides that are scary, and∧ it has rides that are tame.

The Ferris wheel was fun, yet∧ the rollercoaster was scary.

My sister is bringing a friend, but∧ I am bringing a cousin.

 *Check It*

Use a current or corrected draft of your work to practice joining clauses expressing similar ideas.

✔ **SCAN** Mentor Texts. Notice how professional writers present complex ideas.

✔ **READ** your draft. Mark any clauses that can be joined.

✔ **REVISE** your sentences. Rewrite any clauses that can be joined to form a compound sentence.

GAME PLAN Use commas to set off nonessential elements of sentences.

APPOSITIVE If an appositive is not essential to the meaning of a sentence, it should be set off by commas.

The town picnic,∧ <u>a big event,</u>∧ has been held at the park for the past 30 years.

PARTICIPIAL PHRASE A participial phrase not essential to the meaning of a sentence is set off by commas.

I waited for my friend,∧ <u>running late again,</u>∧ at the park entrance.

ADJECTIVAL CLAUSE Use commas to set off an adjectival clause if it is not essential to the meaning of a sentence.

My home town,∧ <u>which has been around for 120 years,</u>∧ has a population of 2,000.

 **Check It**

Use a current or completed draft of your work to practice using commas correctly with nonessential elements.

✔ **SCAN** Mentor Texts. Notice how professional writers use commas to set off nonessential elements.

✔ **IDENTIFY** nonessential elements. Did you use commas to indicate these words, phrases, or clauses?

✔ **REVISE** your sentences. Use commas to set off nonessential elements.

Tech Tip

When you cut part of a sentence and paste it to another, be sure to include the correct punctuation. Proofread these sentences carefully.

LEARN MORE
- See Chapter 25, Punctuation, pages 563–565
- See Writing Coach Online

12

Unnecessary Shift in Verb Tense

Tech Tip

When you cut text from one section to paste to another, the new sentence may have verbs that are not consistent in tense. Proofread revised sentences to make sure they use consistent tenses.

LEARN MORE

• See Chapter 9, Persuasion, pages 188–189
• See Writing Coach Online

GAME PLAN Use consistent verb tenses in your work. Shift tenses only to show that one event comes before or after another.

ACTIONS OCCURRING AT THE SAME TIME Use consistent tenses to show actions that occur at the same time.

I walked to the beach, and I ~~play~~ ∧played in the sand.

I see my best friend in the hall, and I ~~tried~~ ∧try to get her attention.

ACTIONS OCCURRING AT DIFFERENT TIMES If actions occur at different times, you can switch from one tense to another. You may use a time word or phrase to show the shift in tense.

Yesterday, Sarah visted relatives in California; today she ~~flew~~ ∧flies home.

A few hours ago Jeffrey saw a raccoon in his yard; now he ~~saw~~ ∧sees a rabbit.

 Check It

Use a current or completed draft of your work to practice using consistent tenses.

✓ **SCAN** Mentor Text. Notice how professional writers use consistent tenses within a sentence.

✓ **IDENTIFY** possible mistakes. Mark any unnecessary shift in verb tense within a sentence.

✓ **USE** your textbook. Consult the grammar section of your textbook if you are not sure you have used consistent tenses.

GAME PLAN Use a comma before a coordinating conjunction to separate two or more main clauses in a compound sentence.

MAIN CLAUSES Place a comma before a coordinating conjunction (e.g. *and, but, or, nor, yet, so, for*) in a compound sentence.

My cousin Charlotte is starting college this year,∧and she wants to study Italian.

Reba's uncle was supposed to arrive at her house tonight,∧but his flight was canceled.

BRIEF CLAUSES The main clauses in some compound sentences are brief and do not need a comma if the meaning is clear.

Rita is tall and Keiko is short.

SINGLE WORDS Commas should *not* be used to separate single words that are joined by a conjunction.

We bought red, and yellow paint.

He took the baseballs, and bats to practice.

Tech Tip

Be careful when you create a compound sentence by cutting and pasting from different parts of a sentence or paragraph. Remember to include a comma to separate the main clauses.

LEARN MORE
- See Chapter 25, Punctuation, pages 556, 559
- See Writing Coach Online

 *Check It*

Use a current or completed draft of your work to practice using commas in compound sentences.

✓ **SCAN** your draft. Look for compound sentences.

✓ **IDENTIFY** missing commas. Mark any compound sentences that should be punctuated with a comma.

✓ **REVISE** your sentences. Add commas before coordinating conjunctions to separate main clauses.

14

Unnecessary or Missing Apostrophe

Tech Tip

Proofread your draft carefully. Not all computer grammar checkers will point out incorrect uses of apostrophes.

LEARN MORE

- See Chapter 22, Using Pronouns, pages 504, 507
- See Chapter 25, Punctuation, pages 593–597
- See Writing Coach Online

GAME PLAN Use apostrophes correctly to show possession.

SINGULAR NOUNS To show the possessive case of most singular nouns, add an apostrophe and *-s*.

 Adara's figure skating routine was the best one they saw.

PLURAL NOUNS Add an apostrophe to show the possessive case for most plural nouns ending in *-s* or *-es*. For plural nouns that do not end in *-s* or *-es*, add an apostrophe and *-s*.

 The ducks' quacks could be heard across the pond.

The workmen's tools were all stored in the shed.

POSSESSIVE PRONOUNS Possessive pronouns (e.g., *his, hers, its, our, their*) show possession without the use of an apostrophe. Do not confuse *its* and *it's*. The word *its* shows possession, but the word *it's* means "it is."

 You can tell by ~~it's~~ its name that ~~his'~~ his store sells books.

Check It

Use a current or completed draft of your work to practice showing possession.

✔ **SCAN** Mentor Texts. Notice when professional writers use apostrophes to indicate possession.

✔ **IDENTIFY** possible mistakes. Mark each apostrophe in your draft. Did you use them correctly to show possession?

✔ **REVISE** your sentences. Make sure to delete any apostrophes you used with possessive pronouns.

15

Run-on Sentence

GAME PLAN Use correct punctuation to avoid run-on sentences. A run-on sentence is two or more sentences punctuated as if they were a single sentence.

FUSED SENTENCE A fused sentence contains two or more sentences joined with no punctuation. To correct a fused sentence, place a period or an end mark between the main clauses.

He wanted to be a part of the musical, but he couldn't ~~sing the~~ sing. The drama teacher suggested that he be part of the stage crew.

Why did Jan try out for the volleyball ~~team she~~ team? She wanted to play basketball.

RUN-ON SENTENCE Place a comma and a coordinating conjunction between main clauses to avoid run-on sentences.

Raj was excited to go skateboarding, but he was also nervous because he had never tried it before.

✔ Check It

Use a current or completed draft of your work to practice correcting run-on sentences.

✔ **SCAN** your draft. Look for run-on sentences.

✔ **IDENTIFY** missing punctuation. Mark sentences that might need a period or another end mark to separate main clauses.

✔ **REVISE** your sentences. When correcting fused sentences, vary your sentence structure.

Tech Tip

Remember to proofread your work. Not all grammar checkers identify run-on sentences.

LEARN MORE
- See Chapter 20, Effective Sentences, pages 451–455
- See Writing Coach Online

16

Comma Splice

LEARN MORE

- See Chapter 20, Effective Sentences, pages 451–455
- See Chapter 25, Punctuation, pages 556–557
- See Writing Coach Online

GAME PLAN Use correct punctuation to avoid comma splices. A comma splice happens when two or more complete sentences are joined only with a comma.

PERIOD Replace the comma with a period (and capitalize the following word) to separate two complete thoughts.

 I read the book three times, I learned something new each time.

SEMICOLON Replace the comma with a semicolon if the ideas are similar.

 Tara made baked apples for dessert, her family loved them.

COORDINATING CONJUNCTION A comma splice can be corrected by placing a coordinating conjunction (e.g., *and, or, but, yet, nor*) after the comma.

 I wanted to go with them, yet something was holding me back.

✓ Check It

Use a current or completed draft of your work to practice correcting comma splices.

✔ **READ** carefully. Take time to read your draft carefully. Have someone else read your work for a double-check.

✔ **IDENTIFY** possible mistakes. Mark any comma splices you find.

✔ **REVISE** your sentences. Fix comma splices in different ways to vary your sentence structure.

17

Lack of Pronoun-Antecedent Agreement

GAME PLAN Check that pronouns agree with their antecedents in number, person, and gender. When the gender is not specified, the pronoun must still agree in number.

GENDER NEUTRAL ANTECEDENTS When gender is not specific, use *his or her* to refer to the singular antecedent.

Each teammate must return ~~their~~ his or her uniform after the game.

OR, NOR, AND When two or more singular antecedents are joined by *or* or *nor*, use a singular personal pronoun. Use a plural personal pronoun when two or more antecedents are joined by *and*.

Ren <u>or</u> Dara will finish ~~their~~ her history paper first.

Brian <u>and</u> Yoshi will ride together to ~~his~~ their basketball game.

INDEFINITE PRONOUNS A plural personal pronoun must agree with a plural indefinite pronoun. A singular personal pronoun must agree with a singular indefinite pronoun.

<u>Both</u> of the boys want to go somewhere warm for ~~his~~ their vacation.

<u>One</u> of the hostesses was late for ~~their~~ her shift.

Tech Tip

Be careful when you cut and paste text from one sentence to another. Check that the pronouns agree with the antecedents in the new sentences you create.

LEARN MORE
- See Chapter 23, Making Words Agree, pages 529–532
- See Writing Coach Online

 *Check It*

Use a current or completed draft of your work to practice pronoun-antecedent agreement.

✓ **READ** carefully. Take time to read your draft carefully. For a double-check, have someone else read your work.

✓ **IDENTIFY** possible mistakes. Mark any pronouns that do not agree with their antecedents in a sentence.

✓ **USE** your textbook. Check the grammar section of your textbook if you are not sure whether your pronouns and antecedents agree.

18

Poorly Integrated Quotation

Tech Tip

Sometimes you might cut a quote from one sentence and paste it in another. Remember to revise the surrounding sentence to integrate the quote into the text.

LEARN MORE
- See Chapter 25, Punctuation, pages 575–583
- See Writing Coach Online

GAME PLAN Quotations should flow smoothly into the sentence that surrounds them. Add information to explain and link quotes to the rest of your work.

QUOTE IN A SENTENCE Prepare the reader for the information contained in the quote by introducing the quote's idea.

The critic∧spoke about the film's success: "Never before have I seen so much excitement about a movie" (Rico 8).

Jeremiah says∧the play was not rehearsed: "The characters did not seem to know their lines."

QUOTE AS A SENTENCE Place an introductory phrase before or after a quotation that stands alone. In most cases, this phrase should identify the quote's author or speaker.

∧According to Ms. Feldman, "The donation drive covered the expenses for the school's addition" (Kahn 19).

✓ Check It

Use a current or completed draft of your work to practice integrating quotations.

✔ **SCAN Mentor Texts.** Notice how professional writers integrate quotations into their work.

✔ **IDENTIFY quotes.** Mark each quote in your work. Does each quote flow smoothly with the surrounding sentence?

✔ **REVISE your sentences.** Add information as needed to explain and introduce quotes.

GAME PLAN Use hyphens correctly in your writing, including with compound words and compound adjectives.

COMPOUND WORDS Hyphens can connect two or more words that are used as one compound word. Some compound words do not require a hyphen. Check a current dictionary if you are not sure about hyphenating a word.

The ~~ten year old~~ ten-year-old boy asked for a ~~basket-ball~~ basketball.

Her ~~soninlaw~~ son-in-law is taking his daughter to the ~~play-ground~~ playground.

COMPOUND ADJECTIVES A compound adjective that appears before a noun should be hyphenated. Remember, do not hyphenate a compound proper noun acting as an adjective. Also, do not hyphenate a compound adjective that has a word ending in *-ly*.

The ~~right handed~~ right-handed pitcher is the best on the softball team.

I prefer ~~Central-American~~ Central American cuisine.

The ~~happily-smiling~~ happily smiling student just made the basketball team.

✓ Check It

Use a current or completed draft of your work to practice hyphenating words.

✓ **IDENTIFY** possible errors. Mark any compound adjectives before a noun that are not hyphenated.

✓ **REVISE** your sentences. Add a hyphen to words that should be hyphenated.

✓ **USE** a dictionary. Check a dictionary if you are not sure if a word should be hyphenated.

Tech Tip

The automatic hyphenation setting in word processors causes words at the end of a line of text to hyphenate automatically. Be sure that this setting is turned off when you are writing an essay.

LEARN MORE
- See Chapter 25, Punctuation, pages 587–592
- See Writing Coach Online

20

Sentence Fragment

GAME PLAN Use complete sentences when writing. Make sure you have a subject and a complete verb in each and that each sentence expresses a complete thought.

LACKING A SUBJECT OR VERB A complete sentence must have a subject and a complete verb.

His dog always barks at squirrels. ~~And~~ ˄The dog tries to chase them, too!

Miguel ˄is turning 12 this month.

SUBORDINATE CLAUSE A subordinate clause cannot stand on its own as a complete sentence because it does not express a complete thought.

Another baseball was hit over the fence. ~~After~~ ˄after we had already lost three baseballs behind it!

Zane asked his teacher if he could borrow the book. ~~Because~~ ˄because he wanted to read it at home.

Tech Tip

Sometimes, when you cut text from a sentence and paste it to another, you may miss cutting the whole sentence. Make sure you have both a subject and a verb in the new sentences.

LEARN MORE
- See Chapter 20, Effective Sentences, pages 446–450
- See Writing Coach Online

 Check It

Use a current or completed draft of your work to practice writing complete sentences.

✔ **SCAN** your draft. Look for incomplete sentences.

✔ **IDENTIFY** missing words. Mark sentences that have missing subjects or verbs.

✔ **REVISE** your sentences. Rewrite any sentences that are missing subjects or verbs, or are subordinate clauses standing on their own.

NOUNS and PRONOUNS

Well-chosen nouns can help your readers picture the people, places, things, and ideas in your writing.

CHAPTER 13

WRITE GUY *Jeff Anderson, M.Ed.*

WHAT DO YOU NOTICE?

Search for the nouns as you zoom in on these sentences from the story "Stray" by Cynthia Rylant.

MENTOR TEXT

> The puppy stopped in the road, wagging its tail timidly, trembling with shyness and cold.
> Doris trudged through the yard, went up the shoveled drive and met the dog.

Now, ask yourself the following questions:

- Which nouns name people, which nouns name places, and which nouns name things in these sentences?
- How can you decide whether the word *shyness* is an abstract or a concrete noun?

Doris is a noun that names a person. The words *road*, *yard*, and *drive* are all nouns that name places. The words *puppy*, *tail*, and *dog* are all nouns that name things. *Shyness* is an abstract noun because you can't recognize it through your five senses. It is a noun that names an idea.

Grammar for Writers Nouns are a powerful tool writers use to tell what they have observed or what they are thinking. Choose the right noun to exactly describe people, places, things, and ideas in your writing.

What's a noun that begins with the letter L?

Lunch! Now that's a noun I can sink my teeth into.

13.1 Nouns

Nouns are naming words. Words such as *friend*, *sky*, *dog*, *love*, *courage*, and *Seattle* are nouns.

WRITING COACH

Online

www.phwritingcoach.com

Grammar Tutorials

Brush up on your Grammar skills with these animated videos.

Grammar Practice

Practice your grammar skills with Writing Coach Online.

Grammar Games

Test your knowledge of grammar in this fast-paced interactive video game.

RULE 13.1.1

A **noun** names something.

Most nouns fall into four main groups.

People, Places, Things, and Ideas

The nouns in the chart are grouped under four headings. You may know most of the nouns under the first three headings. You may not have realized that all the words in the fourth group are nouns.

PEOPLE	PLACES	THINGS	IDEAS
veterinarian	Lake Mead	bumblebee	strength
Dr. Robinson	classroom	collar	honesty
Americans	kennel	motorcycle	willingness
leader	Bunker Hill	notebook	obedience

See Practice 13.1A

Concrete and Abstract Nouns

Nouns may be classified as **concrete** or **abstract.** In the chart above, *People*, *Places*, and *Things* are concrete nouns. *Ideas* are abstract nouns.

RULE 13.1.2

A **concrete noun** names something that can be recognized through any of the five senses. An **abstract noun** names something that cannot be recognized through the senses.

CONCRETE NOUNS			
pencil	dog	tractor	river
ABSTRACT NOUNS			
courage	fun	honor	exploration

See Practice 13.1B

Collective Nouns

A few nouns name groups of people or things. A *pack*, for example, is "a group of dogs or other animals that travel together." These nouns are called **collective nouns.**

> **A collective noun** names a group of people or things.

See Practice 13.1C

RULE 13.1.3

COLLECTIVE NOUNS		
club	herd	army
troop	orchestra	committee
class	team	group

Count and Non-count Nouns

Nouns can be grouped as **count** or **non-count** nouns.

> **Count nouns** name things that can be counted. **Non-count nouns** name things that cannot be counted.

RULE 13.1.4

See Practice 13.1D
See Practice 13.1E
See Practice 13.1F

COUNT NOUNS	NON-COUNT NOUNS
orange	thunder
bench	rice
street	grass

Count nouns can take an article and can be plural.

EXAMPLE an orange   the orange   three oranges

Non-count nouns do not take an indefinite article (*a* or *an*) and cannot be plural:

EXAMPLES We heard thunder last night.
(*not* We heard *a* thunder last night.)

He needs clothing for the camping trip.
(*not* He needs clothing**s** for the camping trip.)

Read the sentences. Then, write the nouns in each sentence.

EXAMPLE   An ostrich is a type of bird.

ANSWER   *ostrich, type, bird*

1. Borneo is one of the largest islands in the world.

2. The zoo is a good place to learn about animals.

3. One of our neighbors has two dogs and a turtle.

4. Australia is sometimes called the land of parrots.

5. In winter, the sun sets earlier and days are shorter.

6. All planes have wings and a tail.

7. A bird may collect sticks, string, leaves, or rocks to build a nest.

8. Clouds are formed from droplets of water.

9. Each spring, bees pollinate the plants on many farms.

10. Many trees lose their leaves in the autumn.

Read the sentences. Then, write the nouns in each sentence and label each one *concrete* or *abstract*.

EXAMPLE   The nurse used humor to cheer her patients.

ANSWER   *nurse* — *concrete*
humor — *abstract*
patients — *concrete*

11. The eager students wanted to learn about their futures.

12. His story was written on lined paper.

13. Actors must have active imaginations.

14. The carnival caused excitement throughout the school.

15. Some animals cannot live in a cold climate.

16. Many young people voted in the election.

17. Exercise is an important activity for both children and adults.

18. Engineers often find enjoyment in solving math problems.

19. Most people have a fear of public speaking.

20. Firefighters show amazing courage when they race into a burning building.

SPEAKING APPLICATION

In a small group, brainstorm a short list of abstract nouns (two or three more nouns than group members). Then, have each person choose one of the nouns and use it in a sentence.

WRITING APPLICATION

Write two sentences and include one concrete and one abstract noun in each sentence.

PRACTICE 13.1C > Finding Collective Nouns

Read the pairs of nouns. Each pair includes one collective noun. Write the collective noun.

EXAMPLE   child, family

ANSWER   *family*

1. elephant, herd
2. student, class
3. employee, staff
4. team, player
5. coin, collection
6. Senate, Senator
7. panel, juror
8. soprano, choir
9. faculty, teacher
10. club, member

PRACTICE 13.1D > Identifying Count and Non-count Nouns

Read the sentences. Then, list the count and non-count nouns. One sentence has only count nouns.

EXAMPLE   We crammed our luggage into the car.

ANSWER   *count noun — car*
non-count noun — luggage

11. We heard thunder before the storm began.
12. My little sister began to play hockey when she was ten years old.
13. All living things need oxygen.
14. There is too much furniture to fit into the room.
15. If you like to dance, you will love our neighborhood's block parties.
16. Has the mail come yet?
17. When they saw a skunk on the grass by the sidewalk, they waited to leave the house.
18. Traffic on the highway is always heavy on weekends.
19. Honesty is the best policy.
20. Everyone in the city lost electricity during the blackout.

SPEAKING APPLICATION

With a partner, take turns telling about a game you watched recently. Your partner should listen for and name two collective nouns, two count nouns, and two non-count nouns you used.

WRITING APPLICATION

Write three sentences and include one of the following in each: a collective noun, a count noun, and a non-count noun. Read your sentences out loud to a partner. Have your partner name the non-count nouns you used.

PRACTICE 13.1E ▷ **Using Non-count Nouns**

Read the sentence and the two word choices that follow it. Write the sentence using the word that is a non-count noun.

EXAMPLE   We are having _____ with the sauce. (pasta, steak)

ANSWER   *We are having pasta with the sauce.*

1. The school is replacing the _____ in the media center. (copiers, equipment)

2. We will play _____ on the field on Saturday. (soccer, games)

3. Danica needs to get some _____ from the store. (bananas, fruit)

4. At her party, my sister served _____. (lemonade, sandwiches)

5. Some _____ will be displayed at the art fair. (earrings, jewelry)

6. The museum has many pieces of fine _____. (art, paintings)

7. I found _____ in the attic. (toys, paint)

8. The test will cover the _____ we learned in the chapter. (information, facts)

9. Max has jazz band _____. (knowledge, instruments)

10. The dish was served on a bed of _____. (peas, rice)

PRACTICE 13.1F ▷ **Recognizing Non-count Nouns**

Read the sentence. Find and write the non-count noun. Then, write a sentence using that noun.

EXAMPLE   Jamie heard your laughter in the room down the hall.

ANSWER   *laughter— His jokes always bring laughter.*

11. Arturo has been lifting weights to build his strength.

12. We re-use shopping bags to save paper.

13. Marissa needs to install new software on her computer.

14. My brother plays volleyball every week.

15. The table is covered with a layer of dust.

16. Sometimes it is impossible to hide tears of sadness.

17. If you cook rice too long, it gets sticky.

18. All night long, music blared through the open window.

19. It is not good to use too much salt when you cook.

20. The company stopped production because no one was buying the car.

SPEAKING APPLICATION

In a small group, talk about different sports. Choose a recorder to take notes. Review the notes and identify non-count nouns. Then, each person writes two sentences using non-count nouns and reads the sentences to the group.

WRITING APPLICATION

Think about your favorite foods. Write three sentences about food. Include a non-count noun in each one. Read your sentences to a partner, who should identify your non-count nouns.

Test Warm-Up

DIRECTIONS
Read the introduction and the passage that follows. Then, answer
the questions to show that you can use and understand the
function of non-count nouns in reading and writing.

The paragraph tells what happens when James offers to get food. Read the paragraph and think about the changes you would suggest as a peer editor. When you finish reading, answer the questions that follow.

James Almost Meets Disaster

(1) Because of a bad weather, flights were delayed, and people were sitting around the airport waiting for information. (2) James offered to go for tacos. (3) His sister, Tamara, promised to watch the luggages. (4) Dad gave James ten dollar and asked for cheddar cheeses on his taco. (5) James went to the food stand and ordered. (6) Then, he remembered milk for his baby brother. (7) Finally, balancing a full tray, James searched the crowd for his family and nearly knocked over a garbage can. (8) What a big mess that would have been with foods flying everywhere!

---

1 What change, if any, should be made in sentence 1?

  A Change *weather* to **weathers**

  B Change *a* to **the**

  C Change *information* to **informations**

  D Make no change

2 What is the BEST way to combine sentences 2 and 3?

  F James offered to go for tacos, his sister, Tamara, promised to watch the luggages.

  G James offered to go for tacos while his sister, Tamara, promised to watch the luggage.

  H James offered to go for taco, because his sister, Tamara, promised to watch the luggage.

  J James offered to go for tacos because his sister, Tamara, promised to watch the luggages.

3 How should sentence 4 be revised?

  A Dad gave James ten dollars and asked for cheddar cheeses on his taco.

  B Dad gave James moneys and asked for cheddar cheeses on his taco.

  C Dad gave James ten dollars and asked for cheddar cheese on his taco.

  D Dad gave James ten dollar and asked for cheddar cheese on his taco.

4 What change, if any, should be made to sentence 8?

  F Change *mess* to **messes**

  G Change *big* to **bigs**

  H Change *foods* to **food**

  J Make no change

Recognizing Compound Nouns

Some nouns are made up of two or more words. *Classroom* is a **compound noun** made up of *class* and *room*.

> A **compound noun** is one noun made by joining two or more words.

Compound nouns are written in three different ways: as single words, as hyphenated words, and as two or more separate words.

COMPOUND NOUNS		
SINGLE WORDS	HYPHENATED WORDS	SEPARATE WORDS
crossbar	by-product	dinner jacket
firefighter	right-hander	pole vault
thunderstorm	middle-distance	pen pal
classroom	mother-in-law	chief justice

See Practice 13.1G

Using Common and Proper Nouns

All nouns can be divided into two large groups: **common nouns** and **proper nouns.**

> A **common noun** names any one of a class of people, places, things, or ideas. A **proper noun** names a specific person, place, thing, or idea.

Common nouns are not capitalized. Proper nouns are always capitalized.

COMMON NOUNS	PROPER NOUNS
inventor	Alexander Graham Bell
village	Tarrytown
story	"The Tell-Tale Heart"
organization	American Red Cross
idea	Germ Theory of Disease

See Practice 13.1H

Neliä

PRACTICE 13.1G Identifying Compound Nouns

Read the sentences. Then, write the compound nouns, and draw a line between the words that make up each compound noun.

EXAMPLE We have a doghouse in the yard.

ANSWER *dog | house*

1. We built our campsite on the hilltop.
2. In high school we will study more science.
3. Wildflowers covered the countryside.
4. Always wear your seat belt when in a car.
5. Fireflies flickered in the moonlight.
6. Many children start day care at an early age.
7. Mr. Nguyen's brother-in-law is a firefighter.
8. Tomorrow we'll slide our homemade rowboat into the lake.
9. My grandfather used to play basketball.
10. All you need for this trip are a fishing pole and sunglasses.

PRACTICE 13.1H Using Common and Proper Nouns

Read the sentences. Then, rewrite them, replacing the underlined words with proper nouns.

EXAMPLE My class took a trip to the city last month.

ANSWER *My class took a trip to Atlanta last April.*

11. He pointed to an ocean on the classroom globe.
12. We saw a planet through the telescope.
13. Yesterday, I heard someone speaking a foreign language.
14. That store is my favorite store at the mall.
15. We went to the zoo.
16. When I started school, I met the teacher.
17. In class, we studied a country.
18. I would love to see a game at the sports stadium.
19. I walked slowly along the street, which is near my house.
20. I really enjoyed reading a book.

SPEAKING APPLICATION

With a partner, name as many things as you can related to your classroom and school that are compound nouns. Take turns saying how the parts create meaning. For example, *wastebasket* is a basket for waste.

WRITING APPLICATION

Write two or three sentences about places in and around your town. Use proper nouns to name places (streets, stores, parks, and so on) that you know or visit.

13.2 Pronouns

Pronouns are words that take the place of nouns. They are used rather than repeating a noun again and again. Pronouns make sentences clearer and more interesting.

RULE 13.2.1 A **pronoun** is a word that takes the place of a noun or a group of words acting as a noun.

Imagine, for example, that you are writing about Aunt Jenny. If you were using only nouns, you might write the following sentence:

WITH NOUNS
Aunt Jenny was late because **Aunt Jenny** had waited for **Aunt Jenny's** computer technician.

WITH PRONOUNS
Aunt Jenny was late because **she** had waited for **her** computer technician.

Sometimes a pronoun takes the place of a noun in the same sentence.

EXAMPLES
My father opened **his** files first.
pronoun

Many people say exercise has helped **them** .
pronoun

A pronoun can also take the place of a noun used in an earlier sentence.

EXAMPLES
My father opened his e-mail first. **He** couldn't wait any longer.
pronoun

Students must take a science class. **They** can choose biology or ecology.
pronoun

A pronoun may take the place of an entire group of words.

EXAMPLE
Trying to make the team is hard work. **It** takes hours of practice every day.
pronoun

Antecedents of Pronouns

The word or group of words that a pronoun replaces or refers to is called an **antecedent.**

> An **antecedent** is the noun (or group of words acting as a noun) to which a pronoun refers.

EXAMPLES   The **firefighters** described how **they** did **their**
              antecedent   *pronoun*   *pronoun*
jobs.

Finally, the **rescue worker** reappeared. **She**
              antecedent   *pronoun*
seemed to be unharmed.

How Kim was rescued is amazing. **It** is a story
    antecedent   *pronoun*
that will be told often.

Although **he** was known as an expert software
          pronoun
developer, **Darryl** enjoyed selling computers.
              antecedent

See Practice 13.2A

Some kinds of pronouns do not have any antecedent.

EXAMPLES   **Everyone** knows what the truth is.
              indefinite pronoun

Who will represent the class at the town-wide
interrogative pronoun
school meeting?

See Practice 13.2B

The pronouns *everyone* and *who* do not have a specific antecedent because their meaning is clear without one.

PRACTICE 13.2A ▷ Recognizing Pronouns and Antecedents

Read the sentences. Then, write each pronoun and its antecedent.

EXAMPLE   Many people are interested in dogs and their care.

ANSWER   *their, dogs*

1. The children wanted to play, so they grabbed the ball.
2. Dad said he would be working in the basement.
3. Lianna thought she would like to try out for the school play.
4. That car is known for its reliability.
5. Most people can remember their phone numbers.
6. The teacher asked if Joseph had seen her ruler.
7. The squirrel looked as if it couldn't find any acorns.
8. The mayor knew that his job included balancing the budget.
9. My mother said the car on television is just like hers.
10. The students understood that they needed to finish the assignment.

PRACTICE 13.2B ▷ Supplying Pronouns for Antecedents

Read the sentences. Then, write each sentence, filling in the blank with the appropriate pronoun. Correctly identify and underline the antecedent of the pronoun you supply.

EXAMPLE   Did Michael bring _____ camera?

ANSWER   *Did <u>Michael</u> bring his camera?*

11. I like reading books. _____ always give me new ideas.
12. If I left the cupboard open, could you close _____ for me?
13. Farmer Johnson discovered that _____ liked organic farming.
14. Ahmed and Sepida went to _____ rooms to do homework.
15. Rosa wanted everyone to see _____ paintings.
16. Washington, D.C., is famous for _____ great monuments.
17. My mom is a great cook. I wonder how _____ learned to cook.
18. I returned the dress because _____ didn't fit.
19. By early autumn, the tree had lost all _____ leaves.
20. Billy ran because he was afraid the bus would leave without _____.

SPEAKING APPLICATION

With a partner, take turns telling about people you know. Your partner should listen for three pronouns and correctly identify the antecedents.

WRITING APPLICATION

Write two pairs of short sentences, using a noun in the first sentence of the pair and an appropriate pronoun in the second. Do not use the same pronoun twice.

Recognizing Personal Pronouns

The pronouns used most often are **personal pronouns**.

> **Personal pronouns** refer to (1) the person speaking or writing, (2) the person listening or reading, or (3) the topic (person, place, thing, or idea) being discussed or written about.

The first-person pronouns *I, me, my, mine, we, us, our,* and *ours* refer to the person or persons speaking or writing.

EXAMPLES   **I** like the new design.

Please give **us** an example.

The second-person pronouns *you, your,* and *yours* refer to the person or persons spoken or written to.

EXAMPLES   **You** will see the photo.

Your friend is at the door.

The third-person pronouns *he, him, his, she, her, hers, it, its, they, them, their,* and *theirs* refer to the person, place, thing, or idea being spoken or written about.

EXAMPLES   **He** wants to listen to the radio show.

They wrote letters to the editor.

Some personal pronouns show possession. Although they can function as adjectives, they are still identified as personal pronouns because they take the place of possessive nouns.

EXAMPLES   **Mary's** town paper comes out weekly.
possessive noun

Her town paper comes out weekly.
possessive pronoun

The chart on the next page presents the personal pronouns.

PERSONAL PRONOUNS		
	SINGULAR	PLURAL
First person	I, me, my, mine	we, us, our, ours
Second person	you, your, yours	you, your, yours
Third person	he, him, his, she, her, hers, it, its	they, them, their, theirs

See Practice 13.2C

Reflexive and Intensive Pronouns

The ending *-self* or *-selves* can be added to some pronouns to form **reflexive** or **intensive pronouns.** These two types of pronouns look the same, but they function differently within a sentence.

REFLEXIVE AND INTENSIVE PRONOUNS		
	SINGULAR	PLURAL
First person	myself	ourselves
Second person	yourself	yourselves
Third person	himself, herself, itself	themselves

RULE 13.2.4

A reflexive pronoun directs the action of the verb toward its subject. Reflexive pronouns point back to a noun or pronoun earlier in the sentence.

A reflexive pronoun is essential to the meaning of a sentence.

REFLEXIVE   **Joy** helped **herself** to some turkey.
             noun   reflexive pronoun

                 They poured **themselves** some milk.
             pronoun   reflexive pronoun

See Practice 13.2D

RULE 13.2.5

An intensive pronoun simply adds emphasis to a noun or pronoun in the same sentence.

An intensive pronoun is not essential to the meaning of the sentence.

INTENSIVE   The mayor **herself** attended the carnival.

PRACTICE 13.2C **Recognizing Personal Pronouns**

Read the sentences. Then, write the personal pronouns in each sentence.

EXAMPLE   We took a trip to San Antonio, Texas, last summer.

ANSWER   *We*

1. I like having dinner with my family.

2. The neighbors say that ours is the nicest garden.

3. Is that T-shirt yours or mine?

4. Mom and Dad trusted us, and we didn't disappoint them.

5. Luis asked his mother to remind him to return the library books.

6. We forgot to bring food, but Carla and Shaun gave us some of theirs.

7. You can put your books over there.

8. Dad and Tim handed the usher their entrance tickets.

9. Do you want me to come along too?

10. My parents said they were going to a movie.

PRACTICE 13.2D **Supplying Reflexive and Intensive Pronouns**

Read the sentences. Write the reflexive or intensive pronoun that completes each sentence.

EXAMPLE   I painted that painting _____.

ANSWER   *myself*

11. We cooked this meal _____.

12. The coach _____ was amazed at the team's playing.

13. Those students painted the room _____.

14. Adam called the dentist _____.

15. Kim said she could do it by _____.

16. Allow _____ enough time for research.

17. The map _____ wasn't that detailed.

18. Help _____ to the free samples.

19. The trip _____ took one week.

20. The drivers congratulated _____.

SPEAKING APPLICATION

In a small group, have one person say a personal pronoun and the next person use it in a sentence. Additional pronouns may be used, as long as the one given is used.

WRITING APPLICATION

Write three sentences, each one using a reflexive or intensive pronoun to relate something done by friends or family members.

Demonstrative Pronouns

Demonstrative pronouns point to people, places, and things, much as you point to them with your finger.

RULE 13.2.6

> A **demonstrative pronoun** points to a specific person, place, or thing.

There are two singular and two plural demonstrative pronouns.

DEMONSTRATIVE PRONOUNS			
SINGULAR		PLURAL	
this	that	these	those

This and *these* point to what is near the speaker or writer. *That* and *those* point to what is more distant.

NEAR   **This** is the desk where I sit.

These are my favorite books.

FAR   Is **that** the cafeteria down the hall?

Those are my sandwiches.

See Practice 13.2E

Using Relative Pronouns

Relative pronouns are connecting words.

RULE 13.2.7

> A **relative pronoun** begins a subordinate clause and connects it to another idea in the same sentence.

There are five main relative pronouns.

RELATIVE PRONOUNS				
that	which	who	whom	whose

The chart on the next page gives examples of relative pronouns connecting subordinate clauses to independent clauses. (See Chapter 19 to find out more about relative pronouns and clauses.)

INDEPENDENT CLAUSES	SUBORDINATE CLAUSES
Here is the book	that Betsy lost.
Dino bought our old house,	which needs many repairs.
She is a singer	who has an unusual range.
Is this the man	whom you saw earlier?
She is the one	whose house has a fire alarm.
This is the show	that he describes in the newspaper.
Tippy found the ball	that was under the chair.

See Practice 13.2F

Interrogative Pronouns

To interrogate means "to ask questions."

An **interrogative pronoun** is used to begin a question.

13.2.8 RULE

All five interrogative pronouns begin with *w*.

INTERROGATIVE PRONOUNS				
what	which	who	whom	whose

Most interrogative pronouns do not have antecedents.

EXAMPLES **What** did the doctor say?

Which is the best treatment?

Who wants to go with me?

From **whom** will you receive the best advice?

See Practice 13.2G **Whose** is this painting?

Indefinite Pronouns

RULE 13.2.9

> An **indefinite pronoun** refers to a person, place, thing, or idea that is not specifically named.

EXAMPLES   **Everything** is ready for the field trip.

Everyone wants to see the medical center.

Anyone can learn to play tennis.

Something fell out of the cabinet when I opened it.

Among its other uses, an indefinite pronoun can function as an adjective or as the subject of a sentence. If it functions as an adjective, it is called an indefinite adjective.

ADJECTIVE   **Both** students want to be nurses.

SUBJECT   **Both** want to be nurses.

A few indefinite pronouns can be either singular or plural, depending on their use in the sentence.

INDEFINITE PRONOUNS			
SINGULAR		**PLURAL**	**SINGULAR OR PLURAL**
another	much	both	all
anybody	neither	few	any
anyone	nobody	many	more
anything	no one	others	most
each	nothing	several	none
either	one		some
everybody	other		
everyone	somebody		
everything	someone		
little	something		

See Practice 13.2H

See Practice 13.2I

See Practice 13.2J

PRACTICE 13.2E > **Identifying Demonstrative Pronouns**

Read the sentences. Then, write the demonstrative pronoun and the noun to which it refers.

EXAMPLE   This is an old camera.

ANSWER   *This, camera*

1. These are the new basketball uniforms.

2. This is a copy of the letter.

3. Do you know if those are the photographs that were chosen for the yearbook?

4. This is my favorite meal of the week.

5. That was a loud noise we heard during the play.

6. These are the blankets for the children in the hospital.

7. This is an amazing biography.

8. That was the house where my mom lived when she was my age.

9. Yes, these are my boots.

10. I think those are the two songs from the musical that Mrs. Brennan likes the most.

PRACTICE 13.2F > **Supplying Relative Pronouns**

Read the sentences. Then, write the correct relative pronoun for each sentence.

EXAMPLE   Rick Carson, _____ the players like, is leaving soon.

ANSWER   *whom*

11. The plumber, _____ has worked for twenty years, is scheduled for the job.

12. Players _____ like Stephanie want to join her team.

13. The team _____ they want to join hasn't won many games.

14. I met a writer _____ students adore.

15. The message, _____ Marcus is sending, will surprise everyone.

16. The driver, _____ car has a flat tire, is looking for a ride.

17. The only person _____ can solve the problem is gone.

18. Vanessa, _____ office is huge, is holding the meeting there.

19. The other horse _____ will race today is a palomino.

20. My grandmother, _____ we call every week, is coming to visit this summer.

SPEAKING APPLICATION

With a partner, take turns telling about a recent event you attended. Your partner should listen for and name two demonstrative and two relative pronouns you used.

WRITING APPLICATION

Write five sentences, including one of the following relative pronouns in each: *that, which, who, whom,* and *whose.*

PRACTICE 13.2G > Identifying Interrogative Pronouns

Read the sentences. Then, write the interrogative pronoun in each sentence.

EXAMPLE   Who invented the telephone?

ANSWER   *Who*

1. What was your sister's assignment?
2. Who will play soccer after school today?
3. Which is your dad's office?
4. Who called the fire station?
5. What were the reasons given?
6. Whose is this coat?
7. What are the answers to these questions?
8. With whom are you going to the library?
9. Which is the most interesting radio show?
10. What will happen next?

PRACTICE 13.2H > Supplying Indefinite Pronouns

Read the sentences. Then, write an appropriate indefinite pronoun (e.g., *all*, *both*, *nothing*, *anything*) for each sentence.

EXAMPLE   Would _____ close the door, please?

ANSWER   *someone*

11. Did _____ new happen while I was gone?
12. _____ must have moved the plants.
13. I'm sure _____ will be there tonight.
14. _____ of the copies of the book I need are missing!
15. There's _____ we can do about the squeak in that wheel.
16. Can _____ join this club?
17. I think there's _____ funny going on here.
18. If the one you want is gone, then pick _____.
19. Briana and Chai are here, but where are the _____?
20. _____ girls want to play shortstop, but only one of the two girls knows how to play the position.

SPEAKING APPLICATION

With a partner, take turns acting like a newspaper reporter conducting an interview. Ask at least four questions that use interrogative pronouns. Your partner should answer each of the questions, using one of the indefinite pronouns (e.g., *all*, *both*, *nothing*, *anything*) in each answer.

WRITING APPLICATION

Write a short paragraph about a story you have read that you think others should read. Use at least four indefinite pronouns (e.g., *all*, *both*, *nothing*, *anything*). Then, read your sentences aloud to a partner. Have your partner identify the indefinite pronouns you used.

PRACTICE 13.2I ▷ **Recognizing Indefinite Pronouns**

Read the sentence. Write the indefinite pronoun. Then, write another sentence using the same indefinite pronoun.

EXAMPLE   Several of these options will work.

ANSWER   *several — Several of us are working on the neighborhood clean-up.*

1. Rob wants nothing to do with networking on the Internet.

2. Some went to the party last night.

3. Last night, somebody left the lights on downstairs.

4. Ms. Johnson wants everyone to sign up for a committee.

5. Mom said we can bring both of the dogs to the lake on Saturday.

6. I want none of your silliness right now.

7. All of the computers are in use.

8. That bike is the one I want to get.

9. Jacqueline asked if she could do anything to help.

10. Only a few are in the auditorium so far.

PRACTICE 13.2J ▷ **Supplying Indefinite Pronouns**

Read the sentences. Then, complete each sentence, filling in the blank with an indefinite pronoun. Identify the pronoun as singular or plural.

EXAMPLE   _____ of the students has become ill.

ANSWER   *another — singular*

11. Have you finished _____ of the leftovers?

12. _____ of the parents is coming on Friday.

13. I checked, but _____ is in the kitchen.

14. _____ of the twins are at the movies.

15. _____ of the books on the list are in the library.

16. We are ready for the presentation, so _____ remains to be done.

17. They accumulated _____ of their wealth illegally.

18. Have you done _____ about finding a summer job?

19. It took _____ hours to build that table.

20. The new girl invited _____ to her party.

SPEAKING APPLICATION

With a partner, talk about several television series. Use indefinite pronouns to explain the reasons you like certain ones. Then, write four sentences, each using one of these indefinite pronouns: *all*, *both*, *nothing*, and *anything*.

WRITING APPLICATION

Write a paragraph about music you enjoy listening to. Use the indefinite pronouns *all*, *both*, *nothing*, and *anything* in your paragraph. Then, read your paragraph to a partner. Your partner should identify the indefinite pronouns that you used.

Test Warm-Up

DIRECTIONS
Read the introduction and the passage that follows. Then, answer the questions to show that you can use and understand the function of indefinite pronouns in reading and writing.

The narrator writes about coming to bat during a close baseball game. Read the paragraph and think about the changes you would suggest as a peer editor. When you finish reading, answer the questions that follow.

The Bottom of the Ninth

(1) Because nothing can happen in baseball, until the very last inning, all is not yet lost. (2) My team is at bat and behind by one point in the bottom of the ninth inning. (3) Julio picks up his bat and takes a few practice swings. (4) He grabs another bat, so something is wrong. (5) Then, he hits a grounder and beats the throw. (6) I step up to the plate. (7) Everyone in the stands yell. (8) I connect, and the ball sails over the fence for a home run, proving that no one is impossible in this game!

---

1 What change, if any, should be made in sentence 1?

  A Change *nothing* to **anything**

  B Change *all* to **most**

  C Change *all* to **nothing**

  D Make no change

2 What change, if any, should be made in sentence 4?

  F Change *another* to **other**

  G Change *something* to **nothing**

  H Change *something* to **anything**

  J Make no change

3 What is the BEST way to combine sentences 6 and 7?

  A As I step up to the plate, everyone in the stands yells.

  B I step up to the plate all in the stands yell.

  C As I stepped up to the plate, anyone in the stands yells.

  D I stepped to the plate as both in the stands yells.

4 What change, if any, should be made in sentence 8?

  F Change *no one* to **someone**

  G Change *no one* to **nothing**

  H Change *no one* to **none**

  J Make no change

VERBS

When you write, choose verbs that show exactly what someone or something is doing.

WRITE GUY *Jeff Anderson, M.Ed.*

WHAT DO YOU NOTICE?

Chase down some verbs as you zoom in on these sentences from the story "The Tail" by Joyce Hansen.

MENTOR TEXT

> I spotted Keisha and Yvonne walking into the playground. Junior tagged behind me and Naomi as we went to meet them.

Now, ask yourself the following questions:

- Who performs the action of the verb *spotted* in the first sentence, and who receives the action?
- Do the verbs *tagged* and *went* in the second sentence have receivers for their actions?

The narrator *I* is the one who *spotted*, and *Keisha and Yvonne* are the ones who were spotted. *Keisha and Yvonne* receive the action. *Spotted* is a transitive verb because the receivers of the action are named. The verbs *tagged* and *went* do not have receivers of their action, so they are intransitive verbs.

Grammar for Writers Think of verbs as the muscles that make your sentences move. When you use verbs that describe action, your writing is lively and interesting.

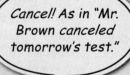

Name an action verb that you hope or expect to hear today.

Cancel! As in "Mr. Brown *canceled* tomorrow's test."

14.1 Action Verbs

Verbs such as *walk, sailed, played, migrate, raced, crossed, learn,* and *arrive* all show some kind of action.

RULE 14.1.1

An **action verb** tells what action someone or something is performing.

EXAMPLES   Father **carries** the ladder.

The ship **chugged** into the harbor.

I **believe** it will snow.

Sandor **remembered** to bring his puzzle.

The verb *carries* explains what Father does with the ladder. The verb *chugged* tells what the ship did. The verb *believe* explains my action about the weather. The verb *remembered* explains Sandor's action with the puzzle.

Some actions, such as *carries* or *chugged,* can be seen. Some actions, such as *believe* or *remembered,* cannot be seen.

See Practice 14.1A

Using Transitive Verbs

RULE 14.1.2

An action verb is **transitive** if the receiver of the action is named in the sentence. The receiver of the action is called the **object** of the verb.

EXAMPLES   Pete **opened** the **window** with great difficulty.
                        verb   object

The truck suddenly **hit** the **trashcan**.
                                    verb   object

In the first example, *opened* is transitive because the object of the verb—*window*—names what Pete opened. In the second example, *hit* is transitive because the object of the verb—*trashcan*—tells what the truck hit.

Using Intransitive Verbs

> An action verb is **intransitive** if there is no receiver of the action named in the sentence. An intransitive verb does not have an object.

RULE 14.1.3

EXAMPLES

The race **began**.

The bus driver **raced** through the traffic light.

Seventh grade students **gathered** in the gym.

The clock alarm **rang** at eight o'clock.

Some action verbs can be transitive or intransitive. You need to determine if the verb has an object or not.

TRANSITIVE VERB   Kyra **painted** the **front door**.

INTRANSITIVE VERB   The artist **painted** in his studio.

TRANSITIVE VERB   The captain **sailed** the **ship**.

INTRANSITIVE VERB   The ship **sailed** out to sea.

TRANSITIVE VERB   The teacher **rang** the **bell**.

See Practice 14.1B   INTRANSITIVE VERB   The bell **rang** for class to begin.

PRACTICE 14.1A	Finding Action Verbs

Read the sentences. Then, write each action verb.

EXAMPLE I see a cocoon on that tree branch.

ANSWER *see*

1. For breakfast, my mom usually eats cereal.
2. I saw an interesting show about Australia.
3. Traffic slows dramatically during rush hour.
4. The potter creates bowls out of clay.
5. Sometimes I forget my password for the computer.
6. Our flowers bloomed this weekend.
7. She said it would be a good movie.
8. My parents encourage my interest in music.
9. The new books arrived last week.
10. I walked the dog after dinner last night.

PRACTICE 14.1B	Identifying Transitive and Intransitive Verbs

Read the sentences. Write each verb and label it *transitive* or *intransitive*.

EXAMPLE Lisa rode her bike down the hill.

ANSWER *rode* — transitive

11. The post office stands near the corner of Main Street and Hill Street.
12. The sun shone throughout the day.
13. A heavy blanket covered the bed.
14. The marathon runners came from many cities.
15. My brother threw his clothes into the washing machine.
16. I created small toys to take to the children.
17. Redwood trees grow amazingly tall.
18. Most animals protect their young.
19. The big balloon rose into the air.
20. We found the perfect place for a picnic.

SPEAKING APPLICATION

With a partner, take turns telling about something you enjoy doing on the weekend. Your partner should listen for and name three action verbs.

WRITING APPLICATION

Write two pairs of short sentences. In each pair, write one sentence using a transitive verb and one using an intransitive, in any order. For example, "I planted a flower. The flower grew."

14.2 Linking Verbs

Some widely used verbs do not show action. They are called **linking verbs**.

RULE
14.2.1

A **linking verb** is a verb that connects a subject with a word that describes or identifies it.

EXAMPLES

IDENTIFIES

Sheridan **was** a Union **general**.
subject — linking verb — predicate nominative

IDENTIFIES

The **winners** **were** **Tony and I**.
subject — linking verb — predicate nominative

DESCRIBES

We **felt** extremely **tired** after all our running.
subject — linking verb — predicate adjective

Recognizing Forms of *Be*

In English, the most common linking verb is *be.* This verb has many forms.

FORMS OF *BE*		
am	can be	has been
are	could be	have been
is	may be	had been
was	might be	could have been
were	must be	may have been
am being	shall be	might have been
are being	should be	must have been
is being	will be	shall have been
was being	would be	should have been
were being		will have been
		would have been

Using Other Linking Verbs

Several other verbs also function as linking verbs. They connect the parts of a sentence in the same way as the forms of *be*. In the sentence below, *calm* describes *chief*.

DESCRIBES

EXAMPLE The **chief** **remained** **calm** during the battle.
         subject   linking verb   predicate
                                   adjective

OTHER LINKING VERBS		
appear	look	sound
become	remain	stay
feel	seem	taste
grow	smell	turn

Action Verb or Linking Verb?

Some verbs can be used either as linking verbs or action verbs.

LINKING The water **looked** polluted.
         (*Looked* links *water* and *polluted.*)

ACTION   The inspectors **looked** at the water.
         (The inspectors performed an action.)

LINKING The people **grew** unhappy.
         (*Grew* links *people* and *unhappy.*)

ACTION   The people **grew** poor crops.
         (The people performed an action.)

To test whether a verb is a linking verb or an action verb, replace the verb with *is, am,* or *are.* If the sentence still makes sense, then the verb is a linking verb.

EXAMPLE The people **are** unhappy.
         linking verb

See Practice 14.2A
See Practice 14.2B
See Practice 14.2C
See Practice 14.2D

PRACTICE 14.2A **Identifying Action Verbs and Linking Verbs**

Read the sentences. Write the verb in each sentence, and label it either *action* or *linking*. One sentence has two verbs.

EXAMPLE   The coach called to the skaters.

ANSWER   *called* — action

1. The driver was unhappy with his car.
2. Sheila waved to the neighbors.
3. The players heard the coach's voice.
4. I don't feel very well.
5. The job you did looks really professional.
6. The two boys raced to the corner.
7. The sun shone on the new snow.
8. This story is about a lost rabbit.
9. We all helped Mom with the dishes.
10. They were happy with their grades.

PRACTICE 14.2B **Using *Be* and Other Linking Verbs**

Read the pairs of words below. For each pair of words, write a sentence that uses a linking verb to connect them.

EXAMPLE   Patrick   busy

ANSWER   *Patrick looked busy as he prepared for the party.*

11. homework   easy
12. Sondra   puzzled
13. door   locked
14. Felipe   surprised
15. food   good
16. sweater   warm
17. idea   interesting
18. day   cloudy
19. puppy   happy
20. Alicia   careful

SPEAKING APPLICATION

With a partner, take turns telling about something you read about or saw on television. Your partner should listen for and name two linking verbs and two action verbs you used.

WRITING APPLICATION

Choose three different linking verbs, other than *be* verbs. Write three sentences, each one using a different linking verb.

| PRACTICE 14.2C > **Identifying Verbs** |

Read the sentences. Choose the verb in parentheses that makes sense in the sentence. Write it and label it *action* or *linking*.

EXAMPLE   A tornado _____ the town twice. (struck, was)

ANSWER   *struck*— action

1. We _____ three miles yesterday. (became, hiked)

2. The puzzle _____ easy enough. (looks, questions)

3. The location _____ a problem for us. (moves, remains)

4. The duck _____ into the water. (plunged, is)

5. The pelican _____ away with a fish in its bill. (was, flew)

6. The flowers _____ fresh for a week. (stayed, swayed)

7. We _____ the celebrity on Fifth Avenue. (are, glimpsed)

8. The crackers _____ stale. (grew, reached)

9. We _____ money to help the victims of the flood. (collected, appeared)

10. The stew _____ too salty. (swallowed, tasted)

| PRACTICE 14.2D > **Using Action Verbs and Linking Verbs** |

Read the verbs. For each verb, write a sentence using the verb as an action verb or a linking verb, as indicated in parentheses.

EXAMPLE   feel (linking)

ANSWER   *Sam feels nervous about the upcoming race.*

11. become (linking)

12. remain (linking)

13. smell (action)

14. smell (linking)

15. taste (linking)

16. feel (action)

17. feels (linking)

18. seem (linking)

19. look (action)

20. look (linking)

SPEAKING APPLICATION

With a partner, take turns talking about pets. Then, write two sentences with action verbs and two sentences with linking verbs. Use action verbs for what pets do and linking verbs for their appearance. Finally, read your sentences to your partner, who will tell which verbs are action verbs and which are linking verbs.

WRITING APPLICATION

Write a short description of an imaginary animal. Use at least two action and two linking verbs. Then, exchange papers with a partner. Your partner should circle the action verbs and underline the linking verbs.

Test Warm-Up

DIRECTIONS
Read the introduction and the passage that follows. Then, answer the questions to show that you can use and understand the function of action verbs and linking verbs in reading and writing.

One student wrote a report about a strange and comical animal. Read the paragraph and think about the changes you would suggest as a peer editor. When you finish reading, answer the questions that follow.

Comedians of the Animal Kingdom

(1) Wildebeests are the comedians of the animal kingdom. (2) From the front they look like an ox, but from the back they look like a horse. (3) Most of the time, they are strange because they groan and make loud noises. (4) If startled by a human, they throw back their large heads. (5) They kick up their heels. (6) Wildebeests are in large groups and travel in search of food and water. (7) Many tourists are on safari enjoy watching them.

---

1 What change, if any, should be made in sentence 1?

  A Change *are* to **sound**

  B Change *are* to an action verb

  C Change *are* to **look**

  D Make no change

2 What change should be made to clarify sentence 3?

  F Change *are* to **feel**

  G Change *are* to **sound**

  H Change *are* to **taste**

  J Change *are* to **eat**

3 What change, if any, should be made to sentence 6?

  A Change *travel* to **grow**

  B Change *are* to **remain**

  C Change *are* to **grow**

  D Make no change

4 What is the BEST way to revise sentence 7?

  F Many tourists are looking for them on safari.

  G They enjoy watching tourists on safari.

  H Many wildebeest enjoy safaris and tourists watching them.

  J Many tourists on safari enjoy watching them.

14.3 Helping Verbs

Sometimes, a verb in a sentence is just one word. Often, however, a verb will be made up of several words. This type of verb is called a **verb phrase**.

WRITING COACH
Online
www.phwritingcoach.com

Grammar Practice
Practice your grammar skills with Writing Coach Online.

Grammar Games
Test your knowledge of grammar in this fast-paced interactive video game.

RULE
14.3.1

> **Helping verbs** are added before another verb to make a **verb phrase**.

Notice how these helping verbs change the meaning of the verb *run*.

EXAMPLES   run   **might have** run

            had run   **should have** run

            will have run   **will be** running

Recognizing Helping Verbs

Forms of *Be* Forms of *be* are often used as helping verbs.

SOME FORMS OF *BE* USED AS HELPING VERBS	
HELPING VERBS	**MAIN VERBS**
am	growing
has been	warned
was being	told
will be	reminded
will have been	waiting
is	opening
was being	trained
should be	written
had been	sent
might have been	played

See Practice 14.3A

Other Helping Verbs Many different verb phrases can be formed using one or more of these helping verbs. The chart below shows just a few.

HELPING VERBS	MAIN VERBS	VERB PHRASES
do	remember	do remember
has	written	has written
would	hope	would hope
shall	see	shall see
can	believe	can believe
could	finish	could finish
may	attempt	may attempt
must have	thought	must have thought
should have	grown	should have grown
might	win	might win
will	jump	will jump
have	planned	have planned
does	want	does want

Sometimes the words in a verb phrase are separated by other words, such as *not* or *certainly*. The parts of the verb phrase in certain types of questions may also be separated.

WORDS SEPARATED

She **could** certainly **have come** earlier.

This **has** not **happened** before.

Marie **has** certainly not **contacted** us.

He **had** carefully **kept** all the records.

Did you ever **expect** to see an elephant?

When **will** we **open** our presents?

Can they really **build** their own home?

They **must** not **have taken** the bus.

Would you ever **want** to go skiing?

See Practice 14.3B

PRACTICE 14.3A > **Identifying Helping and Main Verbs**

Read the sentences. Write *main verb* if the underlined verb is a main verb. Write *helping verb* if it is a helping verb.

EXAMPLE   For weeks now, the weather <u>has</u> been cold and windy.

ANSWER   *helping verb*

1. The school construction <u>was</u> finished in August.

2. They must <u>have</u> believed they were doing the right thing.

3. The children had been <u>told</u> not to go there.

4. You <u>should</u> have seen their faces.

5. If I hadn't called the fire department, the house might have <u>burned</u> down.

6. I have <u>been</u> studying for three hours.

7. By the time we get home, the flowers may have <u>bloomed</u>.

8. The new sewing machine <u>does</u> work.

9. If you had missed the bus, you would have <u>been</u> late.

10. It's spring, and the birds <u>are</u> returning.

PRACTICE 14.3B > **Using Verb Phrases**

Read the verb phrases. Use each verb phrase in an original sentence.

EXAMPLE   were going

ANSWER   We *were going* to the movies.

11. had been dancing

12. must have known

13. might have finished

14. could stay

15. will study

16. have learned

17. did go

18. should rain

19. was growing

20. do wonder

SPEAKING APPLICATION

With a partner, discuss something you've learned in history class. Use helping verbs when you talk. Your partner should listen for and name two examples of helping verbs, along with the main verbs they help.

WRITING APPLICATION

Write three sentences about how things might have been different. You may use any main verbs and any additional helping verbs, but you should choose three of the following: *would, should, could, might,* or *may.*

ADJECTIVES *and* ADVERBS

Make your writing more vivid by using adjectives to describe people, places, and things.

WRITE GUY *Jeff Anderson, M.Ed.*

WHAT DO YOU NOTICE?

Look for adjectives as you zoom in on these sentences from Russell Baker's autobiographical essay "Hard as Nails."

MENTOR TEXT

> Deems was short and plump and had curly brown hair. He owned a car and a light gray suit and always wore a necktie and a white shirt.

Now, ask yourself the following questions:

- In the first sentence, which adjectives modify the proper noun *Deems*, and which two adjectives in a row modify the noun *hair*?
- Which adjective in the second sentence modifies the noun *suit*?

The author describes Deems using the adjectives *short* and *plump* and uses the adjectives *curly* and *brown* to describe Deems's hair. The adjective *gray* modifies the noun *suit*. The word *light* is an adverb, rather than an adjective, because it modifies *gray*.

Grammar for Writers An artist crafts a picture with paint, but a writer uses words to create a picture in the reader's mind. Use a variety of adjectives to help bring your writing to life.

Which two adjectives best describe your book bag?

I only need one: heavy!

15.1 Adjectives

Adjectives are words that make language come alive by adding description or information.

Adjectives help make nouns more specific. For example, *car* is a general word, but a *red two-door car* is more specific. Adjectives such as *red* and *two-door* make nouns and pronouns clearer and more vivid.

RULE 15.1.1

> An **adjective** is a word that describes a noun or pronoun.

Adjectives are often called *modifiers*, because they modify, or change, the meaning of a noun or pronoun. You can use more than one adjective to modify a noun or pronoun. Notice how *game* is modified by each set of adjectives below.

EXAMPLES

old-fashioned game

new video game

children's word game

first baseball game

Adjectives answer several questions about nouns and pronouns. They tell *What kind? Which one? How many?* or *How much?* Numeral adjectives, such as *eleven,* tell exactly how many. In the chart below, notice how adjectives answer these questions.

WHAT KIND?	WHICH ONE?	HOW MANY?	HOW MUCH?
brick house	that judge	one daffodil	no time
white paper	each answer	several roses	enough raisins
serious argument	those sisters	both brothers	many hobbies
colorful shirts	this student	four books	some teams

WRITING COACH

Online

www.phwritingcoach.com

Grammar Tutorials

Brush up on your Grammar skills with these animated videos.

Grammar Practice

Practice your grammar skills with Writing Coach Online.

Grammar Games

Test your knowledge of grammar in this fast-paced interactive video game.

Adjective Position An adjective usually comes before the noun it modifies, as do all the adjectives in the chart on the previous page. Sometimes, however, adjectives come after the nouns they modify.

EXAMPLES
The legal system, **serious** and **complex**, is sometimes hard to understand.
noun · adjective · adjective

The room, **narrow** and **dark**, frightened us.
noun · adjective · adjective

Graphics, **large** and **colorful**, covered the screen.
noun · adjective · adjective

Adjectives that modify pronouns usually come after linking verbs. Sometimes, however, adjectives may come before the pronoun.

AFTER
They were **quiet** and **thoughtful**.
pronoun · adjective · adjective

They are **happy** and **talkative**.
pronoun · adjective · adjective

She is **talented**.
pronoun · adjective

BEFORE
Tall and **elegant**, **she** walked into the room.
adjective · adjective · pronoun

Quiet and **sullen**, **he** sat in a corner.
adjective · adjective · pronoun

Intelligent and **active**, **they** won the tournament.
adjective · adjective · pronoun

See Practice 15.1A
See Practice 15.1B

PRACTICE 15.1A ▷ **Identifying Adjectives**

Read the sentences. Then, write each adjective and list which question it answers. (*What kind? Which one? How many? How much?*)

EXAMPLE   Many people enjoy classical music.

ANSWER   *Many* — How much?
classical — What kind?

1. Australia is home to several unusual animals.

2. The parrot is a clever, friendly bird.

3. That music class was divided into four groups.

4. Some bright colors attract bees.

5. Nitrogen is an important chemical for all plants.

6. Some young people enjoy sports.

7. Eight advanced students went to the science museum.

8. In winter, bright days often bring cold weather.

9. Those little kittens went to five owners.

10. I think red paint will show up best on the gray wall.

PRACTICE 15.1B ▷ **Identifying Adjectives and Words They Modify**

Read the sentences. Then, write the adjectives and the words they modify.

EXAMPLE   Outside the dark house, the sky was blue and cloudless.

ANSWER   *dark, house*
blue, sky
cloudless, sky

11. The ground was covered with the sharp, fragrant needles from the tall pines.

12. It took a long time to build a huge, modern store.

13. The old dirt road was rocky and bumpy.

14. If one person leads, a thousand other people may follow.

15. A hollow tree makes a good place for some birds to nest.

16. The right attitude can make a big difference in many competitions.

17. The water, cool and inviting, tempted us to stop for a short swim.

18. The long blue skirt looks best with the red and white shirt.

19. Most people want a safe, reliable car.

20. Five heavy sweaters will not fit in a little cardboard box.

SPEAKING APPLICATION

With a partner, take turns describing a park near your home or school. Use adjectives to make your description more specific. Your partner should listen for and name three adjectives you used and what they modified.

WRITING APPLICATION

Write three sentences describing what you might see in a store you like. Use adjectives to help readers "see" what you are describing.

Articles

Three frequently used adjectives are the words *a, an,* and *the.*
They are called **articles.** Articles can be **definite** or **indefinite.**
Both types indicate that a noun will soon follow.

> *The* is a **definite article.** It points to a specific person, place,
> thing, or idea. *A* and *an* are **indefinite articles.** They point
> to any member of a group of similar people, places, things, or
> ideas.

DEFINITE   Mr. Ryan is **the** man to call. (a specific person)

Go into **the** gym. (a specific place)

I want to play **the** game. (a specific thing)

INDEFINITE   I want to see **a** game. (any game)

Please take **an** apple. (any apple)

You should see **a** teacher for help. (any teacher)

A is used before consonant sounds. *An* is used before vowel
sounds. You choose between *a* and *an* based on sound. Some
letters are tricky. The letter *h,* a consonant, may sound like either
a consonant or a vowel. The letters *o* and *u* are vowels, but they
may sometimes sound like consonants.

USING *A* AND *AN*	
A WITH CONSONANT SOUNDS	**AN WITH VOWEL SOUNDS**
a blue hat	an endangered water bird
a happy time (*h* sound)	an honest person (no *h* sound)
a one-way street (*w* sound)	an old map (*o* sound)
a unicorn (*y* sound)	an uncle (*u* sound)
a taxi	an opportunity
a pineapple	an angry look
a university (*y* sound)	an eraser

See Practice 15.1C

PRACTICE 15.1C > **Identifying Definite and Indefinite Articles**

Read the sentences. Then, write the articles, and label them *definite* or *indefinite*.

EXAMPLE   A pair of cardinals built their nest in the tree outside my bedroom window.

ANSWER   *A* — indefinite
          the — definite

1. During an average summer day in Antarctica, the temperature is around 20 degrees.

2. The children drew pictures of a waterfall they had seen in an encyclopedia.

3. Javier took a look through the telescope and saw one of the moon's craters.

4. An elephant is quite a sight in the jungles of Southeast Asia.

5. The first time I saw a shooting star, I didn't know what to think.

6. When visiting a new city for the first time, it is important to have a good map.

7. At the zoo, I hoped to see a lion or tiger, but I also wanted to visit the monkey house.

8. It is important when studying a subject like history to remember that the stories are about real people.

9. An unforgettable scene in the movie is when the hero saves a whole town from disaster.

10. After the storm, the clouds parted, and there was a beautiful rainbow.

SPEAKING APPLICATION

With a partner, discuss why picking the correct article—definite or indefinite—is important. Take turns creating examples that show how meaning changes with different articles: "A teacher talked to me" and "The teacher talked to me."

WRITING APPLICATION

Write three sentences, leaving blank spaces where there should be articles. Exchange papers with a partner and fill in the missing articles in each other's papers. Discuss whether the articles chosen were the ones the writer intended.

Using Proper Adjectives

A **proper adjective** begins with a capital letter. There are two types of proper adjectives.

> A **proper adjective** is (1) a proper noun used as an adjective or (2) an adjective formed from a proper noun.

15.1.3 RULE

A proper noun used as an adjective does *not* change its form. It is merely placed in front of another noun.

PROPER NOUNS	USED AS PROPER ADJECTIVES
Thanksgiving	Thanksgiving dinner (*Which* dinner?)
Florida	Florida wetlands (*Which* wetlands?)
December	December weather (*What kind* of weather?)

When an adjective is formed from a proper noun, the proper noun will change its form. Notice that endings such as *-n*, *-ern*, *-ian*, or *-ese* have been added to the proper nouns in the chart below or the spelling has been changed.

PROPER NOUNS	PROPER ADJECTIVES FORMED FROM PROPER NOUNS
America	American history (*Which kind* of history?)
Japan	Japanese cities (*Which* cities?)
Norway	Norwegian legends (*Which* legends?)
Inca	Incan empire (*Which* empire?)
South	Southern hospitality (*Which* hospitality?)

See Practice 15.1D

Using Nouns as Adjectives

Nouns can sometimes be used as adjectives. A noun used as an adjective usually comes directly before another noun and answers the question *What kind?* or *Which one?*

NOUNS	USED AS ADJECTIVES
shoe	a shoe salesperson (*What kind* of salesperson?)
waterfowl	the waterfowl refuge (*Which* refuge?)
court	a court date (*What kind* of date?)
morning	a morning appointment (*What kind* of appointment?)

Using Compound Adjectives

Adjectives, like nouns, can be compound.

RULE 15.1.4

> A **compound adjective** is made up of more than one word.

Most **compound adjectives** are written as hyphenated words. Some are written as combined words, as in "a *runaway* horse." If you are unsure about how to write a compound adjective, look up the word in a dictionary.

HYPHENATED	COMBINED
a well-known actress	a featherweight boxer
a full-time job	a freshwater lake
snow-covered mountains	a sideways glance
one-sided opinions	heartbreaking news
so-called experts	a nearsighted witness

See Practice 15.1E

PRACTICE 15.1D > Using Proper Adjectives

Read each group of words. Then, rewrite the words to include a proper adjective before the underlined noun.

EXAMPLE   a <u>shop</u> in Morocco

ANSWER   *a Moroccan shop*

1. a <u>visitor</u> from Russia
2. <u>birds</u> from South America
3. an <u>invention</u> from Australia
4. <u>food</u> from Mexico
5. <u>salmon</u> from Alaska
6. the <u>flag</u> of Britain
7. a <u>castle</u> built by a German
8. <u>pepper</u> from Brazil
9. the <u>artwork</u> of China
10. <u>pyramids</u> in Egypt

PRACTICE 15.1E > Recognizing Nouns Used as Adjectives

Read the sentences. Write the noun, proper noun, or compound noun used as an adjective. Then, write the noun that the adjective modifies.

EXAMPLE   He enjoyed watching the trains in the railroad yard.

ANSWER   *railroad, yard*

11. December weather is usually cold.
12. The laptop computer might work.
13. We built a stone fireplace.
14. The Lincoln exhibit leaves soon.
15. It looked like a scene from a Dickens novel.
16. I need a guide to Chicago restaurants.
17. Both sides signed the cease-fire treaty.
18. Would you like to visit a South Pacific island?
19. The steel blade gleamed in the dim light.
20. The story came from a newspaper reporter.

SPEAKING APPLICATION

With a partner, take turns describing places around the world that interest you, being sure to use proper adjectives or proper nouns as adjectives. Your partner should listen for and name three or more of the adjectives.

WRITING APPLICATION

Write three sentences and include three of the following: a noun used as an adjective, a compound noun used as an adjective, a proper noun used as an adjective, or a proper adjective.

Practice   335

Using Pronouns as Adjectives

Pronouns, like nouns, can sometimes be used as adjectives.

15.1.5 ▷

> **A pronoun becomes an adjective if it modifies a noun.**

EXAMPLES   We see the ducklings on **this** side of the pond.

Which ducks are the males?

In the first example, the demonstrative pronoun *this* modifies *side*, and in the second example, the interrogative pronoun *which* modifies *ducks*.

Using Possessive Nouns and Pronouns as Adjectives

The following personal pronouns are often **possessive adjectives:** *my, your, her, his, its, our,* and *their*. They are adjectives because they come before nouns and answer the question *Which one?* They are pronouns because they have antecedents.

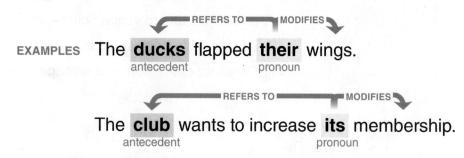

EXAMPLES   The **ducks** flapped **their** wings.
              antecedent   pronoun

The **club** wants to increase **its** membership.
     antecedent   pronoun

In the first example, *their* is an adjective because it modifies *wings*. At the same time, it is a pronoun because it refers to the antecedent *ducks*.

In the second example, *its* is an adjective because it modifies *membership*. The word *its* is also a pronoun because it refers to the antecedent *club*.

Note About Possessive Nouns Possessive nouns function as adjectives when they modify a noun.

EXAMPLES   The pond is on **Mrs. Smith's** property.

The **duck's** feathers are colorful.

See Practice 15.1F

Using Demonstrative Adjectives

This, *that*, *these*, and *those*—the four demonstrative pronouns—can also be **demonstrative adjectives.**

PRONOUN	We saw **that**.
ADJECTIVE	**That** lake is home to many geese.
PRONOUN	What are **these**?
ADJECTIVE	**These** gulls are searching for food.

Using Interrogative Adjectives

Which, *what*, and *whose*—three of the interrogative pronouns—can be **interrogative adjectives.**

PRONOUN	**Which** do you think he will choose?
ADJECTIVE	**Which** parrot do you think he will buy?
PRONOUN	**Whose** can that be?
ADJECTIVE	**Whose** macaw can that be?

Using Indefinite Adjectives

A number of indefinite pronouns—*both*, *few*, *many*, *each*, *most*, and *all*, among others—can also be used as **indefinite adjectives.**

PRONOUN	I bought one of **each**.
ADJECTIVE	**Each** judge writes an opinion.
PRONOUN	I don't want **any**.
ADJECTIVE	I don't want **any** help.

See Practice 15.1G

Recognizing Possessive Nouns and Pronouns Used as Adjectives

Read the sentences. Then, write the possessive noun or pronoun used as an adjective in each sentence.

EXAMPLE   Dad almost forgot his wallet this morning.

ANSWER   *his*

1. I walked by Mr. Levin's house.

2. Mom let me wear her bracelet.

3. The Sanchez children are going to visit their grandmother.

4. Mrs. Kamora's brownies are the best.

5. Why don't you bring your dog with you?

6. When we studied about Jamestown, I enjoyed John Smith's story.

7. Mr. Madorsky let me use his lawn mower.

8. Mrs. Cleary asked the three of us to talk about our vacations.

9. Freddie Johnson's home run tied the game.

10. Did you want me to show you my photographs?

Identifying Demonstrative, Interrogative, and Indefinite Adjectives

Read the sentences. Then, write the adjective in each sentence and label it *demonstrative,* *interrogative,* or *indefinite*.

EXAMPLE   These shoes don't fit me anymore.

ANSWER   *These* — demonstrative

11. Which color do you think looks best on me?

12. Does this dress make me look too young?

13. That bowl will hold the fruit we bought.

14. I have only a few dollars, but I think it's enough.

15. What vegetable should I serve with fish?

16. Most doctors encourage people to eat right.

17. Call and find out if both boys are coming for dinner.

18. I wonder if those shirts will fit Johnny.

19. Whose books are those on the table?

20. Do you have many adventure movies in your collection?

SPEAKING APPLICATION

With a partner, take turns talking about something you or someone you know collects. Your partner should listen for and name two possessive pronouns.

WRITING APPLICATION

Write three or four sentences about your neighborhood. Write about people's houses, pets, and anything else that would give you an opportunity to use possessive nouns and possessive pronouns as adjectives.

15.2 Adverbs

Adverbs can modify three different parts of speech. They make the meaning of verbs, adjectives, or other adverbs more precise.

RULE
15.2.1

> An **adverb** modifies a verb, an adjective, or another adverb.

Although adverbs may modify adjectives and other adverbs, they generally modify verbs.

Using Adverbs That Modify Verbs

Adverbs that modify verbs will answer one of these four questions: *Where? When? In what way? To what extent?* These adverbs are also known as *adverbs of place, adverbs of time, adverbs of manner,* and *adverbs of degree*.

WRITING COACH

Online

www.phwritingcoach.com

Grammar Tutorials
Brush up on your Grammar skills with these animated videos.

Grammar Practice
Practice your grammar skills with Writing Coach Online.

Grammar Games
Test your knowledge of grammar in this fast-paced interactive video game.

ADVERBS THAT MODIFY VERBS			
WHERE?	**WHEN?**	**IN WHAT WAY?**	**TO WHAT EXTENT?**
push upward	will leave soon	works carefully	hardly ate
fell there	comes daily	speaks well	really surprised
stay nearby	swims often	chews noisily	almost cried
go outside	exhibits yearly	acted willingly	partly finished
is here	report later	walk quietly	nearly won
jump away	come tomorrow	smiled happily	fully agree
drove down	went yesterday	moved gracefully	totally oppose

Negative adverbs, such as *not, never,* and *nowhere,* also modify verbs.

EXAMPLES   Helen **never** **arrived** at the party.
                         adverb   verb

I **could** **not** **answer** the question.
  verb   adverb   verb

The trail in the forest **led** **nowhere**.
                          verb   adverb

See Practice 15.2A

Using Adverbs That Modify Adjectives

An adverb modifying an adjective answers only one question:
To what extent?

> When adverbs modify adjectives or adverbs, they answer the question *To what extent?*

ADVERBS THAT MODIFY ADJECTIVES	
very upset	extremely tall
definitely wrong	not hungry

EXAMPLE　Forests can be **very** **beautiful**.

The adverb *very* modifies the adjective *beautiful*.

EXAMPLE　The building is **extremely** **tall**.

The adverb *extremely* modifies the adjective *tall*.

Adverbs Modifying Other Adverbs

When adverbs modify other adverbs, they again answer the question *To what extent?*

ADVERBS MODIFYING ADVERBS	
traveled less slowly	move very cautiously
lost too easily	lived almost happily

EXAMPLE　The raccoon and beaver are **hardly** **ever** seen in dry areas of the forest.

The adverb *hardly* modifies the adverb *ever*.

EXAMPLE　When running, I get tired **too** **quickly**.

The adverb *too* modifies the adverb *quickly*.

See Practice 15.2B

PRACTICE 15.2A **Identifying How Adverbs Modify Verbs**

Read the sentences. Write the adverb in each sentence and list what question it answers. (*When? Where? In what way? To what extent?*)

EXAMPLE Put the table there.

ANSWER *there* — Where?

1. I hope this friendship never ends.

2. Carnations will grow well in this garden.

3. Rhonda seemed extremely excited at the fair.

4. Yesterday, I saw a bird fly out of the library.

5. Carlos seems very upset.

6. Jeffrey did his chores carelessly.

7. Mrs. Shapiro can take us home later.

8. You should put your boots outside.

9. Celia works on her science fair project happily.

10. Bring the flowers here.

PRACTICE 15.2B **Recognizing Adverbs and Words They Modify**

Read the sentences. Write the word that each underlined adverb modifies. Then, write whether that word is a *verb*, an *adjective*, or an *adverb*.

EXAMPLE In 1950, <u>very</u> few people had televisions.

ANSWER *few* — *adjective*

11. By mid-afternoon, we had <u>successfully</u> completed our snow fort.

12. We washed the dishes <u>very</u> carefully.

13. The two scientists were <u>extremely</u> precise when recording their discoveries.

14. In the early days of airplane travel, flying was <u>quite</u> dangerous.

15. Some stuntmen have been injured <u>rather</u> seriously while making movies.

16. When we finally saw a gas station, the car's gas tank was <u>nearly</u> empty.

17. My grandmother returned <u>safely</u> from her first ride in a boat.

18. This book on rare animals is <u>definitely</u> interesting.

19. Did you know you can fly <u>nonstop</u> from Chicago to Beijing?

20. My sister <u>hardly</u> ever forgets to feed the dog.

SPEAKING APPLICATION

With a partner, take turns talking about activities you do regularly. Your partner should listen for three adverbs you use and say which question each adverb answers.

WRITING APPLICATION

Write three sentences about someone you admire—from your life or from history. Modify at least one verb, one adjective, and one adverb with an adverb.

Finding Adverbs in Sentences

Adverbs can be found in different places in sentences. The chart below shows examples of possible locations for adverbs. Arrows point to the words that the adverbs modify.

LOCATION OF ADVERBS IN SENTENCES	
LOCATION	EXAMPLE
At the beginning of a sentence	Silently, she approached the ocean.
At the end of a sentence	She approached the ocean silently.
Before a verb	She silently approached the ocean.
After a verb	She tiptoed silently into the ocean.
Between parts of a verb phrase	She had silently entered the ocean.
Before an adjective	Her father was always quiet.
Before another adverb	Her father spoke rather quietly.

Conjunctive adverbs **Conjunctive adverbs** are adverbs that join independent clauses. (See Chapter 17 for more about conjunctive adverbs.)

EXAMPLES   She injured her leg; **therefore**, she couldn't play in

                                            conjunctive adverb

the game.

Ben predicted his score in the game; **however**,

                                                          conjunctive adverb

his prediction was not accurate.

See Practice 15.2C

Adverb or Adjective?

Some words can function as adverbs or as adjectives, depending on their use in a sentence.

> If a noun or pronoun is modified by a word, that modifying word is an **adjective.** If a verb, adjective, or adverb is modified by a word, that modifying word is an **adverb.**

15.2.3 **RULE**

An adjective will modify a noun or pronoun and will answer one of the questions *What kind? Which one? How many?* or *How much?*

An adverb will modify a verb, an adjective, or another adverb and will answer one of the questions *Where? When? In what way?* or *To what extent?*

ADVERB MODIFYING VERB

Lumberjacks **work** **hard**.
_____verb____adverb

When the wolves reached the clearing,

they **turned** **right**.
_____verb_____adverb

ADJECTIVE MODIFYING NOUN

Lumberjacks accomplish **hard** **tasks**.
_____adjective__noun

The **right** **side** of the road is a good spot
___adjective__noun
to view the wolves safely.

While most words ending in *-ly* are adverbs, some are not. Several adjectives also end in *-ly.* These adjectives are formed by adding *-ly* to nouns.

ADJECTIVES WITH -LY ENDINGS

a **kingly** feast

a **friendly** person

See Practice 15.2D
See Practice 15.2E
See Practice 15.2F

EXAMPLES

At the restaurant, we enjoyed a **kingly** feast.

I like Andrew; he is such a **friendly** person.

Read the sentences. Then, write each adverb and the word or words it modifies.

EXAMPLE   The chair was amazingly old and had almost broken when it was moved.

ANSWER   *amazingly, old*
          almost, had broken

1. The hiker slowly climbed the very steep trail.

2. Suddenly, we came to a garden where flowers had been carefully planted.

3. Spring always seems nicer after a really harsh winter.

4. Our team easily defeated our rivals.

5. The mountains looked especially beautiful on that wonderfully sunny day.

6. Eventually, the boys learned that the plans they had quickly made would not work.

7. My mom gently placed the kitten directly behind my sister.

8. Noisily, the chickens rushed toward the recently filled feed bin.

9. The marathon runners crossed the finish line wearily.

10. We often return to the place where we had luckily found a good campsite.

Read the sentences. Then, write whether each underlined word is an *adjective* or an *adverb*.

EXAMPLE   He answered <u>wisely</u>.

ANSWER   *adverb*

11. The fever is gone, and the doctor says Billy is <u>well</u>.

12. She loves ballet, and she dances <u>well</u>.

13. He worked <u>hard</u> at the math problems.

14. The farmer broke up the <u>hard</u> dirt.

15. Anna and Chen were there by 4:00, but Sasha arrived <u>later</u>.

16. They decided to take a <u>later</u> bus.

17. There's an <u>outside</u> chance we'll make it to the playoffs.

18. If you want to play ball, you need to play <u>outside</u>.

19. He held the book <u>close</u> to the light.

20. That was a <u>close</u> race!

SPEAKING APPLICATION

With a partner, take turns telling about an interesting book you recently read. Your partner should listen for and name three adverbs you used.

WRITING APPLICATION

Write two pairs of sentences, using the same word in each sentence of a pair—once as an adverb and once as an adjective.

PRACTICE 15.2E **Identifying Adjectives and Adverbs**

Read the sentences. Write the adverb or the adjective in each sentence and label it.

EXAMPLE   He took a straight path to his friend's house.

ANSWER   *straight* — adjective

1. My answer on the test was wrong.

2. Justin reads fast when he likes the book.

3. The milk tastes sour to me.

4. He writes harshly about his childhood in the memoir.

5. There was dew on the grass in the early sunshine.

6. Arte finished entirely on his own.

7. Lilianna speaks unkindly of no one.

8. The check will go straight into the bank.

9. Ancient pieces of gold were found by the archaeologists.

10. Her necklace is beautiful.

PRACTICE 15.2F **Recognizing Adverbs and Adjectives**

Read the sentences. Find at least one adverb and one adjective in each. Write the words and label them *adverb* or *adjective*.

EXAMPLE   Lee wisely stopped before spending his last dollar.

ANSWER   *wisely* — adverb
            last — adjective

11. Her mother carefully ties Kesi's long hair with ribbon.

12. The concert was really extraordinary.

13. She shouted out in a very loud voice to warn me.

14. Roz is going home early to watch her new baby sister.

15. He will never walk to school on a rainy day.

16. Early risers like to watch the sun come up slowly over the horizon.

17. This is certainly the best meal that I ever ate.

18. Ryan proudly introduced the opening act in the show.

19. The snake's skin is incredibly smooth.

20. Our school is growing more rapidly every year.

SPEAKING APPLICATION

Take turns with a partner. Describe what you do after school. Your partner will identify all the adjectives and adverbs that you use in your description.

WRITING APPLICATION

Write a brief paragraph about an experience you had recently. Use at least three adjectives and three adverbs. Exchange papers with a partner. Your partner should underline all the adjectives and circle all the adverbs in your paragraph.

Test Warm-Up

DIRECTIONS
Read the introduction and the passage that follows. Then, answer the questions to show that you can use and understand the function of adjectives and adverbs in reading and writing.

Tom wrote this paragraph about his neighbor, Ms. Flowers. Read the paragraph and think about the changes you would suggest as a peer editor. When you finish reading, answer the questions that follow.

Keeping in Touch

(1) Early Monday morning, I was walking quick because the bus usually pulled up at 7:30. (2) As I looked across the dusty road at the tiny old cottage, I wondered about its owner, Ms. Flowers. (3) It was a real long time since I had seen her. (4) When I was little, she told me marvelous stories and the stories were adventure. (5) I decided to visit her after school. (6) She has a rock collection. (7) I will take her a rock that I found, and it was unusual.

---

1 What change, if any, should be made in sentence 1?

  A Add a comma before *Monday*

  B Change *quick* to **quickly**

  C Change *usually* to **usual**

  D Make no change

2 What change, if any, should be made in sentence 3?

  F Change *real* to **really**

  G Add a comma before *since*

  H Change *long* to **longly**

  J Make no change

3 What is the BEST way to revise sentence 4?

  A When I was little, she told me marvelous stories and the stories were adventures.

  B When I was little, she told me marvelous adventure stories.

  C When I was little, she told me adventures that were stories.

  D When I was little she told me marvelous stories and adventures.

4 What is the BEST way to combine sentences 6 and 7?

  F She has a rock collection. I will take her an unusually rock that I found.

  G She has a rock collection, and I will take her a rock that I found, unusual.

  H She has a rock collection, so I will take her an unusual rock that I found.

  J She has a rock collection, so I will take her a rock that I found unusually.

PREPOSITIONS

Use prepositions in your writing to make connections between words and ideas clearer.

CHAPTER 16

WRITE GUY *Jeff Anderson, M.Ed.*

WHAT DO YOU NOTICE?

Look for prepositions as you zoom in on these lines from the play *The Phantom Tollbooth* by Susan Nanus, based on the book by Norton Juster.

MENTOR TEXT

> In this box are the letters of the alphabet. With them you can form all the words you will ever need to help you overcome the obstacles that may stand in your path.

Now, ask yourself the following questions:

- Which preposition shows the relationship between the letters and the box, and which preposition connects the word *letters* to the phrase *the alphabet*?
- Which preposition connects *stand* to *your path*?

The preposition *in* shows the location of the letters; they are inside the box. The preposition *of* connects *letters* and *the alphabet*. The preposition *in* connects *stand* and *your path* to show where someone might stand.

Grammar for Writers Making clear connections between words and ideas is an essential part of a writer's task. Think of prepositions as strings you use to tie together different parts of your writing.

Yesterday, my sister told me to balance a book in my head.

Wait a minute. She meant on your head!

16.1 Prepositions

Prepositions function as connectors, relating one word to another within a sentence.

WRITING COACH

Online

www.phwritingcoach.com

They allow a speaker or writer to express the link between separate items. **Prepositions** can convey information about location, time, or direction or provide details.

Grammar Tutorials

Brush up on your Grammar skills with these animated videos.

Grammar Practice

Practice your grammar skills with Writing Coach Online.

Grammar Games

Test your knowledge of grammar in this fast-paced interactive video game.

RULE 16.1.1

> A **preposition** relates the noun or pronoun following it to another word in the sentence.

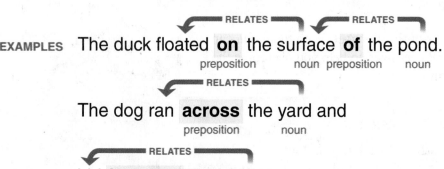

EXAMPLES

The duck floated **on** the surface **of** the pond.
preposition   noun   preposition   noun

The dog ran **across** the yard and
preposition   noun

hid **between** the bushes.
preposition   noun

In the first example, the duck floated where? (on the surface) It was the surface of what? (the pond) In the second example, the dog ran where? (across the yard) The dog hid where? (between the bushes)

FIFTY COMMON PREPOSITIONS				
about	behind	during	off	to
above	below	except	on	toward
across	beneath	for	onto	under
after	beside	from	opposite	underneath
against	besides	in	out	until
along	between	inside	outside	up
among	beyond	into	over	upon
around	but	like	past	with
at	by	near	since	within
before	down	of	through	without

See Practice 16.1A

Compound Prepositions Prepositions consisting of more than one word are called **compound prepositions.** Some of them are listed in the chart below:

COMPOUND PREPOSITIONS		
according to	by means of	instead of
ahead of	in addition to	in view of
apart from	in back of	next to
aside from	in front of	on account of
as of	in place of	on top of
because of	in spite of	out of

See Practice 16.1B

Because prepositions have different meanings, using a particular preposition will affect the way other words in a sentence relate to one another. In the first sentence, for example, notice how each preposition changes the relationship between *parade* and *City Hall.*

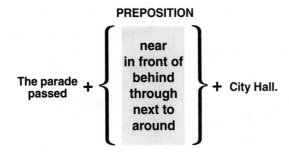

In this sentence, the preposition changes the relationship between *girls* and *gym.*

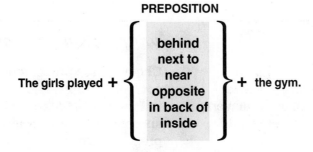

PRACTICE 16.1A **Identifying Prepositions**

Read the sentences. Write the preposition in each sentence. Then, write the function of the preposition (to convey *location*, *time*, or *direction*, or to provide *details*).

EXAMPLE   Just tie a string around the middle.

ANSWER   *around* — location

1. Some people live on islands.

2. The ball got stuck underneath the car.

3. We heard a large crash in the next room.

4. Put the wood beside the fireplace.

5. Finally, the boat disappeared beyond the horizon.

6. Have you thought of a topic?

7. We were excited to find that it had snowed during the night.

8. There are mountains, valleys, and volcanoes under the sea.

9. We left before sunrise to go fishing.

10. There was a high fence between the two yards.

PRACTICE 16.1B **Identifying Compound Prepositions**

Read the sentences. Then, write the compound preposition in each sentence.

EXAMPLE   They worked hard and finished ahead of schedule.

ANSWER   *ahead of*

11. I'll have a salad instead of the soup.

12. Because of the storm, we have to go home.

13. Put the small picture in front of the larger one.

14. Some really fabulous food comes out of my mom's kitchen.

15. In addition to herbs, we planted several vegetables.

16. Don't get too far ahead of your sister.

17. The fire extinguisher is next to the fire alarm.

18. In back of the school, there's a large playing field.

19. The coach communicated by means of hand signals.

20. The game was canceled on account of rain.

SPEAKING APPLICATION

With a partner, take turns discussing a ball game, using prepositions to describe where players are in relation to the ball, other players, or positions on the field. Your partner should listen for and name four prepositions.

WRITING APPLICATION

Choose three prepositions and three compound prepositions from the sentences in Practice 16.1A and Practice 16.1B. Write six sentences of your own, using a different preposition or compound preposition in each to convey location, time, or direction, or to provide details.

Prepositions Used in Sentences

A preposition is never used by itself in a sentence. Instead, it appears as part of a phrase containing one or more other words.

> A **preposition** in a sentence always introduces a **prepositional phrase.**

Prepositional Phrases

A **prepositional phrase** is a group of words that begins with a preposition and ends with a noun or pronoun. The noun or pronoun following the preposition is the **object of the preposition.**

Some prepositional phrases contain just two words—the preposition and its object. Others are longer because they contain modifiers.

EXAMPLES

in **water**
preposition object

from the solar **system**
preposition object

in place of the old, broken **antenna**
preposition object

inside the large, modern **stadium**
preposition object

with **us**
preposition object

according to the new **coach**
preposition object

See Practice 16.1C
See Practice 16.1D
See Practice 16.1E
See Practice 16.1F
See Practice 16.1H

Prepositional phrases convey information about location, time, or direction or provide details. (See Chapter 23 to learn about prepositional phrases and their influence on subject–verb agreement.)

Preposition or Adverb?

Some words can be used either as prepositions or as adverbs. The following chart lists some examples. When the word is used as a preposition, it begins a prepositional phrase and is followed by the object of the preposition. If the word has no object, it is probably being used as an adverb.

PREPOSITION OR ADVERB		
above	inside	outside
after	nearby	past
around	opposite	underneath
before	out	within

PREPOSITION The broken panel was **outside** the spacecraft.

ADVERB The astronauts slowly stepped **outside**.

PREPOSITION He appeared **before** the court.

ADVERB I had not realized that **before**.

PREPOSITION The ball flew **past** third base.

ADVERB The umpire ran **past** quickly.

PREPOSITION They sat **inside** the dugout.

ADVERB Please come **inside** soon.

PREPOSITION The umpire stands **behind** the catcher.

ADVERB Harry stayed **behind**.

See Practice 16.1G

PREPOSITION The team lined up **nearby** the water fountain.

ADVERB Please play **nearby**.

PRACTICE 16.1C **Recognizing Prepositional Phrases**

Read the sentences. Write the prepositional phrase in each sentence, and underline the object of the preposition. Then, write the function of the prepositional phrase (to convey *location*, *time*, or *direction*, or to provide *details*).

EXAMPLE   I read it in the Sunday newspaper.

ANSWER   *in the Sunday newspaper—location*

1. During recess, we played soccer.

2. He parked the car in front of their house.

3. The teacher hung the calendar near the clock.

4. He saved his money to buy a new pair of shoes.

5. A submarine can travel beneath the water's surface.

6. Maria will be going in place of Jolene.

7. The baker turned the flour into bread.

8. Wildflowers had bloomed along the path.

9. He pushed hard against the door but found it wouldn't open.

10. The nature photographer hiked through the old forest.

PRACTICE 16.1D **Distinguishing Prepositions and Prepositional Phrases**

Read the sentences. Write the prepositional phrases. Then, underline the preposition in each phrase.

EXAMPLE   Just leave the package inside the screen door.

ANSWER   *inside the screen door*

11. He wondered if he could climb over the fence.

12. Across from the store, there's a mailbox.

13. School was canceled today because of the snow.

14. The students gathered outside the classroom.

15. In the closet, you'll find extra blankets.

16. He put a flag on top of the fort.

17. We drove toward the next town.

18. Underneath the porch, the rabbit felt safe.

19. Dad helped me look for my lost homework.

20. Is there anything interesting on television?

SPEAKING APPLICATION

With a partner, take turns describing your location. Use at least two prepositional phrases to convey location. Your partner should name the prepositional phrases and the prepositions.

WRITING APPLICATION

Write three sentences about your neighborhood. Use at least one prepositional phrase in each sentence to convey location, time, or direction, or to provide details. Circle the prepositions and underline the objects of the prepositions.

Read and discuss the sentences with a partner. Choose the appropriate preposition or prepositional phrase in parentheses. Then, write the sentences.

EXAMPLE   New tenants moved _____. (into the apartment, with the apartment)

ANSWER   *New tenants moved into the apartment.*

1. Nobody _____ seems ready. (instead of, but me)

2. We left _____ our gear. (across, without)

3. _____ Friday, he made the team. (Next to, As of)

4. Keshia headed _____. (in the wrong direction, against the wrong direction)

5. We expect them soon, _____ the other guests. (by means of, ahead of)

6. _____, I have a meeting. (According to, In addition)

7. Our place is _____ that house. (next to, on top of)

8. _____, we are leaving. (Around five o'clock sharp, At five o'clock sharp)

9. Please put your books _____. (inside your desks, through your desks)

10. The restaurant is _____ the museum and fountain. (among, between)

Read the sentences. Rewrite them adding at least one prepositional phrase to convey location, time, or direction, or to provide details. Then, read your sentences to a partner and discuss the function of your prepositional phrase.

EXAMPLE   Lunch will be served.

ANSWER   *At noon, lunch will be served in the cafeteria.*

11. You can find the post office.

12. Our cat had three kittens.

13. Today is our committee meeting.

14. My little brother was hiding.

15. I take an exercise class.

16. The marathon is this Sunday.

17. Dad bought a new car.

18. Will you come?

19. Tomorrow is the final audition.

20. Dr. Freeman's office will not be open.

SPEAKING APPLICATION

With a partner, talk about your school. Use prepositions and prepositional phrases to convey location, time, or direction, or to provide details. Then, write four sentences about your school using prepositional phrases.

WRITING APPLICATION

Write a paragraph about a store. Use at least five prepositions and prepositional phrases to convey location, time, or direction, or to provide details. Have a partner underline the prepositions and prepositional phrases.

PRACTICE 16.1G **Distinguishing Prepositions and Adverbs**

Read the sentences. Label each underlined word *preposition* or *adverb*.

EXAMPLE   My excitement grew as the day of the party drew <u>near</u>.

ANSWER   *adverb*

1. Leticia was afraid she would be left <u>behind</u>.
2. Is the library <u>behind</u> the school?
3. I left my wet boots <u>by</u> the door.
4. We watched the horses race <u>by</u>.
5. They built a bridge <u>over</u> the stream.
6. If you have time, why don't you come <u>over</u>?
7. He wondered if he'd ever learn what was <u>inside</u> the box.
8. To really appreciate the house, you have to go <u>inside</u>.
9. Stefan asked if he could come <u>along</u>.
10. Be careful that you cut <u>along</u> the dotted line.

PRACTICE 16.1H **Supplying Prepositions and Prepositional Phrases**

Read the sentences. Then, expand each sentence by adding a prepositional phrase that begins with a preposition of your choice, or use one of these prepositions: *in, for, on, of, by, from, with, into, between, through,* or *about*.

EXAMPLE   We watched the dogs play.

ANSWER   *We watched the dogs play in the yard.*

11. There were many clouds.
12. I received a package.
13. May I bring my cat?
14. What did you find out?
15. She found her paper.
16. We saw a groundhog digging.
17. Gabriella put the book down.
18. Jeremy bought a watch.
19. I thought I would look.
20. There is a movie I want to see.

SPEAKING APPLICATION

With a partner, take turns saying a sentence. Use the sentences in Practice 16.1H as models. Have your partner repeat the sentence, adding a prepositional phrase.

WRITING APPLICATION

Use the sentences in Practice 16.1G as models, and write two pairs of sentences. Each pair should have one sentence with a preposition and one sentence in which the same word is used as an adverb.

Test Warm-Up

DIRECTIONS
Read the introduction and the passage that follows. Then, answer the questions to show that you can use and understand the function of prepositions and prepositional phrases in reading and writing.

The following paragraph describes the layout of a community garden. Read the paragraph and think about the changes you would suggest as a peer editor. When you finish reading, answer the questions that follow.

The Community Garden

(1) A group of neighbors planted a garden in a vacant lot across from the fire station. (2) Before winter's end, they dug into the soil and laid out the beds. (3) They planted taller plants like corn near the back. (4) Sunflowers were planted without the tomato plants. (5) Summer squash was sown to the right of the cucumbers and to the left of the lettuce. (6) People said working in the garden was relaxing and fun. (7) The first shoots appeared on about the beginning of April.

---

1 What change should be made in sentence 4?

  A Change *without* to **inside**

  B Change *without* to **next to**

  C Change *planted* to **into**

  D Change *without* to **during**

2 What is the BEST way to rewrite the ideas in sentence 5?

  F Summer squash was sown without the cucumbers or the lettuce.

  G Summer squash was sown inside the cucumbers and the lettuce.

  H Summer squash was sown upon the cucumbers and the lettuce.

  J Summer squash was sown between the cucumbers and the lettuce.

3 What change should be made to clarify sentence 6?

  A Change *People said* to **People never said**

  B Change *People said* to **In spite of the snow,**

  C Change *People said* to **In view of the vegetables,**

  D Change *People said* to **According to people in the group,**

4 What is the BEST way to revise sentence 7?

  F The first shoots appeared around the beginning of April.

  G The first shoots appeared within the beginning of April.

  H The first shoots appeared upon the beginning of April.

  J The first shoots appeared under the beginning of April.

CHAPTER 17

CONJUNCTIONS *and* INTERJECTIONS

Use conjunctions to connect and highlight important ideas in your writing; add interjections to help create emotion.

WRITE GUY *Jeff Anderson, M.Ed.*

WHAT DO YOU NOTICE?

Watch for conjunctions as you zoom in on these sentences from the book *The Pigman & Me* by Paul Zindel.

MENTOR TEXT

> Life does that to us a lot. Just when we think something awful's going to happen one way, it throws you a curve and the something awful happens another way.

Now, ask yourself the following questions:

- Which idea does the subordinating conjunction *when* introduce?
- Which groups of words does the coordinating conjunction *and* link in the second sentence?

The subordinating conjunction *when* introduces the dependent idea *we think something awful's going to happen one way.* The main idea is *it throws you a curve and the something awful happens another way.* The coordinating conjunction *and* links *it throws you a curve* with *the something awful happens another way.*

Grammar for Writers You can add variety to your writing by placing a subordinating conjunction, such as *if*, in different locations in a sentence. *If it snows, they will cancel school. They will cancel school if it snows.*

I think I'll have a conjunction for lunch.

Okay. Are you having the soup and sandwich with a salad or vegetable?

17.1 Conjunctions

Conjunctions are like links in a chain: They help you join words and ideas.

WRITING COACH
Online
www.phwritingcoach.com

Grammar Tutorials
Brush up on your Grammar skills with these animated videos.

Grammar Practice
Practice your grammar skills with Writing Coach Online.

Grammar Games
Test your knowledge of grammar in this fast-paced interactive video game.

RULE 17.1.1

> A **conjunction** connects words or groups of words.

Conjunctions fall into three groups: **Coordinating conjunctions, correlative conjunctions,** and **subordinating conjunctions.**

Coordinating Conjunctions

RULE 17.1.2

> **Coordinating conjunctions** connect words of the same kind, such as two or more nouns or verbs. They can also connect larger groups of words, such as prepositional phrases or even complete sentences.

COORDINATING CONJUNCTIONS						
and	but	for	nor	or	so	yet

In the following examples, notice the coordinating conjunctions that connect the highlighted words.

Connecting Nouns	My cousin and his wife left today for a trip to Washington, D.C.
Connecting Verbs	They printed directions but forgot to bring them.
Connecting Prepositional Phrases	Put the luggage onto the doorstep or into the garage.
Connecting Two Sentences	The flowers were blooming, yet it was still cold outside.

See Practice 17.1A

Correlative Conjunctions

Correlative conjunctions are *pairs* of words that connect similar kinds of words or groups of words.

CORRELATIVE CONJUNCTIONS		
both . . . and	neither . . . nor	whether . . . or
either . . . or	not only . . . but also	

Notice the correlative conjunctions in the following examples.

Connecting Nouns	Either the van or the bus will pick us up.
Connecting Pronouns	Neither he nor she is to be blamed.
Connecting Verbs	Every morning, she both runs and swims.
Connecting Prepositional Phrases	She'll come—whether by train or by plane, I can't say.
Connecting Two Clauses	Not only do they sing, but also they dance.

See Practice 17.1B

Subordinating Conjunctions

Subordinating conjunctions connect two ideas by making one idea dependent on the other.

17.1.3 RULE

FREQUENTLY USED SUBORDINATING CONJUNCTIONS				
after	as soon as	if	though	whenever
although	as though	in order that	till	where
as	because	since	unless	wherever
as if	before	so that	until	while
as long as	even though	than	when	

The Dependent Idea The subordinating conjunction always introduces the dependent idea. The subordinating conjunction connects the dependent idea to the main idea.

EXAMPLES   I did the planning **after** he made the date.

When he rested, he felt better.

The examples show that the main idea can come at the beginning or at the end of the sentence. When the dependent idea comes first, it must be separated from the main idea with a comma. If the dependent idea comes second, no comma is necessary.

See Practice 17.1C
See Practice 17.1D
See Practice 17.1E

Conjunctive Adverbs

Conjunctive adverbs are used as conjunctions to connect complete ideas. They are often used as transitions, connecting different ideas by showing comparisons, contrasts, or results.

Transitional Words and Phrases The transitional words in the chart below, and transitional phrases such as *on the contrary* and *in addition,* are used in writing to provide coherence and improve organization.

CONJUNCTIVE ADVERBS			
accordingly	consequently	indeed	otherwise
again	finally	instead	then
also	furthermore	moreover	therefore
besides	however	nevertheless	thus

Notice the punctuation that is used before and after the conjunctive adverb in the following example. (See Chapter 25 for more about punctuation with conjunctive adverbs.)

EXAMPLE   The film was great; **however**, I prefer the play.

See Practice 17.1F
See Practice 17.1G
See Practice 17.1H
See Practice 17.1I
See Practice 17.1J

PRACTICE 17.1A Supplying Coordinating Conjunctions

Read the sentences. Then, write each sentence, replacing the blank with a coordinating conjunction that makes sense in the sentence.

EXAMPLE   Was Mr. Kim born in Korea _____ the United States?

ANSWER   *Was Mr. Kim born in Korea or the United States?*

1. We weren't on time for the first show, _____ we went to the second show.

2. I like mustard _____ relish on my hot dog.

3. The necklace was expensive _____ seemed worth every penny.

4. We could not score a goal, _____ could we stop our opponents from scoring.

5. You may choose a sandwich _____ a burrito.

6. Marcel wanted to see his friends, _____ he went to their house.

7. The skater showed great skill _____ obvious confidence.

8. Put the key on a chain, _____ you might lose it.

9. Serena doesn't like algebra, _____ she does like geometry.

10. Flowers need water _____ sunlight in order to grow.

PRACTICE 17.1B Writing Sentences With Correlative Conjunctions

Write ten sentences, using each of the correlative conjunctions below.

EXAMPLE   both . . . and

ANSWER   *Both my sister and my brother went camping last weekend.*

Both her mom and her dad attended the school conference.

11. both . . . and

12. neither . . . nor

13. not only . . . but also

14. either . . . or

15. whether . . . or

16. both . . . and

17. neither . . . nor

18. not only . . . but also

19. either . . . or

20. whether . . . or

SPEAKING APPLICATION

With a partner, take turns talking about what you do when you have free time. Your partner should listen for and name three coordinating conjunctions.

WRITING APPLICATION

Write a short paragraph about someone you admire. Use two or more coordinating conjunctions and at least one correlative conjunction in your paragraph.

Identifying Subordinating Conjunctions

Read the sentences. Then, write the subordinating conjunction (e.g., *while*, *because*, *although*, *if*) in each sentence.

EXAMPLE   You can go to the park after you finish your chores.

ANSWER   *after*

1. Before a plane takes off, there is a safety check.
2. I wanted to see the movie because my friends all liked it.
3. As soon as I finish this math problem, I'll help you with your homework.
4. Unless we get a little more wind, we won't be able to fly our kites today.
5. I can make the sauce while you boil the pasta.
6. My sister makes friends wherever she goes.
7. If you do that, the teacher will be upset.
8. We worked hard on the snow fort although we knew it would soon melt.
9. Put those books on the lower shelves so that younger children can reach them.
10. Whenever you need me, just call.

Using Subordinating Conjunctions

Read each sentence. Then, rewrite it, using the subordinating conjunction indicated in parentheses to create a complete sentence with a dependent idea. Discuss with a partner the function of each subordinating conjunction.

EXAMPLE   Alexa won't be able to go swimming. (unless)

ANSWER   *Alexa won't be able to go swimming unless she cleans her room.*

11. I bring a book with me. (whenever)
12. It's possible to see the stars. (if)
13. Coach called time out. (even though)
14. A car should come to a complete stop. (when)
15. We're stuck inside. (until)
16. Mrs. Dumont needed a pair of red shoes. (because)
17. Latrice played the song over and over again. (while)
18. I've been depositing money into a savings account. (since)
19. The neighborhood kids stopped traffic. (so that)
20. Greg got a haircut. (as soon as)

SPEAKING APPLICATION

With a partner, take turns talking about a story you read. Use two subordinating conjunctions. Your partner should listen for and name the subordinating conjunctions.

WRITING APPLICATION

Write a short paragraph about your favorite time of year. Use subordinating conjunctions in at least three of the sentences in your paragraph. Be sure to punctuate your sentences correctly.

PRACTICE 17.1E > Using Subordinating Conjunctions

Read the sentences. Write a sentence combining the two sentences in each item. Use a subordinating conjunction and underline it.

EXAMPLE   He worked hard. He has not finished the assignment.

ANSWER   *Even though he worked hard, he has not finished the assignment.*

1. We are going to the store. What can we get for you?

2. Please come over and help us. Your guests leave.

3. It is early. We thought we would go to a movie.

4. We cannot write the paper. The research is done.

5. Your package must have arrived. We were on vacation.

6. I must send the payment. The order is filled.

7. The house is on that street. Jake can find it.

8. We needed some rest. We had a vacation.

9. The cat always tries to sneak out. We close the door immediately.

10. We have energy left. We will keep working.

PRACTICE 17.1F > Identifying Conjunctive Adverbs

Read the sentences. Then, identify the conjunctive adverb in each sentence.

EXAMPLE   You must do your homework; otherwise, you cannot go.

ANSWER   *otherwise*

11. Brooke cleaned her room; then, she weeded the garden.

12. Chen memorized the U.S. Constitution; consequently, he passed the test.

13. Alicia got up at six o'clock to work; also, she got to bed much later than usual.

14. Evie forgot; however, Mom remembered.

15. You have only 20 minutes; thus, you must plan your time well.

16. Check the paper for misspelled words; furthermore, proofread for commas.

17. Maia did not set her alarm; therefore, she overslept and missed the bus.

18. Humans may land on Mars some day; indeed, they may build colonies there.

19. Meteors look like a streak of light; nevertheless, they are called shooting stars.

20. We practiced every day; finally, we were ready.

SPEAKING APPLICATION

With a partner, discuss a project you enjoyed. Use subordinating conjunctions and conjunctive adverbs. Then, write two sentences based on your conversation. Use a subordinating conjunction in one and a conjunctive adverb in the other.

WRITING APPLICATION

Write a paragraph explaining how you solved a problem. Use at least two subordinating conjunctions and one conjunctive adverb. Read your paragraph to a partner. Your partner should identify the subordinating conjunctions and conjunctive adverb.

Read the sentences. Write the sentences, supplying a conjunctive adverb, such as *consequently*, *furthermore*, and *indeed*, and the correct punctuation.

EXAMPLE Noah got another hit _____ he leads the league in home runs.

ANSWER *Noah got another hit; consequently, he leads the league in home runs.*

1. William sings well _____ he has taken dancing lessons for years.

2. The construction was completed on schedule _____ the charges were not high.

3. Jessica got the flu _____ she missed the party.

4. Ella is a good swimmer _____ she is a better runner.

5. The twins like to fish _____ they are vacationing at a lake this summer.

6. Finish washing the car first _____ do not leave here until the car is spotless.

7. We decided not to go shopping _____ we are going to the game.

8. The library needs money to buy books _____ it could use a media center.

9. The company had to economize _____ it closed seven stores.

10. We waited to learn who made the team _____ the list was posted today.

Read the sentences. Identify the conjunctive adverbs. Then, write sentences using the conjunctive adverbs.

EXAMPLE The paper is due Friday; furthermore, it must be neat.

ANSWER *furthermore — The movie is my favorite; furthermore, it won an award.*

11. Taxes were increased; consequently, teachers could be rehired.

12. We auditioned for the talent show; moreover, we were chosen.

13. I do not want to move; indeed, I dread it.

14. The first section on the test was easy; however, the second was difficult.

15. The flight was long; finally, we arrived.

16. The pool needs scrubbing; furthermore, the chlorine should be tested.

17. Mom did not go to college; instead, she attended trade school.

18. I may try out for the drama club; otherwise, I will join the debate team.

19. Kofi disagrees with the policy; thus, he wrote a letter to the editor.

20. Saul will shop for tennis shoes; moreover, he needs socks.

SPEAKING APPLICATION

With a partner, talk about what it takes to be on a team. Use conjunctive adverbs. Then, based on your conversation, write three sentences with conjunctive adverbs.

WRITING APPLICATION

Write five sentences about school assignments. Use a conjunctive adverb in each one. Read your sentences aloud to a partner. Have your partner identify the conjunctive adverbs.

PRACTICE 17.1I > **Identifying Transitional Words and Phrases**

Read the sentences. Then, write the transitional word or phrase in each sentence and use it in a new sentence. Read your sentences to a partner and discuss if your sentences are correct.

EXAMPLE   Besides being fun, after-school sports promote health.

ANSWER   *besides; Besides being wet, I'm also hungry.*

1. As a rule, caution should be used at all times.

2. On the contrary, uniforms help keep students focused on their studies.

3. First of all, scientists studied migrating birds.

4. As a result, many biking clubs were started.

5. In addition to flour, we need to add salt.

6. In fact, there are many ways to save money.

7. Therefore, we should leave immediately.

8. As usual, it is important to remember the source of the information.

9. For example, a science class might visit the local wetlands.

10. Moreover, trees are an important source of carbon dioxide.

PRACTICE 17.1J > **Writing With Transitional Words and Phrases**

Write a sentence for each of the transitional words and phrases provided. Then, read your sentences to a partner who should tell you if you have used the transitional words or phrases correctly.

EXAMPLE   as well as

ANSWER   *As well as being tasty, orange juice contains vitamin C.*

11. as a result

12. in addition to

13. therefore

14. moreover

15. for example

16. on the contrary

17. as usual

18. in order to

19. first of all

20. besides

SPEAKING APPLICATION

With a partner, debate the issue of global warming. Use transitional words and phrases such as *on the contrary* and *in addition to*. Make a list of the transitions you used in your debate.

WRITING APPLICATION

Write a paragraph explaining why you are for or against field trips during the school week. Use at least three transitional words and phrases such as *on the contrary* and *in addition to* to state the reasons for your position. Read your paragraph aloud to a partner. Your partner should identify the transitional words and phrases in your paragraph.

Test Warm-Up

DIRECTIONS

Read the introduction and the passage that follows. Then, answer the questions to show that you can use and understand the function of transitional words and phrases in reading and writing.

Tyrell wrote this paragraph about the benefits of learning a foreign language. Read the paragraph and think about the changes you would suggest as a peer editor. When you finish reading, answer the questions that follow.

Learning a Foreign Language

(1) Learning a foreign language has many benefits. (2) You can speak to people from different countries. (3) This makes travelling more enriching. (4) Therefore, you can speak to people from different cultures in your own country. (5) This can help you make new friends. (6) Many people say that foreign language is confusing. (7) Learning the grammar of a foreign language helps you understand English grammar. (8) For example, there are many benefits to learning a foreign language.

---

1 How should sentence 2 be revised?

A Otherwise, you can speak to people from different countries.

B Besides, you can speak to people from different countries.

C However, you can speak to people from different countries.

D First of all, you can speak to people from different countries.

2 How should sentence 4 be clarified?

F Change *Therefore* to **As a result**

G Change *Therefore* to **Moreover**

H Change *Therefore* to **Nevertheless**

J Change *Therefore* to **As a rule**

3 How should sentence 7 be revised?

A However, learning the grammar of a foreign language helps you understand English grammar.

B On the contrary, learning the grammar of a foreign language helps you understand English grammar.

C Accordingly learning the grammar of a foreign language helps you understand English grammar.

D Furthermore, learning the grammar of a foreign language helps you understand English grammar.

4 How should sentence 8 be clarified?

F Change *For example* to **Consequently**

G Change *For example* to **Instead**

H Change *For example* to **Besides**

J Change *For example* to **As well as**

17.2 Interjections

The **interjection** is the part of speech that is used the least. Its only use is to express feelings or emotions.

WRITING COACH

www.phwritingcoach.com

Grammar Tutorials
Brush up on your Grammar skills with these animated videos.

Grammar Practice
Practice your grammar skills with Writing Coach Online.

Grammar Games
Test your knowledge of grammar in this fast-paced interactive video game.

> **An interjection** expresses feeling or emotion and functions independently from the rest of a sentence.

RULE 17.2.1

An interjection has no grammatical relationship to any other word in a sentence. It is, therefore, set off from the rest of the sentence with a comma or an exclamation mark.

Interjections can express different feelings or emotions.

JOY	**Wow!** I can't believe you won the race.
SURPRISE	**Oh**, I didn't expect to hear from you.
PAIN	**Ouch!** That hurts.
IMPATIENCE	**Hey!** How long do they expect me to wait?
HESITATION	I, **uh**, think we should leave now.

Interjections are used more in speech than in writing. They are informal, rather than formal, expressions. When you do see them in writing, they are often included in dialogue. The following chart lists words often used as interjections.

INTERJECTIONS			
ah	gosh	nonsense	ugh
aha	great	oh	uh
alas	heavens	oops	um
boy	hey	ouch	well
darn	huh	psst	what
eureka	hurray	shh	whew
fine	my	terrible	wonderful
golly	never	terrific	wow

See Practice 17.2A
See Practice 17.2B

PRACTICE 17.2A > Identifying Interjections

Read the sentences. Write the interjection in each sentence. Then, write what emotion the interjection conveys.

EXAMPLE   Hey! Get out of there now!

ANSWER   *Hey* — *anger*

1. Ugh! That medicine tastes awful.
2. Oh! That's not what was supposed to happen.
3. Wonderful! You got straight A's!
4. Aha, that's where you hid it.
5. Nonsense! You should not believe everything you read in the newspapers.
6. Alas, he never returned from that last voyage.
7. Whew! I didn't think we were going to make it.
8. Darn! Why didn't I remember there was a test today?
9. Ah, these boots help my feet stay warm.
10. I, uh, don't want to go to that restaurant.

PRACTICE 17.2B > Supplying Interjections

Read the sentences. Rewrite each sentence, using an appropriate interjection in place of the feeling shown in parentheses. Use a comma or an exclamation mark after each interjection.

EXAMPLE   (joy) Our football team won the championship.

ANSWER   *Hurray!* *Our football team won the championship.*

11. (impatience) I can't believe you were late again.
12. (pain) Be careful taking off the bandage.
13. (relief) I thought that test would never end.
14. (surprise) I didn't expect to see you here.
15. (anger) Get those dogs away from our picnic.
16. (pleasure) The Kramers are coming for dinner.
17. (disgust) What is that smell coming from the science lab?
18. (wonder) That was an amazing fireworks display!
19. (discovery) Now we see what you were trying to do.
20. (disbelief) I don't believe anyone would do that.

SPEAKING APPLICATION

With a partner, take turns talking about things that happen at school. Your partner should listen to each comment and respond with an interjection. For example, one person might say, "There is a test today," and the other might respond, "Ugh!"

WRITING APPLICATION

Write three sentences that include appropriate interjections. You can use interjections from Practice 17.2A and Practice 17.2B or from the list in the lesson.

PRACTICE 1 ▶ Writing Sentences With Nouns

Write five sentences, each using one of the following kinds of nouns. Circle those nouns, and underline any other nouns you use.

1. a common noun that names a person
2. a proper noun that names a place
3. an abstract noun
4. a single-word compound noun
5. a collective noun

PRACTICE 2 ▶ Identifying Pronouns

Read the sentences. Then, write the pronouns that each sentence contains. Label each pronoun *personal*, *reflexive*, *intensive*, *demonstrative*, *relative*, *interrogative*, or *indefinite*.

1. Uncle Rob, who lives in Spain, is visiting us.
2. Whose picture is this?
3. Jo herself had no idea that a party was planned.
4. Everyone likes this new invention of mine.
5. Sometimes I picture myself as a famous writer.
6. Why didn't anyone say that?
7. Who will the star himself take to the Oscars?
8. Jan, who is good in math, is our club's treasurer.
9. Something in the food gave me a stomachache.
10. Mom often talks to herself when she is happy.

PRACTICE 3 ▶ Using Action and Linking Verbs

Write two sentences for each word below. In the first sentence, use the word as an action verb; in the second sentence, use it as a linking verb.

1. sound
2. grow
3. look
4. feel
5. appear

PRACTICE 4 ▶ Identifying Helping Verbs and Main Verbs in Verb Phrases

Read the sentences. Write the complete verb phrase in each sentence. Then, label the parts of each verb phrase *helping* or *main*.

1. The twins have finished all their homework.
2. The train will arrive at 5:00 P.M.
3. I had been reading a short story.
4. She has worked hard for the medal.
5. The essay will be completed in twenty minutes.
6. Everyone can join in the chorus.
7. I will tell you a secret.
8. The game has been finished for some time now.
9. We had seen the rainbow yesterday.
10. I should have started my project sooner.

Continued on next page ▶

Cumulative Review Chapters 13–17

PRACTICE 5 > **Revising Sentences With Adjectives and Adverbs**

Read the sentences. Then, rewrite each sentence by adding at least one adjective to modify a noun or a pronoun or one adverb to modify a verb, an adjective, or another adverb.

1. Inez lost her umbrella.
2. The boy rides his bicycle to school.
3. The child screams loudly.
4. A beautiful bird perched on the fence.
5. It was cloudy until noon.
6. The truck sped through the night.
7. Shadows fell on the mountainside.
8. Someone whispered in the back of the room.
9. The neon lights glowed like stars in the sky.
10. Have you seen an adventure film?

PRACTICE 6 > **Writing Sentences With Prepositions and Adverbs**

Write ten sentences about running or runners. In your first five sentences, use the prepositional phrases in items 1–5. In your next five sentences, use the words in items 6–10 as adverbs.

1. before the race
2. inside the stadium
3. around the track
4. behind the others
5. up a hill
6. before
7. inside
8. around
9. behind
10. up

PRACTICE 7 > **Identifying Conjunctions**

Read the sentences. Then, identify each underlined word or pair of words as a *coordinating conjunction*, a *subordinating conjunction*, *correlative conjunctions*, or a *conjunctive adverb*.

1. My pet hamster escaped, <u>but</u> Mom found it.
2. We applauded wildly <u>when</u> the concert ended.
3. <u>Either</u> Pedro <u>or</u> Lucy will trade seats with me.
4. I play soccer; <u>however</u>, I rarely watch it on television.
5. My sister <u>and</u> brother walk to school with me.

PRACTICE 8 > **Revising to Include Interjections**

Rewrite the following dialogue, adding interjections to help show the speakers' emotions. Use either a comma or an exclamation mark after each interjection.

JUAN: Do you remember walking on the beach?

TARA: The sun was just beginning to set. It was so beautiful.

JUAN: Maybe we can go again next summer.

TARA: We'll see. But I sure wish it were summer now. I hate this cold weather.

JUAN: Be patient.

TARA: I guess you are right.

JUAN: It won't be long before we will be complaining that it is too hot.

CHAPTER 18

BASIC SENTENCE PARTS

Carefully select your subjects and verbs to create interesting and surprising sentences.

WRITE GUY *Jeff Anderson, M.Ed.*

WHAT DO YOU NOTICE?

Spot the subjects and verbs as you zoom in on these lines from the poem "The Walrus and the Carpenter" by Lewis Carroll.

MENTOR TEXT

> The Walrus and the Carpenter
>   Were walking close at hand:
> They wept like anything to see
>   Such quantities of sand ...

Now, ask yourself the following questions:

- Which two nouns form the compound subject in these lines?
- Which verb shows the subjects' actions?

The proper nouns *Walrus* and *Carpenter* form the compound subject. The verb *were walking* shows their action. You can tell that the proper nouns function as a compound subject because the conjunction *and* connects them. Also notice the second pair of lines, in which the pronoun *They* is the subject of the verb *wept*.

Grammar for Writers Use a variety of conjunctions in your writing. The Walrus and the Carpenter are linked by *and*, but you can also use *or* to form a compound subject. For example, you could write, "Either my brother *or* my sister will make lunch today."

You and I share the same subjects at school.

That makes us a compound subject.

18.1 The Basic Sentence

There are many kinds of sentences. Some are short; others are long. Some are simple, and others are more complex. In order to be considered complete, a sentence must have two things: a subject and a verb.

The Two Basic Parts of a Sentence

Every sentence, regardless of its length, must have a subject and a verb.

RULE 18.1.1 A complete **sentence** contains a subject and a verb and expresses a complete thought.

The Subject

A sentence must have a **subject.** Most subjects are nouns or pronouns. The subject is usually, but not always, found near the beginning of the sentence.

RULE 18.1.2 The **subject** of a sentence is the word or group of words that names the person, place, thing, or idea that performs the action or is described. It answers the question *Who?* or *What?* before the verb.

EXAMPLES   The **cat** is hungry.

Mrs. Meow broke her dish.

She knows several tricks.

A **string** is her favorite toy.

The noun *cat* is the subject in the first sentence. It tells *what* is hungry. In the next sentence, the proper noun *Mrs. Meow* tells *who* broke her dish. The pronoun *she* in the third sentence tells *who* knows several tricks.

WRITING COACH

Online

www.phwritingcoach.com

Grammar Tutorials
Brush up on your Grammar skills with these animated videos.

Grammar Practice
Practice your grammar skills with Writing Coach Online.

Grammar Games
Test your knowledge of grammar in this fast-paced interactive video game.

The Verb

As one of the basic parts of a sentence, the **verb** tells something about the subject.

> The **verb** in a sentence tells what the subject does, what is done to the subject, or what the condition of the subject is.

18.1.3 RULE

EXAMPLES

My cat **won** a ribbon.

The award **was given** in a big ceremony.

He **seems** tired now.

See Practice 18.1A

Won tells what *my cat* did. *Was given* explains what was done with *the award*. *Seems*, a linking verb, tells something about the condition of *he* by linking the subject to *tired*.

Using Subjects and Verbs to Express Complete Thoughts

Every basic sentence must express a complete thought.

> A sentence is a group of words with a subject and a verb that expresses a complete thought and can stand by itself and still make sense.

18.1.4 RULE

INCOMPLETE THOUGHT

in the basket in the hall

(This group of words cannot stand by itself as a sentence.)

This incomplete thought contains two prepositional phrases. The phrases can become a sentence only after *both* a subject and a verb are added to them.

COMPLETE THOUGHT

The **kittens** **are** in the basket in the hall.
  subject   verb

(This group of words can stand by itself as a sentence.)

See Practice 18.1B

In grammar, incomplete thoughts are often called **fragments.**

PRACTICE 18.1A > Finding Subjects and Verbs

Read the sentences. Write the subject and verb of each sentence.

EXAMPLE   Charlie watched the train go by.

ANSWER   *Charlie, watched*

1. The horses pulled the wagon.
2. We finished the assignment.
3. The hot sand burned our feet.
4. Your brother is very sick.
5. A crowd gathered around the guitar player.
6. Jake lives near a lake.
7. Volunteers collected donations.
8. She put the books back onto the shelf.
9. Mikhail came here from Russia.
10. Sondra was glad to be included.

PRACTICE 18.1B > Recognizing Complete Thoughts

Read the following groups of words. If a group of words expresses a complete thought, write *complete.* If a group of words expresses an incomplete thought, write *incomplete.*

EXAMPLE   Outside, behind the barn.

ANSWER   *incomplete*

11. We enjoyed the baseball game.
12. Ducks near the pond.
13. In the evening, after sunset.
14. The storm came in quickly.
15. The garden in full bloom.
16. Leaving the doctor's office.
17. They went to the store.
18. Our cat ate the fish.
19. On the kitchen counter.
20. Everyone came home early.

SPEAKING APPLICATION

With a partner, take turns talking about an activity you enjoy. Your partner should listen for and name two subjects and two verbs.

WRITING APPLICATION

Write a short paragraph about your favorite class. Underline the subject in each sentence, and underline the verb twice.

18.2 Complete Subjects and Predicates

Have you ever seen tiles laid on a floor? First, a line is drawn in the center of the room. One tile is placed to the left of the line, and another is placed to the right. Then, more tiles are added in the same way: one to the left and one to the right.

Imagine that the first tile on the left is a subject and the first tile on the right is a verb. You would then have a subject and a verb separated by a vertical line, as shown in the example.

EXAMPLE   **Fur** | **flew** .

Now, in the same way that you would add a few more tiles if you were tiling a floor, add a few more words.

EXAMPLE   Ginger **fur** | **flew** through the air.

At this point, you could add still more words.

EXAMPLE   Oscar's long ginger **fur** | **flew** through the air in clumps and bunches.

The centerline is important in laying tiles. It is just as important in dividing these sentences into two parts. All the words to the left of the line in the preceding examples are part of the **complete subject.** The main noun in the complete subject, *fur*, is often called the **simple subject.**

> The **complete subject** of a sentence consists of the subject and any words related to it.

18.2.1 RULE

As in the examples above, the complete subject may be just one word—*fur*—or several words—*Oscar's ginger fur.*

Look at the example sentences again, plus one with new words added.

EXAMPLES   Ginger **fur** | **flew** through the air.

Oscar's ginger **fur** | **flew** through the air in clumps.

Oscar's ginger **fur** | **had flown** through the air during his grooming.

All the words to the right of the line in the preceding examples are part of the **complete predicate.** The verb *flew*, or a verb phrase such as *had flown*, on the other hand, is often called the **simple predicate.**

See Practice 18.2A

See Practice 18.2A

RULE 18.2.2

> The **complete predicate** of a sentence consists of the verb and any words related to it.

As the examples show, a complete predicate may be just the verb itself or the verb and several other words.

Many sentences do not divide so neatly into subject and predicate. Look at the subjects and predicates in the following sentences.

EXAMPLES   **After the picnic**, our **family** **went home**.

With the rising temperature, the **snow** **began to melt**.

In these sentences, part of the predicate comes *before* the subject, and the rest of the predicate follows the subject.

As you have seen, a complete simple sentence contains a simple subject and a simple predicate. In addition, a complete simple sentence expresses a complete thought.

See Practice 18.2B

PRACTICE 18.2A > **Identifying Complete
Subjects and Predicates**

Read the sentences. Rewrite each sentence,
and draw a vertical line between the complete
subject and the complete predicate. Then,
underline the subject once and the verb twice.

EXAMPLE   A few leaves remained on the tree.

ANSWER   A few _leaves_ | <u>remained</u> on the tree.

1. The Russian ballerina twirled across the
stage.

2. The second week of class seems more
difficult.

3. Workers from the factory usually walk home
for lunch.

4. My rusting old car needs a lot of work.

5. Our science teacher planned the next day's
experiment.

6. The woman at the bakery sometimes gives
me a sample of their bread.

7. The test results came back today.

8. My father told me I could go to the movies.

9. The white tiger is my favorite animal at
the zoo.

10. Almost nobody went outside today.

PRACTICE 18.2B > **Writing Complete Sentences**

Read the items. Each item contains either a
complete subject or a complete predicate. Rewrite
each item along with the missing part to create
complete sentences.

EXAMPLE   Flowers of every kind _____.

ANSWER   _Flowers of every kind_ **crowded the
gardens.**

11. _____ covered the ground completely.

12. That man in a suit _____.

13. _____ was on her way to the store.

14. The new movie theater _____.

15. _____ includes an instruction manual.

16. All the students from our school _____.

17. _____ usually carry their books in a backpack.

18. My favorite subject in school _____.

19. The firefighters _____.

20. The snow from yesterday's storm _____.

SPEAKING APPLICATION

With a partner, create sentences with complete
subjects and complete predicates. Take turns
talking about things that take place at school.
One person offers a complete subject, and the
other adds a complete predicate.

WRITING APPLICATION

Write three sentences about a favorite activity.
Draw a vertical line between the complete
subject and complete predicate of each
sentence.

18.3 Compound Subjects and Compound Verbs

Some sentences have more than one subject. Some have more than one verb.

WRITING COACH
Online
www.phwritingcoach.com

Grammar Tutorials
Brush up on your Grammar skills with these animated videos.

Grammar Practice
Practice your grammar skills with Writing Coach Online.

Grammar Games
Test your knowledge of grammar in this fast-paced interactive video game.

Recognizing Compound Subjects

A sentence containing more than one subject is said to have a **compound subject.**

RULE 18.3.1

> A **compound subject** is two or more subjects that have the same verb and are joined by a conjunction such as *and* or *or.*

EXAMPLES

Cats and kittens **are** popular as pets.
  compound subject   verb

Cats, dogs, and other pets **can learn** to live
        compound subject   verb
together.

Recognizing Compound Verbs

A sentence with two or more verbs is said to have a **compound verb.**

RULE 18.3.2

> A **compound verb** is two or more verbs that have the same subject and are joined by a conjunction such as *and* or *or.*

EXAMPLES

The **project** **may succeed or fail**.
     subject   compound verb

She **writes, performs, and directs** her plays.
subject   compound verb

Sometimes a sentence will have both a compound subject and a compound verb.

EXAMPLE

Jane and Sharon **sang and danced** on
   compound subject   compound verb
the stage.

See Practice 18.3A
See Practice 18.3B

PRACTICE 18.3A > **Recognizing Compound Subjects and
Compound Verbs**

Read the sentences. Write the compound subject and/or the
compound verb in each sentence.

EXAMPLE   My dog dashed out of the house, raced across the
             lawn, and happily rolled in the fallen leaves.

ANSWER   *dashed, raced, and rolled* — compound verb

1. My brother, sister, and I went out for dinner last night.

2. The old trees creaked and groaned as the temperature
   dropped.

3. Our softball teams practice and play on the community
   baseball diamond.

4. My sister and my brother made their beds, had breakfast,
   and headed for school.

5. The manager and supervisor discuss all job applicants and
   make a decision.

6. Before going to the store, my mom always checks the cupboard,
   looks in the refrigerator, and writes a shopping list.

7. Clarice, Juana, Bethany, and Valeria tried out for the part of
   Juliet in the school play.

8. The doctor and radiologist examined the X-rays, consulted a
   specialist, and planned possible treatments.

9. The spectators and the judges applauded the brilliant
   ice-skating routine during the Olympics.

10. As part of their community service, the boys picked up trash,
    trimmed bushes, and gathered cans and glass for recycling.

SPEAKING APPLICATION

With a partner, describe
a day at the zoo (real or
imagined). Your partner
should listen for and
identify sentences that
use compound subjects or
compound verbs.

WRITING APPLICATION

Use the sentences in
Practice 18.3A as models,
and write two sentences
of your own, one with a
compound subject and one
with a compound verb.

Practice   379

PRACTICE 18.3B > **Combining Sentences With Compound
Subjects and Compound Verbs**

Read the sentences. Combine each pair of sentences by using
compound subjects or compound verbs.

EXAMPLE   Yesterday, I went to the store with my mom.

Yesterday, I also went to the post office with
my mom.

ANSWER   *Yesterday, I went to the store and the post office
with my mom.*

1. Today, my father will clean out the garage. Today, my father
will also mow the lawn.

2. Last week, my aunt went to the movie theater for a special
showing of old films. My mom went to the movie theater
with her.

3. Exercising is good for your health. Eating a balanced diet is
also good for your health.

4. Whenever I get the chance, I go through my mom's cookbooks.
I choose recipes I would like to try.

5. Members of the soccer team often stay late after school to
practice. Members of the baseball team also stay late after
school to practice.

6. The new kittens were curious about their new surroundings.
They explored every part of the house.

7. Fire trucks passed before the gathered crowds during the
big parade. Floats, horses, and bands also passed before the
gathered crowds during the big parade.

8. Sitting in the library, Larissa read a book to prepare for
writing a report. Larissa took notes to prepare for writing
a report.

9. My grandparents are going to eat at that new restaurant
on the corner. My parents are going to go with them.

10. Many people take the train to work. Many people drive
to work.

With a partner, talk about a
sport you enjoy playing or
watching. Have compound
subjects and/or compound
verbs in your sentences.
Your partner should listen
for and identify sentences
with compound subjects
and/or compound verbs.

WRITING APPLICATION

Write two short sentences
about something you do at
school. Then, combine the
two short sentences into
one longer sentence that
has a compound subject
and/or compound verb.

18.4 Hard-to-Find Subjects

It can be difficult to identify simple subjects in certain sentences. These sentences do not follow **normal word order** in which the subject comes before the verb. Sometimes the subject will follow the verb or part of a verb phrase. This is called **inverted word order.** Questions are often presented in inverted word order.

| NORMAL WORD ORDER | The **concert** **will begin** at 8:30 P.M. |
| | subject   verb |

| INVERTED WORD ORDER | When **will** the **concert** **begin**? |
| | verb   subject   verb |

Sometimes the subject will not actually be stated in the sentence. It will be understood to be the pronoun *you.* This is often true in sentences that express commands or requests.

The Subject of a Command or Request

When a sentence commands or requests someone to do something, the subject is often unstated.

> **The subject of a command or request is understood to be the pronoun *you.***

18.4.1 RULE

COMMANDS OR REQUESTS	HOW THE SENTENCES ARE UNDERSTOOD
Stop!	You stop!
Begin at once.	You begin at once.
Please come here.	You please come here.
Audrey, make a list.	Audrey, you make a list.
Bob, get the tickets.	Bob, you get the tickets.

Even though a command or request may begin with the name of the person spoken to, the subject is still understood to be *you.*

See Practice 18.4A

Finding Subjects in Questions

Questions are often presented in inverted word order. You will usually find the subject in the middle of the sentence.

RULE 18.4.2

In questions, the subject often follows the verb.

Some questions in inverted word order begin with the words *what*, *whom*, *when*, *where*, *why*, and *how*. Others begin with the verb itself or with a helping verb.

EXAMPLES   How **are** the **kittens** today?

Did you feed them in the morning?

Have you found homes for all of them yet?

If you ever have trouble finding the subject in a question, use this trick: Change the question into a statement. The subject will then appear in normal word order before the verb.

QUESTIONS	REWORDED AS STATEMENTS
How are the pups today?	The pups are how today.
What did the doctor say?	The doctor did say what.
Were the labels ready?	The labels were ready.
Did she bring her camera with her?	She did bring her camera with her.

Not every question is in inverted word order. Some are in normal word order, with the subject before the verb. Questions beginning with *who*, *whose*, or *which* often follow normal word order.

EXAMPLES   **Who has** the camera?

Whose **story won** the writing contest?

Which **painting should win** the contest?

See Practice 18.4B

PRACTICE 18.4A ▶ **Identifying Subjects in Commands or Requests**

Read the sentences. Write the subject of each sentence.

EXAMPLE   Get the tools I left in the garage.

ANSWER   *you*

1. Get the clothes out of the washing machine.
2. Place the books onto the correct shelves.
3. Please, close the door.
4. Juwan, bring me that globe.
5. Don't forget to take an umbrella.
6. Come to the window so I can see you.
7. Jason and Keiko, put these boxes in the car.
8. For dessert, order whatever looks good.
9. Jena, get me five eggs from the refrigerator.
10. Bring the soup to a boil.

PRACTICE 18.4B ▶ **Identifying Subjects in Questions**

Read the questions. Write the subject of each question. If you have trouble finding the subject in a question, change the question into a statement.

EXAMPLE   Are the girls coming with us?

ANSWER   *girls*

11. Did you remember to lock the back door?
12. Are dogs allowed in your apartment?
13. Is it too late to buy tickets?
14. Will Daniel and Felicia be in the play?
15. Can Stefan bring his guitar?
16. Has everyone signed the petition?
17. Were the Donovans at the party?
18. Was Fernando ready for school?
19. Would your parents let you go to the dance?
20. Did the teacher explain the project to you?

SPEAKING APPLICATION

With a partner, take turns role-playing a coach or teacher getting players or students to do things. Your partner should listen for and identify commands and questions and name the subject.

WRITING APPLICATION

Write a short series of instructions for carrying out a task, such as making soup or turning on a computer. Include at least two command/request sentences.

Finding the Subject in Sentences Beginning With *There* or *Here*

Sentences beginning with *there* or *here* are usually in inverted word order.

> ***There* or *here* is never the subject of a sentence.**

There can be used to start a sentence.

SENTENCE
STARTER

There are two musicians from Texas in the band.

There or *here* can also be used as an adverb at the beginning of sentences. As adverbs, these two words point out *where* and modify the verbs.

ADVERB

There goes the famous rock star.

Here are the invitations to the party.

Be alert to sentences beginning with *there* and *here*. They are probably in inverted word order, with the verb appearing before the subject. If you cannot find the subject, reword the sentence in normal word order. If *there* is just a sentence starter, you can drop it from your reworded sentence.

SENTENCES BEGINNING WITH *THERE* OR *HERE*	REWORDED WITH SUBJECT BEFORE VERB
There is a mistake in the ad for the show.	A mistake is in the ad for the show.
Here comes the star of the show.	The star of the show comes here.

See Practice 18.4C

Finding the Subject in Sentences Inverted for Emphasis

Sometimes a subject is intentionally put after its verb to draw attention to the subject.

> **In some sentences, the subject follows the verb in order to emphasize the subject, or make it stand out.**

In the following examples, notice how the order of the words builds suspense by leading up to the subject.

EXAMPLES

In the midst of the crowd outside the theater

stood the **star**.
  verb   subject

Soaring high above the crowd **was** a huge
 verb   verb

bald eagle.
  subject

Hiding under the bedspread **were** my two
 verb   verb

orange **kittens**.
     subject

You can reword sentences such as these in normal word order to make it easier to find the subject.

INVERTED WORD ORDER	REWORDED WITH SUBJECT BEFORE VERB
In the midst of the crowd outside the theater stood the star.	The star stood in the midst of the crowd outside the theater.
Soaring high above the crowd was a huge bald eagle.	A huge bald eagle was soaring high above the crowd.
Hiding under the bedspread were my two orange kittens.	My two orange kittens were hiding under the bedspread.

See Practice 18.4D

PRACTICE 18.4C **Identifying Subjects in Sentences Beginning With *Here* or *There***

Read the sentences. Write the subject of each sentence.

EXAMPLE   Here is our library.

ANSWER   *library*

1. There goes the deliveryman.
2. Here is your jacket.
3. There is a fly near my soup.
4. Here are the guidebooks for our trip.
5. There were the Johnsons, in that car.
6. Here was a story to make you think.
7. There is a great musician playing on television.
8. Here comes the first rain of the month.
9. There lies the mystery behind this event.
10. Here is the information you requested.

PRACTICE 18.4D **Identifying Subjects in Sentences Inverted for Emphasis**

Read the sentences. Write the subject of each sentence.

EXAMPLE   At the end of the road stood a crumbling house.

ANSWER   *house*

11. On the shores of the lake grew a magnificent tree.
12. In late August came the worst hurricane.
13. Right there in the driveway was the car I liked.
14. As I had feared, on the desk lay a math test.
15. In the carefully tended garden bloomed the most splendid roses.
16. In the middle of the Pacific Ocean are many islands.
17. Near the east coast of Australia lies a spectacular reef.
18. Behind the hedges waits the hunting fox.
19. By the side of the road was a strange sign.
20. On the stove simmers some stew.

SPEAKING APPLICATION

With a partner, take turns talking about a movie you saw. Be sure to start two or three sentences with *there* or *here*. Your partner should listen for and identify the subjects of the sentences.

WRITING APPLICATION

Write two sentences in normal word order. You may write on any topic that interests you. Then, rewrite the sentences in inverted order.

18.5 Complements

Often, a subject and verb alone can express a complete thought. For example, *Birds fly* can stand by itself as a sentence, even though it contains only two words, a subject and a verb. Other times, however, the thought begun by a subject and its verb must be completed with other words. For example, *Toni bought, The eyewitness told, Our mechanic is, Richard feels,* and *Marco seems* all contain a subject and verb, but none expresses a complete thought. All these ideas need **complements.**

> **A complement** is a word or group of words that completes the meaning of a sentence.

RULE 18.5.1

Complements are usually nouns, pronouns, or adjectives. They are located right after or very close to the verb. The complements are shown below in blue. The complements answer questions about the subject or verb in order to complete the sentence.

DIFFERENT KINDS OF COMPLEMENTS

Toni bought cars.
subject verb complement

The eyewitness told us the story.
subject verb complements

Our mechanic is a genius.
subject verb complement

Richard feels sad.
subject verb complement

Marco seems happy.
subject verb complement

This section will describe three types of complements: **direct objects, indirect objects,** and **subject complements.** All complements add information about the subjects or verbs in the sentence. They paint a clearer picture that helps the reader understand the writer's thoughts.

Recognizing Direct Objects

Direct objects follow action verbs.

> A **direct object** is a noun or pronoun that receives the action of a verb.

You can find a direct object by asking *What?* or *Whom?* after an action verb.

EXAMPLES My older **brother** **found** a grass **snake**.
subject   verb   direct object

I **called** **Ricky** early in the day.
subject verb direct object

My dog **Champ** **likes** a good **scratch**
subject   verb   direct object
on his belly.

Snake, Ricky, and *scratch* are the direct objects of the verbs in the examples. In the first sentence, *snake* answers the question *Found what?* In the second sentence, *Ricky* answers the question *Called whom?* In the third sentence, *scratch* answers the question *Likes what?*

Compound Direct Objects

Like subjects and verbs, direct objects can be compound. That is, one verb can have two or more direct objects.

EXAMPLES The **lizard** **eats** **crickets** and other **bugs**.
subject verb direct object   direct object

The **committee** **chose** **Mrs. Franks**,
subject   verb   direct object

Mr. Lynch, and **Ms. Chin** to organize the
direct object   direct object
reptile show.

See Practice 18.5A
See Practice 18.5B

PRACTICE 18.5A **Recognizing Direct Objects**

Read the sentences. Write the direct object or the compound direct object in each sentence.

EXAMPLE   He loved building models.

ANSWER   *models*

1. Maria baked bread.
2. My friends brought gifts to the party.
3. Bears eat plants and meat.
4. The Carlisle twins raise rabbits.
5. Freddy strummed the guitar.
6. Mr. Sanchez speaks Spanish, English, and German.
7. The plant known as the Venus flytrap catches insects.
8. Sasha's older brother studied math and science.
9. The female kangaroo carries her young in a pouch.
10. We all ordered salad, chicken, and potatoes.

PRACTICE 18.5B **Adding Complements**

Read the sentences. Rewrite the sentences, and fill in the blanks with appropriate direct objects. Use both nouns and pronouns.

EXAMPLE   Marcus found his ____.

ANSWER   *Marcus found his* key.

11. Chandar saw ____ at the fair.
12. Estancia played the ____.
13. Jeffrey dug a ____.
14. The two boys visited ____.
15. Carly and Selene knitted ____.
16. I carefully watered ____ each morning.
17. Frankie asked ____ for a pencil.
18. Hey, Tommy, throw me that ____.
19. Michael's dad cooked a great ____.
20. Cecily scanned the ____.

SPEAKING APPLICATION

With a partner, discuss a hobby you have or would like to have. Your partner should listen for and name two direct objects.

WRITING APPLICATION

Write a short paragraph about packing for a trip. Make sure two or more sentences contain direct objects. Underline the direct object or direct objects in each sentence.

Distinguishing Between Direct Objects, Adverbs, and Objects of Prepositions

Not all action verbs have direct objects. Be careful not to confuse a direct object with an adverb or with the object of a preposition. If you are unsure if a word or phrase is a direct object, ask yourself who or what is receiving the action of the verb.

RULE

18.5.3

> **A direct object is never an adverb or the noun or pronoun at the end of a prepositional phrase.**

Compare the following examples. Notice that the action verb *drove* has a direct object in only the first sentence.

EXAMPLES

Joanne **drove** her new **sports car**.
  subject   verb   direct object

Joanne **drove** **quickly**.
  subject   verb   adverb

Joanne **drove** **through the town**.
  subject   verb   prepositional phrase

Each example shows a very common sentence type. The first consists of a subject, a verb, and a direct object. The compound noun *sports car* is the direct object of the verb *drove*.

The second example consists of a subject, a verb, and an adverb. Nothing after the verb in the sentence answers the question *What?* so there is no direct object. *Quickly* modifies the verb and tells *how* Joanne drove.

The third example consists of a subject, a verb, and a prepositional phrase. Again, no noun or pronoun answers the question *What?* after the verb. The prepositional phrase tells *where* Joanne drove.

Notice also that a single sentence can contain more than one of these three parts.

EXAMPLE

Joanne drove her new **sports car** **quickly**
                       direct object   adverb
through the town.
 prepositional phrase

See Practice 18.5C

Finding Direct Objects in Questions

In normal word order, a direct object follows a verb. In questions that are in inverted word order, however, the direct object often appears before the verb and subject.

> **A direct object in a question will sometimes be found before the verb.**

In the following chart, questions are paired with sentences reworded in normal word order. Direct objects are highlighted in pink, subjects are highlighted in yellow, and verbs are highlighted in orange. Compare the positions of the direct objects in each.

QUESTIONS	REWORDED IN NORMAL WORD ORDER
What did Mary play at her recital?	Mary did play what at her recital.
Which car did he drive to school today?	He did drive which car to school today.
What does a snake eat?	A snake does eat what.
Which T-shirt do you like, the purple one or the green striped one?	You do like which T-shirt, the purple one or the green striped one.
Whom did you meet in the cafeteria?	You did meet whom in the cafeteria.

In each of the five questions, the direct object appears before, rather than after, the verb. To locate the direct object in a question, put the sentence into normal word order with the subject appearing before the verb. Then, the direct object will be found in its usual position after the verb.

See Practice 18.5D

PRACTICE 18.5C **Distinguishing Direct Object, Adverb, and Object of a Preposition**

Read the sentences. Label each underlined word *DO* for direct object, *ADV* for adverb, or *OP* for object of a preposition.

EXAMPLE   Melissa walked through <u>town</u>.

ANSWER   *OP*

1. The jeweler polished the <u>bracelet</u>.
2. The squirrels ran up the <u>tree</u>.
3. Pedro carried the <u>groceries</u> into the house.
4. Tonight, the girls played <u>happily</u>.
5. The farmer walked into the <u>barn</u>.
6. The painter worked <u>quickly</u>.
7. Mr. Shapiro washed his <u>dog</u> today.
8. The willow tree swayed <u>gracefully</u>.
9. The children ran across the <u>field</u>.
10. The Nguyen family opened a new <u>restaurant</u>.

PRACTICE 18.5D **Finding Direct Objects in Questions**

Read the questions. Write the direct object in each question.

EXAMPLE   What will you wear tonight?

ANSWER   *What*

11. Whom did you talk to at the bank?
12. What are you reading for your book report?
13. Which shoes should I take?
14. Whom did Dennis ask to the dance?
15. What will Kerri make for the bake sale?
16. Which class should I take first?
17. What did you throw out?
18. Whom will you be inviting to your party?
19. Which flavor do you like best?
20. What do squirrels do with the nuts they gather?

SPEAKING APPLICATION

With a partner, take turns asking questions about planning a party. Include at least two questions with direct objects. Your partner should listen for and name the direct objects.

WRITING APPLICATION

Use Practice 18.5C as a model, and write three sentences: one with a direct object following the verb, one with a prepositional phrase, and one with an adverb. As with the practice, write *DO*, *ADV*, or *OP* after each sentence.

Recognizing Indirect Objects

Sentences with a direct object may also contain another kind of complement, called an **indirect object.** A sentence cannot have an indirect object unless it has a direct object.

> An **indirect object** is a noun or pronoun that comes after an action verb and before a direct object. It names the person or thing to which something is given or for which something is done.

An indirect object answers the questions *To* or *for whom?* or *To* or *for what?* after an action verb. To find an indirect object, find the direct object first. Then, ask the appropriate question.

EXAMPLE   Shrini's **mom** **told** **them** the **story**.
                           indirect object   direct object

(Told *what?* [*story*])
(Told the story *to whom?* [*them*])

Keep in mind the following pattern: *Subject + Verb + Indirect Object + Direct Object.* An indirect object will almost always come between the verb and the direct object in a sentence.

Compound Indirect Objects

Like a subject, verb, or direct object, an indirect object can be compound.

EXAMPLES   **Dave** **assigned** each **car and truck** a
              subject   verb   compound indirect object
new **parking place**.
          direct object
(Assigned *what?* [*parking place*])
(Assigned a parking place *to what?* [*car and truck*])

Mom **offered** **my sister and me** **sandwiches**
  subject   verb   compound indirect object   compound direct object
and milk.

(Offered *what?* [*sandwiches* and *milk*])
(Offered *sandwiches to whom?* [*my sister and me*])

See Practice 18.5E

Distinguishing Between Indirect Objects and Objects of Prepositions

Do not confuse an indirect object with the object of a preposition.

> **An indirect object never follows the preposition *to* or *for* in a sentence.**

Compare the following examples.

EXAMPLES
Father bought **him** a **car**.
indirect   direct
object   object

Father bought a **car** for **him**.
direct   object of
object   preposition

In the first example above, *him* is an indirect object. It comes after the verb *bought* and before the direct object *car*. In the second example, *him* is the object of the preposition *for* and follows the direct object *car*.

EXAMPLES
Paul gave **Jerome** a **sandwich**.
indirect object   direct object

Paul gave a **sandwich** to **Jerome**.
direct object   object of
                     preposition

To find the indirect object in the first example above, you must first find the direct object. Ask yourself what Paul gave. He gave a sandwich, so *sandwich* is the direct object. Then, ask yourself to whom Paul gave the sandwich. He gave it to *Jerome*, so *Jerome* is the indirect object.

Use the same questions in the second example. Again, *sandwich* is the direct object of *gave*; however, *Jerome* is no longer the indirect object. Instead, it is the object of the preposition *to*.

See Practice 18.5F

PRACTICE 18.5E ▷ Recognizing Indirect Objects

Read the sentences. Write the indirect object in each sentence.

EXAMPLE   I brought Mom the paper.

ANSWER   *Mom*

1. Miguel threw Charlie the ball.
2. The Riveras got their dog a new collar.
3. Terry brought the kittens their dinner.
4. The company gave my dad a promotion.
5. Sheila bought her mother flowers.
6. Mom made us costumes for the play.
7. I gave my report a title page.
8. Kelly offered me money for my old bicycle.
9. The committee awarded the project a blue ribbon.
10. The park ranger gave the tourists directions.

PRACTICE 18.5F ▷ Distinguishing Indirect Object and Object of a Preposition

Read the sentences. Write whether the underlined word is an *indirect object* or an *object of a preposition*.

EXAMPLE   John threw the ball to <u>Ravi</u>.

ANSWER   *object of a preposition*

11. Johanna got a birthday card from her <u>grandmother</u>.
12. The baker brought <u>us</u> the bread we ordered.
13. Victoria gave the message to <u>Martina</u>.
14. Mom and I planned a party for <u>him</u>.
15. Our neighbor found <u>me</u> a job.
16. We fed the <u>seals</u> fish.
17. The artist showed her sketch to <u>me</u>.
18. Justin brought his <u>mother</u> a scarf.
19. Gina borrowed a dress from <u>me</u>.
20. My brother sent <u>me</u> a letter from camp.

SPEAKING APPLICATION

With a partner, talk about errands you or family members run regularly, such as trips to the store or library. Be sure to use indirect objects at least two times. Your partner should listen for and name the indirect objects.

WRITING APPLICATION

Write two sentences with indirect objects. Then, rewrite the sentences so that the indirect objects become objects of prepositions. Use the sentences in Practice 18.5F to help you with ideas.

Subject Complements

Both direct objects and indirect objects are complements used with action verbs. Linking verbs, however, have a different kind of complement called a **subject complement.** Like direct and indirect objects, subject complements add information to a sentence. However, subject complements give readers more information about the subject of the sentence, not the verb.

A **subject complement** is a noun, pronoun, or adjective that follows a linking verb and provides important details about the subject.

Predicate Nouns and Pronouns

Both nouns and pronouns are sometimes used as subject complements after linking verbs.

A **predicate noun** or **predicate pronoun** follows a linking verb and renames or identifies the subject of the sentence.

It is easy to recognize predicate nouns and predicate pronouns. The linking verb acts much like an equal sign between the subject and the noun or pronoun that follows the verb. Both the subject and the predicate noun or pronoun refer to the same person or thing.

EXAMPLES

Ronnie **will be** the **captain** of our team.
   subject   verb   predicate noun

(The predicate noun *captain* renames the subject *Ronnie.*)

Ford's first **car** **was** the **Model A**.
      subject   verb   predicate noun

(The predicate noun *Model A* identifies the subject *car.*)

The two **winners** **are** **they**.
     subject   verb predicate pronoun

(The predicate pronoun *they* identifies the subject *winners.*)   See Practice 18.5G

Predicate Adjectives

A **predicate adjective** can also follow a linking verb.

> **A predicate adjective** follows a linking verb and describes the subject of the sentence.

A predicate adjective is considered part of the complete predicate of a sentence because it comes after a linking verb. In spite of this, a predicate adjective does not modify the words in the predicate. Instead, it describes the noun or pronoun that serves as the subject of the linking verb.

EXAMPLES

The **flight** to Houston **was** **swift** .
　　subject　　　　　　　　verb　predicate adjective

(The predicate adjective *swift* describes the subject *flight.*)

The **salesperson** **seems** very **efficient** .
　　subject　　　　　　verb　　　　predicate adjective

(The predicate adjective *efficient* describes the subject *salesperson*.)

Predicate Adjectives and Their Comparative and Superlative Forms

The comparative form of the predicate adjective is used when two items are being compared. The superlative form is used when three or more items are being compared.

Use *-er* or *more* to form the comparative degree of most one- or two-syllable predicate adjectives. Use *-est* or *most* to form the superlative of most one- or two-syllable predicate adjectives. When the superlative form is used, the article *the* is often added.

See Practice 18.5H

EXAMPLES

The **flight** to Houston **was** **swifter** than the flight
　　subject　　　　　　verb　predicate adjective
to Dallas.

The **flight** to San Antonio **was** the **swiftest** of
　　subject　　　　　　　　　verb　　predicate adjective
the three flights.

(For adjectives ending in y, replace the y with -ier and -iest.)

Three or More Syllables

Use *more* and *most* for predicate adjectives with three or more syllables.

EXAMPLES   The Houston **airport** **seemed** more **congested**
subject   verb   predicate adjective
than the Dallas airport.

The New York **airport** **seemed** the most **congested**
subject   verb   predicate adjective
of all three airports.

That **oak tree** **looks** more **beautiful** than that maple tree.
subject   verb   predicate adjective

That **dogwood** **looks** the most **beautiful** of all three trees.
subject   verb   predicate adjective

This **trip** **was** more **fun** than last year's trip.
subject verb   predicate adjective

The **trip** to New York **was** the most **fun** of all the trips.
subject   verb   predicate adjective

Compound Subject Complements

Like other sentence parts, subject complements can be compound.

A compound subject complement consists of two or more
predicate nouns, pronouns, or adjectives joined by a conjunction
such as *and* or *or.*

EXAMPLES   My two best **friends** **are** **Phil and Mark**.
subject   verb compound predicate noun

The **highway** **seems** **slick and icy**.
subject   verb   compound predicate adjective

The **dessert** **was** **apples and oranges**.
subject   verb   compound predicate noun

The two **dogs** **are** **wet and muddy**.
subject   verb compound predicate adjective

The **caller** **might have been** **he or she**.
subject   verb   compound predicate pronoun

398   Complements

PRACTICE 18.5G Identifying Predicate Nouns and Predicate Pronouns

Read the sentences. Write the predicate noun or predicate pronoun in each sentence.

EXAMPLE   My mom is a psychologist.

ANSWER   *psychologist*

1. The Komodo dragon is the largest lizard.
2. A loud voice announced, "It is I."
3. The man in the uniform was captain of the ship.
4. Rome is a city with a lot of history.
5. My favorite fruit is a peach.
6. That tree is a birch.
7. Margo is a good singer.
8. The caterpillar had become a butterfly.
9. The winner is he.
10. Even after his injury, Paco remained our best player.

PRACTICE 18.5H Recognizing Comparative and Superlative Predicate Adjectives

Read the sentences. Write sentences using the comparative and superlative forms of the predicate adjective. Discuss the function of each predicate adjective in its comparative and superlative form with a partner.

EXAMPLE   The steps are slippery after the rain.

ANSWER   *The first step is more slippery than the second one.*

The top step is the most slippery of the three.

11. Miguel is particular about his appearance.
12. Kelsey seems friendly.
13. That detail is important.
14. The last lesson was valuable.
15. Leticia's eyes are blue.
16. The crossing at the stoplight had been hazardous.
17. Diamonds are hard.
18. The chicken casserole is appetizing.
19. Their house design is traditional.
20. Watermelon is juicy.

SPEAKING APPLICATION

In a small group, share memorable experiences. Use comparative and superlative predicate adjectives. Then, make a list of your adjectives and read the list. Discuss the function of these comparative or superlative forms and write a sentence for each.

WRITING APPLICATION

Write a paragraph about characters in a book. Use comparative and superlative forms of predicate adjectives. Read your paragraph to a partner. Have your partner identify the predicate adjectives and explain the forms.

Test Warm-Up

DIRECTIONS

Read the introduction and the passage that follows. Then, answer the questions to show that you can use and understand the function of predicate adjectives and their comparative and superlative forms in reading and writing.

Morgan wrote this paragraph to describe a school celebration. Read the paragraph and think about the changes you would suggest as a peer editor. When you finish reading, answer the questions that follow.

The Best Party Ever

(1) Our school had a party to celebrate winning the trivia contest with Jefferson Middle School. (2) It was a big victory for us since the questions were most challenging than the ones in our earlier contests. (3) Everyone says that Andrea planned a party that became the all-time best. (4) No one could agree about which of the dozen treats was more deliciouser. (5) The sandwiches were great. (6) The lasagna was flavorfuler. (7) In my opinion, the salad was more scrumptious of all.

---

1 What change, if any, should be made in sentence 2?

  A Add *more* before **most**

  B Change *most* to **more**

  C Add a comma after *challenging*

  D Make no change

2 What is the BEST way to revise sentence 4?

  F No one could agree about which of the dozen treats was more delicious.

  G No one could agree about which of the dozen treats was most delicious.

  H No one could agree about which of the dozen treats was more delicious of all.

  J No one could agree about which of the dozen treats was most deliciouser.

3 What is the BEST way to combine sentences 5 and 6?

  A The sandwiches were great, but the lasagna was more flavorful.

  B The sandwiches were great, the lasagna was more flavorfulest.

  C The sandwiches were more great, but the lasagna was more flavorful.

  D The sandwiches were more great, and the lasagna was more flavorful.

4 What is the BEST way to revise sentence 7?

  F In my opinion, the salad was more scrumptiouser of all.

  G In my opinion, the salad was most scrumptiouser of all.

  H In my opinion, the salad was most scrumptious of all.

  J In my opinion, the salad was scrumptious of all.

CHAPTER 19

PHRASES *and* CLAUSES

Understanding how to build sentences using phrases and clauses will help add variety to your writing.

WRITE GUY *Jeff Anderson, M.Ed.*

WHAT DO YOU NOTICE?

Look for phrases as you zoom in on sentences from the play *The Phantom Toll Booth* by Susan Nanus, based on the book by Norton Juster.

MENTOR TEXT

> This is Dictionopolis, a happy kingdom, advantageously located in the foothills of Confusion and caressed by gentle breezes from the Sea of Knowledge. Today, by royal proclamation, is Market Day.

Now, ask yourself the following questions:

- What purpose does the appositive phrase *a happy kingdom* serve in the first sentence?
- What are the prepositional phrases in the first sentence?

The appositive phrase *a happy kingdom* provides readers with more information about Dictionopolis. The five prepositional phrases in the first sentence are *in the foothills, of Confusion, by gentle breezes, from the Sea,* and *of Knowledge.*

Grammar for Writers Writers can use phrases to add more information to their sentences. Be sure to place phrases carefully in your sentences so that they modify the correct words.

Are phrases always short?

It depends on who their parents are.

19.1 Phrases

Sentences are usually built with more than just a subject and a verb. **Phrases** play an important role in sentences by adding more information.

WRITING COACH

Online
www.phwritingcoach.com

Grammar Tutorials
Brush up on your Grammar skills with these animated videos.

Grammar Practice
Practice your grammar skills with Writing Coach Online.

Grammar Games
Test your knowledge of grammar in this fast-paced interactive video game.

RULE 19.1.1

> A **phrase** is a group of words that functions in a sentence as a single part of speech. Phrases do not contain a subject and a verb.

Prepositional Phrases

A **prepositional phrase** has at least two parts, a preposition and a noun or pronoun that is the object of the preposition.

EXAMPLES

near **airports**
 prep   object

around **trees**
 prep   object

The object of the preposition may be modified by one or more adjectives.

EXAMPLES

near busy urban **airports**
 prep adj   adj   object

around lovely green **trees**
 prep   adj   adj   object

The object may also be a compound, consisting of two or more objects connected by a conjunction such as *and* or *nor*.

EXAMPLES

near busy urban **highways** and **airports**
 prep adj   adj   object   object

around lovely green **trees** and **grass**
 prep   adj   adj   object   object

In a sentence, some prepositional phrases can act as adjectives that modify a noun or pronoun. Other prepositional phrases can act as adverbs that modify a verb, adjective, or adverb.

See Practice 19.1A

Using Prepositional Phrases That Act as Adjectives

A prepositional phrase that acts as an adjective in a sentence is called an **adjective phrase** or **adjectival phrase.**

> An **adjective phrase** or **adjectival phrase** is a prepositional phrase that modifies a noun or pronoun by telling *what kind* or *which one.*

19.1.2

RULE

Unlike one-word adjectives, which usually come before the nouns or pronouns they modify, adjectival phrases usually come after the nouns or pronouns they modify.

ONE-WORD ADJECTIVES	ADJECTIVAL PHRASES
The asphalt roadway began there.	The roadway with two lanes began there.
The angry rancher stopped us.	The rancher with the angry face stopped us.

Adjectival phrases answer the same questions as one-word adjectives do. *What kind* of roadway began there? *Which* rancher stopped us?

USES OF ADJECTIVAL PHRASES	
Modifying a Subject	The sound of the wind scared us.
Modifying a Direct Object	It rattled windows in the room.

When two adjectival phrases appear in a row, the second phrase may modify the object of the preposition in the first phrase or both phrases may modify the same noun or pronoun.

ADJECTIVAL PHRASES IN A ROW	
Modifying the Object of a Preposition	The weather vane on the roof of the barn spun wildly.
Modifying the Same Noun	There was a smell of rain in the air.

See Practice 19.1B

Using Prepositional Phrases That Act as Adverbs

A prepositional phrase that acts as an adverb modifies the same parts of speech as a one-word adverb does.

RULE 19.1.3

> An **adverbial phrase** or **adverb phrase** is a prepositional phrase that modifies a verb, an adjective, or an adverb. Adverbial phrases point out *where, when, in what way,* or *to what extent.*

Adverbial phrases are used in the same way as one-word adverbs, but they sometimes provide more precise details.

ONE-WORD ADVERBS	ADVERBIAL PHRASES
Bring your saddle here .	Bring your saddle to the barn .
The parade began early .	The parade began at exactly eleven o'clock .

Adverbial phrases can modify verbs, adjectives, and adverbs.

USES OF ADVERBIAL PHRASES	
Modifying a Verb	Raindrops fell in heavy torrents . (Fell *in what way?*)
Modifying an Adjective	The day was warm for December . (Warm *in what way?*)
Modifying an Adverb	The rain fell softly, for a monsoon storm . (Softly *in what way?*)

Adverbial phrases, unlike adjectival phrases, are not always located near the words they modify in a sentence.

MODIFIES

EXAMPLE   **During the storm**, ranchers chased the herd.

Two or more adverbial phrases can also be located in different parts of the sentence and still modify the same word.

MODIFIES   MODIFIES

EXAMPLE   **In an instant**, a tornado tore **through our house.**

See Practice 19.1C
See Practice 19.1D

PRACTICE 19.1A > **Identifying Prepositional Phrases**

Read the sentences. Then, write the prepositional phrase in each sentence and underline the object of the preposition. Then, write the function of the prepositional phrase (to convey *location*, *time*, or *direction*, or to provide *details*).

EXAMPLE   Stories exist in all societies.

ANSWER   *in all societies* — details

1. I found the professor in the chemistry lab.

2. Can you get my shirts from the cleaners?

3. She parked her bike in front of the store.

4. The advanced math concept was beyond his understanding.

5. They ran around the backyard.

6. The two baby girls were snug under the soft, warm, pink blanket.

7. I left the rake inside the tool shed.

8. The road runs between a forest and the river.

9. She read a history book during the first study period.

10. He backed his car into the neighbor's garage.

PRACTICE 19.1B > **Identifying Adjectival Phrases**

Read the sentences. Then, write the adjectival phrase in each sentence. One sentence has two adjectival phrases.

EXAMPLE   The door to his office is locked.

ANSWER   *to his office*

11. The road toward the east is the one we will take.

12. Many of these books have great plots.

13. I want the one between the red and gray bicycles.

14. That's the birthday present from my grandmother.

15. The bed with the firm mattress was most comfortable.

16. The store at the corner has that magazine.

17. The sound of rushing water helped us find the waterfall.

18. I'm buying food for a friend with allergies.

19. This would be a great day for kite flying.

20. I bought a book about Booker T. Washington.

SPEAKING APPLICATION

With a partner, take turns talking about a trip to a store. Use at least four prepositional phrases (to convey *location*, *time*, or *direction*, or to provide *details*) including two adjectival phrases to describe something about the trip, such as where the store is, what it's like, or things you might buy there. Your partner should listen for and identify the prepositional phrases.

WRITING APPLICATION

Write a short paragraph about a trip into the country. Use prepositional phrases (to convey *location*, *time*, or *direction*, or to provide *details*) including adjectival phrases to describe the things you might see, hear, or experience.

PRACTICE 19.1C Identifying Adverbial Phrases

Read the sentences. Then, write the adverbial phrase in each sentence. One sentence has two adverbial phrases.

EXAMPLE   Mother worried about our safety.

ANSWER   *about our safety*

1. We crossed Lake Michigan on a ferry.
2. The glasses fell with a loud crash.
3. He stood in the rain.
4. The children spoke in hushed voices.
5. Carlotta plays on the soccer team.
6. In the morning, before sunrise, my mom starts making breakfast.
7. The ball rolled under the table.
8. Put those groceries in the cupboard.
9. The rain came down with increasing fury.
10. Craig and Aaron ran toward the cheering crowd.

PRACTICE 19.1D Writing Adjectival and Adverbial Phrases

Read the sentences. Then, rewrite the sentences by adding adjectival or adverbial phrases, as directed in parentheses.

EXAMPLE   Close the door. (adjectival phrase)

ANSWER   *Close the door to the basement.*

11. Many rivers flow. (adverbial phrase)
12. I would like a jacket. (adjectival phrase)
13. We went swimming. (adverbial phrase)
14. Jena works at the drugstore. (adverbial phrase)
15. The bicycle looks great. (adjectival phrase)
16. The forest is where we hike. (adjectival phrase)
17. The football team practices. (adverbial phrase)
18. I bought a wooden box. (adjectival phrase)
19. Some pieces are missing. (adjectival phrase)
20. We read the directions. (adverbial phrase)

SPEAKING APPLICATION

With a partner, discuss the climate where you live. Use at least one adjectival phrase and one adverbial phrase to describe different types of weather you experience. Your partner should listen for and identify the adjectival and adverbial phrases.

WRITING APPLICATION

Write a short paragraph about a visit to an amusement park. Use at least one adjectival phrase and one adverbial phrase to describe what you do and what you see.

Using Appositives and Appositive Phrases

Appositives, like adjectival phrases, give information about nouns or pronouns.

> An **appositive** is a noun or pronoun placed after another noun or pronoun to identify, rename, or explain the preceding word.

RULE 19.1.4

Appositives are very useful in writing because they give additional information without using many words.

EXAMPLES   The conquistador **Francisco de Coronado** led an expedition looking for gold.

I admire the poet **Robert Frost** .

An appositive with its own modifiers creates an **appositive phrase.**

> An **appositive phrase** is a noun or pronoun with modifiers. It is placed next to a noun or pronoun and adds information or details.

RULE 19.1.5

The modifiers in an appositive phrase can be adjectives or adjectival phrases.

EXAMPLES   Uncle Jim, my **favorite** **uncle** , plays the piano.
adjective   noun

In the hall is a painting, a **mural** **in many bright colors** .
noun   adj phrase

Appositives and appositive phrases can also be a compound.

See Practice 19.1E
See Practice 19.1F

EXAMPLE   Volunteers, **boys** and **girls** , work together.
compound noun

PRACTICE 19.1E > Identifying Appositives and Appositive Phrases

Read the sentences. Then, write the appositive or appositive phrase in each sentence.

EXAMPLE   My cousin, Sarah Donnelly, is a veterinarian at our local zoo.

ANSWER   *Sarah Donnelly*

1. The Wright brothers, bicycle mechanics, built the first successful airplane.

2. I enjoy music written by the composer Mozart.

3. We took flowers to Mrs. Tran, our neighbor.

4. Alaska, the largest state in the nation, covers more than 500,000 square miles.

5. My mom's cousin, Misha, will be visiting.

6. Kanji, one of Japan's three alphabets, was adapted from Chinese characters.

7. Placido Domingo, the great Spanish singer, will be performing here next week.

8. America's Jazz Age, the 1920s, saw a growing appreciation of African American art and music.

9. This story was told by Isaac Asimov, the great science fiction writer.

10. Marsupials, animals that carry their young in pouches, include kangaroos and koalas.

PRACTICE 19.1F > Combining Sentences With Appositive Phrases

Read the sentences. Combine each pair of sentences by using an appositive phrase.

EXAMPLE   He won first prize. First prize is a trip to Hawaii.

ANSWER   *He won first prize, a trip to Hawaii.*

11. Samuel Adams was an American patriot. Samuel Adams entered Harvard at the age of 14.

12. Ancient Greeks played the lyre. The lyre is a stringed instrument.

13. Thistles are plants with purple flowers. The thistle is the national flower of Scotland.

14. Apples are members of the rose family. Apples have white and pink flowers.

15. Sequoyah was a Cherokee. Sequoyah invented an alphabet for the Cherokee people.

16. The fourth Thursday in November is Thanksgiving. It is a national holiday.

17. A diamond is the hardest mineral in the world. A diamond is a form of pure carbon.

18. Dr. Martin Luther King Jr. was a civil rights leader. Dr. King was a great speaker.

19. The pomegranate is a tart fruit. The pomegranate has many seeds.

20. The poem is about a gosling. A gosling is a young goose.

SPEAKING APPLICATION

With a partner, take turns telling about something you learned at school. Use two appositive phrases. Your partner should listen for and identify the appositive phrases.

WRITING APPLICATION

Write three sentences about a person or people you have studied. In each sentence, include an appositive phrase that adds information to the sentence.

Using Verbals and Verbal Phrases

A **verbal** is any verb form that is used in a sentence not as a verb but as another part of speech.

Like verbs, verbals can be modified by an adverb or adverbial phrase. They can also be followed by a complement. A verbal used with a modifier or a complement is called a **verbal phrase.**

Participles

Participles are verb forms with two basic uses. When they are used with helping verbs, they are verbs. When they are used alone to modify nouns or pronouns, they become adjectives.

> A **participle** is a form of a verb that is often used as an adjective.

There are two kinds of participles, **present participles** and **past participles.** Each kind can be recognized by its ending.

All present participles end in *-ing.*

EXAMPLES   talking   doing   eating   wanting

Most past participles end either in *-ed* or in *-d.*

EXAMPLES   opened   jumped   played   moved

Other past participles end in *-n, -t, -en*, or another irregular ending.

EXAMPLES   grown   felt   bought   eaten   held

Both present and past participles can be used in sentences as adjectives. They tell *what kind* or *which one.*

PRESENT PARTICIPLES	PAST PARTICIPLES
He arranged a walking tour.	Chilled fruit tastes good.
The dancing bears were a delight.	He was, by then, a grown man.

See Practice 19.1G

Participle or Verb?

Sometimes, verb phrases (verbs with helping verbs) are confused with participles. A verb phrase always begins with a helping verb. A participle used as an adjective stands by itself and modifies a noun or pronoun.

VERB PHRASES	PARTICIPLES
The car was racing around the curve.	The racing car crashed into the wall.
Early settlers may have traveled on this road.	The traveled road led to the sea.

Participial Phrases

A participle can be expanded into a participial phrase by adding a complement or modifier.

RULE 19.1.7

> **A participial phrase** is a present or past participle and its modifiers. The entire phrase acts as an adjective in a sentence.

Participial phrases can be formed by adding an adverb, an adverbial phrase, or a complement to a participle.

EXAMPLES   The instructor, **speaking slowly**, explained the use of skis.

The esteemed poet, **honored by the award**, expressed his thanks.

The first participial phrase contains the adverb *slowly* added to the participle *speaking*. The second includes the adverbial phrase *by the award* added to the participle *honored*.

A participial phrase can also be placed at the beginning of a sentence. The phrase is usually followed by a comma.

EXAMPLE   **Honored by the award**, the esteemed poet expressed his thanks.

See Practice 19.1H
See Practice 19.1I
See Practice 19.1J

PRACTICE 19.1G **Identifying Present and Past Participles**

Read the sentences. Then, write the participle in each sentence and label it *present participle* or *past participle*.

EXAMPLE   Holding onto the railing, the toddler went down the stairs.

ANSWER   *Holding* — present participle

1. The rabbit, hopping across the yard, saw the cat.

2. The only people allowed in the classroom are students.

3. The actors, dressed in funny costumes, sprint across the stage.

4. Rushing down the hall, the doctor responds to an emergency.

5. Chess is a challenging game.

6. The picture drawn in charcoal wins first prize in the art contest.

7. The bird hurt in the storm couldn't return to its nest.

8. During the scavenger hunt, the best clue was the map hidden under the statue.

9. Neil's new running shoes were uncomfortable.

10. The laughter spreading through the audience almost brings the play to a halt.

PRACTICE 19.1H **Distinguishing Verbs and Participles**

Read the sentences. Then, write *verb* or *participle* for the underlined word in each sentence.

EXAMPLE   The woman <u>standing</u> in the corridor is the school principal.

ANSWER   *participle*

11. Those <u>participating</u> in the game were eager to start.

12. The airplane had <u>landed</u> twenty minutes early.

13. <u>Dripping</u> steadily, the leak filled the bucket in no time at all.

14. She was <u>learning</u> to play the guitar after school.

15. Greg <u>showed</u> up without any warning.

16. The plot of the mystery, <u>taken</u> from a recent news story, was familiar to everyone.

17. The trees <u>cleared</u> from the land were used to make wood for furniture.

18. The mayor is <u>defending</u> the new budget.

19. There were <u>varying</u> opinions on the success of the play.

20. The number of goals <u>scored</u> during the period was the highest of the season.

SPEAKING APPLICATION

With a partner, take turns describing a character in a book, movie, or television show. Use at least one present or past participle. Your partner should listen for and name the participle and tell whether it is present or past.

WRITING APPLICATION

Use sentence 13 as a model, and write one sentence with a participle. Then, use sentence 18 as a model, and write one sentence with a verb.

PRACTICE 19.1I ▷ **Identifying Participial Phrases**

Read the sentences. Then, write the participial phrase in each sentence. Underline the participle.

EXAMPLE   Snakes found in South America are often poisonous.

ANSWER   *found in South America*

1. Told around the campfire, the stories seemed particularly exciting.

2. Letters sent by airmail arrive faster.

3. Saltwater crocodiles, measuring up to 25 feet in length, are the largest reptiles.

4. Originating in Africa, many folktales about animals are shared around the world.

5. Heading into the wind, the geese began their flight.

6. The pecans grown in Texas are some of the best.

7. The boys, ignoring all warnings, walked onto the ice-covered pond.

8. This plant, related to the lily, is easy to grow.

9. Climbing the tree, the camper had a better view of her surroundings.

10. Impressed by the student's interest, the teacher let him use the microscope.

PRACTICE 19.1J ▷ **Combining Sentences Using Participial Phrases**

Read the sentences. Combine each pair of sentences by using a participial phrase.

EXAMPLE   Cassie was trusted by the students. She was elected class president.

ANSWER   *Trusted by the students, Cassie was elected class president.*

11. The weeds were growing quickly. The weeds soon overtook the small garden.

12. The students entered the auditorium. The principal followed the students.

13. The tulips were the first to bloom. The tulips were responding to the sunshine.

14. The music box was carved from wood. The music box created a warm, rich sound.

15. Everyone recognized the captain. The captain could not avoid the press.

16. Emma was laughing happily. Emma raced toward the ocean.

17. The kite was caught by the wind. The kite swooped and dove gracefully.

18. My mom shut the window. The noise outside annoyed her.

19. The critics praised the author's first book. The book sold well.

20. Carl stood silently watching the cheetah. Carl held his breath.

SPEAKING APPLICATION

With a partner, take turns talking positively about someone you know. Use two participial phrases. Your partner should listen for and identify the participial phrases.

WRITING APPLICATION

Write three sentences about an animal you have seen or read about. Include a participial phrase in each sentence to add information about the animal's appearance or behavior.

Gerunds

Like present participles, **gerunds** end in *-ing*. While present participles are used as adjectives, gerunds can be used as subjects, direct objects, predicate nouns, and objects of prepositions.

> A **gerund** is a form of a verb that acts as a noun.

USE OF GERUNDS IN SENTENCES	
Subject	Remodeling keeps the builders busy.
Direct Object	Michael enjoys painting.
Predicate Noun	His favorite sport is fishing.
Object of a Preposition	Lucille never gets tired of singing.

Gerund Phrases

Gerunds can also be part of a phrase.

> A **gerund phrase** is a gerund with modifiers or a complement, all acting together as a noun.

This chart shows how gerunds are expanded to form gerund phrases.

FORMING GERUND PHRASES	
Gerund With Adjectives	The loud, shrill howling continued all morning.
Gerund With Direct Object	Reading science fiction inspired many screenwriters.
Gerund With Prepositional Phrase	He helped the police by telling about his experience.
Gerund With Adverb and Prepositional Phrase	The dancers astound spectators by dancing skillfully across the stage in perfect symmetry.

See Practice 19.1K
See Practice 19.1L

Infinitives

Infinitives are verb forms that are used as nouns, adjectives, and adverbs. Like participles and gerunds, they can be combined with other words to form phrases.

> **An infinitive** is a verb form that can be used as a noun, an adjective, or an adverb. The word *to* usually appears before the verb.

EXAMPLES   It is important **to listen**.

He is the one **to ask**.

To stay calm can be difficult.

Infinitive Phrases

> **An infinitive phrase** is an infinitive with modifiers or a complement, all acting together as a single part of speech.

EXAMPLES   It is important **to listen carefully**.

It is not polite **to listen through a keyhole**.

They want **to give you a present**.

An **infinitive phrase** can be used in a sentence as a noun, an adjective, or an adverb. As a noun, an infinitive phrase can function as a subject, an object, or an appositive.

USES OF INFINITIVES	
Used as a Subject	To speak slowly is important.
Used as an Object	She tried to speak slowly.
Used as an Appositive	His suggestion, to speak slowly, was appreciated.
Used as an Adjective	It was her goal to speak slowly.
Used as an Adverb	It isn't always easy to speak slowly when you are excited.

See Practice 19.1M

See Practice 19.1N

PRACTICE 19.1K **Identifying Gerund Phrases**

Read the sentences. Then, write the gerund phrase from each sentence, and underline the gerund. Remember to include all modifiers with the phrase.

EXAMPLE   The constant dripping began to bother me.

ANSWER   *The constant <u>dripping</u>*

1. Moving gracefully is important in women's gymnastics.
2. He gained confidence from his running.
3. Studying for the math exam took two hours.
4. The first step is buying the right equipment.
5. Rocking the crib might get the baby to sleep.
6. Chandra took off the bandages without considering the consequences.
7. Studying weather patterns helps scientists forecast the weather.
8. Use a sharp knife when cutting the vegetables.
9. The sweet, cheerful chirping of the birds told me spring was coming soon.
10. Counting your change is always a good idea.

PRACTICE 19.1L **Writing Gerunds and Gerund Phrases**

Read the sentences. Then, rewrite each sentence, completing it with a gerund or gerund phrase.

EXAMPLE   In the summer, I do a lot of _____.

ANSWER   *In the summer, I do a lot of swimming.*

11. I enjoy _____ for bargains.
12. _____ helped prepare me for the English test.
13. It's important to use the right tools when _____.
14. My mom regretted _____ that dress.
15. The _____ could be heard for miles.
16. When the hikers returned, they told us about _____.
17. _____ can really mess up the kitchen.
18. He gained satisfaction from _____.
19. The most fun activity in the winter is _____.
20. _____ is the first step in making soup.

SPEAKING APPLICATION

With a partner, discuss activities you enjoy doing on weekends. Make sure to use at least two gerunds as you speak. Your partner should listen for and name two gerunds.

WRITING APPLICATION

Use gerund phrases and write three sentences about the summer. Vary the position of the gerund phrases; don't have them all at the beginning or the end of the sentences.

PRACTICE 19.1M Identifying Infinitives and Infinitive Phrases

Read the sentences. Then, write the infinitive phrase from each sentence, and underline the infinitive. Also write *noun*, *adjective*, or *adverb* to describe each infinitive phrase.

EXAMPLE   The easiest way to get there is through the woods.

ANSWER   *to get there* — adjective

1. To find the solution to the puzzle was Katrina's goal.
2. You can trust Miguel to hold the baby gently.
3. The Kim family came from North Korea to the United States to escape communism.
4. Sarai has a paper to write before Friday.
5. John's goal is to speak in front of a large group.
6. To see our grandmother smiling was reassuring.
7. Their plan to build a new house will be challenging.
8. My mom went to buy groceries.
9. We all wanted to go to the beach.
10. The project to raise money for hungry children was successful.

PRACTICE 19.1N Writing Infinitives and Infinitive Phrases

Read the sentences. Then, rewrite each sentence, completing it with an infinitive or an infinitive phrase.

EXAMPLE   Last summer we went _____ our favorite cousins.

ANSWER   *Last summer we went to visit our favorite cousins.*

11. His plan _____ was approved.
12. The class wanted _____ for Earth Day.
13. _____ is really unforgettable.
14. Marsha's dream is _____.
15. Why don't you ask your friends _____?
16. _____ was all that Clara had planned for the evening.
17. Don't you have a report _____?
18. The proposal _____ was put up for a vote.
19. _____ made everyone happy.
20. Grandfather wanted _____ after he retired.

SPEAKING APPLICATION

With a partner, take turns talking about school assignments. Use the sentences in Practice 19.1M as models to help you include two infinitive phrases. Your partner should listen for and identify the infinitive phrases.

WRITING APPLICATION

Use the sentences in Practice 19.1M as models, and write three sentences about everyday life that include infinitive phrases.

19.2 Clauses

Clauses are the basic structural unit of a sentence.

RULE 19.2.1

A **clause** is a group of words with its own subject and verb.

There are two basic kinds of clauses, **main** or **independent clauses** and **subordinate clauses**.

RULE 19.2.2

A **main** or **independent clause** has a subject and a verb and can stand by itself as a complete sentence.

As you can see in the examples below, a main clause can be long or short. All main clauses express a complete thought and can stand by themselves as complete sentences.

EXAMPLES

The **air** **vibrated**.
subject   verb

Early in the day, **he** **began** playing the cello.
subject   verb

RULE 19.2.3

A **subordinate clause,** also known as a dependent clause, has a subject and a verb but cannot stand by itself as a complete sentence. It is only part of a sentence.

SUBORDINATE CLAUSES

after **she** **performed** her solo
subject   verb

while the **band** **practiced** in the garage
subject   verb

After reading a subordinate clause, you will still need more information to have a complete sentence.

Subordinate clauses begin with **subordinating conjunctions** or **relative pronouns.**

Some subordinate clauses begin with **subordinating conjunctions,** such as *if, since, when, although, after, because,* and *while.* Others begin with **relative pronouns,** such as *who, which,* or *that.* These words are clues that the clause may not be able to stand alone. Notice how the addition of subordinating words changes the meaning of the main clauses in the examples below.

COMPARING TWO KINDS OF CLAUSES	
MAIN	**SUBORDINATE**
He arrives this morning.	*when* he arrives this morning
This mosque has a golden dome.	*because* the mosque has a golden dome
I planted the seeds.	the seeds *that* I planted

In order to form a complete thought, a subordinate clause must be combined with a main clause.

EXAMPLES

After she performed her piece , Debbie felt
       subordinate clause   main clause

relieved.

The audience applauded **after Debbie performed**
      main clause   subordinate clause

her piece .

It was Debbie **who was asked to perform first** .
  main clause   subordinate clause

When he arrives this morning , Tom needs to
    subordinate clause   main clause

go right to the nurse.

See Practice 19.2A
See Practice 19.2B

PRACTICE 19.2A Identifying Main and Subordinate Clauses

Read the clauses. Then, write whether each clause is a *main clause* or a *subordinate clause*.

EXAMPLE   Because archaeology is a science.

ANSWER   *subordinate clause*

1. Where many seashells are found.

2. The rules of the game are easy.

3. After the third person walked across the hall.

4. Which meant someone had to call for help immediately.

5. Until the storm finally passed.

6. The team listened intently to the coach's words.

7. He worked hard.

8. That was hiding in plain sight on the lowest bookshelf in the library.

9. Whose paper was about to rip apart.

10. It seemed unbelievable to most listeners.

PRACTICE 19.2B Identifying and Using Main and Subordinate Clauses

Read the clauses. Write *main clause* or *subordinate clause* for each clause. Then, expand each subordinate clause into a complete sentence by adding a main clause.

EXAMPLE   Since the snowstorm ended.

ANSWER   *subordinate clause*
           We have been shoveling the driveway since the snowstorm ended.

11. When you are ready.

12. Every day is a new opportunity.

13. Although it was hot and sunny outside.

14. If the trumpet solo is easy enough to learn.

15. Jumping over a hurdle is difficult.

16. All the mail arrived safely.

17. After he arrived.

18. Ambulance driving is dangerous.

19. Even babies respond to smiles.

20. Who worked every weekend for a month.

SPEAKING APPLICATION

With a partner, take turns saying a subordinate clause. Your partner should expand the subordinate clause into a complete sentence by adding a main clause.

WRITING APPLICATION

Write three complete sentences about what you did at school today. Include a main clause and a subordinate clause. Circle the main clause and underline the subordinate clause in each sentence.

Practice   419

Adjectival Clauses

A subordinate clause will sometimes act as an adjective in a sentence. An adjectival clause or adjective clause is a dependent clause and can not stand on its own.

RULE 19.2.5

> An **adjectival clause** or **adjective clause** is a subordinate clause that modifies a noun or a pronoun.

Like one-word adjectives and adjectival phrases, **adjectival clauses** tell *what kind* or *which one*.

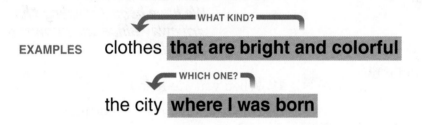

EXAMPLES

WHAT KIND?
clothes **that are bright and colorful**

WHICH ONE?
the city **where I was born**

Recognizing Adjectival Clauses
Most adjectival clauses begin with the words *that, which, who, whom,* and *whose.* Sometimes an adjectival clause begins with a subordinating conjunction, such as *since, where,* or *when.* In the chart below, the adjectival clauses are hightlighted in pink.

ADJECTIVAL CLAUSES
The teacher whom I asked for help stayed after school to work with me. (*Which* teacher?)
The talent show, which was advertised in the local paper, is tomorrow. (*Which* talent show?)
In the years since she started playing, Maia has become an accomplished pianist. (*Which* years?)
I hid my treasure box in the small closet where no one usually goes. (*Which* closet?)
We visited the museum that honors veterans of World War II. (*Which* museum?)
The museum whose exhibits include aircraft carriers is located in our town. (*Which* museum?)

See Practice 19.2C

Combining Sentences With Adjectival Clauses

Two sentences can be combined into one sentence by changing one of them into an adjectival clause. Sometimes you will need to add a relative pronoun or subordinating conjunction to make the sentence read correctly. In the sentences below, the adjectival clauses are highlighted in pink.

TWO SENTENCES	COMBINED WITH AN ADJECTIVAL CLAUSE
My history teacher has written books on the American Revolution. My history teacher is a famous scholar.	My history teacher, who has written books on the American Revolution, is a famous scholar.
We visited the history museum. The history museum is Tori's favorite museum.	We visited the history museum, which is Tori's favorite.
We decided to shop in Don's Grocery. We usually get the best bargains there.	We decided to shop in Don's Grocery, where we usually get the best bargains.
Paula visited her cousin last summer. Paula's cousin lives on a farm in Kansas.	Paula visited her cousin, who lives on a farm in Kansas, last summer.
Every summer, Elizabeth goes to a camp. Her camp is on a beautiful lake.	Every summer, Elizabeth goes to a camp that is on a beautiful lake.

See Practice 19.2D

PRACTICE 19.2C Identifying Adjectival Clauses

Read the sentences. Then, write the adjectival clause in each sentence. One sentence has two adjectival clauses.

EXAMPLE   The book, which my sister lent me, was totally engrossing.

ANSWER   *which my sister lent me*

1. The fish that Sam saw at the aquarium were incredibly colorful.

2. The movie scared my cousin, who asked if we could leave.

3. Your dog, whose bark is loud, is actually a nice dog, isn't he?

4. Heather's neighbors, whom she had not seen in many days, had been away on vacation.

5. The violinist who will be the soloist tonight is originally from Poland.

6. Jerry's great-grandmother, whom he never met, was the person who named him.

7. She had a strong preference for recipes that were easy to follow.

8. The path, which no one ever took, was overgrown and almost impassable.

9. The house where the playwright was born is now a tourist site.

10. Until now, the era when technological innovation was the greatest was the Industrial Revolution.

PRACTICE 19.2D Combining Sentences Using Adjectival Clauses

Read the sentences. Combine the pairs of sentences by changing one of them into an adjectival clause.

EXAMPLE   Kyle and Marcus ran indoors. They were dying of thirst.

ANSWER   *Kyle and Marcus, who were dying of thirst, ran indoors.*

11. The middle school held a science fair. The science fair was a great success.

12. The thunderstorm ruined the picnic. The picnic was for the softball team.

13. Tarik's cousin was visiting from Louisiana. Tarik hosted a Fourth of July party.

14. The dentist examined my teeth. The dentist was happy I had no cavities.

15. A snake startled me. The snake was slithering in the grass.

16. The babies' mothers leave the room. Babies often start crying.

17. Adam ran his eighth marathon last year. Adam is in good shape.

18. The firehouse was just rebuilt. The firehouse is ready to house a new engine.

19. Talia was the last to arrive. Talia did not know anyone.

20. The letter was waiting for him at home. The letter was an acceptance letter.

SPEAKING APPLICATION

With a partner, take turns describing something in the classroom. Use at least one adjectival clause. Your partner should listen for and identify the adjectival clause.

WRITING APPLICATION

Use the sentences in Practice 19.2D as models, and write two pairs of sentences. Then, for each pair, combine the sentences by changing one of them into an adjectival clause.

Adverbial Clauses

Subordinate clauses can also be used as adverbs. Adverbial clauses or adverb clauses are dependent clauses.

> An **adverbial clause** or **adverb clause** is a subordinate clause that modifies a verb, an adjective, or an adverb.

Adverbial clauses can answer any of the following questions about the words they modify: *Where? When? In what manner? To what extent? Under what conditions?* or *Why?*

ADVERBIAL CLAUSES	
Modifying Verbs	Put the package wherever you find room. (Put *where?*)
	The concert will begin when the conductor enters. (Will begin *when?*)
	Leo spoke as if he were frightened. (Spoke *in what manner?*)
	I will have lemonade if you do too. (Will have *under what conditions?*)
Modifying an Adjective	I am tired because I have been chopping wood all day. (Tired *why?*)
Modifying an Adverb	She knows more than the other engineers do. (More *to what extent?*)

Recognizing Adverbial Clauses

> **A subordinating conjunction** introduces an adverbial clause.

A **subordinating conjunction** always introduces an adverbial clause. In a sentence, the conjunction will usually appear in one of two places—either at the beginning, when the adverbial clause begins the sentence, or in the middle, connecting the independent clause to the subordinate clause. In the examples on the next page, the subordinating conjunctions are highlighted in purple.

EXAMPLES **Because** you will get home late, I will prepare dinner.

I will prepare dinner **because** you will get home late.

Whenever you are late, I expect you to call.

I expect you to call **whenever** you are late.

Common Subordinating Conjunctions

Here are the most common subordinating conjunctions. Knowing them can help you recognize adverbial clauses.

COMMON SUBORDINATING CONJUNCTIONS		
after	even though	unless
although	if	until
as	in order that	when
as if	since	whenever
as long as	so that	where
because	than	wherever
before	though	while

Elliptical Adverbial Clauses

In certain adverbial clauses, words are left out. These clauses are said to be elliptical.

RULE

19.2.8

In an **elliptical adverbial clause,** the verb or the subject and verb are understood rather than stated.

Many elliptical adverbial clauses are introduced by one of two subordinating conjunctions, *as* or *than*. In the following examples, the understood words have been added in parentheses. The first elliptical adverbial clause is missing a verb; the second is missing a subject and a verb.

EXAMPLES My brother can eat as much **as I** (can eat).

I liked this book more **than** (I liked) **that one**.

See Practice 19.2E

See Practice 19.2F

PRACTICE 19.2E **Identifying Adverbial Clauses and Recognizing Elliptical Adverbial Clauses**

Read the sentences. Then, write the adverbial clauses. For any of the adverbial clauses that are elliptical, add the understood words in parentheses.

EXAMPLE   I enjoyed Barcelona more than Madrid.

ANSWER   *than (I enjoyed) Madrid*

1. Not all countries have the same laws as the United States.

2. David wore boots so that his feet would not get wet in the rain.

3. Christine will not see her family again until after New Year's Day.

4. As long as the weather is good, we can have our picnic!

5. I liked this book more than that one.

6. China's population is larger than Japan's.

7. As the years go by, my aunt's eyesight worsens.

8. Carmen spent more time in France than in Germany.

9. When she arrived at the station, Sherri phoned.

10. Because I was tired, I didn't mind that everyone went home.

PRACTICE 19.2F **Combining Sentences With Adverbial Clauses**

Read the sentences. Combine each pair of sentences by changing one of them into an adverbial clause. Use an appropriate subordinating conjunction, and drop or change words as necessary.

EXAMPLE   I want to keep walking. My feet hurt.

ANSWER   *I want to keep walking even though my feet hurt.*

11. We watched a movie. We ate dinner.

12. We stayed home. There was a blizzard.

13. Jorge put a gate across the door. His puppy could not get into the kitchen.

14. Many people celebrated. The new president was inaugurated.

15. I will do the cooking. The dishes get washed and put away.

16. This book is interesting. It describes the history of baseball.

17. The carpenter began working. The oak boards had not yet been delivered.

18. Jeremy left the meeting. It was still going on.

19. Monica recognized her uncle. She had not seen him in five years.

20. I wanted to stay. I could continue to take notes.

SPEAKING APPLICATION

With a partner, take turns discussing two books that you read. Use Sentence 5 as a model, and say which book you liked more than the other. Your partner should listen for and identify the adverbial clause.

WRITING APPLICATION

Use the sentences in Practice 19.2F as models, and write two pairs of sentences. For each pair, combine the two sentences by changing one of them into an adverbial clause using an appropriate subordinating conjunction.

19.3 Classifying Sentences by Structure

All sentences can be classified according to the number and kinds of clauses they contain.

The Simple Sentence

The **simple sentence** is the most common type of sentence structure.

RULE 19.3.1

> A **simple sentence** consists of a single independent clause.

Simple sentences vary in length. Some are quite short; others can be several lines long. All simple sentences, however, contain just one subject and one verb. They may also contain adjectives, adverbs, complements, and phrases in different combinations.

Simple sentences can also have various compound parts. They can have a compound subject, a compound verb, or both. Sometimes, they will also have other compound elements, such as a compound direct object or a compound phrase.

All of the following sentences are simple sentences.

TYPES OF SIMPLE SENTENCES	
With One Subject and Verb	The rain came.
With a Compound Subject	Rain and snow are common.
With a Compound Verb	The door squeaked and rattled.
With a Compound Subject and Compound Verb	My mother and father said good-bye and left on vacation.
With a Compound Direct Object	He opened the letter and the box. direct object direct object
With a Compound Prepositional Phrase	It can rain from the east or from the west. prep phrase prep phrase

A simple sentence never has a subordinate clause, and it never has more than one main or independent clause.

WRITING COACH

Online

www.phwritingcoach.com

Grammar Tutorials

Brush up on your Grammar skills with these animated videos.

Grammar Practice

Practice your grammar skills with Writing Coach Online.

Grammar Games

Test your knowledge of grammar in this fast-paced interactive video game.

The Compound Sentence

A **compound sentence** is made up of more than one simple sentence.

> A **compound sentence** consists of two or more main or independent clauses.

19.3.2 RULE

In most compound sentences, the main or independent clauses are joined by a comma and a coordinating conjunction (*and, but, for, nor, or, so,* or *yet*). They may also be connected with a semicolon (;) or a colon (:).

EXAMPLES   **Jamal** **organized** a two-day music festival **,** **and** eight **bands** **agreed** to play.

All the bands **performed** on the first day **;** **two** **were missing** the second day.

See Practice 19.3A
See Practice 19.3B

Notice in both of the preceding examples that there are two separate and complete main clauses, each with its own subject and verb. Like simple sentences, compound sentences never contain subordinate clauses.

The Complex Sentence

Complex sentences contain subordinate clauses, which can be either adjectival clauses or adverbial clauses.

> A **complex sentence** consists of one main or independent clause and one or more subordinate clauses.

19.3.3 RULE

In a complex sentence, the independent clause is often called the **main clause.** The main clause has its own subject and verb, as does each subordinate clause.

In a complex sentence, the main clause can stand alone as a simple sentence. The subordinate clause cannot stand alone as a sentence.

EXAMPLES

January 26, 1950, is the day **that India adopted**
  main clause   subordinate clause

its constitution .

Because the day is so important, **many of the**
         subordinate clause

festivities are official .
         main clause

In some complex sentences, the main clause is split by a subordinate clause that acts as an adjective.

EXAMPLE

Schoolchildren , **who have the day**

off , **participate in an exciting parade** .

See Practice 19.3C
See Practice 19.3D
See Practice 19.3E
See Practice 19.3F

The two parts of the main clause form one main clause: *Schoolchildren participate in an exciting parade.*

The Compound-Complex Sentence

A **compound-complex sentence,** as the name indicates, contains the elements of both a compound sentence and a complex sentence.

> A **compound-complex sentence** consists of two or more main or independent clauses and one or more subordinate clauses.

EXAMPLE

As he was leaving for school ,
         subordinate clause

Larry remembered to take his lunch , but
              main clause

he forgot the report **that he had finished the**
         main clause   subordinate clause

night before .

 **PRACTICE 19.3A** **Distinguishing Simple and Compound Sentences**

Read the sentences. Then, write *simple* or *compound* for each sentence.

EXAMPLE   Students will perform the school musical at the end of March.

ANSWER   *simple*

1. The parrots flew out of the forest.

2. The lions and tigers were in separate cages, but they ate at the same time.

3. My mom went on a business trip to San Francisco, so I did not see her.

4. The train puffed and chugged up the hill.

5. The Pony Express carried mail across the West.

6. My grandfather and my dad measured the wall, yet the refrigerator did not quite fit.

7. My brother mowed Mrs. Clausen's lawn and trimmed her hedges.

8. Last night's snowstorm kept us from going to school today, but we should be back in school tomorrow.

9. My sister and her friends wanted to go to a museum, so they planned a trip for next Tuesday.

10. The plane arrived ten minutes early.

PRACTICE 19.3B **Combining Simple Sentences to Form Compound Sentences**

Read the sentences. Combine the pairs of simple sentences to form compound sentences.

EXAMPLE   The sun was hot. The water was cold.

ANSWER   *The sun was hot, but the water was cold.*

11. Dad found a worm in the apple. He threw out the apple.

12. The snow was falling. The children were catching the snowflakes.

13. Eva cried and stamped her feet. Dad still would not let her see that movie.

14. Johnny and Carlos ran to school. The twins followed them.

15. My sister wanted to live in a warmer climate. She moved to Texas.

16. We must fix the roof. The rain will get in.

17. Latisha and Samuel finished their homework. They may go out to play.

18. The rain began to come down. I opened my umbrella.

19. We tried to get tickets for the play. The box office was closed.

20. Mrs. Baez just arrived for dinner. I heard her car door close.

SPEAKING APPLICATION

With a partner, take turns talking about chores you do around your house. Use one compound sentence. Your partner should listen for and identify two main clauses.

WRITING APPLICATION

Write three compound sentences about activities you do after school. Underline the main clauses.

Read the sentences. Then, label each sentence *complex* or *not complex*.

EXAMPLE   Kim had never had a pet, so her parents gave her one for her birthday.

ANSWER   *not complex*

1. Before she entered a room, the nurse checked to see that she had everything.
2. Mom sent me to the store to buy noodles and celery.
3. Until the Johnsons get home, Marcie is caring for their cats.
4. We had better hurry, or we will miss the train.
5. I did not pass the test, which means I have to take it over.
6. Janine trained hard for the race, though she did not expect to win.
7. Last week we visited five cities in three states.
8. Because Celine was celebrating her birthday, we all brought gifts.
9. If you get an *A* on the test, you may go to the fair.
10. We should have reached Grandmother's house by now.

Read the sentences. Then, label each sentence *compound* or *complex*.

EXAMPLE   When the bird landed on the branch, Shelby took a photograph.

ANSWER   *complex*

11. I went to the grocery store, and Dad went to the hardware store.
12. Cory chose to write about Australia because he wanted to learn about kangaroos.
13. If we find we are running late, we can call a taxi.
14. Loraine and Brandon enjoy basketball, and they play often.
15. While Mom and Aunt Grace fixed dinner, Dad and Uncle Sal fixed the television set.
16. Felicia is very good at math, and she wants to study math in college.
17. Juwan enjoys fishing, and he often goes fishing with his brothers.
18. When I have enough money for a new bicycle, I will give you the old one.
19. Because clouds were gathering, Mom made us go inside.
20. We took photographs of the waterfall; we wanted to remember its beauty.

SPEAKING APPLICATION

With a partner, take turns discussing a movie you saw recently. Use at least two complex sentences to show the relationships between events. Your partner should listen for and identify two subordinate clauses.

WRITING APPLICATION

Write a brief summary of a story you recently read. Include at least two complex sentences to show how events or actions are related.

PRACTICE 19.3E **Combining Sentences and Identifying the Structure**

Read the sentences. Combine the two sentences in each item, and write a compound or a complex sentence. Identify your sentence as compound or complex.

EXAMPLE   The tickets are expensive. All of them are sold.

ANSWER   *The tickets are expensive, yet all of them are sold.* — compound

1. The television star saw the photographers. He waved.

2. We have a dog and two kittens. We adopted them from the shelter.

3. My brother joined the Army. He is in training for nine weeks.

4. Nicholas started telling the same old stories. Olivia left.

5. Timothy read two books by Cynthia Rylant. She is his favorite writer.

6. Sondra comes over every day. She must feel at home here.

7. Logan's voice shook. He was cold or nervous.

8. The door slammed. There was no wind.

9. We lost the championship game. It was close until the ninth inning.

10. I did not go rock climbing yesterday. I did not go hiking either.

PRACTICE 19.3F **Writing Compound and Complex Sentences**

Read each simple sentence. Then, write a new compound or complex sentence by adding to it.

EXAMPLE   Daisy has never gotten straight A's.

ANSWER   *Although Daisy has never gotten straight A's, she could do it.*

11. The waitress took our order.

12. You can find a coupon for a free meal in the newspaper.

13. Apples are a good buy in October.

14. Little Mikey wants to be a basketball player.

15. My ballet lesson is at 4 o'clock.

16. My grandparents are coming from Florida.

17. Our town does not have an airport.

18. Ana has read her favorite book three times.

19. Nichole swims across the lake.

20. You can visit the historic landmark.

SPEAKING APPLICATION

With a partner, talk about teachers you admire at your school. Use compound and complex sentences to describe them. Then, write one compound and two complex sentences about another adult you respect.

WRITING APPLICATION

Write a short paragraph about a place. It can be a nearby shop or a faraway spot. Use two compound sentences and two complex sentences. Read your paragraph to a partner, who identifies the structures of the sentences.

Test Warm-Up

DIRECTIONS

Read the introduction and the passage that follows. Then, answer the questions to show that you can use and understand the function of compound and complex sentences in reading and writing.

Monica wrote the following paragraph about her cat, Callie. Read the paragraph and think about the changes you would suggest as a peer editor. When you finish reading, answer the questions that follow.

Callie's Adventurous Day

(1) After getting the mail yesterday I put food in my cat's bowl. (2) Callie is always hungry, and she usually comes to gobble up food. (3) This time she didn't but I had homework and had to get back to it. (4) After a while, I checked her bowl to find it still full, and I became worried. (5) I opened the front door. (6) There she was. (7) She ran inside and dashed toward the kitchen. (8) I was so busy Callie was gone for two hours before I noticed.

---

1 What change, if any, should be made in sentence 1?

  A Delete the word *After*

  B Add the word **and** after *yesterday*

  C Add a comma after *yesterday*

  D Make no change

2 What change should be made in sentence 3?

  F Add a comma after *time*

  G Add a comma after *didn't*

  H Add a comma after *homework*

  J Add a semicolon after *homework*

3 What is the BEST way to combine sentences 5 and 6?

  A I opened the front door, and there she was.

  B I opened the front door, there she was.

  C I opened the front door although there she was.

  D Even though I opened the front door, there she was.

4 What is the BEST way to revise sentence 8?

  F I was so busy because Callie was gone for two hours before I noticed.

  G That I was so busy Callie was gone for two hours before I noticed.

  H I was so busy, but Callie was gone for two hours before I noticed.

  J Because I was so busy, Callie was gone for two hours before I noticed.

CHAPTER 20

EFFECTIVE SENTENCES

Using a variety of sentences will add interest to your writing and help it flow smoothly.

WRITE GUY *Jeff Anderson, M.Ed.*

WHAT DO YOU NOTICE?

Check out different types of sentences as you zoom in on these lines from the poem "April Rain Song" by Langston Hughes.

MENTOR TEXT

> Let the rain beat upon your head with silver liquid drops.
> Let the rain sing you a lullaby.
>
> The rain makes still pools on the sidewalk.
> The rain makes running pools in the gutter.

Now, ask yourself the following questions:

- Which sentences give a command or an order?
- Which sentences state or declare a fact or an idea?

The first and second sentences are imperative; they command the reader to do something. The third and fourth sentences are declarative; they state a fact. Both imperative and declarative sentences usually end with a period.

Grammar for Writers Writers use different types of sentences to say what they really mean. Effective sentences give readers a strong sense of the writer's voice and message.

I look great today.

How very declarative of you to say so.

20.1 Classifying the Four Functions of a Sentence

Sentences can be classified according to what they do. Some sentences present facts or information in a direct way, while others pose questions to the reader or listener. Still others present orders or directions. A fourth type of sentence expresses strong emotion.

WRITING COACH

Online

www.phwritingcoach.com

Grammar Tutorials
Brush up on your Grammar skills with these animated videos.

Grammar Practice
Practice your grammar skills with Writing Coach Online.

Grammar Games
Test your knowledge of grammar in this fast-paced interactive video game.

These four types of sentences are called **declarative, interrogative, imperative,** and **exclamatory.** As well as having a different purpose, each type of sentence is constructed in a different way.

The type of sentence you are writing determines the punctuation mark you use to end the sentence. The three end marks are the **period (.),** the **question mark (?),** and the **exclamation mark (!).**

The **declarative sentence** is the most common type of sentence. It is used to state, or "declare," ideas, facts, or opinions.

RULE 20.1.1

> A **declarative sentence** states, or declares, an idea and ends with a period.

DECLARATIVE   Soccer is a team sport.

Golf is a sport that can be played throughout a lifetime.

Although most schools fund team sports, many students choose to participate in individual sports.

Interrogative means "asking." An **interrogative sentence** is a question. Interrogative sentences often begin with *who, what, when, why, how,* or *how many.* They end with a question mark.

> **An interrogative sentence asks a question and ends with a question mark.**

INTERROGATIVE   What is your time in the half-mile run?

Where is the county track meet being held?

Who is the fastest runner on the track team?

> **An imperative sentence gives an order, or command, or a direction and ends with either a period or an exclamation mark.**

The word *imperative* comes from the Latin word that means "commanding." **Imperative sentences** are commands or directions. Most imperative sentences start with a verb. In this type of sentence, the subject is understood to be *you*.

IMPERATIVE   Follow my instructions carefully.

Run as hard as you can!

Notice the punctuation at the end of these examples. In the first sentence, the period suggests that a mild command is being given in an ordinary tone of voice. The exclamation mark at the end of the second sentence suggests a strong command, one given in a loud voice.

> **An exclamatory sentence conveys strong emotion and ends with an exclamation mark.**

See Practice 20.1A

See Practice 20.1B

See Practice 20.1C

See Practice 20.1D

Exclaim means "to shout out." **Exclamatory sentences** are used to "shout out" emotions such as happiness, fear, delight, or anger.

EXCLAMATORY   She's going to crash into that hurdle!

What an outstanding runner she is!

Identifying Four Types of Sentences

Read the sentences. Then, identify each type of sentence by writing *declarative*, *interrogative*, *imperative*, or *exclamatory*.

EXAMPLE   The blue whale is the largest animal on Earth.

ANSWER   *declarative*

1. Cashews originated in South America.

2. How much does an elephant eat every day?

3. Clarence Birdseye invented a method for freezing foods.

4. Jupiter is absolutely immense!

5. Put your luggage on the conveyor belt.

6. Where do birds go in the winter?

7. When the island Krakatoa exploded, it was heard more than 2,000 miles away!

8. More people drink water than drink milk.

9. When will the next storm occur?

10. Please read the sign out front.

Punctuating Four Types of Sentences

Read the sentences. Then, rewrite each sentence, adding the correct end punctuation.

EXAMPLE   Where is the post office

ANSWER   *Where is the post office?*

11. Are there any peaches today

12. He looked at the stars

13. I can't believe you did that

14. How will we get to school

15. Tell us about the Arctic

16. Is that the right answer

17. That's terrible

18. Don't forget your coat

19. When will they get here

20. I sing in the school chorus

SPEAKING APPLICATION

With a partner, take turns talking about something that surprised you. Include at least three different types of sentences in your discussion. Your partner should listen for and identify the three types of sentences.

WRITING APPLICATION

Write four sentences on any topics you wish. Make one declarative, one exclamatory, one interrogative, and one imperative. Be sure to punctuate them correctly.

PRACTICE 20.1C Writing Four Types of Sentences

Read the topics. For each topic, write the type of sentence specified in parentheses. Be sure to use the appropriate end punctuation.

EXAMPLE   weather (exclamatory)

ANSWER   *The weather is so cold!*

1. sun (declarative)

2. bicycle (interrogative)

3. door (imperative)

4. astronaut (declarative)

5. whales (exclamatory)

6. vacation (interrogative)

7. books (imperative)

8. forest (declarative)

9. solar eclipse (exclamatory)

10. restaurant (interrogative)

PRACTICE 20.1D Revising Four Types of Sentences

Read the sentences. Rewrite each sentence, changing it to the type of sentence specified in parentheses. Be sure to use the appropriate end punctuation.

EXAMPLE   You can watch a caterpillar. (interrogative)

ANSWER   *Can you watch a caterpillar?*

11. Can you go to the library? (declarative)

12. That mountain is so high! (interrogative)

13. Don't clouds sometimes look like cotton balls? (declarative)

14. Are elephants really big? (exclamatory)

15. Dad went to the hardware store. (interrogative)

16. Why don't you look where you're going? (imperative)

17. Those are her favorite shoes. (interrogative)

18. Would you please close the window? (imperative)

19. Is summer vacation starting soon? (declarative)

20. Is that ice dangerously thin? (exclamatory)

SPEAKING APPLICATION

With a partner, take turns giving orders, as if you were a coach. Give at least two orders each, using imperative sentences. Then, turn the orders into requests, using interrogative sentences.

WRITING APPLICATION

Write a short paragraph about something in nature that you find interesting. Begin with a question. Then, answer the question with at least one declarative and one exclamatory sentence.

20.2 Combining Sentences

Good writing should include sentences of varying lengths and complexity to create a flow of ideas. One way to achieve sentence variety is to combine sentences to express two or more related ideas or pieces of information in a single sentence.

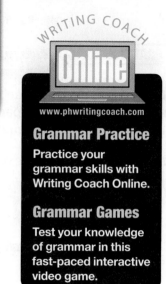

Look at the example below. Then, look at how the ideas are combined in different ways.

EXAMPLE   We went to the zoo. We saw monkeys.

COMBINED   We went to the zoo and saw monkeys.

                We saw monkeys when we went to the zoo.

Combining Sentence Parts

RULE
20.2.1

Sentences can be combined by using a **compound subject**, a **compound verb**, or a **compound object**.

EXAMPLE   Moira enjoyed watching the monkeys.

                Tom enjoyed watching the monkeys.

COMPOUND SUBJECT   **Moira** and **Tom** enjoyed watching the monkeys.

EXAMPLE   Lisa played the game.

                Lisa won a stuffed animal.

COMPOUND VERB   Lisa **played** the game and **won** a stuffed animal.

EXAMPLE   Scott rode the roller coaster.

                Scott rode the Ferris wheel.

COMPOUND OBJECT   Scott rode the **roller coaster** and the **Ferris wheel** .

See Practice 20.2A

Joining Clauses

A **compound sentence** consists of two or more main or independent clauses. (See Chapter 19 for more information about clauses.) Use a compound sentence when combining related ideas of equal weight.

To create a compound sentence, join two main clauses with a comma and a coordinating conjunction. Common conjunctions include *and, but, nor, for, so, or,* and *yet.* You can also link the two sentences with a semicolon (;) if they are closely related.

Grammar
Game Plan

Sentences can be combined by joining two main clauses to create a **compound sentence.**

EXAMPLE	The wind whipped against our faces. The screams of other riders excited us.
COMPOUND SENTENCE	The wind whipped against our faces, and the screams of other riders excited us.
EXAMPLE	The ride lasted just a few minutes. My stomach churned for several hours.
COMPOUND SENTENCE	The ride lasted just a few minutes, but my stomach churned for several hours.
EXAMPLE	The roller coaster is such fun. It's very popular.
COMPOUND SENTENCE	The roller coaster is such fun; it's very popular.
EXAMPLE	I'm so tired when I leave the amusement park. I can't wait to come back again.
COMPOUND SENTENCE	I'm so tired when I leave the amusement park, yet I can't wait to come back again.

See Practice 20.2B

Sentences can be combined by changing one of them into a subordinate clause.

A **complex sentence** consists of one **main** or **independent clause** and one or more **subordinate clauses.** (See Chapter 19 for more information about clauses.) Combine sentences into a complex sentence to emphasize that one of the ideas in the sentence depends on the other. A subordinating conjunction will help readers understand the relationship. Common subordinating conjunctions are *after, although, because, before, since,* and *unless.* Generally no punctuation is required when a main and a subordinate clause are combined. When the subordinate clause comes first, a comma is needed. (See Chapter 25 for more information on punctuation.)

EXAMPLE   We were frightened. The ride went so fast.

COMBINED   We were frightened because the ride went so fast.

See Practice 20.2C

Sentences can be combined by changing one of them into a phrase.

When combining sentences in which one of the sentences simply adds details, change one of the sentences into a **phrase.**

EXAMPLE   My family is leaving to go on vacation.
            We are leaving in the morning.

COMBINED   My family is leaving in the morning to go on vacation.

EXAMPLE   My mother packed a picnic basket.
            It was filled with sandwiches.

COMBINED   My mother packed a picnic basket filled with sandwiches.

See Practice 20.2D

PRACTICE 20.2A Combining Sentences Using Compound Subjects, Verbs, and Objects

Read the sentences. Combine the sentences in each group into a single sentence. Identify each combination as *compound subject*, *compound verb*, or *compound object*.

EXAMPLE   Tanner went to the drugstore. Marcie went to the drugstore, too.

ANSWER   *Tanner and Marcie went to the drugstore.* — compound subject

1. Claudio typed his report. Claudio also printed out his report.

2. Paul tried out for the play. Liam tried out for the play. Rubin tried out for the play.

3. Sari wrote a poem. Sari wrote a short story.

4. Yesterday my grandmother called. She invited me to visit for the weekend.

5. Jordan plays golf. Shelly plays golf, too.

6. My sister likes fruit. She also likes vegetables.

7. I need to paint the model cars. I need to paint the model planes, too.

8. The bake sale raised a lot of money. The car wash raised a lot of money, too.

9. My dog chased the ball. My dog caught the ball.

10. My mom is planning our trip to the museum. My dad is helping her.

PRACTICE 20.2B Combining Sentences Using Main Clauses

Read the sentences. Combine each pair into a compound sentence using the coordinating conjunction in parentheses. Be sure to use correct punctuation for compound sentences.

EXAMPLE   Penguins look awkward on land. They are graceful in the water. (but)

ANSWER   *Penguins look awkward on land, but they are graceful in the water.*

11. I went to the department store. I found the outfit I needed for band. (and)

12. We needed milk. I went to the store. (so)

13. My sister really likes math. My brother does not like math. (but)

14. In this recipe, we add peppers to the sauce. This makes the sauce spicy. (;)

15. We could go to the movies. We could go to the dance. (or)

16. A tadpole grows legs. Its tail disappears. (and)

17. We missed the bus. We took a taxi. (so)

18. My brother is feeling better. It will still be a while before he is well. (but)

19. Our class came in from recess. It was time for lunch. (;)

20. The flowers are beginning to come up. The trees are turning green. (and)

SPEAKING APPLICATION

With a partner, take turns talking about foods you like. Your partner should listen for and name three conjunctions you use.

WRITING APPLICATION

Write three sentences about the kinds of stories you most enjoy reading. Make sure your sentences combine main clauses or contain a compound verb, subject, or object.

PRACTICE 20.2C Combining Sentences Using Subordinate Clauses

Read the sentences. Combine each pair by changing one sentence into a subordinate clause, using the subordinating conjunction in parentheses. Be sure to use the correct punctuation for complex sentences.

EXAMPLE   Cleo is going to the game. Then, she is going to Sue's house. (after)

ANSWER   *After Cleo goes to the game, she is going to Sue's house.*

1. I need to get the house cleaned. Mom comes home tonight. (before)

2. The doctor told Rory he should not run. Rory decided to enter the race. (although)

3. Dad went to the hardware store. We needed batteries. (because)

4. I have to stay inside. I have to get my homework done. (until)

5. The birds start building nests. We know it's spring. (when)

6. Liana took extra science classes. She can get into the advanced class. (so that)

7. You finish your chores. You may leave. (if)

8. Stefan got an *A* on the test. He studied very hard. (because)

9. I'm baking potatoes. I'm making soup. (while)

10. Pedro got the soccer ball. A game of soccer started. (after)

PRACTICE 20.2D Combining Sentences Using Phrases

Read the sentences. Combine each pair of sentences by changing one into a phrase.

EXAMPLE   Mrs. Shankar led the class through the museum. Mrs. Shankar is a dinosaur expert.

ANSWER   *Mrs. Shankar, a dinosaur expert, led the class through the museum.*

11. Ann plays the flute. She plays in the band.

12. Today, we meet Mr. Beale. He is the coach.

13. Jun took his model plane to the park. He wanted to see it fly.

14. Frank Lloyd Wright was a famous architect. He designed this house.

15. We wanted to pick the flowers. The flowers covered the meadow.

16. Shelby knew everyone. Shelby could not go anywhere without seeing friends.

17. The dog was eager for its dinner. It ran to its bowl.

18. The paper's travel section is interesting. The section is edited by Mr. Keller.

19. The children were laughing excitedly. The children played on the swings.

20. The actress walked toward the stage. Her costar followed her.

SPEAKING APPLICATION

With a partner, take turns talking about something you saw on television. Use at least three subordinating conjunctions. Your partner should listen for and name the conjunctions.

WRITING APPLICATION

Write three sentences about a place you visited recently (a museum, park, or friend's house). In each sentence, use a phrase (any kind) to add information.

20.3 Varying Sentences

When you vary the length and form of the sentences you write, you are able to create a rhythm, achieve an effect, or emphasize the connections between ideas.

WRITING COACH

Online
www.phwritingcoach.com

Grammar Practice

Practice your grammar skills with Writing Coach Online.

Grammar Games

Test your knowledge of grammar in this fast-paced interactive video game.

There are several ways you can introduce variety into the sentences you write.

> **Varying the length of sentences makes writing lively and interesting to read.**

20.3.1

RULE

Varying Sentence Length

Reading too many long sentences in a row can be just as uninteresting as reading too many short sentences in a row. When you want to emphasize a point or surprise a reader, insert a short, direct sentence to interrupt the flow of several long sentences.

EXAMPLE   Otters are expert swimmers and divers, swimming at an average speed of seven miles per hour and staying underwater for up to two minutes. Unlike muskrats or beavers, otters barely make a ripple when swimming or a splash when diving. **Otters are even waterproof.** When they are underwater, a flap of skin covering their ears and nose closes to keep them watertight.

You can also break some longer sentences into shorter sentences. If the longer sentence contains two or more ideas, you can break up the ideas into separate sentences. However, if a longer sentence contains only one main idea, you should not break it apart.

LONGER SENTENCE   Many animals in the world fear snakes, but the mongoose does not.

TWO SENTENCES   Many animals in the world fear snakes. The mongoose does not.

See Practice 20.3A

Varying Sentence Beginnings

Another way to create variety is by changing from the usual subject–verb order in a sentence.

RULE
20.3.2

Sentence beginnings can also be varied by reversing the traditional subject–verb order or starting the sentence with an adverb or a phrase.

EXAMPLES

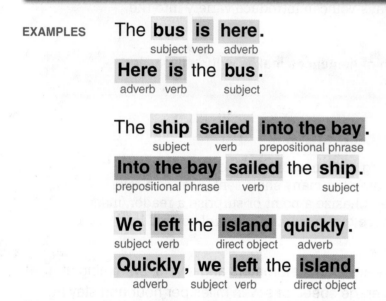

The **bus** **is** **here**.
subject   verb   adverb

Here **is** the **bus**.
adverb   verb   subject

The **ship** **sailed** **into the bay**.
subject   verb   prepositional phrase

Into the bay **sailed** the **ship**.
prepositional phrase   verb   subject

We **left** the **island** **quickly**.
subject verb   direct object adverb

Quickly, **we** **left** the **island**.
adverb   subject verb   direct object

Another way to vary your sentences is to begin them in different ways. For instance, you can start sentences with different parts of speech.

See Practice 20.3B

WAYS TO VARY SENTENCE BEGINNINGS	
Start with a noun.	**Birdhouses**, surprisingly, are not difficult to make.
Start with an adverb.	**Surprisingly**, birdhouses are not difficult to make.
Start with an infinitive.	**To make birdhouses** is, surprisingly, not difficult.
Start with a gerund.	**Making birdhouses** is, surprisingly, not difficult.
Start with a prepositional phrase.	**For a skilled carpenter**, making birdhouses is not difficult.

PRACTICE 20.3A ▶ Varying Sentence Length

Read the sentences. Rewrite each long compound sentence as two or more shorter sentences.

EXAMPLE   During vacation, we went to the circus, and we also swam, and we visited a museum.

ANSWER   *During vacation, we went to the circus. We also swam, and we visited a museum.*

1. We could not stop the dripping, nor could we turn off the water, so we put a bucket under the leak.

2. Australia has many interesting animals, such as wombats and koalas, and they carry their young in pouches.

3. My sister went to summer camp, and my brother went to summer school, and I am going to make money mowing lawns.

4. In the movie, the hero captures the bad guy, but at the end the bad guy escapes, so I think there will be another movie.

5. Bethany came to the United States from England, and she speaks with an English accent.

PRACTICE 20.3B ▶ Varying Sentence Beginnings

Read the sentences. Rewrite each sentence, changing the beginning as specified in parentheses. If there are two sentences, combine them, using one of the sentences to help you create the specified beginning.

EXAMPLE   Repairing the bike will cost money. It is unfortunate. (Begin with an adverb)

ANSWER   *Unfortunately,* repairing the bike will cost money.

6. It takes a lot of practice to learn how to swim well. (Begin with a gerund.)

7. I found the wallet I lost during our hike. That was lucky. (Begin with an adverb.)

8. The film star strutted into the room. (Reverse the subject-verb order.)

9. Modern car engines can be confusing for anyone who does not know the cars. (Begin with a prepositional phrase.)

10. When you are planning a big project like this, you need lots of advice. (Begin with an infinitive.)

SPEAKING APPLICATION

With a partner, read aloud two of the long sentences in Practice 20.3A. Then, read the way you broke up the long sentences. Tell your partner why you think it was good to break up the sentences.

WRITING APPLICATION

Write three sentences about people you know. Vary the sentence beginnings, or use inverted order. You may look at Practice 20.3B to remind you of how sentence beginnings can be varied.

20.4 Avoiding Sentence Problems

Recognizing problems with sentences will help you avoid and fix any problems in your writing.

WRITING COACH

Online

www.phwritingcoach.com

Grammar Practice
Practice your grammar skills with Writing Coach Online.

Grammar Games
Test your knowledge of grammar in this fast-paced interactive video game.

Correcting Fragments

Some groups of words—even though they have a capital letter at the beginning and a period at the end—are not complete sentences. They are **fragments.**

RULE
20.4.1

> **A fragment** is a group of words that does not express a complete thought.

A fragment can be a group of words that includes a possible subject but no verb. A fragment could also be a group of words that includes a possible verb but no subject. It can even be a group of words that contains no subject and no verb. Fragments can be turned into complete sentences by adding a subject, a verb, or both.

FRAGMENTS	COMPLETE SENTENCES
felt happy and relaxed	**I** felt happy and relaxed. (A subject is added.)
the train around the bend	The train **was coming** around the bend. (A verb is added.)
in the early evening	The **flight** **arrived** in the early evening. (A subject and verb are added.)

See Practice 20.4A

Correcting Phrase Fragments A **phrase fragment** cannot stand alone because it does not have both a subject and a verb.

RULE
20.4.2

> **A phrase fragment** should not be capitalized and punctuated as if it were a sentence.

A phrase fragment can be corrected in one of two ways: (1) by adding it to a nearby sentence or (2) by adding whatever is needed to make it a complete sentence.

PHRASE FRAGMENT	The travelers rode camels. **on the morning of March 4**
ADDED TO OTHER SENTENCE	The travelers rode camels **on the morning of March 4**.
PHRASE FRAGMENT	They rode the camels for hours. **parched by the hot sun**
COMPLETE SENTENCES	They rode the camels for hours. They were **parched by the hot sun**.

CHANGING PHRASE FRAGMENTS INTO SENTENCES	
PHRASE FRAGMENT	**COMPLETE SENTENCE**
in the ancient tomb	The treasure was found **in the ancient tomb**.
laughing at her father's jokes	Helen enjoyed **laughing at her father's jokes**.
to play soccer	Elana learned **to play soccer**.

See Practice 20.4B

Correcting Clause Fragments

All clauses have subjects and verbs, but some cannot stand alone as sentences.

> A **subordinate clause** should not be capitalized and punctuated as if it were a sentence.

Subordinate clauses do not express complete thoughts. Although a subordinate adjective or adverb clause has a subject and a verb, it cannot stand by itself as a sentence. (See Chapter 19 for more information about subordinate clauses and the words that begin them.)

Like phrase fragments, **clause fragments** can usually be corrected in either of two ways: (1) by attaching the fragment to a nearby sentence or (2) by adding whatever words are needed to turn the fragment into a sentence.

CLAUSE FRAGMENT	The audience left the concert hall. **after the band finished playing**
COMPLETE SENTENCE	**After the band finished playing** , the audience left the concert hall.
CLAUSE FRAGMENT	The class enjoyed the poem. **that I recited to them as part of my oral report on horses**
COMPLETE SENTENCE	The class enjoyed the poem **that I recited to them as part of my oral report on horses** .
CLAUSE FRAGMENT	I'll give my report today. **as long as you give yours, too**
COMPLETE SENTENCE	I'll give my report today **as long as you give yours, too** .

To change a clause fragment into a sentence by the second method, you must add an independent clause to the fragment.

CHANGING CLAUSE FRAGMENTS INTO SENTENCES	
CLAUSE FRAGMENT	**COMPLETE SENTENCE**
that you requested	I returned the book **that you requested** . The book **that you requested** has been returned.
when he began shouting	I looked up in surprise **when he began shouting.** **When he began shouting** , I looked up in surprise.
what she was thinking	I could not figure out **what she was thinking** .

See Practice 20.4C
See Practice 20.4D

PRACTICE 20.4A **Recognizing Fragments**

Read the groups of words. Then, write whether each group of words is a *sentence* or a *fragment*.

EXAMPLE   In the swimming pool.

ANSWER   *fragment*

1. When you arrive.
2. Dad went to work.
3. Because of the rain.
4. A really good idea.
5. Tomorrow is a new day.
6. Mom washed the dog.
7. Cat in a tree.
8. Spring always returns.
9. Without your raincoat.
10. The car is turning.

PRACTICE 20.4B **Changing Phrase Fragments Into Sentences**

Read the phrase fragments. Then, use each fragment in a sentence.

EXAMPLE   to the library

ANSWER   *I need to go to the library.*

11. at the zoo
12. to open the box
13. around the school
14. finding my books
15. to build that model
16. after the ride
17. taking the bird food
18. in the classroom
19. to climb that tree
20. trading baseball cards

SPEAKING APPLICATION

With a partner, take turns creating phrases. Your partner should listen to the phrase and then turn the phrase into a sentence.

WRITING APPLICATION

Write three sentences about what the yard of your home or school is like and what is found there. Use at least two phrases. Underline the phrases in the sentences.

PRACTICE 20.4C > **Changing Clause Fragments Into Sentences**

Read the clause fragments. Then, use each fragment in a sentence.

EXAMPLE   that we bought yesterday

ANSWER   *Bring me the magazine* that we bought yesterday.

1. as soon as you finish your work
2. while my little brother played
3. even though he was tired
4. because they usually get lost
5. as long as you are here
6. before the sun rises
7. until Dad gets home
8. unless it rains
9. although it seemed late
10. whenever Grandmother visits

PRACTICE 20.4D > **Changing Fragments Into Sentences**

Read the groups of words. If a group of words is a fragment, use it in a sentence. If a group of words is already a sentence, write *sentence*.

EXAMPLE   Looking for their dog.

ANSWER   *I saw the neighbors* looking for their dog.

11. When the bell rings.
12. To find a dress.
13. We found good seats.
14. To finish the project.
15. The snow melted.
16. Eating the leftovers.
17. The library has magazines.
18. We could go with them.
19. To draw a picture.
20. The stairs creaked.

SPEAKING APPLICATION

With a partner, take turns choosing two clause fragments from Practice 20.4D. Read the clause fragment out loud, changing one word in the fragment. Your partner should reply with a sentence using the changed fragment.

WRITING APPLICATION

Write a short paragraph about the plot or action of a movie or book you enjoyed. Include at least two clause fragments as you relate what happened. Then, exchange papers with a partner. Your partner should identify and underline the clause fragments.

Run-on Sentences

A fragment is an incomplete sentence. A **run-on,** on the other hand, is two or more complete sentences that are punctuated as though they were one sentence.

Find It / FIX IT

15

Grammar
Game Plan

> A **run-on** is two or more complete sentences that are not properly joined or separated.

20.4.4   RULE

Run-ons are usually the result of carelessness. Check your sentences carefully to see where one sentence ends and the next one begins.

Two Kinds of Run-ons

There are two kinds of run-ons. The first one is made up of two sentences that are run together without any punctuation between them. This is called a **fused sentence.**

The second type of run-on consists of two or more sentences separated by only a comma. This type of run-on is called a **comma splice.**

FUSED SENTENCES   I flew out of my bed I ran into the hall.

The Lions ran for two touchdowns they won the game.

COMMA SPLICE   Everyone in the house was up, the smoke alarm had gone off.

The Lions have a great offensive team, they also have a great defensive team.

Find It / FIX IT

16

Grammar
Game Plan

See Practice 20.4E

A good way to distinguish between a run-on and a sentence is to read the words aloud. Your ear will tell you whether you have one or two complete thoughts and whether you need to make a complete break between the thoughts.

Three Ways to Correct Run-ons

There are three ways to correct run-on sentences. You can use end marks, commas and coordinating conjunctions, or semicolons.

Using End Marks

Periods, question marks, and exclamation marks are useful to fix run-on sentences.

> **Use an end mark to separate a run-on sentence into two sentences.**

Sometimes the best way to correct a run-on is to use an end mark to split the run-on into two shorter but complete sentences. End marks help your reader pause and group your ideas more effectively.

RUN-ON	On Saturday Jill plays softball, Luis has band practice.
CORRECTED	On Saturday Jill plays softball. Luis has band practice.
RUN-ON	Hurry up we don't want to be late.
CORRECTED	Hurry up! We don't want to be late.
RUN-ON	Are you going to the game I'll meet you there.
CORRECTED	Are you going to the game? I'll meet you there.
RUN-ON	Where have you been, I've been waiting for you for two hours!
CORRECTED	Where have you been? I've been waiting for you for two hours!

Using Commas and Coordinating Conjunctions

Sometimes the two parts of a run-on are related and should be combined into a compound sentence.

> **Use a comma and a coordinating conjunction to combine two independent clauses into a compound sentence.**

To separate the clauses properly, use both a comma and a coordinating conjunction. The most common coordinating conjunctions are *and, but, or, for, nor,* and *yet.* Before you separate a sentence into parts, though, be sure each part expresses a complete thought.

RUN-ON	I want to buy some new shoes, I need more money.
CORRECTED	I want to buy some new shoes, but I need more money.
RUN-ON	The shoes I have are too tight, their heels are worn out.
CORRECTED	The shoes I have are too tight, and their heels are worn out.

Using Semicolons
You can sometimes use a semicolon to connect the two parts of a run-on into a correct sentence.

> **Use a semicolon to connect two closely related ideas into one sentence.**

Use a semicolon only when the ideas in both parts of the sentence are closely related.

RUN-ON	The first train to Houston leaves at 6:05, the express doesn't leave until an hour later.
CORRECTED	The first train to Houston leaves at 6:05; the express doesn't leave until an hour later.

See Practice 20.4F
See Practice 20.4G
See Practice 20.4H

Read the groups of words. Then, write whether each group is a *sentence* or a *run-on*.

EXAMPLE   Rachel Carson was a biologist she wrote about nature.

ANSWER   *run-on*

1. George Washington is called the Father of Our Country he was our first president.

2. Many people visit Italy because there is so much art, history, and good food there.

3. Elsa was an African lion, she became famous because of the book *Born Free*.

4. Isadora Duncan was a dancer, she danced in many countries.

5. Ruth Streeter was the first woman to hold the rank of major in the Marine Corps.

6. Squanto was a Native American who helped the Pilgrims he spoke English.

7. When Columbus first tasted hot chili peppers, he called them "violent fruit."

8. Cashews are related to poison ivy, they originally came from Brazil.

9. Benjamin Carson liked learning about science, he became a leading surgeon.

10. Grace Hopper was one of the world's first software engineers.

Read the sentences. Rewrite each run-on sentence to correct the problem.

EXAMPLE   The shepherd led the sheep he took them to a grassy field.

ANSWER   *The shepherd led the sheep. He took them to a grassy field.*

11. The herb rosemary is good in food it is also used as a symbol of remembrance.

12. Booker T. Washington wrote *Up from Slavery*, it is a book about his early life.

13. Gus and Romero are good friends they go everywhere together.

14. Quito is the capital of Ecuador, it is in the northern half of the country.

15. We hurried to the train station we were late.

16. Alaska is our largest state, Rhode Island is our smallest state.

17. Bananas are green when they are shipped they turn yellow as they ripen.

18. Shandra and Lacey went to the school carnival they had a lot of fun.

19. On Memorial Day, the nation honors its heroes it recalls their bravery.

20. James Naismith invented basketball in 1891, he used peach baskets for the game.

SPEAKING APPLICATION

With a partner, take turns reading the run-ons in Practice 20.4F out loud. Talk about how speaking the run-ons out loud helps you hear where the sentences should end.

WRITING APPLICATION

Choose two run-ons from Practice 20.4F, and rewrite them. This time, feel free to reverse the order of the clauses or add more words. Be sure you don't have any run-ons when you're done.

PRACTICE 20.4G **Recognizing and Correcting Run-ons**

Read the sentences. Then, rewrite each run-on sentence to correct the problem. If the sentence is not a run-on, write *correct*.

EXAMPLE   Uncle Mike lives in Boston, he visits us often.

ANSWER   *Uncle Mike lives in Boston, but he visits us often.*

1. Mom gives us oatmeal for breakfast; she says that it is good for us.

2. My sister likes sports my brother likes fixing things.

3. Aunt Grace gave us that painting she likes art.

4. Jose's dog is not a terrier It is a hound.

5. Gabriela was born in California, but now she lives in Texas.

6. I stumbled in the cafeteria, and my tray went flying.

7. Mom taught school in Dallas, Dad built roads in Austin.

8. The waves were rough our sailboat was tossed around.

9. The beach was covered with shells Diana added many to her collection.

10. I got a bad sunburn Diana got a deep tan.

PRACTICE 20.4H **Correcting Run-ons**

Read the sentences. Then, rewrite each sentence, correcting each run-on using a comma and a coordinating conjunction (e.g., *and, but, so, or, for, nor,* and *yet*).

EXAMPLE   The mail came, there was nothing for me.

ANSWER   *The mail came, but there was nothing for me.*

11. Earl has to write a paper, he has to study for a test.

12. Mr. Heriard was trying to fix the fence he ran out of wood.

13. The show must be sold out there are people standing in the back.

14. Diana woke up late she missed her plane.

15. Dad can make pizza he can make quiche.

16. Use red pens for editing use black pens for final drafts.

17. I went I didn't want to.

18. Jackson was hungry he didn't want to eat the chicken salad.

19. Mallory had to walk to school her bike has a flat tire.

20. We can leave Friday night, we can leave Saturday morning.

SPEAKING APPLICATION

Choose a paragraph from a book. Take turns with a partner. Read your paragraphs aloud without stopping for punctuation. Discuss how reading without punctuation interferes with understanding. Then, read the paragraphs correctly.

WRITING APPLICATION

Rewrite three run-ons from Practice 20.4H in another way. Remember that there are three ways to correct a run-on. Try reversing the order of the clauses and adding more words.

Test Warm-Up

DIRECTIONS
Read the introduction and the passage that follows. Then, answer the questions to show that you can recognize and correct run-on sentences in reading and writing.

David wrote this paragraph for a report about the Civil War between the North (the Union) and the South (the Confederacy). Read the paragraph and think about the changes you would suggest as a peer editor. When you finish reading, answer the questions that follow.

The Civil War

(1) Eleven states in the South withdrew from the Union. their secession led to the Civil War. (2) Confederate soldiers fired the first shots on Fort Sumter. (3) Both sides in the war had excellent generals. (4) Robert E. Lee led the Confederate forces; Ulysses S. Grant led the Union forces. (5) The North had advantages and more people lived there and industry was better developed, too. (6) The turning point came when the Union forces won a battle at Gettysburg the conflict lasted four years and cost many lives.

---

1 What change, if any, should be made in sentence 1?

  A Add a comma after **South**

  B Change the period after **Union** to a comma

  C Change the period after **Union** to a semicolon

  D Make no change

2 What change, if any, should be made in sentence 4?

  F Add a comma after **Lee**

  G Change the semicolon to a comma

  H Delete the semicolon

  J Make no change

3 What is the BEST way to revise sentence 5?

  A The North had advantages. More people lived there, and industry was better developed, too.

  B The North had advantages; more people; industry was better developed, too.

  C The North had advantages, because more people lived there, industry was better developed, too.

  D The North had advantages, more people lived there and industry was better developed, too.

4 What change should be made in sentence 6?

  F Add a period after **came**

  G Add a semicolon after **Gettysburg**

  H Add a semicolon after **won**

  J Add a comma after **Gettysburg**

Properly Placing Modifiers

If a phrase or clause acting as an adjective or adverb is not placed
near the word it modifies, it may seem to modify a different word.
Then the sentence may seem unclear or odd.

> A **modifier** should be placed as close as possible to the word
> it describes.

20.4.8 RULE

A modifier placed too far away from the word it describes is
called a **misplaced modifier.**

MISPLACED
MODIFIER
We rented a boat at the lake **with an outboard
motor** .

The misplaced phrase *with an outboard motor* makes it seem as
though the lake has an outboard motor.

PROPERLY
PLACED
MODIFIER
At the lake, we rented a boat **with an outboard
motor** .

Below is a different type of misplaced modifier that is sometimes
called a **dangling modifier.** A dangling modifier at the beginning
of a sentence causes the sentence to be unclear.

DANGLING
MODIFIER
Walking on the beach , the sand felt hot
under our feet.

In this sentence, *walking on the beach* should modify a person or
people. Instead, it incorrectly modifies *sand*.

CORRECTED
Walking on the beach , we felt the hot sand
under our feet.

See Practice 20.4I
See Practice 20.4J

PRACTICE 20.4I **Revising to Correct Misplaced Modifiers**

Read the sentences. Then, rewrite each sentence to correct the underlined misplaced modifier.

EXAMPLE   A woman was walking a dog <u>in a blue dress</u>.

ANSWER   *A woman in a blue dress was walking a dog.*

1. I found the book after looking in three rooms <u>that I need for class</u>.

2. The boy is my brother <u>in the red shirt</u>.

3. The shopping list seemed long <u>that Dad wrote</u>.

4. <u>Crushed at the bottom of the box</u>, Eileen saw her hat.

5. The bottle fell and broke <u>full of perfume</u>.

6. We knew the music would be played <u>that we liked</u>.

7. Ari's report was fascinating <u>about reptiles</u>.

8. We left our car at the shop <u>with a flat tire</u>.

9. The purse was lost <u>that had her wallet</u>.

10. <u>On the top shelf</u>, my sister found her favorite book.

PRACTICE 20.4J **Recognizing and Correcting Misplaced Modifiers**

Read the sentences. If a sentence has a misplaced modifier, rewrite the sentence so the modifier is properly placed. If a sentence is correct, write *correct*.

EXAMPLE   Covered in flowers, Marilyn admired the hillside.

ANSWER   *Marilyn admired the hillside covered in flowers.*

11. My sister found a sweater in the closet that does not belong to her.

12. Running across the yard, the grass tickled our bare feet.

13. Carrying the luggage outside, Dad began to pack the car for our trip.

14. Sizzling on the grill, Carlos smells the food.

15. Please discuss the information that is enclosed with your friends.

16. I like the car with leather seats.

17. My neighbors have a fence behind the house with a gate.

18. Trying three different keys, the front door was finally unlocked.

19. Leaving his book unfinished, the writer decided to write a short story.

20. Hopping beside the lake I saw a frog.

SPEAKING APPLICATION

With a partner, take turns describing a place you have studied or seen in a movie. Use modifiers to add detail. Your partner should listen for and identify modifiers and what they modify.

WRITING APPLICATION

Write a short paragraph about clothes that are currently in style. Include at least two modifiers to add detail, taking care to properly place the modifiers.

Avoiding Double Negatives

Negative words, such as *nothing* and *not*, are used to deny or to say *no*. Some people mistakenly use **double negatives**—two negative words—when only one is needed.

> **Avoid writing sentences that contain double negatives.**

20.4.9 RULE

In the following examples, negative words are highlighted. The first sentence in each example contains double negatives. The corrected sentences show two ways to correct each double-negative sentence.

DOUBLE NEGATIVES	The lightning **didn't** damage **nothing**.
CORRECTED SENTENCES	The lightning **didn't** damage anything.
	The lightning damaged **nothing**.
DOUBLE NEGATIVES	I **haven't no** time now.
CORRECTED SENTENCES	I **haven't** any time now.
	I have **no** time now.
DOUBLE NEGATIVES	She **never** told us **nothing** about the storm.
CORRECTED SENTENCES	She **never** told us anything about the storm.
	She told us **nothing** about the storm.
DOUBLE NEGATIVES	A few clouds **don't** bother **no one**.
CORRECTED SENTENCES	A few clouds **don't** bother anyone.
	A few clouds bother **no one**.
DOUBLE NEGATIVES	Janice **didn't** invite **nobody**.
CORRECTED SENTENCES	Janice **didn't** invite anybody.
	Janice invited **nobody**.

See Practice 20.4K
See Practice 20.4L

PRACTICE 20.4K > **Using Negatives Correctly**

Read the sentences. Then, write the word in parentheses that makes each sentence negative without creating a double negative.

EXAMPLE   The coach (can, can't) find no one to be quarterback.

ANSWER   *can*

1. The new box of pencils wasn't (anywhere, nowhere) in my room.

2. Maria (has, hasn't) said nothing about her visit to her grandmother's.

3. Henry didn't know (nobody, anybody) at the party.

4. I don't like (none, any) of the television shows this season.

5. I (would, wouldn't) do nothing to hurt my little brother.

6. Our house (is, isn't) nowhere near the grocery store.

7. This magazine doesn't have (anything, nothing) about the parade.

8. We (had, hadn't) never thought that my sister would get a poem published.

9. No one (can, can't) get into our clubhouse.

10. They didn't (never, ever) go away on vacation.

PRACTICE 20.4L > **Revising to Correct Double Negatives**

Read the sentences. Then, rewrite each sentence to correct the double negative.

EXAMPLE   I don't have no interest in that.

ANSWER   *I have no interest in that.*

11. We don't want nobody to go in there.

12. Mom can't find her rolling pin nowhere.

13. I didn't have nothing to do with it.

14. My brother can't never remember his password for that Web site.

15. My sister didn't take none of her books to school.

16. You haven't said nothing about your band concert.

17. The movie stars didn't want to pose for no photographers.

18. We didn't tell nobody about the secret room.

19. I can't find no one to go to the store with me.

20. She didn't go nowhere near the place.

SPEAKING APPLICATION

With a partner, take turns talking about things that should not happen, such as breaking rules at home or failing to take safety precautions. Your partner should listen for and identify negatives and whether they are used correctly.

WRITING APPLICATION

Write two negative sentences about things you have seen happen—or not happen. Be sure to use the negatives correctly.

Avoiding Common Usage Problems

Find It/ FIX IT
1
Grammar
Game Plan

Find It/ FIX IT
5
Grammar
Game Plan

This section contains fifteen common usage problems in alphabetical order. Some are expressions that you should avoid in both your speaking and your writing. Others are words that are often confused because of similar spellings or meanings.

(1) accept, except   Do not confuse the spelling of these words. *Accept*, a verb, means "to take what is offered" or "to agree to." *Except*, a preposition, means "leaving out" or "other than."

VERB	She **accepted** the gift generously.
PREPOSITION	She gave everyone a gift **except** me.

(2) advice, advise   Do not confuse the spelling of these related words. *Advice*, a noun, means "an opinion." *Advise*, a verb, means "to give an opinion."

NOUN	My friend gave me **advice** about hotels in Rome.
VERB	My friend **advised** me to find a good guide.

(3) affect, effect   *Affect*, a verb, means "to influence" or "to cause a change in." *Effect*, usually a noun, means "result."

VERB	The sandstorm **affected** my eyes.
NOUN	What is the **effect** of getting sand in your ears?

(4) at   Do not use *at* after *where*.

INCORRECT	Do you know **where** he is **at**?
CORRECT	Do you know **where** he is?

(5) because   Do not use *because* after *the reason*. Eliminate one or the other.

INCORRECT	**The reason** I am sad is **because** our trip was canceled.
CORRECT	I am sad **because** our trip was canceled.
	The **reason** I am sad is **that** our trip was canceled.

(6) beside, besides These two prepositions have different meanings and cannot be interchanged. *Beside* means "at the side of" or "close to." *Besides* means "in addition to."

EXAMPLES   We picnicked **beside** the Mississippi River.

No one **besides** us had blankets to sit on.

(7) different from, different than *Different from* is preferred over *different than.*

EXAMPLE   The monkeys were **different from** what I had expected.

(8) farther, further *Farther* is used to refer to distance. *Further* means "additional" or "to a greater degree or extent."

EXAMPLES   We walked much **farther** than he did.
After he raised his voice, I listened no **further** .

(9) in, into *In* refers to position. *Into* suggests motion.

POSITION   The tourists are **in** the history museum.
MOTION   They walked **into** the room of famous documents.

(10) kind of, sort of Do not use *kind of* or *sort of* to mean "rather" or "somewhat."

INCORRECT   This CD of jazz music is **sort of** new.
CORRECT   This CD of jazz music is **rather** new.

(11) like *Like*, a preposition, means "similar to" or "in the same way as." It should be followed by an object. Do not use *like* before a subject and a verb. Use *as* or *that* instead.

PREPOSITION   The pyramids looked **like** giant triangles.
INCORRECT   This stew doesn't taste **like** it should.
CORRECT   This stew doesn't taste **as** it should.

(12) that, which, who   *That* and *which* refer to things. *Who* refers only to people.

THINGS	The photograph **that** I took won first prize.
PEOPLE	The dancer **who** performed is my cousin.

(13) their, there, they're   Do not confuse the spelling of these three words. *Their,* a possessive adjective, always modifies a noun. *There* is usually used as a sentence starter or as an adverb. *They're* is a contraction of *they are.*

POSSESSIVE ADJECTIVE	The tourists boarded **their** bus.
SENTENCE STARTER	**There** are many tours available.
ADVERB	The tour guide is standing over **there**.
CONTRACTION	**They're** trying to board the bus now.

(14) to, too, two   Do not confuse the spelling of these words. *To* plus a noun creates a prepositional phrase. *To* plus a verb creates an infinitive. *Too* is an adverb and modifies verbs, adjectives, and other adverbs. *Two* is a number.

PREPOSITION	**to** the house	**to** Florida
INFINITIVE	**to** meet	**to** hide
ADVERB	**too** sad	**too** quickly
NUMBER	**two** clouds	**two** dolphins

(15) when, where, why   Do not use *when,* *where,* or *why* directly after a linking verb such as *is.* Reword the sentence.

INCORRECT	To see the Alamo is **why** we came to Texas.
CORRECT	We came to Texas to see the Alamo.
INCORRECT	In the evening is **when** I walk my dog.
CORRECT	I walk my dog in the evening.

See Practice 20.4M
See Practice 20.4N
See Practice 20.4O
See Practice 20.4P

Read the sentences. Then, write the word in parentheses that best completes each sentence.

EXAMPLE   When the shipment arrived, I (accepted, excepted) the package.

ANSWER   *accepted*

1. The neighbors invited us to (their, they're) house.

2. I thought Mom would be the best one to (advise, advice) me on the science project.

3. It is (to, too) cold to go out without a coat.

4. The news did not seem to (affect, effect) my sister as much as I thought it would.

5. When it is sunny, my cat loves to sleep (beside, besides) the window.

6. Our team hiked two miles (further, farther).

7. Anita is the only one (that, who) knows the combination to the lock.

8. Moisha followed Juan (into, in) the hall.

9. Everyone is here (accept, except) Lisa.

10. The football player carried the ball for only (to, two) yards.

Read the sentences. If the underlined word is used correctly, write *correct*. If the word is incorrect, write the correct word.

EXAMPLE   The moonlight had a lovely <u>affect</u> on the scene.

ANSWER   *effect*

11. The results of the experiment were different <u>than</u> what I expected.

12. I would like to have your <u>advise</u> on this issue.

13. My sister does not know how to <u>except</u> a compliment.

14. My dog loves sleeping <u>beside</u> the fireplace.

15. This food is <u>kind of</u> good.

16. The milk did not smell <u>like</u> it should.

17. I want to discuss this <u>further</u>.

18. I called Derek and Carlos, and <u>their</u> bringing food for the party.

19. This is the friend <u>that</u> went with me to the concert.

20. The stars that night looked <u>like</u> diamonds on black velvet.

SPEAKING APPLICATION

With a partner, choose four sentences from Practice 20.4M. Take turns making up new sentences that correctly use the word that *was not* the right choice in the practice. Your partner should listen and confirm that the word was used correctly.

WRITING APPLICATION

Write a short paragraph about an event in your life that was a surprise. Correctly use at least three words from Practice 20.4M and Practice 20.4N in your paragraph.

PRACTICE 20.4O ▷ Recognizing and Correcting Usage Problems

Read the sentences. Then, if a sentence has a usage problem, rewrite it to correct the problem. If a sentence is correct, write *correct*.

EXAMPLE   Your sandwich is different than mine.

ANSWER   *Your sandwich is different from mine.*

1. Maybe this police officer can tell us where we are at.

2. The reason I want to go is because I'll see Mark.

3. The restaurant was farther away than I thought.

4. This book is kind of interesting.

5. The costumes we rented do not fit like they should.

6. To try out for the play is why I came.

7. The woman who interviewed me is named Carlotta.

8. Five o'clock is when we are supposed to arrive.

9. Grandma and Grandpa invited me to stay at they're house.

10. I loved the special affects in that movie.

PRACTICE 20.4P ▷ Avoiding Usage Problems

Read the pairs of words. For each pair of words, write two sentences that are related in meaning.

EXAMPLE   there, their

ANSWER   *My friends invited me to **their** party. I put my gift over **there**.*

11. accept, except

12. there, they're

13. advise, advice

14. two, too

15. affect, effect

16. beside, besides

17. farther, further

18. who, that

19. into, in

20. like, as

SPEAKING APPLICATION

With a partner, talk about a place you would like to visit. Use two or three words from Practice 20.4O and Practice 20.4P to include in your discussion. Your partner should listen for the words and say whether they were used correctly.

WRITING APPLICATION

Write a very brief story (three or four sentences) about a cat or dog. Choose four "problem" words or phrases from Practice 20.4O and Practice 20.4P, and use them correctly in the story.

PRACTICE 1 Using Complete Subjects and Predicates

Each item below contains only a complete subject or a complete predicate. Rewrite each item, making a sentence by adding the missing part indicated in parentheses.

1. The set for the school play (add a predicate).

2. (add a subject) played three songs at halftime.

3. The substitute teacher (add a predicate).

4. Was (add a subject) hard to fix?

5. My favorite science project (add a predicate).

6. (add a subject) ran through the streets.

7. The local library (add a predicate).

8. (add a subject) left an enormous mess.

9. The girl and her family (add a predicate).

10. (add a subject) competed in the tournament.

PRACTICE 2 Using Direct Objects

Rewrite each incomplete sentence, supplying a direct object where indicated in parentheses. You may also include the article *a*, *an*, or *the* or another modifier along with the direct object.

1. Lions eat (direct object).

2. The workers are building (direct object).

3. On a clear night, Jill studies (direct object).

4. Nick designs (direct object) for a living.

5. Brianna put (direct object) in the refrigerator.

6. I asked (direct object) for a ride home.

7. We saw (direct object) at the street fair.

8. Yesterday, Dan met (direct object) at the zoo.

9. Our teacher gave us (direct object).

10. Who put (direct object) on the chessboard?

PRACTICE 3 Identifying Indirect Objects

Read the sentences. Then, write the indirect object in each sentence. If there is no indirect object, write *none*.

1. The police officer gave the driver a ticket.

2. I told them the story.

3. My father bought himself a new suit.

4. Nadia saved money for a new camera.

5. Please bring me a glass of water.

6. The magician showed us a new trick.

7. Miranda offered the concert tickets to Jake.

8. I wish you a happy birthday.

9. The interviewer asked Jon several questions.

10. Who gave her the new umbrella?

PRACTICE 4 Identifying Subject Complements

Read the sentences. Then, write the subject complement in each sentence. Also indicate whether it is a *predicate noun*, *predicate pronoun*, or *predicate adjective*.

1. The bus ride to the museum seemed long.

2. Maya Angelou is a famous poet.

3. The girls looked unhappy about the situation.

4. Pete will be the president of our class.

5. The person with the highest score is you.

6. She has been mayor for more than six years.

7. Of all the singers, the most talented one is you.

8. Please do not be upset with me.

9. That loud boom was not really anything.

10. Are we late for our piano lessons?

PRACTICE 5 ▷ **Using Prepositional Phrases**

Read the sentences. Then, rewrite each sentence, supplying the type of prepositional phrase indicated in parentheses.

1. The team practiced. (Add an adjectival phrase.)

2. Jojo flew a kite. (Add an adverbial phrase.)

3. The odor was strong. (Add an adjectival phrase.)

4. Mom baked bread. (Add an adverbial phrase.)

5. She twirled her baton. (Add an adverbial phrase.)

PRACTICE 6 ▷ **Identifying Appositive, Participial, Gerund, and Infinitive Phrases**

Read the sentences. Then, write whether the underlined phrase in each sentence is an *appositive phrase*, a *participial phrase*, a *gerund phrase*, or an *infinitive phrase*.

1. Perry loves singing in the choir.

2. Frightened by the noise, the bull charged.

3. We went to the roof to gaze at the stars.

4. The storm, a strong hurricane, devastated the city of Galveston.

5. The birds flocking to the trees were all crows.

6. The coach needs to find another strategy.

7. A Missouri native, Mark Twain in later life lived in Connecticut.

8. Cooking Mexican food is just one of my many interests.

9. Running swiftly, Jesse won the race.

10. Bev wants to find a good hiking trail.

PRACTICE 7 ▷ **Recognizing Main and Subordinate Clauses**

Read the sentences. Then, write and label the *main clause* and the *subordinate clause* in each sentence.

1. After he stayed up all night, Nick yawned all morning.

2. Nobody answered when I rang the bell at the front door.

3. Judge Levy, who lives down the road, always invites us to his annual summer barbecue.

4. Because she sews so well, Mrs. Sanchez helped with the costumes for the school play.

5. Over the winter, moths attacked the wool sweater that I bought last year.

PRACTICE 8 ▷ **Combining Sentences With Subordinate Clauses**

Read the sentences. Combine each pair of sentences by turning one into a subordinate clause. Then, underline the subordinate clause, and indicate whether it is an *adjectival clause* or an *adverbial clause*.

1. My brother works late at the radio station. He gets home after midnight.

2. My sister is in the second grade. She is the youngest member of my family.

3. I searched the library shelves. I finally found an interesting book.

4. The town pool opens in June. It has a lifeguard staff of high school students.

5. My head aches. Toby is playing the trumpet again.

Continued on next page ▶

Cumulative Review   Chapters 18–20

PRACTICE 9 ▷ Writing Sentences

For each item, write the indicated type of sentence, using the words provided.

1. Write a compound sentence using *the athlete* as one of the subjects.

2. Write a declarative sentence using *a flower* as the subject.

3. Write a complex sentence using *was tired* as one of the verbs.

4. Write an exclamatory sentence using the word *exciting*.

5. Write an imperative sentence using *wait* as the verb.

PRACTICE 10 ▷ Combining Sentences

Read the sentences. Combine each pair of sentences by using compound structures. Indicate whether your sentence contains a *compound subject*, a *compound verb*, or a *compound object*, or whether it is a *compound sentence.*

1. Gregory plays the guitar. Mackenzie also plays the guitar.

2. I add milk to my cereal. I add fruit to my cereal too.

3. Barb wanted a new bicycle for her birthday. Her mom gave her a new sweater instead.

4. The painter chooses his paints carefully. He mixes them carefully as well.

5. We may travel to Dallas by train. We may travel to Dallas by bus.

PRACTICE 11 ▷ Revising to Correct Fragments and Run-ons

Read each group of words. If it is a fragment, use it in a sentence. If it is a run-on, correct the run-on. If it is a sentence that needs no correction, write *correct.*

1. The bank teller standing at her window.

2. The soup was pretty tasteless, I ate it anyway.

3. Aunt Meg pays for my dance classes.

4. The color is wrong you need a paler blue.

5. Unless you have the package delivered.

PRACTICE 12 ▷ Revising to Correct Common Usage Problems

Read the sentences. Then, rewrite each sentence to correct misplaced modifiers, double negatives, and other usage problems.

1. Everyone accept Thomas went on the class trip.

2. The medical researchers studied the affects of the new treatment.

3. Twinkling overhead, I thought the stars looked awesome.

4. Many years ago, my grandmother gave me some good advise.

5. I didn't learn nothing new at the meeting.

6. The reason I am so cranky is because I had too little sleep last night.

7. Our teacher told us about earthquakes and volcanoes in our science class.

8. Their doing they're homework in the kitchen.

9. Did anyone beside you and me volunteer to help with the decorations?

10. The trees should be planted further apart.

USING VERBS

Knowing how to use verb tenses will help you convey the correct timing of actions in your writing.

CHAPTER 21

WRITE GUY *Jeff Anderson, M.Ed.*

WHAT DO YOU NOTICE?

Take a snapshot of the verbs as you zoom in on these sentences from the story "The Circuit" by Francisco Jiménez.

MENTOR TEXT

> I was completely soaked in sweat and my mouth felt as if I had been chewing on a handkerchief. I walked over to the end of the row, picked up the jug of water we had brought, and began drinking.

Now, ask yourself the following questions:

- What about the verbs *walked* and *picked* shows that the action takes place in the past?
- How are the verbs *felt* and *began* different from *walked* and *picked*?

The *-ed* ending on the regular verbs *walk* and *pick* shows that the action takes place in the past. The irregular verbs *felt* and *began* also show action that takes place in the past. However, these irregular verbs are spelled differently than their present tenses: *feel* and *begin*.

Grammar for Writers Using carefully chosen verbs and their correct tenses helps a writer convey when actions happen. Be sure to use correct tenses of regular and irregular verbs.

I felt all mixed up this morning, but now I feel fine.

And your irregular verbs are in good shape, too!

469

21.1 The Four Principal Parts of Verbs

Verbs have different tenses to express time. The tense of the verb *walk* in the sentence "They *walk* very fast" expresses action in the present. In "They *walked* too far from home," the tense of the verb shows that the action happened in the past. In "They *will walk* home from school," the verb expresses action in the future. These forms of verbs are known as **tenses.**

A verb's **tense** shows the time of the action or state of being that is being described. To use the tenses of a verb correctly, you must know the **principal parts** of the verb.

RULE 21.1.1

> A verb has four **principal parts: the present,** the **present participle,** the **past,** and the **past participle.**

THE FOUR PRINCIPAL PARTS OF *WALK*			
PRESENT	**PRESENT PARTICIPLE**	**PAST**	**PAST PARTICIPLE**
walk	(am) walking	walked	(have) walked

The first principal part, called the present, is the form of a verb that is listed in a dictionary. The present participle and the past participle must be combined with helping verbs before they can be used as verbs in sentences. The result will always be a verb phrase.

EXAMPLES   He **walks** toward us in a hurry.

June **was walking** behind us a minute ago.

They **walked** to the park.

We **have walked** three miles in the last hour.

The way the past and past participle of a verb are formed shows whether the verb is **regular** or **irregular.**

Using Regular Verbs

Most verbs are **regular,** which means that their past and past participle forms follow a standard, predictable pattern.

> The past and past participle of a **regular verb** are formed by adding **-ed** or **-d** to the present form.

To form the past and past participle of a regular verb such as *chirp* or *hover*, you simply add *-ed* to the present. With regular verbs that already end in *e*—verbs such as *move* and *charge*—you simply add *-d* to the present.

PRINCIPAL PARTS OF REGULAR VERBS			
PRESENT	PRESENT PARTICIPLE	PAST	PAST PARTICIPLE
call	(am) calling	called	(have) called
change	(am) changing	changed	(have) changed
charge	(am) charging	charged	(have) charged
chirp	(am) chirping	chirped	(have) chirped
contain	(am) containing	contained	(have) contained
describe	(am) describing	described	(have) described
fix	(am) fixing	fixed	(have) fixed
hover	(am) hovering	hovered	(have) hovered
jump	(am) jumping	jumped	(have) jumped
lift	(am) lifting	lifted	(have) lifted
look	(am) looking	looked	(have) looked
move	(am) moving	moved	(have) moved
play	(am) playing	played	(have) played
save	(am) saving	saved	(have) saved
serve	(am) serving	served	(have) served
ski	(am) skiing	skied	(have) skied
talk	(am) talking	talked	(have) talked
type	(am) typing	typed	(have) typed
visit	(am) visiting	visited	(have) visited
walk	(am) walking	walked	(have) walked

See Practice 21.1A
See Practice 21.1B

PRACTICE 21.1A Identifying the Principal Parts of Regular Verbs

Read the sentences. Then, label each underlined verb *present*, *present participle*, *past*, or *past participle*.

EXAMPLE   I <u>enjoy</u> seeing a full moon.

ANSWER   *present*

1. When Dad has time, he <u>walks</u> to the train station.

2. My grandmother has <u>lived</u> in the same house for 70 years.

3. Our dog is <u>chasing</u> snowflakes in the backyard.

4. The teacher <u>assigned</u> three pages of homework.

5. The baseball players have <u>used</u> the same equipment for three seasons now.

6. Katrina <u>wants</u> a new microscope.

7. At a Chinese restaurant, I <u>tasted</u> shrimp for the first time.

8. Band members are <u>washing</u> cars to raise money.

9. I have never <u>climbed</u> a tree that tall.

10. My brother is always <u>looking</u> for a new hobby.

PRACTICE 21.1B Supplying the Principal Parts of Regular Verbs

Read the verbs. Write and label the four principal parts of each verb. Use a form of the helping verb *be* with the present participle and a form of the helping verb *have* with the past participle.

EXAMPLE   rely

ANSWER   *rely* — present
is relying — present participle
relied — past
has relied — past participle

11. drop

12. hurry

13. ask

14. move

15. search

16. flap

17. serve

18. knock

19. close

20. divide

SPEAKING APPLICATION

With a partner, take turns talking about current events. Use at least three of the principal verb parts as you talk. Your partner should listen for and name the principal parts of at least three of the verbs you use.

WRITING APPLICATION

Write a short paragraph about friends or family members. Use all four principal verb parts in your sentences.

Using Irregular Verbs

While most verbs are regular, many very common verbs are **irregular**—their past and past participle forms do not follow a predictable pattern.

> The past and past participle of an **irregular verb** are not formed by adding *-ed* or *-d* to the present tense form.

IRREGULAR VERBS WITH THE SAME PAST AND PAST PARTICIPLE			
PRESENT	PRESENT PARTICIPLE	PAST	PAST PARTICIPLE
bring	(am) bringing	brought	(have) brought
build	(am) building	built	(have) built
buy	(am) buying	bought	(have) bought
catch	(am) catching	caught	(have) caught
fight	(am) fighting	fought	(have) fought
find	(am) finding	found	(have) found
get	(am) getting	got	(have) got *or* (have) gotten
hold	(am) holding	held	(have) held
lay	(am) laying	laid	(have) laid
lead	(am) leading	led	(have) led
lose	(am) losing	lost	(have) lost
pay	(am) paying	paid	(have) paid
say	(am) saying	said	(have) said
sit	(am) sitting	sat	(have) sat
sleep	(am) sleeping	slept	(have) slept
spin	(am) spinning	spun	(have) spun
stand	(am) standing	stood	(have) stood
stick	(am) sticking	stuck	(have) stuck
swing	(am) swinging	swung	(have) swung
teach	(am) teaching	taught	(have) taught
win	(am) winning	won	(have) won

Check a dictionary whenever you are in doubt about the correct form of an irregular verb.

IRREGULAR VERBS WITH THE SAME PRESENT, PAST, AND PAST PARTICIPLE			
PRESENT	PRESENT PARTICIPLE	PAST	PAST PARTICIPLE
bid	(am) bidding	bid	(have) bid
burst	(am) bursting	burst	(have) burst
cost	(am) costing	cost	(have) cost
hurt	(am) hurting	hurt	(have) hurt
put	(am) putting	put	(have) put
set	(am) setting	set	(have) set

IRREGULAR VERBS THAT CHANGE IN OTHER WAYS			
PRESENT	PRESENT PARTICIPLE	PAST	PAST PARTICIPLE
arise	(am) arising	arose	(have) arisen
be, am, is, are	(am) being	was, were	(have) been
bear	(am) bearing	bore	(have) borne
beat	(am) beating	beat	(have) beaten
begin	(am) beginning	began	(have) begun
blow	(am) blowing	blew	(have) blown
break	(am) breaking	broke	(have) broken
choose	(am) choosing	chose	(have) chosen
come	(am) coming	came	(have) come
do	(am) doing	did	(have) done
draw	(am) drawing	drew	(have) drawn
drink	(am) drinking	drank	(have) drunk
drive	(am) driving	drove	(have) driven
eat	(am) eating	ate	(have) eaten
fall	(am) falling	fell	(have) fallen
fly	(am) flying	flew	(have) flown
forget	(am) forgetting	forgot	(have) forgotten
freeze	(am) freezing	froze	(have) frozen
give	(am) giving	gave	(have) given
go	(am) going	went	(have) gone

IRREGULAR VERBS THAT CHANGE IN OTHER WAYS (CONTINUED)			
PRESENT	**PRESENT PARTICIPLE**	**PAST**	**PAST PARTICIPLE**
grow	(am) growing	grew	(have) grown
have, has	am having	had	(have) had
know	(am) knowing	knew	(have) known
lie	(am) lying	lay	(have) lain
ride	(am) riding	rode	(have) ridden
ring	(am) ringing	rang	(have) rung
rise	(am) rising	rose	(have) risen
run	(am) running	ran	(have) run
see	(am) seeing	saw	(have) seen
shake	(am) shaking	shook	(have) shaken
sing	(am) singing	sang	(have) sung
sink	(am) sinking	sank	(have) sunk
speak	(am) speaking	spoke	(have) spoken
spring	(am) springing	sprang	(have) sprung
strive	(am) striving	strove	(have) striven
swear	(am) swearing	swore	(have) sworn
swim	(am) swimming	swam	(have) swum
take	(am) taking	took	(have) taken
tear	(am) tearing	tore	(have) torn
throw	(am) throwing	threw	(have) thrown
wear	(am) wearing	wore	(have) worn
weave	(am) weaving	wove	(have) woven
write	(am) writing	wrote	(have) written

See Practice 21.1C
See Practice 21.1D
See Practice 21.1E
See Practice 21.1F

As you can see, there are many irregular verbs. For most of these verbs, you should memorize the different forms. Whenever you are not sure of which form of an irregular verb to use, check a dictionary.

PRACTICE 21.1C ▷ **Supplying the Principal Parts of Irregular Verbs**

Read the verbs. Write and label the four principal parts of each verb. Use a form of the helping verb *be* with the present participle and a form of the helping verb *have* with the past participle.

EXAMPLE   stick

ANSWER   *stick* — present

          is sticking — present participle

          stuck — past

          have stuck — past participle

1. hold
2. spin
3. cost
4. grow
5. sing
6. write
7. bring
8. lead
9. sit
10. swim

PRACTICE 21.1D ▷ **Choosing the Correct Form of Irregular Verbs**

Read the sentences. Then, choose and write the form of the verb in parentheses that correctly completes each sentence.

EXAMPLE   I have (tore, torn) the paper in half.

ANSWER   *torn*

11. Sheila (brung, brought) fruit to the picnic.
12. Which one (cost, costed) the most?
13. We wanted to see the sunrise, so everyone had (arose, arisen) while it was still dark.
14. Carlos (choosed, chose) to perform a difficult piece of music.
15. The water was cool, and we (drank, drunk) our fill.
16. Celeste had never (flew, flown) in a plane before.
17. The town (builded, built) a new government office.
18. If we had (knew, known) then what we know now, things would have been different.
19. They have (sank, sunk) the toy boats.
20. You have (wore, worn) that same shirt three days in a row.

SPEAKING APPLICATION

With a partner, choose two irregular verbs from Practice 21.1C. Take turns using the different parts of each verb in sentences. Your partner should listen for and name which principal part of the verb you have used.

WRITING APPLICATION

Choose one of the irregular verbs from Practice 21.1C and 21.1D. Write four sentences, each one with a different principal part of the verb you selected.

PRACTICE 21.1E **Using Irregular Verbs**

Read the sentences. Rewrite each sentence, using the form of the verb in parentheses that correctly completes the sentence.

EXAMPLE I wish I had (know) you were coming.

ANSWER *I wish I had* **known** *you were coming.*

1. My mom (teach) math for ten years.

2. It (hurt) more yesterday than it does today.

3. Because the wind had (blow) all night, there were no leaves left on the trees.

4. My great-grandfather (fly) a plane in World War II.

5. The potted plants would have (freeze) if we had left them out last night.

6. The carpenters (build) a stage for the spring play.

7. What I should have (say) is, "Please."

8. Grandmother had (write) a letter, and she wanted me to mail it for her.

9. I (see) a four-leaf clover yesterday.

10. My cousin had (drive) all night to join us for Thanksgiving dinner.

PRACTICE 21.1F **Revising for Irregular Verbs**

Read the sentences. Then, if the underlined verb is in the correct form, write *correct*. If it is not, rewrite the sentence with the correct verb form.

EXAMPLE We wished we could have <u>layed</u> there in the sun all day.

ANSWER *We wished we could have* **lain** *there in the sun all day.*

11. They <u>knowed</u> I was coming.

12. My little sister has <u>grew</u> three inches since her last birthday.

13. When the baseball hit the window, the glass <u>broke</u>.

14. The bell at the fire department <u>ringed</u>.

15. We <u>ate</u> dinner at a restaurant near the park.

16. We should have <u>took</u> an extra blanket.

17. We had <u>shaken</u> all the sand out of the blanket before packing it.

18. My brother <u>catched</u> the fly ball.

19. My teacher had <u>spoke</u> to me about the project before class began.

20. My sister <u>swore</u> not to tell anyone about the surprise party.

SPEAKING APPLICATION

With a partner, take turns saying irregular verbs from Practice 21.1E. Your partner should then state one of the other principal parts of the verb and use it in a sentence.

WRITING APPLICATION

Write three or four sentences about what last autumn was like where you live. Use the past and past participle of two or three irregular verbs in your sentences. You may scan the list of words in Practice 21.1E and 21.1F for ideas.

21.2 The Six Tenses of Verbs

In English, verbs have six **tenses**: the **present**, the **past**, the **future**, the **present perfect**, the **past perfect**, and the **future perfect**.

WRITING COACH

Online

www.phwritingcoach.com

Grammar Tutorials
Brush up on your Grammar skills with these animated videos.

Grammar Practice
Practice your grammar skills with Writing Coach Online.

Grammar Games
Test your knowledge of grammar in this fast-paced interactive video game.

RULE 21.2.1

The **tense** of a verb shows the time of the action or state of being.

Every tense has both **basic** forms and **progressive** forms.

Identifying the Basic Forms of the Six Tenses

The chart below shows the **basic** forms of the six tenses, using *begin* as an example. The first column gives the name of each tense. The second column gives the basic form of *begin* in all six tenses. The third column gives the principal part needed to form each tense. Only three of the four principal parts are used in the basic forms: the present, the past, and the past participle.

BASIC FORMS OF THE SIX TENSES OF *BEGIN*		
TENSE	**BASIC FORM**	**PRINCIPAL PART USED**
Present	I begin.	Present
Past	I began.	Past
Future	I will begin.	Present
Present Perfect	I have begun.	Past Participle
Past Perfect	I had begun.	Past Participle
Future Perfect	I will have begun.	Past Participle

Study the chart carefully. First, learn the names of the tenses. Then, learn the principal parts needed to form them. Notice also that the last four tenses need helping verbs.

As you have already learned, some verbs form their tenses in a regular, predictable pattern. Other verbs use an irregular pattern. *Begin* is an example of an irregular verb.

See Practice 21.2A

Conjugating the Basic Forms of Verbs

A helpful way to become familiar with all the forms of a verb is by **conjugating** it.

> A **conjugation** is a list of the singular and plural forms of a verb in a particular tense.

Each tense in a conjugation has six forms that fit with first-, second-, and third-person forms of the personal pronouns. These forms may change for each personal pronoun, and they may change for each tense.

To conjugate any verb, begin by listing its principal parts. For example, the principal parts of the verb *go* are *go, going, went,* and *gone*. The following chart shows the conjugation of all the basic forms of *go* in all six tenses. Notice that the forms of the helping verbs may also change for each personal pronoun and tense.

CONJUGATION OF THE BASIC FORMS OF *GO*		
TENSE	**SINGULAR**	**PLURAL**
Present	I go. You go. He, she, or it goes.	We go. You go. They go.
Past	I went. You went. He, she, or it went.	We went. You went. They went.
Future	I will go. You will go. He, she, or it will go.	We will go. You will go. They will go.
Present Perfect	I have gone. You have gone. He, she, or it has gone.	We have gone. You have gone. They have gone.
Past Perfect	I had gone. You had gone. He, she, or it had gone.	We had gone. You had gone. They had gone.
Future Perfect	I will have gone. You will have gone. He, she, or it will have gone.	We will have gone. You will have gone. They will have gone.

See Practice 21.2B

Conjugating *Be*

The verb *be* is an important verb to know how to conjugate. It is both the most common and the most irregular verb in the English language. You will use the basic forms of *be* when you conjugate the progressive forms of verbs later in this section.

PRINCIPAL PARTS OF *BE*			
PRESENT	PRESENT PARTICIPLE	PAST	PAST PARTICIPLE
be	being	was	been

Once you know the principal parts of *be*, you can conjugate all of the basic forms of *be*.

CONJUGATION OF THE BASIC FORMS OF *BE*		
TENSE	SINGULAR	PLURAL
Present	I am. You are. He, she, or it is.	We are. You are. They are.
Past	I was. You were. He, she, or it was.	We were. You were. They were.
Future	I will be. You will be. He, she, or it will be.	We will be. You will be. They will be.
Present Perfect	I have been. You have been. He, she, or it has been.	We have been. You have been. They have been.
Past Perfect	I had been. You had been. He, she, or it had been.	We had been. You had been. They had been.
Future Perfect	I will have been. You will have been. He, she, or it will have been.	We will have been. You will have been. They will have been.

See Practice 21.2C
See Practice 21.2D

PRACTICE 21.2A **Identifying Present, Past, and Future Tenses of Verbs**

Read the sentences. Then, label each underlined verb *present*, *past*, or *future*.

EXAMPLE   Storm clouds <u>linger</u> above the mountains.

ANSWER   *present*

1. Tomorrow we <u>will wash</u> the car.
2. My brother just <u>swept</u> the driveway yesterday.
3. I <u>check</u> my e-mail every day after school.
4. Chandra <u>touched</u> the rabbit's soft fur.
5. After this winter, we <u>will welcome</u> spring.
6. Miguel <u>brought</u> two friends to the party.
7. The bells <u>ring</u> each morning.
8. This summer I <u>will learn</u> how to swim.
9. This bucket <u>holds</u> five gallons.
10. The weather <u>will turn</u> cool this weekend.

PRACTICE 21.2B **Identifying Perfect Tenses of Verbs**

Read the sentences. Then, write the verb in each sentence, and label it *present perfect*, *past perfect*, or *future perfect*.

EXAMPLE   The end of summer had come so much faster than I expected.

ANSWER   *had come* — *past perfect*

11. I wish I had known there was a test today.
12. By this time next year, Kendra will have finished high school.
13. We have bought a copy of my favorite author's new book.
14. My mom has started a new job.
15. I had brought a salad to the luncheon.
16. Carly had planted the flowers in the window.
17. Our town has benefited from recycling.
18. By 10 P.M., the kids will have come home from the school dance.
19. The days had begun to get longer.
20. The Jacksons have built a porch on the back of their house.

SPEAKING APPLICATION

With a partner, take turns talking about school. Talk about something you did last year, something you are doing now, and something you hope to do next year. Your partner should listen for and name one past-, one present-, and one future-tense verb.

WRITING APPLICATION

Write a short paragraph about a hobby or interest you have had for a while. Write about what you have been doing with it and what you hope you will be doing in the future. Use a perfect tense verb at least once.

PRACTICE 21.2C ▶ Forming Verb Tenses

Read the sentences, which are all in the present tense. Then, rewrite each sentence, changing it to the tense indicated in parentheses.

EXAMPLE   My sister holds the kitten. (past perfect)

ANSWER   My sister *had held* the kitten.

1. The teacher gives homework. (future)

2. The painters put the final coat of paint on the house. (present perfect)

3. We bring Aunt Shelby to every concert. (past)

4. The Boy Scout troop begins the service project. (future perfect)

5. We drink the juice. (past perfect)

6. You eat dinner with your family. (past)

7. Carlo completes the assignment. (future perfect)

8. They run in a marathon. (future)

9. Maureen chooses a science class. (past perfect)

10. Some say history repeats itself. (present perfect)

PRACTICE 21.2D ▶ Using Verb Tenses Correctly

Read the sentences. Then, write the verb in parentheses that correctly completes each sentence.

EXAMPLE   Tomorrow (will be, was) another day.

ANSWER   *will be*

11. By this time next year, Geo (will complete, will have completed) his degree.

12. Everything would change, now that Jill (chose, had chosen) to stay.

13. Rafael (will bring, will have brought) his brother to the party tonight.

14. We (ate, will eat) lunch at Grandma's yesterday.

15. They (had drunk, drink) all the milk by the time we got there.

16. The teacher said that everyone (has done, does) well this week.

17. Cooking (existed, exists) before people began recording history.

18. My mom (writes, had written) a note to my dad every morning.

19. I (will come, have come) to your party this afternoon.

20. My brother (carries, carried) the groceries in for my aunt when she came home.

SPEAKING APPLICATION

With a partner, take turns talking about holidays you celebrate. Talk about what you have done for past holidays, what you might be planning, and what you hope to do in the future. Your partner should listen for and name three verbs in perfect tenses.

WRITING APPLICATION

Write three sentences about school. One sentence should use a verb in the past perfect tense; one, a verb in the present perfect tense; and one, a verb in the future perfect tense.

Recognizing the Progressive Tense of Verbs

The six tenses of *go* and *be* in their basic forms were shown in the charts earlier in this section. Each of these tenses also has a progressive tense or form. The progressive form describes an event that is in progress. In contrast, the basic forms of a verb describe events that have a definite beginning and end.

> The **progressive tense,** or form, of a verb shows an action or condition that is ongoing.

All six of the progressive tenses of a verb are made using just one principal part: the present participle. This is the principal part that ends in *-ing*. Then, the correct form of *be* is added to create the progressive tense or form.

Progressive Tenses of *Sing*

PROGRESSIVE TENSE = be + present participle

PRESENT   I am singing in the chorus.
           be present participle

PAST   I was singing in practice all last week.
          be present participle

FUTURE   I will be singing in this weekend's concert.
            be   present participle

PRESENT PERFECT   I have been singing since I was a young child.
                     be   present participle

PAST PERFECT   I had been singing only in the chorus, but now
                  be   present participle
I also sing solos.

FUTURE PERFECT   I will have been singing in the chorus for ten
                    be   present participle
years by the time I graduate.

Conjugating Progressive Tenses

To create the progressive tenses or forms of a verb, you must know the basic forms of *be*.

RULE **21.2.4**

> To conjugate the **progressive** forms of a verb, add the present participle of the verb to a conjugation of the basic forms of *be*.

A complete conjugation of the basic forms of *be* is shown earlier in this section. Compare that conjugation with the following conjugation of the progressive forms of *go*. You will notice that, even though the present participle form of the verb does not change, the form of the helping verb does change. It is the form of *be* that tells you whether the action or condition is taking place in the past, present, or future.

CONJUGATION OF THE PROGRESSIVE FORMS OF *GO*		
TENSE	SINGULAR	PLURAL
Present Progressive	I am going. You are going. He, she, it is going.	We are going. You are going. They are going.
Past Progressive	I was going. You were going. He, she, it was going.	We were going. You were going. They were going.
Future Progressive	I will be going. You will be going. He, she, it will be going.	We will be going. You will be going. They will be going.
Present Perfect Progressive	I have been going. You have been going. He, she, it has been going.	We have been going. You have been going. They have been going.
Past Perfect Progressive	I had been going. You had been going. He, she, it had been going.	We had been going. You had been going. They had been going.
Future Perfect Progressive	I will have been going. You will have been going. He, she, it will have been going.	We will have been going. You will have been going. They will have been going.

See Practice 21.2E

See Practice 21.2F

PRACTICE 21.2E > **Identifying the Progressive Tenses of Verbs**

Read the sentences. Then, write whether the underlined verb tense in each sentence is *present progressive, past progressive, future progressive, present perfect progressive, past perfect progressive,* or *future perfect progressive.*

EXAMPLE   The wind <u>was blowing</u> across the prairie.

ANSWER   *past progressive*

1. The sun <u>is rising</u> over the ocean.

2. Jenny and Charlotte <u>were watching</u> the younger children play.

3. That movie <u>will be showing</u> at a theater next week.

4. I <u>had been looking</u> for a watch just like that.

5. The sky <u>was turning</u> from pink to orange.

6. I <u>have been cooking</u> all day.

7. The jet soon <u>will be soaring</u> high above Earth.

8. The students <u>had been practicing</u> their parts in the play for weeks.

9. Celia <u>is bringing</u> her cousin.

10. By next Wednesday, they <u>will have been dancing</u> together for two years!

PRACTICE 21.2F > **Using Progressive Tenses of Verbs**

Read the sentences. Then, rewrite each one as a complete sentence, using the tense of the verb in parentheses.

EXAMPLE   Candace _____ her vacation. (*plan,* present progressive)

ANSWER   *Candace **is planning** her vacation.*

11. Meta's story _____ more exciting. (*become,* present progressive)

12. José _____ the architecture. (*admire,* past progressive)

13. Liana _____ in New Mexico. (*live,* present perfect progressive)

14. They _____ while they study. (*eat,* future progressive)

15. Mr. Jung _____ before the alarm went off. (*sleep,* past perfect progressive)

16. I _____ for 12 hours by the time I reach China. (*fly,* future perfect progressive)

17. The author _____ her new book. (*sign,* past progressive)

18. Rosa _____ the sunshine. (*enjoy,* present progressive)

19. Dwayne _____ lawns since he was ten. (*mow,* present perfect progressive)

20. My puppy _____ on the bed. (*sleep,* past perfect progressive)

SPEAKING APPLICATION

With a partner, take turns talking about current events. Use progressive tenses of verbs. Your partner should listen for and name two progressive tense verbs.

WRITING APPLICATION

Write a brief summary of a story or book you enjoyed. Use progressive tenses of verbs in at least two sentences of the summary.

Identifying Active and Passive Voice

Just as verbs change tense to show time, they may also change form to show whether or not the subject of the verb is performing an action.

RULE **21.2.5**

> The **voice** of a verb shows whether or not the subject is performing the action.

In English, most verbs have two **voices: active,** to show that the subject is performing an action, and **passive,** to show that the subject is having an action performed on it.

RULE **21.2.6**

> A verb is in the **active voice** when its subject performs the action.

ACTIVE
VOICE

Sharon **plays** the piano.

Bob **photographed** the debate team.

In each example above, the subject performs the action, so it is said to be in the active voice.

RULE **21.2.7**

> A verb is in the **passive voice** when its subject does not perform the action.

PASSIVE
VOICE

The piano **is being played** by Sharon.

The debate team **was photographed** by Bob.

See Practice 21.2G

In each example above, the person doing the action becomes the object of the preposition *by* and is no longer the subject. Both subjects—*piano* and *team*—are receivers rather than performers of the action. When the subject is acted upon, the verb is said to be in the passive voice.

Forming the Tenses of Passive Verbs

A passive verb always has two parts.

> **A passive verb** is always a verb phrase made from a form of *be* plus a past participle.

The following chart shows a conjugation of the passive forms of the verb *report* with the pronoun *it.*

CONJUGATION OF THE PASSIVE FORMS OF *REPORT*	
TENSE	PASSIVE FORM
Present	It is reported.
Past	It was reported.
Future	It will be reported.
Present Perfect	It has been reported.
Past Perfect	It had been reported.
Future Perfect	It will have been reported.

While there are uses for the passive voice, most writing is more lively when it is in the active voice. Think about how to change each sentence below to the active voice. Follow the pattern in the first two examples.

PASSIVE   It **is decided** to bring the car.

ACTIVE   We **have decided** to bring the car.

PASSIVE   It **was decided** to bring the car.

ACTIVE   We **decided** to bring the car.

PASSIVE   It **will be decided** Tuesday if we should bring the car.

It **has been decided** to bring the car.

It **had been decided** that we will need the car.

It **will have been decided** if we need the car.

Using Active and Passive Voices

Each of the two voices has its proper use in English.

RULE 21.2.9

> Use the **active voice** whenever possible.

Sentences with active verbs are less wordy and more forceful than those with passive verbs. Compare, for example, the following sentences. Notice the different number of words each sentence needs to report the same information.

ACTIVE   Students **conducted** a taste test.

PASSIVE   A taste test **was conducted** by students.

Although you should use the active voice in most of your writing, there will be times when you will need to use the passive voice.

RULE 21.2.10

> Use the **passive voice** to emphasize the receiver of an action rather than the performer of an action.

In the following example, the receiver of the action is the subject *candidate*. It is the *voters* (the direct object) who are actually performing the action.

See Practice 21.2H

See Practice 21.2I

See Practice 21.2J

EMPHASIS
ON RECEIVER   The candidate **was supported** by the voters.

The passive voice should also be used when there is no performer of the action.

RULE 21.2.11

> Use the **passive voice** to point out the receiver of an action when the performer is unknown or not named in the sentence.

PERFORMER   The report **was ordered** last year.
UNKNOWN

PRACTICE 21.2G **Distinguishing Active and Passive Voice**

Read the sentences. Then, write *AV* if the underlined verb is in active voice or *PV* if the verb is in passive voice.

EXAMPLE The ball <u>was thrown</u> to first base.

ANSWER *PV*

1. Sondra <u>opened</u> the door for Mrs. Santos.

2. Jason said that the book <u>was dropped</u> by Celia.

3. The event <u>is being covered</u> by a rookie reporter.

4. I <u>juggled</u> two jobs while studying for my college exams.

5. Christine <u>was awakened</u> by her alarm clock at 6:00 A.M.

6. The kitten <u>lapped</u> up the spilled milk.

7. Lexie quickly <u>drank</u> three glasses of water.

8. The results of the election <u>pleased</u> the candidate.

9. The baby <u>was comforted</u> by its mother's voice.

10. Janet <u>helped</u> her little brother with his chores.

PRACTICE 21.2H **Revising to Use Active Voice**

Read the sentences. Then, rewrite each sentence that is in passive voice so that it is in active voice. If the sentence is already in active voice, write *active*. Discuss your answers with a partner to determine if they are correct.

EXAMPLE This song was written by Jackie.

ANSWER *Jackie wrote this song.*

11. I found a hat that I like.

12. The movie was made by a French director.

13. I went bowling yesterday.

14. The actors were applauded by the audience.

15. The snake warmed itself in the sun.

16. Sammy and Keisha were helped by Richard.

17. The show continued without further interruption.

18. The computer was fixed by the technician.

19. Ten items were scanned by the cashier.

20. Madison jogged around the park.

SPEAKING APPLICATION

With a partner, take turns saying one sentence in active voice and one sentence in passive voice. Use the sentences in Practice 21.2H as models to create your sentences. Your partner should listen to the two sentences and identify which sentence is in active voice and which is in passive voice.

WRITING APPLICATION

Write at least two sentences in passive voice about an activity you enjoy. Then, rewrite the sentences so they are in active voice.

PRACTICE 21.2I ▷ Recognizing Voice

Read the sentences. Then, write whether the underlined verb is in active voice or passive voice. Rewrite the sentences that are in passive voice to ones that are in active voice. Discuss the changes that you made with a partner.

EXAMPLE   The flag <u>was carried</u> by a guard.

ANSWER   *passive — A guard carried the flag.*

EXAMPLE   The school board <u>selected</u> a new superintendent a week ago.

ANSWER   *active*

1. The instructor <u>scheduled</u> the art classes for Saturdays.

2. The overdue book <u>was returned</u> to the library by my brother.

3. The last cat <u>was adopted</u> by the Perrys.

4. Jeff <u>wears</u> those worn-out jeans with his oldest sweatshirt.

5. The class <u>elected</u> Jorge.

6. The movers <u>broke</u> the picture frame by putting a heavy box on it.

7. That quilt <u>was made</u> by my aunt.

8. Those houses in Green Acres <u>are being built</u> by Quality Construction Services.

9. The teacher <u>warned</u> you about being late.

10. The delivery service <u>brings</u> Mom's packages.

PRACTICE 21.2J ▷ Revising Passive Voice

Read the sentences. Then, rewrite the sentences in the active voice. Check your revised sentences by reading them aloud to a partner.

EXAMPLE   The editorial in the school paper about traffic was written by me.

ANSWER   *I wrote the editorial in the school paper about traffic.*

11. The race car that came in first was driven by an expert.

12. The trash was picked up at 7 A.M. by the trash collectors.

13. Our dog, Hamilton, was chased by a coyote last night.

14. The door was locked by me.

15. Mom made the salad, but the spaghetti was made by Uncle Tony.

16. The play was written by Ms. Robinson, and Mr. Jeter directed it.

17. Our computer issue was solved by the Internet support team.

18. The party was planned by the twins, Jeremy and Jessica.

19. An increase in teachers' salaries was approved by the school board.

20. My grandfather has been treated for years by a team of doctors.

SPEAKING APPLICATION

Discuss with a partner when to use passive voice and when to use active voice. Each partner writes one sentence in active voice and one sentence in passive voice. Then, partners check each other's work.

WRITING APPLICATION

Write a paragraph about a sculpture or painting you have seen. Use at least one appropriate sentence in passive voice. Then, have a partner read your paragraph and identify your sentence in passive voice. Discuss how active voice makes sentences stronger.

Test Warm-Up

DIRECTIONS
Read the introduction and the passage that follows. Then, answer the questions to show that you can use and understand the function of active and passive voice in reading and writing.

Sydney wrote this paragraph about her soccer game. Read the paragraph and think about the changes you would suggest as a peer editor. When you finish reading, answer the questions that follow.

I Love Soccer!

(1) On Saturday, I think all of us were nervous to be playing the soccer champions from last season, but we were encouraged by our coach. (2) We got the ball and dribbled down the field. (3) Kofi is good at trapping, and we hung on. (4) A great kick was made by Andra to score a point. (5) Another point was scored by Brianna in the first half, and in the second half the winds died down, and that calmed all of us. (6) In the end, we were up 4 to 2, and a victory had been won!

---

1 What change, if any, should be made in sentence 1?

  A Change *were nervous* to **were being nervous**

  B Change *we were encouraged* to **we encouraged**

  C Change *we were encouraged by our coach* to **our coach encouraged us**

  D Make no change

2 How should sentence 4 be revised in the active voice?

  F A great kick was made by Andra; a point was scored.

  G To score a point, a great kick was made.

  H Andra made a great kick to score a point.

  J Andra made a great kick, and a point was scored by her.

3 What is the BEST way to revise sentence 5?

  A Another point was scored by Brianna in the first half. In the second half, we were calmed by the winds dying down.

  B Brianna scored another point in the first half. In the second half, the winds died down, and that calmed all of us.

  C Brianna scored another point in the first half. In the second half, the winds died down and were calmed by all of us.

  D Another point was scored by Brianna in the first half. In the second half, dying down were the winds that calmed all of us.

4 What change, if any, should be made in sentence 6?

  F Change *a victory had been* to **we**

  G Change *were* to **had been**

  H Add **by us** after *won*

  J Make no change

Moods of Verbs

Verbs in English also use **mood** to describe the status of an action.

> There are three moods for English verbs: the **indicative mood,** the **subjunctive mood,** and the **imperative mood.**

The **indicative mood** indicates, or states, something. It is also used to ask questions. The **subjunctive mood** describes a wish or a condition that may be contrary to fact.

INDICATIVE MOOD	SUBJUNCTIVE MOOD
Melanie **is** in my class.	I wish Joanna **were** in my class.
Jared **has** a new telescope.	If he **had brought** it to camp, we could have looked at the stars.
I **would** like to be president of the debating club.	If I **were** president of the debating club, I would be fair to everyone.

The subjunctive mood can be used to describe situations that are unlikely to happen or not possible. It is often used in clauses that begin with *if* or *that*. In these cases, use the plural form of the verb.

EXAMPLES   If I **were** you, I would leave for home after the rain stops.

(I am not you, so the situation is not possible.)

Mary wishes that she **were** on vacation now.

(She is not going until next month, so the situation is not possible.)

The **imperative** mood states a request or command and always uses the present tense. A mild imperative is followed by a period; a strong imperative is followed by an exclamation point.

EXAMPLES   **Call** me after school. Please **don't** forget.

Watch out for that broken window!

See Practice 21.2K

See Practice 21.2L

Notice that the subject, *you*, is understood but omitted.

PRACTICE 21.2K ▷ **Identifying Moods of Verbs**

Read the sentences. Then, write *indicative,* *subjunctive,* or *imperative* for the mood of the underlined verb in each sentence.

EXAMPLE   Please <u>close</u> the door.

ANSWER   *imperative*

1. I wish I <u>were</u> taller.
2. Lisa <u>is bringing</u> the popcorn tonight.
3. <u>Don't forget</u> your gloves.
4. If I <u>were</u> you, I would think carefully about your choice.
5. Mom and Dad <u>are going</u> out for dinner.
6. <u>Come</u> in for dinner now.
7. If it <u>were</u> up to me, we would take a different path.
8. Carla <u>has</u> a new bicycle.
9. I wish Dad <u>were</u> here now.
10. <u>Send</u> your grandmother a thank-you note.

PRACTICE 21.2L ▷ **Writing Sentences to Express Mood**

Read the verbs. Then, write sentences using the different moods of verbs as indicated below.

EXAMPLE   drink (imperative)

ANSWER   *Please drink some water.*

11. were (subjunctive)
12. will bring (indicative)
13. open (imperative)
14. went (indicative)
15. had been (subjunctive)
16. put (imperative)
17. ran (indicative)
18. could hear (subjunctive)
19. are leaving (indicative)
20. finish (imperative)

SPEAKING APPLICATION

With a partner, take turns talking about what you might like to do if things were different. Your partner should confirm whether you are using the subjunctive mood correctly.

WRITING APPLICATION

Write a short paragraph about what you would like to do if you were older. Use the subjunctive mood at least twice.

21.3 Troublesome Verbs

The following verbs cause problems for many speakers and writers of English. Some of the problems involve using the principal parts of certain verbs. Others involve learning to distinguish between the meanings of certain confusing pairs of verbs.

WRITING COACH

Online

www.phwritingcoach.com

Grammar Practice
Practice your grammar skills with Writing Coach Online.

Grammar Games
Test your knowledge of grammar in this fast-paced interactive video game.

(1) *ain't* *Ain't* is not considered standard English. Avoid using it in speaking and in writing.

INCORRECT   He **ain't** the first to explore this island.

CORRECT   He **isn't** the first to explore this island.

(2) *did, done* Remember that *done* is a past participle and can be used as a verb only with a helping verb such as *have* or *has*. Instead of using *done* without a helping verb, use *did*.

INCORRECT   I already **done** my history project.

CORRECT   I already **did** my history project.

                I **have** already **done** my history project.

See Practice 21.3A

(3) *dragged, drug* *Drag* is a regular verb. Its principal parts are *drag, dragging, dragged,* and *dragged. Drug* is never correct as the past or past participle of *drag.*

INCORRECT   The sailor **drug** the heavy box.

CORRECT   The sailor **dragged** the heavy box.

(4) *gone, went* *Gone* is the past participle of *go* and can be used as a verb only with a helping verb such as *have* or *has. Went* is the past tense of *go* and is never used with a helping verb.

INCORRECT   Jean and Frank **gone** to the museum.

                We **should have went** along with them.

CORRECT   Jean and Frank **went** (or **have gone**) to the museum.

                We **should have gone** along with them.

(5) *have, of* The words *have* and *of* often sound very similar. Be careful not to write *of* when you mean the helping verb *have* or its contraction *'ve*.

INCORRECT	Columbus should **of** continued on.
CORRECT	Columbus should **have** (or **should've**) continued on.

(6) *lay, lie* These verbs look and sound almost alike and have similar meanings. The first step in distinguishing between *lay* and *lie* is to memorize the principal parts of both verbs.

PRINCIPAL PARTS				
	lay	laying	laid	laid
	lie	lying	lay	lain

Lay usually means "to put (something) down" or "to place (something)." It is almost always followed by a direct object. *Lie* means "to rest in a reclining position" or "to be situated." This verb is used to show the position of a person, place, or thing. *Lie* is never followed by a direct object.

EXAMPLES	The captain **lays** his glasses on the desk.
	The sailors must **lie** down in bunks.

Pay special attention to the past tense of *lay* and *lie*. *Lay* is the past tense of *lie*. The past tense of *lay* is *laid*.

PRESENT TENSE OF *LAY*	I **lay** the map on the table.
PAST TENSE OF *LAY*	The sailors **laid** their uniforms on their bunks.
PAST TENSE OF *LIE*	The sailor **lay** down on his bunk.

See Practice 21.3B

(7) *leave, let* *Leave* means "to allow to remain." *Let* means "to permit." Do not reverse the meanings.

INCORRECT	**Leave** me think in peace! **Let** the poor dog alone!
CORRECT	**Let** me think in peace! **Leave** the poor dog alone!

(8) *raise, rise* *Raise* can mean "to lift (something) upward," "to build (something)," or "to increase (something)." It is usually followed by a direct object. *Rise* is not usually followed by a direct object. This verb means "to get up," "to go up," or "to be increased."

EXAMPLES   **Raise** the anchor so we can cast off.

The sailors must **rise** before five in the morning.

(9) *saw, seen* *Seen* is a past participle and can be used as a verb only with a helping verb such as *have* or *has*.

INCORRECT   I **seen** that exhibit last year.

CORRECT   I **saw** that exhibit last year.

(10) *says, said* A common mistake in reporting what someone said is to use *says* (present tense) rather than *said* (past tense).

INCORRECT   The captain **says**, "I need to sit down."

CORRECT   The captain **said**, "I need to sit down."

(11) *set, sit* The first step in learning to distinguish between *set* and *sit* is to become thoroughly familiar with their principal parts.

PRINCIPAL PARTS

set	setting	set	set
sit	sitting	sat	sat

Set means "to put (something) in a certain place or position." It is usually followed by a direct object. *Sit* usually means "to be seated" or "to rest." It is usually not followed by a direct object.

EXAMPLES   He **set** the cup on the coaster.

We **have set** the plants safely in the cargo bay.

Mona **sat** in the captain's chair.

The parrot **has sat** on the perch since it ate.

See Practice 21.3C
See Practice 21.3D

PRACTICE 21.3A **Using *Did* and *Done***

Read the sentences. Then, for each sentence, if *did* or *done* is used correctly, write *correct*. If it is not, write *incorrect*.

EXAMPLE   My brother done something really dangerous.

ANSWER   *incorrect*

1. We did all our homework.

2. We have did what we could to help.

3. Mom has done enough work for today.

4. I done a good job washing the car.

5. Celeste will have done everything necessary.

6. My little brother did his homework without my help.

7. Getting exercise done a lot to improve my health.

8. We have done all our shopping for the party.

9. Carmen has already did the painting.

10. We did invite Michelle and Carlos.

PRACTICE 21.3B **Using *Lay* and *Lie***

Read the sentences. Then, choose and write the correct form of the verb from the pair in parentheses.

EXAMPLE   Our cats love (lain, lying) near the heater.

ANSWER   *lying*

11. He carefully (laid, laying) the tray on the table.

12. Why don't you (lying, lie) down for a while?

13. They were (laying, laid) out their clothes for the next day.

14. You have (lay, lain) there all day!

15. She should (lie, lay) down on the couch to rest.

16. Most chickens (laid, lay) an egg every day.

17. There is a book (lying, laid) on my desk.

18. Yesterday, I (lay, lie) on the lawn, enjoying the smell of cut grass.

19. Jamal isn't feeling well and is (lying, lain) on the bed in the nurse's office.

20. The snow (lay, laid) thick and deep on the field last week.

SPEAKING APPLICATION

With a partner, take turns talking about activities that you do around your home. Use at least two of the verbs practiced on this page. Your partner should confirm whether the verbs were used correctly.

WRITING APPLICATION

Write three sentences about chores you do around your home. In your sentences, use *did* or *done* (you may use both), as well as at least one tense of *lay*.

PRACTICE 21.3C > Using *Set* and *Sit*

Read the sentences. Then, choose and write the correct form of the verb from the pair in parentheses.

EXAMPLE   I'll just (set, sit) right here until you come back.

ANSWER   *sit*

1. You can just (set, setting) it on the table.

2. If you (sat, sit) very still, you may see birds at the feeder.

3. Dad was (sitting, setting) the bags of sand in the truck when his back started to hurt.

4. The students (sat, set) in silence, waiting for the concert to begin.

5. I left the shopping list (setting, sitting) on the counter.

6. Cassie (set, sat) the books on the cart.

7. This weekend, we will be (sitting, setting) the cornerstone for the new library.

8. Our dog loves to (set, sit) on the sofa.

9. The waiter (sit, set) the bowl of soup down carefully.

10. My little brother (sit, sat) happily in the middle of the pile of toys.

PRACTICE 21.3D > Using Troublesome Verbs

Read the sentences. If the underlined verb is used correctly, write *correct*. If it is not, rewrite the sentence using the correct verb.

EXAMPLE   I <u>seen</u> a good place for a picnic.

ANSWER   *I saw a good place for a picnic.*

11. Mom <u>dragged</u> my brother to the barber for a haircut.

12. Have you <u>did</u> the research for your social studies project?

13. My sister wants to <u>raise</u> vegetables this summer.

14. The coach should <u>have</u> sent in a different player.

15. <u>Leave</u> that cut alone, or it won't heal.

16. The teacher gave us an assignment, and then he <u>says</u> it's due tomorrow.

17. Justin and Cleo <u>gone</u> to the zoo with their friends.

18. We <u>seen</u> someone riding an elephant.

19. <u>Leave</u> me sit here for a while.

20. You should have <u>gone</u> on the class trip.

SPEAKING APPLICATION

With a partner, take turns describing an exciting event. Use at least two of the troublesome verbs. Your partner should confirm whether you are using the verbs correctly.

WRITING APPLICATION

Write a short paragraph about a visit to a zoo (real or imagined). Use at least two of the troublesome verbs in your paragraph.

USING PRONOUNS

Using the correct types of pronouns will help make your writing flow smoothly.

CHAPTER 22

WRITE GUY *Jeff Anderson, M.Ed.*

WHAT DO YOU NOTICE?

Focus on the pronouns as you zoom in on these sentences from the speech "Stage Fright" by Mark Twain.

MENTOR TEXT

> My knees were shaking so that I didn't know whether I could stand up. If there is an awful, horrible malady in the world, it is stage fright—and seasickness. They are a pair.

Now, ask yourself the following questions:

- In the first sentence, how do the pronouns *my* and *I* help you figure out whose knees were shaking?
- In the third sentence, how can you tell what the pronoun *they* refers to?

In the first sentence, the pronoun *I* shows that the text is written in the first person. Therefore, the pronoun *my* shows that the narrator is describing his own knees. The pronoun *they* in the third sentence is plural. In the previous sentence, the author says there is one horrible malady, stage fright. Then he adds seasickness. Therefore, *they* refers to both *stage fright* and *seasickness*.

Grammar for Writers Writers use pronouns to avoid awkward repetition. For example, it sounds clumsy to say, "Dave forgot Dave's homework, so Dave's mother brought it to school for Dave." Instead you could say, "Dave forgot *his* homework, so *his* mother brought it to school for *him*."

I'd like to share my pronouns with you.

Thanks! That would make them ours.

22.1 Recognizing Cases of Personal Pronouns

In Chapter 1, you learned that personal pronouns can be arranged in three groups: first person, second person, and third person. Pronouns can also be grouped by their **cases.**

WRITING COACH

Online

www.phwritingcoach.com

Grammar Practice
Practice your grammar skills with Writing Coach Online.

Grammar Games
Test your knowledge of grammar in this fast-paced interactive video game.

RULE
22.1.1

> English has three cases: **nominative, objective,** and **possessive.**

The chart below shows the personal pronouns grouped according to the three cases. The case shows whether a pronoun is being used as a subject, an object, or a possessive.

THE THREE CASES OF PERSONAL PRONOUNS	
NOMINATIVE CASE	**USE IN A SENTENCE**
I, we, you, he, she, it, they	subject of a verb predicate pronoun
OBJECTIVE CASE	**USE IN A SENTENCE**
me, us, you, him, her, it, them	indirect object object of a preposition direct object
POSSESSIVE CASE	**USE IN A SENTENCE**
my, mine, our, ours, your, yours, his, her, hers, its, their, theirs	to show ownership

SUBJECT OF A VERB	**We** wanted badly to see the game.
PREDICATE PRONOUN	The winner is **she**.
INDIRECT OBJECT	Please give **me** the ball.
OBJECT OF A PREPOSITION	Please show the photograph to **me**.
DIRECT OBJECT	A basketball hit **him** on the head.
TO SHOW OWNERSHIP	That is **my** jacket, not **yours**.

See Practice 22.1A
See Practice 22.1B

PRACTICE 22.1A ▷ **Identifying Cases of Personal Pronouns**

Read the sentences. Then, identify the case of each underlined personal pronoun by writing *nominative*, *objective*, or *possessive*.

EXAMPLE   <u>They</u> wanted to go to the store.

ANSWER   *nominative*

1. Celeste offered <u>me</u> a chair.
2. Stanley made <u>his</u> way to the back of the bus.
3. <u>We</u> tried to get tickets for that concert.
4. Why did you invite <u>them</u>?
5. The person at the door announced, "It is <u>I</u>."
6. I grabbed my purse, and Mom grabbed <u>hers</u>.
7. Did you give the boxes to <u>him</u>?
8. I reminded Jena and Phil to bring <u>their</u> notebooks.
9. <u>He</u> went to the movies.
10. We can do it; just leave it to <u>us</u>.

PRACTICE 22.1B ▷ **Identifying Pronoun Cases and Uses**

Read the sentences. Write the case of each underlined pronoun. Then, label it *subject of a verb*, *predicate pronoun*, *direct object*, *indirect object*, or *object of a preposition*.

EXAMPLE   Ravi gave <u>her</u> the signed permission slip.

ANSWER   *objective, indirect object*

11. Carlos grabbed the ball and threw <u>it</u> to first base.
12. <u>She</u> carried the bottles to the recycling bin.
13. It was <u>they</u> who built the snow fort.
14. <u>Mine</u> was the first one picked.
15. Melanie handed the pile of papers to <u>me</u>.
16. After the tornado, <u>we</u> went outside to check for damage.
17. Chandra passed <u>him</u> the list.
18. My grocery cart ran into <u>his</u>.
19. The guide sent <u>them</u> to the information desk.
20. I wondered if it was <u>he</u> who had fixed the window.

SPEAKING APPLICATION

With a partner, take turns talking about things you do with your friends or classmates. Your partner should listen for and name at least two different cases of pronouns.

WRITING APPLICATION

Write three sentences about your family or friends. Use the nominative case in one sentence, the objective in one, and the possessive in one.

The Nominative Case

Personal pronouns in the nominative case have two uses.

RULE 22.1.2

> Use the **nominative** case for (1) the subject of a verb and (2) a predicate pronoun.

Note that predicate pronouns follow linking verbs. Pronouns that follow linking verbs should be in the nominative case. The linking verbs are highlighted in orange in the examples below.

SUBJECTS	**She** hopes to be on our team.
	Excitedly, **they** prepared for the game.
PREDICATE PRONOUNS	It **was I** who suggested a picnic.
	The best players **are she** and Mark.

Checking for Errors in the Nominative Case
People seldom forget to use the nominative case for a pronoun that is used by itself as a subject. Problems sometimes arise, however, when the pronoun is part of a compound subject.

INCORRECT	John and **me** played jacks.
CORRECT	John and **I** played jacks.

To make sure you are using the correct case of the pronoun in a compound subject, isolate the pronoun and the verb in the sentence. *Me played jacks* is obviously wrong, so the nominative case *I* should be used instead.

If the sentence is in verb–subject order, rearrange it into subject–verb order, and then isolate the pronoun and verb.

INCORRECT	Are you and **her** going to the dance?
REARRANGED	You and **?** are going to the dance.
CORRECT	Are you and **she** going to the dance?

See Practice 22.1C
See Practice 22.1D

The Objective Case

Personal pronouns in the objective case have three uses.

> Use the **objective** case for (1) a direct object, (2) an indirect object, and (3) the object of a preposition.

DIRECT OBJECT	Frank's comment on the game upset **me**.
	The referee penalized **her**.
INDIRECT OBJECT	Tell **her** the good news.
	My friend gave **me** highlights of the game.
OBJECT OF PREPOSITION	Our team captain voted for **him**.
	The players swarmed around **me**.

Checking for Errors in the Objective Case

As with the nominative case, people seldom forget to use the objective case for a pronoun that is used by itself as a direct object, indirect object, or object of a preposition. Problems may arise, however, when the pronoun is part of a compound object.

INCORRECT	The players swarmed around Lucy and **I**.
CORRECT	The players swarmed around Lucy and **me**.

To make sure you are using the correct case of the pronoun in a compound object, use only the pronoun with the rest of the sentence. *The players swarmed around I* is obviously wrong, so the objective case *me* should be used instead.

If the sentence is in verb–subject order, rearrange it into subject–verb order.

INCORRECT	Did my mother give Toby and **she** a drink?
REARRANGED	My mother gave Toby and **?** a drink.
CORRECT	Did my mother give Toby and **her** a drink?

See Practice 22.1E
See Practice 22.1F

The Possessive Case

Personal pronouns in the possessive case show ownership of one sort or another.

> Use the **possessive** case of personal pronouns before nouns to show possession. In addition, certain personal pronouns may also be used by themselves to indicate possession.

BEFORE NOUNS	The team won **its** game.
	Chris held **my** baseball glove.
BY THEMSELVES	Is this marble **yours** or **mine**?
	Hers was the best score.

Checking for Errors in the Possessive Case

Personal pronouns in the possessive case are never written with an apostrophe because they already show ownership. Keep this in mind, especially with possessive pronouns that end in *s*.

INCORRECT	These seats are **our's**, not **their's**.
CORRECT	These seats are **ours**, not **theirs**.

When the pronoun *it* is followed by an apostrophe and an *s*, the word becomes *it's,* which is a contraction of *it is*. The possessive pronoun *its* does not have an apostrophe.

CONTRACTION	**It's** going to rain.
POSSESSIVE PRONOUN	The team loves **its** uniform.

To check if you need the contraction *it's* or the possessive pronoun *its*, substitute *it is* and reread the sentence.

INCORRECT	My sweater has lost **it's** button.
CORRECT	My sweater has lost **its** button.

See Practice 22.1G

See Practice 22.1H

PRACTICE 22.1C > **Identifying Nominative Case Pronouns**

Read the sentences. Write the correct pronoun from the choices in parentheses. Then, label the pronoun *subject of a verb* or *predicate pronoun*.

EXAMPLE   It was (them, they) who brought the food.

ANSWER   *they* — predicate pronoun

1. Justin and (me, I) went to the soccer game.

2. It was (she, her) who finished first.

3. I saw the twins, and (they, them) were headed for home.

4. I asked Pedro if it was Bill and (him, he) who found the lost dog.

5. Either Tonya or (her, she) will come to get you.

6. Weren't you and (they, them) trying out for basketball?

7. It was (we, us) who came up with the idea.

8. (He, Him) and I wanted to find a new game.

9. The Steins and (us, we) are going to see a play.

10. It is (I, me) who drew the winning picture.

PRACTICE 22.1D > **Using Nominative Case Pronouns**

Read the sentences. Write the pronoun that is in the nominative case. Then, write a new sentence using the pronoun.

EXAMPLE   Are Erin and she prepared for the test?

ANSWER   *she; Are Erin and she here in the room?*

11. Luke and I are best friends.

12. Jim and he will call us at noon.

13. We should call your friend right now.

14. The first person in line is he.

15. Angel and she are partners for today.

16. We should offer to help Ms. Roberts with her errands.

17. Will he go with me to the dentist?

18. Did they stay past your bedtime?

19. Believe it or not, the first to arrive was she.

20. Jasmine and I will co-chair the meeting.

SPEAKING APPLICATION

With a partner, take turns talking about a movie or television show you enjoyed. Your partner should listen for and name at least two nominative pronouns.

WRITING APPLICATION

Write three sentences about the characters in a book you have read. Include at least two nominative case pronouns.

Using Objective Case Pronouns

Read the sentences. Write an objective pronoun to correctly complete each sentence. Then, label each pronoun *direct object*, *indirect object*, or *object of a preposition*.

EXAMPLE   Jonas sat beside _____.

ANSWER   *her — object of a preposition*

1. Ali handed _____ the book.

2. The guide directed _____ to the entrance.

3. From the plane, I gazed down at the land under _____.

4. I recommended _____ for the job.

5. Dad gave _____ gift certificates.

6. I sent a letter to _____.

7. My grandmother bought _____ the book I wanted.

8. Tina got in line in front of _____.

9. Mom made _____ costumes for the play.

10. We found _____ in the basement.

Writing Sentences With Objective Case Pronouns

Read the sentences. Write the pronoun or pronouns in each sentence that are in the objective case. Write your own sentence using the objective pronoun or pronouns.

EXAMPLE   Take the salad and bring some plates for us.

ANSWER   *us; Bring us some forks, also.*

11. Our warm jackets give us protection from the cold.

12. He brought them his bike to borrow for a week.

13. Are you going with her and him tonight?

14. Since we made the mistake, please forgive us.

15. They gave him and us their tickets.

16. When did he tell them about the mistake?

17. Evie and Taylor will be riding with us.

18. You should thank her for the gift.

19. My aunt sent me and her sweaters.

20. Will you please tell him that I am running late?

SPEAKING APPLICATION

With a partner, talk about things you and your family members do to help each other. Your partner should listen for and name three objective pronouns you used.

WRITING APPLICATION

Write three sentences. In each sentence, use compound subjects or compound objects that include only pronouns. Check to make sure that both pronouns in a compound subject or object are correct.

PRACTICE 22.1G > **Using Possessive Case Pronouns**

Read the sentences. Write the correct pronoun from the choices in parentheses.

EXAMPLE   That backpack is (my, mine).

ANSWER   *mine*

1. My brother and I gathered (our, ours) books.

2. A bird builds (it's, its) nest in the spring.

3. The Corrigans invited us to (their, theirs) house.

4. Those dresses are (her's, hers).

5. It's (your, yours) turn to play.

6. Sandra brought her DVDs, and the twins brought (their, theirs).

7. The teacher pointed to (my, mine) project.

8. It turned out those shoes weren't (ours, our's).

9. I could tell the dog was friendly because it wagged (it's, its) tail.

10. My brother asked if I had seen (him, his) baseball glove.

PRACTICE 22.1H > **Revising to Correct Pronoun Errors**

Read the sentences. For each sentence with a pronoun error, write the incorrect pronoun. Then, rewrite the sentence with the correct pronoun. If a sentence has no pronoun error, write *correct*.

EXAMPLE   It was us who won the contest.

ANSWER   *us; It was we who won the contest.*

11. Claudia and him went to the museum.

12. A chick has to peck it's way out of the egg.

13. It was he who reached the top of the hill first.

14. Mom gave my sister and I our lunches.

15. Our class thought the prize was our's.

16. I sent you and she a letter.

17. My dad took the Johnsons and us to the movies.

18. Was it them who decorated the room?

19. I thought it was mine, but Jena said it was her.

20. John and me went to the game.

SPEAKING APPLICATION

With a partner, talk about things that belong to you or your family. Your partner should listen for and name three possessive pronouns you used.

WRITING APPLICATION

Write a paragraph about things in your home. Describe who uses them most often. Use three possessive pronouns. Read your paragraph aloud to a partner. Your partner should identify the possessive pronouns.

Test Warm-Up

DIRECTIONS
Read the introduction and the passage that follows. Then, answer the questions to show that you can use and understand the function of nominative, objective, and possessive case pronouns in reading and writing.

Cassie wrote the following paragraph about her family's ideas for using a new room. Read the paragraph and think about the changes you would suggest as a peer editor. When you finish reading, answer the questions that follow.

What Should It Be?

(1) My dad says he wants to add a room to ours house. (2) He took a survey to find out how each of us would use the space. (3) My older brothers want a station for playing them games. (4) Mom wants a corner for her craft materials. (5) My twin sister thinks us need a table. (6) We could use it for casual meals. (7) Dad wants a place for the spectacular sound system Mom gave him last year. (8) As for mine, I wonder how all of this will fit in one room.

---

1 What change, if any, should be made in sentence 1?

A Add a comma after *says*

B Change *ours* to **our**

C Change *ours* to **our's**

D Make no change

2 What is the BEST way to revise sentence 3?

F My older brothers want a station for playing their games.

G My older brothers want a station for playing them's games.

H My older brothers want a station for playing they games.

J My older brothers want a station for playing they's games.

3 What is the BEST way to revise sentence 5?

A My twin sister thinks us needs a table.

B My twin sister thinks we need a table.

C My twin sister thinks we's need a table.

D My twin sister thinks our need a table.

4 What change, if any, should be made in sentence 8?

F Change *mine* to **my**

G Change *mine* to **me**

H Change *mine* to **you**

J Make no change

Cases of *Who* and *Whom* The pronouns *who* and *whom* are often confused. *Who* is a nominative case pronoun, and *whom* is an objective case pronoun. *Who* and *whom* have two common uses in sentences: They can be used in questions or to begin subordinate clauses in complex sentences.

> **Use *who* for the subject of a verb. Use *whom* for (1) the direct object of a verb and (2) the object of a preposition.**

22.1.5 RULE

You will often find *who* used as the subject of a question. *Who* may also be used as the subject of a subordinate clause in a complex sentence.

SUBJECT IN A QUESTION	**Who** hit the most home runs?
SUBJECT IN A SUBORDINATE CLAUSE	I admire the player **who** hit the most home runs.

The following examples show *whom* used in questions.

DIRECT OBJECT	**Whom** did he see at the game?
OBJECT OF PREPOSITION	From **whom** is she getting the new softball?

Questions that include *whom* are generally in inverted word order, with the verb appearing before the subject. If you reword the first example in subject–verb word order, you will see that *whom* is the direct object of the verb *did see: He did see whom?* In the second example, *whom* is the object of the preposition *from: She is getting the new softball from whom?*

Subordinate clauses that begin with *whom* can be rearranged to show that the pronoun is a direct object.

EXAMPLE	I will invite all the people **whom** he met at school.
REARRANGED SUBORDINATE CLAUSE	He met **whom** at school.

See Practice 22.1I
See Practice 22.1J

PRACTICE 22.1I ▷ **Identifying the Correct Use of Who and Whom**

Read the sentences. Write the pronoun in parentheses that correctly completes each sentence.

EXAMPLE   With (who, whom) are you going?

ANSWER   *whom*

1. (Who, Whom) brought the potato salad?

2. They told me (who, whom) it was at the door.

3. Anna is the one from (who, whom) I got this book.

4. The ball rolled toward (who, whom)?

5. (Who, whom) are you?

6. I met the friend (who, whom) you brought to the party.

7. You and (who, whom) else are going tonight?

8. Jeff is the one from (who, whom) I heard the news.

9. That is the coach (who, whom) will lead us to victory.

10. The teacher introduced (who, whom) to the class?

PRACTICE 22.1J ▷ **Revising to Correct Who and Whom**

Read the sentences. Then, if a sentence uses *who* or *whom* incorrectly, rewrite the sentence with the correct pronoun form. If a sentence has no pronoun error, write *correct*.

EXAMPLE   I wondered to who I should give it.

ANSWER   *I wondered to **whom** I should give it.*

11. May I ask whom is calling?

12. That's the aunt from whom I get my sense of humor.

13. You mailed a letter to who?

14. That is the person who I met yesterday.

15. If you don't come to the meeting, who will?

16. Besides Mom, whom else is bringing salad?

17. The teacher sent who to the principal's office?

18. With whom were you dancing last night?

19. Whom is at the door?

20. The books were given to him and who else?

SPEAKING APPLICATION

With a partner, take turns asking questions about giving and receiving (for example, "Who gave you that?"). Your partner should listen for and confirm whether you used *who* or *whom* correctly.

WRITING APPLICATION

Write two or three sentences about planning a party. Use *who* in one sentence and *whom* in one sentence.

CHAPTER 23

MAKING WORDS AGREE

Making subjects agree with verbs and pronouns with the words for which they stand will help you write clear sentences.

WRITE GUY *Jeff Anderson, M.Ed.*

WHAT DO YOU NOTICE?

Pay attention to agreement as you zoom in on these lines from the poem "Wilbur Wright and Orville Wright" by Rosemary and Stephen Vincent Benét.

MENTOR TEXT

—And kingdoms may forget their kings
And dogs forget their bites,
But, not till Man forgets his wings,
Will men forget the Wrights.

Now, ask yourself the following questions:

- How can you tell that the verb *forget* agrees with the subject *dogs* in the second line?

- Why do the poets use the pronouns *their* and *his* in the second and third lines?

Because *dogs* is a plural subject and *forget* is a plural verb, they agree with each other. While nouns ending in *-s* or *-es* are usually plural, verbs without *-s* or *-es* endings are usually plural. The poets use the plural pronoun *their* to indicate that the bites belong to the dogs. Because *dogs* is a plural noun, *their* is used instead of *its*. The poets use the singular pronoun *his* to indicate that the wings belong to Man. Because *Man* is a masculine noun, *his* is used instead of *her*.

Grammar for Writers Sentences flow smoothly when subjects and verbs agree and when pronouns match the words for which they stand.

How can you help subjects and verbs to agree?

You always give them the same number.

511

23.1 Subject-Verb Agreement

For a sentence to be correct, its subject and verb must match each other, or agree. Subject–verb agreement has one main rule.

RULE 23.1.1

> **The subject and verb in a sentence must agree in number.**

In grammar, the concept of **number** is simple. The number of a word can be either **singular** or **plural.** A singular word indicates *one.* A plural word indicates *more than one.* In English, only nouns, pronouns, and verbs have number.

Singular and Plural Subjects

Most of the time, it is easy to tell whether a simple subject, such as a noun or pronoun, is singular or plural. That is because most nouns are made plural by adding *-s* or *-es* to their singular form.

EXAMPLES

custom	custom**s**
bell	bell**s**
box	box**es**
tax	tax**es**

Some nouns form plurals in irregular ways.

EXAMPLES

knife	**knives**
mouse	**mice**
child	**children**
goose	**geese**

Pronouns also have different forms to indicate singular and plural. For example, the pronouns *I, he, she, it,* and *this* are singular. *We, they,* and *these* are plural. *You, who,* and *some* can be either singular or plural.

Singular and Plural Verbs

Like nouns, verbs have singular and plural forms. Problems involving number in verbs normally involve the third-person forms in the present tense (*she wants, they want*) and certain forms of the verb *be* (*I am, he is* or *was, we are* or *were*).

The chart shows all the basic forms of several different verbs in the present tense.

SINGULAR AND PLURAL VERBS IN THE PRESENT TENSE		
SINGULAR		PLURAL
First and Second Person	**Third Person**	**First, Second, and Third Person**
(I, you) send	(he, she, it) sends	(we, you, they) send
(I, you) go	(he, she, it) goes	(we, you, they) go
(I, you) look	(he, she, it) looks	(we, you, they) look
(I, you) dance	(he, she, it) dances	(we, you, they) dance
(I, you) visit	(he, she, it) visits	(we, you, they) visit
(I, you) work	(he, she, it) works	(we, you, they) work
(I, you) run	(he, she, it) runs	(we, you, they) run
(I, you) discuss	(he, she, it) discusses	(we, you, they) discuss
(I, you) vote	(he, she, it) votes	(we, you, they) vote
(I, you) choose	(he, she, it) chooses	(we, you, they) choose
(I, you) learn	(he, she, it) learns	(we, you, they) learn

Notice that the form of the verb changes only in the third-person singular, when an *-s* or *-es* is added to the verb. Unlike nouns, which usually become plural when *-s* or *-es* is added, verbs with *-s* or *-es* added to them are singular.

The helping verb *be* may also indicate whether a verb is singular or plural. The following chart shows only those forms of the verb *be* that are always singular.

FORMS OF THE HELPING VERB *BE* THAT ARE ALWAYS SINGULAR			
am	is	was	has been

Making Verbs Agree With Singular and Plural Subjects

To check subject–verb agreement, determine the number of the subject. Then, make sure the verb has the same number.

SINGULAR
SUBJECT
AND VERB

Jeff **enjoys** the beach.

She **was** here earlier today.

PLURAL
SUBJECT
AND VERB

Surfers **enjoy** the beach.

They **were** here earlier today.

> **A prepositional phrase that comes between a subject and its verb does not affect subject–verb agreement.**

Often, a subject is separated from its verb by a prepositional phrase. In these cases, it is important to remember that the object of a preposition is never the subject of a sentence.

INCORRECT

The **arrival** of the firefighters **have caused** much excitement at the picnic.

CORRECT

The **arrival** of the firefighters **has caused** much excitement at the picnic.

INCORRECT

The **cheers** of the crowd **was heard** several blocks away.

CORRECT

The **cheers** of the crowd **were heard** several blocks away.

In the first example, the subject is *arrival,* not *firefighters,* which is the object of the preposition *of.* Because *arrival* is singular, the singular verb *has caused* must be used. In the second example, the subject is the plural *cheers,* not *crowd*; therefore, it takes the plural verb *were heard.*

See Practice 23.1A
See Practice 23.1B

PRACTICE 23.1A **Making Subjects and Verbs Agree**

Read the sentences. Write the verb in parentheses that agrees with the subject. Then, label the subject *singular* or *plural*. Be sure to think about prepositional phrases and their influence on subject-verb agreement.

EXAMPLE   They (is, are) on time.

ANSWER   *are* — *plural*

1. This tree (provides, provide) a home for birds and squirrels.

2. The girls (plays, play) basketball after school.

3. The progress of the group of students (was, were) slowed by the weather.

4. The boys (thinks, think) math is easy.

5. Derek (believe, believes) it is bad to litter.

6. Members of the band (is, are) raising money for new uniforms.

7. She (meets, meet) her friends every Friday for dinner.

8. The pecans in the box (is, are) ready to sell.

9. Twila (wants, want) to study ballet.

10. We (sees, see) the clouds in the distance.

PRACTICE 23.1B **Revising for Subject-Verb Agreement**

Read the sentences. Then, if a sentence has an error in subject-verb agreement, rewrite the sentence correctly. If a sentence has no error, write *correct*.

EXAMPLE   We is excited about vacation.

ANSWER   *We **are** excited about vacation.*

11. They brings their lunches to school.

12. The girls in this group have decided on a project.

13. One of the police officers have a radio.

14. The flowers in the garden is starting to bloom.

15. My friends plans to go to college.

16. The players on that team practice every day.

17. The Smiths' dog barks at everyone.

18. I'll be happy when I gets home.

19. The cost of ten rides is fifteen dollars.

20. My sister often borrow my clothes.

SPEAKING APPLICATION

With a partner, take turns talking about teams or groups and individual members of those teams or groups. Your partner should listen for and identify at least one singular subject and one plural subject and the verbs that agree with them.

WRITING APPLICATION

Write three sentences about school activities. In one sentence, have a singular subject; in one, a plural subject; and in one, a subject with a prepositional phrase between the subject and the verb. Make sure subjects and verbs agree.

Subject-Verb Agreement in Simple and Compound Sentences

Both simple and compound sentences must follow the rules of subject-verb agreement.

RULE 23.1.3

> **In a simple sentence, the subject and verb must agree. In a compound sentence, the subject and verb in each main clause must agree.**

A simple sentence has one main clause. A main clause contains one subject and one verb and can stand alone as a sentence. A singular subject takes a singular verb. A plural subject takes a plural verb.

SIMPLE SENTENCE
Carla **sends** text messages every day after school.

The singular subject *Carla* takes the singular verb *sends*.

SIMPLE SENTENCE
We **are** not allowed to send text messages in school.

The plural subject *We* takes the plural verb *are*.

A compound sentence has two or more main clauses linked by a comma and a coordinating conjunction, such as *and, but, or, nor, for, so,* and *yet.*

You can also link the two sentences with a semicolon if they are closely related. In a compound sentence, the subject and verb in each main clause must agree.

See Practice 23.1C
See Practice 23.1D
See Practice 23.1E
See Practice 23.1F

COMPOUND SENTENCE
Carlos **walks** on the field, and the **fans** **cheer**.

In the first main clause, the singular subject *Carlos* takes the singular verb *walks*. In the second main clause, the plural subject *fans* takes the plural verb *cheer.*

COMPOUND SENTENCE
Luis **leaves** the game early, so **he** **misses** the final touchdown.

The singular subject *Luis* takes the singular verb *leaves*. The singular subject *he* takes the singular verb *misses*.

PRACTICE 23.1C **Recognizing Subject-Verb Agreement**

Read the sentences. Rewrite the sentences using correct subject-verb agreement, choosing the correct verb in parentheses. Then, identify the sentences as simple or compound.

EXAMPLE   The bus (stop, stops) at every corner, but often no one gets on.

ANSWER   *The bus **stops** at every corner, but often no one gets on. — compound*

1. Bethany (sing, sings) in the chorus, and she (play, plays) the piano.

2. Emmett (do, does) not like flying in an airplane.

3. The Festival of Lights (is, are) beginning on Friday.

4. The celebration (take, takes) place near the lake.

5. Mom never (ask, asks) for help, so she (has, have) to be tired.

6. My grandparents (travel, travels) every summer.

7. Aunt Kay (buy, buys) many clothes, and Uncle Joe (complain, complains).

8. A hero (show, shows) courage.

9. Drivers (was, were) honking their horns, but the truck did not move.

10. The rainy season (arrive, arrives) every summer in June.

PRACTICE 23.1D **Revising for Subject-Verb Agreement**

Read the sentences. Then, if a sentence has errors in subject-verb agreement, rewrite the sentence correctly. If the sentence has no error, write *correct*. Identify each sentence as simple or compound.

EXAMPLE   The books belongs here, and the pencils go there.

ANSWER   *The books **belong** here, and the pencils go there. — compound*

11. The campers was asleep by nine o'clock.

12. The sun rises in the East, and it set in the West.

13. The sky is clear, and the Big Dipper is visible.

14. My shoes is under the bed, and yours is in the closet.

15. Either your paper was finished on time, or it was not.

16. Mosquitoes are everywhere, for we has a lot of rain.

17. The new furniture is coming tomorrow.

18. You needs to put up the decorations before the party tomorrow night.

19. The new shirt is too big, and the shoes are too tight.

20. My mom bike to the park, but we likes to walk.

SPEAKING APPLICATION

With a partner, compare the different ways animals look and move. Use verbs that agree with subjects. Then, write two simple sentences and one compound sentence about animals. Use correct subject-verb agreement.

WRITING APPLICATION

Use the examples on this page to write your own simple and compound sentences with correct subject-verb agreement. Read your sentences aloud to a partner. Your partner should check the subject-verb agreement.

PRACTICE 23.1E ▶ Using Subject-Verb Agreement

Read the sentences. Choose the correct verb for subject-verb agreement. Then, rewrite each item, adding a conjunction, to make a compound sentence.

EXAMPLE   Saul and Vernon do the yard work. Brandon _____ the dishes. (do, does)

ANSWER   *Saul and Vernon do the yard work,* ***but Brandon does the dishes.***

1. My neighborhood _____ quiet. Shops are nearby. (is, are)

2. The beds _____ in storage. The apartment remains empty. (is, are)

3. Venus _____ brightly. The moon is even brighter. (shines, shine)

4. The boys like Connor. He _____ to be friendly. (seems, seem)

5. The vegetables are too salty. The meat _____ delicious. (tastes, taste)

6. This perfume _____ awful. The other bottles are fine. (smells, smell)

7. They like push-ups. I _____ aerobics. (like, likes)

8. Angela and Julio both _____ with water colors. Aleta uses acrylics. (paints, paint)

9. Jake and Em exercise every day. Lisa _____ only twice a week. (exercises, exercise)

10. Carrie and Grace go skiing. Annie _____ snowboarding. (prefers, prefer)

PRACTICE 23.1F ▶ Using Subject-Verb Agreement in Simple and Compound Sentences

Read the sentences. Then, rewrite each sentence using correct subject-verb agreement.

EXAMPLE   The programs on television this summer are comedy reruns, or they is reality shows.

ANSWER   *The programs on television this summer are comedy reruns, or they* ***are*** *reality shows.*

11. Shirts is on sale until Saturday, but I have no cash.

12. The performance was not sold out, so the actors was disappointed.

13. Several stores close at nine, but the mall stay open until ten.

14. The hurricane threaten Florida, yet Texas is not under a warning.

15. Baskets are on display in aisle one, and sculptures is in aisle two.

16. The rule is clear, and Bo and Max is wrong.

17. That snake is a rattlesnake, or it look like one.

18. I choose light colors, but my best friend like dark navy.

19. The answer was hard to find, for the problem were not clearly stated.

20. The umpire makes good calls, or the fans is unhappy.

SPEAKING APPLICATION

In a small group, talk about healthy foods your family likes to eat. Then, write one simple sentence and two compound sentences about food. Use correct subject-verb agreement.

WRITING APPLICATION

Write simple and compound sentences of your own using correct subject-verb agreement. With a partner, identify the sentence types and tell how the subjects and verbs agree.

Test Warm-Up

DIRECTIONS
Read the introduction and the passage that follows. Then, answer the questions to show that you can use and understand the function of subject-verb agreement in simple and compound sentences in reading and writing.

Alejandro wrote this paragraph for his report about Brazil. Read the paragraph and think about the changes you would suggest as a peer editor. When you finish reading, answer the questions that follow.

Brazil

(1) Brazil is the largest country in South America. (2) It has miles of coast, and the land cover almost half of South America. (3) There are plains, mountains, and rain forests. (4) Its major river, the Amazon, are the second longest river in the world. (5) It has many kinds of wildlife. (6) Its golden lion tamarin monkeys are most unusual animals. (7) They has manes that make them look a bit like lions. (8) They is tiny in size.

---

1 What change should be made in sentence 2?

A Change *has* to **have**

B Change *and* to **therefore**

C Change *cover* to **covers**

D Change *miles* to **mile**

2 What change, if any, should be made in sentence 3?

F Change *are* to **is**

G Add a comma after **are**

H Change *are* to **be**

J Make no change

3 What is the BEST way to revise sentence 4?

A Its major river, the Amazon, is the second longest river in the world.

B Its major river, the Amazon, are the second longest rivers in the world.

C Their major river, the Amazon, and are the second longest river in the world.

D Their major rivers, the Amazon, are the second longest river in the world.

4 What is the BEST way to combine sentences 7 and 8?

F They has manes that make them look a bit like lions, but they are tiny in size.

G They has manes that make them look a bit like lions, but they is tiny in size.

H They have manes that make them look a bit like lions, but they are tiny in size.

J They have manes that make them look a bit like lions, but they is tiny in size.

Making Verbs Agree With Collective Nouns

Collective nouns—such as *assembly, audience, class, club,* and *committee*—name groups of people or things. Collective nouns are challenging as subjects because they can take either singular or plural verbs. The number of the verb depends on the meaning of the collective noun in the sentence.

RULE 23.1.4

Use a singular verb with a collective noun acting as a single unit. Use a plural verb when the individual members of the group are acting individually.

SINGULAR	The **committee votes** on issues.
PLURAL	The **committee have split** their votes.

SINGULAR	The chess **club plans** a tournament.
PLURAL	The chess **club were pleased** with their games.

SINGULAR	The **class plants** a vegetable garden.
PLURAL	The **class have divided** the responsibilities of planting among the members.

SINGULAR	The scout **troop marches** in the parade.
PLURAL	The scout **troop have earned** badges in many areas.

SINGULAR	The **audience applauds** after the show.
PLURAL	The **audience squirm** in their seats.

See Practice 23.1G
See Practice 23.1H

PRACTICE 23.1G ▷ Making Verbs Agree With Collective Nouns

Read the sentences. Then, write the verb in parentheses that agrees with the subject.

EXAMPLE   After a game, the team (changes, change) their clothes before going home.

ANSWER   *change*

1. Once the assignment is given, the class (opens, open) their books.

2. I read that the army (trains, train) recruits very well.

3. The audience (doesn't, don't) enjoy the movie.

4. A group of students (plans, plan) the annual bake sale.

5. The jury (disagrees, disagree) among themselves.

6. The band (travels, travel) by bus.

7. The cleaning crew (begins, begin) their different tasks.

8. A swarm of bees (is, are) moving across the field.

9. The family (takes, take) their places around the table.

10. The company (relies, rely) on the honesty of its employees.

PRACTICE 23.1H ▷ Revising for Agreement Between Verbs and Collective Nouns

Read the sentences. Then, if a sentence has an error in subject-verb agreement, rewrite the sentence correctly. If a sentence has no error, write *correct*.

EXAMPLE   The cast learns their lines for the play.

ANSWER   *The cast **learn** their lines for the play.*

11. Congress vote on a tax bill tomorrow.

12. The majority think their rights are protected.

13. The committee often argues among themselves.

14. The jury come to a verdict.

15. The team practice or read while they wait.

16. This bunch of bananas look good.

17. The class begins their research reports.

18. The Girl Scout troop says the Pledge of Allegiance.

19. The student council help set rules.

20. The whole herd waits at the gate.

SPEAKING APPLICATION

With a partner, take turns talking about groups you know about, such as school clubs or community groups. Your partner should listen for and name two collective nouns you used. Discuss why the noun is singular or plural.

WRITING APPLICATION

Write three sentences, in the present tense, using these collective nouns as subjects: *committee*, *team*, and *class*. Label the subjects *plural* or *singular*.

Making Verbs Agree With Compound Subjects

A **compound subject** refers to two or more subjects that share a verb. Compound subjects are connected by conjunctions such as *and, or,* or *nor.*

EXAMPLES   The **museums** and **historical sites** in
            compound subject
            Philadelphia **attract** many visitors.
                         plural verb

            Either **Robert** or **Jennifer** **knows** the way to the
                   compound subject   singular
                                           verb
            bus stop.

            Neither the **Liberty Bell** nor **Independence**
                        compound subject
            Hall **disappoints** tourists.
                     singular
                     verb

A number of rules can help you choose the right verb to use with a compound subject.

Compound Subjects Joined by *And*

RULE 23.1.5 When a compound subject is connected by *and*, the verb that follows is usually plural.

EXAMPLE   **Austin** and **Dallas** **are** my favorite Texas cities.
            compound subject   plural
                                     verb

There is an exception to this rule: If the parts of a compound subject are thought of as one person or thing, the subject is singular and takes a singular verb.

EXAMPLES   **Spaghetti and meatballs** **is** my favorite meal.
            compound subject   singular
                                        verb

            Salt and pepper **is** on the table.
            compound subject   singular
                                verb

RULE

Compound Subjects Joined by *Or* or *Nor*

> **When two singular subjects are joined by *or* or *nor*, use a singular verb. When two plural subjects are joined by *or* or *nor*, use a plural verb.**

23.1.6 RULE

SINGULAR   A **car** or a **train** **provides** good transportation to
                    compound subject   singular
                                                 verb
             the city.

PLURAL   Neither **children** nor **adults** **like** to wait in line.
                         compound subject   plural verb

In the first example, *or* joins two singular subjects. Although two vehicles make up the compound subject, the subject does not take a plural verb. Either a car or a train provides good transportation, not both of them.

> **When a compound subject is made up of one singular and one plural subject joined by *or* or *nor*, the verb agrees with the subject closer to it.**

23.1.7 RULE

EXAMPLES   Either the **monuments** or the **White House**
                           plural subject   singular subject

             is interesting to see.
             singular verb

             Either the **White House** or the **monuments**
                          singular subject   plural subject

             are interesting to see.
             plural verb

See Practice 23.1I
See Practice 23.1J

Agreement in Inverted Sentences

In most sentences, the subject comes before the verb. Sometimes, however, this order is turned around, or **inverted.** In other sentences, the helping verb comes before the subject even though the main verb follows the subject.

When a subject comes after the verb, the subject and verb still must agree with each other in number.

EXAMPLE **Do** the historical **attractions** in Boston sound
plural verb   plural subject

exciting to you?

Sentences Beginning With a Prepositional Phrase
In sentences that begin with a prepositional phrase, the object of the preposition may look like a subject, even though it is not.

EXAMPLE Along the shore **were** many nervous **soldiers**.
plural verb   plural subject

In this example, the plural verb *were* agrees with the plural subject *soldiers*. The singular noun *shore* is the object of the preposition *along*.

Sentences Beginning With *There* or *Here*
Sentences beginning with *there* or *here* are almost always in inverted word order.

EXAMPLES There **were** several **books** about holidays.
plural verb   plural subject

Here **is** the latest **book** about holidays.
singular verb   singular subject

The contractions *there's* and *here's* both contain the singular verb *is*: *there is* and *here is*. Do not use these contractions as plural subjects.

INCORRECT Here**'s** the **keys** to the house.

CORRECT Here **are** the **keys** to the house.

Questions With Inverted Word Order
Many questions are also written in inverted word order.

EXAMPLE Where **are** the **keys** to the house?
plural verb plural subject

524 **Making Words Agree**

PRACTICE 23.1I ▷ Making Verbs Agree With Compound Subjects

Read the sentences. Then, write the verb in parentheses that agrees with the subject.

EXAMPLE   Chloe and Emily (is, are) going to dance class.

ANSWER   *are*

1. Either Jason or Kevin (needs, need) to bring the basketball.

2. Weeding and watering (is, are) important parts of gardening.

3. Neither students nor teachers (enjoys, enjoy) fire drills.

4. Macaroni and cheese (is, are) easy to make.

5. My dog and the neighbor's cat (acts, act) like friends.

6. A bus or a taxi (leaves, leave) for the airport every few minutes.

7. Neither the coach nor the players (is, are) ready for this game.

8. The budding trees and the new grass (promises, promise) that spring is near.

9. Either the frills or the lace (needs, need) to be taken off the dress.

10. The canned vegetables and soup (goes, go) into the cupboard.

PRACTICE 23.1J ▷ Revising for Agreement Between Verbs and Compound Subjects

Read the sentences. Then, if a sentence has an error in subject-verb agreement, rewrite the sentence correctly. If a sentence has no error, write *correct*.

EXAMPLE   A button or hook are needed for that skirt.

ANSWER   *A button or hook is needed for that skirt.*

11. Skiing and skating is winter sports.

12. Neither the parents nor the children wants that rule.

13. The gathering clouds and rising wind signal an approaching storm.

14. Either dirt or sand are needed for planting these seeds.

15. The eggs and milk goes into the refrigerator.

16. Neither the hippo nor the elephant seems to notice the zoo's visitors.

17. The maps and guidebook helps us find our way.

18. The museum or aquarium offer classes.

19. Peanut butter and jelly is my favorite sandwich.

20. Either the band or the chorus have a bake sale today.

SPEAKING APPLICATION

With a partner, talk about shopping for food. What sorts of things fill the shopping cart? Where are they found? Your partner should listen for and name three compound subjects and note whether the verbs agree.

WRITING APPLICATION

Write three sentences about your favorite season of the year. Use compound subjects in each sentence. Make sure the verbs agree with the subjects.

Verb Agreement With Indefinite Pronouns

Indefinite pronouns refer to people, places, or things in a general way.

> When an **indefinite pronoun** is the subject of a sentence, the verb must agree in number with the pronoun.

INDEFINITE PRONOUNS				
SINGULAR			PLURAL	SINGULAR OR PLURAL
anybody	everyone	nothing	both	all
anyone	everything	one	few	any
anything	much	other	many	more
each	neither	somebody	several	most
either	nobody	someone	others	none
everybody	no one	something		some

Indefinite Pronouns That Are Always Singular

Indefinite pronouns that are always singular take singular verbs. Do not be misled by a prepositional phrase that follows an indefinite pronoun. The singular verb agrees with the indefinite pronoun, not with the object of the preposition.

EXAMPLES

Each of the basketball team banners **is** blue
singular subject   singular verb
and white.

Either of the hats **is** warm.
singular subject   singular verb

Everyone in the first five rows **was** delighted
singular subject   singular verb
by the play.

Each of the boys **plays** on a town team.
singular subject   singular verb

Indefinite Pronouns That Are Always Plural

Indefinite pronouns that are always plural are used with plural verbs.

EXAMPLE **Both** of my suitcases **are** in the closet.
plural subject   plural verb

Many **are waiting** until it gets cooler
plural subject   plural verb

to go out.

Several **have** not **started** their projects yet.
plural subject plural verb

Few **have chosen** a gift yet.
plural subject   plural verb

Indefinite Pronouns That May Be Either Singular or Plural

Many indefinite pronouns can take either a singular or a plural verb.

> **The number of the indefinite pronoun is the same as the number of its referent, or the noun to which it refers.**

23.1.10 RULE

The indefinite pronoun is singular if the referent is singular. If the referent is plural, the indefinite pronoun is plural.

SINGULAR **Some** of the **milk** **is** frozen.

PLURAL **Some** of the **apples** **are** frozen, too.

In the examples above, *some* is singular when it refers to *milk,* but plural when it refers to *apples.*

SINGULAR **All** of my **money** **is** gone.

PLURAL **All** of these **presents** **are** for you.

See Practice 23.1K
See Practice 23.1L
In these examples, *all* is singular when it refers to *money,* but plural when it refers to *presents.*

PRACTICE 23.1K > **Making Verbs Agree With Indefinite Pronouns**

Read the sentences. Then, write the verb in parentheses that agrees with the subject.

EXAMPLE   Few (is, are) chosen for this honor.

ANSWER   *are*

1. Nothing (happens, happen) at school on Sundays.

2. Both (is, are) good choices.

3. Many of us (likes, like) Chinese food.

4. Each of the participants (gets, get) a certificate.

5. Everything (depends, depend) on teamwork.

6. All of the eggs (is, are) broken.

7. Most of the lake (freezes, freeze) in the winter.

8. Everyone (knows, know) what to do.

9. Several (is, are) going to appear at the event.

10. Anything (happens, happen) at these games.

PRACTICE 23.1L > **Revising for Agreement Between Verbs and Indefinite Pronouns**

Read the sentences. Then, if a sentence has an error in subject-verb agreement, rewrite the sentence correctly. If a sentence has no error, write *correct*.

EXAMPLE   Each of the balloons float.

ANSWER   *Each of the balloons floats.*

11. I don't think anybody come here now.

12. Both of the glasses broke when shipped.

13. Let me know if anything happen.

14. Others disagrees with the idea.

15. On a good team, everyone works together.

16. Most of the work end today.

17. Several has already volunteered.

18. Nothing is on the table.

19. Each of the shirts need ironing.

20. All of the students is early.

SPEAKING APPLICATION

With a partner, take turns talking about events that occur in your town or school. Your partner should listen for and name two indefinite pronouns and note whether the verbs agree.

WRITING APPLICATION

Write three sentences using at least three of the following indefinite pronouns: *some, most, all, both, others, many, each, everyone, nothing, anybody,* and *anything*. Make sure the verbs agree with the pronouns you choose.

23.2 Agreement Between Pronouns and Antecedents

An **antecedent** is the word or words for which a pronoun stands. A pronoun's antecedent may be a noun, a group of words acting as a noun, or even another pronoun. As with subjects and verbs, pronouns should agree with their antecedents.

Find It/ FIX IT

17

Grammar
Game Plan

Making Personal Pronouns and Antecedents Agree

WRITING COACH

Online

www.phwritingcoach.com

Grammar Practice

Practice your grammar skills with Writing Coach Online.

Grammar Games

Test your knowledge of grammar in this fast-paced interactive video game.

Person tells whether a pronoun refers to the person speaking (first person), the person spoken to (second person), or the person, place, or thing spoken about (third person). **Number** tells whether the pronoun is singular or plural. **Gender** tells whether a third-person-singular antecedent is masculine or feminine.

> **A personal pronoun must agree with its antecedent in person, number, and gender.**

23.2.1 | **RULE**

EXAMPLE   I told **David** to bring a bathing suit with **him**.

In this example, the pronoun *him* is third person and singular. It agrees with its masculine antecedent, *David*.

Avoiding Shifts in Person

A personal pronoun must have the same person as its antecedent. Otherwise, the meaning of the sentence is unclear.

INCORRECT   The **skydivers** know **we** must check the

parachutes before takeoff.
(Who must check the parachutes? *We* must.)

CORRECT   The **skydivers** know **they** must check the

parachutes before takeoff.
(Who must check the parachutes? *The skydivers* must.)

As you can see, a shift in the person of the personal pronoun can make it unclear who is going to check the parachutes.

Pronoun–Antecedent Agreement   529

Avoiding Problems With Number and Gender

Making pronouns and antecedents agree in number and gender can be difficult. Problems may arise when the antecedent is a collective noun, when the antecedent is a compound joined by *or* or *nor*, or when the gender of the antecedent is not known.

Making Pronouns Agree in Number With Collective Nouns
Collective nouns are challenging because they can take either singular or plural pronouns. The number of the pronoun depends on the meaning of the collective noun in the sentence.

> **Use a singular pronoun to refer to a collective noun that names a group that is acting as a single unit. Use a plural pronoun to refer to a collective noun when the members or parts of a group are acting individually.**

SINGULAR   The **class showed its** joy with a cheer.

PLURAL   The **class voted** for **their** favorite candidates.

In the first example above, the class is acting as a single unit when it shows its joy, so the singular pronoun, *its*, refers to *class*. In the second example, each member of the class is voting individually, so the plural pronoun, *their*, refers to *class*.

Making Pronouns Agree in Number With Compound Nouns

> **Use a singular personal pronoun to refer to two or more singular antecedents joined by *or* or *nor*. Use a plural pronoun with two or more singular antecedents joined by *and*.**

Two or more singular antecedents joined by *or* or *nor* must have a singular pronoun, just as they must have a singular verb.

INCORRECT   **Becca** or **Megan** will take **their** backpack.

CORRECT   **Becca** or **Megan** will take **her** backpack.

CORRECT   **Becca** and **Megan** will take **their** backpacks.

Avoiding Problems With Gender

When the gender of a third-person-singular antecedent is not known, you can make the pronoun agree with its antecedent in one of three ways:

(1) Use *he or she, him or her,* or *his or hers.*

(2) Rewrite the sentence so that the antecedent and pronoun are both plural.

(3) Rewrite the sentence to eliminate the pronoun.

Traditionally, the masculine pronouns *he* and *his* have been used to stand for both males and females. Today, using *he or she* and *him or her* is preferred. If any of these corrections seem awkward to you, rewrite the sentence.

Making Personal Pronouns and Indefinite Pronouns Agree

Indefinite pronouns are words such as *each, everybody, either,* and *one.* Pay special attention to the number of a personal pronoun when the antecedent is a singular indefinite pronoun.

> **Use a singular personal pronoun when its antecedent is a singular indefinite pronoun.**

Do not be misled by a prepositional phrase that follows an indefinite pronoun. The personal pronoun agrees with the indefinite pronoun, not with the object of the preposition.

INCORRECT   **One** of the cats has lost **their** collar.

CORRECT   **One** of the cats has lost **its** collar.

INCORRECT   **Everyone** in the two groups expressed **their** opinion.

CORRECT   **Everyone** in the two groups expressed **his or her** opinion.

See Practice 23.2A
See Practice 23.2B   CORRECT   **All** of the groups expressed **their** opinions.

PRACTICE 23.2A > **Making Pronouns and Antecedents Agree**

Read the sentences. Then, write the pronoun in parentheses that agrees with its antecedent.

EXAMPLE   Marcia went to the store, and Carmine went with (him, her).

ANSWER   *her*

1. Each player took (his or her, their) place on the field.

2. This shirt is too small, so (it, they) must be returned.

3. I told my brother to bring the binoculars with (him, them).

4. Either Ramon or Danny will present (his, their) project next.

5. The firefighters worked hard, and (he, they) soon had the fire under control.

6. Marissa needed money and asked (her, his) father for ten dollars.

7. If most of the group want to go, (it, they) should go.

8. Both the builder and the designer gave (his, their) opinions.

9. Each of the dogs buried (its, their) bone.

10. Neither Sandra nor Letitia got (her, their) homework done.

PRACTICE 23.2B > **Revising for Pronoun-Antecedent Agreement**

Read the sentences. If a sentence has an error in pronoun-antecedent agreement, rewrite the sentence correctly. Then, circle the pronoun and underline its antecedent. If a sentence has no error, write *correct*.

EXAMPLE   Each child wears a name tag they decorated.

ANSWER   *Each* <u>child</u> *wears a name tag* (he or she) *decorated.*

11. The boys must wear jackets at his school dance.

12. Juanita or Mary will get a prize for their project.

13. We asked the police officers if they could tell us how to get home.

14. Phillip and Pedro said he would help.

15. Everyone took their books home.

16. Jason and Steve will bring their baseball mitts.

17. My older sister likes their job.

18. Neither Gina nor Jessica wanted their project to be late.

19. Bella and I said we would happily share our ideas with the group.

20. Each student will read the essay they wrote.

SPEAKING APPLICATION

With a partner, take turns talking about places you or your family regularly goes to (for fun or errands). Your partner should listen for and name three pronouns and their antecedents and note if they agree.

WRITING APPLICATION

Choose three sentences from Practice 23.2B and rewrite each one so that a different pronoun is correct. You may change the number or gender of the antecedents or change conjunctions to accomplish this.

CHAPTER 24

USING MODIFIERS

Knowing how to use different forms of adjectives and adverbs to make comparisons will enrich the descriptions in your writing.

WRITE GUY *Jeff Anderson, M.Ed.*

WHAT DO YOU NOTICE?

Look for modifiers as you zoom in on these sentences from the essay "Jackie Robinson: Justice at Last" by Geoffrey C. Ward and Ken Burns.

MENTOR TEXT

> Slowly his teammates accepted him, realizing that he was the spark that made them a winning team. No one was more daring on the base paths or better with the glove.

Now, ask yourself the following questions:

- In the second sentence, why do the authors use the word *more* instead of adding another ending to the adjective *daring*?
- Why do the authors use the adjective *better* instead of *best* in the second sentence?

For most one- and two-syllable modifiers, you add *-er* or *-est* to make a comparison. However, adding either ending to *daring* sounds awkward; *more* or *most* is used to make the comparison instead. *Better* is used to make a comparison between two people, while *best* is used to compare three or more people. The authors said that no *one* player on the team was more talented with the glove than Jackie Robinson, so they used *better*. If they had compared Robinson to *all* players, they would have used *best*.

Grammar for Writers Writers can create vivid images when they use adjectives and adverbs to make comparisons. Check how many you are comparing to make sure you use the right form.

I'm the best player on the team.

Do you think of yourself as superlative, too?

24.1 Comparisons Using Adjectives and Adverbs

You may recall that adjectives and adverbs are **modifiers.** Adjectives can modify nouns or pronouns. Adverbs can modify verbs, adjectives, or other adverbs. You can use modifiers to make comparisons.

WRITING COACH

Online

www.phwritingcoach.com

Grammar Tutorials

Brush up on your Grammar skills with these animated videos.

Grammar Practice

Practice your grammar skills with Writing Coach Online.

Grammar Games

Test your knowledge of grammar in this fast-paced interactive video game.

Three Forms of Comparison

Modifiers change their form when they show comparison. These different forms are called **forms,** or **degrees, of comparison.**

RULE 24.1.1

> Most adjectives and adverbs have three forms, or degrees, of comparison: **positive, comparative,** and **superlative.**

The **positive degree** is used when no comparison is being made. This is the form of a word that is listed in a dictionary. The **comparative degree** is used when two items are being compared. The **superlative degree** is used when three or more items are being compared. When the superlative degree is used, the article *the* is often added.

DEGREE	ADJECTIVE	ADVERB
Positive	The hermit crab moved into a **large** shell.	Sue ran **fast.**
Comparative	Soon, it will need a **larger** shell.	Sue ran **faster** than Mari.
Superlative	The crab is living in the **largest** shell it has ever had.	Of the three runners, Sue ran the **fastest.**

Like verbs, adjectives and adverbs change forms in different ways. Some adjectives and adverbs change in regular ways, or according to predictable patterns. As you can see in the chart above, *large* and *fast* form their comparative and superlative degrees regularly, by adding *-er* and *-est* to their positive form.

Regular Modifiers With One or Two Syllables

Most modifiers are **regular**—their degrees of comparison are formed in predictable ways.

> Use *-er* or *more* to form the comparative degree and use *-est* or *most* to form the superlative degree of most one- and two-syllable modifiers.

COMPARATIVE AND SUPERLATIVE DEGREES FORMED WITH *-ER* AND *-EST*		
POSITIVE	COMPARATIVE	SUPERLATIVE
deep	deeper	deepest
fast	faster	fastest
friendly	friendlier	friendliest
narrow	narrower	narrowest
sunny	sunnier	sunniest

Use *more* to form a modifier's comparative degree when adding *-er* sounds awkward. Use *most* to form a modifier's superlative degree when adding *-est* sounds awkward.

COMPARATIVE AND SUPERLATIVE DEGREES FORMED WITH *MORE* AND *MOST*		
POSITIVE	COMPARATIVE	SUPERLATIVE
careful	more careful	most careful
complete	more complete	most complete
handsome	more handsome	most handsome
often	more often	most often
quietly	more quietly	most quietly

More and *most* should not be used when the result sounds awkward, however. If you are not sure which form to use, check a dictionary. Most dictionaries list modifiers formed with *-er* and *-est*.

See Practice 24.1A

Regular Modifiers With Three or More Syllables

Modifiers for words with three or more syllables follow the same rules.

RULE 24.1.3

Use *more* and *most* to form the comparative and superlative degrees of all modifiers of three or more syllables. Do not use *-er* or *-est* with modifiers of more than two syllables.

DEGREES OF MODIFIERS WITH THREE OR MORE SYLLABLES		
POSTIVE	COMPARATIVE	SUPERLATIVE
expensive	more expensive	most expensive
flexible	more flexible	most flexible

Adverbs Ending in *-ly*

To modify most adverbs ending in *-ly*, use *more* or *most*.

RULE 24.1.4

Use *more* to form the comparative degree and *most* to form the superlative degree of most adverbs ending in *-ly*.

EXAMPLES   quickly, more quickly, most quickly

gracefully, more gracefully, most gracefully

Using *Less* and *Least*

Less and *least* can show decreasing comparisons.

RULE 24.1.5

Use *less* with a modifier to form the decreasing comparative degree and *least* to form the decreasing superlative degree.

EXAMPLES   flexible, less flexible, least flexible

quickly, less quickly, least quickly

See Practice 24.1B

PRACTICE 24.1A **Forming Comparatives and Superlatives of One- and Two-Syllable Modifiers**

Read the modifiers. Write the comparative and superlative forms of each modifier.

EXAMPLE   soft

ANSWER   *softer, softest*

1. cool
2. happy
3. willing
4. long
5. slowly
6. young
7. small
8. shiny
9. alert
10. straight

PRACTICE 24.1B **Using Forms of Modifiers**

Read the sentences. Then, write each sentence, using the form of the modifier specified in parentheses.

EXAMPLE   I am the _____ of the three children. (*old*, superlative)

ANSWER   *I am the **oldest** of the three children.*

11. Callie has the _____ shoe collection. (*fabulous*, superlative)
12. An apple would be a _____ choice. (*healthy*, comparative)
13. A computer is _____ than a typewriter. (*efficient*, comparative)
14. Coach was _____ than usual. (*angry*, comparative)
15. Johnny is the _____ of their children. (*young*, superlative)
16. Claire is my _____ friend. (*funny*, superlative)
17. Are there stars _____ than our sun? (*bright*, comparative)
18. The little boy ran _____ than his brother. (*slowly*, comparative)
19. I got there _____ than you. (*soon*, comparative)
20. What is the _____ way to the park? (*quick*, superlative)

SPEAKING APPLICATION

With a partner, talk about athletes you have seen or know about. Use modifiers to compare their performances or skills. Your partner should listen for and name at least two modifiers used in the comparative or superlative form.

WRITING APPLICATION

Write three or four sentences about animals you have seen or read about. Use modifiers to compare the animals' appearance, behavior, or other characteristics. Underline modifiers that are in the comparative or superlative form.

Irregular Adjectives and Adverbs

A few adjectives and adverbs are irregular.

RULE 24.1.6 Memorize the comparative and superlative forms of adjectives and adverbs that have irregular spellings.

The chart lists the most common irregular modifiers.

DEGREES OF IRREGULAR ADJECTIVES AND ADVERBS		
POSITIVE	**COMPARATIVE**	**SUPERLATIVE**
bad (adjective)	worse	worst
badly (adverb)	worse	worst
far (distance)	farther	farthest
far (extent)	further	furthest
good (adjective)	better	best
well (adverb)	better	best
many	more	most
much	more	most

When you are unsure about how a modifier forms its degrees of comparison, check a dictionary.

See Practice 24.1C

Using Comparative and Superlative Degrees

Keep these rules in mind when you use the comparative and superlative degrees.

RULE 24.1.7 Use the comparative degree to compare *two* people, places, or things. Use the superlative degree to compare *three or more* people, places, or things.

Usually, you do not need to mention specific numbers when you are making a comparison. Other words in the sentence should help make the meaning clear whether you are comparing two items or three or more items.

EXAMPLES   The captain felt **better** once all the

crew were safely on shore.

The rescue team completed the practice session

in their **best** time this week.

Pay particular attention to the modifiers you use when you are comparing just two items. Do not use the superlative degree with fewer than three items.

INCORRECT   Of their two practice runs, that one was **best**.

CORRECT   Of their two practice runs, that one was **better**.

INCORRECT   They were the **fastest** of the two teams

competing.

CORRECT   They were the **faster** of the two teams competing.

Do not make double comparisons. Do not use both *-er* and *more* to form the comparative degree or both *-est* and *most* to form the superlative degree. Also, be sure not to use *-er, more,* and *most* with an irregular modifier.

RULE 24.1.8

INCORRECT   That student ran the **most fastest**.

CORRECT   That student ran the **fastest**.

INCORRECT   The thunderstorm was **more worse** than the one

last summer.

CORRECT   The thunderstorm was **worse** than the one last

See Practice 24.1D   summer.

PRACTICE 24.1C Forming Comparatives and Superlatives of Irregular Adjectives and Adverbs

Read the modifiers. Write the comparative and superlative forms of each modifier.

EXAMPLE   good (adjective)

ANSWER   *better, best*

1. far (distance)

2. bad (adjective)

3. many

4. badly (adverb)

5. far (extent)

6. well (adverb)

7. much

PRACTICE 24.1D Using Comparatives and Superlatives of Irregular Adjectives and Adverbs

Read the sentences. Then, write each sentence, using the form of the modifier in parentheses.

EXAMPLE   He walked _____ than anyone else. (*far*, comparative)

ANSWER   He walked *farther* than anyone else.

8. This is the _____ cold he has ever had. (*bad*, superlative)

9. He looks _____ like his father. (*much*, comparative)

10. This is the _____ work you have done so far. (*good*, superlative)

11. He played _____ before he got a new coach. (*badly*, comparative)

12. She has the _____ books. (*many*, superlative)

13. He did _____ on the test than he expected. (*well*, comparative)

14. After the dog in the story died, I could not read _____. (*far*, comparative)

15. That is the _____ price. (*good*, comparative)

16. Do you have _____ envelopes? (*many*, comparative)

17. Of the two, that is the _____. (*bad*, comparative)

SPEAKING APPLICATION

With a partner, take turns talking about a competition (cooking, music, sports, or another) that you have seen on television. Whom did you like? Who should have won? Your partner should listen for and confirm the correct use of irregular modifiers.

WRITING APPLICATION

Write three sentences describing a place in nature you have visited or seen in pictures. Use at least two modifiers in either the comparative or superlative form. One modifier should be three or more syllables, and one should be irregular.

Making Logical Comparisons

In most situations, you will have no problem forming the degrees of modifiers and using them correctly in sentences. Sometimes, however, you may find that the way you have phrased a sentence makes your comparison unclear. You will then need to think about the words you have chosen and revise your sentence, making sure that your comparison is logical.

> **When you make a comparison, be sure you are comparing things that have clear similarities.**

RULE 24.1.9

Balanced Comparisons

Most comparisons make a statement or ask a question about the way in which similar things are either alike or different.

EXAMPLE   Is **Chesapeake Bay** **deeper** than **Puget Sound**?
(Both bodies of water have depths that can be measured and compared.)

Because the sentence compares depth to depth, the comparison is balanced. Problems can occur, however, when a sentence compares dissimilar things. For example, it would be illogical to compare the depth of one bay to the shape of another bay. Depth and shape are not similar things and cannot be compared meaningfully.

ILLOGICAL   The **plants in our garden** are **prettier** than **your garden**.
(*Plants* and a *garden* cannot be logically compared.)

LOGICAL   The **plants in our garden** are **prettier** than the **plants in your garden**.
(Two sets of plants can be logically compared.)

> **Make sure that your sentences compare only similar items.**

RULE 24.1.10

An unbalanced comparison is usually the result of carelessness. The writer may have simply left something out. Read the following incorrect sentences carefully.

INCORRECT	**Building a ship** is **harder** than a **house**. The **number of shipwrecks** near the East Coast is **larger** than the **West Coast**.

In the first sentence, building a ship is mistakenly compared to a house. In the second sentence, events are compared to a place. Both sentences can easily be corrected to make the comparisons balanced.

CORRECT	**Building a ship** is **harder** than **building a house**. The **number of shipwrecks** near the East Coast is **larger** than the **number** near the West Coast.

See Practice 24.1E

Other and *Else* in Comparisons

Another common error in writing comparisons is to compare something to itself.

RULE 24.1.11

> When comparing one of a group to the rest of the group, make sure your sentence contains the word *other* or *else*.

Adding *other* or *else* can make a comparison clear. For example, in the second sentence below, because the *United States* is itself a country, it cannot logically be compared to *all countries*. It must be compared to *all other countries*.

PROBLEM SENTENCES	CORRECTED SENTENCES
A salvor is someone who returns an abandoned or sunken ship to shore before anyone.	A salvor is someone who returns an abandoned or sunken ship to shore before anyone else.
U.S. laws may allow a salvor to collect a larger reward than any country's laws do.	U.S. laws may allow a salvor to collect a larger reward than any other country's laws do.

See Practice 24.1F

PRACTICE 24.1E > Making Balanced Comparisons

Read the sentences. Rewrite each sentence, correcting the unbalanced comparison.

EXAMPLE   My dad's car is newer than your dad.

ANSWER   *My dad's car is newer than your dad's car.*

1. Our school library is bigger than their school.

2. The number of tigers in Asia is larger than zoos.

3. My brother's bicycle is faster than your brother.

4. The amount of money I owe is less than him.

5. The high school's playing field is nicer than the university.

6. There are fewer students in this classroom than that classroom.

7. Mariana's project is more complicated than Ciara.

8. The paint on this wall is drier than that wall.

9. This store's prices are lower than that store.

10. The distance this bus has traveled is longer than that bus.

PRACTICE 24.1F > Using *Other* and *Else* to Make Comparisons

Read the sentences. Rewrite each sentence, adding *other* or *else* to make the comparisons more logical.

EXAMPLE   Russia is bigger than any country.

ANSWER   *Russia is bigger than any* **other** *country.*

11. My brother is better at math than anyone.

12. I think the rose is lovelier than any flower.

13. My grandfather is older than anyone in our family.

14. The Pacific Ocean is bigger than any ocean.

15. Rafael studied harder than anyone in class.

16. Our park is cleaner than any park in the state.

17. This chair is more comfortable than anything.

18. She practiced longer than anyone on the team.

19. I was earlier than anyone.

20. My sister draws better than anyone in my family.

SPEAKING APPLICATION

With a partner, take turns talking about sports. Compare the sports or athletes, making sure that your comparisons are balanced and correct. Your partner should listen for and name any comparisons you might need to fix.

WRITING APPLICATION

Write three sentences comparing current clothing styles with images you have seen of past styles. One sentence should have a balanced comparison, and one should have either *else* or *other* to complete the comparison.

24.2 Troublesome Adjectives and Adverbs

The common adjectives and adverbs listed below often cause problems in both speaking and writing.

WRITING COACH

Online

www.phwritingcoach.com

Grammar Practice
Practice your grammar skills with Writing Coach Online.

Grammar Games
Test your knowledge of grammar in this fast-paced interactive video game.

(1) bad and badly   *Bad* is an adjective. Use it after linking verbs, such as *are, appear, feel, look,* and *sound. Badly* is an adverb. Use it after action verbs, such as *act, behave, do,* and *perform.*

INCORRECT	Jan looked **badly** after the trip.
CORRECT	Jan looked **bad** after the trip.

INCORRECT	I did **bad** on the test.
CORRECT	I did **badly** on the test.

(2) good and well   *Good* is an adjective. *Well* can be either an adjective or an adverb, depending on its meaning. A common mistake is the use of *good* after an action verb. Use the adverb *well* instead.

INCORRECT	The children behaved **good** all day.
	The apple tastes **well**.

CORRECT	The children behaved **well** all day.
	The apple tastes **good**.

As adjectives, *good* and *well* have slightly different meanings, which are often confused. *Well* usually refers simply to health.

EXAMPLES	Janet felt **good** after the hike.
	The fresh bread smells **good**.
	That puppy is not **well**.

(3) *fewer and less* Use the adjective *fewer* to answer the question, "How many?" Use the adjective *less* to answer the question, "How much?"

HOW MANY	**fewer** calories	**fewer** chores
HOW MUCH	**less** food	**less** work

(4) *just* When used as an adverb, *just* often means "no more than." When *just* has this meaning, place it right before the word it logically modifies.

INCORRECT	Do you **just** want **one baked potato**?
CORRECT	Do you want **just** **one baked potato**?

(5) *only* The position of *only* in a sentence sometimes affects the sentence's entire meaning. Consider the meaning of these sentences.

EXAMPLES

Only she answered that question.
(Nobody else answered that question.)

She **only** answered the question.
(She did nothing else with the question.)

She answered **only** that question.
(She answered that question and no other question.)

Mistakes involving *only* usually occur when its placement in a sentence makes the meaning unclear.

UNCLEAR	**Only** take advice from me.
BETTER	Take advice **only** from me. (not from anyone else)
	Take **only** advice from me. (nothing but advice)

See Practice 24.2A
See Practice 24.2B
See Practice 24.2C
See Practice 24.2D

Using *Bad* and *Badly*, *Good* and *Well*

Read the sentences. Write the word in parentheses that correctly completes each sentence.

EXAMPLE   I did (good, well) on the test.

ANSWER   *well*

1. He performed (bad, badly) during the concert.
2. We expected a (good, well) outcome.
3. I felt (bad, badly) about the competition results.
4. The projection equipment worked (good, well).
5. The garbage is beginning to smell (bad, badly).
6. The sets for the play look really (good, well).
7. Dad's car is running (bad, badly).
8. Did your brother finish (good, well) in the race?
9. Our dog (bad, badly) needs to be bathed.
10. The warm sunshine feels (good, well).

Revising for Troublesome Modifiers

Read the sentences. Rewrite the sentences that contain errors in the use of modifiers. If a sentence has no error, write *correct*.

EXAMPLE   The baking bread smells well.

ANSWER   *The baking bread smells good.*

11. The pollution is badly in this town.
12. A warm blanket feels good on a cold night.
13. These bruises still hurt bad.
14. I did good in yesterday's race.
15. Everyone felt bad about the coach leaving.
16. My brothers work good together.
17. This yellow dress looks badly on me.
18. I was sick for a while, but I'm well now.
19. The plumber did the work bad.
20. Everything the chef made was well.

SPEAKING APPLICATION

With a partner, take turns talking about a movie you enjoyed. Did the actors perform well or badly? Was the story good or bad? Your partner should listen for and confirm that you have used these troublesome modifiers correctly.

WRITING APPLICATION

Write three or four sentences about characters in a story you like. What do they do? How do they do it? Use at least three of the following: *well, good, bad,* and *badly.* Be sure to use them correctly in your sentences.

PRACTICE 24.2C > **Using *Fewer* and *Less***

Read the sentences. Rewrite the sentences using *fewer* or *less* correctly.

EXAMPLE   Toddlers have (fewer, less) chores than teenagers.

ANSWER   Toddlers have *fewer* chores than teenagers.

1. The school can purchase (fewer, less) equipment this year.

2. Shannon made (fewer, less) sandwiches than usual.

3. She served (fewer, less) food to avoid leftovers again.

4. Aiden has thrown (fewer, less) pitches this season than last season.

5. We will face (fewer, less) opponents this year.

6. Right now Sophie has (fewer, less) money in the bank.

7. Mom put (fewer, less) rice on my plate than Dan's.

8. Diego has (fewer, less) bad habits than Adam.

9. My sister's high school has (fewer, less) rules than our middle school.

10. I answered (fewer, less) questions correctly on the test than Liam.

PRACTICE 24.2D > **Using *Just* and *Only***

Read the sentences. If the placement of *just* or *only* makes sense, write *correct*. If not, rewrite the sentence with the correct placement of modifiers.

EXAMPLE   Do you only know one song, or can you play many?

ANSWER   *Do you know only one song, or can you play many?*

11. Ava just has one pencil, and it is broken.

12. Our house has only four rooms, yet it is perfect for Dad and me.

13. There will be no test today because only the teacher has three exam books.

14. Only two of us went to the movie, but we both liked it.

15. I need one word only to complete this puzzle.

16. I need to find just one more item to win the scavenger hunt.

17. One person only came to the meeting, so it was cancelled.

18. Lila only went to Alaska with a thin coat.

19. Do you just want one egg for breakfast?

20. Did you finish just one chapter?

SPEAKING APPLICATION

With a partner, talk about a time when you did not have enough of something. Use examples of *fewer, less, just,* and *only*. Write a sentence for each of the words and use it correctly. Discuss your sentences with a partner.

WRITING APPLICATION

Write a paragraph about making sandwiches without the ingredients you need. Use examples of *fewer, less, just,* and *only*. Have a partner check your understanding of the words.

Test Warm-Up

DIRECTIONS
**Read the introduction and the passage that follows. Then,
answer the questions to show that you can use and understand
the function of troublesome adjectives and adverbs in reading
and writing.**

*Paige wrote this paragraph for a column about crafts in the school
newspaper. Read the paragraph and think about the changes you would
suggest as a peer editor. When you finish reading, answer the questions
that follow.*

Be a Sculptor

(1) Papier-mâché makes a great animal sculpture. (2) Besides balloons
for the base, you only need water, flour, paint, and brushes. (3) Mix the flour
with water to make a paste that looks like glue. (4) You will need fewer
flour than water. (5) If your mixture is too thick, just add a little water.
(6) Tear newspaper into strips, and soak the strips in the paste. (7) Then,
put them over the balloon. (8) Try only to add a few layers at a time.
(9) It will dry good. (10) Once dry, paint your sculpture with whatever
colors you choose.

---

1 What change, if any, should be made in
sentence 2?

  A Move *only* to follow *paint*

  B Move *only* to come before *you*

  C Move *only* to follow *need*

  D Make no change

2 What change, if any, should be made in
sentence 4?

  F Change *fewer* to **less**

  G Change *fewer* to **only**

  H Add **just** before *fewer*

  J Make no change

3 How should sentence 5 be revised?

  A If your mixture is just too thick, just add
a little water.

  B If your mixture is too thick, add just a
little water.

  C If your mixture is too thick, add a little
water, just.

  D If your only mixture is too thick, add just
a little water.

4 What is the BEST way to combine
sentences 8 and 9?

  F Try to add only a few layers at a time so
it will dry good.

  G Only try to add a few layers at a time so
it will dry good.

  H Only try to add a few layers at a time so
it will dry well.

  J Try to add only a few layers at a time, so
it will dry well.

 **PRACTICE 1** > **Identifying Verb Tenses**

Read the sentences. For each sentence, write whether the verb is in the *present, past, future, present perfect, past perfect*, or *future perfect* tense. Also indicate if the verb is *progressive*.

1. Lureen sings in the choir.

2. The new restaurant opened on Friday.

3. Mrs. Macy has operated a crane at a construction site before.

4. The secretary of state will visit India.

5. By noon, Samantha will have been working on the project for six hours.

6. My father is stuffing the turkey for our Thanksgiving dinner.

7. Jeff Jackson had once starred in a musical version of *Old Yeller*.

8. The Lopez family will be leaving shortly on their vacation.

9. Elizabeth had been dancing for years.

10. Ten trumpeters were marching with the band.

PRACTICE 2 > **Revising to Use Active Voice**

Read the sentences. Then, rewrite each sentence in passive voice so that it is in active voice. If a sentence is already in active voice, write *active*.

1. The best music is played by that salsa band.

2. The poem was written by Emily Dickinson.

3. The Tremonts live in a large house by the lake.

4. This award is shared by all the people involved in our great film.

5. Todd is leaving for Denver tomorrow.

PRACTICE 3 > **Using Verbs Correctly**

Read the sentences. Then, rewrite the sentences to correct any incorrect verb tenses. If a sentence has no errors, write *correct*.

1. A week ago, Lawrence run his best time on the track.

2. Last Saturday the phone rung all afternoon.

3. The concert has finally begun.

4. Yesterday I accidentally lay my books at the bottom of the wrong locker.

5. I always sit a vase of flowers in the center of the table.

6. Bonnie finally done her homework.

7. At the grand opening last week, Cindy says to me, "Calm down."

8. Mrs. Menendez has spoke to me about the problem with the microphones.

9. I seen the Memorial Day parade for the first time last May.

10. All day the monkeys have swinged in the trees.

PRACTICE 4 > **Identifying Pronoun Cases and Uses**

Read the sentences. Write whether each underlined pronoun is in the *nominative, objective*, or *possessive* case. Then, write whether it is used as a *subject*, a *predicate pronoun*, a *direct object*, an *indirect object*, or the *object of a preposition*.

1. Polly talked to <u>him</u> for two hours.

2. The teacher gave <u>her</u> a high grade.

3. <u>Mine</u> is the jacket with the fake fur trim.

4. Pedro showed <u>us</u> around the computer room.

5. The winners were Robin and <u>I</u>.

Continued on next page ▶

Cumulative Review   Chapters 21–24

PRACTICE 5 **Using Pronouns Correctly**

Read the sentences. Then, rewrite the sentences to correct any incorrect pronouns. If a sentence has no errors, write *correct*.

1. Us and Roberto went to the library.
2. The shopkeeper gave Yvonne and I a discount.
3. Whom did Anthony invite to the party?
4. The cat ate it's dinner.
5. The newest counselors were Sonya and me.
6. Ali is the one who the team appointed as leader.
7. There was an agreement between Lou and she.
8. The house at the end of the street is their's.
9. The problem worries Christine and he.
10. Young people do not know whom that actor is.

PRACTICE 6 **Revising for Subject–Verb Agreement**

Read the sentences. Then, rewrite the sentences to correct any errors in subject-verb agreement. If a sentence has no errors, write *correct*.

1. A book of poems sit on the shelf.
2. Each of the members belong to other clubs too.
3. Neither Miranda nor I like radio talk shows.
4. The family sometimes argues at dinner.
5. None of the triplets are in my class.
6. Cara and Leslie enjoy scuba diving.
7. The manager or her assistants greets shoppers.
8. Do Jane or Randy come here after school?
9. The committee have named her as treasurer.
10. Macaroni and cheese are my favorite dish.

PRACTICE 7 **Revising for Pronoun–Antecedent Agreement**

Read the sentences. Then, rewrite the sentences to correct any errors in pronoun-antecedent agreement. If a sentence has no errors, write *correct*.

1. Each of the girls spent their money on magazines.
2. Several of the runners had their blisters treated.
3. Nate takes a class where you learn yoga.
4. Neither the dog nor the cat ate their food.
5. Back then, everyone had their shoes polished.
6. Belle and Natalie finished their homework.
7. Both of the horses had scars on its legs.
8. Either Jane or Ann wore lip balm on her lips.
9. None of the workers did his or her own cooking.
10. Everybody remembered his or her manners.

PRACTICE 8 **Using Modifiers Correctly**

Read the sentences. Then, rewrite the sentences to correct any errors involving modifiers. If a sentence has no errors, write *correct*.

1. Less people visit the museum on weekdays.
2. Of the three papers, hers is the most good.
3. Stuart did good in his first attempt.
4. You can walk more far in comfortable shoes.
5. Of the two villains, who is badder?
6. Pearl is the prettiest cat we have ever owned.
7. Many office workers only work on weekdays.
8. The stale crackers taste really badly.
9. Most border collies are smarter than any dogs.
10. How bad did she perform in the play?

CHAPTER 25

PUNCTUATION

Each punctuation mark plays an important role in making your writing understandable and unified.

WRITE GUY *Jeff Anderson, M.Ed.*

WHAT DO YOU NOTICE?

Keep track of commas as you zoom in on these sentences from the story "Why the Tortoise's Shell Is Not Smooth" by Chinua Achebe.

MENTOR TEXT

> When all the birds had gathered together, they set off in a body. Tortoise was very happy as he flew among the birds, and he was soon chosen as the man to speak for the party because he was a great orator.

Now, ask yourself the following questions:

- Why does the author use a comma after *together*?
- Why is a comma needed before *and* in the second sentence?

The first sentence begins with the subordinate clause *when all the birds had gathered together*. Therefore, a comma is needed after *together* to separate the subordinate clause from the main or independent clause that follows. In the second sentence, a comma is needed before the conjunction *and* because there are complete thoughts on either side of it.

Grammar for Writers Well-placed commas can help readers follow your ideas. When in doubt about whether to use a comma, read the sentence aloud. If you come to a brief pause, that might be a place where the rules call for a comma.

Stop! I forgot a comma!

Commas are for pauses, not for stops.

25.1 End Marks

End marks signal the end or conclusion of a sentence, word, or phrase. There are three end marks: the **period (.)**, the **question mark (?)**, and the **exclamation mark (!)**.

Using Periods

A **period** indicates the end of a sentence or an abbreviation.

RULE 25.1.1

Use a period to end a **declarative** sentence—a statement of fact or opinion.

DECLARATIVE SENTENCE   This is a beautiful park.

RULE 25.1.2

Use a period to end most **imperative** sentences—sentences that give directions or commands.

IMPERATIVE SENTENCE   Finish reading the chapter.

RULE 25.1.3

Use a period to end a sentence that contains an **indirect question**.

An **indirect question** restates a question in a declarative sentence. It does not give the speaker's exact words.

INDIRECT QUESTION   Mae asked me if I could stay.

RULE 25.1.4

Use a period after most **abbreviations** and **initials**.

ABBREVIATIONS   Gov. Mrs. Rd. in. Jr.

INITIALS   E. B. White   Robin F. Brancato

Note: The abbreviation for *inch, in.,* is the only measurement abbreviation that uses a period after it.

When a sentence ends with an abbreviation that uses a period, do not put a second period at the end.

EXAMPLE   Be sure to include Jack Jenkins Jr.

> **Do not use periods with acronyms, words formed with the first or first few letters of a series of words.**

EXAMPLES   USA   United States of America

                 UN   United Nations

Using Question Marks

A **question mark** follows a word, phrase, or sentence that asks a question.

> **Use a question mark after an interrogative sentence—one that asks a direct question.**

INTERROGATIVE   Do snakes hatch from eggs?
SENTENCES
                       Would you like to come over?

Sometimes a single word or brief phrase is used to ask a direct question. This type of question is punctuated as though it were a complete sentence because the words that are left out are easily understood.

> **Use a question mark after a word or phrase that asks a question.**

EXAMPLES   Many small birds build false nests. Why?

See Practice 25.1A   Let's meet for lunch. Where?

Using Exclamation Marks

Use an exclamation mark to end a word, phrase, or sentence that shows strong emotion.

EXAMPLES

Look at that huge vulture **!**

Watch out **!**

Use an exclamation mark after an imperative sentence that gives a forceful or urgent command.

IMPERATIVE SENTENCE

Don't spill the water **!**

Let's go **!**

While imperative sentences containing forceful commands often end with an exclamation mark, mild imperatives should end with a period.

MILD IMPERATIVES

Please sit down **.**

Go to the store for me tomorrow **.**

Use an exclamation mark after an interjection that expresses strong emotion.

INTERJECTIONS

Wow **!** That was a great throw.

Oh **!** Look what I found.

Exclamation marks should not be used too often. Overusing them reduces their emotional effect and makes writing less effective.

See Practice 25.1B

PRACTICE 25.1A **Using Question Marks and Periods**

Read the sentences. Rewrite each sentence, adding missing question marks and periods.

EXAMPLE   Dr Smith checked my heart rate
ANSWER   *Dr. Smith checked my heart rate.*

1. Mrs Cohen lives at 14 Maple Rd
2. Have you read anything by C S Lewis
3. Molly asked if I had 18 in of string
4. Has Mr Martinez arrived yet
5. Mrs Jones lives across the street
6. He lives at 20 Elm St
7. I need to practice before the game
8. We read about Dr Martin Luther King Jr
9. Where are they going on vacation
10. Did Mr Nguyen receive his package

PRACTICE 25.1B **Using Exclamation Marks and Periods**

Read the sentences. Rewrite each sentence, adding missing exclamation marks and periods.

EXAMPLE   Clean your room
ANSWER   *Clean your room!*

11. Please turn to page five
12. Wow That was a good catch
13. Dr Amir's house is so large
14. J R R Tolkien wrote *The Hobbit*
15. That's terrible
16. Oh I didn't know you were here
17. Watch out
18. I walked from 12 Oak St to 12 Central Rd
19. Hey I'd like some privacy, please
20. They were amazing

SPEAKING APPLICATION

With a partner, read the following sentences aloud. Use your voices to show how the different punctuation changes meaning. *Close the door. Close the door! Bring it here. Bring it here!* Discuss what the exclamation mark adds to the sentences.

WRITING APPLICATION

Write three or four sentences about working in the kitchen. Use a question mark in one, a period in another, and an exclamation mark in another.

25.2 Commas

End marks signal a full stop. **Commas** signal a brief pause.
A comma may be used to separate elements in a sentence or to
set off part of a sentence. Include a comma in your writing when
you want your reader to group information in your sentence.

Using Commas in Compound Sentences

A **compound sentence** consists of two or more main or
independent clauses that are joined by a coordinating
conjunction, such as *and, but, for, nor, or, so,* or *yet.*

RULE 25.2.1

> Use a comma before the conjunction to separate two main or
> independent clauses in a **compound sentence.**

COMPOUND
SENTENCE

Chimpanzees are full grown at age five**,**
but their mothers still take care of them.

Use a comma before a conjunction only when there are complete
sentences on both sides of the conjunction. If the conjunction
joins single words, phrases, or subordinate clauses, do not use a
comma.

SINGLE WORDS

Heat and sand are common desert features.

PHRASES

Teri likes both green apples and red apples.

SUBORDINATE
CLAUSES

They have decided that you should study more
and that they will check on you.

See Practice 25.2A
See Practice 25.2B

In some compound sentences, the main or independent clauses
are very brief, and the meaning is clear. When this occurs, the
comma before the conjunction may be omitted.

EXAMPLE

Jon listened carefully but he heard nothing.

Avoiding Comma Splices

A **comma splice** occurs when two or more sentences have been
joined with only a comma between them.

25.2.2 RULE

> Avoid **comma splices** by making sure all of your ideas are properly linked.

INCORRECT   The snow clumped on the trees, many branches snapped under its weight.

CORRECT   The snow clumped on the trees. Many branches snapped under its weight.

Using Commas in a Series

Sometimes, a sentence lists a number of single words or groups of words. When three or more of these items are listed, the list is called a **series.** Separate the items in a series with commas.

25.2.3 RULE

> Use commas to separate three or more words, phrases, or clauses in a **series.**

A comma follows each of the items except the last one in a series. The conjunction *and* or *or* is added after the last comma.

SERIES OF WORDS   The desert animals included camels, toads, gerbils, and insects.

SERIES OF PHRASES   The treasure map directed them over the dunes, into the oasis, and past the palm tree.

There are two exceptions to this rule. If each item except the last one in a series is followed by a conjunction, do not use commas. Also, do not use a comma to separate groups of words that are considered to be one item.

EXAMPLES   I visited castles and museums and forts.

Every table in the diner was set with a knife and fork, a cup and saucer, and salt and pepper.

See Practice 25.2C

Using Commas Between Adjectives

Sometimes, two or more adjectives are placed before the noun they describe.

RULE 25.2.4

> **Use commas to separate adjectives of equal rank.**

There are two ways to tell whether adjectives in a sentence are of equal rank:

- If the word *and* can be placed between the adjectives without changing the meaning, the adjectives are of equal rank.

- If the order of the adjectives can be changed, they are of equal rank.

EXAMPLE A smooth, round stone was cupped in her hand.
(*A smooth and round stone* does not change the sentence's meaning. *A round, smooth stone* also does not change the meaning.)

RULE 25.2.5

> **Do not use commas to separate adjectives that must appear in a specific order.**

Do not use a comma if adding *and* or changing the order of the adjectives would result in a sentence that makes no sense.

INCORRECT It will take three and brief hours to reach the park.

INCORRECT It will take brief three hours to reach the park.

CORRECT It will take three brief hours to reach the park.

RULE 25.2.6

> **Do not use a comma to separate the last adjective in a series from the noun it modifies.**

INCORRECT A large, gentle, camel stood by the road.

CORRECT A large, gentle camel stood by the road.

See Practice 25.2D

PRACTICE 25.2A Using Commas in Compound Sentences

Read the sentences. Rewrite each compound sentence, adding commas where they are needed.

EXAMPLE Julie will meet us at the field and she will bring the soccer ball.

ANSWER *Julie will meet us at the field, and she will bring the soccer ball.*

1. I don't know how to skate but I can learn.

2. Angela wants to go to the store but she has to stay home.

3. Mom and Dad fixed dinner and my sister and I washed the dishes.

4. We will have to get up at dawn for we must start early.

5. Joseph won't be here Monday nor will he be here Tuesday.

6. Tony and Chen went to a movie but Michelle went to a concert.

7. You could paint the fence now or you could wait until later.

8. I wanted to go yet something held me back.

9. I have to do my work so I'll see you later.

10. We need to fix this bike or I won't be in the race.

PRACTICE 25.2B Writing Compound Sentences Using Commas

Read the sentences. Combine the two simple sentences to create a compound sentence. Use a comma and the coordinating conjunction in parentheses.

EXAMPLE The dogs are playing in the yard. The cat is asleep near the fire. (and)

ANSWER *The dogs are playing in the yard, and the cat is asleep near the fire.*

11. Zoey wanted to have pizza. Gabrielle wanted ravioli. (but)

12. Exercise is an important factor in good health. Nutrition is also important. (and)

13. Sean is quarterback on the team. His brother is the punter. (and)

14. Mrs. Spencer won't eat meat. She is a vegetarian. (for)

15. It may have been a great car once. Now it is rusty and old. (but)

16. I registered for the art class. Charlotte registered, too. (so)

17. The speaker was nervous. Maybe he was afraid. (or)

18. The mail came. I got the letter. (so)

19. Kyle skipped pracrice. He forgot to go. (or)

20. Kevin wanted to buy a computer. Something changed his mind. (yet)

SPEAKING APPLICATION

With a partner, use the compound sentences on this page as models to write three compound sentences of your own. Then, read your sentences aloud. Discuss how natural pauses in speaking help you remember where to place commas in compound sentences.

WRITING APPLICATION

Write three compound sentences about your favorite meal. Be sure to use commas correctly. Then, trade papers with a partner and correct any errors in the use of commas.

PRACTICE 25.2C **Using Commas in a Series**

Read the sentences. Rewrite each sentence, adding commas as needed.

EXAMPLE   She looked under the desk behind the dresser and in the closet.

ANSWER   *She looked under the desk, behind the dresser, and in the closet.*

1. I had a sandwich milk and an apple for lunch.

2. Florence Rome and Venice are cities in Italy.

3. At the museum I like the mummies dinosaurs fossils and old jewelry.

4. I wrote the letter folded it and mailed it.

5. Mom could not decide whether she wanted pears peaches or grapes.

6. Justin prepared the soil planted the seeds and watered the garden.

7. The menu offered macaroni and cheese salad and spaghetti with meatballs.

8. Our dog ran across the lawn through the gate and into the street.

9. My sister used flowers grasses and ferns in the arrangement.

10. This year I'm taking math Spanish English science and history.

PRACTICE 25.2D **Using Commas Between Adjectives**

Read the sentences. Rewrite the sentences, adding commas where necessary. If no comma is needed, write *correct*.

EXAMPLE   That large heavy book is an atlas

ANSWER   *That large, heavy book is an atlas.*

11. Rows of healthy tall sunflowers filled the field.

12. The little Boston terrier ran up to the fence.

13. Australia's wild rugged scenery is fascinating.

14. I need a small gift box.

15. This wet rich land is good for growing rice.

16. The new music teacher seems very young.

17. Arizona's hot dry climate appeals to many people.

18. The sunset offered bright beautiful colors.

19. There are just four short blocks until we reach home.

20. The deep cold lake looked refreshing.

SPEAKING APPLICATION

With a partner, pick two sentences from Practice 25.2D that needed to be fixed and two that were correct. Read the sentences aloud, reversing the order of the adjectives. Talk about how you can tell when a group of adjectives doesn't need commas.

WRITING APPLICATION

Write a brief description of someplace you have visited. Include at least two different instances in which commas are needed, such as in a compound sentence and between adjectives.

Using Commas After Introductory Words, Phrases, and Clauses

When a sentence begins with an introductory word, phrase, or other structures, that word or phrase is usually separated from the rest of the sentence by a comma.

> Use a comma after most introductory words, phrases, or dependent clauses.

25.2.7

RULE

KINDS OF INTRODUCTORY MATERIAL	
Introductory Word	Hey, give me your camera quickly before the kangaroo moves.
	Pete, please bring me my shoes and socks.
	Well, I certainly didn't expect that to happen.
	Tomi, where are you?
Introductory Phrase	To conserve water, some plants drop their leaves.
	With Mark gone, Jake didn't know how he would get home.
	In the center of the city, you will see many skyscrapers.
	To visit Japan, you need a passport.
Introductory Adverbial Clause	Although the alarm had gone off, the police arrived too late.
	When the mice got into the garage, they ate the birdseed.
	When the home team entered the stadium, the crowd loudly cheered every player.

When a prepositional phrase of only two words begins a sentence, a comma is not absolutely necessary.

EXAMPLES At night we heard the crickets.

In July we go to the lake.

For hours she patiently waited for the plane.

See Practice 25.2E

Using Commas With Parenthetical Expressions

A **parenthetical expression** is a word or phrase that is not essential to the meaning of the sentence. These words or phrases generally add extra information to the basic sentence.

RULE 25.2.8

> Use commas to set off **parenthetical expressions** from the rest of the sentence.

A parenthetical expression in the middle of a sentence needs two commas. A parenthetical expression at the end of a sentence needs only one.

KINDS OF PARENTHETICAL EXPRESSIONS	
Names of People Being Addressed	Listen carefully , Lucinda , while I explain. Don't be late , Randy.
Certain Adverbs	The sand dune , therefore , is several meters higher. Your answer is incorrect , however.
Common Expressions	They believe in her ability , of course. She was not given enough credit , in my opinion.
Contrasting Expressions	The decision should be mine , not yours. These flowers , not those , are ready to be picked.

See Practice 25.2F

See Practice 25.2G

Using Commas With Nonessential Expressions

To determine when a phrase or clause should be set off with commas, decide whether the phrase or clause is **essential** or **nonessential** to the meaning of the sentence. Nonessential expressions can be left out without changing the meaning of the sentence.

> Use commas to set off **nonessential** expressions from the main clause. Do not set off **essential** material with commas.

Appositives and Appositive Phrases

Appositives are often set off with commas, but only when their meaning is not essential to the sentence. In the first example below, the appositive *Sahara* is not set off with commas because it clarifies which movie is being discussed.

Find It/ FIX IT

7

Grammar
Game Plan

ESSENTIAL	The 1943 movie *Sahara* takes place in North Africa.
NONESSENTIAL	*Sahara*, a 1943 movie, takes place in North Africa.

Participial Phrases

Like appositives, participial phrases are set off with commas when their meaning is nonessential. In the first example below, *waiting in the van* is essential because it tells which man is the guide.

Find It/ FIX IT

11

Grammar
Game Plan

ESSENTIAL	The man waiting in the van is our guide.
NONESSENTIAL	Pat, waiting in the van, asked us to hurry.

Adjectival Clauses

Adjectival clauses, too, are set off with commas only if they are nonessential. In the second example below, *who could lead us to the playing field* is nonessential because it adds information about Darius. The main clause in the sentence is about people cheering, not about what Darius can do.

ESSENTIAL	We need someone who can lead us to the playing field.
NONESSENTIAL	We cheered enthusiastically for Darius, who could lead us to the playing field.

See Practice 25.2H

Using Commas After Introductory Words, Phrases, or Clauses

Read the sentences. Rewrite each sentence, adding the comma needed after the introductory word, phrase, or clause.

EXAMPLE   If you are done with the book put it back.

ANSWER   *If you are done with the book, put it back.*

1. No I do not think we have any left.

2. After you finish eating you may go outside.

3. Jerome are you going to the library?

4. With just two days left we had to work faster on our project.

5. My that was a big yawn.

6. Whether or not he is here we are leaving.

7. Well I'm not sure that's why he's going.

8. In the sequel to the movie there were even more special effects.

9. Sherry tell us about your voice lessons.

10. Even though we were late we still got in.

Proofreading a Passage for Commas

Read the paragraph. Rewrite the paragraph, adding commas where they are needed.

EXAMPLE   To earn some money during the summer I decided to make and sell necklaces. Well sometimes events surprise you.

ANSWER   *To earn some money during the summer, I decided to make and sell necklaces. Well, sometimes events surprise you.*

When I first started this project I thought it would last one summer. I wanted to buy beads make necklaces and sell them at craft fairs. Well it was a lot of work. I bought hundreds of beads and I began stringing them. The beads were red blue gold silver and green. Some were metal but others were glass or stone. Although I liked all the different kinds of beads the blue glass beads were among my favorites. I made forty necklaces that first summer but I could have sold more. Once I started I could not stop. It has now been three years and I am still making and selling necklaces.

SPEAKING APPLICATION

With a partner, read this sentence aloud: *In the new book I found a story about spiders.* Discuss where the comma should go and why a comma would help someone reading the sentence.

WRITING APPLICATION

Write three sentences about activities you do in school or at home. Start each sentence with an introductory word, phrase, or clause that requires a comma.

PRACTICE 25.2G **Using Commas With Parenthetical Expressions**

Read the sentences. Rewrite each sentence, adding commas as needed to set off parenthetical expressions.

EXAMPLE   That play will be I think a success.

ANSWER   *That play will be, I think, a success.*

1. Do you think Tyler that you would like to go?
2. The information however is out of date.
3. I wanted red not purple.
4. When you arrive Manny let me know.
5. She thinks she is right of course.
6. That is a blue jay not a robin.
7. The outcome therefore can be predicted.
8. Well Anita what do you think?
9. I wanted fruit not yogurt.
10. You will need to clean up the mess however.

PRACTICE 25.2H **Using Commas With Nonessential Expressions**

Read the sentences. Rewrite the sentences, adding commas where necessary. If a sentence is punctuated correctly, write *correct*.

EXAMPLE   My brother staring at his feet mumbled an apology.

ANSWER   *My brother, staring at his feet, mumbled an apology.*

11. George Washington our first president took his oath of office on April 30, 1789.
12. The wallaby and the kangaroo carry their young in pouches.
13. Our guide standing on the hilltop waved to us to follow.
14. The phone a wonderful invention really changed communication.
15. The 1893 World's Fair was held in Chicago.
16. The Komodo dragon the world's largest lizard is found in Indonesia.
17. The man handing out papers is our teacher.
18. That table a real antique was made by my great-grandfather.
19. My sister standing on tiptoe could just reach the bottom shelf.
20. Seeing a dentist regularly is important.

SPEAKING APPLICATION

With a partner, act as if you are trying out for a play and the sentences in Practice 25.2G are your lines. Take turns reading the lines aloud. Talk about how hard it would be to read a script with no punctuation.

WRITING APPLICATION

Rewrite three of the correct sentences in Practice 25.2H so that they need commas. You may rearrange words or add words of your own so that the sentences now require commas.

Practice   565

Using Commas With Dates and Geographical Names

Dates usually have several parts, including months, days, and years. Commas prevent dates from being unclear.

RULE 25.2.10 When a date is made up of three parts, use a comma after each item, except in the case of a month followed by a day.

Notice in the examples that commas are not used to set off a month followed by a numeral standing for a day. Commas are used when both the month and the date are used as an appositive to rename a day of the week.

EXAMPLES   On July 12, 1979, Aunt Mei arrived in this country with just a few possessions.

Tuesday, March 18, was carefully circled on his calendar.

When a date contains only a month and a year, commas are unnecessary.

EXAMPLES   I will graduate in June 2010.

Most of the storms we experienced in March 2011 dropped a lot of snow.

RULE 25.2.11 When a geographical name is made up of a city and a state, use a comma after each item.

EXAMPLES   They lived in Marietta, Georgia, for several years and then moved to Sarasota, Florida.

Mari went to Santa Fe, New Mexico, to visit the many art galleries in the area.

See Practice 25.2I

Using Commas in Numbers

Numbers of one hundred or less and numbers made up of two words (for example, *three thousand*) are generally spelled out in words. Other large numbers (for example, 8,463) are written in numerals. Commas make large numbers easier to read.

> **With large numbers of more than three digits, count from the right and add a comma to the left of every third digit to separate it from every fourth digit.**

RULE 25.2.12

EXAMPLES

2,532 bricks

749,000 birds

a population of 1,806,421

> **Use commas with three or more numbers written in a series.**

RULE 25.2.13

EXAMPLES

Read pages 123, 124, and 125 carefully.

The groups originally had 101, 103, and 107 members.

> **Do not use a comma with ZIP Codes, telephone numbers, page numbers, years, serial numbers, or house numbers.**

RULE 25.2.14

ZIP CODE	14878
TELEPHONE NUMBER	(607) 555-1328
PAGE NUMBER	on page 1817
YEAR	the year 2010
SERIAL NUMBER	402 36 4113
HOUSE NUMBER	1801 Houston Street

See Practice 25.2J

PRACTICE 25.2I — Using Commas in Dates and Geographical Names

Read the sentences. Rewrite each sentence, adding commas where they are needed.

EXAMPLE	On June 21 1788 the United States Constitution went into effect.
ANSWER	*On June 21, 1788, the United States Constitution went into effect.*

1. Friday March 12 is the date of our meeting.

2. St. Augustine Florida is the oldest city in the United States.

3. Mr. and Mrs. Sanchez were married on November 12 1988.

4. We visited Philadelphia Pennsylvania.

5. On July 20 1969 American astronauts first set foot on the moon.

6. We met on Tuesday November 5 in Boston Massachusetts.

7. The Wright brothers made their historic flight on December 17 1903.

8. Austin Texas was named for Stephen Austin.

9. On Wednesday February 24 we will be moving to Denver Colorado.

10. It is almost two thousand miles from Atlanta Georgia to Los Angeles California.

PRACTICE 25.2J — Using Commas in Numbers

Read the items. Rewrite each item, adding commas where needed. If no commas are needed, write *correct*.

EXAMPLE	1874 miles
ANSWER	*1,874 miles*

11. 2142 hours

12. a population of 4709875

13. 1629 West Street

14. 1945580 seconds

15. ZIP Code 07960

16. 295943 minutes

17. 24321 days

18. page 1024

19. 397000 trees

20. the year 1993

WRITING APPLICATION

Write three sentences with dates and place names. You may use places or dates that have meaning for you or any dates or places. Be sure to use commas correctly.

WRITING APPLICATION

Write one sentence that contains a number that requires a comma. Then, write one sentence with a number that does not require a comma.

Using Commas With Addresses and in Letters

Commas are also used in addresses, salutations of friendly letters, and closings of friendly or business letters.

> **Use a comma after each item in an address made up of two or more parts.**

In the following example, commas are placed after the name, street, and city. There is no comma between the state and the ZIP Code.

EXAMPLE   She is writing to Helen Till, 1402 Cray Street, Carey, Ohio 43316.

Fewer commas are needed when an address is written in a letter or on an envelope.

EXAMPLE   Maxwell Hunnicutt
54 Monmouth Avenue
Dallas, Texas 75243

> **Use a comma after the salutation in a personal letter and after the closing in all letters.**

See Practice 25.2K
See Practice 25.2L

SALUTATION   Dear Shawn,   CLOSING   Sincerely,

Using Commas With Direct Quotations

Commas are also used to separate **direct quotations** from other phrases in a sentence.

> **Use commas to set off a direct quotation from the rest of a sentence.**

EXAMPLES   Bret said, "Hold the door open."

"I can't," Lorna replied, "because my arms are full."

PRACTICE 25.2K > Using Commas in Addresses and Letters

Read the items. Rewrite each item, adding commas where needed. If no commas are needed, write *correct*.

EXAMPLE   Dear Grandmother

ANSWER   *Dear Grandmother,*

1. 52 Hampton Road

2. With love

3. Dear Janice

4. Santa Barbara, California 93103

5. Yours truly

6. He is writing to Ellen Green 1219 Main Street Wheeling Illinois 60090.

7. Dearest Daddy

8. Sincerely

9. 846 Howland Drive

10. James Paige
    479 Ashton Court
    Richmond VA 23173

PRACTICE 25.2L > Revising a Letter by Adding Commas

Read the letter. Rewrite the letter, adding commas where necessary.

EXAMPLE   I like to use pencils pens and markers when I draw.

ANSWER   *I like to use pencils, pens, and markers when I draw.*

Mr. Xavier Martinez Jr.
48 Felton Way
Houston Texas 77020

October 16 2010

Dear Mr. Martinez

Thank you for the pens markers ribbons and glue. They were exactly what I needed and now I can start my project. Mr. Smith my art teacher loves my ideas for the project. Thanks to you I shall be able to do it right.

Your friend

Carlos

SPEAKING APPLICATION

With a partner, talk about the people to whom you might write a personal letter. Look at the examples in Practice 25.2K, and come up with some salutations of your own—ones that would be followed by a comma.

WRITING APPLICATION

Write a sentence that includes your full address, using proper punctuation. Then, write your address as if you were addressing an envelope.

25.3 Semicolons and Colons

The **semicolon (;)** joins related **independent clauses** and signals a longer pause than a comma. The **colon (:)** is used to introduce lists of items and in other special situations.

WRITING COACH

Online

www.phwritingcoach.com

Grammar Tutorials

Brush up on your Grammar skills with these animated videos.

Grammar Practice

Practice your grammar skills with Writing Coach Online.

Grammar Games

Test your knowledge of grammar in this fast-paced interactive video game.

Using Semicolons to Join Independent Clauses

Sometimes two **independent clauses** are so closely connected in meaning that they make up a single sentence, rather than two separate sentences.

> Use a **semicolon** to join related **independent clauses** that are not joined by the conjunctions *and, or, nor, for, but, so,* or *yet.*

25.3.1 RULE

INDEPENDENT CLAUSES	The fire began with a tossed match.
	Jamestown was burned in 1676.
CLAUSES JOINED BY SEMICOLONS	The fire began with a tossed match**;** all of Jamestown began to burn.

A semicolon should be used only when there is a close relationship between the two independent clauses. If the clauses are not very closely related, they should be written as separate sentences with a period or another end mark to separate them or joined with a coordinating conjunction.

Note that when a sentence contains three or more related independent clauses, they may still be separated with semicolons.

| EXAMPLES | The birds vanished**;** the sky grew dark**;** the little pond was still. |
| | Marie won the backstroke events**;** Tamara won the freestyle events**;** Jana won the butterfly. |

Using Semicolons to Join Clauses Separated by Conjunctive
Adverbs or Transitional Expressions

Semicolons help writers show how their ideas connect.

> **Use a semicolon to join independent clauses separated by
> either a conjunctive adverb or a transitional expression.**

CONJUNCTIVE ADVERBS	*also, besides, consequently, first, furthermore, however, indeed, instead, moreover, nevertheless, otherwise, second, then, therefore, thus*
TRANSITIONAL EXPRESSIONS	*as a result, at this time, for instance, in fact, on the other hand, that is*

EXAMPLE

We were impressed with Martin's knowledge of history ; **indeed** , he was very well informed about colonization.

Remember to place a comma after the conjunctive adverb or
transitional expression. The comma sets off the conjunctive
adverb or transitional expression, which acts as an introductory
expression to the second clause.

Using Semicolons to Avoid Confusion

Sometimes, to avoid confusion, semicolons are used to separate
items in a series.

> **Consider the use of semicolons to avoid confusion when items
> in a series already contain commas.**

Place a semicolon after all but the last complete item in a series.

EXAMPLES

The fans , cheering ; the band , playing loudly ; and
the cheerleaders , yelling , helped inspire the team to
play well.

Three important dates in this year are April 30 , 2011 ;
May 10 , 2011 ; and June 7 , 2011.

See Practice 25.3A

Using Colons

The **colon (:)** is used to introduce lists of items and in certain special situations.

Use a colon after an independent clause to introduce a list of items.

RULE 25.3.4

The independent clause that comes before the colon often includes the words *the following, as follows, these,* or *those.*

EXAMPLE   Some orchids grow only in the following countries: Costa Rica, Peru, and Brazil.

Remember to use commas to separate three or more items in a series.

In most cases, do not use a colon after a verb, and never use a colon after a preposition.

RULE 25.3.5

INCORRECT   Veronica always orders: soup, salad, and dessert.

CORRECT   Veronica always orders soup, salad, and dessert.

Use a colon to introduce a long or formal quotation.

RULE 25.3.6

EXAMPLE   The sign clearly states the law: "Dogs within the park boundaries must be leashed at all times."

SOME ADDITIONAL USES OF THE COLON	
To Separate Hours and Minutes	3:15 P.M. 9:45 A.M.
After the Salutation in a Business Letter	Gentlemen: Dear Miss Robinson:
On Warnings and Labels	Warning: The ice is thin. Note: Shake before using. Caution: Children Playing

See Practice 25.3B

PRACTICE 25.3A **Using Semicolons**

Read the sentences. Rewrite each sentence, adding any necessary semicolons.

EXAMPLE   We won the game everyone celebrated the victory.

ANSWER   *We won the game; everyone celebrated the victory.*

1. I watched television last night consequently, I did not do very well on today's test.

2. My dad is a great cook I really like his food.

3. I was really tired the bed was soft I fell asleep quickly.

4. We were sorry to lose the tree on the other hand, the garden gets more sun.

5. The book was good I liked the characters the plot was exciting.

6. There were total lunar eclipses on March 3, 2007 September 11, 2007 and February 21, 2008.

7. Dad wants to watch a movie Mom wants to watch a travel program.

8. We have one dog, a mutt one cat, a stray and two birds, a canary and a parakeet.

9. There is really nothing on television besides, I need to do some work on my project.

10. The swimming race started the swimmers dove into the pool.

PRACTICE 25.3B **Using Colons**

Read the items. Rewrite each item, adding any necessary colons. If no colon is needed, write *correct.*

EXAMPLE   I need the following for school, pencils, notebooks, paper, and a ruler.

ANSWER   *I need the following for school: pencils, notebooks, paper, and a ruler.*

11. Can you bring me some bread, peanut butter, and milk?

12. Here's what goes in the fruit basket, peaches, apples, and grapes.

13. I wrote a note to Grandmother, thanking her for my birthday present.

14. The judge made the rules clear "You must not discuss this case with anyone."

15. We ordered soup, salad, chicken, and potatoes.

16. Warning Keep away from heat.

17. Mom and Dad want to get started by 900 A.M.

18. I want a bike; my brother wants a scooter.

19. Dear Sir

20. Put these on the shopping list, milk, carrots, lettuce, bread.

WRITING APPLICATION

Write three sentences about a big event you saw or heard about. Use semicolons in at least two different ways in your description of the event.

WRITING APPLICATION

Write two sentences that require colons. One sentence should include a list, and one should include a time of day.

25.4 Quotation Marks, Underlining, and Italics

Quotation marks (" ") set off direct quotations, dialogue, and certain types of titles. Other types of titles may be **underlined** or set in *italics,* a slanted type style.

Find It/ FIX IT

6

Grammar
Game Plan

Using Quotation Marks With Quotations

Quotation marks identify the spoken or written words of others. A **direct quotation** represents a person's exact speech or thoughts. An **indirect quotation** reports the general meaning of what a person said or thought.

Both types of quotations are acceptable when you write. Direct quotations, however, generally result in a livelier writing style.

Direct quotations should be enclosed in quotation marks.

25.4.1 RULE

EXAMPLES   Kate said, "Williamsburg had the first theater."

"Where is the key?" asked Caroline.

Indirect quotations do not require quotation marks.

25.4.2 RULE

EXAMPLES   Margo said that she would take the dog out.

Don wondered why the president hadn't called him with the results of the election.

Using Direct Quotations With Introductory, Concluding, and Interrupting Expressions

Commas help you set off introductory information so that your reader understands who is speaking. Writers usually identify a speaker by using words such as *he asked* or *she said* with a quotation. These expressions can introduce, conclude, or interrupt a quotation.

Find It/ FIX IT

18

Grammar
Game Plan

Direct Quotations With Introductory Expressions

Commas are also used to indicate where **introductory expressions** end.

When an **introductory expression** precedes a direct quotation, place a comma after the introductory expression, and write the quotation as a full sentence. Be sure to leave a space between the comma and the quotation mark.

EXAMPLES The guide explained, "All historical buildings should be treated with respect."

The coach warned, "If you don't show up for every practice, you won't play in the game."

If an introductory expression is very long, set it off with a colon instead of a comma.

EXAMPLE At the end of the practice, Sarah spoke of her dreams: "I hope to be able to run the final leg in the relay by my senior year."

Direct Quotations With Concluding Expressions

Direct quotations may sometimes end with **concluding expressions.**

When a **concluding expression** follows a direct quotation, write the quotation as a full sentence ending with a comma, question mark, or exclamation mark inside the quotation mark. Then, write the concluding expression. Be sure to use end punctuation to close the sentence.

Concluding expressions are not complete sentences; therefore, they do not begin with capital letters. Notice also that the closing quotation marks are always placed outside the punctuation at the end of direct quotations followed by a concluding expression.

EXAMPLE "Could you show us one of the houses?" interrupted Barney.

Direct Quotations With Interrupting Expressions

You may use an interrupting expression in a direct quotation, which is also called a **divided quotation.** Interrupting expressions help writers clarify who is speaking and can also break up a long quotation.

> When the direct quotation of one sentence is interrupted, end the first part of the direct quotation with a comma and a quotation mark. Place a comma after the **interrupting expression,** and then use a new set of quotation marks to enclose the rest of the quotation. Be sure to leave a space after the final quotation mark.

EXAMPLES "What would we have done," asked Corrina, "if we had lived in the path of the tornado?"

"If you get a new bicycle," my mother warned, "you'll have to remember to lock it up."

Do not capitalize the first word of the second part of the sentence.

> When two sentences in a direct quotation are separated by an **interrupting expression,** end the first quoted sentence with a comma, question mark, or exclamation mark and a quotation mark. Place a period after the interrupter, and then write the second quoted sentence as a full quotation.

See Practice 25.4A
See Practice 25.4B

EXAMPLES "Did you see those rooms?" asked Mark. "Can you imagine having such a large house?"

"I know I had my keys when I left," Jane said. "They are probably in my pocket."

PRACTICE 25.4A ▷ Using Quotation Marks With Direct Quotations

Read the sentences. If the sentence contains a direct quotation, write *D*. If it contains an indirect quotation, write *I*. Then, rewrite each sentence that contains a direct quotation, adding the quotation marks where needed.

EXAMPLE   Marlene said, I do not know anything about fishing.

ANSWER   *D — Marlene said, "I do not know anything about fishing."*

1. Jason asked me if I knew the answer.

2. We went to the movies last night, Brianna said.

3. Rafael told us he knew a shortcut.

4. We heard from Mr. Smith that there would be no more watermelon at the fruit stand.

5. Just wait, Gail said, and I will get it for you.

6. I need help with math, my brother said.

7. Justine shared with everyone her hope that she would get a new bike.

8. Mrs. Johnson yelled, Look out for that car!

9. There is room for one more, Mr. Chen said.

10. I was told that the Taylor twins were going to compete in the race.

PRACTICE 25.4B ▷ Punctuating With Expressions

Read the sentences. Rewrite each sentence adding commas and quotation marks where needed. Be sure to use correct spacing for quotations.

EXAMPLE   We will have a visit from a firefighter the teacher announced.

ANSWER   *"We will have a visit from a firefighter," the teacher announced.*

11. Coach said We will get in an extra practice this week.

12. A tadpole grows into a frog Miss Jenner explained.

13. When will my car be ready? Dad asked.

14. Hold still Mom said or your haircut will not be right.

15. The old fisherman said There are no trout in these waters now.

16. I prefer country music said Melanie.

17. The principal announced There will be a fire drill today.

18. Let me go with you my brother begged.

19. Why Anna asked would you not tell me about the party?

20. Dad shouted Turn that music down.

SPEAKING APPLICATION

With a partner, read aloud two or three of the direct quotations in Practice 25.4A and 25.4B. Only read the part that should be within quotations. Talk about why using quotation marks, proper punctuation, and spacing makes sense.

WRITING APPLICATION

Write a four-sentence conversation between two friends who are planning to go to lunch together. Vary the location of the expressions within the sentences. Make sure to use proper punctuation and spacing for quotations.

Find It/FIX IT

6

Grammar Game Plan

Using Quotation Marks With Other Punctuation Marks

You have seen that a comma or period used with a direct quotation goes inside the final quotation mark. In some cases, however, end marks should be placed outside of quotation marks.

> **Always place a comma or a period inside the final quotation mark. Leave a space after the final quotation mark.**

25.4.7 **RULE**

EXAMPLES "This area needs work , " Mrs. Finch said .

She added , "It looks like you're living in a junkyard, not a room . "

> **Place a question mark or an exclamation mark inside the final quotation mark if the end mark is part of the quotation. Do not use an additional end mark outside the quotation marks.**

25.4.8 **RULE**

EXAMPLES Joe asked , "Didn't I already clean that room ? "

Salvatore , his brother , protested loudly , "I helped rebuild three buildings last summer ! "

> **Place a question mark or exclamation mark outside the final quotation mark if the end mark is part of the entire sentence, not part of the quotation.**

25.4.9 **RULE**

EXAMPLES Did he say , "You have wasted your entire day " ?

See Practice 25.4C

I can't believe he said , "I like taking tests " !

Using Single Quotation Marks for Quotations Within Quotations

Double quotation marks are used to enclose the main quotation. The rules for using commas and end marks with **single quotation marks (' ')** are the same as they are with double quotation marks.

Single quotation marks are used to separate a quote that appears inside of another quotation.

> Use **single quotation marks** to set off a quotation within a quotation.

EXAMPLES "Did you mean to say, 'That's my cat,' or 'That's my hat'?" Lori asked.

Steve said, "I thought I heard him yell, 'Fire!' That's why I ran out the door."

Punctuating Explanatory Material Within Quotes

Sometimes it is necessary to add information to a quotation that explains the quote more fully. In that case, brackets tell your reader which information came from the original speaker and which came from someone else. (See Section 25.7 for more information on brackets.)

> Use brackets to enclose an explanation located within a quotation to show that the explanation is not part of the original quotation.

EXAMPLE The mayor said, "This bridge is more than a link between two communities [Oceanville and Riverton]."

"We [the students of Center High School] wish to express our support of the student council." See Practice 25.4D

PRACTICE 25.4C > Using Quotation Marks With Other Punctuation Marks

Read the sentences. Decide whether the missing punctuation goes inside or outside the quotation marks. Then, rewrite the sentences, using the proper punctuation and spacing for quotations.

EXAMPLE   "When will he arrive" she asked.

ANSWER   *"When will he arrive?" she asked.*

1. "Come right home afterwards" Dad instructed.

2. Our teacher asked, "Who knows where the equator is"

3. Didn't Mom say, "No television tonight"

4. I heard Lacie scream, "Look out"

5. "Do you like this bowl" the potter asked.

6. I can't believe you said, "No"

7. "Bread is easy to make" Wally stated.

8. Coach said, "We have a good chance of getting to the finals"

9. What did you mean by, "It's all over now"

10. "Ouch" cried Jill. "Did you have to pull the bandage off so fast"

PRACTICE 25.4D > Punctuating Quotations Within Quotations and Explanatory Material

Read the sentences. Rewrite each sentence, using single quotation marks or brackets where needed. Be sure to use the proper punctuation and spacing.

EXAMPLE   Marcia asked, "Do you remember when he said, I'll take care of it?"

ANSWER   *Marcia asked, "Do you remember when he said, 'I'll take care of it'?"*

11. The teacher said, "Please say to the museum guide, Thank you for the tour."

12. "Did she say, I can help you?" Mom asked.

13. Coach shouted, "Next person who says, We can't win, does twenty push-ups."

14. "Did he say, I'm too busy?" Maria asked.

15. "He declared, It's so good to see you, when he saw me at the concert," Betsy said.

16. "Did he say, I found my keys?" Carlos asked.

17. Denise related, "Nikki asked, What am I doing here?"

18. "Which subject biology or math do you like better?" the teacher wondered.

19. Ravi reported, "My father said, You should have known better."

20. Stella demanded, "Why did she say, I wouldn't go anywhere with you?"

WRITING APPLICATION

Write three sentences of a conversation you might have with someone at school. Be sure to use the proper punctuation and spacing for quotations.

WRITING APPLICATION

Write an imagined conversation between two people. Each "speaker" should quote something or someone within his or her own statement. Be sure to use the proper punctuation and spacing for quotations.

Using Quotation Marks for Dialogue

A conversation between two or more people is called a **dialogue.** Adding dialogue makes your writing lively because it brings different points of view into your work. It makes your work sound like speech, so dialogue makes your reader feel involved in the scene you describe.

RULE
25.4.12

> When you are writing a **dialogue,** indent to begin a new paragraph with each change of speaker. Also be sure to add quotation marks around a speaker's words. When a new speaker is quoted, be sure to indicate the change to your reader by adding information that identifies the new speaker.

EXAMPLE

"Will you be going with us on the family trip again this summer?" Noreen asked her cousin.

Gwen hesitated before answering. "I'm afraid so. My parents think I enjoy the experience of traveling with our whole family."

"You fooled me, too," Noreen replied. "Maybe the trip will be better this year. I think we're going to places that have large parks. If we're lucky, we might even be able to go on a few rides."

"Well, at least it can't be any worse," sighed Gwen. "On the last trip, we waited in line for one hour at three different historic homes in one day!"

"I remember those lines," said Noreen. "Didn't you get sunburned while we were waiting?"

Notice that the quotations within each sentence are properly punctuated and spaced. Also, note that paragraph spacing separates each change of speaker.

See Practice 25.4E
See Practice 25.4F

PRACTICE 25.4E **Using Quotation Marks in Dialogue**

Read the dialogue. Then, rewrite the dialogue. Use proper spacing for quotations and create additional paragraphs where needed. Be sure to use quotation marks and other punctuation correctly.

EXAMPLE   What do you know about the United States Constitution the teacher asked. Keisha answered, I think the U.S. Constitution explains how our government works.

ANSWER   *"What do you know about the U.S. Constitution?" the teacher asked.*

Keisha answered, "I think the U.S. Constitution explains how our government works."

Attention please the teacher said. We will be starting a new project today. Will this be something we do at home Melanie asked. No the teacher responded we will be able to work on it during class time. Is it a history project asked Francisco. Yes it will be about the U.S. Constitution the teacher said. Sarah blurted out I know the opening We the people of the United States . . . Very good, Sarah the teacher said. Now turn to page 498 in your books, and let's read about the writing of the Constitution. Those writers must have been really smart Noah added.

PRACTICE 25.4F **Revising Dialogue for Punctuation and Paragraphs**

Read the dialogue. Then, rewrite the dialogue. Add quotation marks and other punctuation, and begin new paragraphs where needed.

EXAMPLE   I asked my mom Is there a new museum exhibit? My mom answered Yes, there's one that just opened last week.

ANSWER   *I asked my mom, "Is there a new museum exhibit?"*

My mom answered, "Yes, there's one that just opened last week."

The museum has a new exhibit the guide told us. It's on the third floor, if you'd like to see it. What is in the exhibit my brother asked. It has Egyptian mummies the guide said and wooden carvings from their tombs. There are also photographs of where the mummies were found. Great! I love anything from Egypt said my dad. So do I added my mom. I chimed in That makes three of us, so let's go. There is an elevator on the left the guide advised. Thank you for telling us about this my dad said, heading for the elevator.

SPEAKING APPLICATION

With a partner, take turns reading a few lines of your corrected dialogues. Talk about why you think there is a new paragraph each time the speaker changes.

WRITING APPLICATION

Write a brief dialogue between two friends planning their weekend. Write enough dialogue so that you have to start a new paragraph. Add quotation marks using the proper punctuation and spacing.

Using Quotation Marks in Titles

Quotation marks are generally used to set off the titles of shorter works.

 RULE 25.4.13

> Use **quotation marks** to enclose the titles of short written works and around the title of a work that is mentioned as part of a collection.

WRITTEN WORKS THAT USE QUOTATION MARKS	
Title of a Short Story	"The Gift of the Magi"
Chapter From a Book	"The Test Is in the Tasting" from *No-Work Garden Book*
Title of a Short Poem	"Lucy"
Title of an Article	"How to Build a Birdhouse"
Title Mentioned as Part of a Collection	"Uncle Vanya" in *Eight Great Comedies*

 RULE 25.4.14

> Use **quotation marks** around the titles of episodes in a television or radio series, songs, and parts of a long musical composition.

ARTISTIC WORKS THAT USE QUOTATION MARKS	
Title of an Episode	"The Nile" from *Cousteau Odyssey*
Title of a Song	"The Best Things in Life Are Free"
Title of a Part of a Long Musical Work	"The Storm" from the *William Tell Overture*

Using Underlining and Italics in Titles

Underlining and **italics** help make titles and other special words and names stand out in your writing. Underlining is used only in handwritten or typewritten material. In printed material, italic (slanted) print is used instead of underlining.

UNDERLINING   <u>The Hobbit</u>   ITALICS   *The Hobbit*

Underline or **italicize** the titles of long written works and publications that are published as a single work.

RULE

WRITTEN WORKS THAT ARE UNDERLINED OR ITALICIZED	
Title of a Book or Play	*War and Peace, Guys and Dolls*
Title of a Long Poem	*Paradise Lost*
Title of a Magazine or Newspaper	*People, The New York Times*

See Practice 25.4G

See Practice 25.4H

Underline or **italicize** the titles of movies, television and radio series, long works of music, and art.

25.4.16

RULE

ARTISTIC WORKS THAT ARE UNDERLINED OR ITALICIZED	
Title of a Movie	*Notting Hill*
Title of a Television Series	*Friends*
Title of a Long Work of Music	*Surprise Symphony*
Title of a Music Album	*TJ's Greatest Hits*
Title of a Painting	*Mona Lisa*
Title of a Sculpture	*The Thinker*

Underline or **italicize** the names of air, sea, and spacecraft.

25.4.17

RULE

EXAMPLES   *Gemini 5*   the *Titanic*

Underline or **italicize** words and letters used as names for themselves and foreign words.

25.4.18

RULE

EXAMPLES   How do you spell *alligator*?

A Japanese *obento* is a homemade lunch.

PRACTICE 25.4G ▷ **Underlining Titles, Names, and Words**

Read the sentences. Rewrite each sentence, underlining titles, names, and words where needed. You can use italics if you are typing your answers.

EXAMPLE   I read Charlotte's Web in fifth grade.

ANSWER   *I read Charlotte's Web in fifth grade.*

1. Have you read the book Beauty and the Beast?

2. I just read all seven books of The Chronicles of Narnia.

3. My dad reads The New York Times.

4. What does duplex mean?

5. I enjoy watching Best Westerns on television.

6. The play Romeo and Juliet always makes me cry.

7. Write noun and pronoun at the top of the page.

8. I learned that merci is French for "thank you."

9. Did you like the book Waltzing Australia?

10. The aircraft carrier Intrepid is now a floating museum.

PRACTICE 25.4H ▷ **Using Underlining and Quotation Marks**

Read the sentences. Rewrite each sentence, enclosing the titles in quotation marks or underlining them. You can use italics if you are typing your answers.

EXAMPLE   I read the article The Titanic.

ANSWER   *I read the article "The Titanic."*

11. Robert Frost's short poem Out, Out is in this collection.

12. I read the article The Spice Is Right in North Shore Magazine.

13. My brother loves the short story The Tell-Tale Heart.

14. Isn't the song Ol' Man River from the musical Showboat?

15. Did you see the Live and Learn episode of the television show Happy Days?

16. The encyclopedia has a biographical article titled Stephen F. Austin.

17. I love the song Yesterday.

18. Aquarium is my favorite part of the musical work The Carnival of the Animals.

19. Did you ever hear the song What a Wonderful World by Louis Armstrong?

20. I think Just You Wait is the funniest song in the musical My Fair Lady.

SPEAKING APPLICATION

With a partner, say a few sentences that need underlining or quotation marks. Discuss which seems to draw more attention to a word or title, the underlining or the quotation marks.

WRITING APPLICATION

Write three sentences recommending things a friend should read or see. Use proper mechanics, including quotation marks, and underlining or italics for book titles.

25.5 Hyphens

Hyphens (-) are used to combine words and to show a connection between the syllables of words that are broken at the ends of lines.

Using Hyphens in Numbers

Hyphens are used to join compound numbers and fractions.

> **Use a hyphen when you write two-word numbers from twenty-one through ninety-nine.**

RULE
25.5.1

EXAMPLES   seventy-eight   thirty-five

> **Use a hyphen when you use a fraction as an adjective but not when you use a fraction as a noun.**

RULE
25.5.2

ADJECTIVE   This glass is two-thirds full.

NOUN   Two thirds of the members were present.

Using Hyphens for Prefixes and Suffixes

Many words with common prefixes are no longer hyphenated. The following prefixes are often used before proper nouns: *ante-*, *anti-*, *post-*, *pre-*, *pro-*, and *un-*. Check a dictionary when you are unsure about using a hyphen.

> **Use a hyphen after a prefix that is followed by a proper noun or adjective.**

RULE
25.5.3

EXAMPLES   pre-Columbian   mid-August

> **Use a hyphen in words with the prefixes *all-*, *ex-*, and *self-* and the suffix *-elect*.**

RULE
25.5.4

EXAMPLES   all-American   mayor-elect

Hyphens   587

Using Hyphens in Compound Words

Compound words are two or more words that must be read together to create a single idea.

Use a **hyphen** to connect two or more nouns that are used as one compound word, unless the dictionary gives a different spelling.

EXAMPLES   great-grandfather   secretary-treasurer

Using Hyphens With Compound Modifiers

Hyphens help your reader group information properly.

Use a hyphen to connect a **compound modifier** that comes before a noun. Do not use a hyphen with a compound modifier that includes a word ending in *-ly* or in a compound proper adjective.

EXAMPLE   Cass was a big-hearted dog lover.

INCORRECT   clearly-written text   West-Indian music

CORRECT   clearly written text   West Indian music

A hyphen is not necessary when a compound modifier follows the noun it describes.

MODIFIER
BEFORE NOUN   They traveled in well-equipped wagons.

MODIFIER
AFTER NOUN   They traveled in wagons that were well equipped.

However, if a dictionary spells a word with a hyphen, the word must always be hyphenated, even when it follows a noun.

EXAMPLE   The design is up-to-date.

See Practice 25.5A
See Practice 25.5B

PRACTICE 25.5A > **Using Hyphens in Numbers and Words**

Read the following phrases. Then, write each phrase, adding hyphens where needed.

EXAMPLE   thirty five days

ANSWER   *thirty-five days*

1. the country's president elect
2. forty three pages
3. Mom's father in law
4. mid December party
5. three fourths full
6. seventy four miles
7. half price sale
8. self appointed leader
9. twenty one years ago
10. hard earned reward

PRACTICE 25.5B > **Proofreading for Hyphens**

Read the sentences. Rewrite each sentence, adding hyphens where needed.

EXAMPLE   We are the all district champions.

ANSWER   *We are the all-district champions.*

11. There were thirty two sets of clearly written instructions.
12. The project is three fourths done.
13. My dad's brother in law is an ex Marine.
14. The pro freedom rally was attended by the governor elect.
15. He bought twenty eight high definition DVDs.
16. Prices are one third off at the mid June sale.
17. It was the top selling movie of the summer.
18. I inherited my great grandmother's well worn cookbook.
19. It's another forty seven miles to the highway exit.
20. Please complete the self evaluation form.

SPEAKING APPLICATION

Go through the lesson and create your own example for each rule of hyphen usage.

WRITING APPLICATION

Write three or four sentences about a trip to a store or shopping mall. Use three different applications of hyphens (numbers, compound words, compound modifiers, and so on) in your sentences.

Using Hyphens at the Ends of Lines

Hyphens serve a useful purpose when they are used to divide words at the ends of lines. They should not, however, be used more often than is necessary because they can make reading feel choppy.

RULE

25.5.7

Avoid dividing words at the end of a line whenever possible. If a word must be divided, always divide it between syllables.

EXAMPLE   The soccer coach's pep talks are usually quite unin-
spiring and short.

Check a dictionary if you are unsure how a word is divided into syllables. Looking up the word *seriously*, for example, you would find that its syllables are *se-ri-ous-ly*.

RULE

25.5.8

A hyphen used to divide a word should never be placed at the beginning of the second line. It must be placed at the end of the first line.

INCORRECT   Knock down this par

-tition.

CORRECT   Knock down this par-

tition.

Using Hyphens Correctly to Divide Words

One-syllable words cannot be divided.

RULE

25.5.9

Do *not* divide one-syllable words even if they seem long or sound like words with two syllables.

INCORRECT   sch-ool   bru-ised   thro-ugh

CORRECT   school   bruised   through

Do *not* divide a word so that a single letter stands alone.

RULE 25.5.10

INCORRECT   a‑mid   ver‑y   o‑kay

CORRECT   amid   very   okay

Also avoid placing *-ed* at the beginning of a new line.

INCORRECT   The school awards ceremony was halt‑
ed by the blackout.

CORRECT   The school awards ceremony was
halted by the blackout.

Avoid dividing proper nouns or proper adjectives.

RULE 25.5.11

INCORRECT   Eliza‑beth   Ger‑man

CORRECT   Elizabeth   German

Divide a hyphenated word only immediately following the existing hyphen.

RULE 25.5.12

INCORRECT   It was a post‑sea‑
son soccer game.

See Practice 25.5C
See Practice 25.5D

CORRECT   It was a post‑
season soccer game.

PRACTICE 25.5C Using Hyphens to Divide Words

Read the following words. Rewrite each word, and draw vertical lines between syllables that can be divided at the end of a line. Do nothing to words that cannot be divided.

EXAMPLE responsible

ANSWER *re | spon | si | ble*

1. insurance
2. wary
3. tasteless
4. forward
5. English
6. uninteresting
7. parted
8. Audrey
9. stunned
10. undoubtedly

PRACTICE 25.5D Using Hyphens in Words in Sentences

Read the sentences. If a word has been divided correctly, write *correct*. If not, rewrite the sentence, dividing the word correctly or writing it as one word if it cannot be divided.

EXAMPLE I was absent from today's Fre-nch class.

ANSWER *I was absent from today's French class.*

11. The animal in that story is imag-inary.
12. The news showed the pro-Amer-ican forces winning.
13. I thought you would be bringing Kar-en with you.
14. It had rained for days, but it stopped even-tually.
15. Losing the game to a rival school end-ed our hopes of a district championship.
16. All the musicians were on hand for the pre-concert rehearsal.
17. Everyone gasped when I fell, but I was o-kay.
18. For the potluck, Christina had bro-ught a casserole.
19. The math book said we should multi-ply first, and then divide.
20. On the map, we located the Rus-sian city of Moscow.

WRITING APPLICATION

Think of long words you know, and write them down. Then, divide them into syllables. Check a dictionary if necessary.

WRITING APPLICATION

Choose three of the rules for dividing words with hyphens. For each of the rules, write a sentence that puts the rule into practice.

25.6 Apostrophes

The **apostrophe (')** is used to show possession or ownership.
It is also used in shortened forms of words called contractions.
In a contraction, the apostrophe marks the place where letters
have been omitted.

Using Apostrophes With Possessive Nouns

Apostrophes are used with nouns to show ownership or
possession.

> **Add an apostrophe and -s to show the possessive case of most
> singular nouns and plural nouns that do not end in -s or -es.**

 25.6.1 RULE

EXAMPLES   My dog's favorite toy is a ball.

The men's trek up Mt. Everest was strenuous.

Even when a singular noun already ends in *-s*, you can usually
add an apostrophe and *-s* to show possession.

EXAMPLE   An iris's colors are often purple and white.

In classical or ancient names that end in *-s*, it is common to omit
the final *-s* to make pronunciation easier.

EXAMPLE   Odysseus' voyages were dangerous.

> **Add an apostrophe to show the possessive case of plural
> nouns ending in -s or -es. Do not add an -s.**

25.6.2 RULE

EXAMPLE   The bears' den is hidden in the mountains.

Add an apostrophe and -*s* (or just an apostrophe if the word is a plural ending in -*s*) to the last word of a compound noun to form the possessive.

25.6.3

EXAMPLES   the Girl Scouts' cookie sale

my sister-in-law's car

See Practice 25.6A

Using Apostrophes With Pronouns

Both indefinite and personal pronouns can show possession.

Use an apostrophe and -*s* with indefinite pronouns to show possession.

25.6.4

EXAMPLES   another's preference   nobody else's business

Do not use an apostrophe with possessive personal pronouns.

25.6.5

POSSESSIVE PERSONAL PRONOUNS		
	SINGULAR	PLURAL
First Person	my, mine	our, ours
Second Person	your, yours	your, yours
Third Person	his; her, hers; its	their, theirs

Some of these pronouns act as adjectives.

EXAMPLES   The spider caught a fly in its web.

Our house is for sale.

Others act as subjects, objects, and subject complements.

EXAMPLES   Mine is the yellow crayon.

Someone broke yours.

See Practice 25.6B

Using Apostrophes With Contractions

Contractions are used in informal speech and writing, especially in dialogue because they create the sound of speech.

> Use an **apostrophe** in a **contraction** to show where one or more letters have been omitted.

25.6.6 RULE

COMMON CONTRACTIONS		
Verb + *not*	is not = isn't	cannot = can't
Noun or Pronoun + *will*	I will = I'll	we will = we'll
Noun or Pronoun + *be*	you are = you're	Andy is = Andy's
Noun or Pronoun + *would*	she would = she'd	who would = who'd

> Avoid using contractions in formal speech and writing.

25.6.7 RULE

Contractions may be used in dialogue and in informal speech and writing, but they should be avoided in formal usage.

INFORMAL WRITING   What's the solution?

FORMAL WRITING   What is the solution?

Using Apostrophes to Create Plurals

Do not use an apostrophe to form plurals, except in specific instances.

> Use an **apostrophe** and -*s* to create the plural form of a letter, numeral, or a word used as a name for itself.

25.6.8 RULE

See Practice 25.6C
See Practice 25.6D

EXAMPLES   Mind your *p*'s and *q*'s.

Remember your *please*'s, please.

Read each phrase. Write the possessive form of each item.

EXAMPLE   the book of Charles

ANSWER   *Charles's book*

1. the collar of the shirt
2. the project of the student
3. the songs of the children
4. the decision of the judges
5. the mooing of the cow
6. the suggestion of my mom
7. the bicycle of Marcus
8. the efforts of the women
9. the chirping of the sparrows
10. the pocket watch of my great-grandfather

Read the sentences. If all pronouns in a sentence are used correctly, write *correct*. If one or more pronouns are used incorrectly, rewrite the sentence correctly.

EXAMPLE   We found everyone else's name tag, but not her's.

ANSWER   *We found everyone else's name tag, but not* **hers.**

11. We respected one anothers privacy.
12. Celeste wanted her books, not his.
13. We have ours, but where are their's?
14. This must be someone's ruler.
15. If it is not hers, whose is it?
16. Is this anybodys lunch?
17. One must be careful where one puts one's glasses.
18. It is your turn now, but soon it will be our's.
19. Josh asked if his' bicycle had been found.
20. Everyone was asked if the watch was his or hers.

SPEAKING APPLICATION

With a partner, take turns reading aloud the possessive forms you wrote in Practice 25.6A. Compare the ending sound of *judges/judges'* and *Marcus/Marcus's*. Talk about how what you hear matches what you wrote.

WRITING APPLICATION

Write three or four sentences about things you and your friends or family own. Use possessive forms of a singular noun, a plural noun, and at least one pronoun.

PRACTICE 25.6C Using Apostrophes in Contractions

Read the sentences. Each sentence contains a word group that can be written as a contraction. Write the contractions.

EXAMPLE   I cannot find my hat.

ANSWER   *can't*

1. Who is coming to dinner?

2. I will get the front door.

3. More homework is not what I wanted.

4. She would like to see you.

5. You are welcome to come in.

6. Stella is planning on coming to the play.

7. The twins are not able to do that.

8. He would make a good catcher.

9. That will be enough.

10. Do not slam the door.

PRACTICE 25.6D Proofreading for Apostrophes

Read the sentences. Rewrite each sentence, adding apostrophes where needed.

EXAMPLE   I cant be responsible for my youngest brothers behavior.

ANSWER   *I can't be responsible for my youngest brother's behavior.*

11. Everyones supposed to bring his or her own lunch.

12. Well try to come, but its not easy to get away from work.

13. Id like to introduce you to Cindy, Bonnies cousin.

14. Theyll bring sandwiches if youll bring salad.

15. Is this someones jacket?

16. My moms new sweater isnt the right size.

17. The paint in the doctors office wasnt dry.

18. If youre in this area, stop by.

19. Hed fix Tylers bike if he could, but its too badly damaged.

20. They wont let us open Seans mail.

SPEAKING APPLICATION

With a partner, read aloud the original form of two or three sentences in Practice 25.6C. Then, say the sentence aloud, using contractions. Talk about which form sounds more like regular speech.

WRITING APPLICATION

Write two sentences about interesting people you know or have read about. Use both possessives (nouns or pronouns) and contractions in your sentences.

25.7 Parentheses and Brackets

Parentheses and **brackets** enclose explanations or other information that may be omitted from the rest of the sentence without changing its basic meaning or construction.

Parentheses

Parentheses are used to separate information from the rest of a sentence or paragraph.

RULE 25.7.1

> Use **parentheses** to set off explanations or other information that is loosely related to the rest of the sentence.

EXAMPLE   During the Civil War **(** 1861–1865 **)** he helped soldiers stay in touch with their families.

RULE 25.7.2

> A **parenthetical sentence** within another sentence should not begin with a capital letter unless the parenthetical sentence begins with a word that should be capitalized.

EXAMPLE   Tickets for the play **(** click here to see the schedule **)** go on sale Thursday.

RULE 25.7.3

> A **parenthetical sentence** within another sentence may end with a question mark or exclamation mark if applicable, but it should not end with a period.

INCORRECT   Tickets for the play **(** click here to see the schedule **.)** go on sale Thursday **.**

CORRECT   Tickets for the play **(** they haven't posted the schedule yet **!)** go on sale Thursday **.**

Parenthetical Sentences That Stand on Their Own
Parenthetical sentences add information to another sentence or a paragraph.

> **A parenthetical sentence** that stands on its own should begin with a capital letter and end with an end mark before the closing parenthesis.

RULE 25.7.4

EXAMPLE Tickets for the play go on sale Thursday **.**

(Click here to see the schedule **.**)

Brackets

Brackets have one major use: to enclose a word or words in a quotation that were not spoken by the person or source that is quoted.

> Use **brackets** to enclose an explanation located within a quote to show that the explanation is not part of the original quote.

RULE 25.7.5

EXAMPLE An eyewitness to the inaugural celebration said, "I have not seen such excitement since the last landslide victory [in 2008]."

> Use **brackets** to enclose an explanation that is located within parenthetical text.

RULE 25.7.6

EXAMPLE George Washington (the first president of the United States [1789–1797]) was known for his leadership and honesty.

See Practice 25.7A
See Practice 25.7B

Parentheses and Brackets

PRACTICE 25.7A **Using Parentheses and Brackets**

Read the sentences. Rewrite each sentence, using parentheses or brackets where appropriate.

EXAMPLE   Alaska was once called Seward's Folly. It was bought by William Seward.

ANSWER   *Alaska was once called Seward's Folly. (It was bought by William Seward.)*

1. The United States entered the war World War II in 1941.

2. Georgia O'Keeffe 1887–1986 was an American artist.

3. My mom said, "I remember my last year of school 1989 as if it were yesterday."

4. Clara Barton's organization the American Red Cross was started in 1881.

5. Franklin Roosevelt was president of the United States for longer than anyone else four terms 1933–1945.

6. Our teacher said, "By that time two o'clock you should all be finished."

PRACTICE 25.7B **Proofreading for Parentheses and Brackets**

Read the sentences. Rewrite each sentence, using parentheses or brackets where appropriate.

EXAMPLE   We picked fourteen baskets of apples count them! at the orchard.

ANSWER   *We picked fourteen baskets of apples (count them!) at the orchard.*

7. Two presidents, John Quincy Adams 1825–1829 and George W. Bush 2001–2009, were sons of earlier presidents.

8. Emily Dickinson 1830–1886 wrote, "Tell all the Truth but tell it slant."

9. Wolfgang Amadeus Mozart wrote more than 40 symphonies in his short life 36 years.

10. "The actor's Lee Upshaw portrayal of a loner will both move and upset you," wrote the movie reviewer.

11. Benjamin Franklin 1706–1790 offered this tip for a good life: "Early to bed and early to rise, makes a man healthy, wealthy, and wise still good advice today."

12. During World War II 1941–1945, many American women Rosie the riveter, for example took the place of men in factories.

SPEAKING APPLICATION

With a partner, take turns reading sentences in Practice 25.7B, leaving out the parts in parentheses or brackets. Discuss what taking out the information does to the sentence.

WRITING APPLICATION

Write three sentences about a period of history or a historical event that interests you. Use parentheses or brackets to add information to your sentences.

Punctuation

25.8 Ellipses and Dashes

An **ellipsis** (. . .) shows where words have been omitted from a quoted passage. It can also mark a pause in dialogue. A **dash** (—) shows a strong, sudden break in thought or speech.

Using the Ellipsis

An **ellipsis** consists of three evenly spaced periods, or ellipsis points, in a row. There is a space before the first ellipsis point, between ellipsis points, and after the last ellipsis point. The plural form of the word *ellipsis* is *ellipses.*

> Use an **ellipsis** to show where words have been omitted from a quoted passage. Including an ellipsis shows the reader that the writer has chosen to omit some information.

RULE 25.8.1

QUOTED PASSAGE	"Four score and seven years ago our fathers brought forth on this continent a new nation conceived in liberty and dedicated to the proposition that all men are created equal." –Abraham Lincoln, *The Gettysburg Address,* November 19, 1863
QUOTED PASSAGE WITH WORDS OMITTED	"Fourscore and seven years ago our fathers brought forth . . . a new nation . . . dedicated to the proposition that all men are created equal."

Ellipses in Advertising

Ellipses are commonly used in ads for movies and other media. When you see an ellipsis in an ad, think about what might have been omitted. You might want to find the original review because the ad might be giving a different impression from what the reviewer intended.

ORIGINAL REVIEW	"It is amazing that anyone would think this was a love story."
AD WORDING	" . . . amazing . . . love story"

RULE 25.8.2

Use an **ellipsis** to mark a pause in a dialogue or speech.

EXAMPLE   "But, in a larger sense, we can not dedicate **...** we can not consecrate **...** we can not hallow **...** this ground."

RULE 25.8.3

It is not necessary to use an **ellipsis** to show an omission at the beginning of material you are quoting. However, if you choose to omit any words *within* material you quote, you must use an ellipsis to show where information has been omitted.

UNNECESSARY   " **...** Now we are engaged in a great civil war, testing whether that nation, or any nation, so conceived and so dedicated, can long endure."

CORRECT   "Now we are engaged in a great civil war, testing whether that nation, or any nation so conceived and so dedicated, can long endure."

RULE 25.8.4

Use an **ellipsis** in the middle of the sentence to show an omission, pause, interruption, or incomplete statement.

EXAMPLE   "But, in a larger sense, we cannot dedicate **...** this ground."

RULE 25.8.5

Use an **ellipsis** and an end mark at the end of the sentence to show an omission, pause, or incomplete statement.

EXAMPLE   "I wonder how we are ever going to finish this project. Maybe we could **. ...** "

If you omit words from a source you are quoting, omit the punctuation that accompanies the words unless it is correct in your sentence.

Punctuation

Dashes

Like commas and parentheses, **dashes** separate certain words, phrases, or clauses from the rest of the sentence or paragraph. Dashes, however, signal a stronger, more sudden interruption in thought or speech than commas or parentheses. A dash may also take the place of certain words before an explanation.

> **Use a dash to show a strong, sudden break in thought or speech.**

RULE **25.8.6**

EXAMPLE   I can't believe how many free throws my brother missed—I don't even want to think about it!

If the interrupting expression is in the middle of the sentence, use a dash on either side of it to set it off from the rest of the sentence.

EXAMPLE   I read an article—I forget who wrote it—about renewable energy sources.

> **Use a dash in place of *in other words, namely,* or *that is* before an explanation.**

RULE **25.8.7**

EXAMPLES   Ruth plays ball for one purpose—to win.

To see his jersey hanging from the rafters—this was his greatest dream.

Dashes can also be used to set off nonessential appositives or modifiers.

EXAMPLE   The selfish player—a "star" who is concerned mainly with his own glory—will not pass the ball.

See Practice 25.8D

Read the sentences. For each sentence, tell whether ellipses (or ellipses points) are used to indicate a *pause*, an *interruption*, or an *omission*.

EXAMPLE   Mom said, "Don't go . . . ," but I didn't hear the rest.

ANSWER   *omission*

1. I'm not sure . . . perhaps we should wait.

2. "We hold these truths to be self-evident . . . endowed . . . with certain . . . rights . . . ."

3. "I pledge allegiance to the flag . . . and to the republic . . . ."

4. Gosh . . . I . . . uh . . . I'm not sure.

5. This is important . . . really important . . . maybe the most important thing I've ever done.

6. I love the song that begins, "O beautiful for spacious skies . . . ."

7. Wait . . . please . . . I can't do this alone.

8. I heard, "Read page 280 through . . . ," but I didn't catch the final page number.

9. "We the people of the United States . . . do ordain and establish this Constitution . . . ."

10. I was slowing down . . . and I wasn't sure . . . I would make it.

Read the sentences. Identify where the ellipses belong in the sentences. Rewrite the sentences using ellipses to show the pause, the interruption, or the omission.

EXAMPLE   "Huh what are you trying to say?" asked Zach.

ANSWER   *"Huh . . . what are you trying to say?" asked Zach.*

11. Jada spoke hesitantly, "Well I guess what if?"

12. My favorite Emily Dickinson poem begins, "I dwell in Possibility."

13. MARSHA (*to FAITH*): It's time to FAITH (*breaking in*): You're wrong!

14. "What is your point please say something," Millie begged.

15. "we shall pay any price, bear any burden" comes from John F. Kennedy's Inaugural Address.

16. "That's one small step" was the beginning of Neil Armstrong's message to America when he stepped on the moon.

17. "Oh no you can't come?"

18. "Oops there goes the glass of water."

19. "Let me think did you notice anything unusual?"

20. Superb handling Roomy trunk Fuel economy What more could you want?

WRITING APPLICATION

Write three sentences using ellipses to indicate omissions, interruptions, or incomplete statements. Explain the purpose of the ellipses in each sentence.

WRITING APPLICATION

Write a short dialogue between characters in a story or play. Use ellipses to show pauses, interruptions, or omissions in the conversation. Read the dialogue aloud with a partner, paying attention to the ellipses.

PRACTICE 25.8C ▷ Using Ellipses

Read each statement. Then, rewrite each sentence adding ellipses where appropriate. Write whether the ellipses indicate an omission, an interruption, or an incomplete statement.

EXAMPLE   That outfit looks too What would you call it?

ANSWER   *That outfit looks too . . . What would you call it?*—incomplete statement or omission

1. Stop I can't understand what you're saying.

2. This motor is I know what's wrong.

3. We can't present the award without see if you can find him.

4. Your term paper is good, but it needs

5. Love is special. Love is

6. I'm not sure Could you say that again?

7. Jason where do I know him from?

8. Wait until I OK, I'm finished.

9. I wonder if we could

10. Look over there quick!

PRACTICE 25.8D ▷ Using Dashes

Read the sentences. Rewrite each sentence, adding dashes where they are needed.

EXAMPLE   It was important so important, in fact, I couldn't let anything stop me.

ANSWER   *It was important—so important, in fact, I couldn't let anything stop me.*

11. The United States had a mission to be the first to the moon.

12. I would like to show you my collection of hey, what was that?

13. We went to a store I don't remember which one to look for a dress.

14. I have one purpose in life to become a scientist.

15. See you tomorrow oh, don't forget to take the handouts.

16. He needed a job even a part-time one for the money.

17. We saw a movie I don't remember the title on Saturday.

18. We'll talk after class you do have time, don't you? about our plans.

19. She came for a reason to clean up this place.

20. When we go and we will go you can come with us.

SPEAKING APPLICATION

With a partner, take turns reading the new sentences created in Practice 25.8C. Discuss whether your new sentences show omissions, interruptions, or incomplete statements. Then, practice reading sentences containing ellipses with proper expression.

WRITING APPLICATION

Write two sentences about your weekend. In each sentence, use a dash to show a sudden break in thought or speech or to replace *in other words, namely,* or *that is* before an explanation.

Test Warm-Up

DIRECTIONS
Read the introduction and the passage that follows. Then, answer the questions to show that you can recognize and use punctuation marks, including ellipses, to indicate omissions and interruptions or incomplete statements.

Erin wrote this dialogue about Ashley and her mother for a class play. Read the paragraph and think about the changes you would suggest as a peer editor. When you finish reading, answer the questions that follow.

Getting Serious About Grades

(1) Ashley and her mother, Mrs. Holland, are discussing new rules. (2) Mrs. Holland is unhappy about Ashley's grades, and Ashley doesn't think the rules are fair. (3) "You must be home my decision is final every day by four o'clock. (4) You cannot text or watch television until your homework is done. (5) Is that clear?" said Mrs. Holland. (6) "But . . . Mom" (7) "No . . . it's time way past time for you to get serious about school." (8) Ashley spoke quietly, "Well . . . I see your point but." (9) "No more buts . . . ." replied Mrs. Holland, leaving the room.

1 What is the BEST way to revise sentence 3?

A "You must be home . . . my decision is final every day by four o'clock.

B "You must be home my decision is final every . . . day by four o'clock.

C "You must be—home my decision is final every day and by four o'clock.

D "You will be home—my decision is final— every day by four o'clock.

2 What change, if any, should be made in sentence 6?

F Delete the ellipsis

G Use a lowercase *M* on *Mom*

H Add ellipses after *Mom*

J Make no change

3 What is the BEST way to revise sentence 7?

A "No. It's time, way past time, for you to get serious about school."

B "No . . . it's time—way past time for you, to get serious about school."

C "No . . . it's time—way—past time—for you to get serious about school."

D "No . . . it's time—way past time—for you to get serious about school."

4 What change should be made in sentence 8?

F Add a comma after *well*

G Add ellipses after *but*

H Add ellipses after *see*

J Add a dash after *point*

CHAPTER 26

CAPITALIZATION

Knowing which words to capitalize will make the content of your writing clearer and easier to read.

WRITE GUY *Jeff Anderson, M.Ed.*

WHAT DO YOU NOTICE?

Search for examples of capitalization as you zoom in on sentences from the story "Stray" by Cynthia Rylant.

MENTOR TEXT

> In January, a puppy wandered onto the property of Mr. Amos Lacey and his wife, Mamie, and their daughter, Doris.

Now, ask yourself the following questions:

- Why is the word *January* capitalized?
- Why does the abbreviation *Mr.* begin with a capital letter?

The word *January* is capitalized because it names a specific period of time. The abbreviation *Mr.* begins with a capital letter because it stands for *Mister,* which is part of Amos Lacey's name. *Mamie* and *Doris* are capitalized because they are also proper nouns that name specific people.

Grammar for Writers Knowing the rules of capitalization helps a writer signal the start of a new sentence and present specific people, places, things, and events accurately. Be sure to check your writing for words that need to be capitalized.

What is the capital of Texas?

I'm sure it's the letter T.

26.1 Using Capitalization

Capital letters are used for the first words in all sentences and in many quotations. They are also used for the word *I*, no matter what its position is in a sentence.

The Word *I*

RULE 26.1.1

> **The pronoun *I* is always capitalized.**

EXAMPLE   **I** worked for two years as a clerk before **I** received a promotion.

Sentences

One of the most common uses of a capital letter is to signal the beginning of a sentence. The first word in a sentence must begin with a capital letter.

RULE 26.1.2

> **Capitalize the first word in declarative, interrogative, imperative, and exclamatory sentences.**

DECLARATIVE   **S**trong gusts of wind made it dangerous to drive on the bridge.

INTERROGATIVE   **W**ho found the clue leading to the suspect's arrest?

IMPERATIVE   **T**hink carefully before you decide.

EXCLAMATORY   **W**hat an amazing coincidence this is!

Sometimes only part of a sentence is written. The rest of the sentence is understood. In these cases, a capital is still needed for the first word.

EXAMPLES   **W**hen?   **W**hy not?   **C**ertainly!

Capitalization

Quotations

A capital letter also signals the first word in a **direct quotation,** a person's exact words.

> **Capitalize the first word in a quotation if the quotation is a complete sentence.**

RULE 26.1.3

EXAMPLES   Several people shouted, "**S**top the bus!"

"**S**he really wants to see that movie," Arlene confided.

My father asked, "**W**hen will you be home?"

> **When a quotation consists of one complete sentence in two parts, only capitalize the first part of the quotation.**

RULE 26.1.4

EXAMPLES   "**H**ow much longer," asked Brian, "**i**s this speech going to last?"

"**T**he Hawaiian islands, " she said, "**h**ave so many birds and flowers that are not found anywhere else."

> **If a quotation contains more than one sentence, the first word of each sentence begins with a capital.**

RULE 26.1.5

EXAMPLES   "**P**lease distribute these maps to everyone," said the director. "**T**hey show the location of each exhibit."

"**R**emember to bring your calculator," said the teacher. "**Y**ou will need it for class tomorrow."

See Practice 26.1A
See Practice 26.1B

PRACTICE 26.1A Supplying Capitalization

Read the sentences. Rewrite each sentence, adding the missing capitals.

EXAMPLE   he and i went to the movies.

ANSWER   *He* and *I* went to the movies.

1. Mom said, "you need to finish that."

2. are we going to get there soon?

3. Jason asked, "when will we arrive?"

4. the container read, "do not shake. do not place near heat."

5. who? what? when was this decided?

6. the Schmidts said i could use their pool.

7. when i was younger, i wanted to be a doctor.

8. the teacher announced, "there will be no test next week."

9. Dad said, "we might go, but it depends on the weather."

10. my sister warned, "if i were you, i would keep quiet."

PRACTICE 26.1B Proofreading for Capitalization

Read the sentences. Rewrite each sentence, adding the missing capitals.

EXAMPLE   "is it true?" i asked.

ANSWER   "*Is* it true?" *I* asked.

11. when was your father born?

12. the coach said, "this is a new season. everything is different."

13. Sarah and i went to the park.

14. the health reporter wrote, "avoid sugar."

15. mom asked, "could you bring me two eggs?"

16. "when i was young," my grandma said, "we didn't have a television."

17. steel made it possible to build skyscrapers.

18. Greg said, "when i'm older, i want to go to college."

19. the librarian said, "please keep your voices down."

20. "what is that?" he wondered.

WRITING APPLICATION

Write three sentences: one declarative, one interrogative, and one exclamatory. Use capitalization correctly in each sentence.

WRITING APPLICATION

Write three sentences about your family or friends. Include a quotation in each sentence. Use capitalization correctly.

Using Capitalization for Proper Nouns

An important use of capital letters is to show that a word is a **proper noun.** Proper nouns name specific people, places, or things.

> Capitalize all **proper nouns.**

RULE 26.1.6

EXAMPLES
Joe **S**mith
Joshua **T**ree **N**ational **M**onument
Tappan **Z**ee **B**ridge
Eiffel **T**ower

Names of People

> Capitalize each part of a person's full name, including initials.

RULE 26.1.7

EXAMPLES
Margaret **R**ose **W**indsor
Brian **J**. **T**. **J**ameson
L. **T**. **C**ornwall

When a last name has two parts and the first part is *Mac, Mc, O',* or *St.,* the second part of the last name must also be capitalized.

EXAMPLES
Mac**I**ntosh
Mc**M**urphy
O'**C**onnor
St. **J**ohn

For two-part last names that do not begin with *Mac, Mc, O',* or *St.,* the capitalization varies. Check a reliable source, such as a biographical dictionary, for the correct spelling.

See Practice 26.1C

Geographical Places

Any specific geographical location listed on a map should be capitalized.

> **Capitalize geographical names.**

GEOGRAPHICAL NAMES	
Streets	Warren Street, Carlton Avenue, Interstate 10
Cities	Baltimore, London, Memphis, Tokyo
States	Arizona, Florida, Hawaii, Idaho
Nations	Italy, Canada, Kenya, France, Peru, South Korea
Continents	North America, Asia, Africa, Antarctica
Deserts	Sahara, Negev, Mojave
Mountains	Mount Everest, Rocky Mountains
Regions	Great Plains, Appalachian Highlands, Northwest
Islands	Canary Islands, Fiji Islands
Rivers	Mississippi River, Amazon River
Lakes	Lake Michigan, Great Salt Lake, Lake Erie
Bays	Hudson Bay, Baffin Bay, Biscayne Bay
Seas	Black Sea, Mediterranean Sea, North Sea
Oceans	Atlantic Ocean, Arctic Ocean

Regions and Map Directions

Names of regions, such as the South and the Northeast, are capitalized because they refer to a specific geographical location. Map directions that do not refer to a specific geographical location are not capitalized.

> **Do not capitalize compass points, such as north, southwest, or east, when they simply refer to direction.**

REGION   We spent our vacation in the **S**outheast.

DIRECTION   Our boat headed **n**orth on the river.

Specific Events and Time Periods

> Capitalize the names of specific events, periods of time, and documents.

The following chart contains examples of events, periods of time, and documents that require capitalization.

SPECIFIC EVENTS AND TIMES	
Historical Periods	Age of Enlightenment, Middle Ages, the Renaissance
Historical Events	World War II, Boston Tea Party, Battle of Lexington
Documents	Bill of Rights, Treaty of Paris, Declaration of Independence
Days	Wednesday, Saturday
Months	December, October
Holidays	Thanksgiving, Labor Day
Religious Days	Christmas, Passover, Ramadan
Special Events	Fiddlers' Convention, Boston Marathon, Super Bowl

Names of Seasons
The names of the seasons are an exception to this rule.
Even though they name a specific period of time, the seasons of the year are not capitalized unless they are part of a title or an event name.

SEASONS   The most popular color this **f**all is rust.

The students traveled in the **s**ummer.

TITLE   During a hot **s**ummer, I read *The Long **W**inter.*

EVENT   It was so cold at the **M**ontana **S**pring Festival that

See Practice 26.1D   it felt like **w**inter.

PRACTICE 26.1C **Using Capitalization for Names of People**

Read the sentences. Write each name, adding the missing capitals.

EXAMPLE   Our third president was thomas jefferson.

ANSWER   *Thomas Jefferson*

1. ulysses s. grant was a general during the Civil War.

2. The inventor who perfected a machine to cut wheat was cyrus mccormick.

3. Do you like the writing of j.r.r. tolkien?

4. orville and wilbur wright built and flew the first successful airplane.

5. sandra day o'connor was the first woman appointed to the Supreme Court.

6. The first African American secretary of state was colin powell.

7. President ronald reagan helped bring the Cold War to an end.

8. harriet beecher stowe wrote a book that helped Americans realize the cruelty of slavery.

9. *Winnie the Pooh* was written by a. a. milne.

10. When pocahontas married john rolfe, it helped create peace in Jamestown.

PRACTICE 26.1D **Using Capitalization for Geographical Places, Specific Events, and Time Periods**

Read the sentences. Write the name of each geographical place, specific event, and time period, adding the missing capitals.

EXAMPLE   The mississippi river is the longest river in the united states.

ANSWER   *Mississippi River, United States*

11. My aunt visited london, england, in June.

12. We are studying about south america.

13. Have you ever visited the blue ridge mountains?

14. The nile river flows through egypt.

15. The weather in the northeast can be cold.

16. I enjoyed studying renaissance paintings at the museum.

17. The pacific ocean is the largest ocean.

18. We drove across pennsylvania, ohio, and indiana.

19. The gobi desert covers the southern part of mongolia.

20. Last year, my favorite baseball team won the world series.

WRITING APPLICATION

Write three sentences about people who played a part in the history of the United States. Be sure to capitalize the names correctly.

WRITING APPLICATION

Write three sentences about places you have studied or would like to visit. Be sure to capitalize geographical names correctly.

Specific Groups

Proper nouns that name specific groups also require capitalization.

> **Capitalize the names of various organizations, government bodies, political parties, and nationalities, as well as the languages spoken by different groups.**

26.1.11 RULE

EXAMPLES   The ambassadors attended the first session of the **A**ustrian **P**arliament.

She delivered a brief address in **J**apanese and received warm applause.

Three **E**agle **S**couts demonstrated search and rescue techniques.

The proper nouns shown in the chart are groups with which many people are familiar. All specific groups, however, must be capitalized, even if they are not well known.

See Practice 26.1E

SPECIFIC GROUPS	
Clubs	**K**iwanis **C**lub **R**otary **C**lub
Organizations	**N**ational **G**overnors **A**ssociation **N**ational **O**rganization for **W**omen
Institutions	**M**assachusetts **I**nstitute of **T**echnology **S**mithsonian **I**nstitution
Businesses	**S**imon **C**hemical **C**orporation **F**ido's **F**avorite **P**et **F**oods
Government Bodies	**U**nited **S**tates **C**ongress **S**upreme **C**ourt
Political Parties	**D**emocrats **R**epublican **P**arty
Nationalities	**C**hinese, **G**erman **N**igerian, **I**ranian
Languages	**E**nglish, **S**panish **K**orean, **S**wahili

Religious References

Use capitals for the names of the religions of the world and certain other words related to religion.

RULE 26.1.12

> **Capitalize references to religions, deities, and religious scriptures.**

The following chart presents words related to five of the world's major religions. Next to each religion are examples of some of the related religious words that must be capitalized. Note that the name of each religion is also capitalized.

RELIGIOUS REFERENCES	
Christianity	God, Lord, Father, Holy Spirit, Bible, books of the Bible (Genesis, Deuteronomy, Psalms, and so on)
Judaism	Lord, Father, Prophets, Torah, Talmud, Midrash
Islam	Allah, Prophet, Mohammed, Qur'an
Hinduism	Brahma, Bhagavad Gita, Vedas
Buddhism	Buddha, Mahayana, Hinayana

Note in the following examples, however, that the words *god* and *goddess* in references to mythology are not capitalized. A god's or goddess's name, however, is capitalized.

EXAMPLES In Roman mythology, the supreme god was Jupiter.

The goddess Juno was the wife of Jupiter and was the goddess of women.

Specific Places and Items

Monuments, memorials, buildings, celestial bodies, awards, the names of specific vehicles, and trademarked products should be capitalized.

Capitalize the names of specific places and items.

OTHER SPECIAL PLACES AND ITEMS	
Monuments	Statue of Liberty Washington Monument
Memorials	Winston Churchill Memorial Vietnam Veterans Memorial
Buildings	Houston Museum of Fine Arts Empire State Building the Capitol Building (in Washington, D.C.)
Celestial Bodies (except the moon and sun)	Earth, Milky Way Jupiter, Aries
Awards	Newbery Medal Nobel Peace Prize
Air, Sea, and Space Craft	Spirit of St. Louis Monitor Voyager 2 Metroliner
Trademarked Brands	Krazy Korn Eco-Friendly Cleanser
Names	Zenox Kermit the Frog the Great Houdini

Capitalize the names of awards.

Notice that *the* is not capitalized in these examples.

EXAMPLES   the Academy Awards

the Fulbright Scholarship

the Pulitzer Prize

See Practice 26.1F   the Medal of Honor

PRACTICE 26.1E > **Using Capitalization for Groups and Organizations**

Read the sentences. Write each group or organization, adding the missing capitals.

EXAMPLE   My brother joined the boy scouts.

ANSWER   *Boy Scouts*

1. My dad is a member of the american medical association.

2. Do you know who represents you in congress?

3. We flew on capital airlines to California.

4. Our state is divided between democrats and republicans.

5. The north central high school basketball team is one of the best teams in the state.

6. The midwest writers association held a meeting on Tuesday.

7. Both girl scouts and boy scouts were in the parade.

8. He has cuban, russian, and indian neighbors.

9. Instead of a house of representatives, England has a house of commons.

10. Mariano speaks both english and spanish.

PRACTICE 26.1F > **Using Capitalization for Religious References and Specific Items and Places**

Read the sentences. Write each term that should be capitalized, adding the missing capitals.

EXAMPLE   A planet close to earth is mars.

ANSWER   *Earth, Mars*

11. I wanted to visit the washington monument.

12. genesis is the first book in the bible.

13. The museum of science and industry has wonderful displays.

14. In islam, people read the qur'an.

15. The largest of the planets is jupiter.

16. The pulitzer prize is awarded for great writing.

17. The jewish torah makes up part of the christian bible.

18. The holocaust memorial attracts many visitors.

19. The apollo 11 spacecraft landed on the moon on July 20, 1969.

20. In India, there are more hindu temples than buddhist temples.

WRITING APPLICATION

Write two sentences about organizations to which you, friends, or family members belong, including clubs, businesses, and schools. Be sure to use the correct capitalization for the names of the organizations.

WRITING APPLICATION

Choose an organization that you would like to join, either now or in the future. Write three sentences about why you would like to be a member. Be careful to use the correct capitalization of the organization.

Using Capitalization for Proper Adjectives

When a proper noun or a form of a proper noun is used to describe another noun, it is called a **proper adjective.** Proper adjectives usually need a capital letter.

> **Capitalize most proper adjectives.**

In the following examples, notice that both proper nouns and proper adjectives are capitalized. Common nouns that are modified by proper adjectives, however, are not capitalized.

PROPER NOUNS	**W**orld **W**ar I
	Canada
PROPER ADJECTIVES	a **W**orld **W**ar I **b**attle
	a **C**anadian **f**lag

The names of some countries and states must be modified to be used as proper adjectives. For example, something from Kenya is Kenyan, someone from Texas is Texan, a chair from Spain is a Spanish chair, and a building in France is a French building.

Brand Names as Adjectives

Trademarked brand names are considered to be proper nouns. If you use a brand name to describe a common noun, the brand name becomes a proper adjective. In this case, capitalize only the proper adjective and not the common noun.

> **Capitalize brand names used as adjectives.**

PROPER NOUN	**H**ealthy **G**rains
PROPER ADJECTIVE	**H**ealthy **G**rains **c**ereal

Notice that only the proper adjective *Healthy Grains* is capitalized. The word *cereal* is not capitalized because it is a common noun; it is not part of the trademarked name.

See Practice 26.1G

Using Capitalization for Titles of People

A person's title shows his or her relationship to other people. Whether a title is capitalized often depends on how it is used in a sentence.

Social and Professional Titles
Social and professional titles may be written before a person's name or used alone in place of a person's name.

> Capitalize the title of a person when the title is followed by the person's name or when it is used in place of a person's name in direct address.

BEFORE A NAME **D**etective O'Toole and **D**octor Perkins have arrived.

IN DIRECT ADDRESS Look, **S**ergeant, the fingerprints match!

TITLES OF PEOPLE	
Social	**M**ister, **M**adam or **M**adame, **M**iss, **M**s., **S**ir
Business	**D**octor, **P**rofessor, **S**uperintendent
Religious	**R**everend, **F**ather, **R**abbi, **B**ishop, **S**ister
Military	**P**rivate, **E**nsign, **C**aptain, **G**eneral, **A**dmiral
Government	**P**resident, **S**enator, **R**epresentative, **G**overnor, **M**ayor, **P**rince, **Q**ueen, **K**ing

In most cases, do not capitalize titles that are used alone or that follow a person's name—especially if the title is preceded by the articles *a, an,* or *the.*

EXAMPLES Samantha Rodgers, the **d**octor on call, will be able to see you.

Tell your **s**enator how you feel about the issue.

My cousin Ralph, who is a **p**rivate in the army, will be home on leave soon.

Government Officials

> **Capitalize the titles of government officials when they immediately precede the name of specific officials. If no person is named, these titles should be written in lowercase.**

EXAMPLES

President **O**bama will answer questions from reporters after the speech.

The club **p**resident will answer questions after the speech.

Mayor **W**alker will speak to the people about conserving energy.

The **m**ayor of a large city is responsible for energy conservation and planning.

Note: Certain honorary titles are always capitalized, even if the title is not used with a proper name or direct address. These titles include the First Lady of the United States, Speaker of the House of Representatives, Queen Mother of England, and the Prince of Wales.

Titles for Family Relationships

> **Capitalize titles showing family relationships when the title is used with the person's name or as the person's name—except when the title comes after a possessive noun or pronoun.**

BEFORE A NAME

We respect **U**ncle Frank's opinion.

IN PLACE OF A NAME

Is **G**randmother going?

AFTER POSSESSIVES

Alan's **f**ather is the team captain.

See Practice 26.1H

Notice that the family title *father* used in the last example is not capitalized because it is used after the possessive word *Alan's*.

PRACTICE 26.1G > **Using Capitalization for Proper Adjectives**

Read the sentences. Write the proper adjectives, adding the correct capitalization.

EXAMPLE   Have you ever been to a french restaurant?

ANSWER   *French*

1. Each morning, they raise the american flag.

2. The soldier talked about a vietnam war battle he fought in.

3. We watched a spanish-language film.

4. I prefer the krazy corn brand of chips.

5. The conference was in the russian capital.

6. He was a world war II hero.

7. The japanese-influenced architecture was lovely.

8. I like chinese food.

9. That book won the newbery medal award.

10. Were you on time for your german class?

PRACTICE 26.1H > **Using Capitalization for Titles of People**

Read the sentences. If the title in each sentence is correctly capitalized, write *correct*. If it is not, rewrite the title correctly.

EXAMPLE   I met representative Dan Rutherford at the rally.

ANSWER   *Representative*

11. In England, queen Elizabeth has reigned for more than fifty years.

12. There is a sergeant on duty now.

13. He was talking with miss Jenner and mister Chen.

14. When she fell, we had to rush Juanita to doctor Pradesh's office.

15. We wondered what it was like to be a professor at that college.

16. Both general Patton and admiral Nimitz won important battles during World War II.

17. Look, Senator, they have begun the session.

18. The reverend Joel Sarnoff officiated at the wedding ceremony.

19. The sign on the door said Governor David Johnson.

20. Straighten up, private; no slouching on duty.

WRITING APPLICATION

Write two sentences about places or events in your social studies book. Include in each sentence something that is modified by a proper adjective.

WRITING APPLICATION

Think of everyone you know at school, at home, and anywhere else. Write people's names with their titles. Be careful to capitalize titles correctly.

Using Capitalization for Titles of Works

Capital letters are used for the titles of things such as written works, pieces of art, and school courses.

> **Capitalize the first word and all other key words in the titles of books, newspapers, magazines, short stories, poems, plays, movies, songs, and artworks.**

26.1.20 RULE

Do not capitalize articles (*a, an, the*), prepositions (*of, to*), and conjunctions (*and, but*) that are fewer than four letters long unless they begin a title. Verbs and personal pronouns, no matter how short, are always capitalized in titles.

EXAMPLE   "**O**verdoing **I**t" by Anton Chekhov

> **Capitalize the title of a school course when it is followed by a course number or when it refers to a language. Otherwise, do not capitalize school subjects.**

26.1.21 RULE

EXAMPLES   **F**rench   **H**istory 420   **A**lgebra II

I have **a**lgebra this morning.

Using Capitalization in Letters

Several parts of friendly and business letters are capitalized.

> **In the heading, capitalize the street, city, state, and the month.**

26.1.22 RULE

EXAMPLES   **M**ain **S**treet   **N**ewton   **O**hio   **M**ay

> **In the salutation, capitalize the first word, any title, and the name of the person or group mentioned. In the closing, capitalize the first word.**

26.1.23 RULE

See Practice 26.1I

See Practice 26.1J

SALUTATIONS   **M**y **d**ear **S**usan,   **D**ear **U**ncle **S**teve,

CLOSINGS   **Y**our **f**riend,   **Y**ours **t**ruly,   **L**ove,

PRACTICE 26.1I	**Using Capitalization for Titles of Things**

Read the sentences. Write the titles, adding the correct capitalization.

EXAMPLE   We subscribe to *national geographic* magazine.

ANSWER   *National Geographic*

1. I looked it up in the *encyclopedia international*.

2. Have you read the story "the tortoise and the hare"?

3. We watched the movie *the lion king*.

4. Pearl S. Buck wrote *the good earth*.

5. She performed "the star-spangled banner."

6. Da Vinci's painting *the last supper* is in Italy.

7. My dad reads *the daily express*.

8. I signed up for history 101.

9. My parents saw the play *the merchant of venice*.

10. I like the poem "the man from snowy river."

PRACTICE 26.1J	**Using Capitalization for Titles of Things**

Read the sentences. Rewrite each sentence, adding the missing capitals.

EXAMPLE   After lunch, I will take a quiz in spanish.

ANSWER   *After lunch, I will take a quiz in Spanish.*

11. I signed up for an english class.

12. *The phantom of the opera* is a popular musical.

13. He sang "pennies from heaven."

14. Did you see the movie *cinderella story*?

15. Mark Twain is the author of *the adventures of tom sawyer*.

16. She will be taking german.

17. Rudyard Kipling wrote "the sing-song of old man kangaroo."

18. The *daily herald* is our local paper.

19. Have you ever seen the painting *the potato eaters*?

20. My dad read me the poem "the charge of the light brigade."

WRITING APPLICATION

Write three sentences about the things you like to read. Be careful to capitalize titles correctly.

WRITING APPLICATION

Write a brief paragraph about the types of entertainment available in your area. Think of museums, movies, plays, and concerts, and then name the things you might see in these places or at these events. Be sure to check for correct capitalization.

Using Capitalization in Abbreviations, Acronyms, and Initials

An **abbreviation** is a shortened form of a word or phrase. An **acronym** is an abbreviation of a phrase that takes one or more letters from each word in the phrase being abbreviated.

See Practice 26.1K
See Practice 26.1L
See Practice 26.1M
See Practice 26.1N

> In general, capitalize **abbreviations, acronyms,** and **initials** if the words or names they stand for are capitalized.

RULE 26.1.24

INITIALS	**E. B.** White
TITLES	**R**ev. Martin Luther King **J**r.
ACADEMIC DEGREES	Mei Yan, **M.D.**, Ben King, **Ph.D.**
ACRONYMS	**NASA**, **UNICEF**

Abbreviations for most units of measurement are not capitalized.

EXAMPLES	**f**t (feet)		**t**sp (teaspoon)

> Capitalize **abbreviations** that appear in addresses.

RULE 26.1.25

Use a two-letter state abbreviation without periods when the abbreviation is followed by a ZIP code. Capitalize both letters of the state abbreviation.

EXAMPLE	Austin, **TX** 78701

> Capitalize **acronyms** that stand for proper nouns, such as businesses, government bodies, and organizations.

RULE 26.1.26

Spell out the name of an organization and include its acronym in parentheses the first time you use it. Use only the acronym in later references.

EXAMPLE	You may have heard of the Internal Revenue Service (**IRS**). The **IRS** collects federal taxes.

Read the sentences. Write each abbreviation, adding the missing capitals.

EXAMPLE Have you seen mt. Rushmore?

ANSWER *Mt.*

1. I addressed the letter to mr. William Park.

2. Did dr. Hill examine Mark's leg for any broken bones?

3. Benjamin O. Davis jr. organized the Tuskegee Airmen.

4. We visited st. Augustine, Florida.

5. Ben Carson, m.d., is one of the country's leading surgeons.

6. Her address is Cambridge, Ma 01773.

7. According to a Gallup poll, rev. Billy Graham is one of the country's most admired people.

8. The flag that inspired "The Star-Spangled Banner" flew over ft. McHenry.

9. His new address is Los Angeles, ca 90001.

10. Karen Phillips, ph.d., is the new professor in the economics department.

Read the sentences. Then, rewrite each sentence using the correct capitalization for abbreviations.

EXAMPLE After being away for six months, lt. Inez Ray wanted to see her friends.

ANSWER *After being away for six months, Lt. Inez Ray wanted to see her friends.*

11. My appointment next week is with Lucia Martinez, m.d.

12. My teacher, ms. Collins, is working on her ed.d. in educational administration.

13. The seat of our government is Washington, d.c.

14. My letter is addressed to mr. James Peabody in San Antonio, tx.

15. The recipe calls for 8 Oz. of milk.

16. On all major holidays, the nyse closes, and no stocks are traded.

17. Mr. Calvin Percy jr. has been appointed president of gwc Industries.

18. Send the check to Chicago, il, and not Phoenix, az.

19. My baby brother has this long name: Elijah Thomas Welby jr.

20. My aunt lives at 2350 Park, nw, in St. Petersburg.

WRITING APPLICATION

Write a complete address, real or imagined. Include at least three abbreviations in the address. Make sure abbreviations are capitalized correctly.

WRITING APPLICATION

Write the names of people and companies—real or imagined—using the following abbreviations: *Mr., Co., Hon., Inc.,* and *Rev.* Write at least three sentences using the names.

PRACTICE 26.1M **Using Capitalization for Initials and Acronyms**

Read the sentences. Write the initials and acronyms, adding the missing capitals.

EXAMPLE   The central intelligence agency (cia) gathers and analyzes information.

ANSWER   *Central Intelligence Agency (CIA)*

1. Some great science fiction stories were written by h. g. Wells.

2. I need a map of the usa.

3. He's a member of the cap (civil air patrol).

4. nasa (national aeronautics and space administration) is the government agency for space exploration.

5. The Chicago transit authority (cta) is a city government department.

6. The women's army corps (wac) was active during World War II.

7. The spca (society for the prevention of cruelty to animals) has an important job protecting animals.

8. Many drivers are members of the American automobile association (aaa).

9. Madame c. j. Walker was the first African American woman to become a millionaire.

10. The environmental protection agency (epa) monitors pollution levels.

PRACTICE 26.1N **Using Capitalization for Initials and Acronyms**

Read the sentences. Rewrite each sentence using the correct capitalization for the initial or the acronym.

EXAMPLE   Harry Potter's creator is j. k. Rowling.

ANSWER   *Harry Potter's creator is J. K. Rowling.*

11. My dad is going to school at night to get his mba.

12. Mr. j. m. Smith was once a coach for an nba team.

13. Another ufo was sighted over Texas last month.

14. The United States and Canada are members of nato.

15. My mom is in charge of r&d for the Belmont Corp.

16. My best friend is named Kathryn Christine, but her dad calls her k. c.

17. The ceo, Charles s. Grayson, signed the letter.

18. My aunt's favorite mystery writer is p. d. James.

19. Grandfather likes to watch the news on the bbc.

20. We used to belong to an hmo for our healthcare.

WRITING APPLICATION

Use initials that stand for words to make up names for three organizations or companies. Then write three sentences with the new names. Use sentence context to help readers understand what the initials mean.

WRITING APPLICATION

Look up the following acronyms: HUD, VFW, USMC. Write the full names of the organizations.

Test Warm-Up

DIRECTIONS

Read the introduction and the passage that follows. Then, answer the questions to show that you can use and understand the function of capitalization for abbreviations, initials, and acronyms in reading and writing.

Noah wrote this paragraph about his plan to write a letter. Read the paragraph and think about the changes you would suggest as a peer editor. When you finish reading, answer the questions that follow.

Spacesuits and Photos From Space

(1) My homework assignment in ms Russell's class is to write a letter to request information. (2) I am interested in space exploration. (3) I went to the nasa Internet site. (4) It's amazing! (5) The public can borrow real spacesuits, scale models of space shuttles, and photos of Earth from space. (6) We have an annual science fair at l.b. Johnson High School, and I am going to write a letter to see how I can plan an exhibit. (7) My letter will be mailed to NASA Johnson Space Center, 2101 NASA pkwy. 1, Houston, Tx 77058.

---

1 What change, if any, should be made in sentence 1?

A Change *ms* to **MS**

B Change *ms* to **Ms**.

C Capitalize the word *class*

D Make no change

2 What is the BEST way to combine sentences 2 and 3?

F I am interested in space exploration, so I went to the nasa Internet site.

G I am interested in space exploration, so I went to the Nasa Internet site.

H I am interested in space exploration, so I went to the NASA Internet site.

J I am interested in space exploration, so I went to the nasa Internets Site.

3 How should sentence 6 be revised?

A Change *Johnson* to **johnson**

B Capitalize the word *exhibit*

C Capitalize the initials *l.b.*

D Capitalize the words *science fair*

4 What is the BEST way to revise sentence 7?

F I will mail my letter to NASA Johnson Space Center, 2101 NASA Pkwy. 1, Houston, tx 77058.

G My letter should be mailed to nasa Johnson Space Center, 2101 nasa Pkwy. 1, Houston, tx 77058.

H My letter should be mailed to NASA Johnson Space Center, 2101 NASA pkwy. 1 Houston, TX 77058.

J I will mail my letter to NASA Johnson Space Center, 2101 NASA Pkwy. 1, Houston, TX 77058.

Using Periods, Question Marks, and Exclamation Marks

Read the sentences. Then, rewrite the sentences, adding periods, question marks, and exclamation marks where needed.

1. Are you going to the dog show
2. Please help me with the dishes
3. What a wonderful teacher she is
4. Mr Wu lives in Richmond
5. He asked if he could borrow the lawn mower
6. Many people visit the UN each year
7. Keep your hands away from the hot stove
8. Sabrina hopes to make the team Can she
9. Wow How magnificent the eagle looked
10. Will you be joining the book club

PRACTICE 2 **Using Commas Correctly**

Read the sentences. Then, rewrite the sentences, adding commas where needed. If a sentence is correct as is, write *correct*.

1. Those pants cost a lot but this shirt costs more.
2. Dirt got on my face in my shoe and on the floor.
3. The thick jagged object was a piece of glass.
4. To prevent snoring breathe through your nose.
5. Jack said "Tell me sir what is the problem?"
6. Exactly 3421 people visited on May 3 2009.
7. The manatee a sea mammal swam nearby.
8. Two white pillars held up the porch roof.
9. I first visited Austin Texas in March 2007.
10. "It must be finished soon of course" said Amy.

PRACTICE 3 **Using Colons, Semicolons, and Quotation Marks**

Read the sentences. Rewrite the sentences, using colons, semicolons, and quotation marks where needed. If a sentence is correct as is, write *correct*.

1. We moved last year, we love our new home.
2. Who said, Give me liberty, or give me death?
3. Bring these items a comb, a brush, and tissues.
4. I'm sorry, said Rose, but I must leave by 430.
5. He won a trophy, however, he soon broke it.
6. How I love the poem Birches!
7. Warning Keep out of the hands of children.
8. Luis likes chicken, rice, and corn.
9. Mia asked, When will this difficult day be over?
10. Native to the Americas are the turkey, a bird, the chipmunk, a rodent, and the tomato, a plant.

PRACTICE 4 **Using Apostrophes Correctly**

Read the sentences. Then, rewrite the sentences, adding or removing apostrophes as needed. If a sentence is correct as is, write *correct*.

1. Mom is deaf and cant hear Mels voice.
2. The horse stays in it's stall when its raining.
3. Silas's bags got mixed up with someone elses.
4. The five top students grades were all As.
5. The myth described the god Zeus' thunderbolts.
6. Donalds prized possession is an 08 yearbook.
7. I'm amazed that you dont tell him hes too loud.
8. Theirs is the best restaurant in town.
9. She couldn't make other plans on Tuesdays.
10. Its hard to tell whats hers and whats yours.

Continued on next page ▶

Using Underlining (or Italics), Hyphens, Dashes, Parentheses, Brackets, and Ellipses

Read the sentences. Then, rewrite the sentences, adding underlining (or italics if you type your answers on a computer), hyphens, dashes, brackets, parentheses, or ellipses. If a sentence is correct as is, write *correct*.

1. Who wrote the novel The Yearling?

2. My sister in law is a happy go lucky person.

3. I asked Bridget she is our new neighbor to be sure to join us at our block party.

4. The film is set during World War II 1939–1945.

5. This is a nicely written essay.

6. Today in court, one person shouted, "She meaning Mrs. Gibbs is guilty!"

7. Americans "pledge allegiance to the flag . . . with liberty and justice for all."

8. The Supreme Court ruled on the case. See page 4 for the actual ruling column 2.

9. The team's goal to win the championship finally seemed within reach.

10. The Pilgrims sailed here on the Mayflower.

PRACTICE 6 ▷ **Using Correct Capitalization**

Read the sentences. Then, rewrite each sentence, using capital letters where they are needed.

1. touring the southwest, we saw the grand canyon.

2. on sunday, reverend sykes gave a fine sermon.

3. the treaty of versailles ended world war I.

4. lewis carroll, a british author, wrote "the walrus and the carpenter."

5. every morning, grandma eats tasty choice cereal.

6. former vice president al gore jr. was awarded the nobel prize.

7. the planet jupiter is named for a roman god.

8. "i met mr. kim," said jo, "when i visited ohio."

9. the norton museum of art is on south olive avenue in west palm beach, florida.

10. the republican party met just north of houston.

11. my sister takes history 101 at yale university.

12. our family visited the lincoln memorial in washington, D.C.

13. "i believe doctor patel is from india," greta said. "he came to the united states in march of 2003."

14. the bible is sacred to christians.

15. was aunt meg in the girl scouts of america?

PRACTICE 7 ▷ **Writing Sentences With Correct Capitalization**

Write a sentence about each of the following people, places, or things. Be sure to use correct capitalization.

1. the governor of your state

2. a local museum or tourist attraction

3. your favorite vacation spot

4. your favorite television show

5. a book that you have enjoyed

RESOURCES FOR
Writing
COACH

WRITING IN THE
Content Areas

Writing in the content areas—math, social studies, science, the arts, and various career and technical studies—is an important tool for learning. The following pages give examples of content area writing along with strategies.

Writing in Math

Prewriting

- **Choosing a Topic** If you have a choice of topics, review your textbook and class notes for ideas, and choose one that interests you.

- **Responding to a Prompt** If you are responding to a prompt, read and then reread the instructions, ensuring that you understand all of the requirements of the assignment.

Drafting

- **State Problems Clearly** Be clear, complete, and accurate in your description of the problem you are analyzing or reporting on. Make sure that you have used technical terms, such as *ratio*, *area*, and *factor*, accurately.

- **Explain Your Solution** Tell readers exactly which mathematical rules or formulas you use in your analysis and why they apply. Clearly spell out each step you take in your reasoning.

- **Use Graphics** By presenting quantitative information in a graph, table, or chart, you make it easier for readers to absorb information. Choose the format appropriate to the material, as follows:

  ✔ **Line Graphs** Use a line graph to show the relationship between two variables, such as time and speed in a problem about a moving object. Clearly label the x- and y-axis with the variable each represents and with the units you are using. Choose units appropriately to make the graph manageable. For example, do not try to represent time in years if you are plotting changes for an entire century; instead, use units of ten years each.

  ✔ **Other Graphs** Use a pie chart to analyze facts about a group, such as the percentage of students who walk to school, the percentage who drive, and the percentage who take the bus. Use a bar graph to compare two or more things at different times or in different categories. Assign a single color to each thing, and use that color consistently for all the bars representing data about that thing.

  ✔ **Tables** Use a table to help readers look up specific values quickly, such as the time the sun sets in each month of the year. Label each column and row with terms that clearly identify the data you are presenting, including the units you are using.

Revising

- **Ensure Accuracy** For accuracy, double-check the formulas you use and the calculations you make.

- **Revise for Traits of Good Writing** Ask yourself the following questions: *How well have I applied mathematical ideas? Does my organizational plan help readers follow my reasoning? Is my voice suitable to my audience and purpose? Have I chosen precise words and used mathematical terms accurately? Are my sentences well constructed and varied? Have I made any errors in grammar, usage, mechanics, and spelling?* Use your answers to help you revise and edit your work.

Writing in Science

Prewriting

- **Choosing a Topic** If you have a choice of topics, look through class notes and your textbook, or conduct a "media flip-through," browsing online articles, or watching television news and documentaries to find a science-related topic.

- **Responding to a Prompt** If you are responding to a prompt, read the instructions carefully, analyzing the requirements and parts of the assignment. Identify key direction words in the prompt or assignment, such as *explain* and *predict*.

- **Gathering Details**
  - ✔ If your assignment requires you to conduct research, search for credible and current sources. Examples of strong sources may include articles in recent issues of science magazines or recently published books. Confirm key facts in more than one source.
  - ✔ If your assignment requires you to conduct an experiment, make sure you follow the guidelines for the experiment accurately. Carefully record the steps you take and the observations you make, and date your notes. Repeat the experiment to confirm results.

Drafting

- **Focus and Elaborate** In your introduction, clearly state your topic. Make sure you tell readers why your topic matters. As you draft, give sufficient details, including background, facts, and examples, to help your readers understand your topic. Summarize your findings and insights in your conclusion.

- **Organize** As you draft, follow a suitable organizational pattern. If you are telling the story of an important scientific breakthrough, consider telling events in chronological order. If you are explaining a natural process, consider discussing causes and the effects that follow from them. If you are defending a solution to a problem, you might give pros and cons, answering each counterargument in turn.

- **Present Data Visually** Consider presenting quantitative information, such as statistics or measurements, in a graph, table, or chart. Choose the format appropriate to the material. (Consult the guidance on visual displays of data under "Use Graphics" on page R2.)

Revising

- **Meet Your Audience's Needs** Identify places in your draft where your audience may need more information, such as additional background, more explanation, or the definition of a technical term. Add the information required.

- **Revise for Traits of Good Writing** Ask yourself the following questions: *How clearly have I presented scientific ideas? Will my organization help a reader see the connections I am making? Is my voice suitable to my audience and purpose? Have I chosen precise words and used technical terms accurately? Are my sentences well constructed and varied? Have I made any errors in grammar, usage, mechanics, and spelling?* Use your answers to revise and edit your work.

FORMS OF SCIENCE WRITING

Lab Report A firsthand report of a scientific experiment, following an appropriate format. A standard lab report includes a statement of the hypothesis, or prediction, that the experiment is designed to test; a list of the materials used; an account of the steps performed; a report of the results observed; and the experimenter's conclusions.

Cause-and-Effect Essay A scientific explanation of the causes and effects involved in natural or technical phenomena, such as solar flares, the digestion of food, or the response of metal to stress.

Technical Procedure Document A step-by-step guide to performing a scientific experiment or performing a technical task involving science. A well-written technical procedure document presents the steps of the procedure in clear order. It breaks steps into substeps and prepares readers by explaining what materials they will need and the time they can expect each step to take.

Response to an Open-Ended Science Prompt A response to a question or writing assignment about science.

Summary of a Science-Related Article A retelling of the main ideas in an article that concerns science or technology, such as an article on a new medical procedure.

Writing in Social Studies

FORMS OF SOCIAL STUDIES WRITING

Social Studies Research Report
An informative paper, based on research, about a historical period or event or about a specific place or culture. A well-written research report draws on a variety of sources to develop and support a thoughtful point of view on the topic. It cites those sources accurately, following an accepted format.

Biographical Essay An overview of the life of a historically important person. A well-written biographical essay reports the life of its subject accurately and clearly explains the importance of his or her contributions.

Historical Overview A survey, or general picture, of a historical period or development, such as the struggle for women's right to vote. A successful historical overview presents the "big picture," covering major events and important aspects of the topic without getting lost in details.

Historical Cause-and-Effect Essay An analysis of the causes and effects of a historical event. A well-written historical explanation makes clear connections between events to help readers follow the explanation.

Prewriting

- **Choosing a Topic** If you have a choice of topics, find a suitable topic by looking through class notes and your textbook. Make a quick list of topics in history, politics, or geography that interest you and choose a topic based on your list.

- **Responding to a Prompt** If you are responding to a prompt, read the instructions carefully, analyzing the requirements and parts of the assignment. Identify key direction words in the prompt or assignment, such as *compare*, *describe*, and *argue*.

- **Gathering Details** If your assignment requires you to conduct research, consult a variety of credible sources. For in-depth research, review both primary sources (documents from the time you are investigating) and secondary sources (accounts by those who analyze or report on the information). If you find contradictions, evaluate the likely reasons for the differences.

Drafting

- **Establish a Thesis or Theme** If you are writing a research report or other informative piece, state your main point about your topic in a thesis statement. Include your thesis statement in your introduction. If you are writing a creative piece, such as a historical skit or short story, identify the theme, or main message, you wish to convey.

- **Support Your Thesis or Theme** Organize your work around your main idea.

  ✔ In a research report, support and develop your thesis with well-chosen, relevant details. First, provide background information your readers will need, and then discuss different subtopics in different sections of the body of your report. Clearly connect each subtopic to your main thesis.

  ✔ In a creative work, develop your theme through the conflict between characters. For example, a conflict between two brothers during the Civil War over which side to fight on might dramatize the theme of divided loyalties. Organize events to build to a climax, or point of greatest excitement, that clearly conveys your message.

Revising

- **Sharpen Your Focus** Review your draft for sections that do not clearly support your thesis or theme, and consider eliminating them. Revise unnecessary repetition of ideas. Ensure that the sequence of ideas or events will help reader comprehension.

- **Revise for Traits of Good Writing** Ask yourself the following questions: *How clearly have I developed my thesis or my theme? Will my organization help a reader follow my development of my thesis or theme? Is my voice suitable to my audience and purpose? Have I chosen precise and vivid words, accurately using terms from the period or place about which I am writing? Are my sentences well constructed and varied? Have I made any errors in grammar, usage, mechanics, and spelling?* Use your answers to revise and edit your work.

Writing About the Arts

Prewriting

Experience the Work Take notes on the subject of each work you will discuss. Consider its mood, or general feeling, and its theme, or insight into life.

- ✔ For visual arts, consider the use of color, light, line (sharp or smooth, smudged or definite), mass (heavy or light), and composition (the arrangement and balance of forms).
- ✔ For music, consider the use of melody, rhythm, harmony, and instrumentation. Also, consider the performers' interpretation of the work.

Drafting

Develop Your Ideas As you draft, support your main ideas, including your insights into or feelings about a work, with relevant details.

Revising

Revise for Traits of Good Writing Ask yourself the following questions: *How clearly do I present my ideas? Will my organization help a reader follow my points? Is my voice suitable to my audience and purpose? Have I chosen precise and vivid words, to describe the works? Are my sentences varied? Have I made any errors in grammar, usage, and mechanics?* Use your answers to revise and edit your work.

Writing in Career and Technical Studies

Prewriting

Choosing a Topic If you have a choice of topics, find a suitable one by looking through class notes and your textbook or by listing your own related projects or experiences.

Drafting

Organize Information As you draft, follow a logical organization. If you are explaining a procedure, list steps in the order that your readers should follow. If they need information about the materials and preparation required, provide that information first. Use formatting (such as headings, numbered steps, and bullet points), graphics (such as diagrams), and transitional words and phrases (such as *first*, *next*, and *if… then*).

Revising

Revise for Traits of Good Writing Ask yourself the following questions: *Have I given readers all the information they will need? Will my organization help a reader follow my points? Is my voice suitable to my audience and purpose? Have I chosen precise words, using technical terms accurately? Are my sentences well constructed? Have I made errors in grammar, usage, and mechanics?* Use your answers to revise and edit your work.

FORMS OF WRITING ABOUT THE ARTS

Research Report on a Trend or Style in Art An informative paper, based on research, about a specific group of artists or trend in the arts.

Biographical Essay An overview of the life of an artist or performer.

Analysis of a Work A detailed description of a work offering insights into its meaning and importance.

Review of a Performance or Exhibit An evaluation of an artistic performance or exhibit.

FORMS OF CAREER AND TECHNICAL WRITING

Technical Procedure Document A step-by-step guide to performing a specialized task, such as wiring a circuit or providing first aid.

Response to an Open-Ended Practical Studies Prompt A response to a question or writing assignment about a task or concept in a specialized field.

Technical Research Report An informative paper, based on research, about a specific topic in a practical field, such as a report on balanced diet in the field of health.

Analysis of a Career An informative paper explaining the requirements for a particular job, along with the responsibilities, salary, benefits, and job opportunities.

WRITING FOR
Media

New technology has created many new ways to communicate. Today, it is easy to contribute information to the Internet and send a variety of messages to friends far and near. You can also share your ideas through photos, illustrations, video, and sound recordings.

Writing for Media gives you an overview of some ways you can use today's technology to create, share, and find information. **Here are the topics you will find in this section:**

- Blogs
- Social Networking
- Widgets and Feeds
- Multimedia Elements
- Podcasts
- Wikis

Blogs

A **blog** is a common form of online writing. The word *blog* is a contraction of *Web log*. Most blogs include a series of entries known as posts. The posts appear in a single column and are displayed in reverse chronological order. That means that the most recent post is at the top of the page. As you scroll down, you will find earlier posts.

Blogs have become increasingly popular. Researchers estimate that 75,000 new blogs are launched every day. Blog authors are often called bloggers. They can use their personal sites to share ideas, songs, videos, photos, and other media. People who read blogs can often post their responses with a comments feature found in each new post.

Because blogs are designed so that they are easy to update, bloggers can post new messages as often as they like, often daily. For some people blogs become a public journal or diary in which they share their thoughts about daily events.

Types of Blogs

Not all blogs are the same. Many blogs have a single author, but others are group projects. These are some common types of blog:

- **Personal blogs** often have a general focus. Bloggers post their thoughts on any topic they find interesting in their daily lives.

- **Topical blogs** focus on a specific theme, such as movie reviews, political news, class assignments, or health-care opportunities.

 WEB SAFETY Using the Internet safely means keeping personal information personal. Never include your address (e-mail or physical), last name, or telephone numbers. Avoid mentioning places you go to often.

Never give out passwords you use to access other Web sites and do not respond to e-mails from people you do not know.

Anatomy of a Blog

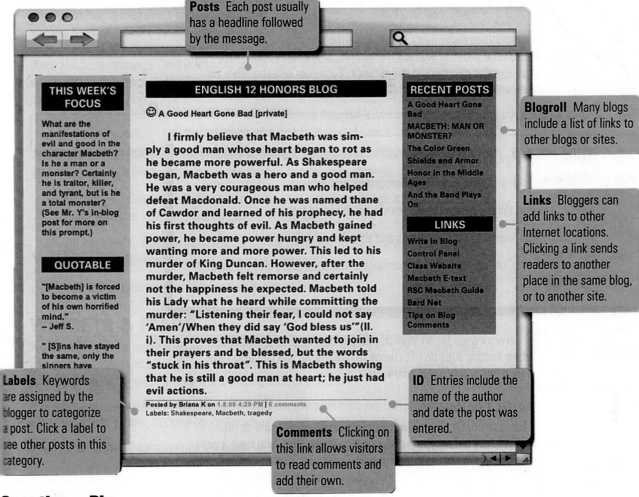

Posts Each post usually has a headline followed by the message.

THIS WEEK'S FOCUS

What are the manifestations of evil and good in the character Macbeth? Is he a man or a monster? Certainly he is traitor, killer, and tyrant, but is he a total monster? (See Mr. Y's in-blog post for more on this prompt.)

QUOTABLE

"[Macbeth] is forced to become a victim of his own horrified mind."
– Jeff S.

"[S]ins have stayed the same, only the sinners have

ENGLISH 12 HONORS BLOG

☺ A Good Heart Gone Bad [private]

   I firmly believe that Macbeth was simply a good man whose heart began to rot as he became more powerful. As Shakespeare began, Macbeth was a hero and a good man. He was a very courageous man who helped defeat Macdonald. Once he was named thane of Cawdor and learned of his prophecy, he had his first thoughts of evil. As Macbeth gained power, he became power hungry and kept wanting more and more power. This led to his murder of King Duncan. However, after the murder, Macbeth felt remorse and certainly not the happiness he expected. Macbeth told his Lady what he heard while committing the murder: "Listening their fear, I could not say 'Amen'/When they did say 'God bless us'"(II. i). This proves that Macbeth wanted to join in their prayers and be blessed, but the words "stuck in his throat". This is Macbeth showing that he is still a good man at heart; he just had evil actions.

Posted by Briana K on 1.8.08 4:29 PM | 6 comments
Labels: Shakespeare, Macbeth, tragedy

RECENT POSTS

A Good Heart Gone Bad
MACBETH: MAN OR MONSTER?
The Color Green
Shields and Armor
Honor in the Middle Ages
And the Band Plays On

LINKS

Write In Blog
Control Panel
Class Website
Macbeth E-text
RSC Macbeth Guide
Bard Net
Tips on Blog Comments

Blogroll Many blogs include a list of links to other blogs or sites.

Links Bloggers can add links to other Internet locations. Clicking a link sends readers to another place in the same blog, or to another site.

Labels Keywords are assigned by the blogger to categorize a post. Click a label to see other posts in this category.

ID Entries include the name of the author and date the post was entered.

Comments Clicking on this link allows visitors to read comments and add their own.

Creating a Blog

Keep these hints and strategies in mind to help you create an interesting and fair blog:

- Focus each blog entry on a single topic.

- Vary the length of your posts. Sometimes, all you need is a line or two to share a quick thought. Other posts will be much longer.

- Choose font colors and styles that can be read easily.

- Many people scan blogs rather than read them closely. You can make your main ideas pop out by using clear or clever headlines and boldfacing key terms.

- Give credit to other people's work and ideas. State the names of people whose ideas you are quoting or add a link to take readers to that person's blog or site.

- If you post comments, try to make them brief and polite.

Social Networking

Social networking means any interaction between members of an online community. People can exchange many different kinds of information, from text and voice messages to video images. Many social network communities allow users to create permanent pages that describe themselves. Users create home pages to express themselves, share ideas about their lives, and post messages to other members in the network. Each user is responsible for adding and updating the content on his or her profile page.

Here are some features you are likely to find on a social network profile:

Features of Profile Pages

- A **biographical description**, including photographs and artwork

- **Lists of favorite things**, such as books, movies, music, and fashions

- **Playable media** elements such as videos and sound recordings

- **Message boards**, or "walls," on which members of the community can exchange messages

Privacy in Social Networks

Social networks allow users to decide how open their profiles will be. Be sure to read introductory information carefully before you register at a new site. Once you have a personal profile page, monitor your privacy settings regularly. Remember that any information you post will be available to anyone in your network.

Users often post messages anonymously or using false names, or pseudonyms. People can also post using someone else's name. Judge all information on the net critically. Do not assume that you know who posted some information simply because you recognize the name of the post author. The rapid speed of communication on the Internet can make it easy to jump to conclusions—be careful to avoid this trap.

You can create a social network page for an individual or a group, such as a school or special interest club. Many hosting sites do not charge to register, so you can also have fun by creating a page for a pet or a fictional character.

Tips for Sending Effective Messages

Technology makes it easy to share ideas quickly, but writing for the Internet poses some special challenges. The writing style for blogs and social networks is often very conversational. In blog posts and comments, instant messages, and e-mails, writers often express themselves very quickly, using relaxed language, short sentences, and abbreviations. However in a face-to-face conversation, we get a lot of information from a speaker's tone of voice and body language. On the Internet, those clues are missing. As a result, Internet writers often use italics or bracketed labels to indicate emotions. Another alternative is using emoticons—strings of characters that give visual clues to indicate emotion.

:-) **smile** (happy)   :-(**frown** (unhappy)   ;-) **wink** (light sarcasm)

Use these strategies to communicate effectively when using technology:

✔ *Before you click Send,* **reread your message** *to make sure that your tone is clear.*

✔ **Do not jump to conclusions**—*ask for clarification first. Make sure you really understand what someone is saying before you respond.*

✔ **Use abbreviations** *your reader will understand.*

Widgets and Feeds

A **widget** is a small application that performs a specific task. You might find widgets that give weather predictions, offer dictionary definitions or translations, provide entertainment such as games, or present a daily word, photograph, or quotation.

A **feed** is a special kind of widget. It displays headlines taken from the latest content on a specific media source. Clicking on the headline will take you to the full article. Many social network communities and other Web sites allow you to personalize your home page by adding widgets and feeds.

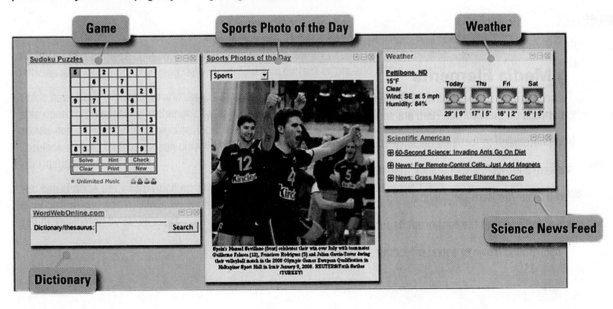

Game **Sports Photo of the Day** **Weather**

Science News Feed

Dictionary

Multimedia Elements

One of the great advantages of communicating on the Internet is that you are not limited to using text only. When you create a Web profile or blog, you can share your ideas using a wide variety of media. In addition to widgets and feeds (see page R9), these media elements can make your Internet communication more entertaining and useful.

GRAPHICS	
Photographs	You can post photographs taken by digital cameras or scanned as files.
Illustrations	Artwork can be created using computer software. You can also use a scanner to post a digital image of a drawing or sketch.
Charts, Graphs, and Maps	Charts and graphs can make statistical information clear. Use spreadsheet software to create these elements. Use Internet sites to find maps of specific places.

VIDEO	
Live Action	Digital video can be recorded by a camera or recorded from another media source.
Animation	Animated videos can also be created using software.

AUDIO	
Music	Many social network communities make it easy to share your favorite music with people who visit your page.
Voice	Use a microphone to add your own voice to your Web page.

Editing Media Elements

You can use software to customize media elements. Open source software is free and available to anyone on the Internet. Here are some things you can do with software:

- **Crop** a photograph to focus on the subject or brighten an image that is too dark.

- **Transform** a drawing's appearance from flat to three-dimensional.

- **Insert** a "You Are Here" arrow on a map.

- **Edit** a video or sound file to shorten its running time.

- **Add** background music or sound effects to a video.

Podcasts

A **podcast** is a digital audio or video recording of a program that is made available on the Internet. Users can replay the podcast on a computer, or download it and replay it on a personal audio player. You might think of podcasts as radio or television programs that you create yourself. They can be embedded on a Web site or fed to a Web page through a podcast widget.

Creating an Effective Podcast

To make a podcast, you will need a recording device, such as a microphone or digital video camera, as well as editing software. Open source editing software is widely available and free of charge. Most audio podcasts are converted into the MP3 format. Here are some tips for creating a podcast that is clear and entertaining:

- **Listen to several podcasts by different authors** to get a feeling for the medium.

- **Make a list** of features and styles you like and also those you want to avoid.

- **Test your microphone** to find the best recording distance. Stand close enough to the microphone so that your voice sounds full, but not so close that you create an echo.

- **Create an outline** that shows your estimated timing for each element.

- **Be prepared** before you record. Rehearse, but do not create a script. Podcasts are best when they have a natural, easy flow.

- **Talk directly to your listeners**. Slow down enough so they can understand you.

- Use software to **edit your podcast before publishing it**. You can edit out mistakes or add additional elements.

You can change the information on a wiki, but be sure your information is correct and clear before you add it. Wikis keep track of all changes, so your work will be recorded and can be evaluated by other users.

Wikis

A **wiki** is a collaborative Web site that lets visitors create, add, remove, and edit content. The term comes from the Hawaiian phrase *wikiwiki*, which means "quick." Web users of a wiki are both the readers and the writers of the site. Some wikis are open to contributions from anyone. Others require visitors to register before they can edit the content. All of the text in these collaborative Web sites was written by people who use the site. Articles are constantly changing, as visitors find and correct errors and improve texts.

Wikis have both advantages and disadvantages as sources of information. They are valuable open forums for the exchange of ideas. The unique collaborative writing process allows entries to change over time. However, entries can also be modified incorrectly. Careless or malicious users can delete good content and add inappropriate or inaccurate information. Wikis may be useful for gathering background information, but should not be used as research resources.

WRITING FOR THE
Workplace

Writing is something many people do every day at work, school, or home. They write letters and reports, do research, plan meetings, and keep track of information in notes.

Writing for the Workplace shows you some models of the following forms of writing:

- **Note Cards**
- **Meeting Agenda**
- **Business Letter**
- **Friendly Letter**

Creating Note Cards

Whether you are working on a research report or gathering information for another purpose, it is helpful to keep your notes on individual cards or in note files on a computer. You will need to make sure that you note your sources on your cards. You can organize information many different ways, but it is most helpful to keep notes of one kind together.

> You can name the **source**, as shown here, or refer to the source by number (e.g., Source 3) if you are using source cards.

> The **topic** is the main focus of the notes.

Topic: Octopus
Source: PBS Web site Accessed 10/15/2010
http://www.pbs.org/wnet/nature/episodes/ the-octopus-show/
a-legend-of-the-deep/2014/

- Acrobatic and shy animals
- Can squeeze into very small spaces to hide or catch food
- Talented swimmers
- Can change color
- Live in all kinds of environments

> *In the notes section focus on the ideas that are most important to your research. Note that these ideas may not always be the main ideas of the selection you are reading. You do not need to write in full sentences. However, you may want to use bullets to make your notes easier to read.*

Writing a Meeting Agenda

When you have a meeting, it is helpful to use an agenda. An agenda tells what will be discussed in the meeting. It tells who is responsible for which topic. It also provides a guide for the amount of time to be spent on each topic.

Book Drive Project Meeting

Saturday, February 6, 2010 2:00 P.M.–6:00 P.M.

Called by Daphne Farkis

Attendees: Bill Aldridge, Erika Cruz, Alexis Chang, Daphne Farkis, Alex Guitierrez, Tiffany Hopper, John Robinson, Sylvie Snopes

> Your meeting will need a **title** that explains the purpose of the meeting.

> You should also include the **date** and **time**.

> This is the person who **called** the meeting. The person often, but not always, leads parts of the meeting.

> The **attendees** are all the people invited to the meeting.

> The **time** provides a guide for how long a topic should be discussed.

> This is the **item**, or **topic**, to be discussed.

> The **owner** is the person who will lead each section of the meeting.

Time	Item	Owner
2:00 P.M.–2:30 P.M.	Welcome and introduction	Daphne
2:30 P.M.–3:30 P.M.	Overview of book drive process	Daphne
3:30 P.M.–4:00 P.M.	Discuss roles and responsibilities	Alexis, All
4:00 P.M.–4:30 P.M.	Break	All
4:30 P.M.–5:00 P.M.	Brainstorm session for flyer ideas	Erika, All
5:00 P.M.–5:30 P.M.	Next steps and deadlines	Daphne, All
5:30 P.M.–6:00 P.M.	Recap and adjournment	Daphne

Writing Business Letters

Business letters are often formal in tone and written for a specific business purpose. They generally follow one of several acceptable formats. In block format, all parts of the letter are at the left margin. All business letters, however, have the same parts: heading, inside address, salutation, body, closing, and signature.

The **heading** shows the writer's address and organization (if any).

The **inside address** indicates where the letter will be sent and the date.

A **salutation**, or **greeting,** is punctuated by a colon. When the specific addressee is not known, use a general greeting such as "To Whom It May Concern."

The **body** of the letter states the writer's purpose. In this case, the writer requests that the class participate in the book drive.

The **closing**, "Sincerely," is common, as are "Best regards," "Yours truly," and "Respectfully yours."

Oscar Diego
Community Book Drive
P.O. Box 34535
Middletown, NY 10941

February 10, 2010
Yin Wallenez
English Teacher
Marsden School
1515 Main River Drive
Middletown, NY 10940

Dear Ms. Wallenez:

We are writing to you to encourage you and your class to join in this year's Community Book Drive. We really appreciated your participation last year and hope you will join us again. As you know, the Community Book Drive gathers books for hundreds of children who otherwise could not afford them. Last year we gathered more than 1,500 books!

Participating this year is simple. Just nominate two members of your class to serve as the book drive leaders. They will post flyers about the book drive around the school and other community areas. They will also be responsible for letting the book drive team leaders know when the drop boxes at your school are getting full.

Please let me know if you are interested. I sure hope that your class will be able to make this year's drive as much of a success as the last! Thanks for your time and consideration.

Sincerely,

Oscar Diego

Oscar Diego • Co-Coordinator, Community Book Drive

Writing Friendly Letters

Friendly letters are less formal than business letters. You can use this form to write to a friend, a family member, or anyone with whom you'd like to communicate in a personal, friendly way. Like business letters, friendly letters have the following parts: heading, inside address, salutation, body, closing, and signature. The purpose of a friendly letter might be:

- to share news and feelings
- to send or answer an invitation
- to express thanks

> The **heading** includes the writer's address and the date on which he or she wrote the letter. In some very casual letters, the writer may not include his or her address.

345 Whitehall Dr.
Beaverton, OR 97005
July 20, 2010

Dear Grandma and Grandpa,

Thank you so much for the journal you sent me. I can't wait to write in it. The cover is gorgeous. Did you know that red is my favorite color? I also love the pen—I can't believe that it is erasable. How cool!

> The **body** of the letter is the main section and contains the message of the letter.

I am having a great summer. I've played soccer a lot and read a lot of books. It sure is hot here, though. Yesterday it was 90 degrees! I know that is nothing compared to summers in Texas, but it is sure hot for us.

Mom says that you are planning a visit for the early fall. I'm really looking forward to it. Maybe you can come watch me play soccer.

Thanks again for the terrific journal.

> Some common **closings** for friendly letters include "Best wishes," "Love," and "Take care."

Love,

Rhonda

MLA Style for Listing Sources

Book with one author	London, Jack. *White Fang.* Clayton: Prestwick, 2007. Print.
Book with two or three authors	Veit, Richard, and Christopher Gould. *Writing, Reading, and Research.* 8th ed. Boston: Wadsworth-Cengage Learning, 2009. Print.
Book prepared by an editor	Twain, Mark. *The Complete Essays of Mark Twain.* Ed. Charles Neider. New York: Da Capo, 2000. Print.
Book with more than three authors or editors	Donald, Robert B., et al. *Writing Clear Essays.* 3rd ed. Upper Saddle River: Prentice, 1996. Print.
A single work from an anthology	Poe, Edgar Allan. "The Fall of the House of Usher." *American Literature: A Chronological Approach.* Ed. Edgar H. Schuster, Anthony Tovatt, and Patricia O. Tovatt. New York: McGraw, 1985. 233–247. Print. [Indicate pages for the entire selection.]
Introduction, foreward, preface, or afterward in a book	Vidal, Gore. Introduction. *Abraham Lincoln: Selected Speeches and Writings.* By Abraham Lincoln. New York: Vintage, 1992. xxi–xxvii. Print.
Signed article in a weekly magazine	Walsh, Brian. "Greening This Old House." *Time* 4 May 2009: 45–47. Print. [For a multi-page article that does not appear on consecutive pages, write only the first page number on which it appears, followed by a plus sign.]
Signed article in a monthly magazine	Fischman, Josh. "A Better Life with Bionics." *National Geographic* Jan. 2010: 34–53. Print.
Unsigned editorial or story	"Wind Power." Editorial. *New York Times* 9 Jan. 2010: A18. Print. [If the editorial or story is signed, begin with the author's name.]
Signed pamphlet	[Treat the pamphlet as though it were a book.]
Audiovisual media, such as films, slide programs, videocassettes, DVDs	*Where the Red Fern Grows.* Dir. Norman Toker. Perf. James Whitmore, Beverly Garland, and Stewart Peterson. 1974. Sterling Entertainment, 1997. DVD.
Radio or TV broadcast transcript	"Texas High School Football Titans Ready for Clash." *Weekend Edition Sunday.* Host Melissa Block. Guests Mike Pesca and Tom Goldman. Natl. Public Radio. KUHF, Houston, 18 Dec. 2009. Print. Transcript.
A single page on a Web site	U.S. Census Bureau: Customer Liaison and Marketing Services Office. "State Facts for Students: Texas." *U.S. Census Bureau.* U.S. Census Bureau, 15 Oct. 2009. Web. 1 Nov. 2009. [Indicate the date of last update if known or use "n.d." if not known. After the medium of publication, include the date you accessed the information. You do not need the URL unless it is the only way to find the page. If needed, include it in angled brackets at the end, i.e. <http://www.census.gov/schools/facts/texas.html >.]
Newspaper	Yardley, Jim. "Hurricane Sweeps into Rural Texas; Cities Are Spared." *New York Times* 23 Aug. 1999: A1. Print. [For a multipage article that does not appear on consecutive pages, write only the first page number on which it appears, followed by a plus sign.]
Personal interview	Jones, Robert. Personal interview. 4 Sept. 2006.
Audio with multiple publishers	Simms, James, ed. *Romeo and Juliet.* By William Shakespeare. Oxford: Attica Cybernetics; London: BBC Education; London: Harper, 1995. CD-ROM.
Signed article from an encyclopedia	Askeland, Donald R. "Welding." *World Book Encyclopedia.* 1991 ed. Print. [For a well known reference, you do not need to include the publisher information, only the edition and year, followed by the medium used.]

Commonly Misspelled Words

The list on this page presents words that cause problems for many people. Some of these words are spelled according to set rules, but others follow no specific rules. As you review this list, check to see how many of the words give you trouble in your own writing.

absence	benefit	conscience	excellent	library	prejudice
absolutely	bicycle	conscientious	exercise	license	previous
accidentally	bought	conscious	experience	lightning	probably
accurate	brief	continuous	explanation	likable	procedure
achievement	brilliant	convenience	extension	literature	proceed
affect	bulletin	coolly	extraordinary	mathematics	pronunciation
agreeable	bury	cooperate	familiar	maximum	realize
aisle	buses	correspondence	fascinating	minimum	really
all right	business	courageous	February	misspell	receipt
allowance	cafeteria	courteous	fiery	naturally	receive
analysis	calendar	criticism	financial	necessary	recognize
analyze	campaign	curiosity	foreign	neighbor	recommend
ancient	canceled	deceive	fourth	niece	rehearse
anniversary	candidate	decision	generally	ninety	repetition
answer	capital	defendant	genuine	noticeable	restaurant
anticipate	capitol	definitely	government	occasion	rhythm
anxiety	career	dependent	grammar	occasionally	sandwich
apologize	cashier	description	guidance	occur	schedule
appearance	category	desert	height	occurred	scissors
appreciate	ceiling	dessert	humorous	occurrence	theater
appropriate	certain	dining	immediately	opinion	truly
argument	changeable	disappointed	immigrant	opportunity	usage
athletic	characteristic	distinguish	independence	parallel	valuable
attendance	clothes	effect	independent	particularly	various
awkward	colonel	eighth	individual	personally	vegetable
bargain	column	embarrass	intelligence	persuade	weight
battery	commercial	enthusiastic	judgment	physician	weird
beautiful	commitment	envelope	knowledge	possibility	whale
beginning	condemn	environment	lawyer	precede	yield
believe	congratulate	especially	legible	preferable	

A

accuracy (ak′yər ə sē) *n.* the state of being without error

alliteration (ə lit′ər ā′shən) *n.* the repetition of beginning sounds in words that are next to or near each other

alternative (ôl tʉr′nə tiv) *n.* another possibility

analysis (ə nal′ə sis) *n.* the process of looking at something closely to understand its meaning, structure, or parts

analyze (an′ə līz) *v.* to look at something carefully to understand its meaning or structure

audience (ô′dē əns) *n.* all the readers of a book or other piece of writing; a group of listeners or viewers

B

believe (bə lēv′) *v.* to accept as true

C

character (kar′ik tər) *n.* a person (or animal) who plays a part in the action of a story, play, or movie

chronological (krän′ə läj′i kəl) *adj.* described or arranged in the order of time, starting with what happened first

citations (sī tā′shənz) *n.* references to sources of information

communicate (kə myü′ni kāt′) *v.* to exchange information

community (kə myü′nə tē) *n.* a group of people who live in the same area or are alike in some way

compare (kəm par′) *v.* to examine the differences and similarities between things

conclusion (kən klü′zhən) *n.* the end of a piece of writing that sums up the main points

consequence (kän′si kwens′) *n.* the result of an action

contrast (kən trast′) *v.* to compare in a way that shows differences

counter-argument (kount′ər är′gyü mənt) *n.* a reason against the original argument

D

demonstrate (dem′ən strāt′) *v.* to make a fact clear by giving proof or evidence

describe (di skrīb′) *v.* to say what something is like

detail (dē′tāl′) *n.* a specific fact or piece of information about something

develop (di vel′əp) *v.* to explain or build an idea or example bit by bit

dialogue (dī′ə lôg′) *n.* a conversation between two or more people in a book, play, or movie

document (däk′yü mənt) *n.* anything printed or written that gives information; *v.* to support ideas with information from sources

E

effect (e fekt′) *n.* the way that something changes because of a separate action

element (el′ə mənt) *n.* one of several parts that make up a whole

evaluate (ē val′yü āt′) *v.* to look into something carefully to assess and judge it

event (ē vent′) *n.* something that happens

evidence (ev′ə dəns) *n.* anything that gives proof or shows something to be true

example (eg zam′pəl) *n.* something typical of a particular group which can be used to represent or help explain

experience (ek spir′ē əns) *n.* the knowledge gained by doing a job or living through a situation; something a person has encountered firsthand; *v.* to have an event or feeling happen to you or to be affected by it

explain (ek splān′) *v.* to make something clear by describing it or giving important details

express (ek spres′) *v.* to say or show thoughts, feelings, or ideas

F

fact (fakt) *n.* a piece of information that can be shown to be true

focus (fō′kəs) *n.* the main topic or most important point; the center of attention

formal (fôr′məl) *adj.* reflecting language that is traditional and correct, not casual

formatting (fôr´mat´ing) *adj.* related to the arrangement of text, images, and graphics on a page

G

genre (zhän´rə) *n.* a type of writing that contains certain features

I

image (im´ij) *n.* a word or phrase in a poem or other kind of writing which appeals to one or more of the five senses

inform (in fôrm´) *v.* to give facts and information

insight (in´sīt´) *n.* a useful, important, deep understanding about a topic

instructions (in struk´shənz) *n.* steps to be followed to accomplish something

interpret (in tur´prət) *v.* to decide on and explain the meaning of something

introduction (in´trə duk´shən) *n.* the part at the beginning of a piece of writing which often tells what the rest will be about

J

judgment (juj´mənt) *n.* an opinion or conclusion formed after careful thought and evaluation

L

logical (läj´i kəl) *adj.* clear and reasonable; based on logic

M

metaphor (met´ə fôr´) *n.* a figure of speech in which something is described as if it were another thing

meter (mēt´ər) *n.* a poem's rhythmic pattern, made by the number of beats in each line

N

narrative (nar´ə tiv) *n.* a story, either fiction or nonfiction

O

onomatopoeia (än´ō mät´ō pē´ə) *n.* the use of words that imitate the sounds they describe

opinion (ə pin´yən) *n.* a belief or view that is not necessarily based on facts

organized (ôr´gə nīzd´) *adj.* the state of being in order

P

plot (plät) *n.* the sequence of events in a story

point of view (point uv vyü) *n.* the perspective from which a story is told; an attitude, position, standpoint, or way of looking at a situation; an opinion

position (pə zish´ən) *n.* a point of view or attitude toward something

purpose (pur´pəs) *n.* the reason that something exists or is done

R

reader-friendly (rēd´ər frend´lē) *adj.* easy for an audience to read and understand

reasoning (rē´zən ing) *n.* the process of reaching a conclusion by looking at the facts

relate (ri lāt´) *v.* to tell, as in to tell a story; to be connected to; to be concerned with

relationship (ri lā´shən ship´) *n.* the way two or more things are connected

relevant (rel´ə vənt) *adj.* closely connected, important, or significant to the matter at hand

reliable (ri lī´ə bəl) *adj.* able to be depended upon

resolution (rez´ə lü´shən) *n.* what happens to resolve the conflict in the plot of a story

respond (ri spänd´) *v.* to say or do something in response; to make an answer

rhyme (rīme) *n.* the repetition of the same sounds at the ends of words, especially in poetry

S

sense (sens) *n.* one of the five abilities of sight, touch, taste, hearing, and smell

sensible (sen´sə bəl) *adj.* having, showing, or a product of good sense and reason

sensory (sen´sər ē) *adj.* of or relating to the five senses

sequence (sē´kwəns) *n.* when a series of things follows each other in a particular order

setting (set´ing) *n.* the time and place of the action in a story or other piece of writing

similar (sim´ə lər) *adj.* alike but not exactly the same

simile (sim´ə lē´) *n.* a sentence or phrase that compares one thing to another, using the words *like* or *as*

standard (stan´dərd) *adj.* used as a basis for comparison

structure (struk´chər) *n.* the way something is organized and put together; *v.* to put together according to a pattern or plan

style (stīl) *n.* a way of doing something; a way of writing

summarize (sum´ə rīz´) *v.* to briefly state the main points or main ideas

suspense (sə spens´) *n.* a feeling of anxiety and uncertainty about what will happen in a story or other piece of writing

T

thesis (thē´sis) *n.* an idea or theory that is stated and then discussed in a logical way

technical (tek´ni kəl) *adj.* related to technology, computers, or applied sciences

topic (täp´ik) *n.* a subject that is written about or discussed

transition (tran zish´ən) *n.* the change from one part, place, or idea to another; in writing, the change between sentences, paragraphs, and ideas

U

understand (un´dər stand´) *v.* to know the meaning of something; to know how someone feels; to know why or how something happens

urgent (ʉr´jənt) *adj.* needing immediate action or attention

V

valid (val´id) *adj.* reasonable and logical, and therefore worth taking seriously; acceptable as true and correct

A

accuracy / exactidud *s.* el estado de no tener errores

alliteration / aliteración *s.* la repetición de los sonidos iniciales de palabras seguidas o cercanas.

alternative / alternativa *s.* otra posibilidad u opción

analysis / análisis *s.* el proceso de examinar algo detenidamente para entender su significado, su estructura o sus partes

analyze / analizar *v.* examinar algo detenidamente para entender su significado o estructura

audience / audiencia, público *s.* los lectores de un libro u otra obra escrita; un grupo de oyentes o espectadores

B

believe / creer *v.* aceptar como la verdad

C

character / personaje *s.* un individuo (humano o animal) que tiene un papel en la acción de un cuento, una obra de teatro o una película

chronological / cronológico *adj.* descrito o arreglado en el orden temporal, empezando con el evento que ocurrió primero

citations / citas *s.* referencias a fuentes de información

communicate / comunicar *v.* intercambiar información

community / comunidad *s.* un grupo de personas que viven en la misma zona o tienen algunas cosas o atributos en común

compare / comparar *v.* examinar las diferencias y semejanzas entre cosas

conclusion / conclusión *s.* el final de una obra escrita que resume las ideas centrales

consequence / consecuencia *s.* el resultado de una acción

contrast / contrastar *v.* comparar dos o más cosas para señalar las diferencias entre ellas

counter-argument / contraargumento *s.* una razón contra el argumento original

D

demonstrate / demostrar *v.* aclarar un hecho por dar pruebas o evidencia

describe / describir *v.* decir cómo es algo

detail / detalle *s.* un dato específico o información específica de algo

develop / desarrollar *v.* explicar o exponer poco a poco una idea o ejemplo

dialogue / diálogo *s.* una conversación entre dos personajes o más en un libro, obra de teatro o película

document / documento *s.* cualquier cosa impresa o escrita que aporta información; documentar *v.* apoyar las ideas con información de fuentes

E

effect / efecto *s.* la manera en la que algo cambia a causa de una acción separada

element / elemento *s.* una de varias partes que forman una totalidad

evaluate / evaluar *v.* investigar algo cuidadosamente para analizarlo y valorarlo

event / evento *s.* algo que ocurre

evidence / pruebas *s.* cualquier cosa que demuestre o indique que algo es cierto

example / ejemplo *s.* algo típico de un grupo particular que se puede usar para representar o aclarar

experience / experiencia *s.* el conocimiento adquirido por hacer un trabajo o sobrevivr una situación; algo que una persona encuentra directamente experimentar *v.* pasar por un evento o sentimiento o ser afectado por un evento o sentimiento

explain / explicar *v.* aclarar algo describiéndolo o dando detalles importantes

express / expresar *v.* decir or mostrar los pensamientos, sentimientos o ideas

F

fact / hecho *s.* un dato que se puede verificar

focus / foco, idea central s. el tema principal o la idea más importante; el centro de atención

formal / formal adj. que refleja lenguaje tradicional y correcto, no informal

formatting / formateo s. la colocación de texto, imágenes y gráficos en una página

G

genre / género s. una clase de escritura que tiene características específicas

I

image / imagen s. una palabra o frase en un poema u otra clase de escritura que atrae uno o más de los cinco sentidos

inform / informar v. dar datos e información

insight / perspicacia s. el profundo entendimiento útil e importante de un tema

instructions / instrucciones s. los pasos que hay que seguir para realizar algo

interpret / interpretar v. determinar y explicar el significado de algo

introduction / introducción s. la parte inicial de una obra escrita que muchas veces cuenta de qué se trata el resto de la obra

J

judgment / juicio s. una opinión o conclusión formada después de una consideración y evaluación cuidadosa

L

logical / lógico adj. claro y razonable; basado en la lógica

M

metaphor / metáfora s. una figura retórica que describe algo como si fuera otra cosa

meter / métrica s. el patrón rítmico de un poema, marcado por el tiempo y ritmo de cada verso

N

narrative / narrativa s. un cuento de ficción o no ficción

O

onomatopoeia / onomatopeya s. el uso de palabras que imitan los sonidos que describen

opinion / opinión s. una creencia o perspectiva que no es necesariamente basada en los hechos

organized / organizado adj. que está ordenado

P

plot / argumento s. la secuencia de eventos en una historia

point of view / punto de vista s. la perspectiva de la cual se cuenta una historia

position / postura s. el punto de vista o la actitud hacia algo

purpose / propósito s. la razón por la cual algo existe o se hace

R

reader-friendly / fácil de leer adj. no complicado, fácil de entender y leer

reasoning / razonamiento s. el proceso de llegar a una conclusión por examinar los hechos

relate / relatar, relacionar v. contar, como contar un cuento; estar conectado con; tratarse de

relationship / relación s. la manera en la que dos cosas o más están conectadas

relevant / relevante adj. conectado estrechamente, importante o significante al asunto en cuestión

reliable / fiable adj. que se puede fiar de la información

resolution / resolución s. lo que ocurre para resolver el conflicto en el argumento de una historia

respond / responder v. decir o hacer algo como respuesta; contestar

rhyme / rima s. la repetición de los mismos sonidos al final de las palabras, especialmente en la poesía

S

sense / sentido s. una de las cinco habilidades de visión, tacto, gusto, audición y olfato

sensible / sensato adj. tener, demostrar o ser un producto de buen sentido y razonamiento

sensory / sensorial *adj.* perteneciente o relativo a los cinco sentidos

sequence / secuencia *s.* cuando una serie de eventos ocurre en un orden determinado

setting / escenario *s.* el lugar y el momento de la acción en un cuento u otra obra escrita

similar / similar *adj.* semejante pero no exactamente igual

simile / simil *s.* una oración o frase que compara una cosa con otra, usando la palabra como (en inglés like o as)

standard / estándar *adj.* usado como base de comparación

structure / estructura *s.* la manera en la que algo está organizado o compuesto; estructurar *v.* organizar o componer según un patrón o plan

style / estilo *s.* una manera de hacer algo; una manera de escribir

summarize / resumir *v.* exponer de una manera breve los puntos o ideas principales

suspense / suspenso *s.* una sensación de ansiedad e incertidumbre sobre lo que va a pasar en una historia u otra obra escrita

T

technical / técnico *adj.* perteneciente o relativo a la tecnología, la informática o las ciencias aplicadas

thesis / tesis *s.* una idea o teoría que se expone y que se discute de una manera lógica

topic / tema *s.* una idea de la cual se escribe y que se discute

transition / transición *s.* el cambio entre partes, lugares y conceptos; en la escritura, el cambio entre oraciones, párrafos e ideas

U

understand / entender *v.* saber el significado de algo; saber cómo se siente alguien; comprender por qué o cómo ocurre algo

urgent / urgente *adj.* requiriendo acción o atención inmediata

V

valid / válido *adj.* razonable y lógico y por lo tanto vale la pena tomarlo en serio; aceptable como verdadero y correcto

Meeting Agenda

Meeting Title: _____

Date: _____

Time: _____

Called by: _____

Attendees: _____

_____

Time	Item	Owner

Cause and Effect Chart

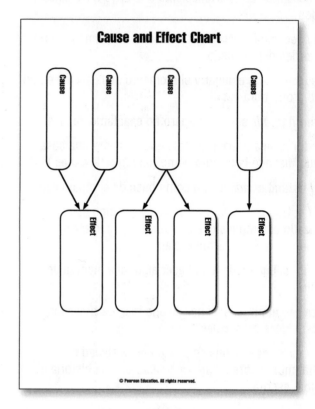

Cluster Diagram

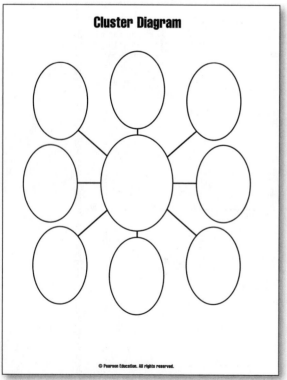

Five Ws Chart

Use these questions as you read, and write important details. Remember, you may not need to answer every question.

Who?	
What?	
When?	
Where?	
Why?	

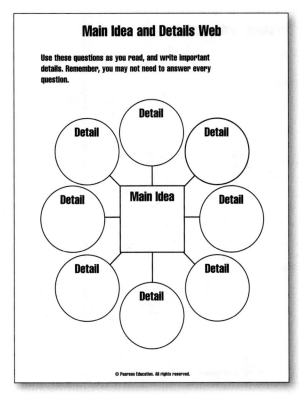

KWL Chart

Topic:		
What I Know	**What I Want to Know**	**What I Learned**

Main Idea and Details Web

Use these questions as you read, and write important details. Remember, you may not need to answer every question.

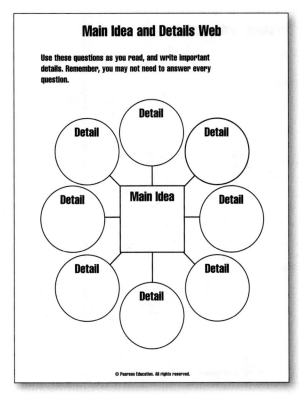

Main Idea, Detail, Detail, Detail, Detail, Detail, Detail, Detail, Detail

Meeting Notes

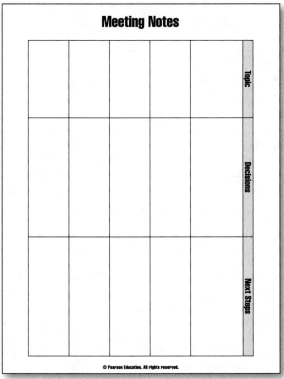

Topic

Decisions

Next Steps

Note Card

Topic:

Source:
-
-
-

Topic:

Source:
-
-
-

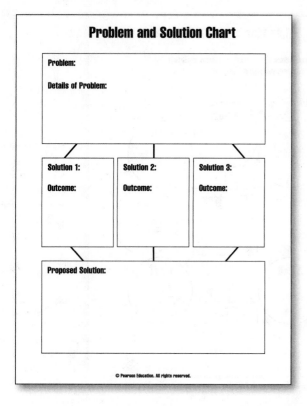

Problem and Solution Chart

Problem:

Details of Problem:

Solution 1:

Outcome:

Solution 2:

Outcome:

Solution 3:

Outcome:

Proposed Solution:

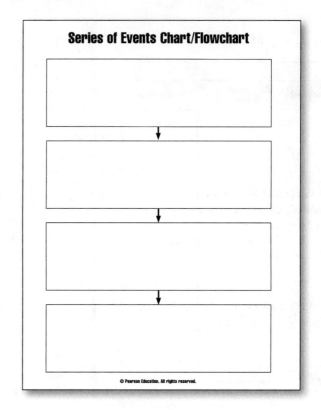

Series of Events Chart/Flowchart

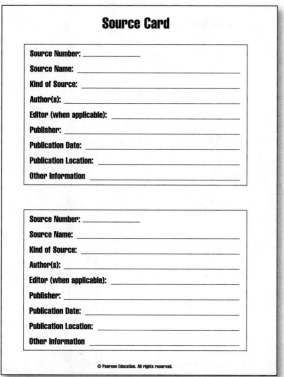

Source Card

Source Number: _____

Source Name: _____

Kind of Source: _____

Author(s): _____

Editor (when applicable): _____

Publisher: _____

Publication Date: _____

Publication Location: _____

Other Information: _____

Source Number: _____

Source Name: _____

Kind of Source: _____

Author(s): _____

Editor (when applicable): _____

Publisher: _____

Publication Date: _____

Publication Location: _____

Other Information: _____

Outline

Topic   I. _____

Subtopic   A. _____

Supporting details

1. _____
2. _____
3. _____
4. _____

Subtopic   B. _____

Supporting details

1. _____
2. _____
3. _____
4. _____

Topic   II. _____

Subtopic   A. _____

Supporting details

1. _____
2. _____
3. _____
4. _____

Subtopic   B. _____

Supporting details

1. _____
2. _____
3. _____
4. _____

Listening and Speaking Handbook

Communication travels between people in many forms. You receive information by listening to others, and you convey information through speaking. The more developed these skills are, the more you will be able to communicate your ideas, as well as to comprehend the ideas of others.

If you improve your listening skills, it will become easier to focus your attention on classroom discussions and to identify important information more accurately. If you develop good speaking skills, you will be better prepared to contribute effectively in group discussions, to give formal presentations with more confidence, and to communicate your feelings and ideas to others more easily.

Listening

Different situations call for different types of listening. Learn more about the four main types of listening—critical, empathic, appreciative, and reflective—in the chart below.

Types of Listening		
Type	**How to Listen**	**Situations**
Critical	Listen for facts and supporting details to understand and evaluate the speaker's message.	Informative or persuasive speeches, class discussions, announcements
Empathic	Imagine yourself in the other person's position, and try to understand what he or she is thinking.	Conversations with friends or family
Appreciative	Identify and analyze aesthetic or artistic elements, such as character development, rhyme, imagery, and descriptive language.	Oral presentations of a poem, dramatic performances
Reflective	Ask questions to get information, and use the speaker's responses to form new questions.	Class or group discussions

This handbook will help you increase your ability in these two key areas of communication.

Steps in a Process Chart

Steps	Details
Step 1:	
Step 2:	
Step 3:	
Step 4:	
Step 5:	

Storyboard

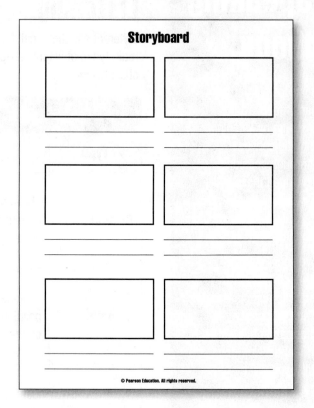

Timeline

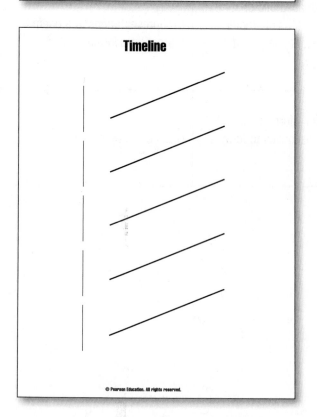

Venn Diagram

Graphic Organizer Handbook

Using Different Types of Questions

A speaker's ideas may not always be clear to you. You may need to ask questions to clarify your understanding. If you understand the different types of questions, you will be able to get the information you need.

- An **open-ended question** does not lead to a single, specific response. Use this question to open up a discussion: "What did you think of the piano recital?"

- A **closed question** leads to a specific response and must be answered with a yes or no: "Did you play a piece by Chopin at your recital?"

- A **factual question** is aimed at getting a particular piece of information and must be answered with facts: "How many years have you been playing the piano?"

Participating in a Group Discussion

In a group discussion, you openly discuss ideas and topics in an informal setting. The group discussions in which you participate will involve, for the most part, your classmates and focus on the subjects you are studying. To get the most out of a group discussion, you need to participate in it.

Use group discussions to express and to listen to ideas in an informal setting.

Communicate Effectively Think about the points you want to make, the order in which you want to make them, the words you will use to express them, and the examples that will support these points before you speak.

Ask Questions Asking questions can help you improve your comprehension of another speaker's ideas. It may also call attention to possible errors in another speaker's points.

Make Relevant Contributions Stay focused on the topic being discussed. Relate comments to your own experience and knowledge, and clearly connect them to your topic. It is important to listen to the points others make so you can build off their ideas. Work to share the connections you see. For example, say whether you agree or disagree, or tell the goup how your ideas connect.

Speaking

Giving a presentation or speech before an audience is generally recognized as public speaking. Effective speakers are well prepared and deliver speeches smoothly and with confidence.

Recognizing Different Kinds of Speeches

There are four main kinds of speeches: informative speeches, persuasive speeches, entertaining speeches, and extemporaneous speeches.

Consider the purpose and audience of your speech before deciding what kind of speech you will give.

- Give an **informative speech** to explain an idea, a process, an object, or an event.

- Give a **persuasive speech** to get your listeners to agree with your position or to take some action. Use formal English when speaking.

- Give an **entertaining speech** to offer your listeners something to enjoy or to amuse them. Use both informal and formal language.

- Give an **extemporaneous speech** when an impromptu occasion arises. It is an informal speech because you do not have a prepared manuscript.

Preparing and Presenting a Speech

If you are asked to deliver a speech, begin choosing a topic that you like or know well. Then, prepare your speech for your audience.

To prepare your speech, research your topic. Make an outline, and use numbered note cards.

Gather Information Use the library and other resources to gather reliable information and to find examples to support your ideas.

Organizing Information Organize your information by writing an outline of main ideas and major details. Then, when you deliver your speech, write the main ideas, major details, quotations, and facts on note cards.

When presenting your speech, use rhetorical forms of language and verbal and nonverbal strategies.

Use Rhetorical Language Repeat key words and phrases to identify your key points. Use active verbs and colorful adjectives to keep your speech interesting. Use parallel phrases to insert a sense of rhythm.

Use Verbal and Nonverbal Strategies Vary the pitch and tone of your voice, and the rate at which you speak. Speak loudly and emphasize key words or phrases. Avoid consistently reading your speech from you notes. Work to maintain eye contact with the audience. As you speak, connect with the audience by using gestures and facial expressions to emphasize key points.

Evaluating a Speech

Evaluating a speech gives you the chance to judge another speaker's skills. It also gives you the opportunity to review and improve your own methods for preparing and presenting a speech.

When you evaluate a speech, you help the speaker and yourself to learn from experience. Listed below are some questions you might ask yourself while evaluating another person's speech or one of your own speeches.

- Did the speaker introduce the topic clearly, develop it well, and conclude it effectively?

- Did the speaker support each main idea with appropriate details?

- Did the speaker approach the platform confidently and establish eye contact with the audience?

- Did the speaker's facial expressions, gestures, and movements appropriately reinforce the words spoken?

- Did the speaker vary the pitch of his or her voice and the rate of his or her speaking?

- Did the speaker enunciate all words clearly?

Listening Critically to a Speech

Hearing happens naturally as sounds reach your ears. Listening, or critical listening, requires that you understand and interpret these sounds.

Critical listening requires preparation, active involvement, and self-evaluation from the listener.

Learning the Listening Process Listening is interactive; the more you involve yourself in the listening process, the more you will understand.

Focus Your Attention Focus your attention on the speaker and block out all distractions—people, noises, and objects. Find out more about the subject that will be discussed beforehand.

Interpret the Information To interpret a speaker's message successfully, you need to identify and understand important information. You might consider listening for repeated words or phrases, pausing momentarily to memorize and/or write key statements, watching non-verbal signals, and combining this new information with what you already know.

Respond to the Speaker's Message Respond to the information you have heard by identifying the larger message of the speech, its most useful points, and your position on the topic.

Index

Note: Page numbers in **boldface** refer to pages where terms are defined; *italicized* page numbers refer to writing applications.

A

Abbreviations
capitalization for, 625, *626, 628*
ending sentence, 553
punctuation, 552

ABCDs of On-Demand Writing (attack the prompt, brainstorm possible answers, choose order of response, detect errors)
compare-and-contrast essays and, *168–169*
interpretative response essays and, *220–221*
I-Search reports and, *254–255*
personal narratives and, *88–89*
persuasive essays and, *194–195*
poetry and, *142–143*
procedural text and, *268–269*
short stories and, *116–117*

Abstract nouns, 294, *296*

Acronyms, 553, 625, *626, 627, 628*

Action verbs, 316, *322, 323*
direct objects and, 388
indirect objects and, 393
types, 317, *318*, 320, *321*
See also Linking verbs

Actions
call to, 24, 85, 182, 186
consequences and, 74, 75, 77, 80, 89, 117, 235
consistent verb tense and, 284

Active voice
identifying, 486
using, 488, *489, 490, 491*

Add. *See* Revision RADaR

Addresses, 569, *570*, 625, 626, 627, R14, R15

Adjectival clauses, 420
combining sentences with, 421, *422*
commas with, 279, 283, 563
set off, with comma, 563

Adjectival phrases, 403, *405–406*

Adjectives, 327, 328–329, *330*
adverbial clauses modifying, 423
versus adverbs, 343, *344*, 345, 346
adverbs that modify, 340
adverbs versus, 343, *344, 345, 346*
articles as, 331
fractions as, versus nouns, 587
indefinite pronouns as, 310
infinitive phrase as, 414, *416*
nouns as, 334, 335, 336, 338
order/rank/series of, 558
pronouns as, 336, *338*
troublesome, 544–545, 546, *547, 548*
types, 333, 334, 336, 337
using commas between, 558, *560*
verb forms as, 409
See also Compound adjectives; Demonstrative adjectives; Indefinite adjectives; Interrogative adjectives; Modifiers; Possessive adjectives; Predicate adjectives; Proper adjectives

Adverbial clauses, 274, 423–424, *425*

Adverbial phrases, 404, *406*

Adverbs, 327, 339, 340
adjectives versus, 343, *344, 345, 346*
adverbial clauses modifying, 423
beginning sentence with, 444
conjunctive, 342, 360, *362*
direct objects versus, 390, *392*
ending in -*ly*, 536
finding, in sentences, 342
infinitive phrase as, 414, 416
prepositions versus, 352, 355
there and *here* as, 384

troublesome, 544–545, *546, 547, 548*
and words they modify, 339–340, *341, 344*
See also Conjunctive adverbs; Modifiers

Advertisements, 19, 24, 173
composition and, 53
ellipses in, 601
See also Persuasive essays

Affixes, 199

Aircraft names, 585, 617

Allegories, 55

Alliteration, 54, 129

Alphabet letters, capitalization of, 623

Alternative viewpoints, 172, 179, 180, 181, 182, 183, 186, 193, 195, 221

Analysis (interpretative response essays), 198, 202–203, 208, 210, 212, 215, 220, 221

Analytical essays, 15, 17, 145, 147
See also Expository writing

Annotated bibliographies.
See Bibliographies

Antecedents
of pronouns, 303, *304*
pronouns in agreement with, 529–531, *532*
third-person singular, 531

Apostrophes, 593–*597*
in contraction, 504, 595, *597*
to create plural form of word, 286, 595, 597
with possessive nouns, 286, 593–594, *596, 598*
with pronoun, 594, *596*
unnecessary/missing, 286

reader's, 7
See also Blogs

K

KWL chart, R25

L

Lab reports, 21

Label warnings, colons in, 573

Language(s)
names of, 615
polite/professional, 198, 257
powerful, 172
rhetorical, R30
See also Figurative language; Vivid
images/language

Leader (in collaborative group), 6

Learning log, 4

Legends/myths, 12, 93

**Legible writing, 84, 138, 139, 165, 190,
248**

Letters
alphabet, capitalization of, 623
written messages
body of, R14, R15
business, 22, R14
closing for, 22, 198, 260, 262, R14,
R15
to editors, 19, 173
friendly, 22, 257, 258–259, 262–
263, R15
greeting/salutation, 22, 198, 260,
263, R14
informal, 257, 260, 261, 262, 263,
266, 267
punctuation in, 569, 570, 573
thank-you letters, 260–261

Letters to authors, 20, 198–221
analysis and, 198, 203, 208, 210, 212,
215, 220, 221
audience and, 199, 201, 205, 210,
211, 212, 213, 216, 217, 219, 221
characteristics of, 198
characters and, 199, 204, 218
conventions and, 214, 215
drafting and, 208–209
editing and, 214–215
evidence and, 198, 202, 203, 206,
207, 208, 209, 210, 211, 212, 215,
218, 219, 220, 221
examples, 202–203
focus and, 204, 205, 208, 209, 211
graphic organizers and, 205, 206,
207, 209, 220
insights and, 198, 211, 212, 218, 219,
221
organization and, 208, 209, 215
plot and, 198, 199, 200, 204
prewriting and, 204–207
publishing and, 216
purpose and, 199, 201, 205, 210, 211,
212, 213, 216, 217, 219, 221
revising and, 210–213
rubric for, 215
setting and, 198
sharing, with school community,
217
thesis statements and, 198, 203, 206,
208, 209, 210, 211, 212, 220, 221
topics and, 204, 205, 216, 217
See also Interpretative response
essays

Lines, 120
See also Poetry

**Linking verbs, 136, 319–320, *321, 322,
323***
predicate pronouns following, 502
subject complement following, 396
See also Action verbs

Listening
listener (in collaborative group), 6
Listening and Speaking
Listening and Speaking Handbook,
R28–R31
types of, R28

Literary elements, 198
See also Characters; Plot; Settings

Literary strategies, 11

Literary/rhetorical devices, 54–55
See also Narrative devices

Literature responses, *See* Interpretative
response essays

Lyric poems, 121

M

Magazines
articles, 17, 147
covers, 192–193
/eZines, informational research
reports and, 249

Main clauses
combining sentences using, 427,
439–440, *441*
commas and, 285, 563
in sentence structure, 417, 418, *419*
See also Independent clauses

Main idea, *See* Ideas

Main verbs, 324–325, *326*

Map directions, 612

Maps, 241, 266, 612, R10

Meaning
sentence meaning, 562–563
word meaning, 199, 273
See also Thoughts, complete/
incomplete

short stories and, 112
thank-you letters and, 261
in writing process (diagram), 30

Punctuation in good writing, 551

Purpose
compare-and-contrast essays and, 147, 153, 158, 160, 161, 166, 167
informational research reports and, 231
letters to authors and, 199, 201, 205, 210, 211, 212, 213
personal narratives and, 78, 80
persuasive essays and, 173, 174, 179, 180, 184, 185, 186, 187, 193
poetry and, 121, 127, 132, 133, 134, 135, 140, 141
prewriting and, 32, 33, 34, 73, 101, 127, 153, 179, 205, 231
short stories and, 93, 101, 106, 108, 109
workplace writing and, 257

Q

Question marks, 553, 555
quotations and, 576–577, 579, 581
sentence function and, 435, 436
to separate run-ons, 452

Questions
direct object in, 391, 392
finding subject in, 382, 383
open-ended, 165, 191, 217, 225, 226, 230, 231, 251, 254, 265
period to end indirect, 552
research, 231. *See also* Informational research reports
types of, R29
who and *whom* in, 509
See also Big Question; Interrogative sentences

Quotation marks, 214, 575, 578
dialogue and, 582, 583

with other punctuation marks, 278, 579, 581, 583
in quotation with expressions, 575–577, 578
titles and, 584, 586
using single, 580, 581

Quotations
capitalization in, 609
colon to introduce long/formal, 573
comma to set off, 569, 570
direct, 214, 235, 240, 241, 251, 252, 275, 278, 569, 570, 575, 577
divided, 577, 578
embedded, 20
explanatory material within (brackets), 580, 581, 599
indirect, 278, 575, 577
with other expressions, 575–577, 578
other quotations within, 580, 581
poorly integrated, 290
punctuation error with, 278
quotation marks to enclose, 575, 578
to show omission in (passage), 601

R

RADaR. *See* Revision RADaR

Radio series titles. *See* Titles

Reader-friendly formatting techniques, 22, 257, 259, 261, 263, 267

Reader's journal, 7
See also Journals

Reading
dramatic reading, 113
out loud (to yourself), 36
writing ideas and, 3

Realistic fiction, 11, 93, 101, 113

Realistic short stories. *See* Short stories

Rearrange. *See* Revision RADaR

Reasoning, sound, 172, 175, 180, 181, 183, 195, 221

References. *See* Citations

Reflecting (on writing), 7, 25, 47, 84, 112, 138, 248

Reflective essays, 10, 67

Reflexive pronouns, 306, 307

Regions, 612

Rehearsal
dramatic reading and, 113
multimedia projects and, 25, 165, 249
poems and, 139

Relative pronouns, 308–309, 311, 418

Religious references/titles, 616, 618, 620

Reorder. *See* Revision RADaR

Repetition (tautology), 55
ballads and, 121
rhyme and, 54, 129
sound devices and, 54
unnecessary, 39, 213

Replace. *See* Revision RADaR

Reports. *See* Informational research reports; *specific reports*

Requests, 381, 383, 492

Research plan, 232

Research questions, 231

Research reports, 21
See also Informational research reports

Research writing, 21, 222–255
forms of, 225
publishing opportunities for, 47
thesis statements and, 21

short story and, 111
See also Active voice; Passive voice

Vowel sound, 331

W

Watching, 3

Web
voice on Web page, R10

Web safety, R7

White space, 54

Widgets, R9

Wikis, R11

Word choice
poetry and, 120
as writing trait, 27, 28, 48, 58, 63
compare-and-contrast essays and, 163
letters to an author and, 215
personal narratives and, 83
persuasive essays and, 189
poetry and, 137
research reports and, 247
short stories and, 111
wrong, 273

Word order
agreement in inverted, 523–524, 525
normal/inverted, 381–382, 383
reversing, for variety, 444, *445*
rewording inverted
to identify pronoun case, 509, 510
to identify subject, 382–385, *386*

Words
commonly misspelled, R17
missing, 281
root words, 199
single, commas separating, 285
word meaning, 199, 273
See also specific types of words

Workplace writing, 22–23, 256–269
characteristics of, 257
example of, 258
forms of, 257
purpose and, 257
reader-friendly formatting techniques and, 22, 257, 259, 261, 263, 267
topics and, 259

Works Cited list, 228, 229, 234, 236, 237, 244, 275

Writing
budgeting time for, 5
building blocks of, 48–52
collaborative, 6, 7
comfortable environment for, 5
cooperative, 6
emotions/feelings and, 87, 91, 119
figurative, 55
finished, 7
free writing versus, 4
genres, 8–25
groups and, 6
ideas. *See* Ideas
legible, 84, 138, 139, 165, 190
materials for, 5
for media. *See* Multimedia projects
motivations for, 2
paragraphs and, 50–52

portfolios and, 7, 84, 112, 138, 164, 248
reflecting on, 7, 25, 47, 84, 112, 138, 248
sentences and, 48–49
topics. *See* Topics
types of, 8–25
ways of, 3
workplace, 22–23, 256–269
See also ABCDs of On-Demand Writing; Compositions; Descriptive essays; Essays; Expository writing; Fiction narration; Interpretative response essays; Nonfiction narration; Persuasive essays; Poetry; Procedural writing; Research writing; Test prompts

Writing process, 30–47
biographical narratives and, 87
diagram of, 30
reasons for using, 31
rubrics and, 28–29
stages in, 30
tips for, 31
See also Drafting; Editing; Prewriting; Publishing; Revising

Writing traits, *26–27, 56–59*
See also Conventions; Ideas; Organization; Sentence fluency; Voice; Word choice

Writing conventions. *See* Conventions

Index of Authors and Titles

Acknowledgments

Grateful acknowledgment is made to the following for copyrighted material:

Brandt & Hochman Literary Agents, Inc.

"Wilbur Wright and Orville Wright" by Stephen Vincent Benet, from *A Book of Americans* by Rosemary and Stephen Vincent Benet. Copyright © 1933 by Rosemary and Stephen Vincent Benet. Copyright renewed © 1961 by Rosemary Carr Benet. Used by permission of Brandt & Hochman Literary Agents, Inc.

Jenny Darling & Associates Pty Ltd.

"A Gentleman's Agreement" by Elizabeth Jolley from *Stories.* Copyright © 1976 Elizabeth Jolley. Used by permission.

Alfred A. Knopf, Inc., A Division of Random House, Inc.

"April Rain Song" from *The Collected Poems of Langston Hughes* by Langston Hughes, edited by Arnold Rampersad with David Roessel, Associate Editor, copyright © 1994 by The Estate of Langston Hughes. Used by permission of Alfred A. Knopf, a division of Random House, Inc.

Neal Levin

"Baby Ate a Microchip" by Neal Levin previously published in *Rolling in the Aisles* (Meadowbrook Press). Copyright © 2004 Neal Levin. Used by permission.

Longman Publishing Group, A Division of Pearson Education, Inc.

Writing in a Second Language" from *Writing: A Guide for College and Beyond (2nd Edition)* by Lester Faigley. Copyright © 2010 by Pearson Education. Used by permission.

National Council of Teachers of English (NCTE)

"Mistakes are a fact of Life: A National Comparative Study" by Andrea A. Lunsford and Karen J. Lunsford translated from *bcs. bedfordstmartins.com/lunsford/PDF/Lunsford_article_Mistakes. pdf.* Copyright © NCTE. Used by permission of National Council of Teachers of English (NCTE).

Harold Ober Associates Incorporated

"April Rain Song" from *The Collected Poems of Langston Hughes* by Langston Hughes, copyright © 1994 by The Estate of Langston Hughes. Used by permission of Harold Ober Associates Incorporated.

Philadelphia Inquirer c/o The YGS Group

"Search for boy and giant chicken will charm young and old" by Sandy Bauers from *Philadelphia Inquirer 9/15/2004, Book Review, Page H.15.* Copyright © 2004 Philadelphia Inquirer. Used by permission.

St. Louis Post-Dispatch

"Individuals Can Make a Difference and Little Things Can Have a Big Impact" by Martha M. Everett. From *St. Louis Post-Dispatch, 6/9/2008.* Copyright © 2008 St. Louis Post-Dispatch. Used by permission.

Viking Penguin, Inc., A division of Penguin Group (USA), Inc.

"Roommates" by Jon Scieszka from *Knucklehead.* Copyright © 2005, 2008 by Jon Scieszka. Used by permission of Viking Children's Books, A Division of Penguin Young Readers Group, A Member of Penguin Group (USA) Inc., 345 Hudson Street, NY, NY 10014. All rights reserved.

Weekly Reader Publishing Group

"Profiles in Caring: Volunteering Provides Teens with Great Experience in Work and in Life" by Kirsten Weir from *Career World, Feb–Mar 2009.* Copyright © Weekly Reader. Used by permission.

Note: Every effort has been made to locate the copyright owner of material reproduced in this component. Omissions brought to our attention will be corrected in subsequent editions.

Image Credits

Illustrations
  Robert Neubecker

All interior photos provided by Jupiter Images. Except

  118: © Corbis/age fotostock; 196: © Stockbroker/age fotostock.